T0202774

Lecture Notes in Artificial Intelligence 11650

Subseries of Lecture Notes in Computer Science

More information about this series at http://www.springer.com/series/1244

Kaspar Althoefer · Jelizaveta Konstantinova ·
Ketao Zhang (Eds.)

Towards Autonomous Robotic Systems

20th Annual Conference, TAROS 2019
London, UK, July 3–5, 2019
Proceedings, Part II

 Springer

Editors
Kaspar Althoefer
Queen Mary University of London
London, UK

Jelizaveta Konstantinova
Queen Mary University of London
London, UK

Ketao Zhang ⓘ
Queen Mary University of London
London, UK

ISSN 0302-9743 ISSN 1611-3349 (electronic)
Lecture Notes in Artificial Intelligence
ISBN 978-3-030-25331-8 ISBN 978-3-030-25332-5 (eBook)
https://doi.org/10.1007/978-3-030-25332-5

LNCS Sublibrary: SL7 – Artificial Intelligence

This Springer imprint is published by the registered company Springer Nature Switzerland AG
The registered company address is: Gewerbestrasse 11, 6330 Cham, Switzerland

Preface

This volume contains the papers presented at TAROS 2019, the 20th Towards Autonomous Robotic Systems (TAROS) Conference, held at Queen Mary University of London, London, UK, during July 3–5, 2019 (https://www.qmul.ac.uk/robotics/events/taros2019/).

TAROS is the longest running UK-hosted international conference on robotics and autonomous systems (RAS), which is aimed at the presentation and discussion of the latest results and methods in autonomous robotics research and applications. The conference offers a friendly environment for robotics researchers and industry to take stock and plan future progress. It welcomes senior researchers and research students alike, and specifically provides opportunities for research students and young research scientists to present their work to the scientific community.

TAROS 2019 was held at Queen Mary University of London, the most inclusive university of its kind. It included an academic conference, industry exhibitions, robot demonstrations, and a conference dinner. The program highlights included:

- Keynote lectures by world-leading experts in robotics, including lectures by Professor Veronique Perdereau from Sorbonne University, France, Dr Francesco Nori from Google DeepMind, UK, and Professor Bruno Siciliano from University of Naples Federico II, Italy.
- IET-sponsored evening lecture by Professor Aude Billard from the Swiss Institute of Technology Lausanne (EPFL), Switzerland.
- Invited talks by Rich Walker from Shadow Robot Company, UK, and Dr Stoyan Smoukov from Queen Mary University of London, UK.
- Oral presentations, covering topics of robotic grippers and manipulation, human–robot interaction, robotic learning, robot navigation, planning and safety, robotic sensing, soft robotics, and mobile and industrial robots.
- Poster presentations, covering topics of swarm and multi-robot system, aerial and space robotics, eversion robots, bio-inspired robots, reconfigurable robots, robot design and testing, and human–robot interaction.
- Presentations of the finalists of the Queen Mary UK Best PhD in Robotics Award.
- Industrial and academic exhibition stands.

TAROS also offers several prizes for papers and posters. In 2019, the following papers were nominated by the Program Committee (PC):

Nominees for Best Paper Prize sponsored by Springer and Frontiers

- Fabian Falck, Kawin Larppichet, Petar Kormushev, "DE VITO: A Dual-arm, High Degree-of-freedom, Lightweight, Inexpensive, Passive Upper-limb Exoskeleton for Robot Teleoperation"
- Paola Ardón, Èric Artau, Ron Petrick, Subramanian Ramamoorthy, Katrin Solveig Lohan, "Reasoning on Grasp-Action Affordances"

- Mathieu Geisert, Thomas Yates, Asil Orgen, Pierre Fernbach, Ioannis Havoutis, "Contact Planning for the ANYmal Quadruped Robot using an Acyclic Reachability-Based Planner"

Nominees for Best Student Paper Prize in memory of Professor Ulrich Nehmzow

- Gerard Canal, Michael Cashmore, Senka Krivic, Guillem Alenyà, Daniele Magazzeni, Carme Torras, Probabilistic Planning for Robotics with ROSPlan
- Faisal ALJaber, Kaspar Althoefer, Light Intensity-Modulated Bending Sensor Fabrication and Performance Test for Shape Sensing
- Ata Otaran, Ildar Farkhatdinov Modeling and Control of Ankle Actuation Platform for Human-Robot Interaction

Nominees for Best Poster Prize sponsored by the Frontiers

- Mohammad Safeea, Pedro Neto, Richard Bearee, "The Third hand, Cobots Assisted Precise Assembly"
- Ranjan Vepa, "Optimal Manoeuver Trajectory Synthesis for Autonomous Space and Aerial Vehicles and Robots"
- Inmo Jang, Joaquin Carrasco Gomez, Andrew Weightman, Barry Lennox, "Intuitive Bare-Hand Teleoperation of a Robotic Manipulator using Virtual Reality and Leap Motion"

Nominees for Best Poster Prize sponsored by the UK-RAS Network

- Fabrizio Putzu, Jelizaveta Konstantinova, Kaspar Althoefer, "Soft particles for granular jamming"
- Cuebong Wong, Erfu Yang, Xiu-Tian Yan, Dongbing Gu, "An Optimal Approach to Anytime Task and Path Planning for Autonomous Mobile Robots in Dynamic Environments"
- Omar Zahra, David Navarro-Alarcon, "A Self-Organizing Network with Varying Density Structure for Characterizing Sensorimotor Transformations in Robotic Systems"

Nominees for IET Prize for Innovation in Robotics

- Shreyus Bagga, Benedikt Maurer, Tom Miller, Luke Quinlan, Lorenzo Silvestri, Dan Wells, Rebecka Winqvist, Mark Zolotas, Yiannis Demiris, "instruMentor: an Interactive Robot for Musical Instrument Tutoring"
- Ahmed Hassan, Hareesh Godaba, Kaspar Althoefer, "Design analysis of a fabric based lightweight robotic gripper"
- Ketao Zhang, Kaspar Althoefer, "Designing Origami-adapted Deployable Modules for Soft Continuum Arms"

Audience Voted Best Paper Prizes sponsored by the Centre for Advanced Robotics at QMUL (ARQ)

- 1st place: Èric Artau, Paola Ardón, Michael Mistry, Yvan Petillot, "Learning and Composing Primitive Skills for Dual-arm Manipulation"

- 2nd place: Gerard Canal, Michael Cashmore, Senka Krivic, Guillem Alenyà, Daniele Magazzeni, Carme Torras, "Probabilistic Planning for Robotics with ROSPlan"
- 3rd place: Beichen Ding, Andrew Plummer, Pejman Iravani, "Investigating balance control of a hopping bipedal robot"

The PC's Award Panel evaluated the presentations given by the shortlisted candidates during the conference and announced the winners at the award ceremony.

The TAROS 2019 Organizing Committee would like to thank all the authors, reviewers, and the conference sponsors, including the IET, UK-RAS Network, The Alan Turing Institute, Institute of Applied Data Science, Queen Mary University of London, University of Nottingham (The Rolls-Royce UTC in Manufacturing and On-wing Technology), NCNR, Automata, Ocado Technology, Springer and Frontiers in Robotics and AI.

May 2019

Kaspar Althoefer
Jelizaveta Konstantinova
Ketao Zhang

Organization

General Chair

Kaspar Althoefer — Queen Mary University of London, UK

Program Chairs

Jelizaveta Konstantinova	Queen Mary University of London, UK
Ketao Zhang	Queen Mary University of London, UK

Web Chair

Joshua Brown — Queen Mary University of London, UK

TAROS Steering Committee

Chris Melhuish	Bristol Robotics Laboratory, UK
Mark Witkowski	Imperial College London, UK

Program Committee

Akram Alomainy	Queen Mary University of London, UK
Kaspar Althoefer	Queen Mary University of London, UK
Ahmad Ataka	Kings College London, UK
Christos Bergeles	Kings College London, UK
Michael Cashmore	Kings College London, UK
Kerstin Dautenhahn	University of Waterloo, Canada
Yiannis Demiris	Imperial College London, UK
Sanja Dogramadzi	University of the West of England, UK
Venky Dubey	Bournemouth University, UK
Ildar Farkhatdinov	Queen Mary University of London, UK
Manuel Giuliani	University of the West of England, UK
Hareesh Godaba	Queen Mary University of London, UK
Roderich Gross	University of Sheffield, UK
Dongbing Gu	University of Essex, UK
Marc Hanheide	University of Lincoln, UK
Lorenzo Jamone	Queen Mary University of London, UK
Jelizaveta Konstantinova	Queen Mary University of London, UK
Senka Krivic	Kings College London, UK
Barry Lennox	University of Manchester, UK
Honghai Liu	University of Portsmouth, UK
Shan Luo	University of Liverpool, UK

Contents – Part II

Robotic Mapping, Navigation and Planning

Novel Robotic Systems and Applications

Healthcare and Assistive Robotics

An Augmented Reality Environment to Provide Visual Feedback to Amputees During sEMG Data Acquisitions

Francesca Palermo[1,2(✉)], Matteo Cognolato[1,3], Ivan Eggel[1], Manfredo Atzori[1], and Henning Müller[1]

[1] University of Applied Sciences Western Switzerland (HES-SO), Sierre, Switzerland
[2] Queen Mary University of London, London, UK
f.palermo@qmul.ac.uk
[3] Swiss Federal Institute of Technology Zurich (ETH), Zurich, Switzerland

Abstract. Myoelectric hand prostheses have the potential to improve the quality of life of hand amputees. Still, the rejection rate of functional prostheses in the adult population is high. One of the causes is the long time for fitting the prosthesis and the lack of feedback during training. Moreover, prosthesis control is often unnatural and requires mental effort during the training. Virtual and augmented reality devices can help to improve these difficulties and reduce phantom limb pain. Amputees can start training the residual limb muscles with a weightless virtual hand earlier than possible with a real prosthesis. When activating the muscles related to a specific grasp, the subjects receive a visual feedback from the virtual hand. To the best of our knowledge, this work presents one of the first portable augmented reality environment for transradial amputees that combines two devices available on the market: the Microsoft HoloLens and the Thalmic labs Myo. In the augmented environment, rendered by the HoloLens, the user can control a virtual hand with surface electromyography. By using the virtual hand, the user can move objects in augmented reality and train to activate the right muscles for each movement through visual feedback. The environment presented represents a resource for rehabilitation and for scientists. It helps hand amputees to train using prosthetic hands right after the surgery. Scientists can use the environment to develop real time control experiments, without the logistical disadvantages related to dealing with a real prosthetic hand but with the advantages of a realistic visual feedback.

Keywords: Augmented reality · Rehabilitation · sEMG prosthesis

1 Introduction

It is estimated that 1.6 million persons were living without a limb in the United States in 2005 (about 41,000 with an upper limb loss) [25]. This number is expected to more than double by 2050 and to reach a total of 3.6 million people [25]. Amputees have to adapt to the absence of a body part and to deal with

© Springer Nature Switzerland AG 2019
K. Althoefer et al. (Eds.): TAROS 2019, LNAI 11650, pp. 3–14, 2019.
https://doi.org/10.1007/978-3-030-25332-5_1

numerous problems in order to perform daily activities. On the market, hand prostheses with many functions have recently become available. Such prostheses are usually controlled using surface electromyographic (sEMG) signals and specific control strategies. In scientific research (and in a few recent cases also in commercially available prostheses[1]), pattern recognition algorithms were applied to classify hand movements using sEMG data. On hand amputees, movement classification performance of over 90% can be obtained on very few movements (usually fewer than ten) [7,8,19].

Myoelectric hand prosthesis control systems are expected to improve the quality of life of amputees. However, the systems proposed on the market so far are not satisfying for the patients, as they lack intuitive and adaptive real time control. In most cases, the results proposed in scientific research were not translated to clinical practice, mainly due to a lack of robustness and repeatability [4,12,18], as well as differences between the performance of amputees related to clinical parameters [2] that are not often taken into account. In a survey led by Davidson [10] it was shown that of a total of 65 subjects only 28% were satisfied with their functional abilities when using a hand prosthesis. Biddiss and Chau [5] described a rejection rate for electric prostheses of 35% and 23% respectively in paediatric and adult populations. One of the main causes for abandoning sEMG prostheses is the insufficient feedback that users receive during the use of the prosthesis [19]. Furthermore, [21] and [22] concluded that the time that passed between amputation and prostheses fitting has a strong impact on accepting the prosthesis in adults. To address these challenges, Virtual and Augmented Reality (VR/AR) systems can be integrated during the training of hand prostheses use. Virtual reality consists of using an immersive headset (such as the PlayStation VR or Oculus Rift) sometimes combined with controllers. In *virtual reality*, the user is immersed into a fully virtual environment that is completely disconnected from the real world. In such an environment, the user can interact with objects, similarly to what happens in real environments, through the usage of the external controller. In *augmented reality* the real world is enriched with virtual elements, thanks to devices such as smart glasses (e.g. Microsoft HoloLens) or contact lenses (e.g. Emacula contact lenses). While hand prostheses are relatively heavy and can often not be used immediately after surgery, a virtual prosthesis is weightless and can be integrated directly after an amputation with very limited costs. In this way, the subject can train the muscles in the residual limb within the augmented/virtual environment in order to better interact with the future prosthesis. In 1994, Dupont et al. [11] developed a software to train children with upper limb amputation to use myoelectric control. The objective was to open and close the hand until it matched a target. As a result, all the subjects improved their myoelectric control capabilities. Soares et al. [23] developed a virtual myoelectric prosthesis controlled with an Artificial Neural Network (ANN). The outputs of the neural network were used to control the movements of a virtual prosthesis, replicating the movements of the real arm (extension, flexion, pronation and supination). In a related article

---

[1] For example http://www.coaptengineering.com/.

by Lamounier et al. [15] an augmented reality system was added to the previously cited system, showing to the patients a virtual arm in correspondence to the stump on an external screen. Takeuchi et al. [24] developed a virtual reality technology in which amputees could train in a virtual environment. The patients had to grasp a virtual object without breaking it. Thus, the subjects were also able to control the grasping force of the virtual hand. Moreover, the difficulty of the tasks was modified in accordance to the control success rate to better adapt the system to the capabilities of the subjects. Kuttuva et al. [14] developed the composite myokinetic interface-virtual reality (MKI-VR) system composed of a pressure sensor array mounted on an arm sleeve, a trained filter and a virtual hand. Preliminary tests showed that upper-limb amputees were able to grasp and release virtual objects. More recently, augmented reality environments have been developed to give more realistic visual feedback to the subject. Anderson et al. [1] created the Augmented Reality Myoelectric (ARM) Trainer, an augmented reality-based system that provides a natural and engaging interface to train for myoelectric prostheses control. Augmented reality environments have also been used as alternative to the mirror therapy to treat phantom limb pain. Ortiz-Catalan et al. [17] developed an augmented environment in which the virtual limb responds directly to myoelectric activity of the residual limb. During the trial, the sustained level of pain reported by the patient was gradually reduced to completely pain-free periods.

External devices can be used to better interact with augmented and virtual reality systems. The Myo Gesture Control (Thalmic Labs, Canada) is an affordable (approximately 199$) armband containing 8 sEMG sensors, 9 axis Inertial Measurement Units (IMU) and Bluetooth communication. The Myo was successfully tested for pattern recognition-based control systems to classify hand movements on healthy subjects, obtaining a performance comparable to expensive electrodes on the classification of 40 hand movements [20] and high classification accuracy on the classification of 9 movements [16]. One disadvantage of the Myo is however its low sampling frequency (200 Hz) but for the task of detecting the hand movement the influence of this low sampling frequency seems limited. Recently, the Myo was also used to classify hand movements performed by hand amputees, obtaining good results [9].

Following these projects, the goal of the work presented in this paper is to create a new augmented acquisition and training system for hand amputees integrating Microsoft HoloLens (Microsoft, USA) and the Myo armband. To the best of our knowledge, this is one of the first portable implementations of augmented reality to help amputees created using both Microsoft HoloLens and Myo Armband. This environment allows transradial amputees to train in myoelectric control and to receive real-time visual feedback of the performed movements. The flexibility of an augmented reality environment that allows to use virtual 3D holograms in the real environment can also be used to create more interactive and game-based acquisition setups and to simplify the investigation of neurocognitive parameters related to the amputation such as the phantom limb sensation.

2   Methods

2.1   Device Setup

This section presents the equipment used in this work, which includes the following:

- a Dell XPS 13 laptop: the personal computer used to receive the data from the Myo and send it to the HoloLens;
- the Thalmic Labs Myo Gesture Control armband: the wearable device used to recognize the hand movements;
- the Microsoft HoloLens: the augmented reality headset used to display the holographic hand and objects;
- a JETech Bluetooth Mini Keyboard: a bluetooth keyboard allowing the calibration of the Myo armband and the resetting of the virtual scene.

The Myo Gesture Control Armband, developed by *ThalmicLabs*[2] is composed of eight medical grade stainless steel EMG sensors, a nine-axis IMU containing a three-axis gyroscope, a three-axis accelerometer and a three-axis magnetometer. The device is connected to the laptop through Bluetooth. The Myo can recognize 5 predefined hand movements (6 including the rest position): fist, spread finger, wave in, wave out and double tap. The holographic hand is displayed in the Microsoft HoloLens[3]. Microsoft's custom-designed Holographic Processing Unit (HPU) is a TSMC (Taiwan Semiconductor Manufacturing Company)-fabricated 28 nm coprocessor with 24 Tensilica DSP (Digital Signal Processing) cores. The HoloLens has an inertial measurement unit (IMU) (that includes an accelerometer, gyroscope, and a magnetometer), it is also able to recognize voice and gesture commands. The software was developed using the Unity 3D platform[4] that is used for building 2D and 3D games and deploying them on various devices (mobile, VR/AR, consoles, etc.).

2.2   Myo Software

The Myo software aims at continuously receiving the data stream from the Myo and modifying the appearance of the virtual hand accordingly. The Myo armband is provided with a calibration tool and a real-time hand gesture recognition algorithm. The manufacturer does not provide information regarding the classifier and the used time window length. The Myo algorithms and software directly provide the estimated hand pose. The first step was to create a channel to transfer Myo data to the HoloLens. The Myo offers an SDK (Software Development Kit) that allows to easily extract data from the Myo, such as the pose or the quaternions for the rotation. However, the Myo SDK does not support the Universal Windows Platform (UWP) used by the HoloLens. Thus, it

---

[2] https://www.myo.com/.
[3] https://www.microsoft.com/en-us/hololens/.
[4] https://unity3d.com/.

was not possible to send the Myo data to the HoloLens without an appropriate connection between the two devices.

Since the application presented in this paper is designed to work in real-time, the User Datagram Protocol (UDP) was chosen to transmit Myo data to the HoloLens. UDP is suitable for real-time experiments in which a limited delay on data transmission is fundamental, even though it does not guarantee packet delivery and packet duplicate protection. The communication between the Myo and the HoloLens is performed with a custom made script written in C++. It runs on the acquisition laptop to which the Myo is connected via Bluetooth. The script manages the UDP communication using the Windows Socket API. It acquires the Myo hand pose and forearm orientation at 100 Hz using the Myo SDK and it sends the data through the UDP socket to the HoloLens. An assessment of the latency of sending each package from the UDP server and receiving it to the UDP client on the HoloLens was estimated analysing the experimental data and it was found to be 200 ms.

2.3   HoloLens Software

The HoloLens software was developed using Unity3D and Visual Studio 2015 and the scripts were coded in C#. A script implementing an asynchronous UDP communication was adapted from the *hololens-littlebits* github repository[5] and included in the Unity application running on the HoloLens. The Myo sends all the relevant data to the computer and the laptop transmits them to the HoloLens through the UDP connection. The creation of the UDP client is included in the *Main.cs* script that is attached to the *Arm Holder* object in the Unity3D space, which contains the rigged model of a hand. The hand model used in this work is openly available on the bitbucket repository[6]. The *Main.cs* sends the classified grasp to the script *MyoPoseCheck.cs*, while the angles of the rotation are delivered to the *ArmRotation.cs* script. The *Arm Holder* is encapsulated in a primitive capsule GameObject called *Player*. This game object is a Controller type that allows the arm to be moved through the angle obtained from the quaternion provided by the IMU of the Myo and to control the collisions and the object grasping. The Myo armband returns the orientation of the device in quaternion, from which the roll, pitch and yaw angles of the hand are calculated. It is possible to accurately detect the change in orientation of the device, which allows to understand how the user moves his/her forearm. The Bluetooth keyboard is used to calibrate the Myo orientation and to reset the virtual scene at any time by simply pressing the specific keyboard button. The calibration of the orientation returned by the Myo is fundamental to achieve an accurate and reliable orientation control of the virtual hand. The possibility to reset the virtual scene is provided to quickly restart the training trial either after the completion of the task or when some virtual objects are moved too far from the hand. In Fig. 1, a simplified version of the framework used in this project is shown.

---

[5] https://github.com/rondagdag/hololens-littlebits/.
[6] https://bitbucket.org/AngryBurritoCoder/.

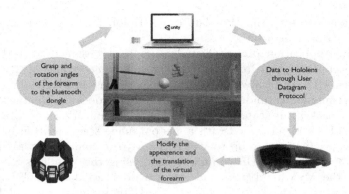

Fig. 1. Overview of the project framework. The Myo sends the classified grasp and the rotation angles to the computer that transmits them to the Microsoft HoloLens through a UDP protocol. The latter displays and modifies the appearance of the virtual hand allowing it to interact with augmented reality objects.

2.4 Virtual Hand Control

The system was designed to give a visual feedback to subjects with transradial amputation for training and data acquisitions purpose. The Myo and HoloLens work in parallel towards this goal. The subjects are asked to wear the Myo and the HoloLens. A calibration of the Myo is performed on the user. Then, the augmented environment starts on the HoloLens, while on the computer the script providing the communication between the Myo and the HoloLens is running. At this point, the HoloLens sets the subject in an augmented reality environment, which renders a table, a set of objects and a hand. The set of objects includes, from right to left: a bottle, a screwdriver, a tennis ball, a pen and a can. The rotation of the real arm can be calibrated with the rotation of the augmented arm by pressing the "K" button on the Bluetooth keyboard, allowing the subject to control the virtual hand with the real forearm. Each predefined gesture classified by the Myo was associated to a grasp chosen among the most important grasps for the activities of daily living (ADL) [6,13]:

- Fist → Power sphere;
- Wave In → Index finger extension;
- Wave Out → Tripod grasp;
- Spread Fingers → Large diameter;
- Rest → Rest.

Figure 2 represents the grasps that can be performed by the virtual hand. The gesture "Double Tap" was not included in this experiment, since it was shown that this hand gesture is not easily recognized in hand amputees [9], likely because it purely based on sEMG data.

Each grasp was associated with a specific object, as described in the following list:

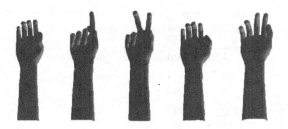

Fig. 2. The set of movements that are performed by the virtual hand. From left to right: power sphere, index finger extension, tripod, large diameter, rest.

- Tennis ball → Power sphere;
- Pen, Screwdriver → Index finger extension;
- Can → Tripod grasp;
- Bottle → Large diameter;

The rotation of the hand is performed acquiring the angles from the quaternion provided by the Inertial Measurement Unit (IMU) of the Myo armband, which allows the user to find a proper position to grasp the desired object. In this augmented reality environment the subjects can visualize the movements they are performing and they can easily train to activate the required muscles to perform each grasp. Whenever the subject feels the need to reset the scene (for instance when an object falls from the table), he/she can press the button "R". Figure 3 shows the holograms in the augmented reality environment.

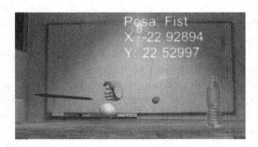

Fig. 3. View of the virtual hand in the augmented set in the real world.

3   Evaluation of the Augmented Reality Environment

The main goal of the framework presented in this paper is to give visual feedback to hand amputees during myoelectric control training. The system was tested on five intact subjects (5 males, average age 30.2 ± 2.94 years old), in order to have a

Table 1. Description of the participants in the Augmented Reality acquisitions. The weight is expressed in kilograms. The length is expressed in centimetres.

Subject	Gender	Age	Height (cm)	Weight (kg)
1	M	35	184	95
2	M	29	185	90
3	M	31	170	60
4	M	28	187	82
5	M	28	180	70

qualitative evaluation of the augmented reality myoelectric control environment and a proof of concept. The details of the 5 subjects are shown in Table 1.

It was previously shown that intact subjects can be used as a proxy measure for amputees in hand movement classification tasks [3], despite the fact that overall results are higher for non-amputees compared to what amputees can reach. Each subject was asked to pick up each object with the virtual hand using a specific grasp starting from the right to the left. At the end of each successfully performed grasp, the system was restarted. The sequence was repeated ten times. Among the set of subjects, Subject 1 and Subject 2 had previously tested the system and had more knowledge on how to perform the tasks. Subject 3 and Subject 4 completed one previous acquisition of three repetitions before the current acquisitions. Finally, Subject 5 completed one trial run before starting the acquisitions to get used to the system. Table 2 presents the average time required to grasp the respective object. The subjects were divided into two categories: experienced subjects (subject 1 and 2) and non-experienced subjects (the remaining ones). It is possible to notice that the time required to grasp an object for the experienced group is, in most of the cases, constant. While in the non-experienced group, the time tends to decrease through the usage of the system. The most difficult object to grasp is the can. This may be related to the fact that this object is positioned below the virtual hand and a double rotation of the arm (horizontal and vertical) is required to grasp it correctly. Nevertheless, with experience the time required to pick it up decreases. Figure 4 shows the total time required to finish one repetition of the acquisition. Each line represents a subject. Raw data are used to better show the learning curve of each subject. A statistical test was performed on the results to check their statistical significance. The non-parametric Friedman test that tests for differences between groups, returned a p-value < 0.001, which indicates that the number of repetitions influences the time required to grasp an object. The results suggest that the augmented reality environment is operational and that the control of virtual hand improves well through training of the users.

Table 2. The table shows the required time to grasp an object in the augmented reality environment. The subjects were divided into experienced and without experience. The second column of the table corresponds to the virtual objects with the respective hand pose. The third one indicates the number of the repetition. A total of ten repetitions were performed on each object. The last column illustrates the required time to grab the object with the respective hand pose activated through the sEMG data of the Myo armband.

Subject	Object	Repetition	Time Required	Subject	Object	Repetition	Time Required
Experienced (Subject 1 Subject 2)	Bottle - Large Diameter	1	0:04	No Experience (Subject 3 Subject 4 Subject 5)	Bottle - Large Diameter	1	0:18
		2	0:07			2	0:05
		3	0:04			3	0:05
		4	0:07			4	0:08
		5	0:04			5	0:04
		6	0:03			6	0:06
		7	0:03			7	0:04
		8	0:04			8	0:02
		9	0:04			9	0:08
		10	0:03			10	0:04
	Screwdriver - Index Finger Extension	1	0:04		Screwdriver - Index Finger Extension	1	0:07
		2	0:01			2	0:03
		3	0:01			3	0:04
		4	0:01			4	0:04
		5	0:01			5	0:07
		6	0:01			6	0:02
		7	0:01			7	0:02
		8	0:01			8	0:02
		9	0:01			9	0:02
		10	0:01			10	0:02
	Ball - Power Sphere	1	0:12		Ball - Power Sphere	1	0:13
		2	0:03			2	0:14
		3	0:04			3	0:07
		4	0:03			4	0:11
		5	0:03			5	0:07
		6	0:02			6	0:07
		7	0:03			7	0:03
		8	0:03			8	0:06
		9	0:03			9	0:05
		10	0:03			10	0:06
	Pen - Index Finger Extension	1	0:02		Pen - Index Finger Extension	1	0:05
		2	0:02			2	0:05
		3	0:03			3	0:04
		4	0:02			4	0:03
		5	0:01			5	0:02
		6	0:02			6	0:03
		7	0:02			7	0:02
		8	0:02			8	0:02
		9	0:01			9	0:02
		10	0:01			10	0:02
	Can - Tripod Grasp	1	0:11		Can - Tripod Grasp	1	0:15
		2	0:08			2	0:09
		3	0:04			3	0:17
		4	0:05			4	0:14
		5	0:04			5	0:09
		6	0:02			6	0:05
		7	0:03			7	0:07
		8	0:04			8	0:18
		9	0:06			9	0:07
		10	0:04			10	0:10

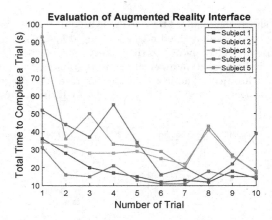

Fig. 4. Results of the Augmented Reality Environment. Each line represents one of the five subjects. The horizontal axis represents the number of the trial performed. On the vertical axis the total time required to complete the corresponding trial is shown. (Color figure online)

4   Conclusions

This work presents an augmented reality environment to provide visual feedback of sEMG activity to amputees when training for using an sEMG hand prosthesis. The environment was developed to allow myoelectric training for prostheses control and research, and to allow sEMG data acquisitions of upper limb amputees. We expect visual feedback to improve results in the training phase compared to an analysis where no feedback is given to the amputees. The environment integrates the immersive headset Microsoft HoloLens and the low-cost sEMG sensor Thalmic Labs Myo. The environment allows to receive real-time visual feedback of diverse hand movements controlled via sEMG. The system can help hand amputees to train using myoelectric prosthetic hands after surgery with visual feedback. It is also capable to help scientific researchers to perform experiments on sEMG and prostheses using an augmented reality environment, which can be easier than dealing with real physical hand prostheses that are very expensive, often heavy and less flexible, as they may need to be made to fit a subject. Grasping some of the objects was more difficult than others, due to differences in the classification performance of movements by the Myo and to the characteristics of the object collider included in the Unity platform. Increasing the size of the collider allowed to make grasping easier.

The software is now planned to be tested on hand amputees. Using amputees in prototype phases is often not considered ethical, as each test creates stress for them when trying to perform the movements, so only well tested setups can be used for experiments with amputees. The raw data of the Myo will also be analyzed with the usage of more complex real time classifiers. This has shown to lead to better results after a training phase and it can also help in the real-time control speed.

References

1. Anderson, F., Bischof, W.F.: Augmented reality improves myoelectric prosthesis training. Int. J. Disabil. Hum. Dev. **13**(3), 349–354 (2014)
2. Atzori, M., et al.: Clinical parameter effect on the capability to control myoelectric robotic prosthetic hands. J. Rehabil. Res. Dev. **53**(3), 345–358 (2016)
3. Atzori, M., Gijsberts, A., Müller, H., Caputo, B.: Classification of hand movements in amputated subjects by semg and accelerometers. In: 2014 36th Annual International Conference of the IEEE Engineering in Medicine and Biology Society (EMBC), pp. 3545–3549. IEEE (2014)
4. Atzori, M., Müller, H.: Control capabilities of myoelectric robotic prostheses by hand amputees: a scientific research and market overview. Front. Syst. Neurosci. **9**, 162 (2015)
5. Biddiss, E.A., Chau, T.T.: Upper limb prosthesis use and abandonment: a survey of the last 25 years. Prosthet. Orthot. Int. **31**(3), 236–257 (2007)
6. Bullock, I.M., Zheng, J.Z., De La Rosa, S., Guertler, C., Dollar, A.M.: Grasp frequency and usage in daily household and machine shop tasks. IEEE Trans. Haptics **6**(3), 296–308 (2013)
7. Castellini, C., Gruppioni, E., Davalli, A., Sandini, G.: Fine detection of grasp force and posture by amputees via surface electromyography. J. Physiol.-Paris **103**(3–5), 255–262 (2009)
8. Cipriani, C., et al.: Online myoelectric control of a dexterous hand prosthesis by transradial amputees. IEEE Trans. Neural Syst. Rehabil. Eng. **19**(3), 260–270 (2011)
9. Cognolato, M., et al.: Hand gesture classification in transradial amputees using the Myo armband classifier. In: 2018 7th IEEE International Conference on Biomedical Robotics and Biomechatronics (Biorob), pp. 156–161. IEEE (2018)
10. Davidson, J.: A survey of the satisfaction of upper limb amputees with their prostheses, their lifestyles, and their abilities. J. Hand Ther. **15**(1), 62–70 (2002)
11. Dupont, A.C., Morin, E.L.: A myoelectric control evaluation and trainer system. IEEE Trans. Rehabil. Eng. **2**(2), 100–107 (1994)
12. Farina, D., et al.: The extraction of neural information from the surface emg for the control of upper-limb prostheses: emerging avenues and challenges. IEEE Trans. Neural Syst. Rehabil. Eng. **22**(4), 797–809 (2014)
13. Jang, C.H., et al.: A survey on activities of daily living and occupations of upper extremity amputees. Ann. Rehabil. Med. **35**(6), 907–921 (2011)
14. Kuttuva, M., Burdea, G., Flint, J., Craelius, W.: Manipulation practice for upper-limb amputees using virtual reality. Presence: Teleoperators Virtual Environ. **14**(2), 175–182 (2005)
15. Lamounier, E., Lopes, K., Cardoso, A., Andrade, A., Soares, A.: On the use of virtual and augmented reality for upper limb prostheses training and simulation. In: 2010 Annual International Conference of the IEEE Engineering in Medicine and Biology Society (EMBC), pp. 2451–2454. IEEE (2010)
16. Mendez, I., et al.: Evaluation of the Myo armband for the classification of hand motions. In: 2017 International Conference on Rehabilitation Robotics (ICORR), pp. 1211–1214. IEEE (2017)
17. Ortiz-Catalan, M., et al.: Phantom motor execution facilitated by machine learning and augmented reality as treatment for phantom limb pain: a single group, clinical trial in patients with chronic intractable phantom limb pain. Lancet **388**(10062), 2885–2894 (2016)

18. Palermo, F., Cognolato, M., Gijsberts, A., Müller, H., Caputo, B., Atzori, M.: Repeatability of grasp recognition for robotic hand prosthesis control based on sEMG data, pp. 1154–1159 (2017)
19. Peerdeman, B., et al.: Myoelectric forearm prostheses: state of the art from a user-centered perspective. J. Rehabil. Res. Dev. 48(6), 719–738 (2011)
20. Pizzolato, S., Tagliapietra, L., Cognolato, M., Reggiani, M., Müller, H., Atzori, M.: Comparison of six electromyography acquisition setups on hand movement classification tasks. PloS one 12(10), e0186132 (2017)
21. Roeschlein, R., Domholdt, E.: Factors related to successful upper extremity prosthetic use. Prosthet. Orthot. Int. 13(1), 14–18 (1989)
22. Silcox, D.H., Rooks, M.D., Vogel, R.R., Fleming, L.L.: Myoelectric prostheses. a long-term follow-up and a study of the use of alternate prostheses. JBJS 75(12), 1781–1789 (1993)
23. Soares, A., Andrade, A., Lamounier, E., Carrijo, R.: The development of a virtual myoelectric prosthesis controlled by an emg pattern recognition system based on neural networks. J. Intell. Inf. Syst. 21(2), 127–141 (2003)
24. Takeuchi, T., Wada, T., Mukobaru, M., Doi, S.: A training system for myoelectric prosthetic hand in virtual environment. In: IEEE/ICME International Conference on Complex Medical Engineering, CME 2007, pp. 1351–1356. IEEE (2007)
25. Ziegler-Graham, K., MacKenzie, E.J., Ephraim, P.L., Travison, T.G., Brookmeyer, R.: Estimating the prevalence of limb loss in the united states: 2005 to 2050. Arch. Phys. Med. Rehabil. 89(3), 422–429 (2008)

LibRob: An Autonomous Assistive Librarian

Costanza Di Veroli, Cao An Le, Thibaud Lemaire, Eliot Makabu,
Abdullahi Nur, Vincent Ooi, Jee Yong Park, Federico Sanna,
Rodrigo Chacon(✉)🆔, and Yiannis Demiris🆔

Imperial College London, South Kensington, London SW7 2AZ, UK
{costanza.di-veroli15,caoan.le15,thibaud.lemaire18,eliot.makabu15,
abdullahi.nur15,vincent.ooi15,jee.park15,fs2215,r.chacon-quesada17,
y.demiris}@imperial.ac.uk

Abstract. This study explores how new robotic systems can help library
users efficiently locate the book they require. A survey conducted among
Imperial College students has shown an absence of a time-efficient and
organised method to find the books they are looking for in the college
library. The solution implemented, LibRob, is an automated assistive
robot that gives guidance to the users in finding the book they are searching for in an interactive manner to deliver a more satisfactory experience.
LibRob is able to process a search request either by speech or by text and
return a list of relevant books by author, subject or title. Once the user
selects the book of interest, LibRob guides them to the shelf containing
the book, then returns to its base station on completion. Experimental
results demonstrate that the robot reduces the time necessary to find a
book by 47.4%, and left 80% of the users satisfied with their experience,
proving that human-robot interactions can greatly improve the efficiency
of basic activities within a library environment.

Keywords: Robot · Library · Human-robot interaction

1 Introduction

University libraries contain a wide
range of written materials readily
available for their users, however
finding physical copies of these materials is not always easy. An obstacle that several library users face
is the process of locating a specific book title within extensive book
collections in a library. In university libraries for example, this process typically requires the user to
manually type the book title on a
computer using the library's search
engine, which returns the library
floor where the book is located and
the book's identification number.
The user is then expected to go find

Fig. 1. LibRob: An autonomous assistive
librarian.

© Springer Nature Switzerland AG 2019
K. Althoefer et al. (Eds.): TAROS 2019, LNAI 11650, pp. 15–26, 2019.
https://doi.org/10.1007/978-3-030-25332-5_2

the shelf that contains the book by themselves. We recently conducted a survey in which students at Imperial College London were asked about how much time they typically spend searching for a book. The results showed that 82% of students spent more than 5 min searching for a book, suggesting that the process by which books are located can be improved in order to give library-users easier access to the available resources.

In this paper we propose the use of an autonomous robot to guide the user directly to the book's location in order to increase library-user's satisfaction while reducing the time needed to locate a book inside the library. We called our solution LIBROB, a robot that receives a book title from the user, searches in the library's database for the relevant books and autonomously guides the user directly to the correct shelf. We implemented an intuitive multi-language enabled graphical user interface (GUI) that is able to communicate with the user through visual feedback and speech synthesis for a better interaction with their users. Furthermore, the user can choose from two available options to input the book title: by text or speech. We tested our platform through experiments conducted in an actual library and involving 40 participants asked to find an specific book. An image showing LIBROB's final design is shown in Fig. 1.

2   Related Work

Robots have already found their application in public libraries, and some significant advances have already been made. One of the most advanced examples is AuRoSS a robotic system capable of navigating a library, scanning the books on the shelves, analysing the result of the scanning process and generating a report based on the latest library database [1]. The scanning and the identification processes are both based on Radio Frequency Identification (RFID) technology. Even though many of the principles are relevant to our project (navigation, book identification, interaction and connection with the database), the aim and human interaction differ fundamentally. AuRoSS's objective is to find misplaced books and send a report to the librarian, without any interaction with the actual users of the library. On the other hand, our study is focused on improving user experience through interactions with the user. Furthermore, AuRoSS is incapable of using the stairs or the elevator, which is an important development aspect for LIBROB as it is being designed to operate in a five-level library.

Another relevant development in this field is the Comprehensive Access to Printed Materials (CAPM) [2]. This is an autonomous mobile robotic library system developed to retrieve items from bookshelves and carry them to scanning stations located in the off-site shelving facility. Again there are similarities that can be used for this project but also crucial differences. The CAPM project does not directly interact with the user and operates in a off-site facility, while LIBROB aims to interact directly with the user and will operate in the actual library. Similar attempts for robotic applications in library environments have also been made in other universities. At Aberystwyth University, a group of students designed Hugh, a robot reported to help library-users find books in the

library by physically taking the user to any book's location while interacting
with speech [3]. Just as Aurora, Hugh also uses RFID to recognise books; but in
contrast it aims at interacting fluently with the users, helping them locate the
books in the library, similarly to what we are trying to achieve [4,5]. At University
of Birmingham, a robot, Bob, has been assigned with the task of monitoring
library spaces, while two robots, Vincent and Nancy were deployed in a public
library in Westport, Connecticut, which were designed to teach computer
programming skills to library users [3].

3   System Description

3.1   Hardware Design

An illustration of LibRob and it's hardware components is shown in Fig. 2.
We selected a PeopleBot mobile robot [6] to be LibRob's base due to its body
dimensions which allow it to move around freely through narrow space between
shelves in libraries. In order to interconnect the electronic devices used to operate
the robot, a wireless router was installed onto the moving base. This router
connects to the library's wireless network and gives LibRob internet and local
network access to allow all the system devices to communicate using ROS [7]. A
tablet sits on top of the robot and plays the role of GUI as well as representing
LibRob's head. A Raspberry Pi 3b + works as motor control unit. In addition,
this unit runs all ROS nodes but the Navigation node, which runs on a remote
laptop due to the relatively low memory performance of the Raspberry Pi. One
SICK LMS200 rangefinder is used as Lidar sensor to scan the robot's surroundings.
Finally, a microphone coupled with an external sound card is used as audio
recording device to help with the speech processing task.

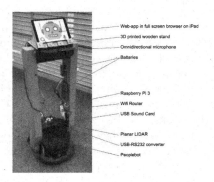

Fig. 2. LibRob's hardware components.

3.2   Software Components

The high-level design of LIBROB's software system is depicted in Fig. 3. The whole system operates around a central ROS node called **Behaviour**. All other nodes in the system primarily communicate with this node, which is in charge of taking the major decisions in the process.

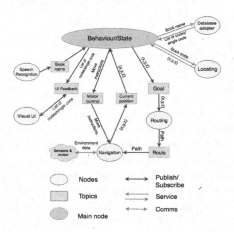

Fig. 3. Software framework diagram.

User Interface. The GUI was implemented as a web application, motivated by the idea of having a cross-platform application that would run on many different devices. The fundamental purpose of the Visual UI node is to make LIBROB more user-friendly, and allow the user to interact with the robot more intuitively.

In a typical interaction between LIBROB and a user, first the user approaches to LIBROB and selects one of the two available options to input a book title (see Fig. 4a): the user can either press the microphone icon and ask for a book by talking to the robot, or press the search icon to type in the book title. A drop-down menu is also available at the bottom of the page to allow for different language options. Indeed, LIBROB is able to communicate in different languages (LIBROB currently support English, French, and Italian). Once LIBROB receives the book title, a list of the books returned by the database is displayed as shown in Fig. 4b. Relevant information about the title, author, floor number, availability and identification code of each book is also provided. The user is able to scroll through the list, find and select the desired book by pressing on the icon next to it (see Fig. 4c). After pressing this icon, LIBROB will start moving towards the destination shelf where the book is located. At this point, LIBROB provides an audio-visual message saying *"let's go!"* to tell the user to follow him. Once LIBROB reaches the book's location, it will announce to the user *"We have arrived at your shelf !"* (see Fig. 4d) and the operation is terminated.

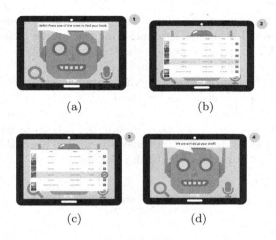

(a)   (b)

(c)   (d)

Fig. 4. LibRob's Graphical user interface.

These specific messages are used for a standard scenario with no issues. However, other types of messages have also been designed to handle different situations, such as when the robot has not found a book, or when the user is trying to interact with it while it is moving. Furthermore, all these messages are available in all supported languages.

Speech Processing Node. With the aim of ensuring the smoothest human-centered interaction, much effort was allocated to the **Speech node**. In order to allow LibRob to communicate with humans naturally, we made use of a combination of three technologies within the field of Speech Processing, namely real-time speech recognition, language translation, and natural language processing. The **Speech node**'s initial goals is to make the speech-to-text conversion of what the user says through speech recognition, and to publish the book request on a ROS topic that would be fed to the **Database Adapter node**. This task was made robust by ensuring it would operate well even in noisy environments and in environments where noise levels may vary. Furthermore, to allow for a more natural communication between LibRob and their users, we added a natural language processing layer to the design, with the use of the *Snips NLU* package. This package is based on a machine learning model trained with many examples of how humans could ask for a book orally [8]. The objective of this layer is to extract semantic information on the presence of a book title or an author's name in the transcribed string, in which case the relevant information is sent as a request. Following the implementation of this natural language processing layer, LibRob was able to understand sentences such as: *"Could you help me find a book on Organic Chemistry written by Alan Turner please?"* or *"I really need a book to study for my Digital Signal Processing exam tomorrow!"*.

Moreover, we decided to add real-time language translation to the **Speech node** to allow users to talk to LibRob in their native language. Thus, depending on whether or not the user requests for a book in English, a language translation to English is performed in the background using the speech translation package from the Python Package Index [9] and the translated string is fed to the natural language processing layer. The same English-trained model is used for any language as it only has to operate with the output of the translation layer. A full work flow of the speech node can be found in Fig. 5. In addition, the **Speech node** is also designed to handle the case where the user has to take the lift to get to the right floor. In this scenario, a background listener is triggered as soon as LIBROB enters the lift to listen continuously until it hears the floor number corresponding to the floor where the book is located.

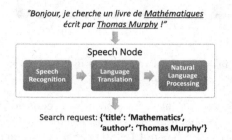

Fig. 5. Work flow of the Speech node. The example input is a French sentence translated as: "Hello, I am looking for a Mathematics book written by Thomas Murphy!"

Database Adapter Node. Determining exactly which book the user is looking for, based on the limited amount of information input during the search process, is crucial to the correct operation of LIBROB. The logical solution to achieve this is to connect the robot with a database where all the relevant information of every book in the library is stored. Due to the large amount of books generally available in a library, storing such a database locally on LIBROB is impractical as it would require a tremendous amount of memory space. The method that is currently used in LIBROB is to run an HTTP request script to the library's database Application Programming Interface (API) which will only return information based on the search performed by the user.

The **Database Adapter node** script can perform the search with title information, author information or both. By adding arguments to the search, it is possible to perform a more specific search. The most important argument added is to limit the search to printed books so that it excludes any journals, articles or e-books. Furthermore, additions or subtractions to the library are recorded and the availability of books is tracked by the library and visible on the API's response. This information can therefore be exploited by LIBROB to enhance the system. The data returned by the search request is then filtered in order to extract the book's title, author, code, floor, availability and thumbnail.

This information is then made available to other LibRob's nodes as required. Figure 6 is an example of one search response returned by the **Database Adapter node** when a search request is given to LibRob.

"title": "Harry Potter and the Order of the Phoenix",
"author": "J.K. Rowling",
"code": "800.ROW",
"floor": "1",
"availability": "True",
"thumbnail": "https://proxy-eu.hosted.exlibrisgroup.comex

Fig. 6. Example of one search response returned by the Database Adapter node for a search request with title key "Harry Potter".

Locator Node. The purpose of the Locator node is to provide the book's location inside the library given it's code. When an user selects a book (see Fig. 4c) the correspondent code obtained by the **Database Adapter node** is passed to the **Locator node**. The **Locator node** then searches through the list of shelves and responds with the book's coordinates that are used as a goal for the **Navigation node**. The relation between book-codes and their positions in the library is made using a file in which only the code of the first book in every shelf together with their corresponding location is stored. Just with this information, a range of all the books contained in an specific shelf can be obtained, giving LibRob all the information needed to take the user to the correct location.

Navigation Node. As the layout of the library does not change often, a map of the library is assumed to be available. We mapped all five floors of Imperial College's central library by constructing the map while driving the robot manually using the on-board Lidar [10]. Maps were manually corrected and normalised such that lifts overlap in different floor maps. An example of the maps used by LibRob is shown in Fig. 7. The robot is localised using ROS's navigation stack [11,12]. In addition, the navigation module also uses the ActionLib library [13] to notify the user that LibRob has reached the book shelf.

Behaviour Node. Figure 8a shows the design of the state machine implemented in the **Behaviour node** and that determines the actions to be taken by LibRob based on received inputs and measurable goals. During the *Idle* state LibRob is waiting for a user to initiate interaction and request a book title. In *Display list of Books* state the database request results are displayed to the user. *Navigate to Book* state uses the assigned shelf coordinates for the user-selected book as a navigation goal. Then, in *Indicate book* state LibRob notifies the user where the book is located. Finally, in the *Return to station* state LibRob uses the station coordinates to navigate back to its original location.

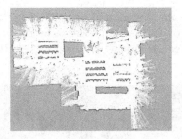

Fig. 7. Map of Imperial College Library's 4th Floor.

To implement the steps taken to navigate to a book on a different floor, the *Navigate to Book* state is separated into multiple sub-states as shown in Fig. 8b, and include the following: in *Move to Lift* state LIBROB navigates to the front of the lift doors. Then, in *Wait for Lift* state LIBROB waits for the indication that the lift doors have opened. In *Enter Lift* state LIBROB enters the lift and finally in *Move to book* state the requested shelf location becomes the new navigation goal.

Fig. 8. State machines of the Behaviour node. (a) Main state machine. (b) Navigation state machine.

4   Experimental Procedure and Evaluation

4.1   Experimental Setup

We conducted experiments at Imperial College's Central Library where 40 volunteers were asked to search for a given book. All participants were students from Imperial College London. Participants were divided in two groups: the control group and the LIBROB group. The control group only had access to the existing library's search system (described in Sect. 1) to search for a book, while the LIBROB group was only allowed to use LIBROB. We compared these two groups in terms of the average time needed to find a book. In addition, we retrieved students' satisfaction and preferred method (speech or text) of inter-action when using LIBROB, the successful against failed attempts of LIBROB to guide a user to requested book and the number of times the user required help to use LIBROB. Consent was obtained from the participants followed by a demographics questionnaire.

To start, participants were asked to find a particular book within the fourth floor of the library. Participants from the control group were given with a lap-top and the library's search system ready to use at the same start position that the robot was placed for participants of the LIBROB group. No training sessions or further instructions were given. Then, participants filled a final ques-tionnaire. Participants from the control group were asked if they would like to see improvements on the current library's search system. Participants from the LIBROB group were presented with four questions regarding (1) perceived use-fulness and (2) how satisfied were they with the robot, (3) how likely they were to use LIBROB again and (4) how intuitive it was for them to use it. All these questions were rated using a scale from 1 to 5. Participants reporting not finding LIBROB useful were asked to further describe the reasons why.

Statistical analysis is performed using two group comparison test (i.e. T-Test). Normally distributed values are represented as means and standard deviations.

Table 1. Demographics of the participants from the experiment ($N = 40$).

Factor	n	%
Gender		
Female	11	27.5
Male	29	72.5
Age (years)		
18–24	37	92.5
25–34	3	7.5
Group		
LibRob	20	50
Control	20	50

4.2 Results

The demographics of the participants are shown in Table 1. Every participant successfully found the book they were asked to find. However, the LIBROB group spent 47.4% less time in doing so, resulting in a reduction of almost half the time as shown in Fig. 9. The average time for the LIBROB group was 91.9 s (SD = 24 s), while for the control group was 174.9 s (SD = 40 s). A T-Test showed that there was a significant difference in the time to find a book (p < 8.191e−09) between both groups. Furthermore, it should be noted that LIBROB also reduces the variance of the search time. This is an expected result as once the user inputs their query, the robot guides them to the right shelf, and the variance in time is only introduced when users need to locate the book within the shelf. Such results confirm that LIBROB helps users to find books faster.

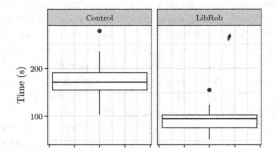

Fig. 9. Experiment results. Time to find a book for each group.

When control group participants were asked if they would like to see improvements on the current library's search system, 85% of participants in the control group stated that they would like to have a better system to find books in the library, suggesting a considerable need for a better solution to locate books in the library. The final questionnaire results for the LIBROB group are summarised in Fig. 10. The results allow us to conclude that LIBROB not only can reduce the time users spend searching a book in the library, but also that, even in cases where the time spent looking for a book was not significantly reduced, it still ensures a positive experience as evidenced by the high rates reported by participants: satisfaction - 80%, usefulness - 70%, willingness to use the robot again - 85% and intuitiveness - 90%. Only 10% of the participants were not immediately sure about how to operate LIBROB, further supporting how intuitive it is to use. Overall, the interactions between the users and LIBROB proved to optimise the book location time and provide a satisfactory experience for the library users.

When comparing the use of text-typing and speech-to-text, only 20% of users used text-typing to search for a book title, suggesting that speech-to-text is the preferred method of interaction with LIBROB. Only three participants reported not being satisfied with the robot. Two of them claimed that LIBROB was too slow or took too long. This was primarily due to the nature of the robot base itself as it has a maximum forward speed of 0.8 m/s, which could feel slow for some users if they are covering considerable distances. The third one was not satisfied with the precision of the indications received, he found that identifying the right shelf was not sufficient, and wanted LIBROB to point precisely at the book. Nevertheless, none of these participants found issues while interacting with the robot or reported LIBROB bringing them to the wrong shelf.

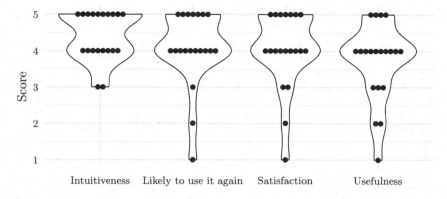

Fig. 10. Responses to the survey presented to the LıbRob group.

5   Conclusions and Future Work

The current version of LıbRob allows the users to be successfully guided towards the book they are looking for. Nevertheless, further improvements are still possible, some of which were already implemented as separate functions. A face recognition algorithm was developed to detect faces of the users through the tablet' s webcam to track their face position and allow LıbRob's eyes to follow them. This functionality has the potential to capture the users' attention and make them feel even more engaged when interacting with LıbRob. Another feature that was not tested in this first prototype is the use of elevators. However, in its current version LıbRob is able to understand when it has arrived to the correct floor as well as entering the elevator and updating the floor map once reaching a new floor. The reason why it was not evaluated in our experiment is due to the lack of an internet connection in the elevator, which is fundamental for the speech recognition package to operate. Pocketsphinx, an offline speech recognition package, was also tested, however the accuracy of the speech recognition was considerably degraded. Finally, some participants suggested the inclusion of a tool to point to the queried book in order to further reduce the time spent looking for it once the shelf has been reached. In order to do so, a method to recognise the book codes on the shelf together with an orientation-controlled laser, the robot could be able to point at the right book.

In conclusion, LıbRob has been successfully implemented and tested. With the results obtained, we confirmed that the time taken for students to locate a book was significantly reduced when they were using LıbRob. Furthermore, the users were overall more satisfied with their experience. In addition, the feedback obtained indicates that many users were happy with the GUI, found it intuitive and felt it enhanced their experience with the library system. While test participants were all Imperial College students and not representative of the general public, we have hopefully demonstrated sufficient evidence that our approach is an efficient solution for this type of application.

References

1. Li, R., Huang, Z., Kurniawan, E., Ho, C.K.: AuRoSS: an autonomous robotic shelf scanning system. In: 2015 IEEE/RSJ International Conference on Intelligent Robots and Systems (IROS), pp. 6100–6105. IEEE (2015)
2. Suthakorn, J., Lee, S., Zhou, Y., Thomas, R., Choudhury, S., Chirikjian, G.S.: A robotic library system for an off-site shelving facility. In: 2002 Proceedings of IEEE International Conference on Robotics and Automation, ICRA 2002, vol. 4, pp. 3589–3594. IEEE (2002)
3. Phillips, D.: Robots in the Library: gauging attitudes towards developments in robotics and AI, and the potential implications for library services. Dissertation C (2017)
4. Meet Hugh, the robot librarian. https://www.aber.ac.uk/en/news/archive/2016/02/title-181095-en.html. Accessed 27 Oct 2018
5. Robot librarian designed by Aberystwyth University students. https://www.times highereducation.com/news/robot-librarian-designed-aberystwyth-university-students. Accessed 27 Oct 2018
6. Activmedia Robotics, L.L.C.: Pioneer 2/PeopleBot^{TM}. Operations Manual. http://www8.cs.umu.se/research/ifor/dl/Product%20info/ActiveMedia/Pioneer%202%20%20PeopleBot%20Operation%20Manual.pdf. Accessed 7 Feb 2019
7. Quigley, M., et al.: ROS: an open-source Robot Operating System. In: ICRA workshop on open source software, vol. 3, no. 3.2 (2009)
8. Coucke, A., et al.: Snips voice platform: an embedded spoken language understanding system for private-by-design voice interfaces. arXiv preprint arXiv:1805.10190, 25 May 2018
9. PyPI. https://pypi.org/project/translation/. Accessed 5 Dec 2018
10. Kohlbrecher, S., Von Stryk, O., Meyer, J., Klingauf, U.: A flexible and scalable slam system with full 3D motion estimation. In: 2011 IEEE International Symposium on Safety, Security, and Rescue Robotics (SSRR), pp. 155–160. IEEE (2011)
11. Navigation. http://wiki.ros.org/navigation. Accessed 8 Feb 2019
12. Zheng, K.: ROS navigation tuning guide. arXiv preprint arXiv:1706.09068. Accessed 27 Jun 2017
13. Actionlib. http://wiki.ros.org/actionlib. Accessed 8 Feb 2019

Robotic-Assisted Ultrasound for Fetal Imaging: Evolution from Single-Arm to Dual-Arm System

Shuangyi Wang[1]([✉]), James Housden[1], Yohan Noh[1],
Davinder Singh[2], Anisha Singh[2], Emily Skelton[3],
Jacqueline Matthew[3], Cornelius Tan[1], Junghwan Back[4],
Lukas Lindenroth[4], Alberto Gomez[1], Nicolas Toussaint[1],
Veronika Zimmer[1], Caroline Knight[5], Tara Fletcher[3], David Lloyd[6],
John Simpson[6], Dharmintra Pasupathy[5], Hongbin Liu[4],
Kaspar Althoefer[7], Joseph Hajnal[1], Reza Razavi[1], and Kawal Rhode[1]

[1] School of Biomedical Engineering & Imaging Sciences,
King's College London, London, UK
shuangyi.wang@kcl.ac.uk
[2] Xtronics Ltd., Gravesend, UK
[3] Women's Ultrasound Guy's and St Thomas' NHS Foundation Trust,
London, UK
[4] Department of Informatics, King's College London, London, UK
[5] Division of Women's Health, Fetal Medicine Unit, Guy's and St Thomas'
NHS Foundation Trust, Women's Health Academic Centre, King's Health
Partners, London, UK
[6] Fetal Cardiology, Evelina Children's Hospital, London, UK
[7] Faculty of Science and Engineering,
Queen Mary University of London, London, UK

Abstract. The development of robotic-assisted extracorporeal ultrasound systems has a long history and a number of projects have been proposed since the 1990s focusing on different technical aspects. These aim to resolve the deficiencies of on-site manual manipulation of hand-held ultrasound probes. This paper presents the recent ongoing developments of a series of bespoke robotic systems, including both single-arm and dual-arm versions, for a project known as intelligent Fetal Imaging and Diagnosis (iFIND). After a brief review of the development history of the extracorporeal ultrasound robotic system used for fetal and abdominal examinations, the specific aim of the iFIND robots, the design evolution, the implementation details of each version, and the initial clinical feedback of the iFIND robot series are presented. Based on the preliminary testing of these newly-proposed robots on 42 volunteers, the successful and reliable working of the mechatronic systems were validated. Analysis of a participant questionnaire indicates a comfortable scanning experience for the volunteers and a good acceptance rate to being scanned by the robots.

© Springer Nature Switzerland AG 2019
K. Althoefer et al. (Eds.): TAROS 2019, LNAI 11650, pp. 27–38, 2019.
https://doi.org/10.1007/978-3-030-25332-5_3

1   Introduction

An extracorporeal robotic ultrasound system refers to the configuration in which the robotic system is constructed to hold and manipulate hand-held ultrasound probes for external examinations. The research interests in motorizing ultrasound systems started in the late 1990s within the European Union, North America, and Japan [1]. This was motivated by the deficiencies of the on-site manual manipulation of hand-held probes, such as difficulties of maintaining accurate probe positioning for long periods of time using human hands [2] and the requirements for experienced sonographers to be on-site [3]. Many of these robotic systems were designed in the typical master-slave config-uration, whereby the master-side sonographer can be in a remote location to perform the examination and a slave-side robot driving the ultrasound probe mimics the movements of the remote sonographer. These systems were mainly designed for diagnostic purposes but a few of them were also aimed at guidance of interventional procedures or open surgeries.

The iFIND (intelligent Fetal Imaging and Diagnosis) project is a recent ongoing research project that relates to the use of robotic system to assist ultrasound exami-nation. Started in 2014, this project aims to improve the accuracy of routine 18–20 week screening in pregnancy by developing new computer-guided ultrasound tech-nologies that will allow screening of fetal abnormalities in an automated and uniform fashion. This was motivated by evidence that the diagnostic accuracy and sensitivity of ultrasound can be limited by technical restraints in the imaging. There is also strong evidence of major regional and hospital-specific variation in prenatal detection rates of major anomalies [4, 5]. Within the aim of the iFIND project, developing new ultra-sound robots, which have the potential to assist and standardize the ultrasound scan, has been set as one of the objectives.

Utilization of robotic systems for fetal and abdominal examinations is one of the biggest research directions in the area of ultrasound robotics as it could include scanning of many possible anatomies and it is also one of the most easily accessible ultrasound scanning areas. One of the early robotic ultrasound systems proposed by Vilchis et al. [6, 7] was a unique robot aiming for abdominal examinations, known as TER. In the design, motor-driven cables were supported on the examination table. These cables translated a circular platform, upon which a mounted robotic wrist gen-erated angular orientation. This early work has had significant influence on subsequent research, such as the work from Masuda et al. [8] a few years later which introduced a platform with jointed legs on a pair of rails. The leg joints along with the raising/lowering of the platform allowed 6-DOF positioning of an ultrasound probe to perform an abdominal scan.

Originally introduced by Gourdon et al. [9] and Arbeille et al. [10], a cage-like probe holder containing a robotic wrist was designed for abdominal examination. The configuration of this robot is unique as it does not include any translational axes, and was instead held in position manually at the region of scanning. The wrist incorporated three rotational axes with a unique remote-centre-of-motion mechanism, allowing a remote ultrasound expert to orient the probe locally. Supported by the European Space Agency (ESA), the projects TERESA [11] and ESTELE [12] have largely tested the proposed robot on transabdominal obstetrical and abdominal examinations for remote diagnosis. The OTELO project, developed by multiple partners within the European Union, utilized similar rotational mechanisms from the previous ESA-funded projects but added additional active translational axes to the design. The emphasis was on light weight and portability when used for general ultrasound examination [13, 14]. The research with this 6-DOF robot included a wide range of topics, such as teleoperation, kinematics, automatic control laws, and ergonomic control.

Studying the development history of extracorporeal ultrasound robots, we identified that there were very limited new bespoke systems proposed in recent years. During this time, new rapid prototyping techniques such as 3D printing have emerged, and these have significantly changed the methods of mechanical design and manufacture. We believe that the use of 3D printing techniques offers new opportunities to design specially-shaped robot structures, which might improve the clinical acceptance and the fundamental safety of an ultrasound robot. Moreover, with the rapidly growing field of image processing and machine learning techniques, some of the fundamental difficulties of processing and interpreting ultrasound images have been addressed, which potentially changes the design requirements of an ultrasound robot, e.g. automation rather than telemedicine. Therefore, we strongly feel that it is timely to introduce a new series of ultrasound robots for the iFIND project. With several versions of robots developed and tested, this paper briefly reports the design evolution and the preliminary clinical feedback of our proposed robots. Compared with most of the previous projects on extra-corporeal ultrasound robots, the robots designed for the iFIND project are a series of robots including single-arm versions manipulating one ultrasound probe and a dual-arm version manipulating two probes simultaneously to explore novel scanning approaches. Additionally, these proposed iFIND robots do not focus on telemedicine but aim to provide a powerful research tool to explore new way of ultrasound imaging.

2 Design Evolution and Implementation

2.1 iFIND Version 1 Robot

The iFIND-v1 robot has a simple Cartesian configuration developed as a proof-of-concept prototype. The robot has seven DOFs with three orthogonal translational axes for global positioning (J_1, J_2, and J_3), three orthogonal rotational axes for orientation adjustments (J_4, J_5, J_7), and an additional translation axis (J_6) at the distal end of the robot to control the accurate contact of the probe with the abdominal surface.

The probe holder mechanism has multiple specially shaped cavities which can include single-axis force sensors based on miniature reflective optoelectronic sensors for the measurement of vertical and side forces applied by the probe to the patient. A similar multiple-axis force sensor based on a simply-supported beam was documented in our previous research [15]. The diagram of the robot, with each joint and the main functional structures labelled, is shown in Fig. 1a along with the final implementation of the system shown in Fig. 1b. For safety management, the iFIND-v1 robot mainly relies on force control using the custom-made force sensor. With the kinematics solved, we implemented conventional robotic control methods and invited sonographers to try the system

30 S. Wang et al.

and collected feedback to guide further developments. It was generally believed that although the system provided several useful functions and can acquire ultrasound images, this industrial-looking robot working in a clinical environment with in-adequate safety features could not be clinically translated.

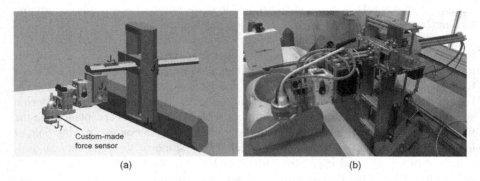

Fig. 1. iFIND-v1 robot: (a) schematic representation with each joint and main structures labelled and (b) final implementation of the robot shown with a fetal ultrasound phantom.

2.2 iFIND Version 2 Robot

Based on the lessons learned from the iFIND-v1 robot, we modified the design substantially by changing the shapes, configurations, mechanisms, and safety management methods of the robot, which led to the design of the iFIND-v2 robot (Fig. 2). The proposed system has a 5-DOF light-weight wrist unit [16] for holding and locally adjusting the probe (J_4, J_5, J_6, J_7, and J_8) and a 2-DOF two-bar arm-based set of parallel link mechanisms (J_2, J_3) with a 1-DOF rotational axis for global positioning (J_1). The specially designed new end-effector is lightweight and has a smaller footprint compared with the end-effector unit for the iFIND-v1 robot.

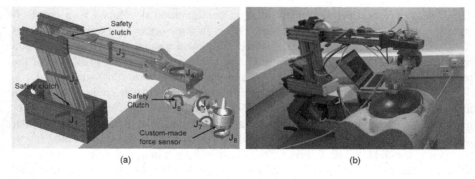

Fig. 2. iFIND-v2 robot: (a) schematic representation with each joint and main structures labelled and (b) final implementation of the robot shown with a fetal ultrasound phantom.

As a result of this design, the total weight of the end-effector unit is less than 2 kg and the length of the end-effector unit is about 25 cm. In terms of functionality of the joints in the new end-effector unit, J_4 can rotate the following structures 360° to allow the US probe to point towards different sides of the scanning area, such as the top, bottom, and sides of the abdomen. J_5 is used to tilt down the probe to align with the surface of the scanning area. The last three orthogonal revolute joints (J_6, J_7, and J_8) are used to control the tilting and axial rotation of the probe, allowing fine adjustments of the probe in a local area. In addition to employing a similar force sensor to that used in the iFIND-v1 robot, the mechanical safety of the iFIND-v2 robot was emphasized with clutch mechanisms incorporated into three joints to limit the allowable force applied to the patient. These would disengage the following links from the joint driven gears when the load exceeds a pre-set threshold [16]. Additionally, gas springs were implemented to lift the robot off the patient if the clutch at the back of the robot arm is triggered.

2.3 iFIND Version 3 Robot

The dual-probe system has been developed directly from our experience with the iFIND-v2 single-arm robot. Several design iterations have been considered with our robotics team, clinical team, and image analysis team working together to determine a suitable design. More consideration was given to the placement of the robot arms over the patient, and how this would affect clinical and patient acceptability, as well as the working space, safety and reliability of the robot. It was agreed that a side-mounted gantry system over the patient, with the two arms attached to the gantry coming in from the side, would be the design goal for the iFIND-v3 dual-probe robot. Based on our experience testing the iFIND-v2 single-arm robot, several changes were made to the mechanical design of some joints. These joints are now made from harder-wearing materials with improved mechanisms, and all safety-critical joints now include mechanical clutches to prevent excessive force being applied.

Some joints have been given a larger movement range, and in particular the final end-effector is able to tilt downwards to almost vertical while keeping the probe in

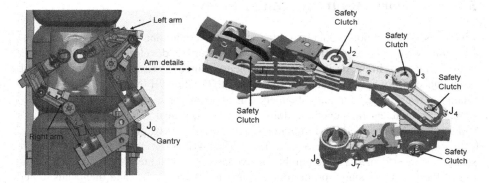

Fig. 3. iFIND-v3 robot: schematic representation with the general dual arm configuration shown (left) and the joint details for one arm shown (right).

contact with the abdomen. This was essential for allowing the flexibility to place the two probes close together and maneuver them through a continuous sweep without the arms colliding. As illustrated in Fig. 3, the final design has 17 DOFs with two arms holding and controlling two ultrasound probes. These include one translational DOF for the gantry (J_0), three rotational DOFs (J_1, J_2, and J_3) for each of the arms, and five rotational DOFs (J_4, J_5, J_6, J_7, and J_8) for each of the end wrist units. The redundant DOFs in the system were designed to allow the two ultrasound probes positioned and orientated flexibly while at the same time not colliding into each other. Compared with the iFIND-v2 robot, each joint was designed to have the capability for housing a homing sensor, which allows the robot to be easily reset to its starting position. This also ensures more consistent positioning accuracy, because the starting position will be known by the control software with greater precision. Additionally, the iFIND-v3 robot is implemented on a trolley system, allowing easy transportation of the device. The final implementation of the iFIND-v3 robot is shown in Fig. 4.

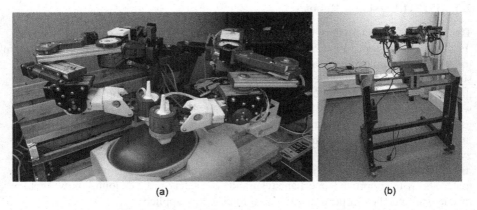

(a)   (b)

Fig. 4. Final implementation of the iFIND-v3 robot: (a) perspective showing the dual-arm configuration with a fetal phantom shown and (b) the trolley system for holding the arms.

3   Preliminary Healthy Volunteer Study

Live tests of the robots with the participation of sonographers, engineers, and most importantly volunteers greatly contributes to the further development of the systems while we are still in the design phase and able to change the configuration of the robot. After successfully and adequately testing the iFIND-v2 and iFIND-v3 robots on a fetal phantom, we applied for and obtained ethical approval to test our robots on non-pregnant volunteers for general abdominal scans. Approval was given by the King's College London local ethics committee (study title: Investigating Robotic Abdominal Ultrasound Imaging, Study reference: HR-17/18-5412). Through this study, we have successfully performed a large number of live tests. The volunteer tests started with the use of the iFIND-v2 single-probe robot, scanning 20 volunteers, and then transitioned to the iFIND-v3 multi-probe robot for testing more advanced features. So far, 22 volunteers have been scanned using the iFIND-v3 robot. The initial technical aim of the volunteer study was to test the reliability of the mechatronic system of the robots, verify the safety management methods, and experiment with potential control and image acquisition schemes. Moreover, the weekly-scheduled volunteer study intends to offer the sonographers and the engineers an opportunity to work as a team to build confidence in using the robot in a realistic scenario and overcome the psychological anxiety of the use of robotic technology in medicine. Most importantly, the volunteer study aimed to collect volunteer's feedback on the experience of being scanned by the robots, which is feedback to our design loop and influences the technical direction of the project.

Volunteer tests using the iFIND-v2 and iFIND-v3 robots are shown in Fig. 5. For the setup, the robotic system was located at the left side of the bed controlled and monitored by the engineer while the sonographer controlled the ultrasound machine on the right side of the bed. For the iFIND-v3 robot, some of the tests involved an imaging workstation to process and display images from both probes. The workstation was located at the head end of the bed where both the sonographers and engineers could observe the two images simultaneously.

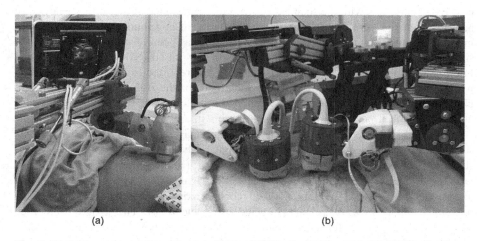

(a)   (b)

Fig. 5. Volunteer tests performed using (a) the iFIND-v2 robot and (b) the iFIND-v3 robot.

The most fundamental test for both robots required the sonographers to give verbal instructions to the engineers, who then controlled the robotic software and manipulated the probe accordingly to acquire standard views for a general abdominal scan. Targets included structures such as the aorta, liver, pancreas, and kidney. This was mainly to test the general reliability of the mechatronic system and focused on collecting volunteers' feedback. Moving forward, we utilized a Kinect scanner to acquire the abdominal surface of the volunteer and imported that into the robot software. Based on the kinematics, the ability of each robot to follow the acquired surface was tested. In this mode, the target positions of the probe were provided by the Kinect scan and the robots manipulated the probes to follow the abdominal surface. For the iFIND-v2 robot, control based on the force and proximity sensors was also tested in some of the sessions. These tests of the technical functionalities, assessed qualitatively, were mainly to verify the correct working of the robotic systems.

For feedback from the volunteers, a questionnaire was designed, and the volunteer was asked to complete and answer the questions using a scale of 0 to 4 after being scanned by the robot. For the given score, 0 represents strongly disagree, 1 represents disagree, 2 represents neutral, 3 represents agree and 4 represents strongly agree. The questions relating to the use of robots are:

- Q1: I felt relaxed about the scan;
- Q2: The scanning robot appeared to be like a typical piece of hospital equipment;
- Q3: I found the appearance of the scanning robot to be appealing;
- Q4: I felt no discomfort during the scan;
- Q5: I felt no pain during the scan;
- Q6: I felt safe during the scan;
- Q7: I enjoyed the scanning experience.

The summary of the results of the questionnaire for the iFIND-v2 and iFIND-v3 robots (20 and 22 participants respectively) are shown in Fig. 6. Most volunteers had positive experiences with the scan except with the appearance of the robots. They were neutral about the attractiveness and their similarity in appearance to hospital equipment. Comparing the two robots, a larger variation has been identified in terms of the similarity in appearance to hospital equipment for the iFIND-v3 dual-arm robot. Importantly, for both robots volunteers felt safe and reported little discomfort or pain while more consistent results have been identified for the iFIND-v3 dual-arm robot. However, there were outliers who did report discomfort, pain, and feeling unsafe for both robots and it could be useful to address this in any later designs.

For the iFIND-v2 robot only, we analysed the images obtainable, compared to the sonographer scanning manually. In each volunteer, the sonographer aimed to capture standard views of the aorta, including the following: pancreas transverse section (TS), left lobe of the liver TS, right lobe of the liver TS, right lobe of liver with right kidney, gallbladder longitudinal section, aorta at coeliac axis and aorta at mid abdominal position. Similar views were then targeted using the robot. The images were then scored by a sonographer for image quality as 'good', 'acceptable' and 'poor' according to the image quality component of the British Medical Ultrasound Society Peer Review Audit Tool 2014 v3 [17].

In total, 252 images were captured, 162 by sonographer and 90 by robot. Images from the first two volunteers were unlabelled and thus excluded from the analysis. The proportion of images with 'good' or 'acceptable' quality was 97.5% for sonographer and 81.1% for the robot, which is a statistically significant difference ($p < 0.001$). Of the images with 'good' or 'acceptable' quality scores, the sonographer achieved a 'good' image in 72.2% of images, while the robot achieved this in 42.5% of images – again a statistically significant difference ($p < 0.001$). When analysed by location, the robot was most often able to acquire the liver, pancreas and abdominal aorta images, which require a central or upper scanning area on the abdomen. It was often unable to acquire images of the gallbladder, kidneys, bladder and spleen, which require probe positions either on the side or caudal end of the abdomen.

■ Score value: 0 ■ Score value: 1 ■ Score value: 2 ■ Score value: 3 ■ Score value: 4

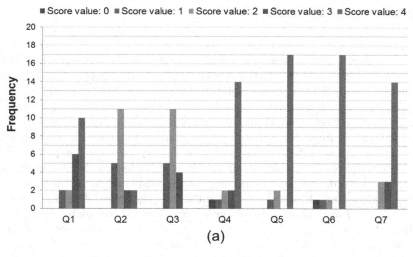

(a)

■ Score value: 0 ■ Score value: 1 ■ Score value: 2 ■ Score value: 3 ■ Score value: 4

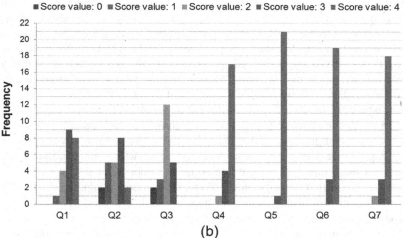

(b)

Fig. 6. Questionnaire results for the robotic ultrasound volunteer tests performed using (a) the iFIND-v2 robot (N = 20) and (b) the iFIND-v3 robot (N = 22).

Comparing only images of the liver, pancreas and abdominal aorta, which the robot was better able to capture, the sonographer achieved a 'good' or 'acceptable' quality in 96.6% of images, whereas the robot achieved this in 90.8% of images. This was not a statistically significant difference (p > 0.05), which suggests the robot is capable holding the probe in contact with the necessary pressure to acquire adequate ultrasound images. However, the sonographer achieved significantly more 'good' images than 'acceptable' compared to the robot (74.4% compared to 52.4% respectively). This may be because of the more difficult indirect control when using the robot, making it harder to achieve the optimum image.

4 Discussion and Conclusions

With the general aim of using robotic technology to assist fetal ultrasound screening, we have developed three versions of the iFIND robots starting with a proof-of-concept prototype, coming to a significantly improved design with a patient-friendly appearance, and eventually finishing at a novel dual-arm robot for simultaneously controlling two ultrasound probes. With much more flexibility to make specially-shaped links and custom joint mechanisms, the iFIND robots look different from many existing robotic arms. The feedback from clinicians and patients indicated that these bespoke links can have positive impacts on the acceptance of using the robot in medicine. In terms of the robot configurations, we encountered great difficulties in finding the best arrangement of the DOFs in the design process and then solving the closed-form kinematics of the resulting configuration. Especially for the iFIND-v3 robot, the collision avoidance of the two arms and the various required arrangements of the two probes have led to a complicated kinematic analysis, which will be presented more technically separately.

In this design evolution process, apart from the technical considerations, one important driving factor was the feedback from the clinicians and patients. We realized that sometimes this is easily left out in the design process where the engineering team builds a robot to its technical expectation but the robot does not meet the expectation of the clinicians and patients in other aspects. Therefore, the iFIND robots were designed in a way that involved the combined inputs from engineers, clinicians, and patients. A number of examples can be found in our designs which were motivated by the clinicians and patients. These include the design of the end-effector unit for the iFIND-v2 robot, where we produced a streamlined 2 kg small unit incorporating five DOFs within 25 cm to improve the patients' and clinicians' acceptance. Similarly, the selection of the configuration of the gantry for the iFIND-v3 robot was based on the patients' inputs that they do not want to be enclosed while being scanned. We can conclude that these inputs are of great importance to our robot design.

In terms of the functionality and testing of the robot, a significant step for this project was to perform healthy volunteer tests in the design process and collect feedback from the volunteers. We realized that the only way to build confidence in using the robots for both engineers and clinicians is to continuously perform live tests. Looking at the results from the questionnaire, it is unsurprised to find out that the robots' appearances still need to be improved cosmetically to be like a piece of hospital equipment, although this is not the primary focus of this project. More importantly, the rest of the questions about comfort of the robots and their psychological effect indicate a good acceptability to be scanned by our robots for ultrasound examination. This is an important proof of our design idea.

When comparing image quality to images acquired by a sonographer, the iFIND-v2 robot was able to achieve a similar proportion of good or acceptable quality images in areas of the abdomen that it could easily reach. The unobtainable images are a limitation of the robot's workspace, which was designed for pregnant patients rather than non-pregnant volunteers. Therefore, the ability to reliably obtain some of the abdominal views is encouraging for the robots' abilities to scan a fetus in a pregnant patient. Currently the image qualities obtained do not reach the highly optimized quality achieved manually by a sonographer. However, this could improve with the development of a more sophisticated user interface, or perhaps automated optimization of the images using image quality feedback. It should also be noticed that the image quality study reported in this paper is still in an early stage while more systematic analyses with improved functionalities of the robot will be followed up for both robots in the future. With the current stage of the robots, it is difficult to compare the performance of the iFIND robots with the existing other robots in terms of the image acquisition quality as very limited clinical evidences in the literature are available for fully-active ultrasound robots used for abdominal scan.

From the technical point of view, we identified that the use of a custom-made mechanical clutch, with ball-spring pairs as the connection method between driven mechanism and the next link structure, is extremely useful. It not only prevents the joint from generating excessive force as a safety control independent of electrical systems and software logic, but also allows the operators and the volunteers to manually rotate each joint and move the robotic arm to other places, which turned out to be very useful in the real clinical scenario.

Working towards the future, we have developed a quality management system to facilitate the documenting and clinical translation of the robots and the goal is to eventually use the iFIND robots on pregnant women as the project is progressing. Importantly combining with the newly-developed image processing methods within the iFIND project, we intend to explore new ways of robotic-assisted ultrasound examination, which includes using the iFIND-v3 dual-arm robots to perform a full sweep of the abdominal area and extract useful information afterwards, compound the two ultrasound images from the two probes in real time to improve the visualization, and automatically detect the region and standard planes of the fetus using advanced machine learning algorithms and feedback to the robot for automatic adjustments.

Acknowledgements. This work was supported by the Welcome Trust IEH Award [102431] and by the Wellcome/EPSRC Centre for Medical Engineering [WT203148/Z/16/Z]. The authors acknowledge financial support from the Department of Health via the National Institute for Health Research (NIHR) comprehensive Biomedical Research Centre award to Guy's & St Thomas' NHS Foundation Trust in partnership with King's College London and King's College Hospital NHS Foundation Trust.

References

1. Priester, A.M., Natarajan, S., Culjat, M.O.: Robotic ultrasound systems in medicine. IEEE Trans. Ultrason. Ferroelectr. Freq. Control **60**, 507–523 (2013)
2. Magnavita, N., Bevilacqua, L., Mirk, P., Fileni, A., Castellino, N.: Work-related musculoskeletal complaints in sonologists. J. Occup. Environ. Med. **41**, 981–988 (1999)
3. LaGrone, L.N., Sadasivam, V., Kushner, A.L., Groen, R.S.: A review of training opportunities for ultrasonography in low and middle income countries. Tropical Med. Int. Health **17**, 808–819 (2012)
4. Kilner, H., Wong, M., Walayat, M.: The antenatal detection rate of major congenital heart disease in Scotland. Scott. Med. J. **56**, 122–124 (2011)

5. Quartermain, M.D., et al.: Variation in prenatal diagnosis of congenital heart disease in infants. Pediatrics **136**, 3783 (2015)
6. Vilchis Gonzales, A., et al.: TER: a system for robotic tele-echography. In: Niessen, Wiro J., Viergever, Max A. (eds.) MICCAI 2001. LNCS, vol. 2208, pp. 326–334. Springer, Heidelberg (2001). https://doi.org/10.1007/3-540-45468-3_39
7. Vilchis, A., Troccaz, J., Cinquin, P., Masuda, K., Pellissier, F.: A new robot architecture for tele-echography. IEEE Trans. Robot. Autom. **19**, 922–926 (2003)
8. Masuda, K., Kimura, E., Tateishi, N., Ishihara, K.: Three dimensional motion mechanism of ultrasound probe and its application for tele-echography system. In: 2001 Proceedings of IEEE/RSJ International Conference on Intelligent Robots and Systems, pp. 1112–1116. IEEE (2001)
9. Gourdon, A., Poignet, P., Poisson, G., Vieyres, P., Marche, P.: A new robotic mechanism for medical application. In: 1999 Proceedings of IEEE/ASME International Conference on Advanced Intelligent Mechatronics, pp. 33–38. IEEE (1999)
10. Arbeille, P., Poisson, G., Vieyres, P., Ayoub, J., Porcher, M., Boulay, J.L.: Echographic examination in isolated sites controlled from an expert center using a 2-D echograph guided by a teleoperated robotic arm. Ultrasound Med. Biol. **29**, 993–1000 (2003)
11. Arbeille, P., Ruiz, J., Herve, P., Chevillot, M., Poisson, G., Perrotin, F.: Fetal tele-echography using a robotic arm and a satellite link. Ultrasound Obstet. Gynecol. **26**, 221–226 (2005)
12. Arbeille, P., Capri, A., Ayoub, J., Kieffer, V., Georgescu, M., Poisson, G.: Use of a robotic arm to perform remote abdominal telesonography. Am. J. Roentgenol. **188**, W317–W322 (2007)
13. Courreges, F., Vieyres, P., Istepanian, R.: Advances in robotic tele-echography services-the OTELO system. In: 2004 26th Annual International Conference of the IEEE Engineering in Medicine and Biology Society, IEMBS 2004, pp. 5371–5374. IEEE (2004)
14. Vieyres, P., Poisson, G., Courrèges, F., Smith-Guerin, N., Novales, C., Arbeille, P.: A tele-operated robotic system for mobile tele-echography: The OTELO project. In: Istepanian, R. S.H., Laxminarayan, S., Pattichis, C.S. (eds.) M-Health. Topics in Biomedical Engineering, pp. 461–473. Springer, Boston (2006)
15. Noh, Y., et al.: Multi-axis force/torque sensor based on simply-supported beam and optoelectronics. Sensors **16**, 1936 (2016)
16. Wang, S., et al.: Design and implementation of a bespoke robotic manipulator for extra-corporeal ultrasound. JoVE **143**, e58811 (2019)
17. https://www.bmus.org/static/uploads/resources/Peer_Review_Audit_Tool_wFYQwtA.pdf

Eduardo: A Low Cost Assistive Robot Development Platform, Featuring a Compliant End Effector

Oliver Smith[✉], Samuel White[✉], and Martin Stoelen

School of Computing, Electronics and Mathematics, University of Plymouth,
Plymouth, UK
{oliver.smith, samuel.white-5}@students.plymouth.ac.uk

Abstract. People with temporary or permanent disabilities often struggle to perform daily tasks, and this loss of agency can cause undue emotional distress. This paper presents "Eduardo" (Fig. 1); a low cost prototype of an assistive robot arm featuring a passive compliant element in the end effector of the arm, to simplify the control of the arm, and ensure the safety of the user during physical interaction. As a demonstration of the prototype, the arm was programmed to comb hair. The robot is envisioned as an open source platform for research into the use of compliance for assistive robots.

Keywords: Low cost · Open source platform ·
Active and passive compliance · Assistive robot arm ·
Robot for the physically impaired

1 Introduction

People with temporary or permanent disabilities often struggle to perform daily tasks that are taken for granted. Conditions [1] such as cerebral palsy, motor neurone disease, muscular dystrophy, introduce problems for even basic tasks like washing, feeding, or grooming. Often, this can cause embarrassment and/or emotional distress through removing one's agency in life.

In this paper we present Eduardo: A low cost, open source, assistive robot arm prototype, designed as a development platform for research into the use of compliance for assistive robots. We implement a passive complaint element (PCE) in the design of the end effector, as a means of ensuring user safety during human robot physical interaction. As an example of the robot's capability, we programmed the robot to comb a user's hair, to demonstrate the effectiveness of a compliant end effector, which conformed to the profile of the head in real-time, via the elastic deformation of the PCE. Furthermore, a simple control loop allowed the arm itself to respond to the force applied to the head by the end effector, ensuring that a comb is in contact with the head, but not applying so much force as to cause discomfort.

The assistive robot arm has been designed with the purpose of facilitating research into the use of compliancy for assistive robots. Using low cost off the shelf parts, and

K. Althoefer et al. (Eds.): TAROS 2019, LNAI 11650, pp. 39–48, 2019.
https://doi.org/10.1007/978-3-030-25332-5_4

3D printed components, the arm is viable as a rapid prototyping development platform, and as such, has been made open source.

Fig. 1. The Combing robot

2 Related Work

The idea of using robots to assist the disabled is not new. Feeding devices are already commercially available (e.g. Meal Buddy, My Spoon, The Obi, Meal-Mate) in an established market. Further assistive robots, such as Toyota's Human Support Robot [2] and HERB [3], the "Home Exploring Robot Butler" of the Personal Robotics lab at Carnegie Mellon University, are in development and nearing the point of consumer viability. Finally, Kinova – a robot arm firm, manufacture and sell the JACO assistive robot arm [4], designed to integrate with a wheelchair and assist people with limited or no upper limb mobility in daily tasks (Kinova also sells the previously mentioned Obi feeder). Through partnerships with universities and companies (e.g. Carengie Mellon's personal robotics lab [5], Clearpath robotics [6]), Kinova have established themselves as the leaders in the field of assistive robot arms. However, these robot arms follow the convention of being rigid in their design. As such, they require precise kinematic control in order to interact with any object in the real world.

The application of various methods for creating compliant robots is a fast-growing area of research, and one that potentially offers great improvements to robot arms. Variable stiffness actuators (VSAs) and adjustable compliant actuators are and are seeing potential applications in wearable robotics, prosthetics, walking robots. These actuators feature elastic elements, which can store and release energy, minimise large forces due to shocks, and safely interact with people, when employed to create soft-bodied robots [7].

Existing robot arms featuring compliance include the DLR hand/arm system [8], Anthrob – an anthropomimetic robot arm [9], and the Gummi Arm [10], although it should be noted that these are all research platforms. An exception to this is Baxter, a two-armed industrial robot with an animated face, which uses series elastic actuators in combination with sensors, software control, and soft padding on the exterior shell, to minimise the risk of injury upon collision [11]. As a result, it can share its workspace with humans, making it a collaborative robot. However, Baxter is designed for collaborative use in manufacturing, not as an assistive robot. Its uses compliancy only so far as to minimize impact forces, and cannot control the stiffness for different tasks, making it unsuitable for physical interaction with a human.

3 Design

3.1 Physical Robot Design

Several requirements were taken into consideration during the design of the robot. The robot arm allows for a large workspace, to make it easy for the user to position themselves, and reaches down from overhead, to minimize the risk of accidental collision. The arm is physically capable of reaching both the left and right sides of the head, as well as the front and back. Additionally, the end effector (Fig. 2) is designed to be easily interchangeable, so that other end effectors could be fitted for different purposes, other than combing. The compliant element within the end effector itself is also designed to be interchangeable. Autodesk Fusion 360 was used in the design of the robot. All parts were designed to be easily manufactured quickly and at low cost; through 3D printing and minimal labour.

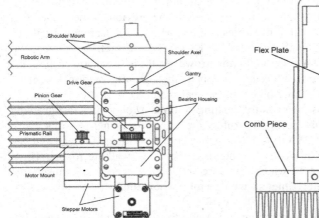

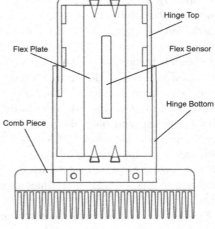

Fig. 2. Prismatic gantry and rail assembly   **Fig. 3.** Compliant end effector design

The parts created include; detachable comb part, end effector lower hinge, end effector upper hinge, flex plate, wrist servo mount, axel to arm mount, bearing housing, prismatic stepper motor mount, pedestal to rail mount and a belt coupler.

The compliant end effector (Fig. 3) is comprised of two hinge pieces that serve as a frame, an interchangeable comb piece and a flex plate. The flex plate is designed to elastically deform when' bent along a single axis. By utilising the natural material properties of PLA (Polylactic acid), and altering the thickness, any desired stiffness in the design could be achieved. This provides the robot with the passive compliance required to safely interact with a participant's head. Affixed to the flex plate is a flex sensor [12], which measures the deformation of the part, and this feedback allows for an active compliant element.

The robot makes use of pre-fabricated parts, including an aluminum arm assembly, with an elbow and two wrist joints, powered by an Alturn AAS-750MG servo and two ADS-967 servos, respectively. The arm was mounted on a pedestal, featuring a counterweighted and stepper controlled vertical prismatic mounting platform.

Nema17 1704HS168A stepper motors were used for the prismatic and shoulder joints, for their high torque and precision, with DRV8825 motor drivers. A custom motor power board was built, to stepper drivers, along with the previously mentioned servo motors (Alturn AAS-750MG servo and two ADS-967). A computer power supply (FSP 300 W micro-ATX) was used to provide a 5 V and 12 V rail for the stepper drivers and servo motor. A laptop (Lenovo G770 i5-2450 M CPU @ 2.50 GHz × 4) was used to communicate with a ST-Nucleo-F429ZI microcontroller, which controlled the motors. Figure 4 illustrates the connections between the electrical systems. The entire system is low cost, being able to be re-produced approximately £200 [13]. Figure 5 shows the final assembly of the completed robot.

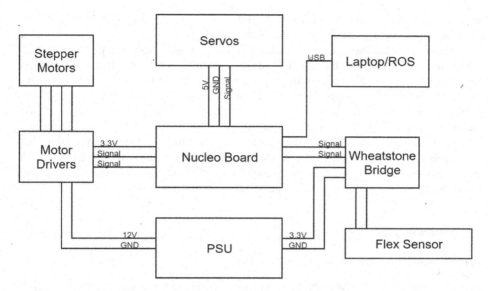

Fig. 4. Electrical system block diagram

Fig. 5. The completed robot arm

3.2   Software

To perform the path planning for the arm, a laptop running Ubuntu 16.04LTS, ROS-Kinetic, and the Moveit! kinematics and motion planning package was used. From the CAD model of the robot, a URDF (Universal Robot Description Format) was created, in turn used by Moveit! to calculate the kinematics of the arm, including collision avoidance, and path planning for the end effector.

The laptop used the ros_serial package to communicate with the microcontroller, which was used to control the stepper and servo motors, as well as adjusting the elbow joint height based on the value of the flex sensor. This meant the joint states of the arm could be sent from the laptop to the microcontroller, and subsequently executed.

To create an active compliant end effector, the microcontroller measures the deformation of the flex plate, by reading the voltage of the flex sensor. The sensor reading is compared against two threshold values, an upper threshold, indicating that too much force is being applied, and a lower threshold indicating too little force, or a loss of contact with the head. In real time, the microcontroller will raise or lower the elbow joint, ensuring that the end effector safely interacts with the user.

4 Experiments

4.1 Testing for Thickness of the Flex Plates

To make sure the robot arm applies an appropriate force to a participant's head, the flex plate has to be tested to find what thickness provides a suitable amount of force. The force applied must be enough to comb a participant's hair effectively, but not so much as to cause injury or discomfort.

The force required to comb hair is not uniform and follows a curve that peaks at approximately 250 mN [14]. The flex plate will have to be soft enough to bend significantly so that the compliant element is functional, while being stiff enough to apply enough force to pass the comb through the hair. By using double the peak force of the combing motion, the end effector will have enough force to comb without injuring the participant. 0.5 N was selected as an appropriate force for testing these parts.

Determining the desired displacement of the flex plate under this force was a matter of approximating the amount of required vertical displacement over a participant's head. Assuming the average human head is 20 cm in diameter, an ideal flex plate would displace half this distance (10 cm) when 0.5 N of force is applied. The end effector will be able to deform around the top half of a participant's head with this range of displacement.

Several tests were performed to determine the thickness of the flex plates that would be appropriate for use in the robot. The first of these tests consisted applying a force of 0.5 N by hanging a 50-g weight on the flex plates of various thicknesses to measure the resultant displacement, shown in Table 1. The 1 mm flex plate averages a deformation of 10 cm, making it an ideal thickness for the compliant end effector.

Table 1. Perpendicular displacements of flex plates with a 0.5 N load

Thickness (mm)	Perpendicular displacement (cm)			
	1st	2nd	3rd	Average
0.25	32	32	33	32.3
0.50	24	22	24	23.3
0.75	20	20	19	19.7
1.00	9	10	11	10.0
1.50	2	2	2	2.0
2.00	1	1	2	1.3

Another experiment was conducted using Fusion 360's Finite Element Analysis (FEA) feature. Using the simulation, a calculated displacement of the flex plates was able to be determined with a 0.5 N force applied to it. Figure 6 shows the simulations.

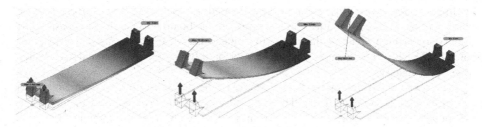

Fig. 6. FEA for displacement of flex plates at 1 mm, 1.5 mm and 2 mm

From this information, it was determined that a flex plate of 1 mm thickness would be the most appropriate, as it displayed bending properties most suited to the robot's function.

4.2 Flex Sensor Voltage Response Test

To acquire valuable data from the flex sensor, a large voltage range is desired. A Wheatstone bridge was used to produce an accurate voltage output with a range of 0–3.1 V, using the full range for the microcontroller analogue input. This gives the highest resolution for the response, increasing accuracy, without overpowering the board.

This signal from the bridge is being sent to the microcontroller board. The input pins of the board can handle a maximum voltage of 3.3 V. Using resistors in the bridge, the maximum output voltage needs to be as close to 3.3 V as possible. This will give the highest resolution for the response, increasing accuracy, without overpowering the board.

Table 2. Voltage response to bend of flex sensor at specific time intervals as it combs across the head

Time (s)	Voltage response (V)			
	1st	2nd	3rd	Average
0	0.0	0.0	0.0	0.00
2	0.7	1.0	0.9	0.87
4	1.5	1.8	1.8	1.70
6	2.2	2.2	2.3	2.23
8	2.2	2.1	1.8	2.03
10	1.9	1.5	1.5	1.63
12	0.0	0.0	0.0	0.00

With an input voltage of 10 V, output voltage of 3.3 V and a flex sensor resistance of 60,000 Ω when fully bent, the following calculation can be done to find resistance of other resistors needed in the Wheatstone bridge.

The exact resistance needed to provide an output voltage of 3.3 V is 121,800 Ω. Finding a resistor like this is impractical. Rounding up to 125,000 Ω gives a close result without going over the voltage limit of the board. The voltage measured is slightly lower than that calculated due to voltage drops caused by resistance of components. The lower voltage is ideal to allow for a buffer for any anomalous voltage spikes that may occur.

In order to determine the voltage response of the flex sensor at given time intervals for a given displacement of the flex plate, an experiment was devised to take measurements. These measurements, shown in Table 2, were used to calibrate the active response of the robotic arm. The voltage data from the experiment was plotted in Fig. 7.

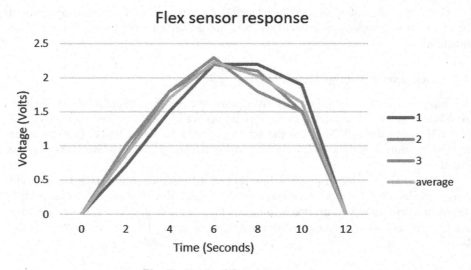

Fig. 7. Graph of flex sensor response

4.3   Combing

Testing the combing function, meant iteratively testing the operation on a participant and making adjustments to the speed and pressure the arm provided as necessary to attain a comfortable experience for the user. The stepper motors running the prismatic element of the arm had a natural upper speed limit. The combing ran close to this limit to make the robot comb at a reasonable speed.

The response of the arm to the PCEwas adjusted as necessary to achieve enough pressure to sufficiently comb hair, but not too much as to cause harm to a participant.

Figure 8 illustrates how the flex plate in the comb assembly deforms on contact with the head. Further, it can be observed the in the first three images the arm adjusts the elbow joint in order to raise the height of the comb, based on the flex sensor reading. Finally, the comb returns to its original state after combing.

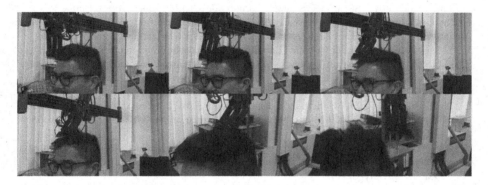

Fig. 8. Sequence of images showing combing in action (in order, top left to bottom right)

5   Conclusion

The robot arm successfully demonstrates the simplicity and effectiveness of integrating passive compliance and active compliance to the end effector of a robot arm. The introduction of a compliant element in the end effector allows for real time deformation upon collision with an object, and as such, allows the robot arm to physically interact with a person's head at minimal risk of injury. Furthermore, this compliance allows the end effector to conform to the profile of a head in real time, eliminating the need for complex real-time motion planning control software. Compared against the existing assistive robots, the Eduardo arm is advantageous in its use of active and passive compliance to provide safe physical interaction.

There is no shortage of further improvements that could be made to this project, as shortcuts were taken in order to create a functioning prototype within the time constraints, and a full list of recommended improvements is available in the GitHub repository [15]. For future work, we recommend research into different types of compliant end effectors (passive verses active, antagonistic pairs and series elastic actuators), as well as different applications with people with disabilities (feeding, washing, clothing).

Finally, the robot arm itself lends itself to further use as a development platform for other research projects. The large workspace (including the vertical prismatic element of the pedestal), construction of the arm using low cost components, interchangeable end effector, and open source software, makes the arm a viable candidate for other institutions to use in their own research projects.

References

1. Ottobock: Common Conditions (2013). https://www.ottobock.co.uk/wheelchairs-seating/common-conditions/
2. Toyota: Toyota Global Newsroom, 16 July 2015. https://newsroom.toyota.co.jp/en/detail/8709541/
3. Srinivasa, S.: HERB 2.0: lessons learned from developing a mobile manipulator for the home, 8 July 2012. https://www.ri.cmu.edu/pub_files/2012/7/SrinivasaEtal11.pdf
4. Robotics, K.: Kinova JACO Assistive Robot Arm, Kinova Robotics (2019). https://www.kinovarobotics.com/en/products/assistive-technologies/kinova-jaco-assistive-robotic-arm
5. C.M. University: Personal Robotics Lab. http://personalrobotics.ri.cmu.edu/
6. Hennessey, M.: Clearpath robotics expands into advanced manipulation with kinova robotics, 9 July 2013. https://www.clearpathrobotics.com/blog/2013/07/clearpath_robot_arm/
7. Ham, R.V., Sugar, T.G., Vanderborght, B., Hollander, K.W., Leferber, D.: Compliant actuator designs, September 2009. https://pdfs.semanticscholar.org/9e80/be2cf92ea3e1f425065cff5f50de710f6300.pdf
8. Braun, D.J., et al.: Robots driven by compliant actuators: optimal control under actuation constraints, 30 July 2013. http://citeseerx.ist.psu.edu/viewdoc/download?doi=10.1.1.420.6774&rep=rep1&type=pdf
9. Jantsch, M., Wittmeier, S., Dalamagkidis, K., Panos, A., Volkart, F., Knoll, A.: Anthrob – a printed anthropomimetic robot, 15–17 October 2013. http://www.cs.cmu.edu/~cga/shoulder/robot2.pdf
10. Stoelen, M.: GummiArm. https://mstoelen.github.io/GummiArm/
11. Robotics, R.: Baxter safety and compliance overview. https://www.active8robots.com/wp-content/uploads/Baxter-Safety-and-Compliance-Overview.pdf
12. Symbol, S.: Flex sensor datasheet. https://cdn-shop.adafruit.com/datasheets/SpectraFlex.pdf
13. Smith, O.: Eduardo Github repository. https://github.com/badmanwillis/Eduardo
14. Kamath, Y.K.: Measurement of combing forces. J. Soc. Cosmet. Chem. **37**, 111–124 (1986)
15. W.S Github Hair Combing Robot Repository: January 2019. https://github.com/badmanwillis/Eduardo/blob/master/parts/Prices.txt

GarmNet: Improving Global with Local Perception for Robotic Laundry Folding

Daniel Fernandes Gomes[1]([✉]) [iD], Shan Luo[1] [iD], and Luis F. Teixeira[2,3] [iD]

[1] Department of Computer Science, University of Liverpool, Liverpool, UK
{danfergo,shan.luo}@liverpool.ac.uk
[2] Faculdade de Engenharia, Universidade do Porto, Porto, Portugal
luisft@fe.up.pt
[3] INESC TEC, Porto, Portugal

Abstract. Developing autonomous assistants to help with domestic tasks is a vital topic in robotics research. Among these tasks, garment folding is one of them that is still far from being achieved mainly due to the large number of possible configurations that a crumpled piece of clothing may exhibit. Research has been done on either estimating the pose of the garment as a whole or detecting the landmarks for grasping separately. However, such works constrain the capability of the robots to perceive the states of the garment by limiting the representations for one single task. In this paper, we propose a novel end-to-end deep learning model named *GarmNet* that is able to simultaneously localize the garment and detect landmarks for grasping. The localization of the garment represents the global information for recognising the category of the garment, whereas the detection of landmarks can facilitate subsequent grasping actions. We train and evaluate our proposed GarmNet model using the CloPeMa Garment dataset that contains 3,330 images of different garment types in different poses. The experiments show that the inclusion of landmark detection (GarmNet-B) can largely improve the garment localization, with an error rate of 24.7% lower. Solutions as ours are important for robotics applications, as these offer scalable to many classes, memory and processing efficient solutions.

Keywords: Garment localization · Landmark detection · Robot laundry folding

1 Introduction

Garment recognition is one necessary capability not only for the automation of tasks involving its manipulation, such as garment folding, within robotic systems [12] but many other applications as well: online e-commerce platforms [20] that make suggestions based on image information [11], intelligent surveillance systems that track people based on the clothing description, etc. However, recognition of clothes, or (highly) deformable objects in general, is a challenging task due to the many poses and deformations that a flexible object may exhibit.

© Springer Nature Switzerland AG 2019
K. Althoefer et al. (Eds.): TAROS 2019, LNAI 11650, pp. 49–61, 2019.
https://doi.org/10.1007/978-3-030-25332-5_5

We consider the scenario wherein an image containing a single piece of clothing, flat, wrinkled and semi-folded exists on a clean background and a robotic system wants to find the garment and good grasping points. Our goal is then to perceive, at the global level, a piece of garment existing in an image, by localizing and classifying it. And, at a local level, by identifying and localizing its landmarks, e.g., neckline-left, right-armpit, right-sleeve-inner, is an image point. Each garment class has a different amount and types of landmarks e.g., towels have four, whereas t-shirts and long t-shirts have both 12. Because of such variances, garment+landmark detection can be formulated using two different approaches: (a) garment finding as object localization, followed by conditional, class specific, landmarks finding, also as object localization. (b) Finding all landmarks existing in the image independently of the garment class as object detection, and the garment piece as object location.

Although approach (a), is a simpler solution to build using off-the-shelf models, and is commonly seen in current literature [10,13], it is more inefficient because: 1. It requires one different sub-model for each garment category, being that many landmarks are shared between garment category e.g., a sleeve of a hoody is similar to a sleeve in a jacket. 2. On the other hand, when using Neural Networks, these work by building more complex representations as its depth increases, through the combinatorial effect of chaining multiple layers together. Therefore, a Network that recognizes a piece of clothing, should in principle, recognize somewhere in its hidden layers some of its landmarks. This means that in approach (a) multiple redundant hidden features are learned, representing extra parameters to be stored in memory, and more operations to be computed during execution time. Adding to this, in the context of robotics e.g., a top view of a laundry bin, the garment global perception might not be possible with good accuracy, but recognizing some local landmarks might be just as valuable for the robot, as it could grasp the piece of clothing by one good landmark and then perform further recognition using the same model.

Therefore, we address the detection of landmarks and classification+localization of garment simultaneously, with a Convolutional Neural Network (CNN) [9] composed of one common trunk and two separate branches. We then introduce a bridge connection that feeds the landmarks detection output into the garment localizer branch, resulting in a decrease from 56.7% to 32.0% in the error rate, that demonstrates the advantages in considering both tasks together. We balance and augment our dataset with Gaussian and hue noise, and perform one last training achieving: 0% and 17.8% error rate on classification and classification+localization respectively; and 36.2% mean Average Precision (mAP) on landmark detection.

2   Related Work

Early works handling clothes happen in Robotics with the folding task, and the problem domain is constrained enough to avoid the necessity of classification i.e., only one type of clothing is considered. In [12] towels are considered, and depth discontinuities are explored to detect its borders and corners. With that information, a PR2 robot is able pick them from a random dropped position and, following a predefined sequence of steps, folds them.

Machine Learning methods are latter used, not only in robotic tasks but other software applications as well e.g., in [20] real-time classification and segmentation of people's clothing appearing in a camera video feed are addressed. However, using the raw image i.e., each pixel is a feature, would result in a low performance results due to the curse of dimensionality, that many Machine Learning (ML) methods suffer from. To overcome this challenge, one common approach is to use the Bag of Visual Words (BoW), that extracts handcrafted features e.g., Scale-Invariant Feature Transform (SIFT) or Histogram of Oriented Gradients (HOG) and feeds these into a classifier e.g., Support Vector Machine (SVM) or k-Nearest Neighbours (k-NN). In [10] the authors use this approach to design a two layer hierarchical classifier to determine the category and grasping point (equivalent to pose, in this work) of a piece of clothing. Other works address the extraction of domain specific features from images. In [19], a set of Gabor filters are used to filter edges magnitude and orientation that are representative of wrinkling and overlaps and with that information, the authors propose three types of features: Position and orientation distribution density, cloth fabric and wrinkle density; and existence of cloth-overlaps.

Deep Learning (DL) Methods. In 2012, AlexNet [8] achieves a notorious improvement of 11% in the ILSVRC2012 image classification competition, when comparing against the next best solution. In [6], to address object detection, region proposal techniques are combined with CNNs, resulting in R-CNN, an hybrid method that combines a CNN with SVMs. Then, in [5], two main improvements are made: the RoI pooling layer is introduced, and the SVM is replaced by a softmax classifier. The improved model Fast R-CNN model is then a two headed CNN, optimized using a multi-task loss, $9\times$ quicker to train and $213\times$ faster test-time. In [16], the authors further introduce Region Proposal Networks (RPNs), making this architecture finally an end-to-end trainable model. Another simpler architecture, YOLO, is introduced in [14] and improved in [15], consisting of only two direct branches on the top of a regular fully CNN: one for positions coordinates regression and another for classes attribution. The system is capable of real-time object detection.

DL in Garment Perception. After the successes using DL methods, some works that address garment perception also explore their potential, mainly considering classification problems. One example is [13], that addresses the same problem as [10]: pose and category recognition. The solution is also similar, a two layer hierarchical classifier. But here, instead of BoW and SVMs, one CNN is used to determine the garment class, followed by a class specific CNN that determines the garment pose index. The authors compare the model against others using hand engineered features and report gains of 3% in accuracy. Similarly, in [1] a robotic system composed of two arms and a RGB-D camera, uses an hierarchy of CNNs with three specialization levels. At a first step one CNN classifies the garment piece, and then two others are used to find the first and second grasping points.

Our Approach. In contrast to these approaches, ours leverages the intrinsic characteristics of CNNs and the architecture patterns from both classification/localization and detection models to perform the global and local perception in one step with a single CNN. Our model can also exploit prior knowledge gained to detect landmarks, to enhance the global garment perception. Our approach is therefore more memory and processing efficient than hierarchical solutions presented above. This happens because, in our approach, lower level layers are shared between the Global and Local perception components, as discussed in Sect. 1. Exploring these intrinsic characteristics of CNNs, in [17], the authors propose Hierarchical Convolutional Neural Networks (H-CNN), to address hierarchical classification. With coarse/top-level classifications being extracted from hidden layers while finer/more-specific classes being predicted by the latest layers of the network.

3   Network Architecture

Our network, **GarmNet**, at a macro level can be summarized into three blocks: **Feature extractor, Landmark detector** and **Garment localizer** (Fig. 1).

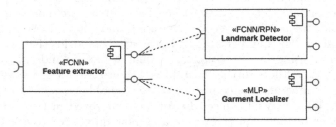

Fig. 1. GarmNet macro view, UML [3] Components Diagram. The architecture is broken into three blocks (components): Feature extractor, Landmark Detector and Garment Localizer; that output: intermediate features at two depths, landmarks classes+localizations and garment class+localization.

Feature Extractor. We implement the feature extraction module with a Fully Convolutional Neural Network (FCNN), a 50-layer ResNet [7]. The model is pre trained on ImageNet [2], to which we remove the last Fully Connected (FC) layers, resulting in a 7×7 output tensor. Yet, because in some cases we have multiple landmarks close to each other, we preferred a larger output size, that would result in a higher number of anchors in the landmark detector. We achieve this by probing the ResNet at the end of the *conv4_x* block, which has an output size of 14×14.

Landmark Detector. Responsible for classifying and localizing all the landmarks present in the image, this module is a small, 3×3, sliding FCNN, similar to the Region Proposal Network (RPN) introduced in [16], and it is implemented with convolutional (CONV) layers. The network is composed by an intermediate 256-d layer, with a rectified linear unit (ReLU) [8] activation, followed by two heads: one for localization and other for classification, see Fig. 2.

The localizer head is a Multi-Layer Perceptron (MLP), that outputs the predicted landmark relative coordinates such that

$$A_{(i,j)} = (s * j, s * i) \tag{1}$$
$$L_{(i,j)} = A_{(i,j)} + O_{(i,j)} \tag{2}$$

where L is a predicted landmark location, A stands for the sliding network position O the localization head output, and s a stride value that we define to spread the base referential (or anchor points, as introduced in [16]) evenly across the input image (we set it as 18, that together with a 26 landmark area matches the 224 image input size).

The classifier head, a convolutional layer with $n + 1$ filters, where n is the number of landmark classes and the plus one answers for background, non positive, landmarks. We apply a *softmax* activation along the depth dimension and, therefore the output of this layer can be interpreted, at each position, as the probability of the associated landmark $L_{(i,j)}$ being of a certain class, or background.

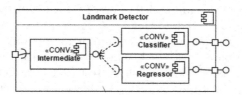

Fig. 2. Landmark detector component, UML [3] representation. After one intermediate branch, two separate branches output 18×18 landmark proposals (classification and location). This block, implemented with convolutional layers, can be interpreted as small fully connected network sliding over the feature extractor output.

Garment Localizer. To perform the localization of the piece of clothing present in the image, we use a two head three-layer fully connected network, similar to the sliding window used for landmark detection. The intermediate layer is a 512-d FC with ReLU activation, followed by the regression and classification heads.

The regression head outputs four values: x, y, with and height; and the classification head outputs n values, where n is the number of garment classes, that we remap to probabilities with a *softmax* activation. We retrieve the predicted landmarks by computing the *argmax* over the classifier output tensor depth dimension, and associating it with the point predicted in same spacial position on the regression head. We further discard all the landmarks that have a confidence value i.e., the value that motivated the argument to be the maximum, lower than 0.5 (Fig. 3).

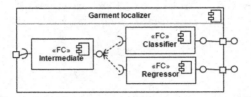

Fig. 3. Garment localizer component, UML [3] representation. Similar to the landmark detector 2, yet fully connected layers are used. The Intermediate layer outputs a 512-d, the classifier a 9-d (one hot encoded classes) and the regressor the 3-d (x,y, with and height) vectors

4   Experiments

Our implementation was performed using Keras[1] framework with the TensorFlow[2] back-end. All experiments were carried out on a laptop, with GPU support enabled, equipped with an Intel(R) Core(TM) i7-6700HQ CPU @ 2.60 GHz, 16 GB DDR4 RAM, and a Nvidia Geforce GTX 1060 6 GB GDDR5 GPU. We initialize kernels with random values drawn from a normal distribution, and bias with ones. Optimization is performed using Adadelta with 1.0 learning, a batch size of 30, and 40 epochs per experiment. At test time our model runs at roughly 30 FPS. For classification and localization evaluation we use error rate, while for detection we use the mean Average Precision metric (mAP) as proposed in [4]. The source code has been made publicly available[3].

4.1   Dataset

We adapt the CTU Color and Depth Image Dataset of Spread Garments [18]. This dataset is divided into two groups: "Flat and wrinkled", with 2050, and "Folded", with 1280 examples. Each example contains one image of a piece of

---

[1] https://keras.io/.
[2] https://www.tensorflow.org/.
[3] https://github.com/danfergo/garment.

clothing placed on a wooden floor and is annotated with the stereo disparity; garment category; interest points coordinates and category; and other meta-information. We merge both groups, and because it only contains information regarding each landmark position, we extend its annotation with the garment bounding box as follows:

$$P_1 = (\min_{\forall l \in L} l_i, \min_{\forall l \in L} l_j) \tag{3}$$

$$P_2 = (\max_{\forall l \in L} l_i, \max_{\forall l \in L} l_j) \tag{4}$$

where L is the set of Landmarks, P_1 and P_2 are the top-left and bottom-right corners of the bounding box. There is a total of 27 landmark categories, distributed among 9 types of garment. Some landmark categories are shared among classes. We then create two splits, with 300 randomly chosen images for validation and the remaining the ones used for training. The remaining 2318, make the training split. Results are reported over the validation split.

4.2   Landmark Detection Anchors

For training the landmark detector heads we transform the landmark locations into small squared areas and follow a strategy similar to the anchor boxes described in [16]. To all the anchor boxes that intercept a landmark box with $IoU > 0.7$, we consider it a positive for the respective class. If it does not intercept any with $IoU \geq 0.3$ we set it to background. Because the ratio between positive and negative anchor boxes is high, we create a binary mask that is used to filter the anchors that effectively are considered in the loss function. This mask selects all the class positive and 10 randomly chosen background anchors.

4.3   Loss Functions

Landmark Detector. For the localization head, we apply the robust loss defined in [16] to all the active anchors that are selectable by the mask, m, described in Sect. 4.2.

$$L_{reg} = m \odot L_{robust}(P, T) \tag{5}$$

$$L_{robust}(P, T) = \begin{cases} (P - T)^2, & P - T < 0.5 \\ |P - T|, & \text{otherwise} \end{cases} \tag{6}$$

For the classification head, we apply the cross-entropy loss function to all active anchors, being that at each anchor the landmark class is one-hot encoded.

$$L_{cls} = m \odot L_{ce}(T, P) \tag{7}$$

Garment Localizer. With the garment classes represented in a one hot encoded vector, we use the cross-entropy loss on the classification head and, for the regression head, we use the mean squared error.

4.4   One Landmark Class per Sample, Constraint

One important peculiarity of landmark detection to consider is the fact that, per image, only one class of landmarks exist. Therefore, we can introduce this constraint into the loss function and promote parameter combinations that tend to predict only one landmark per class. We implement this constraint by also applying cross-entropy over the spacial dimension, resulting in the loss function 8. However, because cross-entropy expects its input to be a probability distribution, we must firstly apply *softmax* accordingly. We therefore, place two *softmax* after the last convolutional layer activation: the first, (regular) depth wise, the second, spacial wise; and pass each output to the correspondent cross-entropy. At test time, we average the two *softmax*, similarly to 8. Because for each garment category, only a few landmarks are active, we further create a second mask, that is the ground-truth max spacial value, and we use it to ignore the loss spacial component for the landmark classes that are not applicable.

$$L_{cls} = \frac{1}{2}\Big[m \odot L_{ce}(T, P) + \max_{w \times h} T \odot L_{ce(spatially)}(T, P)\Big] \tag{8}$$

Although with the spacial constraint loss addition, we achieve a 2% lower detection mAP score, dropping from 37.8% to 35.7%. Yet, we are able to achieve lower duplicated predictions, as illustrated in Fig. 4.

4.5   Using Landmarks Within Garment Localization

We investigate the gains in feeding the landmark detector output features into the garment localize intermediate layer, expecting that these would help better frame the garment bounding box and. We flatten the 18×18 tensor outputted by the classifier block from the landmark detector branch, and concatenate it with the flatten Feature Extractor output, before feeding it to the 512-d intermediate layer, resulting in GarmNet-B, represented in the Fig. 5. With this bridge connection, the network achieves 32.0% classification+localization error rate, a 24.7% improvement when comparing with the individual garment detector training (Table 1).

Table 1. Summary of Classification and Classification+Localization error rates. Garm-Net is our base model, GarmNet-B is the model obtained after the bridge connection introduced in Sect. 4.5 and GarmNet-B (A.D) the latter model optimized using the augmented dataset

	Classification	Classif.+Loca.
GarmNet	0%	56.7%
GarmNet-B	0%	32.0 %
GarmNet-B (A.D.)	0%	17.8%

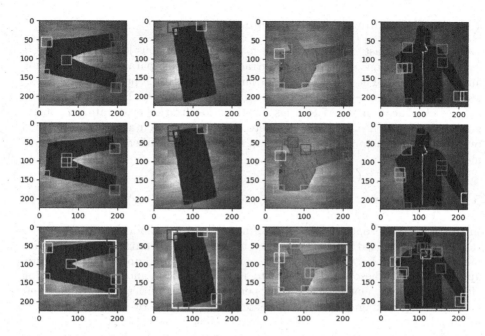

Fig. 4. Representative cases of the result of applying the spacial constraint loss. At the top row, predictions with composed loss, at the middle, without, and the bottom, the ground truth

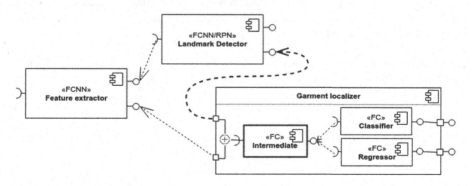

Fig. 5. GarmNet-B (introduced in Sect. 4.5) representation using UML [3]. The output emitted by the classifier block from the Landmark Detector branch is concatenated with the Feature Extractor output before being fed into the intermediate layer

4.6 Final Optimization with Augmented Data

We perform one last training, without loading any previous learned parameters (with the exception of the feature extractor ImageNet parameters) and using augmented data. The data augmentation is achieved by repeating examples of less numerous classes and adding Gaussian and hue noise. The obtained results are: 0% classification and 17.8% classification+localization error rate, and 36.2% landmark detection mAP. The complete classification accuracy can be justified by the almost constant background and the few, often differently colored, garments per class.

5 Conclusion

In this work, we proposed a novel deep neural network model named GarmNet that can be optimized in an end-to-end manner, for performing simultaneous garment local and global perception. Approaches as ours are important for robotics applications, as these offer scalable to many classes, memory and processing efficient solutions, enabling real-time perception capabilities. We evaluate our solution using an augmented dataset assembled using the two collected by CTU during the CloPeMa project [18]. The experiments showed the effectiveness and side effects of introducing domain specific knowledge into the loss function being optimized, at both quantitative and qualitative levels. We finally demonstrate the improvements on garment localization by considering the landmark detection as an intermediate step.

In the future work, more experiments will be done to further optimise the network architecture and its hyper-parameters configuration. A more challenging dataset, with higher number of images and variability e.g., [11], will also be used. Within the context of garment perception for robotic laundry folding, the work will be extended to garment folding with a robot arm-hand setup, supported by the garment perception done in this paper.

Acknowledgment. This work was supported by the EPSRC project "Robotics and Artificial Intelligence for Nuclear (RAIN)" (EP/R026084/1).

A   Appendix

See Table 2.

Table 2. Summary of landmark Classification+Localization, as follows: GarmNet, the results obtained using the base model; GarmNet (S.C), the base model optimized with the spacial constraint (Sect. 4.4); GarmNet-B, the modified model with the bridge connection (4.5); and, GarmNet-B (A.D.), the latter model optimized using augmented dataset.

	GarmNet	GarmNet (S.C.)	GarmNet-B	GarmNet-B (A.D.)
Mean AP	37.8	35.7	34.5	36.1
Left leg outer	38.5	33.7	33.0	38.2
Left leg inner	47.6	39.5	0	44.1
Crotch	46.4	42.5	43.7	34.3
Right leg inner	46.0	42.6	50.5	39.9
Left leg inner	45.3	41.4	43.7	40.9
Top right	62.1	54.7	50.5	55.7
Top left	57.3	58.4	47.8	50
Right sleave inner	44.3	38.7	60.2	37.3
Right sleave outer	38.2	30.4	53.6	42.2
Left sleave inner	43.9	41.5	46.5	48.3
Left selave outer	34.5	30.7	46.0	35.7
Hood right	0	54.5	46.4	0
Hood top	0	0	42.5	40.9
Hood left	56.4	30.9	0	0
Bottom left	38.8	38.2	34.5	40.7
Bottom middle	0	0	0	43.9
Bottom right	38.6	37.1	40	39.9
Right armpit	46.1	41.7	44.7	50.7
Right shoulder	44.0	39.7	47.1	60.2
Neckline right	44.5	32.2	45.0	36.1
Collar right	44.1	38.7	47.2	48.7
Collar left	55.3	48.4	51.9	60.2
Neckline left	34.3	33.8	35.6	36.1
Left shoulder	44.4	39.1	46.7	48.7
Left armpit	43.3	38.8	39.0	37.4
Fold 1	27.5	26.4	27.5	25.2
Fold 2	0	0	0	0

References

1. Corona, E., Alenyà, G., Gabas, A., Torras, C.: Active garment recognition and target grasping point detection using deep learning. Pattern Recogn. **74**, 629–641 (2018). https://doi.org/10.1016/j.patcog.2017.09.042. http://www.sciencedirect.com/science/article/pii/S0031320317303941
2. Deng, J., Dong, W., Socher, R., Li, L.J., Li, K., Fei-Fei, L.: ImageNet: a large-scale hierarchical image database. In: CVPR 2009 (2009)
3. Engels, G., Heckel, R., Sauer, S.: UML—a universal modeling language? In: Nielsen, M., Simpson, D. (eds.) ICATPN 2000. LNCS, vol. 1825, pp. 24–38. Springer, Heidelberg (2000). https://doi.org/10.1007/3-540-44988-4_3
4. Everingham, M., Gool, L., Williams, C.K., Winn, J., Zisserman, A.: The pascal visual object classes (VOC) challenge. Int. J. Comput. Vis. **88**(2), 303–338 (2010). https://doi.org/10.1007/s11263-009-0275-4
5. Girshick, R.B.: Fast R-CNN. CoRR abs/1504.08083 (2015). http://arxiv.org/abs/1504.08083
6. Girshick, R.B., Donahue, J., Darrell, T., Malik, J.: Rich feature hierarchies for accurate object detection and semantic segmentation. CoRR abs/1311.2524 (2013). http://arxiv.org/abs/1311.2524
7. He, K., Zhang, X., Ren, S., Sun, J.: Deep residual learning for image recognition. CoRR abs/1512.03385 (2015). http://arxiv.org/abs/1512.03385
8. Krizhevsky, A., Sutskever, I., Hinton, G.E.: Imagenet classification with deep convolutional neural networks. In: Advances in Neural Information Processing Systems (2012)
9. Lecun, Y., Bengio, Y.: Convolutional networks for images, speech, and time-series. In: The Handbook of Brain Theory and Neural Networks, January 1995
10. Li, Y., Chen, C.F., Allen, P.K.: Recognition of deformable object category and pose. In: Proceedings of the IEEE International Conference on Robotics and Automation (ICRA) (2014)
11. Liu, Z., Luo, P., Qiu, S., Wang, X., Tang, X.: Deepfashion: powering robust clothes recognition and retrieval with rich annotations. In: Proceedings of IEEE Conference on Computer Vision and Pattern Recognition (CVPR), June 2016
12. Maitin-Shepard, J., Cusumano-Towner, M., Lei, J., Abbeel, P.: Cloth grasp point detection based on multiple-view geometric cues with application to robotic towel folding. In: 2010 IEEE International Conference on Robotics and Automation, pp. 2308–2315, May 2010. https://doi.org/10.1109/ROBOT.2010.5509439
13. Mariolis, I., Peleka, G., Kargakos, A., Malassiotis, S.: Pose and category recognition of highly deformable objects using deep learning. In: 2015 International Conference on Advanced Robotics (ICAR), pp. 655–662. IEEE, July 2015. https://doi.org/10.1109/ICAR.2015.7251526. http://ieeexplore.ieee.org/document/7251526/
14. Redmon, J., Divvala, S.K., Girshick, R.B., Farhadi, A.: You only look once: Unified, real-time object detection. CoRR abs/1506.02640 (2015). http://arxiv.org/abs/1506.02640
15. Redmon, J., Farhadi, A.: YOLO9000: better, faster, stronger. CoRR abs/1612.08242 (2016). http://arxiv.org/abs/1612.08242
16. Ren, S., He, K., Girshick, R.B., Sun, J.: Faster R-CNN: towards real-time object detection with region proposal networks. CoRR abs/1506.01497 (2015). http://arxiv.org/abs/1506.01497

17. Seo, Y., Shik Shin, K.: Hierarchical convolutional neural networks for fashion image classification. Expert Syst. Appl. **116**, 328–339 (2019). https://doi.org/10.1016/j.eswa.2018.09.022. http://www.sciencedirect.com/science/article/pii/S095741741 8305992
18. Wagner, L., K.D., Smutný, V.: CTU color and depth image dataset of spread garments. Technical Report CTU-CMP-2013-25, Center for Machine Perception, K13133 FEE Czech Technical University, Prague, Czech Republic, September 2013
19. Yamazaki, K.: Instance recognition of clumped clothing using image features focusing on clothing fabrics and wrinkles. In: 2015 IEEE International Conference on Robotics and Biomimetics, IEEE-ROBIO 2015, pp. 1102–1108 (2016). https://doi.org/10.1109/ROBIO.2015.7418919, http://dx.doi.org/10.1007/s10514-016-9559-z
20. Yang, M., Yu, K.: Real-time clothing recognition in surveillance videos. In: Macq, B., Schelkens, P. (eds.) ICIP, pp. 2937–2940. IEEE (2011). http://dblp.uni-trier.de/db/conf/icip/icip2011.html#YangY11

Soft Robotics and Sensing

Soft Particles for Granular Jamming

Fabrizio Putzu$^{(\boxtimes)}$, Jelizaveta Konstantinova, and Kaspar Althoefer

Centre for Advanced Robotics @ Queen Mary, Queen Mary University
of London, Mile End Road, London E1 4NS, UK
f.putzu@qmul.ac.uk

Abstract. In the last decade, soft robots demonstrated their distinctive advantages compared to 'hard' robots. Soft structures can achieve high dexterity and compliance. However, only low forces can be exerted, and more complicated control strategies are needed. Variable stiffness robots offer an alternative solution to compensate for the downsides of flexible robots. One of the most common approach in the development of variable stiffness robots is the use of granular jamming. In this paper a variable stiffness manipulator based on granular jamming is studied. Here, we propose the use of soft and deformable spherical particles instead of commonly used rigid particles. Further on, we evaluate the performance of the soft particles under vacuum. In addition, a comparison between our approach and the standard approach to granular jamming is presented. The proposed soft particles show good performance in terms of their capability of compacting and squeezing against each other to achieve a high-stiffness robot arm.

Keywords: Soft robotics · Stiffness controllability · Granular jamming ·
Soft particles

1 Introduction

Traditionally, robots are made from rigid components, and, thus, they cannot deform or adapt their shape when facing environmental constraints. This leads to drawbacks when considering safety, especially when the rigid robots are used for the interaction with humans. To overcome such problems, researchers took inspiration from nature to create compliant robot systems. One approach is to create robots from soft materials, such as silicone or fabric – a trend currently emerging in the field of soft robotics. In soft robotics, many researchers try to replicate the motion and movement of soft parts of animals that do not have a rigid skeleton, i.e. the octopus's arm, elephant trunk or worm [5, 6, 8–12]. These types of robots are inherently compliant and capable of adapting their shape to the surrounding environment [1–5]. Due to the compliant structure, soft material robots are excellent candidates for applications requiring safe human robot interaction [6, 7].

The difference between traditional robots inspired by human biology, such as traditional robotics arm, and soft robots inspired by soft nature is the increased dexterity. Robots made of rigid links connected by joints with low Degrees of Freedom (DoF) have low dexterity compared to soft robot that have a theoretical infinite number of DoFs. Silicone and fabric based soft robotic systems mainly, make use of pneumatic

© Springer Nature Switzerland AG 2019
K. Althoefer et al. (Eds.): TAROS 2019, LNAI 11650, pp. 65–74, 2019.
https://doi.org/10.1007/978-3-030-25332-5_6

actuation; when pressurizing specific chambers embedded within the structure, different movements can be achieved such as elongation, bending and twisting [13–15]. The expansion of a or multiple pressurized chambers lead to a deformation and thus the movement of the overall structure.

However, a drawback of these soft technologies is difficulties in position control, the lack of stability and the low exertion forces that can be achieved when compared to rigid structures. However, position control and stability are fundamental requirements for applications such us Minimally Invasive Surgery (MIS) where instruments need to be held in a specific position in order to perform the surgical task required. With traditional component robots' control and navigation are usually easily achieved and many navigation algorithms have been developed [16]. With soft robots especially those that can vary their stiffness this becomes much more complicated. These are disadvantages that need to be overcome; however, advantageously, a variable-stiffness robot does not only have the strength and stability of a rigid structure, but also has the dexterity and compliance of a soft system.

One of the most commonly used approaches to achieve variable stiffness in robotics is tendon-based stiffening. It is achieved by tensioning of the tendons to obtain a stiffer structure [17–20]; one of the main drawbacks of this method is that the stiffness achieved is not uniform along the structure indeed the tip cannot be stiffer than the base. Other methods that are used to achieve stiffening and actuation of soft structures include technologies, such as a thermally activated joints [21] which usually implement Shape Memory Alloy (SMA) wires. The problem with this solution is that it can only achieve binary stiffness, which means that the structure can only be completely soft or completely stiff with no intermediate state. Concentric tube robots [22] are another approach used to achieve variable stiffness devices, but concentric tubes have to compromise their shape in order to change the stiffness.

Granular jamming is an alternative technology that can be used to create variable stiffness manipulators. It is a phenomenon that allows a structure to reversibly pass from a fluid-like state to a rigid-like state and back. This process and relevant examples are presented in the next section.

1.1 Granular Jamming

Granular jamming devices can behave like liquid or solid structures or assume an intermediate state where particles are partially jammed, and the overall structure is still able of movement but with higher stiffness compared to the 'liquid' state. This phenomenon is exploited in a number of robotics applications ranging from grippers, haptic interfaces with force feedback and endoscopic tubes enable the capability to control the stiffness of these systems over a wide range. The jamming of granules or particles occurs when compressed by an outside force, such as the difference between the outside pressure and the inside pressure due to an applied vacuum. The most common design of a device that exploits the granular jamming phenomenon is composed of three main components: (1) a flexible membrane, (2) granules or particles and (3) a vacuum pump.

The membrane is used to improve the tensile performance of the device where granular jamming is used. The membrane can be fabricated from a soft material, such as latex, silicone or fabric. The desired membrane should be thin and soft/flexible enough to guarantee a good contact with the particles when the air is taken out. Different membrane materials were studied, and polythene material showed to be capable of reaching the highest value of stiffness [23]. The usual approach is to fill the membrane with small granules or particles. In order to implement the change of the stiffness of the device the air present in between the particles is pumped out employing an external vacuum pump. Thus, when the particles are free to move the device feels soft and flexible, but when the vacuum is applied the particles are 'jammed' together and the overall structure is stiff and capable of keeping is current shape. For instance, this principle is used in the Universal Gripper (UG) [24], as it is shown in Fig. 1. This gripper is made of a thin latex membrane filled with grounded coffee and connected to a vacuum pump. The operation of this universal gripper is based on three different gripping modes, illustrated in Fig. 1: firstly, static friction from surface contact (Fig. 1 (b)), secondly, geometric constriction from interlocking (Fig. 1(c)), and, thirdly, vacuum suction from an airtight seal (Fig. 1(d)).

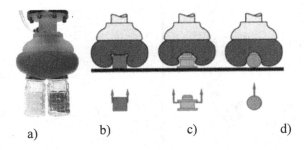

Fig. 1. (a) Universal gripper, (b) UG in static friction gripping, (c) UG in interlocking gripping, (d) UG in vacuum suction gripping [24].

Other researchers exploited the granular jamming principle by embedding granules into haptic devices [25, 26], creating a haptic display with variable stiffness and deformable geometry, as shown in Fig. 2. The haptic device (Fig. 2(a)) consists of four hollow silicone cells which are filled with ground coffee. A combination of different levels of pneumatic and vacuum pressures leads to the creation of different tactile responses varying from soft lumps, via medium-stiff lumps to virtually rigid lumps. The palpation device using a pneumatic actuator and a granular jamming actuator (Fig. 2(b)) consists of a granular jamming chamber and a pneumatic chamber that work simultaneously, simulating the stiffness of different biological tissues [26] (Fig. 3).

Another implementation of the granular jamming phenomenon is proposed in [27], where a novel flexible manipulator capable of high dexterity moving with high speed, strength and articulation is proposed. The importance of the particle's material and also their shape has been well studied in [28–30], but in all cases rigid particles has been used.

The main aspect that we need to consider in order to achieve a good jamming of the particles are shape and size, their interlocking capability, as well as friction between the

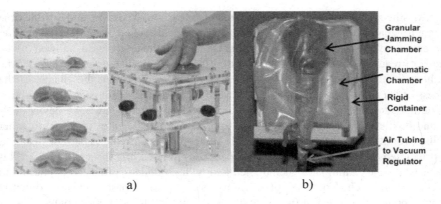

Fig. 2. (a) Haptic jamming array with four hexagonal cells [25], (b) haptic palpation device utilizing granular jamming stiffness feedback actuator [26].

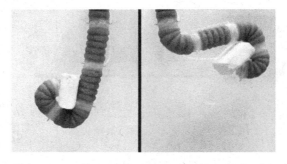

Fig. 3. Granular jammed manipulator proposed by Cheng et al. [27].

particles [28–30]. So far, grounded coffee demonstrates the best capabilities in this context. Granules with high interparticle friction flow less in the 'liquid' state but are considerably stiffer in the jammed state and vice versa. To the best of our knowledge, soft material particles for granular jamming were not explored in detail yet for robotics applications [31]. In this paper we demonstrate the potential of soft and deformable granules for the use in granular jamming. It was found that soft particles enable low friction during interaction, which allow them to flow freely when not jammed and good interlocking capabilities, indeed they are able to squeeze against each other reaching high stiffening.

This paper is organized as follows: the next section describes the design, materials used and fabrication of our manipulator. Section 3 shows the experimental study and evaluation of the soft particles' behavior. Section 4 presents the conclusions and future work.

2 Design and Fabrication

In this paper the granular jamming approach is exploited to create a snake like manipulator. Soft particles were employed and their behavior under vacuum pressure studied. The desired outcome is to have a highly compact structure and evaluate its stiffness. In this section the design and the materials used are presented (Fig. 4).

Fig. 4. Manipulator with soft particles in its jammed state.

To create the external membrane, transparent plastic material has been used. The plastic employed is not stretchable to avoid excessive expansion of the manipulator body; the material thickness is less than 1 mm. In order to fabricate the membrane of the manipulator, the plastic is cut into two rectangles with dimensions of 300 mm by 30 mm; the plastic material is sewn together on three sides using a sewing machine (both sides and the top). The soft particles used in the manipulator are made from Styrofoam. They are extremely lightweight, composed of almost 90% of air, with a diameter ranging from 2 mm to 4 mm. The plastic bag previously created was then filled with soft particles until the plastic bag was loosely filled with particles.

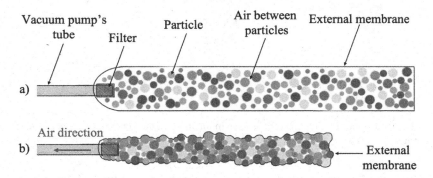

Fig. 5. Two states of the variable stiffness manipulator: (a) manipulator in unjammed state, (b) jammed state of the manipulator.

The dimensions of the assembled structure are 300 mm in length with a diameter of 20 mm. In order to allow the air to be removed from the membrane cavity a vacuum pump is attached to the open end of the sleeve. To avoid the particles to be drawn out of the external plastic membrane and into the vacuum pump, a filter made of cotton textile is applied. The filter does not obstruct the airflow but stops the particles from escaping the external membrane. To measure the vacuum pressure, a manometer is placed between the manipulator and the vacuum pump. A schematic drawing of the setup is shown in Fig. 5.

3   Experimental Study and Results

In order to study how the soft particles, deform under the vacuum force, and how their physical properties (density) can be modulated a set of experiments is carried out.

The deformability of the particles is a crucial point: the more they can compact the higher is the achievable stiffness.

To study the deformability of particles, the Styrofoam spheres are placed in a container with a fixed volume of 0.03 l. One end of the container is closed by an airtight piston, that is able to slide up and down inside the container. The other end of the container is connected to the vacuum pump with the cotton textile filter in between. When the pump is switched on, the air inside the container is sucked out and the particles start to jam. In addition, the piston is moving down and helps to compress the particles. Figure 6 shows the deformation of the Styrofoam under the applied vacuum force of −100 MPa.

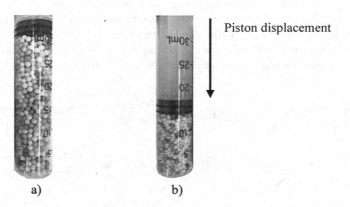

a)   b)

Fig. 6. (a) A container filled with soft particles in unjammed state, (b) same number of particles jammed at −100 MPa.

As a result of the experiment, the overall volume reduced by 50% from 0.03 l to 0.015 l. Figure 7 is a close up view of the particles and shows the behavior of a single particle for different jamming conditions. The selected particle has an initial diameter of 4 mm. When the vacuum force is applied, the deformation of the particles can be easily noted: their diameter reduces when the vacuum force is increased. The deformation of the particle is measured with a Vernier caliper.

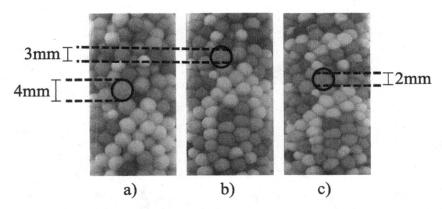

Fig. 7. Behavior of a single particle for different jamming conditions: (a) unjammed particles at atmospheric pressure; (b) particles jammed at −50 MPa, (c) particles jammed at −100 MPa.

With these experiments it can be clearly stated that the density (ρ [kg/m^3]) expressed as:

$$\rho = m/V \,[\text{kg/m}^3],$$

$$(a) \quad \rho = 0.002/3e^{-5} = 66.7\,[\text{kg/m}^3],$$

$$(b) \quad \rho = 0.002/2.25e^{-5} = 88.9\,[\text{kg/m}^3],$$

$$(c) \quad \rho = 0.002/1.5e^{-5} = 133.3\,[\text{kg/m}^3],$$

where m is the mass and V the volume. As it can be seen, density ρ increases by a factor of two from (a) to (c). In this regards an experiment comparing grounded coffee and Styrofoam particles has been carried out.

Grounded coffee is suggested from most of researchers in the field as the best option for granular jamming [24–26], thanks to its large absolute strength and high strength to weight ratio. Furthermore, its irregular surface helps to increase the inter-particle friction.

In the next experiment, the same membrane has been filled with ground coffee, and then with Styrofoam particles and exposed to the same vacuum force of −100 MPa.

The coffee showed a good jamming capability, but the weight plays an important role in this application. The manipulator filled with coffee has a weight of 22 g while the same manipulator filled with Styrofoam particles has a weight of only 2 g thanks to its composition (almost 90% of air). As shown in Figs. 8(a), (b), (c) and (d) the gravitational force (g) forced the ground-coffee-filled robot arm downwards and we observe that the arm filled with coffee particles cannot keep its shape even when vacuumed. On the other hand, the much lighter robot arm filled with Styrofoam particles is able to keep its shape when a vacuum is applied (Figs. 8(f), (g), (h) and (i)) even against the gravitational force.

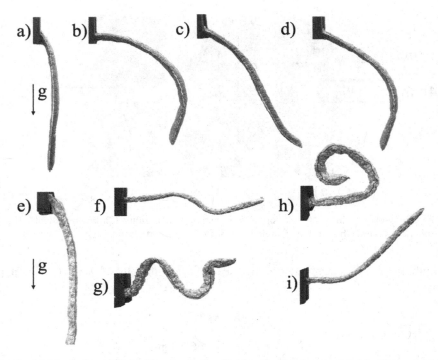

Fig. 8. (a) Manipulator filled with grounded coffee in unjammed state; (b), (c), (d) manipulator filled with grounded coffee in a jammed state different shapes has been tried to be achieved but the elevate weight didn't allowed it. (e) Manipulator filled with soft Styrofoam particles in an unjammed state, (f), (g), (h), (i) manipulator filled with soft Styrofoam particles in a jammed state, thanks to the light weight of the material used it was possible to achieve different configurations. The arrow 'g' represents the direction of the gravitational force.

4   Conclusions and Future Work

In this paper, a novel approach for granular jamming is presented, soft particles have been used instead of the traditional hard particles. The behavior of the soft particles inside an airtight flexible membrane under vacuum was evaluated in an experimental study. A comparison between our approach and what is considered to be the gold standard in granular jamming is presented. The Styrofoam particles showed a better performance thanks to being lightweight and their capability to squeeze against each other significantly increasing the interparticle friction.

The soft Styrofoam particles demonstrate to have a higher specific modulus compared to grounded coffee. The Styrofoam particles are seven times lighter than the coffee particles. Compared to the coffee-based robot arm, the Styrofoam-particle arm is superior in attaining structural shapes when vacuumed.

Having a lighter structure, it is assumed that less forces will be necessary to actuate the manipulator, this will allow to employ smaller motors compared to other approaches and so have a more compact, lightweight and power efficient robotic device.

In the future, we will test particles with different shapes and dimensions and will explore ways to actuate the particle-jammed robot arm.

References

1. Culha, U., Nurzaman, S.G., Clemens, F., Iida, F.: SVAS3: strain vector aided sensorization of soft structures. Sensors **14**(7), 12748–12770 (2014)
2. Pfeifer, R., Gómez, G.: Morphological computation – connecting brain, body, and environment. In: Sendhoff, B., Körner, E., Sporns, O., Ritter, H., Doya, K. (eds.) Creating Brain-Like Intelligence. LNCS (LNAI), vol. 5436, pp. 66–83. Springer, Heidelberg (2009). https://doi.org/10.1007/978-3-642-00616-6_5
3. Sareh, S., Rossiter, J., Conn, A., Drescher, K., Goldstein, R.E.: Swimming like algae: biomimetic soft artificial cilia. J. R. Soc. Interface rsif20120666 (2012)
4. Stilli, A., Wurdemann, H.A., Althoefer, K.: Shrinkable, stiffness-controllable soft manipulator based on a bio-inspired antagonistic actuation principle. In: 2014 IEEE/RSJ International Conference on Intelligent Robots and Systems (IROS 2014), pp. 2476–2481. IEEE (2014)
5. Trivedi, D., Rahn, C.D., Kier, W.M., Walker, I.D.: Soft robotics: Biological inspiration, state of the art, and future research. Appl. Bionics Biomech. **5**(3), 99–117 (2008)
6. Laschi, C., Cianchetti, M., Mazzolai, B., Margheri, L., Follador, M., Dario, P.: Soft robot arm inspired by the octopus. Adv. Robot. **26**(7), 709–727 (2012)
7. Pfeifer, R., Lungarella, M., Iida, F.: The challenges ahead for bio-inspired 'soft' robotics. Commun. ACM **55**(11), 76–87 (2012)
8. Baisch, A.T., Sreetharan, P.S., Wood, R.J.: Biologically-inspired locomotion of a 2 g hexapod robot. In: 2010 IEEE/RSJ International Conference on Intelligent Robots and Systems (IROS), pp. 5360–5365. IEEE (2010)
9. Srivatsan, R.A., Travers, M., Choset, H.: Using lie algebra for shape estimation of medical snake robots. In: 2014 IEEE/RSJ International Conference on Intelligent Robots and Systems (IROS 2014), pp. 3483–3488. IEEE (2014)
10. Tully, S., Kantor, G., Zenati, M.A., Choset, H.: Shape estimation for image-guided surgery with a highly articulated snake robot. In: 2011 IEEE/RSJ International Conference on Intelligent Robots and Systems (IROS), pp. 1353–1358. IEEE (2011)
11. Walker, I.D.: Continuous backbone continuum robot manipulators. ISRN Robot. **2013** (2013)
12. Zhang, Z., Shang, J., Seneci, C., Yang, G.-Z.: Snake robot shape sensing using micro-inertial sensors. In: 2013 IEEE/RSJ International Conference on Intelligent Robots and Systems (IROS), pp. 831–836. IEEE (2013)
13. Manfredi, L., Putzu, F., Guler, S., Huan, Y., Cuschieri, A.: 4 DOFs hollow soft pneumatic actuator – HOSE. Mater. Res. Express (2018)
14. Stilli, A., Wurdemann, H., Althoefer, K.: A novel concept for safe, stiffness-controllable robot links. Soft Robot. **4**(1), 16–22 (2017)
15. Althoefer, K.: Antagonistic actuation and stiffness control in soft inflatable robots. Nat. Rev. Mater. **3**, 76–77 (2018)

16. Althoefer, K.: Neuro-fuzzy path planning for robotic manipulators. Ph.D. thesis, King's College London (1996)
17. Degani, A., et al.: Highly articulated robotic probe for minimally invasive surgery. In: 30th Annual International Conference of the IEEE Engineering in Medicine and Biology Society, vols. 1–8, pp. 3273–3276 (2008)
18. Simaan, N.: Snake-like units using flexible backbones and actuation redundancy for enhanced miniaturization. In: 2005 IEEE International Conference on Robotics and Automation (ICRA), vols. 1–4, pp. 3012–3017 (2005)
19. Camarillo, D.B., et al.: Mechanics modeling of tendon-driven continuum manipulators. IEEE Trans. Robot. **24**, 1262–1273 (2008)
20. Ning, K., Worgotter, F.: A novel concept for building a hyper-redundant chain robot. IEEE Trans. Robot. **25**, 1237–1248 (2009)
21. Cheng, N., et al.: Design and analysis of a soft mobile robot composed of multiple thermally activated joints driven by a single actuator. In: 2010 IEEE International Conference on Robotics and Automation (ICRA), pp. 5207–5212 (2010)
22. Dupont, P.E., et al.: Design and control of concentric-tube robots. IEEE Trans. Robot. **26**, 209–225 (2010)
23. Jiang, A., et al.: Robotic granular jamming: does the membrane matter? Soft Robot. **1**(3), 192–201 (2014)
24. Amend, J., Brown, E., Rodenberg, N., Jaeger, H., Lipson, H.: A positive pressure universal gripper based on the jamming of granular material. IEEE Trans. Robot. **28**(2), 341–350 (2012)
25. Stanley, A.A., Gwilliam, J.C., Okamura, A.M.: Haprtic jamming: a deformable geometry, variable stiffness tactile display using pneumatics and particle jamming. In: World Haptics Conference (WHC), 14–17 April 2013
26. Li, M., et al.: Multi-fingered haptic palpation utilizing granular jamming stiffness feedback actuators. Smart Mater. Struct. **23**(9), 095007 (2014)
27. Cheng, N., et al.: Design and analysis of roust, low-cost, highly articulated manipulator enabled by jamming of granular media. In: International Conference on Robotics and Automation (ICRA), 14–18 May 2012
28. Zuriguel, I., Garcimartín, A., Maza, D., Pugnaloni, L.A., Pastor, J.M.: Jamming during the discharge of granular matter from a silo. Phys. Rev. E **71** (2005)
29. Roux, J.-N.: Geometric origin of mechanical properties of granular materials. Phys. Rev. E **61**(6), 6802–6836 (2000)
30. Corwin, E., Jaeger, H., Nagel, S.: Structural signature of jamming in granular media. Nature **435**(7045), 1075–1078 (2005)
31. van Hecke, M.: Jamming of soft particles: geometry, mechanics, scaling and isostaticity. J. Phys. Condens. Matter **22**(3) (2009)

A K-Nearest Neighbours Based Inverse Sensor Model for Occupancy Mapping

Yu Miao$^{(\boxtimes)}$, Ioannis Georgilas, and Alan Hunter

University of Bath, Claverton Down, Bath BA2 7AY, UK
y.miao@bath.ac.uk

Abstract. OctoMap is a popular 3D mapping framework which can model the data consistently and keep the 3D models compact with the octree. However, the occupancy map derived by OctoMap can be incorrect when the input point clouds are with noisy measurements. Point cloud filters can reduce the noisy data, but it is unreasonable to apply filters in a sparse point cloud. In this paper, we present a k-nearest neighbours (k-NN) based inverse sensor model for occupancy mapping. This method represents the occupancy information of one point with the average distance from the point to its k-NN in the point cloud. The average distances derived by all the points and their corresponding k-NN are assumed to be normally distributed. Our inverse sensor model is presented based on this normal distribution. The proposed approach is able to deal with sparse and noisy point clouds. We implement the model in the OctoMap to carry out experiments in the real environment. The experimental results show that the 3D occupancy map generated by our approach is more reliable than that generated by the inverse sensor model in OctoMap.

Keywords: K-nearest neighbours · Inverse sensor model · Occupancy mapping

1 Introduction

Autonomous vehicles are widely used in military, agricultural, industrial and commercial areas. Robotic mapping as an essential part of the autonomous navigation system is often required in these application scenarios. The process of building a map of the environment while locating a robot itself is referred to as simultaneous localization and mapping (SLAM) [1].

In robotics, point clouds can be obtained by low-cost sensors and are effective in representing the environment [2]. Point clouds usually consist of a great number of points which contain the location data of the environment. The point cloud is a popular data type since it is easily accessible to researchers. Depth sensors such as the LIDAR, stereo cameras and RGB-D cameras can be used to produce point clouds. Point clouds are used for a wide range of research and commercial applications, including mapping, navigation and autonomous driving. With 3D point clouds, a mapping approach for household environments is

© Springer Nature Switzerland AG 2019
K. Althoefer et al. (Eds.): TAROS 2019, LNAI 11650, pp. 75–86, 2019.
https://doi.org/10.1007/978-3-030-25332-5_7

proposed in [3]. Some SLAM systems are also based on point clouds. In [4], a 3D SLAM system for outdoor scenes is presented using laser range data.

The Point Cloud Library (PCL) has been developed for processing point clouds [5]. Many functions such as filtering, registration and segmentation are included in this library. Recently, a popular occupancy mapping approach to map the environment with point clouds is OctoMap [6]. It is an efficient framework for 3D occupancy mapping. However, the map generated by OctoMap can be inaccurate when the point clouds are noisy. Although PCL provides several point cloud filters to remove noisy data, it is unreasonable to apply filters in a sparse point cloud with only a few points.

To solve these problems, we propose a k-nearest neighbours (k-NN) based inverse sensor model for occupancy mapping. We use the average distance from a point to its k-NN to represent the occupancy information of the point. This distance is assumed to be follow the normal distribution. Two neighbouring point clouds are compared to obtain a dynamic normal distribution (Sect. 3.2). With this distribution, a k-NN based inverse sensor model is presented to update the occupancy map (Sect. 3.3). The proposed model is implemented in the OctoMap to illustrate its effectiveness. We test it in a semi-structured environment by generating a 3D occupancy map with the point clouds derived by ORB-SLAM [7] (Sect. 4). The experimental results show that the map generated by our method is more accurate than that derived by the model in OctoMap.

2   Related Work

The processing and mapping methods for point clouds have been investigated in many studies.

The octree is an tree-based data structure in which each node is a cube and has eight child nodes [8]. Due to this hierarchical structure, an octree can quickly expand a large number of nodes by recursively subdividing a node into eight children. Based on the octree structure, PCL is able to index 3D point cloud data efficiently and provide processing algorithms, including point cloud compression, spatial partitioning, neighbour search and spatial change detection [9–11].

OctoMap is a 3D occupancy mapping method, which is based on octrees and probabilistic estimation [6]. OctoMap models the environment by volumetric representation and can keep models compact by implementing octrees. With a clamping update policy to limit the occupancy estimates, OctoMap can rapidly adapt to environment changes.

ORB-SLAM is considered to be the most complete feature-based monocular visual SLAM system and has been extended to stereo visual SLAM [7,12]. It uses ORB features in the mapping process. ORB-SLAM contains three threads, tracking, local mapping and loop closing. They are parallel threads, so ORB-SLAM can run efficiently on a CPU without using a GPU. Bundle adjustment (BA) is performed in both local mapping and loop closing to reduce the projection error of the vision sensor. The map will be updated when the loop is detected.

We implement ORB-SLAM to get point clouds. In ORB-SLAM, keyframes are selected frames to map the environment. Each keyframe contains the camera pose, camera intrinsics and ORB features extracted from the image. Each ORB feature point corresponds to a point on the objects in the environment, so we can get a point cloud by accumulating the feature points in each keyframe. In this paper, the point cloud obtained by ORB features in the keyframe is referred to as the keyframe point cloud.

3   Methodology

The point cloud which contains the points from all the observations is referred to as the map point cloud. In the map point cloud, the average distances from all the points to their corresponding k-NN are assumed to follow the normal distribution. We use these average distances to represent the occupancy information of the points. Our mapping approach first updates the normal distribution and then updates the occupancy map with the k-NN based inverse sensor model. We implement our inverse sensor model in the OctoMap to generate a 3D occupancy map. This section will explain our method in detail.

3.1 Background of OctoMap

OctoMap is an efficient probabilistic framework for 3D occupancy mapping. It has been explained in detail in [6]. The probability $P(n|z_{1:t})$ of a node is modelled by Bayes rule and can be written as

$$P(n|z_{1:t}) = \left[1 + \frac{1 - P(n|z_t)}{P(n|z_t)} \frac{1 - P(n|z_{1:t-1})}{P(n|z_{1:t-1})} \frac{P(n)}{1 - P(n)}\right]^{-1}, \qquad (1)$$

where n is the node, $z_{1:t}$ denotes the set of all sensor measurements acquired from time 1 to time t, $P(n|z_t)$ is the occupied probability given the measurement z_t and $P(n)$ is the prior probability.

In OctoMap, the prior probability $P(n) = 0.5$ and (1) can be simplified by the log-odds notation

$$L(n) = ln\left[\frac{P(n)}{1 - P(n)}\right]. \qquad (2)$$

Then the probability of a node given measurements to time t is

$$L(n|z_{1:t}) = L(n|z_{1:t-1}) + L(n|z_t), \qquad (3)$$

where $L(n|z_t)$ is the inverse sensor model. For any kind of ranging senor, a ray-cast operation will be performed from the sensor origin to the end points. The inverse sensor model in OctoMap is defined as

$$L(n|z_t) = \begin{cases} l_{occ} & \text{if the endpoint is in the node } n \\ l_{free} & \text{if a ray traverses the node } n \end{cases}, \qquad (4)$$

where l_{occ} and l_{free} are the probabilities set to the nodes. A clamping update policy is applied in OctoMap to set lower and upper bounds on the log-odds value.

3.2   Update Normal Distribution

Description of Point Cloud. Normally, the map point cloud can be different at different times. We use new points, disappeared points and affected points to describe the changes in the point cloud. As shown in Fig. 1, the points in the point cloud at time t but not in the point cloud at time $t-1$ are called new points. While the points in the point cloud at time $t-1$ but not in the point cloud at time t are called disappeared points. Due to the changes in the point cloud, some points may have different k-NN or average distances at time $t-1$ and t. These points are called affected points. In Fig. 1, the points selected by the dashed circle are the k-NN of the point in the center.

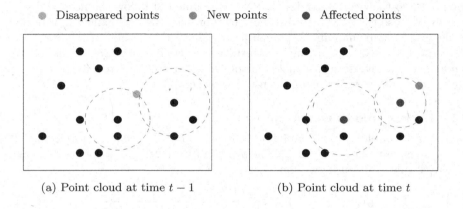

(a) Point cloud at time $t-1$ (b) Point cloud at time t

Fig. 1. Different points in the point cloud

To detect the changes in the map point cloud, the spatial change detection in the PCL is implemented. The points in the point cloud are indexed by the octree structure in PCL. By comparing the octree structures at time $t-1$ and time t, we can get new points and disappeared points. The detection of affected points will be discussed later.

Normal Distribution. To describe how informative one point is, we assume that the average distance from any point to its k-NN is subject to a normal distribution

$$f(s) = \frac{1}{\sqrt{2\pi\sigma^2}} exp\left(-\frac{(s-\mu)^2}{2\sigma^2}\right), \tag{5}$$

where s is the average distance from the point to its k-NN, μ is the mean of average distances derived by all the points and σ is the standard deviation.

To mitigate the impact from noisy or wrong measurements, a limit, s_{limit}, for the average distance is set to remove unreasonable data. The remaining points, called valid points, will be used to calculate the mean and the standard deviation. When the map point cloud changes, the most common way to update the normal distribution is to calculate the mean with all the average distances and then sum the squares of all the deviations from the mean. To avoid this brute force calculation, the method for calculating corrected sums of squares is implemented [13]. This method does not need to store prior data and can reduce rounding errors in the computer implementation [14]. A series of means and standard deviations will be generated when the number of input values grows. Based on the description of the point cloud and the method in [13], we will illustrate how to update the normal distribution.

Add Point to Normal Distribution. At time t, if a point p is a new point or an affected point, we will compare the average distance $s_{p,t}$ of this point with the limit s_{limit}. If $s_{p,t} < s_{limit}$, the following process will be performed

$$N \leftarrow N + 1, \tag{6}$$

$$S \leftarrow S + \frac{N-1}{N}(s_{p,t} - \mu)^2, \tag{7}$$

$$\mu \leftarrow \frac{N-1}{N}\mu + \frac{1}{N}s_{p,t}, \tag{8}$$

where N is the number of valid points and S is the sum of the squares of the deviations of valid points. The sum of squares and the mean are updated after this process. The average distance of the point will be included in the normal distribution.

Erase Point from Normal Distribution. This process is the inverse process of adding a point to the normal distribution. At time t, if a point p is a disappeared point or an affected point, we will compare the average distance $s_{p,t-1}$ of this point with the limit s_{limit}. If $s_{p,t-1} < s_{limit}$, the following process will be performed

$$\mu \leftarrow \frac{N}{N-1}\mu - \frac{1}{N-1}s_{p,t-1}, \tag{9}$$

$$S \leftarrow S - \frac{N-1}{N}(s_{p,t-1} - \mu)^2, \tag{10}$$

$$N \leftarrow N - 1, \tag{11}$$

After this process, the sum of squares and the mean are updated. The average distance of this point will be removed from the normal distribution.

Update Standard Deviation. At time t, after all the new points, disappeared points and affected points have been processed, we are able to update the standard deviation. The standard deviation is

$$\sigma = \sqrt{\frac{S}{N}}. \tag{12}$$

Update Affected Points. This process will search the affected points and update the normal distribution with affected points. Algorithm 1 illustrates the process of searching affected points. Let C_{new}, $C_{disappeared}$ and $C_{affected}$ denote the collections of new points, disappeared points and affected points, respectively. s_{max} is the maximum limit for the affected points searching process. The searching process increases the radius of the circle centred on any point $p \in (C_{new} \bigcup C_{diappeared})$ by step Δr. Lines 10 through 11 exclude new points and affected points in the annulus with inner radius $r - \Delta r$ and outer radius r in the map point cloud at time t. Line 12 updates the average distance from each remaining point to its k-NN. If the distance are different at time $t - 1$ and t, the searching point will be marked as an affected point. Lines 16 and 17 update the normal distribution with affected points. The searching process will stop when the average distance of each searching point in the annulus remains same at time $t - 1$ and t, or $r \geq s_{max}$.

Algorithm 1. Update Affected Points

Input: p, Δr, s_{max}, C_{new}, $\bigcup s_{p,t-1}$, $MapPointCloud_t$, s_{limit}, N, S, μ, σ
Output: N, S, μ, σ

1 $r \leftarrow \Delta r$
2 $C_{previous} \leftarrow \emptyset$
3 $C_{affected} \leftarrow \emptyset$
4 **do**
5      $flagIncreaseRadius \leftarrow false$
6      $C_{temp} \leftarrow SearchPoints(MapPointCloud_t, p, r)$
7   **if** $(C_{temp} - C_{previous} - C_{temp} \bigcap C_{new}) = \emptyset$ **then**
8          $flagIncreaseRadius \leftarrow true$
9   **else**
10   **for** $q \in (C_{temp} - C_{previous} - C_{temp} \bigcap C_{new})$ **do**
11   **if** $q \notin C_{affected}$ **then**
12                 $s_{q,t} \leftarrow UpdateAverageDistance(MapPointCloud_t, q)$
13   **if** $s_{q,t} \neq s_{q,t-1}$ **then**
14                     $flagSameKNN \leftarrow false$
15                     $C_{affected}.insert(q)$
16                     $ErasePointFromNormalDistribution(s_{q,t-1})$
17                     $AddPointFromNormalDistribution(s_{q,t})$
18   **if** $flagIncreaseRadius = false$ **and**
                       $flagSameKNN = false$ **then**
19                       $flagIncreaseRadius \leftarrow true$

20   **if** $flagIncreaseRadius = true$ **then**
21         $r \leftarrow r + \Delta r$
22         $C_{previous} \leftarrow C_{temp}$
23 **while** $flagIncreaseRadius = true$ **and** $r < s_{max}$

Update Normal Distribution. Based on the process of updating affected points, we can update the normal distribution completely. Algorithm 2 presents the complete process of updating the normal distribution. Lines 1 through 4 update the normal distribution with new points and affected points caused by new points. Lines 5 to 7 update the normal distribution with disappeared points and affected points caused by disappeared points. Line 8 calculates the standard deviation.

Algorithm 2. Update Normal Distribution

Input: C_{new}, $C_{disappeared}$, $\bigcup s_{p,t-1}$, $MapPointCloud_t$, s_{limit}, N, S, μ, σ
Output: N, S, μ, σ

1 **for** $p \in C_{new}$ **do**
2 | $s_{p,t} \leftarrow UpdateAverageDistance(MapPointCloud_t, p)$
3 | $AddPointToNormalDistribution(s_{p,t})$
4 |__ $UpdateAffectedPoints(p)$
5 **for** $p \in C_{disappeared}$ **do**
6 | $ErasePointFromNormalDistribution(s_{p,t-1})$
7 |__ $UpdateAffectedPoints(p)$
8 $\sigma \leftarrow \sqrt{S/N}$

3.3   Mapping with k-NN Based Inverse Sensor Model

k-NN Based Inverse Sensor Model. With (5) that the average distance is subject to a normal distribution, we can define a probability function to represent the occupancy information of a point in the point cloud

$$Prob(s_{p,t}) = P_u - \frac{\int_{-\infty}^{s_{p,t}} f(s)ds}{\int_{-\infty}^{w\sigma+\mu} f(s)ds}(P_u - P_w), \tag{13}$$

where w is a scale factor, P_u is the upper limit of the probability and P_w is the corresponding probability when $s_{p,t} = w$. w, P_u and P_w are changeable parameters. The probability will be smaller than P_u since the lower limit of the integral is negative infinity. A point is more relevant to points nearby when it has a higher probability. The noisy data and wrong measurements usually have lower probabilities. In this way, noisy measurements are given lower weights and thus can be filtered out to some extent. We use a similar method as the free nodes update strategy in OctoMap to update free nodes. However, before a ray is cast from the sensor position to the endpoint p, the endpoint must satisfy

$$ln\left[\frac{Prob(s_{p,t})}{1 - Prob(s_{p,t})}\right] > ln\left[\frac{P_w}{1 - P_w}\right]. \tag{14}$$

Then the inverse sensor model can be defined as

$$
L(n|z_t) = \begin{cases} \sum_p ln\left[\dfrac{Prob(s_{p,t})}{1 - Prob(s_{p,t})}\right] & \text{if the end point } p \text{ is in the node } n \\ l_{free} & \text{if a ray traverses the node } n \end{cases}, \quad (15)
$$

where $p \in C_{view}$ and p is in node n. C_{view} is the measurement z_t, the collection of points in the sensor field of view (FOV) at time t. This model considers both the occupancy probability of each point and the number of points in a node. $L(n|z_t)$ tends to be bigger when the points in the node are with higher probabilities and the node contains more points. This also accords with the common sense.

Update Occupancy Map. Algorithm 3 shows the mapping process with the proposed inverse sensor model. x_{sensor} denotes the position of the vision sensor. Lines 3 through 7 update the occupied nodes and prepare for free nodes updates. Line 8 updates the free nodes. Now the map has been updated with the latest observation z_t.

Algorithm 3. Mapping with k-NN Based Inverse Sensor Model

Input: C_{view}, x_{sensor}, $\bigcup L(n|z_{1:t-1})$, $\bigcup s_{p,t}$, w, P_u, P_w
Output: $\bigcup L(n|z_{1:t})$

1 $L(n|z_{1:t}) \leftarrow L(n|z_{1:t-1})$
2 $C_{end} \leftarrow \emptyset$
3 **for** $p \in C_{view}$ **do**
4      $n \leftarrow SearchNode(p)$
5      $L(n|z_{1:t}) \leftarrow L(n|z_{1:t}) + ln\left[Prob(s_{p,t})/(1 - Prob(s_{p,t}))\right]$
6   **if** $ln\left[Prob(s_{p,t})/(1 - Prob(s_{p,t}))\right] > ln\left[P_w/(1 - P_w)\right]$ **then**
7          $C_{end}.insert(p)$
8 $UpdateFreeNodes(x_{sensor}, C_{end})$

---

4 Experimental Results

4.1 Experiment Setup

We run ORB-SLAM with a ZED stereo camera to capture the feature points on a tree (See Fig. 2(a)). To collect enough points to shape the tree, we move the camera around the tree. The trajectory of the camera is approximately a circle of radius 3.5 m. In the end, we use a set of keyframes derived after loop correction to extract a series of keyframe point clouds and poses. With the pose information, the map point clouds can be recovered by accumulating keyframe point clouds. Then the map point clouds are used to update the normal distribution in Sect. 3.2. Each keyframe point cloud can be regarded as an measurement

z_t. So the keyframe point cloud can be used to update the occupancy map with the k-NN based inverse sensor model in Sect. 3.3. When the objects are far away from the camera, the depth measurements can be unreliable. To remove those unreasonable but avoid impacts on the occupancy map, we keep those points whose distances to the camera are within 4 m.

(a) Tree   (b) Reference

Fig. 2. Tree and reference

The ground truth is described by a reference map in which the foliage and the pot are represented by an ellipsoid and an cuboid (See Fig. 2(b)). In this paper, the resolution of the occupancy map is set to 0.1 m. Since the trunks in Fig. 2(a) are partly blocked by the foliage and the grass in the pot, we ignore the trunks in the reference map. The grass is treated as a part of the pot, so the height of the pot in the reference map is greater than the real height. Although the reference is different from the ground truth, we can compare different inverse sensor models by comparing their relative mapping results to the reference.

4.2 Experiment Results

Figure 3(a) shows the camera trajectory derived by ORB-SLAM. Figure 3(b) is the last keyframe point cloud and Fig. 3(c) is the corresponding map point cloud. Figure 3(d) and (e) present the occupied nodes derived by the OctoMap inverse sensor model and the proposed k-NN model, respectively. Figure 3(f) and (g) show the occupancy maps with both free and occupied nodes. The mapping results of the inverse sensor model in OctoMap and the proposed model are compared with the reference map. The occupied nodes in an occupancy map is a shell since the camera cannot observe the inside of an object. Figure 3(h) and (i) are the comparison results of the mapping results and the reference. A number of nodes are attached to the surface of the shell in the reference map and a minor translation occurs between two maps. This is because the measurements from the stereo camera are not accurate enough. To find those nodes that are apparently irrelevant to the map, we inflate the reference above ground by 0.3 m. The ground part and the nodes whose vertical distances to the ground are within 0.3 m are also ignored. The nodes outside the inflated reference map are presented in Fig. 3(j) and (k). These nodes are apparently irrelevant to the ground truth.

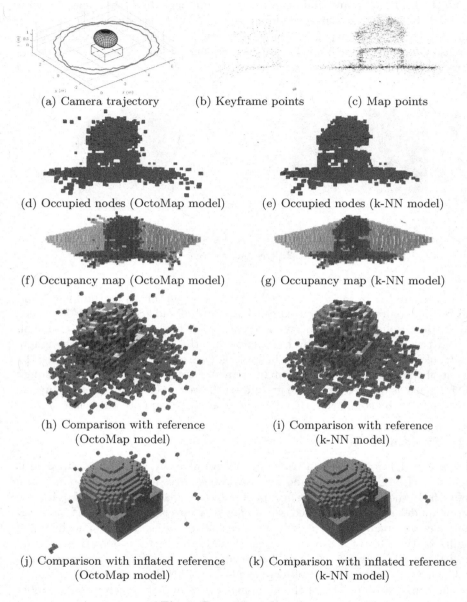

(a) Camera trajectory   (b) Keyframe points   (c) Map points

(d) Occupied nodes (OctoMap model)   (e) Occupied nodes (k-NN model)

(f) Occupancy map (OctoMap model)   (g) Occupancy map (k-NN model)

(h) Comparison with reference   (i) Comparison with reference
(OctoMap model)   (k-NN model)

(j) Comparison with inflated reference   (k) Comparison with inflated reference
(OctoMap model)   (k-NN model)

Fig. 3. Experimental results

Table 1 shows the comparison results of the reference map and the inflated reference map. The total nodes number of the reference shell is 1441. The mapping results of the OctoMap model and the k-NN model share 399 and 387 nodes, respectively. 756 occupied nodes in the map derived by the OctoMap model are either on the reference shell or inside the shell. While the reference shell can cover 703 occupied nodes in the map generated by the k-NN model. The numbers of irrelevant nodes for two maps are 33 and 4, respectively.

Table 1. Comparison with reference

Model	Nodes in reference shell	Nodes covered by reference	Irrelevant nodes
OctoMap model	399	756	33
K-NN model	387	703	4

4.3 Discussion

Sometimes the spatial change detection in PCL cannot detect all the new points and disappeared points. It is possible that the average distance $s_{p,t-1}$ of an affected point and the average distance $s_{p,t}$ of a point in the keyframe point cloud are unknown. In these cases, we process such points as new points.

The experiment in the semi-structured environment shows that our approach can deal with sparse and noisy point clouds. The occupied nodes derived by the k-NN based model are more accurate and with less irrelevant nodes. Due to the noise and wrong measurements in the point cloud, the OctoMap model can branch free nodes even when the measurements are highly irrelevant. While the k-NN based model only generate free nodes with reliable measurements.

Since the point clouds are sparse, and camera measurements and the reference map are not accurate enough, the number of nodes shared by the occupancy map and the reference shell is smaller than the number of the nodes which form the reference shell. In Table 1, the numbers of the k-NN model are slightly smaller than the numbers of the OctoMap model. Because the k-NN based method can filter unreliable points, and the reference map cannot overlap the ground truth completely so that wrong matches may occur between the map derived by the OctoMap model and the reference map.

In this paper, we ignore the influence of the pruning and clamping update policy in the OctoMap when counting the number of nodes. Because it is rare to see pruning and clamping when the input point clouds are sparse.

5 Conclusion

In this paper, we present a k-NN based inverse sensor model for occupancy mapping with an illustration of the update process of the normal distribution and the inverse sensor model. Our approach is reliable even when the input point cloud is noisy and sparse. The mapping result of the k-NN based method is with less irrelevant nodes than that of the OctoMap model. In the future, the performance of the proposed algorithms will be optimized. An map update policy will be developed so that the occupancy map can update accordingly when ORB-SLAM detects loop closure and updates the keyframes. Then the proposed model can be extended to the real-time mapping.

Acknowledgments. Yu Miao thanks University of Bath grant University Research Studentship Award-Engineering and China Scholarship Council grant No. 201706120022 for financial support.

References

1. Robotic mapping. https://en.wikipedia.org/wiki/Robotic_mapping. Accessed 23 Jan 2019
2. Kwon, Y., Kim, D. and Yoon, S.E.: Super ray based updates for occupancy maps. In: Proceedings of the 2016 IEEE International Conference on Robotics and Automation, pp. 4267–4274. IEEE, Stockholm (2016)
3. Rusu, R.B., Marton, Z.C., Blodow, N., Dolha, M., Beetz, M.: Towards 3D point cloud based object maps for household environments. Robot, Auton. Syst. **56**(11), 927–941 (2008)
4. Cole, D.M. and Newman, P.M.: Using laser range data for 3D SLAM in outdoor environments. In: Proceedings of the 2006 IEEE International Conference on Robotics and Automation, pp. 1556–1563. IEEE, Orlando (2006)
5. Rusu, R.B. and Cousins, S.: 3D is here: Point Cloud Library (PCL). In: Proceedings of the 2011 IEEE International Conference on Robotics and Automation, pp. 1–4. IEEE, Shanghai (2011)
6. Hornung, A., Wurm, K.M., Bennewitz, M.: OctoMap: an efficient probabilistic 3D mapping framework based on octrees. Auton. Robots **34**(3), 189–206 (2013)
7. Mur-Artal, R., Montiel, J.M.M., Tardos, J.D.: ORB-SLAM: a versatile and accurate monocular SLAM system. IEEE Trans. Robot. **31**(5), 1147–1163 (2015)
8. Octree. https://en.wikipedia.org/wiki/Octree. Accessed 24 Jan 2019
9. Point Cloud Compression. http://pointclouds.org/documentation/tutorials/compression.php#octree-compression. Accessed 24 Jan 2019
10. Spatial Partitioning and Search Operations with Octrees. http://pointclouds.org/documentation/tutorials/octree.php#octree-search. Accessed 24 Jan 2019
11. Spatial change detection on unorganized point cloud data. http://pointclouds.org/documentation/tutorials/octree_change.php#octree-change-detection. Accessed 24 Jan 2019
12. Taketomi, T., Uchiyama, H., Ikeda, S.: Visual SLAM algorithms: a survey from 2010 to 2016. IPSJ Trans. Comput. Vis. Appl. **9**(1), 16 (2017)
13. Welford, B.P.: Note on a method for calculating corrected sums of squares and products. Technometrics **4**(3), 419–420 (1962)
14. Standard deviation. https://en.wikipedia.org/wiki/Standard_deviation. Accessed 23 Jan 2019

Elastomer-Based Touch Sensor: Visualization of Tactile Pressure Distribution

Wanlin Li[1], Jelizaveta Konstantinova[1], Akram Alomainy[2],
and Kaspar Althoefer[1(✉)]

[1] Centre for Advanced Robotics @ Queen Mary (ARQ), Queen Mary University
of London, Mile End Road, London E1 4NS, UK
{wanlin.li, j.konstantinova, k.althoefer}@qmul.ac.uk
[2] School of Electronic Engineering and Computer Science (EECS), Queen Mary
University of London, Mile End Road, London E1 4NS, UK
a.alomainy@qmul.ac.uk

Abstract. This paper presents an elastomer-based tactile sensor that can sense
the tactile information in the form of pressure distribution. Our proposed sensor
uses a piece of coated elastomer with thin conical pins underneath as the touch
medium. The elastomer consists of 91 pins arranged in a honeycomb pattern,
each pin can be regarded as a tactile sensing element. They are spaced at 1.5 mm
in x and y direction. Each tactile element transfers the applied pressure value into
a circular image pattern which can be captured by a camera placed at the end of
the sensor structure. The applied pressure over the sensing array can be computed by processing the area of each sensing element. MATLAB is used to
process the received images relating the applied pressure to the activated pixels
in each circular pattern of the tactile element, and further visualizing the pressure
distribution on a reconstructed surface of the sensor. This paper presents the
development principle and fabrication process of the proposed sensor. The
experimental results have proven the viability of the sensing concept; the prototype sensor can effectively detect single-point touch caused by objects with
different dimensions and multi-point touch interactions with a spacing of more
than 2.5 mm.

Keywords: Tactile sensor · Elastomer-based

1 Introduction

Tactile sensor development in robotics research is becoming an important aspect since
touch sensing acquires useful information about the physical interaction with the
external environment [1]. The human tactile system is extremely powerful as it consists
of extraordinarily high number of epidermis mechanoreceptors to detect the mechanical
stimulus on the skin. Different kinds of cells are aligned at different depths in human
skin, called Pacinian Corpuscle, Ruffini Corpuscle, Merkel Cells and Meissner's
Corpuscle [2]; these are sensitive to different kinds of mechanical stimuli, such as high-
frequency vibration, static force, low-frequency force and low-frequency vibration. The
human hand is one of the most dexterous parts and the feeling of touch is an essential

© Springer Nature Switzerland AG 2019
K. Althoefer et al. (Eds.): TAROS 2019, LNAI 11650, pp. 87–98, 2019.
https://doi.org/10.1007/978-3-030-25332-5_8

human sensation. Figure 1 shows the cut-away view of a fingertip showing the inter-mediate ridges whose static and dynamic displacement are detected through the skin's mechanoreceptors [3].

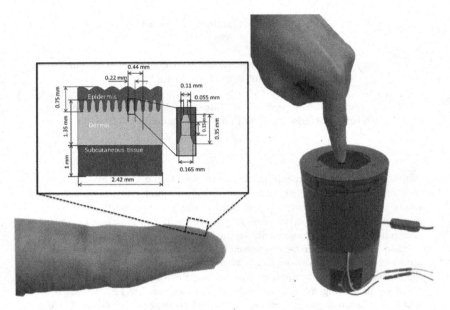

Fig. 1. A simplified elastic model mimicking a cut-away view of the human fingertip. The proposed tactile sensor can be used to create a 3D reconstruction of the sensor membrane. The Figure shown right is a sensory snapshot with its reconstruction shown together with the sensor.

Many biologically-inspired devices are embedded in robotic sensing systems. Today's robotic sensing systems consist of different kinds of tactile sensors [4] including resistive sensors, capacitive sensors, piezoelectric sensors, organic field-effect transistors (OFETs) sensors and optical sensors. These sensors are designed to acquire signals allowing tactile perception similar to the human and assist the robots in manipulation tasks. Tactile sensors can continuously provide tactile information, for instance the direction and the magnitude of forces at all contact points and the information (shape, texture, softness etc.) of the objects they are interacting with.

Optical tactile sensors have attracted plenty of attention from researchers in the past few years [5]. Compared with electromagnetic sensing methods such as resistive-based or capacitive-based sensors that largely require the transmission of electrical signals, optical-based sensors use an optical sensor, such as a high-resolution camera, to capture the information and interpret the deformation of the sensing surface as tactile sensation with the aid of computer vision techniques. Most of the optical sensors use a physical medium which deforms according to the applied force and then indirectly infers the pressure or force information from the deformation.

An ideal optical tactile sensor is required to be a compliant mechanism with a large sensing area and high sensitivity, but with low power consumption [6]. With the rapid development of small cameras and image processing techniques, many optical tactile sensors have been proposed and manufactured. The TacTip [7] is a biologically-inspired sensing and object manipulation device that is inspired by the deformation of the epidermal layers of the human skin. Papillae pins on the inside of the device's skin are tracked by a camera and their movement under external contact can be converted into pressure and shear force. The tactile force sensor in [8] is a fiber optic based tactile array sensor that can detect normal forces and object shapes via nine individual sensing elements made from electromagnetically isolated optical fibers. The optical three-axis tactile sensor in [9] is capable of sensing normal force and shearing force detected from the deformation and displacement of the contact areas of rubber-made conical feelers. GelSight [10] has a soft contact interface, and provides high resolution tactile images of contact geometry, as well as contact force and slip conditions.

This paper introduces an optical-based tactile sensing concept employing a 2D vision system for the acquisition of tactile information, see Fig. 1. The sensor uses a reflective soft opaque elastomer with 91 thin conical pins at one end made of silicone to obtain the spatial pressure distribution when physically interacting with objects. The conical pins are placed in a 3D printed shell that maintains contact with a transparent acrylic plate. Pressure is detected from the integrated binary values of bright pixels calculated from the captured image of the contact areas of the 91 conical pins. We present the design and development process in Sect. 2. The experimental evaluation process is presented in Sect. 3. Conclusions are drawn in Sect. 4.

2 Sensor Design

Our elastomer-based tactile sensor is a biologically-inspired and low-cost device which uses a 3D printed shell and a compliant contact surface (so-called elastomer) as a touch medium to obtain tactile information from stimuli. Figure 2 demonstrates the schematic design of the sensor that is made of several components. The elastomer (1) is made of a silicone material extracted from a 3D printed mold to provide the compliant properties referred as the tip of the sensor. The interior of the elastomer of an array of small reflective pins which are made of silicone mixed with metallic powder. More details of the elastomer will be shown in Sect. 2.1. A web-cam (2) is placed at the bottom of the device to track the pins of the elastomer. A transparent acrylic sheet with 5 mm thickness (3) is placed under the elastomer; this is the supporting plate to provide a solid plate for the camera to observe the deformation of the elastomer during contact. A white LED array (4) is placed inside the 3D printed shell (5) acting as an internal light source to illuminate the elastomer, the light goes through the light-guiding plate (6) which has a 45° angle at the edge towards the pins of the elastomer. The 3D printed sensor base (7) and shell are made of nylon (dyed in black color), the shell acts as a force sensitive structure (so-called flexure) behaving like a spring mechanism due to its build-in cantilever structure. With such a design, the flexure can support as well as stabilize the elastomer during the contact. A cap (8) is screwed onto the top of the sensor to keep the elastomer in place during the interaction with the external environment.

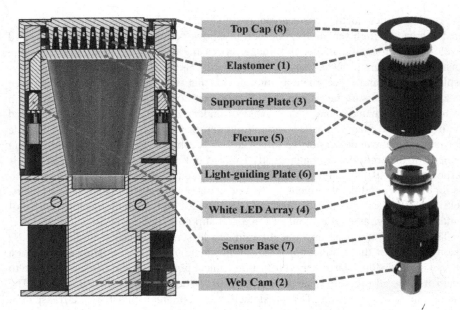

Fig. 2. Elastomer-based tactile sensor design. The left side shows the schematic design and the right side shows the exploded view of the sensor.

2.1 Design and Fabrication of the Elastomer

The elastomer part acts as the touch medium of the device and is composed of an array of pins on the interior of the soft silicone membrane to translate contact information into pin deformation, which can be then presented as the visualization of the tactile data. The array of pins performs a similar mechanical response as the dermal papillae of the human skin under load (see Fig. 3).

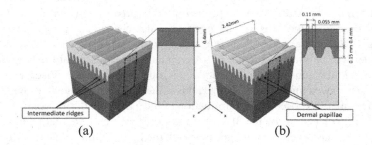

Fig. 3. Depth configuration of (a) the 2D ridge model and (b) the 3D ridge model.

In our proposed research, the elastomer part is composed of two parts: the opaque elastomer base with a hexagonal arrangement of 91 reflective pins underneath and the opaque membrane. The elastomer's properties largely influence the sensitivity of the device, so the pins need to be highly elastic and the membrane is made to be thin, flexible and uniform. Figure 4(a), (b) and (c) shows the manufactured elastomer including both elastomer base and the membrane together with its 3D printed mold. Our mold is made of the material Polylactide (PLA). The layout of the pins is a 2D hexagonal pattern with 91 elements which are 1.5 mm apart. Each conical pin has a height of 11 mm, a diameter of 3 mm at the base and a diameter of 1.25 mm at its tip. These tactile pins are in contact with the transparent supporting plate, facing towards the camera when at rest and will be pushed towards the transparent plate when a load is exerted at the membrane on the top. This leads to a deformation of these conical pins captured by the camera at the base. The tactile information can then be extracted using computer vision methods.

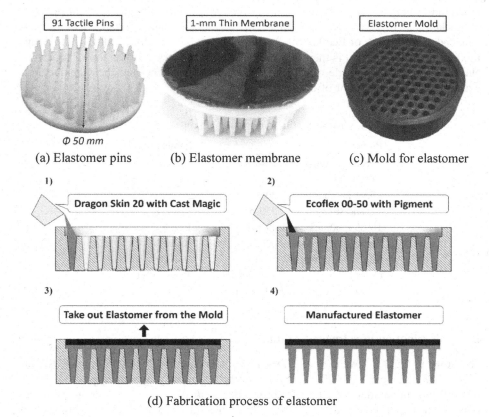

(a) Elastomer pins   (b) Elastomer membrane   (c) Mold for elastomer

(d) Fabrication process of elastomer

Fig. 4. Elastomer description and the fabrication process, with (a) and (b) showing the integrated elastomer. In (c), the mold for manufacturing the elastomer is depicted. In (d), the step-by-step manufacturing process of the elastomer with different parts using different types of silicone materials is shown.

Figure 4(d) demonstrates the fabrication process of the elastomer part. The two types of silicone materials used in our sensor are Dragon Skin 20 and Ecoflex 00-50 from Smooth-on Company. The properties of both silicone types are shown in Table 1. During the molding of the elastomer base with its integrated pins, Silicone Thinner and part A of Dragon Skin 20 are pre-mixed with a weight ratio of 1:5. Silicone Thinner is a non-reactive silicone fluid that can lower the viscosity of platinum cure silicone (Dragon Skin and Ecoflex, in this case), which offers the advantages of making the elastomer de-air faster, as well as letting the liquid mixture better flow over the intricate mold with its many tinny holes. Then part B of Dragon Skin 20 is added into the liquid mixture with the same weight of part A. Silver Bullet Cast Magic Powder is then added to the material with a weight ratio of 1:100 to make the material reflective on its surface. The liquid mixture is put into a conditioning planetary mixer (THINKY ARE-250) to mix and degas. We pour the material into the holes of the mold and about four or five hours later the silicone will be cured and solidified. For the membrane, the layer is required to be thin and opaque to ensure high resolution of the sensor. Opacity helps to exclude any external light interference. Here we use Silc Pig silicone color pigment to blacken the silicone structure. To make the membrane, same colorant Silc Pig black is added to the part A of Ecoflex 00-50 and mix well before adding part B. The liquid mixture of Ecoflex 00-50 is then sent to the mixer and poured on the top of the cured elastomer base that is made of Dragon Skin 20. After 3 h curing, the manufactured elastomer can be taken out of the mold.

Table 1. Elastomer material properties

Property	Dragon Skin 20	Ecoflex 00-50
Specific gravity	1.08 g/cc	1.07 g/cc
Cure time	4 h	3 h
Shore hardness	20 A	00–50
Tensile strength	550 psi	315 psi
100% modulus	49 psi	12 psi
Elongation @ break	620%	980%
Mix ratio by weight	1A:1B	1A:1B
Color	Translucent	Translucent
Mixed viscosity	20000 cps	8000 cps

2.2   Illumination and Image Capture

As shown in Fig. 5(a), we use an LED array which contains 12 white 5 mm LEDs with a 30° viewing angle. All LEDs are soldered on a hollow-ring shaped printed circuit board (PCB) in parallel and the LED array is placed inside of the sensor to generate the inner light source powered by a USB TTL cable. In order to completely block the external light interference, an opaque silicone rubber ring made of Ecoflex 0050 painted with black is placed on top of the light-guiding plate. The size of the hollowed rubber ring has an inner diameter of 55 mm and an outer diameter of 66 mm with 45° angle at one end, which is the same as the light-guiding plate dimension. The light-guiding plate is a 3D printed hollowed cylinder using transparent material VeroClear. It has a 45° angle on top end to guide and reflect the light from LED to the transparent supporting plate (shown in Fig. 2(6)), thus the reflective elastomer pins can be illuminated. The top cap of the sensor also helps to block the light coming from upwards. We use a webcam (Microsoft LifeCam Studio) with a resolution of 640 × 480 pixels and 30 fps to capture the visible area of the elastomer pins. Focusing on the center area of 430 × 430 pixels cropped from the received raw image, tactile information can be processed and visualized in the form of pressure distribution. More details are presented in Sect. 3.1.

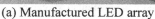

(a) Manufactured LED array   (b) Manufactured opaque rubber ring

Fig. 5. Proposed tactile sensor illumination system. In (a), the LED array provides the inner light source within a closed environment. In (b), an opaque rubber ring is placed within the flexure (Fig. 2(5)) to block the external light interference.

3   Prototype Sensor Performance

3.1   Working Principle of Tactile Sensor

A Matlab model determines the activated area of each tactile sensing element. As is shown in the flowchart of Fig. 6, we firstly read the real-time video information from the web cam. Next, the real-time RGB image is converted to grayscale image and is divided into 91 hexagonal parts based on a uniformly distributed honeycomb layout which enables the detection of activated area for each sensing element. After that the grayscale image is further converted to binary image and a numeric display calculates the quantity of black and white pixels detected from each hexagonal area. Finally, via an interpolation method with the scattered data, we reconstruct a surface of the elastomer membrane based on the activated area of each silicone pin.

When switching on the power, the light is transferred from the source to the unloaded elastomer through the light-guiding plate and the supporting plate. The web cam is placed at the bottom to capture the raw images of the illuminated elastomer. The received images (without load) are displayed by the video output shown in Fig. 7(a), there are 91 pins on one side of the elastomer which are represented as the bright blobs. Then the input image is converted into a grayscale image and divided into 91 hexagonal parts (with a radius of 23 pixels each), see Fig. 7(b). Each hexagon represents one sensing element and all 91 elements can be treated as a tactile array. After thresholding, the grayscale image is converted into a binary image as shown in Fig. 7

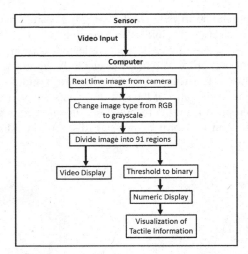

Fig. 6. Flowchart of activated pin areas to tactile information visualization system. The system acquires the input video in 30 frame per second and all the image computations can be processed in real-time.

(c), there is no white blobs when no load is applied as the threshold eliminates the gray color. Once an external contact is applied on the elastomer membrane, the pins are squeezed onto the supporting plate, causing an increase in contact area with the supporting plate for each sensing element. These contact areas are white because of the reflectiveness of the pins and they can pass the threshold and generate the white blobs. Thus, the corresponding sensing area will generate more activated pixels. Figure 7(d), (e), and (f) shows the raw image received by the camera and the corresponding grayscale image and binary image when part of the black membrane (Fig. 4(b)) is touched on its left part. Figure 7(g), (h) and (i) shows the raw image received by the camera and the corresponding grayscale image and binary image when the whole surface of the membrane is touched and pressed.

3.2   Visualization of Tactile Information

The tactile information in terms of pressure distribution is measured in our proposed tactile sensor. The pressure distribution is visualized from the number of activated pixels of all 91 silicone pins. We use the scattered data interpolation method (griddata function in Matlab) to plot the interpolated surface of the elastomer membrane. We apply triangulation-based natural neighbor interpolation which is an efficient tradeoff between linear and cubic method to support 3-D interpolation. The grayscale pressure color map is built when an external contact is applied on the sensor membrane. When there is no contact, the initial reconstruction status of the surface in our method is shown in Fig. 8(a). To evaluate the tactile response of the proposed sensor, several tests including single-point touch, multiple-points touch are applied to the sensor. These tests aim to verify that the system can detect touch. Firstly, we test the single-point

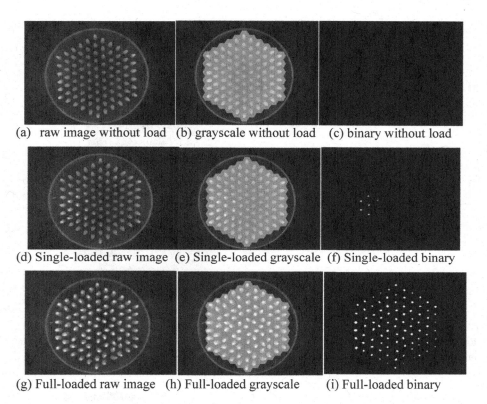

(a) raw image without load   (b) grayscale without load   (c) binary without load

(d) Single-loaded raw image   (e) Single-loaded grayscale   (f) Single-loaded binary

(g) Full-loaded raw image   (h) Full-loaded grayscale   (i) Full-loaded binary

Fig. 7. Camera received image and viewer tool demonstrating the deformation of the reflective elastomer pins.

touch to the sensor as shown in Fig. 8(b). The sensor can detect and visualize the pressure on the reconstructed surface.

Then we test the single-point touch with objects of different dimensions to investigate the touch ability (10 cubes with side length of 2 mm to 20 mm with an increment of 2 mm, see Fig. 9(a)). We segment the sensor membrane into five zones as shown in Fig. 9(b), then we push each cube into each zone and calculate the sum of the activated pixels of the received images and repeat for 10 times. We then calculated the averaged activated pixels of the sensor for each cube under different zones and plot as shown in Fig. 10. The results show that the sensor can detect different size of cubes over its whole surface and can recognize its corresponding dimensions.

Finally, we test with multi-points touch and the sensor is able to detect three-fingers touch as shown in Fig. 11(a). However, a misdetection happens when two fingers are very closed to each other as the sensor regards the touch as a single-point touch. The minimum spacing distance between multi-points is less than 2.5 mm, as is shown in Fig. 11(b).

(a) No pressure is applied to sensor membrane

(b) Single-point contact to sensor membrane

Fig. 8. Reconstructing surface of the sensor membrane displaying the visualized tactile information in form of pressure distribution together with the corresponding pressure test.

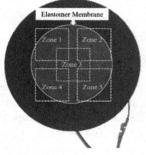

(a) 3D printed test cubes of different sizes   (b) 5 test zones of the membrane

Fig. 9. Setup for different pressure test. In (a), 10 different cubes are made to test the sensor touch ability. In (b), 10 cubes are placed one by one in Zone 1 to Zone 5 respectively and repeated 10 times for each test to record the sensor performance.

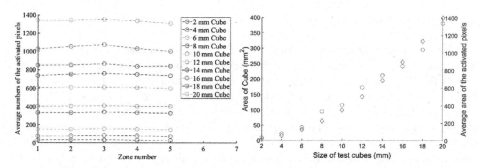

Fig. 10. The figure shown left is average number of the activated pixels while palpating cubes that differ in side length by 2 mm. Each test repeats ten times for data collection. The figure shown right is the average number of the activated pixels of the sensor versus the areas of cubes.

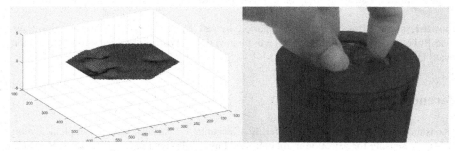

(a)   Successful detection of multi-points contacts

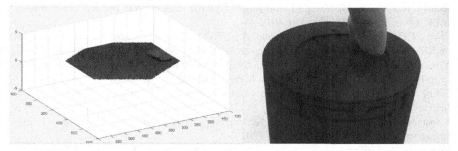

(b)   Failed detection when contact points are less than 2.5 mm away from each other

Fig. 11. Reconstructing surface of the sensor membrane displaying the multi-points contact to the sensor. (a) shows a successful detect of three-point contact with human fingers. Failure happens in (b) when contact points are too closed to each other, specifically less than 2.5 mm.

4   Conclusions

This paper presents a prototype tactile sensor that uses a soft coated elastomer with 91 thin conical pins at one end to sense the tactile information in the form of pressure distribution. The sensor can measure the tactile information over the sensor membrane surface based on a pixel-based method relying on the area change of each reflective conical pin recorded by a camera when a pressure is applied. The fabrication procedure shows the manufacturing of the elastomer using different silicone materials, as well as the other components of the sensor system. Test results show the feasibility of the sensing approach together with the accuracy of the sensor in detecting different objects. The proposed sensor has many advantages, e.g. compliant structure with the use of the elastomer, the sensor only uses one web cam to detect the sensing medium which provides a low-cost manufacturing. Future work will mainly focus on miniaturization of the sensor in order to fit with a wide range of robot arms and hands. An extension of the tactile spatial resolution may also be helpful to increase the sensing capability.

Acknowledgments. This work was supported in part by the EPSRC National Centre for Nuclear Robotics project (EP/R02572X/1), the Innovate UK WormBot project (104059) and the Innovate UK project iGrasp (103676).

References

1. Konstantinova, J., Jiang, A., Althoefer, K., Dasgupta, P., Nanayakkara, T.: Implementation of tactile sensing for palpation in robot-assisted minimally invasive surgery: a review. IEEE Sens. J. **14**(8), 2490–2501 (2014)
2. Dahiya, R.S., Metta, G., Valle, M., Sandini, G.: Tactile sensing–from humans to humanoids. IEEE Trans. Robot. **26**(1), 1–20 (2010)
3. Pham, T.Q., Hoshi, T., Tanaka, Y., Sano, A.: Effect of 3D microstructure of dermal papillae on SED concentration at a mechanoreceptor location. PLoS ONE **12**(12), e0189293 (2017)
4. Yousef, H., Boukallel, M., Althoefer, K.: Tactile sensing for dexterous in-hand manipulation in ro-botics—a review. Sens. Actuators A Phys. **167**(2), 171–187 (2011)
5. Schneiter, L., Sheridan, T.B.: An optical tactile sensor for manipulators. Robot. Comput.-Integr. Manuf. **1**, 65–71 (1984)
6. Konstantinova, J., Stilli, A., Althoefer, K.: Fingertip fiber optical tactile array with two-level spring structure. Sensors **17**(10), 2337 (2017)
7. Winstone, B., Griffiths, G., Pipe, T., Melhuish, C., Rossiter, J.: TACTIP - tactile fingertip device, texture analysis through optical tracking of skin features. In: Lepora, N.F., Mura, A., Krapp, H.G., Verschure, P.F.M.J., Prescott, T.J. (eds.) Living Machines 2013. LNCS (LNAI), vol. 8064, pp. 323–334. Springer, Heidelberg (2013). https://doi.org/10.1007/978-3-642-39802-5_28
8. Xie, H., Jiang, A., Wurdemann, H.A., Liu, H.: Magnetic resonance-compatible tactile force sensor using fiber optics and vision sensor. IEEE Sens. J. **14**(3), 829–838 (2013)
9. Ohka, M., Mitsuya, Y., Higashioka, I., Kabeshita, H.: An experimental optical three-axis tactile sensor for micro-robots. Robotica **23**(4), 457–465 (2005)
10. Yuan, W., Li, R., Srinivasan, M.A., Adelson, E.H.: Measurement of shear and slip with a GelSight tactile sensor. In: 2015 IEEE International Conference on Robotics and Automation (ICRA), pp. 304–311 (2015)

Modelling of a Soft Sensor for Exteroception and Proprioception in a Pneumatically Actuated Soft Robot

Abu Bakar Dawood$^{(\boxtimes)}$, Hareesh Godaba, and Kaspar Althoefer

Center for Advanced Robotics @ Queen Mary University of London,
London, UK
a.dawood@qmul.ac.uk

Abstract. Soft sensors are crucial to enable feedback in soft robots. Soft capacitive sensing is a reliable technology that can be embedded into soft pneumatic robots for obtaining proprioceptive and exteroceptive feedback. In this paper, we model a soft capacitive sensor that measures both the actuated state as well as applied external forces. We develop a Finite Element Model using a multiphysics software (COMSOL®). Using this model, we investigate the change in capacitance with the application of external force, for a range of different internal pressures and strains. We hope this study is helpful in understanding the coupling of internal inputs and external stimuli on the feedback obtained from the sensors and help us design better sensory systems for soft robots.

Keywords: Soft sensor · Hyperelastic materials ·
Proprioception · Exteroception · COMSOL

1 Introduction

Living organisms have always been a source of inspiration for scientific development. Many developments in soft robotics are products of inspiration from soft bodied organisms like octopus [1], jelly fish [2] and plant roots [3]. Unlike soft robots, conventional rigid bodied robots that are employed extensively in industry, lack inherent compliance and adaptability. These rigid bodied robots need to be isolated from human workspaces due to safety hazards posed by them. However soft robots are a more practical solution for safe Human Robot Interaction (HRI) [4]. Due to the complexity of controlling soft robot arms, Finite Element Modelling (FEM) becomes an important area for investigation. FEM, when combined with neural-network or fuzzy-logic methods, can provide solutions to accurately navigate soft robot arms in their environment [5].

Rigid robots often have finite degrees of freedom and are easier to sensorize. Built-in feedback systems provide information of the state of the robot which can be utilized to control the robots effectively. However, in soft robots, the task of obtaining feedback of the forces and positions is a much more complex task due to the infinite number of degrees of freedom of motion of these robots.

© Springer Nature Switzerland AG 2019
K. Althoefer et al. (Eds.): TAROS 2019, LNAI 11650, pp. 99–110, 2019.
https://doi.org/10.1007/978-3-030-25332-5_9

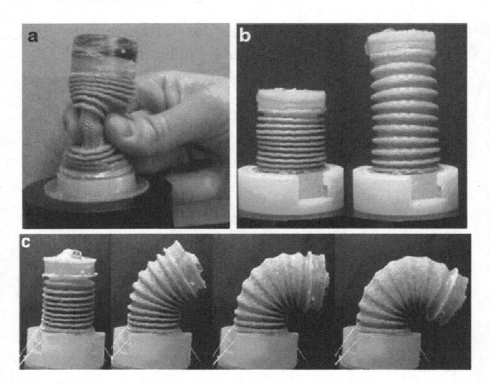

Fig. 1. Stiff-Flop, a medical soft robot [6]. This figure shows the 3 scenarios (a) External pressure, (b) Extension, (c) Bending.

Previous works have utilized Electro-conductive yarn [7], Conductive rubber sensors [8], Elastomer channels filled with Gallium Indium [9, 10], Carbon nanotubes [11, 12] and screen printed liquid metals [13] for shape sensing of soft actuators. Magnetic sensors [14, 15] have also been used for curvature sensing, in bending actuators. However, the sensors need to be isolated from external magnetic fields in the environment. Resistive sensors have also been demonstrated as strain and force sensors. Many resistive sensors, especially filled rubbers, exhibit hysteresis which detrimentally affects sensor reliability. Although sensors utilizing Gallium Indium have been shown to have low hysteresis, however manufacturing of strain sensors with high complexity and at a large scale needs to be addressed. Optical methods such as optical fibers [6, 16, 17] optical wave guides [18], and fiber brag grating [19] have also been used to make reliable strain sensors.

Ozel et al. [20] analyzed soft bending actuation modules integrated with commercially available resistive flex sensor and hall sensor separately and concluded that the magnetic sensor integrated actuation module, showed more repeatability and precision as compared with the resistive sensor. Shintake et al. [21] used carbon black filled elastomer composite to make a multilayered strain sensor having both resistive and capacitive elements. It was established that the performance of capacitive sensing elements was superior to that of the resistive elements due to high linearity, low hysteresis and high repeatability.

Often, we encounter different types of stimuli acting together in soft robots. Figure 1 shows external force acting on a soft actuator and deforming it. Several works have utilized soft sensors to measure multiple senses such as internal pressure and external forces in soft robots. Larson et al. [22] used Ecoflex based sensors to measure change in capacitance with stretch, pneumatic pressure and external force, individually. However, the response because of two or more stimuli acting at the same time in a real environment was not studied. For pressure sensing, both resistance [23, 24] and capacitance based [22, 25] have been extensively used and a combination of different types of sensors have been employed to achieve proprioception and exteroception for soft actuators. Totaro et al. [26] have made a proprioceptive and exteroceptive sensor by utilizing two different sensing technologies in one sensor. Bending was sensed by the change in resistance of thin tracks of gold nanoparticles, implanted by using Supersonic Cluster Beam Implantation (SCBI) while external force was measured by the change in IR intensity within the sensor substrate as measured by a phototransistor. This sensor has showed promising results. However, the integration of this sensor in a soft actuator, different deformations of soft wave guide depending upon different types of indenters, and the dependence of refraction of IR in different materials are yet to be studied in detail.

As we know of these coupling issues, we conduct a detailed investigation of how pressure, force and stretch simultaneously affect the capacitance of a soft capacitor. In this paper we model a soft capacitive sensor under the application of different internal and external stimuli simulated by application of internal pressure and external forces. We study the change in capacitance with stretch and benchmark the results with an analytical model. After benchmarking, the changes in the capacitance under varying internal pressures simulating proprioception is studied. We finally model the changes in capacitance due to application of external forces to a sensor that is stretched and bulged under internal pressure. Understanding the nature of capacitance changes due to application of different modes of stimuli would provide us information that would help us to decouple these modes. We hope that a matrix of these capacitive sensors combined with the knowledge of the effects of various stimuli would be a step forward for proprioceptive and exteroceptive soft robots.

2   Methodology

2.1   Finite Element Modeling

We model the sensor shown in Fig. 2 using COMSOL. The sensor is integrated with the substrate which is analogous to the body of a soft actuator. The inset in Fig. 2 shows the exploded view of the capacitor.

When internal pressure is applied, the bottom layer bulges thereby also expanding the sensor layer. Then the area of sensor increases and the thickness decreases leading to increase in the capacitance. Also, external pressure can be applied onto the sensor causing it to display a change in the capacitance. We model the soft robot body and the

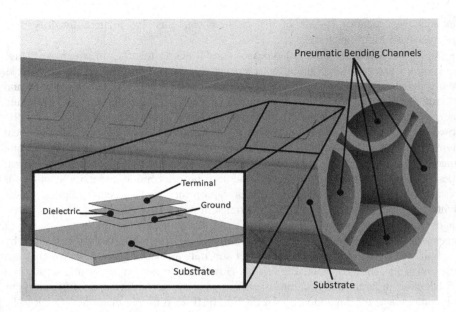

Fig. 2. Cross-sectional area of a pneumatic soft actuator is shown along with the bending channels. Placement of sensor array is also shown integrated with the sensor skin. In-set figure shows the exploded view of the capacitor being modeled.

sensor as dielectric materials with hyperelastic behavior. In our COMSOL® model, the following dimensions were used (Table 1).

Table 1. Dimensions of base and capacitor used in COMSOL Model.

Name	Value
Width_Base	50 [mm]
Depth_Base	40 [mm]
Height_Base	2 [mm]
Width_Cap	20 [mm]
Depth_Cap	16 [mm]
Height_Cap	50 [um]

A predefined fine mesh is used and then customized by using a maximum element size of 0.004 m and a minimum element size of 0.0005 m. The element type used for this model was free tetrahedral. The meshing of the complete model is shown in Fig. 3.

We employ Eco-Flex 00-30 as the material for both the substrate and the sensor. Silicone is selected from the COMSOL® material library as the base material and the relative permittivity ($\varepsilon_r = 2.5$) and bulk modulus ($k = 0.098$ MPa) corresponding to Eco-Flex 00-30 are employed. Hyperelastic material property is then added to the assigned material. Mooney-Rivlin model is selected as the Hyperelastic material model

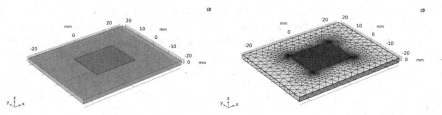

Fig. 3. Figure (a) shows the Soft Capacitive Sensor on a silicone substrate. Thickness of the substrate is 2 mm while the sensor is made up 50 μm thick dielectric layer with upper and lower boundaries defined as terminals. (b) 3D Model showing the free tetrahedral meshing. Maximum element size is 0.004 m and minimum element size is 0.0005 m

and the parameters for the model are calculated by curve fitting the experimental uniaxial stretch-stress data of Eco-Flex 00-30 available in literature [22]. The curve fitting showing the calculated material parameters and experimental stress-stretch values are shown in Fig. 4.

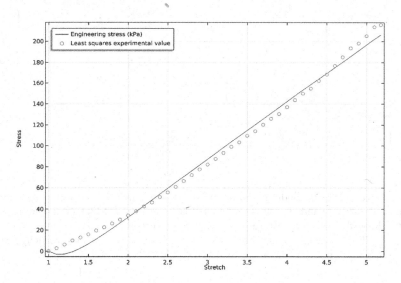

Fig. 4. Curve fitting for calculating Mooney-Rivlin Parameters, green circles show measured stress while the blue line shows stress computed using the material properties that have been fitted to the measured data. (Color figure online)

2.2 Model Validation

We first validate the model by benchmarking the finite element solution with the analytical results for a capacitance change of a soft parallel plate capacitor under uniaxial tension. To study the dependence of capacitance on the stretch of the capacitor, a parametric study was used. The sensor was stretched by fixing one boundary of the base and subjecting the opposite boundary to prescribed displacement constraints. A domain probe was placed on the capacitor to calculate the stretch λ at every step. The base was stretched from 0 to 0.055 m so that λ i.e. the stretch in the capacitor was from 1 to 2 (Fig. 5).

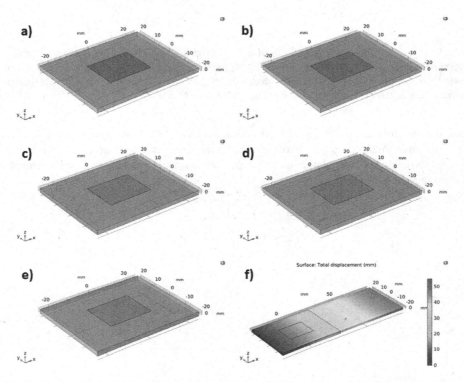

Fig. 5. Setup of boundary conditions for our FEM model. Figure (a) and (b) show the definition of upper and lower boundaries of the dielectric layer as terminal and ground respectively. Figure (c) shows the boundary that was fixed while Fig. (d) shows the boundary that is subjected to prescribed displacements. Figure (e) shows the two boundaries that were partially fixed i-e only in z-direction. Figure (f) shows the total deformation when λ = 2.

The plot of capacitance against stretch obtained from the FEM is shown in Fig. 6.

For analytical modeling of parallel plate capacitor, following parameters were used (Table 2).

The value of stretch was changed from 1 to 2 in increments of 0.1 and the capacitance with respect to the applied stretch is computed using the following equation

$$C = \frac{\varepsilon_r \varepsilon_0 WL}{D} \lambda, \tag{1}$$

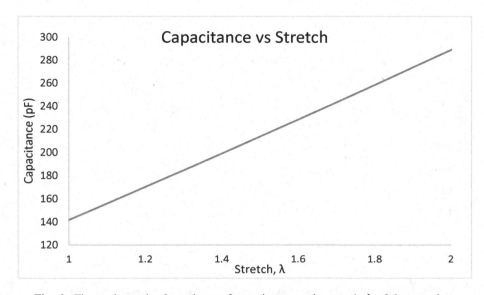

Fig. 6. Figure shows the dependence of capacitance on the stretch, λ of the capacitor.

Table 2. Parameters used for capacitance in analytical modeling.

Name	Expression
Relative permittivity	2.5
Width_Cap	20 [mm]
Depth_Cap	16 [mm]
Thickness_Dielectric	50 [um]

where ε_r and ε_0 are the relative permittivity and dielectric permittivity of free space respectively, W, L and D are the initial width, length and the thickness of the dielectric being stretched, respectively, and λ is the stretch of the dielectric given by the ratio of the resultant length to the initial length. The finite element result for the change of capacitance with stretch is plotted along with the analytical result computed using Eq. (1). The results from FEM analysis compare closely with the results obtained using the analytical model (Fig. 7).

3   Results and Discussion

Internal Pressure and external force being proprioceptive and exteroceptive stimuli respectively, are applied on the same model. The application of pressure on the bottom surface, simulating internal pressure in a soft robot, makes the Eco-Flex substrate inflate, bulging out from the center as shown in Fig. 8a. This bulge increases the area between the capacitive terminals and decreases the dielectric thickness, causing an increase in capacitance. Without external forces, the capacitance is directly related to

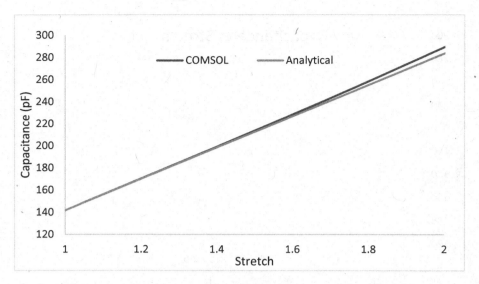

Fig. 7. Comparison of capacitance vs stretch COMSOL and analytical model.

the internal pressure applied, and the capacitance can, hence, be used as a measure of the internal pressure and state of the robot. In the simulations, the internal pressure is increased from 0 to 10 kPa in increments of 1000 Pa. The change in the capacitance with respect to the pressure is shown in Fig. 9.

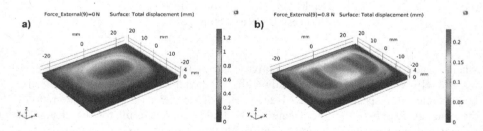

Fig. 8. (a) Bulging in the Ecoflex substrate when internal pressure of 2 kPa is applied. (b) Indentation in the bulge at an instant, when an external force of 0.8 N is applied.

Now, we simulate how applied external forces change the capacitance of the soft capacitor at different levels of internal pressure. At each applied internal pressure, a normal force of 0 to 1 N distributed across the area, is applied to the top surface of the soft capacitor. At $\lambda = 1$, the force range of 0 to 1 N creates a considerable change in capacitance for the trend to be studied. The deformed capacitor approaching the non-deflated state as shown in Fig. 8b. These changes in capacitance for different internal pressures (IP) are shown in Fig. 10.

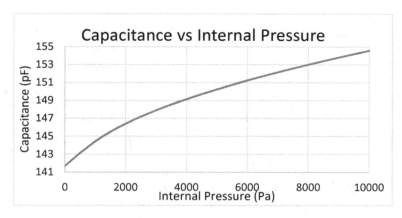

Fig. 9. Change in capacitance when internal pressure of 0 to 10 kPa is applied with no external force in action.

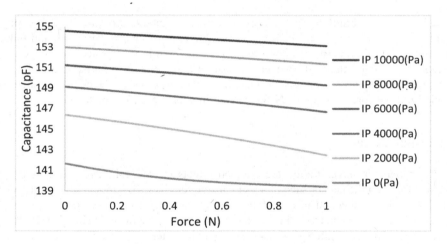

Fig. 10. Effect of external force on capacitance for a series of internal pressures.

Many soft actuators and soft robot links are designed so that application of internal pressure results in linear elongation [6, 27]. The linearly extending actuators also need to sense the strains for proprioception and the external forces for force feedback. To address this scenario, we also simulate the effect of the initial stretch of the soft substrate on the sensor's response to external forces. Change in capacitance due to the soft robotic link stretching and external force being applied simultaneously is a common practical scenario. When the $\lambda = 1$ and an external force is applied to the capacitor, the bulging of the membrane decreases resulting in a decrease in the capacitance as seen in Fig. 11.

When the stretch is increased, the initial bulging due to application of internal pressure decreases. Consequently, the slope of decrease in capacitance with applied force also decreases until the $\lambda = 1.75$. However, when the initial stretch of the

108 A. B. Dawood et al.

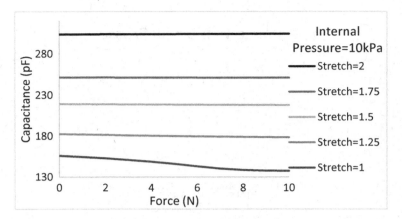

Fig. 11. Effect of external force on capacitance when the stretch changes from 1 to 2 while internal pressure was kept constant at 10 kPa.

capacitor is 2, the bulge in the membrane because of internal pressure is almost negligible, and the external force causes the membrane to reverse in curvature and bulge inwards against the internal pressure causing an increase in the surface area, hence, an increase in the capacitance. However, because of a higher stretch, larger external force is required to achieve a noticeable change in the capacitance. Hence, the range of applied normal force is 0 to 10 N for change in capacitance to be studied.

4 Conclusions

In this paper, we have studied the coupled effects of internal pressure, stretch and external force on the capacitance of a soft capacitive sensor. We model a substrate with a soft capacitor embedded in it, to replicate the case of a soft robot body with a soft capacitive sensor attached to it. Finite element analysis is conducted using COMSOL to calculate the effects of internal pressure, stretch and external force. The changes in the capacitance due to internal pressure relate to the sensor output during proprioception while the changes in the capacitance due to external forces relate to the sensor output during exteroception. The results show that capacitance changes due to applied external forces depend significantly on the internal pressure and stretch of the soft robot body.

This implies that the internal states of the robot body should be identified in order to measure the external interactions for a soft robot with capacitive sensing embedded in the soft body. The coupling between the internal states and the deformations due to external stimuli should be considered when designing sensors for combined proprioception and exteroception of the soft robots.

Acknowledgements. This work was supported in part by the EPSRC National Centre for Nuclear Robotics project (EP/R02572X/1), the Innovate UK WormBot project (104059).

References

1. Shiva, A., et al.: Tendon-based stiffening for a pneumatically actuated soft manipulator. IEEE Robot. Autom. Lett. **1**, 632–637 (2016)
2. Godaba, H., Li, J., Wang, Y., Zhu, J.: A soft jellyfish robot driven by a dielectric elastomer actuator. IEEE Robot. Autom. Lett. **1**, 624–631 (2016)
3. Lucarotti, C., Totaro, M., Sadeghi, A., Mazzolai, B., Beccai, L.: Revealing bending and force in a soft body through a plant root inspired approach. Sci. Rep. **5**, 8788 (2015)
4. Stilli, A., Wurdemann, H.A., Althoefer, K.: A novel concept for safe, stiffness-controllable robot links. Soft Robot. **4**, 16–22 (2017)
5. Althoefer, K.: Neuro-fuzzy path planning for robotic manipulators (1996)
6. Cianchetti, M., et al.: Soft robotics technologies to address shortcomings in today's minimally invasive surgery: the STIFF-FLOP approach. Soft Robot. **1**, 122–131 (2014)
7. Wurdemann, H.A., et al.: Embedded electro-conductive yarn for shape sensing of soft robotic manipulators. In: Proceedings of the Annual International Conference of the IEEE Engineering in Medicine and Biology Society, EMBS (2015)
8. Popa, G.T., et al.: A stretchable, conductive rubber sensor to detect muscle contraction for prosthetic hand control. In: The 6th IEEE International Conference on E-Health and Bioengineering-EHB (2017)
9. White, E.L., Case, J.C., Kramer, R.K.: Multi-element strain gauge modules for soft sensory skins. IEEE Sens. J. **16**, 2607–2616 (2016)
10. White, E.L., Case, J.C., Kramer, R.K.: Multi-mode strain and curvature sensors for soft robotic applications. Sens. Actuators A Phys. **253**, 188–197 (2017)
11. Giffney, T., Bejanin, E., Kurian, A.S., Travas-Sejdic, J., Aw, K.: Highly stretchable printed strain sensors using multi-walled carbon nanotube/silicone rubber composites. Sens. Actuators A Phys. **259**, 44–49 (2017)
12. Christ, J.F., Aliheidari, N., Ameli, A., Pötschke, P.: 3D printed highly elastic strain sensors of multiwalled carbon nanotube/thermoplastic polyurethane nanocomposites. Mater. Des. **131**, 394–401 (2017)
13. Koivikko, A., Raei, E.S., Mosallaei, M., Mäntysalo, M., Sariola, V.: Screen-printed curvature sensors for soft robots. IEEE Sens. J. **18**, 223–230 (2018)
14. Ozel, S., Keskin, N.A., Khea, D., Onal, C.D.: A precise embedded curvature sensor module for soft-bodied robots. Sens. Actuators A Phys. **236**, 349–356 (2015)
15. Luo, M., et al.: Toward modular soft robotics: proprioceptive curvature sensing and sliding-mode control of soft bidirectional bending modules. Soft Robot. **4**, 117–125 (2017)
16. Sareh, S., Noh, Y., Li, M., Ranzani, T., Liu, H., Althoefer, K.: Macrobend optical sensing for pose measurement in soft robot arms. Smart Mater. Struct. (2015)
17. Searle, T.C., Althoefer, K., Seneviratne, L., Liu, H.: An optical curvature sensor for flexible manipulators. In: Proceedings of IEEE International Conference on Robotics and Automation (2013)
18. Zhao, H., O'Brien, K., Li, S., Shepherd, R.F.: Optoelectronically innervated soft prosthetic hand via stretchable optical waveguides. Sci. Robot. (2016)
19. Albert, J., Shao, L.Y., Caucheteur, C.: Tilted fiber Bragg grating sensors (2013)
20. Ozel, S., et al.: A composite soft bending actuation module with integrated curvature sensing. In: Proceedings of IEEE International Conference on Robotics and Automation (2016)
21. Shintake, J., Piskarev, E., Jeong, S.H., Floreano, D.: Ultrastretchable strain sensors using carbon black-filled elastomer composites and comparison of capacitive versus resistive sensors. Adv. Mater. Technol. (2018)

22. Larson, C., et al.: Highly stretchable electroluminescent skin for optical signaling and tactile sensing. Science (80) (2016)
23. Wang, T., et al.: A self-healable, highly stretchable, and solution processable conductive polymer composite for ultrasensitive strain and pressure sensing. Adv. Funct. Mater. (2018)
24. Park, J., et al.: Giant tunneling piezoresistance of composite elastomers with interlocked microdome arrays for ultrasensitive and multimodal electronic skins. ACS Nano **8**, 4689–4697 (2014)
25. Kim, S.Y., Park, S., Park, H.W., Park, D.H., Jeong, Y., Kim, D.H.: Highly sensitive and multimodal all-carbon skin sensors capable of simultaneously detecting tactile and biological stimuli. Adv. Mater. **27**, 4178–4185 (2015)
26. Totaro, M., Mondini, A., Bellacicca, A., Milani, P., Beccai, L.: Integrated simultaneous detection of tactile and bending cues for soft robotics. Soft Robot. **4**, 400–410 (2017)
27. Wurdemann, H., et al.: Integrated soft bending sensor for soft robotic manipulators (2015)

Robotic Mapping, Navigation and Planning

Online Human In-Hand Manipulation Skill Recognition and Learning

Disi Chen[1] , Zhaojie Ju[1(✉)], Dalin Zhou[1], Gongfa Li[2], and Honghai Liu[3]

[1] University of Portsmouth, Portsmouth PO1 3HE, UK
zhaojie.ju@port.ac.uk
[2] Wuhan University of Science and Technology, Wuhan 430080, China
[3] Shanghai Jiao Tong University, Shanghai 200240, China

Abstract. This work intends to contribute to transfer human in-hand manipulation skills to a dexterous prosthetic hand. We proposed a probabilistic framework for both human skill representation and high efficient recognition. Gaussian Mixture Model (GMM) as a probabilistic model, is highly applicable in clustering, data fitting and classification. The human in-hand motions were perceived by a wearable data glove, CyberGlove, the motion trajectory data proposed and represented by GMMs. Firstly, only a certain amount of motion data were used for batch learning the parameters of GMMs. Then, the newly coming data of human motions will help to update the parameters of the GMMs without observation of the historical training data, through our proposed incremental parameter estimation framework. Recognition in the research takes full advantages of the probabilistic model, when the GMMs were trained, the log-likelihood of a candidate trajectory can be used as a measurement to achieve human in-hand manipulation skill recognition. The recognition results of the online trained GMMs show a steady increase in accuracy, which proved that the incremental learning process improved the performance of human in-hand manipulation skill recognition.

Keywords: In-hand manipulation skills · GMMs · Online learning

1 Introduction

The advance of dexterous prosthetic hands, which now highly resemble the structures and functions of human hand. How to endow human hand capabilities to a prosthetic hand is now a cutting edge research topic. In-hand manipulation skills as a certain series skills of a human hand, are defined as capabilities of human to interact with an object within one hand [1], during which the object can be moved/rotated or deformed. Transferring human in-hand manipulation skills by using traditional hard-coding method is tedious and inefficient, therefore Learn from Demonstration (LfD) [2] is widely used for transferring human skill to a prosthesis. based on LfD paradigm, we proposed a online learning model for

Supported by grant of the EU Seventh Framework Programme (Grant No. 611391).

K. Althoefer et al. (Eds.): TAROS 2019, LNAI 11650, pp. 113–122, 2019.
https://doi.org/10.1007/978-3-030-25332-5_10

the human in-hand manipulation skill learning. As for human beings, in-hand manipulation skills are usually learned by us when we grow up and they play an important role in our daily life. However, to acquire these skills is a challenging task for the robot system or the prothesis. Firstly, to percept the motion of human hand in a high precision is difficult, since the structures of human hand are rather complex, with 27 bones and up to 25 degree of freedom (DoF) [3]. The huge amount of sensory information also leaves a gap in analyzing the actions performed by such a complex physical structure. Additionally, collecting a dataset with an ideal number of samples for classifier training, usually requires massive human actions, this both take a lot of memory and tedious human involvement. To overcome the difficulties mentioned above, we proposed a novel online framework for human in-hand manipulation skill learning. In this framework, Gaussian Mixture Models (GMM) with fixed component number [4] were applied for trajectory data representation, an Expectation Maximization (EM) [5] inspired incremental learning algorithm helps to update the parameters of GMMs, which released human candidates from tedious repeating one kind of in-hand manipulation at one time. In this process recognition provides the cue for updating the corresponding GMM in long term learning. We discussed the recognition results based on the motion data of human in-hand manipulations collected by the CyberGlove, to show the performance of our proposed method.

2   Related Work

2.1   In-Hand Motion Capturing

Recently, many literatures studied the human in-hand manipulations [6,7], those researches revealed the relations between the objects and human hands in a kinematic way and gives a guidance for designing a sensory system to collect human motion data in manipulations. There are many sensing systems designed for human hand motion measurement, such as data glove [8], camera system [9,10] and electromyography (EMG) system [11,12]. However, due to the high precision and better anti-interference ability compared with EMG system, data glove proved to be one of the most important sensing devices for in-hand motion perception, which measures the degree of bending of wearer's fingers and sent the corresponding signal to the computer. Kuroda [13] et al., proposed an innovative intelligent low-cost data glove named StrinGlove, which is capable to measure the displacements of all 24 DoF of one human hand with 24 inductcoders and 9 contact sensors. Fahn and Sun [14] presented a data glove with only five sensors properly mounted on the palmer surface, which is able to measure 10 DoF of a hand. Using data glove can not only continuously measure the angles of finger joints, but also record the haptic information on the finger tips. In this paper, we choose Cyberglove (Fig. 1(a)) as the sensor for measuring, since this data glove is capable to capture the movements of fingers and palm with 22 built-in bending angle sensors as shown in Fig. 1(b). The positions of sensors match all the joints on human fingers and the palm, these arrangement of sensors simplified the mapping the movement of human hand to a commercial prosthetic hand, such as i-Limb.

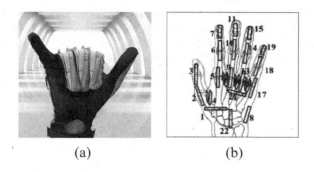

(a)   (b)

Fig. 1. Cyberglove and its sensor positions

2.2   Motion Skill Representation and Learning

Hand motion data of in-hand manipulation are temporal and spatial coupled, with a high dimension. To achieve recognition of in-hand manipulations, representation learning is important in recognition tasks. Statistical modelling is a bunch of powerful tools for representation learning, the models most frequently applied are known as GMMs. Considering the features of human in-hand manipulation data, we introduce GMMs to model the data. Calinon and Billard [15] proposed an approach to teach incrementally human gestures to a humanoid robot, in which the motion data were projected to another space and encoded into a GMM. Kalgaonkar and Raj [16] successfully identified 100 hand gestures based on ultrasound data with a high accuracy using a GMM.

Incremental parameter estimation of GMMs has already been achieved with various methods, most of them assume that novel data arrives in blocks as opposed to a single datum at a time. Hall et al. [17] merged Gaussian components in a pair-wise manner by considering volumes of the corresponding hyperellipsoids. Song and Wang [18] who used the W statistic and the Hotelling's T2 statistic for judging the equivalence of each Gaussian component before merging. However, they do not fully exploit the available probabilistic information. EM-inspired online parameter estimation method will try to explain it in the context of other novel data, affecting the accuracy of the fitting [19].

3   The Incremental Learning Framework for Gaussian Mixture Model

For a compact motion data representation, we resized the time-domain signals of all channels collected by the Cyberglove to be the same length, as shown in Fig. 2, each resized signal $\{\eta_t\}_{t=1}^T$ includes the bending information in the joint space. Firstly, for each in-hand motion, we used the human motion data to build the initial dataset D_{ini} for batch learning the parameters of a 2-dimensional GMM with 5 Gaussian components. Assuming there are m independent trajectories form different channels in one dataset, which is denoted $D_{ini} = \{d_i\}_{i=1}^m$ and for each $d_i = \{(t, \eta_t)\}_{t=1}^T$, where the subscript m is the index of channels and t represents the time step. For a concise representation in the following section, one sample used for training GMM can be denote as $s_t = (t, \eta_t)$. Then, more data from human performance will be collected and processed in the same form, denoted as D_{new}, these newly arrived data will be used for online updating the historical GMMs.

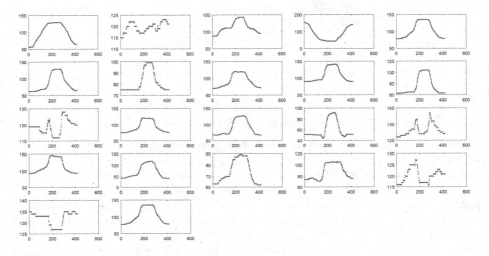

Fig. 2. Resized trajectories from human motion data

3.1   Batch Learning of GMM Using Standard EM Algorithm

The standard EM algorithm was applied to estimate the parameters of each GMM g_m with samples generated by one single channel m. The probability density function (PDF) is,

$$g_m(s_t) = \sum_{k=1}^K P(k)p(s_t|k) = \sum_{k=1}^K \pi_k \mathcal{N}(s_t|\mu_k, \Sigma_k) \tag{1}$$

where $P(k)$ is the prior of each Gaussian component, their value π_k are also called mixing coefficients, s_t is a data point in the trajectory d_i, $p(s_t|k)$ is the conditional PDF of a sample s_t, given k, $\mathcal{N}(\cdot)$ means a 2-dimentional normal distribution in this problem. All the parameters of the model g_m are $\Theta = \{\pi_k, \mu_k, \Sigma_k\}_{k=1}^K$, which were optimized by E-step and M-step in standard

EM algorithm according to maximum Likelihood Estimation (MLE). In E-step, we need to calculate the component likelihoods $p(k|s_t)$,

$$p(k|s_t, \Theta) = \frac{p(s_t, k|\Theta)}{\sum_j^K p(s_t, j|\Theta)} \tag{2}$$

and

$$p(s_t, k|\Theta) = p(s_t|k, \Theta) \cdot p(k|\Theta) = \mathcal{N}(s_t|\mu_k, \Sigma_k) \cdot \pi_k \tag{3}$$

where, the parameters, μ_k, Σ_k and π_k, are either initialized by human or from M-step during last iteration. The EM algorithm stopped when a local optimization reached, the optimal parameter set is Θ_{ini}.

3.2 Incremental Parameter Learning of GMMs

The newly coming data, denoted as D_{new}, usually include new information of the motion. To enroll those new in formation into the GMM, standard EM algorithm needs to explore both the historical data D_{ini} and the new data D_{new} during iteration, this is neither convenient nor practicable. Incremental learning is a considerable way to bridge this gap, it can update the historical parameter set Θ_{ini} without visiting the old dataset D_{ini} only used the data in D_{new}.

Considering that, after training a GMM, the old sample set D_0 is no longer accessible, only the parameters of a GMM are stored in the memory. Then, human continue to perform an action for several times, in each rollout, the trajectory $d_i^{new} \in D_{new}$ is recorded. To incrementally update the GMM, we introduced an assumption, the component likelihood $p(k|s_t)$ is almost do not change when only one new sample s_t^{new} arrives, so we modified the M-step in EM algorithm [5]. The parameter set Θ_{new} can be updated with component likelihoods and Θ_{ini}. For a clear expression, the old component likelihood denoted as $p(k|s_t) = \Phi_k$, the Θ_{new} is updated by,

$$\pi_k^{new} = \frac{\Phi_k + p(k|s_t^{new})}{N_s + 1} \tag{4}$$

$$\mu_k^{new} = \frac{\mu_i \Phi_k + s_t^{new} p(k|s_t^{new})}{\Phi_k + p(k|s_t^{new})} \tag{5}$$

$$\Sigma_k^{new} = \frac{(\Sigma_k + \mu_k \mu_k^\top - \mu_k \mu_k^{new \top} - \mu_k^{new} \mu_k^\top + \mu_k^{new} \mu_k^{new \top}) \Phi_k + (s_t^{new} - \mu_k^{new})(s_t^{new} - \mu_k^{new})^\top p(k|s_t^{new})}{\Phi_k + p(k|s_t^{new})} \tag{6}$$

where N_s is the number of total samples s_t used for learning the historical parameter set Θ_{ini}. When the incremental learning process is finished the up-to-date model can be updated again when new data arrives.

3.3 In-Hand Manipulation Recognition

Manipulation recognition in our experiment settings can be regarded as a classification problem We assume there are L different manipulation motion, for each motion $\mathcal{G}_l$, we trained a set of GMMs to represent trajectories from all the channels, which denoted as $\mathcal{G}_l = \{g_1^l, g_2^l, \ldots, g_M^l\}$. After collecting the trajectories of human in-hand motions, the newly collected data D_{new} will firstly serve as testing set, which also consists of M independent trajectories from different channels on CyberGlove. GMM is a kind of typical probability model, according to the PDF of a GMM, see Eq. (1), the probability of a candidate trajectory $D_{new} = \{d_m\}_{m=1}^M$ generated by the GMM $\mathcal{G}_l$ can be calculated. Therefore, we defined a novel metric, based on log-likelihood, to indicate the possibility $\mathcal{H}(D_{new}|\mathcal{G}_l)$ of a trajectory belonging to any set of GMM $\mathcal{G}_l$,

$$\mathcal{H}(D_{new}|\mathcal{G}_l) = \sum_{m=1}^{M} \left\{ \sum_{t=1}^{T} log[g_m^l(s_t^{new})] \right\} \tag{7}$$

where the formula in the outside summation indicates the log-likelihood of the candidate trajectory [20], while $\mathcal{H}(D_{new}|\mathcal{G}_l)$ is no longer a probability but it can be used to evaluate the possibilities. The following equation shows how to classify D_{new} into a class $\mathcal{G}_l$ belongs to.

$$l = arg \max_{l \in L} \mathcal{H}(D_{new}|\mathcal{G}_l) \tag{8}$$

The results from the above equation will be stored and to guide the online update process.

4   Experiments and Discussions

4.1   Experiment Settings

To evaluate the performance of our proposed framework, we defined 10 different in-hand manipulation skills for human to perform, as shown in Fig. 3. Human candidates were asked to finish those actions wearing a CyberGlove, For example, at the batch learning stage, each action was repeated 10 times by human to get enough data for training the initial GMMs.

In our proposed online learning and recognition framework, as shown in Fig. 4, the learning process can be divided into two stages, the first one is batch learning and the second one is incremental learning. In GMM batch learning phrase, 10 set of trajectory samples of human in-hand manipulation skills D_{ini} are utilised to train an initial GMM. For a fast training, the standard EM algorithm was set to converge when the increment of the log-likelihood is less than 10^{-3}. The training result of a initial GMM is visualized in Fig. 5(a), in which the trajectories consisting of many blue dots are the training samples and the 5 red ellipses visualised the Gaussian functions. After training the parameters of GMMs Θ, the component likelihoods $p(k|s_t)$ and the number of the samples used for training N_s will be stored for recognition the motions in newly arrived human motion data D_{new} and online parameter updating. In incremental learning phrase, the stored parameters will be updated using the algorithm proposed

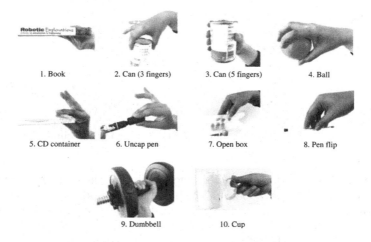

Fig. 3. Pre-defined 10 different in-hand manipulation skills

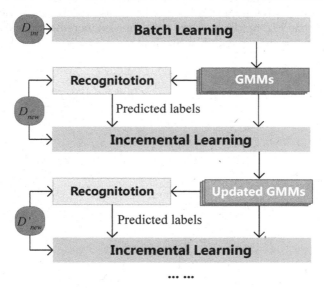

Fig. 4. The overview of online learning framework

in 3.2. Meanwhile, the predicted labels from recognition will guide the data to feed into corresponding GMM set $\mathcal{G}_l$. By this mean, a GMM was updated as shown in Fig. 5(b), where the blue trajectory is the newly arrived human in-hand motion data collected by CyberGlove during human demonstration, the red ellipses are the Gaussian components in old GMM and the blue ellipses indicate the updated ones using proposed incremental learning algorithm.

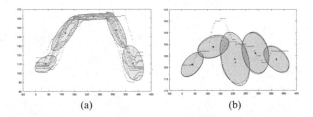

(a)   (b)

Fig. 5. Learning results of a GMM (Color figure online)

The recognition tests are conducted before each time the parameters of GMMs updated (see Fig. 4). However, except the batch learning phrase, no ground truth labels of the newly coming data were provided during online learning for the algorithm to update the correct GMMs with the corresponding sample. The recognition results will decide the new sample belongs which in-hand skill GMM. This experimental setting helps to simulate the long-term learning process in real world application for prosthesis hand. The recognition accuracies witness a steady increase as shown in Fig. 6, which proved the proposed incremental learning framework can achieve a good result in a online learning task.

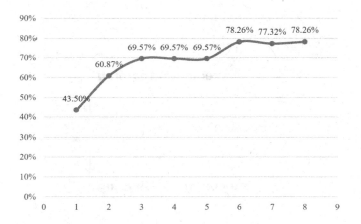

Fig. 6. Learning results of a GMM

5   Conclusion and Future Work

This paper introduced a novel incremental learning framework for in-hand manipulation skill recognition, which can be implemented in transferring human in-hand skills to a dexterous prosthetic hand. We applied GMM for representing the complex human in-hand motion data, the experimental results show the incremental learning process can improve the quality of human in-hand motion representation and optimize the GMMs accuracy with the growth of the model updating times and the data labels predicted by the recognition algorithm. In future work, (a) the GMM can be modified to be more adaptive to various data structures, this require the learning algorithm being able to adjust the number of Gaussian components during learning process. (b) In current framework, online learning needs to count the samples used for training GMM and save the component likelihoods as the extra parameters, this is not suitable for long-term online learning, in the future we are going to optimize the framework to achieve the same functions with less parameters to be stored. (c) Motion recognition is a small step in human in-hand manipulation motion studies, more work can be done based on current framework, for example, applied regression method to generalize trajectories and transfer human skill to robots.

References

1. Yousef, H., Boukallel, M., Althoefer, K.: Tactile sensing for dexterous in-hand manipulation in robotics—a review. Sens. Actuators A Phys. **167**(2), 171–187 (2011)
2. Schaal, S.: Learning from demonstration. In: Advances in Neural Information Processing Systems, pp. 1040–1046 (1997)
3. Ju, Z., Liu, H.: Human hand motion analysis with multisensory information. IEEE/ASME Trans. Mechatron. **19**(2), 456–466 (2014)
4. Chen, D., et al.: An interactive image segmentation method in hand gesture recognition. Sensors **17**(2), 253 (2017)
5. Zhang, Y., Chen, L., Ran, X.: Online incremental EM training of GMM and its application to speech processing applications. In: Signal Processing (ICSP), 2010 IEEE 10th International Conference on Proceeding, pp. 1309–1312. IEEE (2010)
6. Sudsang, A., Srinivasa, N.: Grasping and in-hand manipulation: geometry and algorithms. Algorithmica **26**(3–4), 466–493 (2000)
7. Kondo, M., Ueda, J., Ogasawara, T.: Recognition of in-hand manipulation using contact state transition for multifingered robot hand control. Robot. Auton. Syst. **56**(1), 66–81 (2008)
8. Kumar, P., Verma, J., Prasad, S.: Hand data glove: a wearable real-time device for human-computer interaction. Int. J. Adv. Sci. Technol. 43 (2012)
9. Bendels, G. H., Kahlesz, F., Klein, R.: Towards the next generation of 3D content creation. In: Proceedings of the working conference on Advanced visual interfaces, pp. 283–289. ACM (2004)
10. de La Gorce, M., Paragios, N., Fleet, D. J.: Model-based hand tracking with texture, shading and self-occlusions. In: Computer Vision and Pattern Recognition, 2008, CVPR 2008, IEEE Conference On Proceeding, pp. 1–8. IEEE (2008)
11. Fukuda, O., Tsuji, T., Kaneko, M., Otsuka, A.: A human-assisting manipulator teleoperated by EMG signals and arm motions. IEEE Trans. Robot. Autom. **19**(2), 210–222 (2003)
12. Reddy, N.P., Gupta, V.: Toward direct biocontrol using surface EMG signals: control of finger and wrist joint models. Med. Eng. Phys. **29**(3), 398–403 (2007)
13. Kuroda, T., Tabata, Y., Goto, A., Ikuta, H., Murakami, M.: Consumer price dataglove for sign language recognition. In: Proceedings of 5th International Conference on Disability, Virtual Reality Associated Technologies, Oxford, UK, pp. 253–258 (2004)

14. Fahn, C.S., Sun, H.: Development of a data glove with reducing sensors based on magnetic induction. IEEE Trans. Ind. Electron. **52**(2), 585–594 (2005)
15. Calinon, S., Guenter, F., Billard, A.: On learning, representing, and generalizing a task in a humanoid robot. IEEE Trans. Syst. Man Cybern. Part B (Cybernetics) **37**(2), 286–298 (2007)
16. Kalgaonkar, K., Raj, B.: One-handed gesture recognition using ultrasonic Doppler sonar. In: Acoustics, Speech and Signal Processing, 2009, ICASSP 2009, IEEE International Conference on Proceeding, pp. 1889–1892. IEEE (2009)
17. Hall, P., Marshall, D., Martin, R.: Merging and splitting eigenspace models. IEEE Trans. Pattern Anal. Mach. Intell. **22**(9), 1042–1049 (2000)
18. Song, M., Wang, H.: Highly efficient incremental estimation of Gaussian mixture models for online data stream clustering. In: Intelligent Computing: Theory and Applications III, vol. 5803, pp. 174–184. International Society for Optics and Photonics (2005)
19. Hicks, Y., Hall, P.M., Marshall, D.: A method to add Hidden Markov Models with application to learning articulated motion. In: BMVC, pp. 1–10 (2003)
20. Ju, Z., Liu, H.: A unified fuzzy framework for human-hand motion recognition. IEEE Trans. Fuzzy Syst. **19**(5), 901–913 (2011)

Mapping of Ultra-Wide Band Positional Variance for Indoor Environments

Harry A. G. Pointon$^{(\boxtimes)}$ and Frederic A. Bezombes

Engineering and Technology Research Institute, Liverpool John Moores University,
3 Byrom Street, Liverpool, Merseyside L3 3AF, UK
H.A.Pointon@2016.ljmu.ac.uk

Abstract. This paper presents recent work on the subject of measurement variance in Ultra-Wide Band localisation systems. Recent studies have shown the utility in more rigorous noise characterisation of sensor inputs used in state estimation systems such as the Extended Kalman Filter. This investigation strategy is extended to using data collected during trials of such state estimation algorithms using an Unmanned Ground Vehicle, for the generation of variance maps of the testing environments. The feasibility of building variance models from this data is discussed, and other applications for the information is proposed. As there exist circumstances where the practice of moving the agent around a space incrementally is not practicable, such as in the case of Unmanned Aerial Vehicles, or in restricted spaces, an alternate method is needed. From the results it can be concluded that the use of data collected during standard operation in the environment is not sufficient for initial characterisation of localisation sensors. Initial analysis of this data was also utilised to investigate the effects of environmental factors.

Keywords: Ultra-Wide Band · State estimation ·
Sensor characterisation

1 Introduction

Localisation of robotic systems is often the foundation of their application, whether that be in collision avoidance, data collection, or unsupervised navigation [1,10,14]. The subject is much studied, with focus on the sensing systems employed and the methods used to process and filter the navigation data collected [2,4,5]. Previous work has been conducted to investigate the methods by which this technology may be integrated into existing state estimation systems [10,11]. It has been found that although existing state estimation techniques such as the Extended Kalman Filter (EKF), are capable of dealing with the inherent sensor measurement noise [3], further modifications to the way the sensor measurement variance is represented yield improvements in the estimation [10,11]. This series of work has demonstrated the effectiveness of employing a model in place of a static value, however thus far this function only represents a

© Springer Nature Switzerland AG 2019
K. Althoefer et al. (Eds.): TAROS 2019, LNAI 11650, pp. 123–130, 2019.
https://doi.org/10.1007/978-3-030-25332-5_11

1 dimensional variance model for the UWB system. The next stages in this series of investigations involve alternate modelling methods, and new data collection schemes.

2   Related Works

The current methodology for characterisation of UWB error is to move about the intended environment in increments, collecting samples of sufficient size at each location before moving on. For systems capable of the extended operating time required for characterisation, or spaces whose access is not time limited, this approach is acceptable. However for agents not capable of operating for extended durations or whose operational envelopes prevent this type of practice, this is not practical. Examples of this could be Unmanned Aerial Vehicle (UAV) operations, with limited flight time in comparison to UGVs. Spaces with limited access also present a challenge to this method of working, for example characterisation of sensor systems in situ when operating in nuclear decommissioning sites is not feasible.

Ultra wideband or UWB localisation systems operate through the use of radio frequency (RF) signals sent and received between beacons or "nodes". Each node is capable of both sending and receiving RF signals. Through the use of measured time differences and the known signal transmission speed it is possible to calculate range. Among these works, navigation beacon technology such as the Ultra-Wide Band (UWB) system "Pozyx" has gained popularity [5,9,12]. The variance of UWB measurements has been found to be highly dependent upon a number of factors. As shown by other works, UWB systems are generally noisy and often contain significant outliers [8]. Work on this subject has shown that these factors include the range between beacons and, relative pose between antennas [6,7,11]. There is also evidence to suggest material around the operating environment, and even that in contact with the nodes themselves is a cause of inaccuracy [9]. In the case of the Pozyx system the range is calculated though the Time Of Arrival (TOA) method [13]. However, other systems utilise Time Difference Of Arrival or TDOA, whereby a number of fixed nodes receive the same signal transmitted from a node of unknown location [15]. The time difference between these signal arrivals is used to calculate the position of the unknown node to those of known position. Generally, and in the case of the Pozyx the stationary nodes of known position are referred to as "anchor" nodes, and the node whose position is unknown is referred to as the "rover" node.

3   Methodology

An initial experiment was conducted to investigate the effects of relative orientation on the variance of the UWB range measurements. This testing was conducted using the same experimental methodology as described in [11], over a range of 19 meters in a corridor of similar construction to the space used for testing the EKF system mentioned. For clarity of explanation, the terms, front, back and edge are applied to the UWB nodes, in this case the front is defined as that side to which the antenna is mounted, a visual representation of this may be seen in Fig. 1. The UWB anchor was placed on a tripod at a known location, with the Rover node placed on a separate tripod which was then moved in increments, first facing the Anchor, then facing away, and with its edge towards the Anchor node. Finally a test was run with both nodes facing towards the wall of the corridor and their edges facing each other. These orientations were chosen as they were representative of what is seen during the normal operation for ground vehicles. The Pozyx system in use here will return a 0 RSSI, 0 meter range value if no signal is available when requested, this is noted here as a "dropout" as no range readings is made.

The aim of this investigation is to determine to viability of a UWB sensor variance model as a function of position (x, y) rather than node to node range. In order to obtain this model UWB pose measurements from throughout the space are needed, with an associated ground truth. This ground truth is obtained as shown as described in previous work [10, 11] where a Robotic Total Station (RTS) was deployed.

A Robotic Total Station or RTS is a piece of surveying equipment which extends upon the theodolite system. Conventional theodolites are used for measuring the angle between two points in space, usually from a known reference point. A Total Station (TS) is a similar system, however also includes the capability to measure distances. An RTS is a system capable of remote operation, and onboard logging of points. In the case of this experiment a Trimble S7 RTS is used. The S7 includes actuators in both the vertical and horizontal planes combined with rotary encoders, used in conjunction with the Laser distance measurement system it is capable of taking measurements to sub centimetre accuracy. The benefit of the RTS is the tracking functionality. This system has been shown to effectively provide reliable ground truth measurements for the assessment of sensor systems [10, 11].

The anchor ranges and RTS readings throughout the test were recorded and synchronised through the use of the Robotic Operating System. As described, the UWB measurement reliability is highly dependent upon the initial setup and positioning accuracy of the anchor nodes. To reduce the influence of this, and allow for analysis of variance principally due to system uncertainty the RTS was used to record the anchor positions. This was also used later calculate to the ranges between the rover and anchor nodes from the RTS ground truth measurements. The room layout may be seen in Fig. 2a. The error e is the difference between the RTS ground truth range r and the measured distance r_m using the UWB system at that time-step, thus: $e = r - r_m$. As the RTS measurements are taken at a slower rate than the UWB range readings a linear interpolation is taken after time synchronisation to fill in the missing RTS readings. To cover the most varied locations and orientations between the rover node and the anchors the UGV was driven around the space in raster square patterns, with the fringes facing first in the x and, for later tests the y direction. Speed was constant during the straight portions of the path used in testing. The impact of the velocity of the agent is likely to be negligible if at all noticeable in the readings, as it moves significantly slower than the signal transmitted.

The Pozyx rove node was mounted at a height of 0.4 m on the UGV as shown in Fig. 2b. The Pozyx system was setup in the same way as in our previous works, along with the location of the rover node, as seen in Fig. 2b. The anchor nodes were placed facing inwards of the space, at approximately 1 m from the ground, therefore approximately 0.6 of a meter above the rover node. As discussed previously the cosine error due to the assumption of the space being 2 dimensional is minimal [11]. However, for this case the altitudes of the anchors was taken into account using a 3 dimensional multilateration algorithm, based on Eq. (1), where R is the range between nodes, x, y and z are the Cartesian coordinates of the nodes in question, and those subscripted by i indicate anchor i's position. The Pozyx system allows a number of settings used in the UWB system to be specified. These include the bitrate, which defines the rate of communication, a higher bitrate allows for increased measurement rate. An increase in the bitrate also decreases the range due to the requirement to allow for space between signal transmission and reception. The channel may also be specified, this allows for separate networks to operate independently in the same area. The PRF or Pulse Repetition Frequency also allows the system to operate in 2 modes, therefore with the different channels taken into account 12 networks may operate simultaneously. The Preamble Length (PL) defines the message length, therefore the transmission time. For this investigation the system is configured as described in [10].

$$R = \sqrt{(x - x_i)^2 + (y - y_i)^2 + (z - z_i)^2} \tag{1}$$

Fig. 1. UWB node, lines 1, 2 and 3 represent the top left of the device, the "top side" and the "edge" of the UWB node respectively.

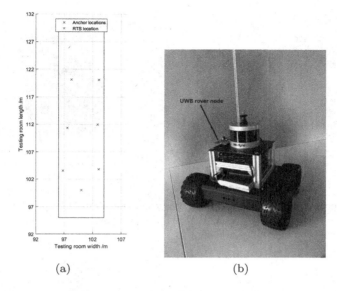

(a)   (b)

Fig. 2. (a) Plan view of the testing space. (b) UGV used for testing, demonstrating the position of the UWB rover node.

4   Results and Analysis

A heatmap was plotted to examine the sensor error throughout the testing area, with colour temperature representing the absolute error of the UWB system at that location. The absolute error was calculated as the sum of the absolute value of both the error in x and y directions. This may be seen in Fig. 3, with both the overall x and y absolute error, and the error of a single anchor's range readings throughout the test. Factors for consideration during the analysis of these figures are that the readings between the areas covered by the UGV are interpolations, of the data assuming a linear relationship, it is worth noting that, in order to negate the requirement for interpolation a very dense raster pattern is needed, which would lead to increased experimental duration, and is therefore impractical to implement. It should also be noted that Fig. 3a, and Fig. 3 show the range error of the UWB system and not the standard deviation. In order to plot this repetitions on the order of hundreds would need to be conducted to gather the required sample size to reliably calculate a standard deviation.

The range error of a single anchor as seen in Fig. 3 and demonstrates an increased occurrence of discrete regions of higher absolute error in the upper left quadrant when compared to the lower right. This is in line with the literature on the subject, which describes a relationship between the relative orientation between nodes and the range measurement error. It may be seen from other experiments that the angle between the anchors and the rover node has a relation with the signal dropouts, as shown in Table 1 and Fig. 4.

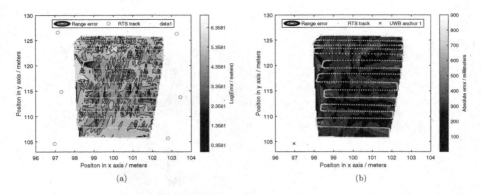

(a)   (b)

Fig. 3. (a) Heatmap of the space with magnitude representing the natural log of the overall, absolute positional error. (b) Heatmap of the space with magnitude representing the absolute range error from anchor 1.

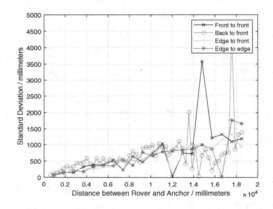

Fig. 4. Comparison of standard deviation in relation to relative orientation between rover - anchor nodes

The sample size of 5000 desired readings was proven as sufficient, and is therefore used here to give a representative example [11]. This relationship also

Table 1. Pozyx measurement dropout rates for differing Rover - anchor orientations out of 5000 intended samples.

Rover - anchor orientation	Dropout rate/% (5000 samples)
Front to front	10.74
Back to front	16.94
Edge to front	10.80
Edge to edge	31.48

extends to the range error, therefore it may be concluded that the experiment run could also show differing measurement errors depending upon the direction of travel. This presents itself as increased error in collinear paths such as those on the left side of Fig. 3b in comparison to those on the right. However this is not demonstrated clearly in Fig. 3a. It may therefore be considered that the relative pose may have an effect upon the range error of the system, however, there is another transient factor which alters the reliability of the UWB range measurement to a greater extent. Further study is required to verify this, however it may be the case that environmental factors or passing people with radio frequency devices, such as mobile phones may be the cause.

5 Conclusion

To conclude, while it may be shown that the tracking of an agent utilising UWB systems for navigation during typical operations is a valid method for demonstrating the areas of increased noise or error, this method is not compatible with the characterisation scheme required for use in sensor measurement variances of state estimation systems. Although the data did give an insight into the areas of increased sensor error, the data did not provide sufficient sample size to accurately, or reliably calculate the variance in any one position without significant repetition. However, one application for this technique could the determination of the effect of other less impactful, or more transient factors on a UWB system, such as environmental factors. Future work should be conducted to investigate the effects of the implementation of a secondary variance model of a space to account for factors not in the primary model. Such a method could involve a pre-existing high-resolution model of the measurement variance, as a function of the most prominent variable, in this case the relation to range. Which is then augmented by an a priori knowledge of the space to correct for factors not accounted for in the model. Such a system would be preferable for UAV systems, which generally lack the endurance for the required flight paths.

References

1. Alarifi, A., et al.: Ultra wideband indoor positioning technologies: analysis and recent advances. Sens. (Switz.) **16**(5), 707 (2016). https://doi.org/10.3390/s16050707. http://www.mdpi.com/1424-8220/16/5/707
2. Gageik, N., Benz, P., Montenegro, S.: Obstacle detection and collision avoidance for a UAV With complementary low-cost sensors. IEEE Access **3**, 599–609 (2015)
3. Guo, K., et al.: Ultra-wideband-based localization for quadcopter navigation. Unmanned Syst. **04**(01), 23–34 (2016). https://doi.org/10.1142/S2301385016400033. http://www.worldscientific.com/doi/abs/10.1142/S2301385016400033
4. Juliá, M., Gil, A., Reinoso, O.: A comparison of path planning strategies for autonomous exploration and mapping of unknown environments. 427–444 (2012). https://doi.org/10.1007/s10514-012-9298-8

5. Kapoor, R., Ramasamy, S., Gardi, A., Sabatini, R.: UAV navigation using signals of opportunity in urban environments: a review. Energy Procedia **110**, 377–383 (2017). https://doi.org/10.1016/J.EGYPRO.2017.03.156. https://www.sciencedirect.com/science/article/pii/S1876610217301868

6. Ledergerber, A., D'Andrea, R.: Ultra-wideband range measurement model with Gaussian processes. In: 2017 IEEE Conference on Control Technology and Applications (CCTA), pp. 1929–1934. IEEE (2017). https://doi.org/10.1109/CCTA.2017.8062738. http://ieeexplore.ieee.org/document/8062738/

7. Ledergerber, A., D'andrea, R.: Calibrating away inaccuracies in ultra wideband range measurements: a maximum likelihood approach. IEEE Access **6**, 78719–78730 (2018). https://doi.org/10.1109/ACCESS.2018.2885195. https://ieeexplore.ieee.org/document/8561287/

8. Liu, J., Pu, J., Sun, L., He, Z.: An approach to robust INS/UWB integrated positioning for autonomous indoor mobile robots. Sensors **19**(4), 950 (2019). https://doi.org/10.3390/s19040950. http://www.mdpi.com/1424-8220/19/4/950

9. Masiero, A., Fissore, F., Vettore, A., Masiero, A., Fissore, F., Vettore, A.: A low cost UWB based solution for direct georeferencing UAV photogrammetry. Remote Sens. **9**(5), 414 (2017). https://doi.org/10.3390/rs9050414. http://www.mdpi.com/2072-4292/9/5/414

10. McLoughlin, B.J., Pointon, H.A., McLoughlin, J.P., Shaw, A., Bezombes, F.A.: Uncertainty characterisation of mobile robot localisation techniques using optical surveying grade instruments. Sens. (Switz.) **18**(7), 2274 (2018). https://doi.org/10.3390/s18072274. http://www.mdpi.com/1424-8220/18/7/2274

11. Pointon, H.A.G., McLoughlin, B.J., Matthews, C., Bezombes, F.A.: Towards a model based sensor measurement variance input for extended Kalman filter state estimation. Drones **3**(1) (2019). https://doi.org/10.3390/drones3010019. http://www.mdpi.com/2504-446X/3/1/19

12. Ridolfi, M., et al.: Experimental evaluation of UWB indoor positioning for sport postures. Sensors **18**(1) (2018). https://doi.org/10.3390/s18010168. http://www.mdpi.com/1424-8220/18/1/168

13. Sookyoi, T.: Experimental analysis of indoor positioning system based on ultra-wideband measurements (2016)

14. Vanegas, F., Gonzalez, F.: Enabling UAV navigation with sensor and environmental uncertainty in cluttered and GPS-denied environments. Sens. (Switz.) **16**(5) (2016). https://doi.org/10.3390/s16050666

15. Wang, J., Raja, A.K., Pang, Z.: Prototyping and experimental comparison of IR-UWB based high precision localization technologies. In: Proceedings of 2015 IEEE 12th International Conference on Ubiquitous Intelligence and Computing, 2015 IEEE 12th International Conference on Advanced and Trusted Computing, 2015 IEEE 15th International Conference on Scalable Computing and Communications, vol. 20, pp. 1187–1192 (2016). https://doi.org/10.1109/UIC-ATC-ScalCom-CBDCom-IoP.2015.216

MoDSeM: Towards Semantic Mapping with Distributed Robots

Gonçalo S. Martins[1]([✉]), João Filipe Ferreira[2,3], David Portugal[2], and Micael S. Couceiro[1]

[1] Ingeniarius, Rua Coronel Veiga Simão, Edifício B CTCV,
3025-307 Coimbra, Portugal
{gondsm,micael}@ingeniarius.pt

[2] Institute of Systems and Robotics, University of Coimbra,
3030-290 Coimbra, Portugal
{jfilipe,davidbsp}@isr.uc.pt

[3] Computational Neuroscience and Cognitive Robotics Group, School of Science and Technology, Nottingham Trent University, Nottingham, UK
joao.ferreira@ntu.ac.uk

Abstract. This paper presents MoDSeM, a software framework for cooperative perception supporting teams of robots. MoDSeM aims to provide a flexible semantic mapping framework able to represent all spatial information perceived in missions involving teams of robots, and to formalize the development of perception software, promoting the implementation of reusable modules that can fit varied team constitutions. We provide an overview of MoDSeM, and describe how it can be applied to multi-robot systems, discussing several sub-problems such as history and memory, or centralized *vs* distributed perception. Aiming to demonstrate the functionality of our prototype, preliminary experiments took place in simulation, using a $100 \times 100 \times 100$ m simulated map to demonstrate its ability to receive, store and retrieve information stored in semantic voxel grids, using ROS as a transport layer and OpenVDB as a grid storage mechanism. Results show the appropriateness of ROS and OpenVDB as a back-end for supporting the prototype, achieving a promising performance in all aspects of the task. Future developments will make use of these results to apply MoDSeM in realistic scenarios, including multi-robot indoor surveillance and precision forestry operations.

Keywords: Artificial Perception · Multi-robot systems · Cooperative perception · Software framework

1 Introduction

Perception is one of the core tasks in Robotics, allowing artificial systems to extract meaningful information from noisy sensor data, which can then be used

This work was supported by the Seguranças robóTicos coOPerativos (STOP, ref. CENTRO-01-0247-FEDER-017562), the Safety, Exploration and Maintenance of Forests with Ecological Robotics (SEMFIRE, ref. CENTRO-01-0247-FEDER-03269) and the Centre of Operations for Rethinking Engineering (CORE, ref. CENTRO-01-0247-FEDER-037082) research projects co-funded by the "Agência Nacional de Inovação" within the Portugal2020 programme.

© Springer Nature Switzerland AG 2019
K. Althoefer et al. (Eds.): TAROS 2019, LNAI 11650, pp. 131–142, 2019.
https://doi.org/10.1007/978-3-030-25332-5_12

to make decisions that impact the operating environment. This includes cooperative perception, in which several agents contribute to the global knowledge of the system by sharing and cooperatively processing data and percepts from one another, combining the sensorial abilities, perspectives and processing power of various agents to achieve better results. The body of work in Artificial Perception is vast, comprising contributions produced for decades, including both scientific contributions and materialization in software. This has led to an undesirable fragmentation of both code and effort in the implementation of perception techniques that tackle each individual problem; several potential solutions exist for many problems, but it is difficult to articulate them with one another to achieve a higher level of functionality in an integrated system.

The **Mo**dular Framework for **D**istributed **S**emantic **M**apping (MoDSeM) provides a semantic mapping approach able to represent all spatial information perceived in autonomous missions involving teams of field robots, aggregating the knowledge of all agents into a unified representation. It also aims to formalize and normalize the development of new perception software, promoting the implementation of modular and reusable software that can be easily swapped in accordance with the sensory abilities of each individual platform. This article presents a conceptual overview of MoDSeM and of preliminary experiments that evaluate the main design choices in a simulated forestry environment, serving as an extension of previous work [11].

The text is structured as follows. Section 2 presents an overview of the state of the art and of the specific contributions of this paper. Section 3 presents an overview of MoDSeM, including its application to multi-robot systems. Section 4 presents our preliminary experiments, results and discussion. Lastly, Sect. 5 summarizes the paper and presents the main premises for future work.

2   Related Work, Novelty and Contributions

MoDSeM's originality and contribution to the field lies in its focus on improving the technology readiness level (TRL) [10] of cooperative perception techniques, enabling them to operate in a coordinated, flexible and seamless manner. While works in perception are abundant, including probabilistic approaches [2] and works on several sub-problems of field robotics such as tree detection [4], crop/weed discrimination [8] or detection of plant disease [13], very few of these techniques are available as easily-reusable software packages. These software packages, which include for instance mapping and localization techniques [6,7][1,2], constitute the most accessible way of testing perception techniques in the field, in conditions as close to real operation as possible. However, these packages represent only a small subsection of the substantial body of work in perception, and are traditionally behind the state of the art. MoDSeM aims to tackle this issue by providing the means to integrate the output of these techniques, to make them usable by heterogeneous teams of robots.

---

[1] https://github.com/OctoMap/octomap.
[2] https://github.com/introlab/rtabmap.

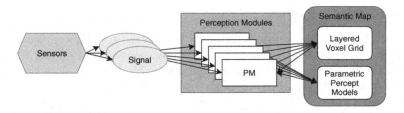

Fig. 1. An overview of the framework. Sensors produce signals, which are passed to independent perception modules. Percepts gathered by these modules are aggregated in a Semantic Map, containing layers for different types of information.

Software frameworks have been developed for generic robots, such as ROS [14], YARP [3] or GenoM3 [9], and also specifically for agriculture and forestry robots [5]. These frameworks focus on improving software portability, standards, common features and assumptions, and serve as an important stepping stone for MoDSeM. However, they do not tackle the particular issues of perception systems, such as achieving a common representation of the world with varying sensor input, or the storage and retrieval of this information, both current and in the past. Past efforts also do not define a development methodology to produce portable perception software, one of the main long-term goals of MoDSeM. To the best of our knowledge, MoDSeM is the first attempt at such a system and methodology applied directly to the problem of perception.

In this paper we aim to show that OpenVDB [12] and ROS [14] are a suitable back-end for MoDSeM by demonstrating that:

– MoDSeM can receive map updates with efficiency that enables real-time use;
– MoDSeM can retrieve data from the map at will, also promoting real-time use.

3   MoDSeM Overview

The framework is split into three blocks, as depicted in Fig. 1:

– The **sensors**, which provide raw signals;
– The **Perception Modules** (PMs) which take these signals and produce percepts, *i.e.* processed information;
– The **Semantic Map** (SM), containing a unified view of the state of the workspace/world.

Sensors produce raw signals, which are used by Perception Modules to produce percepts, in this case information grounded on a spatial reference such as occupancy, presence of people, etc. These are taken as inputs to build a Semantic Map, which can in turn be used by any agent in the team to make decisions or coordinate with others. In this case, each sensor is seen as a mere source of data, which is assumed to be preconfigured and working as needed at the time of execution.

3.1   Perception Modules

In software terms, each Perception Module is expected to be decoupled from all other modules of the system, depending only on sensors and on the Semantic Map itself. Thus, we can ensure that Perception Modules are interchangeable elements of the system, allowing us to swap them at will, depending on the computational power and available sensors on each robot. This allows for great flexibility in the deployment of the framework, enabling modules to be employed in each system without the need to re-design the global representation.

Perception Modules can use the Semantic Map as input, thus making use of the percepts from other techniques. Removing modules from the robot should not impact the remainder of the system. However, this may still result in a cascade reaction, with Perception Modules depending on each others' output for further processing; Perception Module selection should still be a careful process.

3.2   Semantic Map

The semantic map works as a global output of the perception system. It is split into the Layered Voxel Grid (LVG) and the Parametric Percept Models (PPM).

The LVG is composed of a layered volumetric representation of the workspace. Each layer of the LVG is itself a voxel grid, containing information on one aspect of the world, such as occupancy, traversability, relevance to current task, etc. The combination of these layers provides an overview of the state of the world as perceived by the robot team; individually, they provide insight that may be relevant on a particular aspect of the mission. Different Perception Modules can contribute to different layers of the LVG, with for instance a people detector contributing to a people occupancy layer or a mapping technique contributing to a physical occupancy layer. This information can then be used by decision-making routines.

The PPM contains percepts that are represented as parametric models with a spatial representation, thus representing entities without volume, e.g. robot poses or human joint configurations. The PPM complements the LVG's expressive power, allowing the system to represent entities without volume, such as robot poses, human joint configurations, navigation goals, etc.

3.3   History and Memory

At a basic level, perception can be seen as a one-way pipeline: signals are fed into Perception Modules, resulting in percepts. MoDSeM aims to introduce non-linearity in this flow, allowing Perception Modules to access current and past data, including percepts obtained by other Perception Modules. In order to achieve this, two measures are taken:

- Perception Modules are allowed to use the Semantic Map as input;
- Perception Modules are allowed to use **previous versions** of the Semantic Map as input.

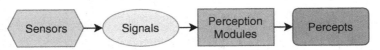

(a) Traditional ROS-based perception techniques implement a linear flow from sensors to percepts; signals are processed and percepts are output.

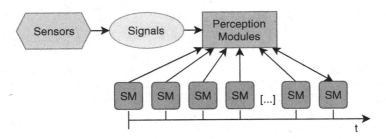

(b) MoDSeM aims to implement a non-linear perception pipeline: Perception Modules can access previous versions of the Semantic Map to execute over previous states.

Fig. 2. Linear data flow compared to MoDSeM's non-linear data flow.

In the first case, Perception Modules are allowed to depend on the Semantic Map and use it as a complement to any signal input they require. Indeed, some Perception Modules are expected to use solely the Semantic Map as input; *e.g.*, a traversability detector could estimate the traversability of the map using only occupancy, movable object and vegetation information.

Additionally, as in Fig. 2, allowing perception modules to use previous version of the SM as input implies that a history of SMs is kept during operation, which would quickly make the its storage infeasible. This can be mitigated in two ways:

- By storing successive differences between the maps as they are generated, as is done in video compression algorithms and source control systems;
- By intelligently choosing which snapshots of the map should be saved, using information-theoretic techniques, avoiding redundant information.

By fine-tuning these two approaches, it should be possible to establish a history in secondary memory with enough granularity to allow Perception Modules that depend on it to operate. For instance, the total system memory to be used by this mechanism can be set as a parameter, guiding the compression and data selection techniques in their optimization of the amount of information stored, as measured by information-theoretic metrics such as entropy.

3.4   ModSeM for Multi-robot Perception

Traditionally, multi-robot perception is achieved in one of two ways (Fig. 3): by propagating raw signals from each robot to a centralized perception server, which then replies with percepts; or by endowing each team member with perceptive

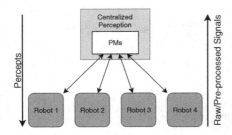
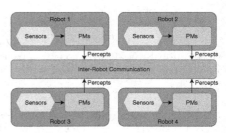

(a) Centralized perception: raw signals are sent to a centralized machine that returns percepts.

(b) Distributed perception: agents contain the necessary perception modules, and propagate percepts to other agents.

Fig. 3. Centralized *vs.* distributed perception.

abilities, as well as the ability to decide when percepts should be propagated among the team. Centralized perception is preferable when the robots in the team contain little processing power and when the communication infrastructure is a non-issue, *i.e.* is always available and can support the necessary bandwidth. On the other hand, distributed perception is the appropriate technique when bandwidth is limited, when robots have heterogeneous needs and capabilities, and when each robot can be endowed with perception abilities that fit its needs. A hybrid approach can be used with heterogeneous teams, when for instance one of the robots is significantly more computationally powerful than other team members, who can unload part of their perceptual load to this team mate. MoDSeM can be used to implement all of these perceptual modalities: The centralized approach is immediately supported, as it involves simply implementing all modules on a single machine; The distributed and hybrid approaches can also be achieved by communicating relevant layers of the Semantic Map among robots, using appropriate tools for multi-robot communication[3].

Figure 4 shows an overview of MoDSeM implemented on a robotic team. In this case, the agent contains its own sensors, processing modules and semantic map. Its Perception Modules include specialized Perception Modules that are used to fuse information received from other agents, to achieve consensus. The agent also contains a selection procedure, which must be configured or endowed with some decision-making ability, which decides which information it should share with other agents, to be sent for inter-robot communication. Specific Perception Modules in each robot can then fuse these representations, achieving consensus and allowing all robots to plan with the same information. Other topologies can also be achieved with the framework, as in Fig. 5. Different topologies are achieved by mixing-and-matching the necessary components, such as Perception Modules and sensors and their configurations, to achieve different use cases.

---

[3] http://wiki.ros.org/multimaster_fkie.

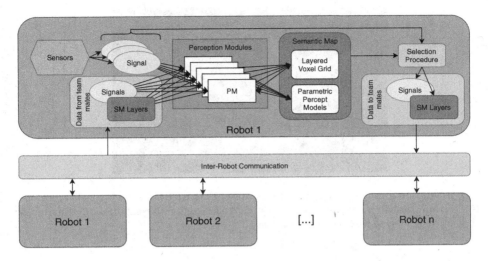

Fig. 4. An overview of a robot team operating with MoDSeM. Each team member can have its own sensors, perception modules and semantic map. These can be shared arbitrarily with the rest of the team, as needed. Each robot is also able to receive signals and Semantic Map layers from other robots, which are used as input by Perception Modules to achieve a unified Semantic Map.

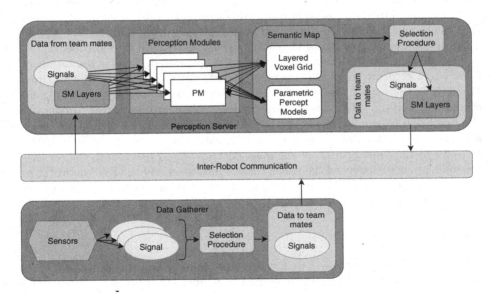

Fig. 5. Different topologies (in addition to the hybrid topology of Fig. 4) for multi-robot perception using MoDSeM. Top: a perception server, which receives information and Semantic Map layers from the team and executes the most expensive perception modules. Bottom: a data gatherer agent, which observes the world with its sensors and sends data for processing in other agents.

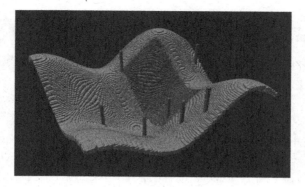

Fig. 6. An illustration of the semantic map used in these tests. Green voxels represent the terrain, brown voxels represent trees and red voxels represent unwanted material that must be cleaned. (Color figure online)

4   Preliminary Experiments

4.1   Experimental Scenario

Tests were developed with the goal of determining the appropriateness of Open-VDB and ROS as a back-end for MoDSeM, exploring the two main functions of the Semantic Map: data insertion retrieval. These constitute the main operations that the semantic map server is expected to perform during runtime, and should operate with enough efficiency that the system can be used in real time.

A realistic, 100-by-100-by-100 m map was generated, with a resolution of 5 cm/voxel, or 20 voxels/m, illustrated in Fig. 6[4], which was populated with three semantic layers with a total of circa 18 million voxels. It was procedurally generated and sent piece-by-piece over ROS to the semantic map server, simulating the operation of a mapping node that advances through the terrain and iteratively updates the global map. At each update, the server was asked for the retrieval of the same portion of the map. Metrics were captured on the server's side and, as such, disregard the travel time of messages over the ROS network; as the final composition of the network is not known, communication details would be subject to change and would not provide insight into the server's function.

4.2   Results

Figure 7 illustrates the time it took to update the map as a function of the size, in occupied points, of the respective update. A linear trend is observable in the data, as was expected given the iterative nature of the insertion procedure. Given that a better than $O(n)$ complexity was unlikely to occur, this is a positive result:

---

[4] Aliasing artefacts can be seen due to the downsampling procedure that must be applied for visualization; it is not possible to represent the near-20-million voxels of the original map in ROS's visualization tool, rviz.

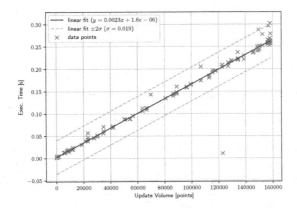

Fig. 7. Time needed to update the map as a function of the size of the update, in occupied points. Data points are represented in blue crosses, a linear regression in read and the boundaries ±2σ in yellow. The clear outlier corresponds to the very first insertion of the map, wherein the full received grid is used. A clear linear relationship can be observed, since points must be introduced one-by-one. (Color figure online)

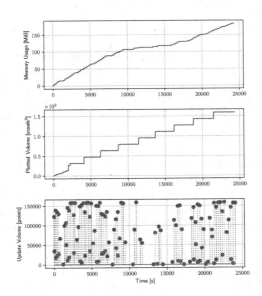

Fig. 8. Evolution of memory usage as updates are received by the server. (Top) represents the total memory usage of the map; (middle) illustrates the volume, in voxels³ of the map; (bottom) shows the update times of non-zero updates, as well as their size in points. A clear relationship between update size, memory usage and mapped volume and update size can be observed.

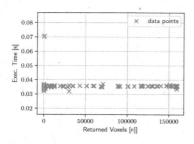 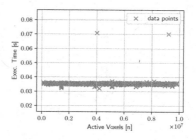

(a) Retrieval time *vs* number of voxels contained in the sub-grid.

(b) Retrieval time *vs* number of active (occupied) voxels in the full map.

Fig. 9. Time taken to retrieve a sub-map (or sub-grid) as a function of (a) the number of voxels contained in the sub-map and (b) the number of voxels active in the full map. We can observe no undesirable relationships between variables.

Table 1. A summary of the current proof-of-concept's performance.

Metric	Best case	Worst case
Map update time	<0.05 s (20,000 points)	0.3 s (160,000 points)
Map retrieval time	~0.035 s (150,000 points)	~0.035 s (150,000 points)
Memory usage	~180 MiB (1.5×10^9 voxels stored)	n/a

the update time of the map is easily predictable knowing the size of the update, and measures can be taken to account for it. At the worst case, the update procedure took 0.3 s for an update of 160,000 points, with best-case updates of less than 20,000 points taking less than 0.05 s to execute ($1.33\times$ faster per point) (Table 1). An update of this dimension is relatively unlikely; it may result, for instance, from an update to the map produced by a mapping node, which would not update at a high enough rate to block the server. It seems unlikely at first sight that such updates would be produced frequently, or at a high enough frequency to overload the server.

Figure 8 illustrates the memory usage of the map as updates are received. Naturally, usage grows when map updates are received, correlating imperfectly with the size of the update. This is to be expected: a re-update of a previously-mapped cell will not occupy extra memory, but simply replace the respective value. The mapped volume also correlates imperfectly with the size in memory and the size of the updates, which is due to the fact that the updates are being sent in blocks which are not completely full, sometimes carrying very little information.

Figure 9 illustrates the performance of the server when retrieving a subsection of the map. There is no relationship between the voxel structure of the grid and the time it takes to retrieve it. In fact, for a constant sub-grid volume, the retrieval time is almost constant and independent of the number of voxels.

4.3 Discussion

Section 2 outlined the claims of this paper, namely that the current prototype would be able to store and retrieve information in an efficient way. In general terms, the current results appear promising. Map update speeds seem fast enough for our purposes, given the size of the updates in the tests and the rate at which they can be expected to be transmitted, and do not seem to pose an immediate limitation. According to our results, update speeds are fast enough that real-time operation is plausibly feasible, thus supporting the first claim.

Retrieval speeds are also found to be acceptable: our results indicate it to be efficient enough for real-time operation, thus supporting the second claim. It depends only on the volume of the sub-grid being retrieved, which indicates its efficiency and allowing its duration to be estimated in advance, potentially providing important insight during the scheduling of map access.

Regarding memory usage, the system appears able to deal both with large and small updates in an efficient manner, maintaining the map in an acceptable (between 150 to 200 MiB in our tests) amount of memory. This demonstrates that basic functionality is possible; OpenVDB and ROS are appropriate back-ends for MoDSeM, and should provide a stable framework for future development.

5 Conclusion

This paper presents the design and ongoing development of MoDSeM, a novel framework for spatial perception. The framework was presented at a conceptual level, outlining its main premises, novelty and applicability. Preliminary experiments confirm the appropriateness of our basic design choices, namely showing that the current prototype is able to store and retrieve information efficiently.

This work will now be extended in several ways. Firstly, MoDSeM's functionalities, as described in Sects. 3 and 3.4 will be implemented and tested with real sensors in real environments, providing actual data for a better performance assessment as well as comparison with state-of-the-art techniques. Secondly, the Perception Module development procedures will be formalized, including guidelines on how to package them in ROS packages and how to conform to MoDSeM's requirements. MoDSeM will then be applied in two real-world target problems: in teams of indoor patrolling robots, in the context of the STOP project[5] for surveillance and inspection, and in heterogeneous teams of field robots for automated forestry tasks in the context of the SEMFIRE project[6] [1].

In the particular case of SEMFIRE, a hybrid approach (as depicted in Fig. 5) will be employed. The SEMFIRE system will include a heterogeneous team of robots, composed of a *Ranger* robot, implemented on a Bobcat T190, and a number of *Scouts*, implemented using custom made UAVs. This hybrid approach will allow us to leverage the larger size of the *Ranger* to deploy higher processing power, onto which the *Scouts* can unload a portion of their perceptual needs.

---

[5] http://stop.ingeniarius.pt/.
[6] http://semfire.ingeniarius.pt/.

References

1. Couceiro, M.S., Portugal, D., Ferreira, J.F., Rocha, R.P.: SEMFIRE: towards a new generation of forestry maintenance multi-robot systems. In: IEEE/SICE International Symposium on System Integration, no. 2 (2019)
2. Ferreira, J.F., Dias, J.: Probabilistic Approaches for Robotic Perception. Springer, Cham (2014). https://doi.org/10.1007/978-3-319-02006-8. https://www.springer.com/us/book/9783319020051
3. Fitzpatrick, P., Ceseracciu, E., Domenichelli, D.E., Paikan, A., Metta, G., Natale, L.: A middle way for robotics middleware. J. Softw. Eng. Robot. 5, 42–49 (2014)
4. Hellström, T., Ostovar, A., Hellström, T., Ostovar, A.: Detection of trees based on quality guided image segmentation. In: Second International Conference on Robotics and Associated High-Technologies and Equipment for Agriculture and forestry (RHEA 2014): New Trends in Mobile Robotics, Perception and Actuation for Agriculture and Forestry, May 2014
5. Hellström, T., Ringdahl, O.: A software framework for agricultural and forestry robotics. In: International Conference on Robotics and Associated High-technologies and Equipment for Agriculture, pp. 171–176 (2012)
6. Hornung, A., Wurm, K.M., Bennewitz, M., Stachniss, C., Burgard, W.: OctoMap: an efficient probabilistic 3D mapping framework based on octrees. Auton. Robot. **34**(3), 189–206 (2013). https://doi.org/10.1007/s10514-012-9321-0
7. Labbé, M., Michaud, F.: RTAB-Map as an open-source lidar and visual simultaneous localization and mapping library for large-scale and long-term online operation. J. Field Robot. (2018). https://doi.org/10.1002/rob.21831
8. Lottes, P., Stachniss, C.: Semi-supervised online visual crop and weed classification in precision farming exploiting plant arrangement. In: 2017 IEEE/RSJ International Conference on Intelligent Robots and Systems (IROS), September 2017, pp. 5155–5161 (2017). https://doi.org/10.1109/IROS.2017.8206403
9. Mallet, A., Pasteur, C., Herrb, M., Lemaignan, S., Ingrand, F.: GenoM3: building middleware-independent robotic components. In: 2010 IEEE International Conference on Robotics and Automation (ICRA), May 2014 (2010). https://doi.org/10.1109/ROBOT.2010.5509539
10. Mankins, J.C.: Technology readiness levels. White Pap. **6**(2), 5 (1995). https://doi.org/10.1080/08956308.2010.11657640
11. Martins, G.S., Ferreira, J.F., Portugal, D., Couceiro, M.S.: MoDSeM: modular framework for distributed semantic mapping. In: The 2nd UK-RAS Conference for PhD Students and Early-Career Researchers on Embedded Intelligence (2019)
12. Museth, K.: VDB: high-resolution sparse volumes with dynamic topography. ACM Trans. Graph. **32**(3), 1–22 (2013). https://doi.org/10.1145/2487228.2487235. http://dl.acm.org/citation.cfm?id=2487228.2487235
13. Oberti, R., Marchi, M., Tirelli, P., Calcante, A., Iriti, M., Borghese, A.N.: Automatic detection of powdery mildew on grapevine leaves by image analysis: optimal view-angle range to increase the sensitivity. Comput. Electron. Agric. **104**, 1–8 (2014). https://doi.org/10.1016/j.compag.2014.03.001
14. Quigley, M., et al.: ROS: an open-source robot operating system. In: ICRA Workshop on Open Source Software (2009). http://www.willowgarage.com/papers/ros-open-source-robot-operating-system

Towards Long-Term Autonomy Based on Temporal Planning

Yaniel Carreno$^{(\boxtimes)}$, Ronald P. A. Petrick, and Yvan Petillot

Edinburgh Centre for Robotics, Heriot-Watt University, Edinburgh, UK
{yc66,r.petrick,y.r.petillot}@hw.ac.uk

Abstract. This paper investigates the application of temporal planning to multiple robots in long-term missions, using the OPTIC and POPF temporal planners. We design a new planning domain, motivated by a realistic indoor-outdoor scenario. In particular, we investigate plan concurrency, makespan and plan generation time in the multi-robot problem and propose a schema which has been shown to improve plan quality while significantly reducing planning time for the multi-agent problem. Experiments are done in simulation using ROS and Gazebo, and demonstrated in missions with concurrent actions. The ROSPlan framework is also extended to work with multiple robots and used to integrate the planners in ROS. OPTIC provides the best overall solution considering the domain complexity and mission execution in the environment.

Keywords: Temporal-planning · Multi-agent · Long-term autonomy

1 Introduction

The implementation of long-term missions using multiple robotic platforms has been increasingly studied in recent years [25,27]. Multi-agent systems are more robust to individual platform failures, present advantages in terms of their overall system capabilities and support the introduction of coordinated actions to solve more challenging tasks. However, the implementation of complex missions for long time periods requires robust planning and execution tools in order to maintain the uninterrupted operation of the robots. Planning is particularly promising to support long-term autonomy since it offers techniques for managing typical problems that arise in highly constrained missions, such as limited power, navigational uncertainty and perception noise.

Automated planning is the process of reasoning about the actions needed to achieve a set of goals. The introduction of multiple robots forces the analysis of the *time-factor* to generate plans in the presence of concurrent actions in the mission. Temporal planning involves explicit representations of time in the planning problem, allowing more realistic modelling of real-world domains that require temporal constraints. Such problems can be addressed using PDDL2.1 [12], an extension of the standard Planning Domain Definition Language (PDDL)

© Springer Nature Switzerland AG 2019
K. Althoefer et al. (Eds.): TAROS 2019, LNAI 11650, pp. 143–154, 2019.
https://doi.org/10.1007/978-3-030-25332-5_13

[15], which adds support for temporal planning through additional language constructs. A number of temporal planners support PDDL2.1 [9,10,20]. However, these planners face problems of scalability, concurrency, or issues with actions' time-slot allocation which have limited their introduction in long-term missions with multiple robots. Two temporal planners are particularly promising for the implementation of complex missions: Forward-Chaining Partial-Order Planning (POPF) [6] and Optimizing Preferences and TIme-dependent Costs (OPTIC) [1]. These planners support numerical fluents, concurrent and exogenous events. POPF is characterised by its ability to find plans with low *makespan*—the time that elapses from the start of plan implementation to the end—while OPTIC's main application is in problems where preferences or time-dependent goal costs define the plan cost. However, whilst different planners have been proposed, identifying a single "optimal" planner able to support long-term missions is a difficult task [24], due to differences in representational power and plan generation efficiency.

In this paper, we explore the application of planning techniques for multi-robot fleets, to enhance long-term autonomy and overall fleet robustness. The main contributions of this work are: (i) the implementation of a realistic domain with high levels of expressiveness that supports the implementation of long-term missions, (ii) the performance comparison of two temporal planners implementing time and resource constrained missions, and (iii) the integration of multiple robots using ROSPlan to implement time sensitive and concurrent tasks. The scenario used for evaluation is a fleet of robots exploring an arena to detect targets, collect data, and transmit information using different timelines (days, hours, minutes). We implement simulations in ROS and Gazebo using TurtleBots to evaluate system performance in a complex environment.

Multi-agent planning techniques broadly address three problems: task allocation, planning, and coordination of robot groups [8]. Although, planning strategies for multi-robot missions have been significantly studied during recent years [21,23,26], few approaches directly consider temporal planning for multi-agent applications. In [7], planning problems are modelled using standard PDDL and then translated to a temporal planning model for generating and distributing plans to individual robots. [24] considers temporal planning for coordinated missions using OPTIC in human interaction applications. [11] introduces the Scotty-Activity planner which provides good results controlling continuous variables in the domain. Moreover, [18,19] successfully implement task allocation based on auction algorithms and temporal constraints. However, the solutions do not support long-term missions due to the robots' resources such as energy are not considered to allocate the tasks or to generate the plan.

There are multiple examples of architectures which support plan execution in robotic systems [5,13,14,16]. However, these approaches employ domain-specific or inflexible language specifications and methodologies, which lead to bespoke implementations not easily ported to new applications. Additionally, a number of frameworks [4,17] experience difficulties connecting high-level causal reasoning and symbolic plan generation with sensor and actuator level reasoning.

A notable exception is ROSPlan [3] which connects the widely used Robot Operating System (ROS) [22] and PDDL2.1. ROSPlan allows different task planners to be embedded in a modular architecture, making it suitable for testing plan feasibility and quality. Prior implementations using ROSPlan have mainly explored the performance of a single agent [2,3], often in simple domains, and have therefore not evaluated ROSPlan's ability to deal with complex temporal and resource constrained missions.

2 Domain Definition

Our planning domain considers problems where a centralised task planner is called to find a plan for a heterogeneous robot fleet. The characteristics of the environment define the type of actions the robotic system can implement. In this work, we use a segmented indoor-outdoor environment for modelling multi-robot real-world problems. Figure 1 (left) shows a map of the scenario, with the robots' initial positions (R_1, R_2, R_3), docking point (DP), transmission centre (TC) and four regions which constitute the mission goals. The tasks are associated with three type of sensors (odometry, camera, and 3D scan), enabling important mission scenarios such as: point of interest exploration, target identification, obstacle detection and image or scan data acquisition. We modelled our domain focusing on the implementation of real-world actions using PDDL.

The domain[1] defines multiple **types**[2] called **robot**, **waypoint**, **sensors**, and **observation_point**. Waypoints situate the vehicle in specific sections of the arena, and the robot executes actions related with the camera and 3D scan sensor in the observation points. The **waypoint** and **observation_point** instances represent the vehicle's position, part of the robot state supporting exploration. These instances have a fixed location defined by the domain designer. The domain also includes **static facts**, such as **dock_at ?wp**, **control_centre_at ?wp** and **observation_at ?o**, representing the DP and TC waypoint positions, and the observation point locations. In addition, **robot_at ?r ?wp** describes the robot's position which changes dynamically. We define 8 **actions** in the domain:

- **navigate(?r, ?wp_init, ?wp_final)**: a durative action which moves the robot ?r from waypoint ?wp_init to waypoint ?wp_final. The action duration depends on the distance between the waypoints.
- **explore_ob(?r, ?wp, ?o)**: a durative action which rotates the robot ?r on the observation point ?o, positioning the vehicle in three different angles exploring 360^0.
- **dock(?r, ?wp_init, ?wp_final)**: a durative action for robot ?r battery recharging. The robot moves from its actual position ?wp_init to waypoint ?wp_final, where it stays during recharging time. In this case ?wp_final is the DP.

---

[1] Domain and problem examples are available at https://github.com/MA-TemporalP.

[2] In the following, we will use ?r to denote a parameter of type **robot**, ?wp a parameter of type **waypoint**, ?o a parameter of type **observation_point**, and ?s a parameter of type **sensors**.

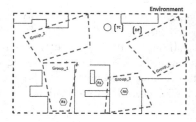

Fig. 1. A depiction of the domain (left) and the RViz simulation environment with multiple robots implementing an exploration mission (right). The docking point (DP) and transmission centre (TC) are static points in the environment. The R_1 (centre of the arena) and R_2 (left side) execute the `navigate_parallel` action moving to different points at the same time.

- undock(?r, ?wp): a durative action to disconnect the robot ?r from the waypoint ?wp (DP). The robot ?r is disconnected when the battery is full.
- send-data(?r, ?wp): a durative action which moves the robot ?r to the waypoint ?wp (TC) simulating the transmission of the acquired information (image and scan readings).
- take-image_data/-sample_data(?r, ?o, ?wp, ?s): durative actions which enable the robot ?r's sensors ?s to capture images, or read and store the scan data, respectively about the observation point ?o.
- target_id(?r, ?o, ?wp, ?s): a durative action which enables the robot ?r's sensors ?s to detect non-static targets near to the waypoint ?wp and take pictures of the targets.

Domain Constraints: The domain includes a number of `functions` associated with the robots' technical characteristics, available resources, and the relationship between object instances. The functions help to define a set of preconditions which constrain the implementation of the actions. We claim the domain supports long-term autonomy and the resulting plans follow representative constraints of real-world missions, in particular, time constraints and resource constraints. For temporal constraints, all the actions associated with point-to-point navigation such as `navigate` and `dock`, depend on the `distance` ?wp_init ?wp_final between the waypoints and the robot `avg_speed` ?r. The implementation time of the other actions is a fixed value. In addition, the domain includes resource constraints which represent preconditions for the implementation of a particular action. For instance, the preconditions of the action `dock` consider the robot ?r's level of `energy` and the `consumption_rate` (c_r) which depends on the robot's characteristics. Furthermore, the execution of the actions `send_data`, `target_id`, and `take -image_data/-sample_data` are determined by the `image_capacity/_data_capacity` ?r of the robot ?r and the actual `sample _image/_data` ?r acquired by the robot. In terms of capability constraints, for each action associated with specific sensors (scan or camera), a new `robot_capable` ?r predicate is added to the list of predicates and included as a precondition. This ensures the agents performing the action have the appropriated sensors for the implementation. All of these constraints support autonomous operation for long time periods, providing the robot with the essential actions it needs to maintain a running system.

3 Multi-vehicle Implementation

Temporal planning is capable of dealing with multi-agent planning problems since time is modelled explicitly: individual actions for different robots can be scheduled and executed in parallel. In ROSPlan only one action execution node is running. This leads to the situation where for the same type of actions, the handler process is blocked until it completes the action on a single robot. Therefore, concurrently dispatched actions are executed sequentially affecting makespan performance. We introduce a new type of action in the domain which allows the implementation of concurrent tasks using ROSPlan. Our domain presents two type of actions:

- **Standard Actions (SA):** The action definition contains one actor (e.g., robot). We can specify multiple robots of the same type in the problem definition to implement multi-agent solutions (e.g., robot_1, ..., robot_n). The planner allocates individual actions to each robot, some of which might be concurrent actions). All the actions described in Sect. 2 are SA.
- **Parallel Actions (PA):** The action definition is associated with multiple actors (e.g., robot_1, ..., robot_n). We do not need to specify multiple robots of the same type in the problem definition to implement multi-agent solutions. The planner simultaneously allocates the action to the robots defined in the action's description, which is intrinsically concurrent. The PDDL PA (actions included in the plan) messages are individually sent to the robots in the action definition for parallel execution.

Figure 2 shows a general representation of the system. The domain and the problem, which specifies the set of goals to achieve during the mission, are inputs to ROSPlan. The framework generates and dispatches the plan using Action Dispatch. ROS nodes were written for actions defined in the domain. This serves as a connection between high-level actions from task planning and low-level robot controls (Actuators). The plan defines a sequence of tasks for each robot delimited for particular time slots. PA solves the problem of sequential execution of the same type of action (same colour), allowing the concurrent execution of the same action type in all the robots (?r_1 to ?r_n) and relaxing the problem by allocating multiple goals. We define 3 parallel actions (navigate_parallel, take_parallel-image_data and take_parallel-sample_data) which are based on the properties of the navigate, take-image_data and take-sample_data actions. The PA implementation splits the total number of goals in multiple groups associated with individual robots. This strategy reduces the risk of collisions, increases the area covered by the agents, relaxes the plan complexity, and helps to guarantee optimality by forcing the robots to reduce distance travelled and mission time implementation.

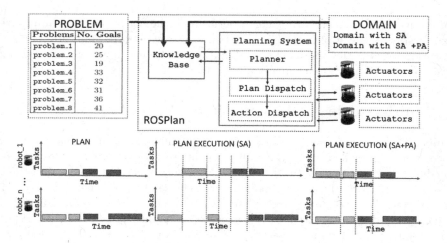

Fig. 2. General representation of the system architecture considering SA and SA+PA in the domain. SA+PA allows the concurrent execution of actions of the same type (same colour) for multiple robots using ROSPlan. The framework does not implement concurrent actions of the same type if we use SA.

Simulation Environment: The simulation environment is implemented in ROS and Gazebo, and uses the ROSPlan package to integrate a planning system with ROS. The simulation world is customised considering the models from Gazebo library and the main environment characteristics established in Fig. 1 (left). We integrate multiple robots (TurtleBots) in the world. The arena was previously mapped using the pre-built ROS package explore_lite. Figure 1 (right) shows the map of the environment in Rviz. The image exposes part of a plan implementation where a set of 2 robots are executing a `navigate_parallel` action. The robots execute the navigation in parallel, exploring different points previously allocated to each robot.

4   Performance Evaluation

Plan generation time and makespan influence the reaction capacity of the robotic system and the optimal implementation of time sensitive tasks. Therefore, the evaluation of the system performance will be based on the analysis of plan solvability, makespan and planning time in order to achieve long-term autonomy. We begin with the evaluation of the domain definition, POPF and OPTIC using a single robot (R_1). This initial analysis allows us to determine the best planner and the optimality of the domain approach. Additionally, we assess the results of multiple robots and the mission execution time using the Gazebo simulator. All the experiments were run on a machine with a 4 GHz processor, limiting the planner to 30 min of CPU for plan generation and 8 GB of memory consumption. The simulations were attempted 10 times for 8 problems of increasing difficulty and we measured the results' average. Figure 2 shows the number of goals to achieve in each problem.

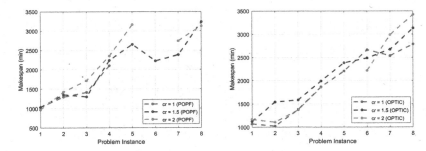

Fig. 3. Plan generation analysis for different values of the consumption_rate (c_r) using POPF (left) and OPTIC (right) for a single robot. The evaluation exhibits the sensitivity of both planners towards numeric variables in the domain definition.

Domain and Planner Evaluation: We first evaluated the planners' ability to cope with changes in the domain's numeric variables, to outline the planners' limitations. Figure 3 shows the plan makespan for 3 different values of consumption_rate. The graphs reveal the sensitivity of both planners towards changes in numeric constraints, which limit the planner's capacity to find a solvable plan in 30 min. However, OPTIC produces solvable plans for almost all problem instances, showing better performance than POPF. Additionally, POPF can be sensitive towards the ordering of object instances, which affects the plan's solvability in large problems. Results indicate that large consumption_rate values can increase the mission time, due to the robot more frequently executing intermediate actions that enhance long-term missions such as battery recharging, which delay the achievement of the goals. The experiments demonstrate that the high level of domain expressiveness makes plan generation largely dependent on the value of the domain variables. However, we avoid discrepancies between the model and the real-world through the inclusion of time and resource constraints. The results also demonstrate the numeric constraints can affect plan generation.

We evaluated planning time and makespan performance for the first solvable plan using consumption_rate of 1.5 and SA. Figure 4 shows plan makespan (left) and plan generation time (right) for a single robot using both planners. We performed the planner comparison using a single robot to simplify the analysis. POPF generates plans with the smallest makespan in most of the problem instances considering the planner cost function is based on achieving the lowest makespan. Nevertheless, planner sensitivity to the ordering of object instances makes the makespan values highly dependent on the goal position which affects the optimality of POPF's plans. In contrast, OPTIC is not affected by goal-ordering phenomena which provides freedom for action allocation in the mission schedule. In addition, OPTIC delivers anytime improvement behaviour of the initial plan which reduces the plan makespan at the expense of increased planning time.

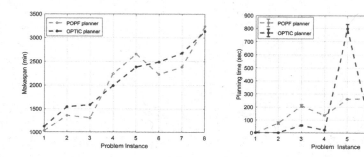

Fig. 4. Plan makespan (left) and plan generation time (right) analysis using OPTIC and POPF for a single robot. Both planners generate similar results in terms of makespan considering the close distance between the goals. OPTIC produces the first solvable plan in the shortest time period.

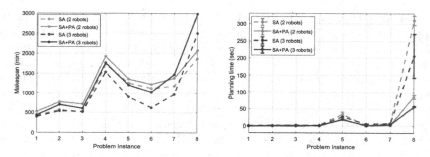

Fig. 5. Plan makespan (left) and plan generation time (right) for two and three robot fleets considering a domain with SA and a domain with SA+PA. Multi-agent implementations relax the mission complexity reducing the makespan and planning time. Missions with SA+PA increases the plan makespan and reduce the planning time respect to plans with just SA.

In terms of planning time, OPTIC achieves the first solvable plan in a shorter time period than POPF in the majority of the problems. OPTIC allows the introduction of other variables in the cost function which improves the plan's performance. In this work, OPTIC's plan utility is based on the minimisation of the *total-time* of the mission and the *total-distance* travelled. The plots indicate the planning time does not only depend on the number of goals. For instance, the time for plan generation for problem_5 is larger than the time used for problem_8 (problem with the largest number of goals). The effect of reducing the total distance travelled influences the plan generation time in problem_5. In problem_5, the robot needs to recharge the battery multiple times and OPTIC has to allocate these actions trying to reduce the distance travelled. The goals are in different regions at similar distances from the docking point (DP) which increases the time spent searching for a solvable plan. We use OPTIC for the multi-agent implementation due to the poor performance of POPF when dealing with numeric changes in the domain definition. Furthermore, POPF shows errors in the temporal place-ment of preconditions and effects and insufficient support of the Action Descrip-tion Language (ADL) which limits the expressiveness of the domain definition. In addition, OPTIC can deal with more complex problems such as preferences in the cost function. For instance, we can limit the implementation of one action to the early execution of another (`sometime-before` (`explore_ob robot_1 wp3 ob_1`) (`send_data robot_1 wp10`)). Therefore, with OPTIC we can constrain the region explored for each robot, reduce energy consumption, avoid collisions, and cover a large area in a short time period.

Multi-agent System Evaluation: Figure 5 shows the plan makespan (left) and plan generation time (right) produced by OPTIC for multi-robot sets using SA and SA+PA in the domain. For SA and SA+PA, the plan makespan is substan-tially reduced with the addition of multiple robots. The allocation of individual actions' schedules for each agent reduces the total mission time and the recur-rence of intermediate actions. From the plot we can define the optimal number of robots to execute the mission in a short time with minimum implementation costs, in this case 2 robots considering the number of mission goals. For multi-agent implementations, plan generation time is also reduced with respect to the single agent solution. The R_3 presents a small number of capabilities (the robot does not have the laser scan sensor) which limits its operation. Therefore, the planning time results for 2 and 3 robots are very similar, revealing the effect of fleet heterogeneity on the planning time and makespan results.

In addition, we compare the results of domains with SA and SA+PA in terms of plan generation. We add PA in the domain to overcome ROSPlan's concurrency problem. PA implements the same type of actions defined in Sect. 2, now including multiple robots. However, the definition of PA increases the action duration time and the number of constraints (i.e., the set of constraints for each robot) which affect the makespan and planning time results. The duration of the PA considers the distance from the robots' positions to the goals and the action duration is calculated based on the largest distance. For SA+PA, the domain includes 8 actions (3 PA and 5 SA), where the SA are the actions non transformed to parallel in Sect. 3. The graph exhibits an overhead of mission time for plans with SA+PA. OPTIC generates shorter plans using SA in the domain. However, the plan execution time overcomes the makespan defined for OPTIC (which will be analysed below) considering ROSPlan is unable to execute in parallel the same action in multiple robots. The planning time performance is considerably improved using SA+PA, since plan complexity is relaxed with the implementation of parallel actions. The reaction capacity of the robotic system is therefore improved, reducing the planning time.

Plan Execution: In this work we also execute our plans using a set of Turtle-Bots in the Gazebo environment. We compare the main differences between the mission time defined by OPTIC (plan makespan) and the real mission implemen-tation time (plan execution time). We proved in early experiments the domain with SA generates plans with shorter makespan than SA+PA. However, the ROSPlan framework dispatches SA of the same type sequentially to different

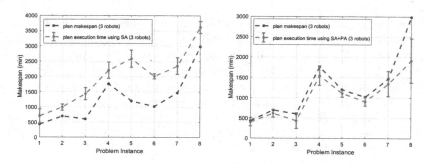

Fig. 6. Plan makespan and plan execution time for three robot fleets using SA (left) and SA+PA (right). The domain with SA+PA allows the implementation of parallel actions giving a correspondence between the times of execution and the plan makespan proposed by OPTIC.

robots which affects the real mission implementation time. Figure 6 shows a comparison of the plan makespan generated by OPTIC and the real mission execution time for a fleet of three robots. Results (left) demonstrate the mission execution times are larger than the plan makespan proposed by the planner for all the problems using just SA. This problem affects the plan's reliability, system robustness and forces the mission replanning due to the real action implementation time is larger than the action duration constraint defined in the domain. In contrast, the inclusion of PA enhances concurrent action implementation with ROSPlan at the expense of an increased makespan. The simulations (right) also indicate the framework effectively deals with concurrent actions during plan execution. The time differences are notably reduced with respect to the solutions with SA in the domain. In addition, we proved the shortest planning time is achieved for plans with PA+SA, which minimises the mission time in case of intermediate replanning. The primary causes for replanning in our experiments are the errors in robot localisation and the agent's incomplete knowledge about the states of the world at all times.

Results demonstrate the plan execution time differs with the plan makespan generated by OPTIC. These differences are based on some particular assumptions made during domain definition. We assume the distance between the points is the Euclidean norm and OPTIC produces a plan based on the shortest path. However, the robots have to avoid obstacles which increases the actual distance travelled and the action duration time. In addition, the action duration considers an average robot speed and our low-level motion planning moves the robot at different speeds depending on a free path between the points. However, these assumptions on the domain definition do not affect the system's capability to work for long-term periods.

5   Conclusions

In this paper we investigated the advantages of temporal planning to implement long-term missions with multiple robots in a highly constrained domain. We found that expressing domains precisely tends to over-complicate the planning problem and increase planning time. Planners can successfully achieve goals while keeping cost functions such as time and resources at levels that allow robots to maintain long-term autonomy. We define an accurate domain to handle any discrepancies between the model and the real (or simulated) world. We evaluated the performance of POPF and OPTIC in a new complex planning domain, and we simulated environments in ROS and Gazebo with different levels of complexity. ROSPlan was used to integrate the planning systems with the low-level controllers for multiple robots. Experiments showed OPTIC's potential for implementing multi-agent missions with different timelines and demonstrated ROSPlan's efficiency during mission execution with multiple vehicles.

References

1. Benton, J., Coles, A.J., Coles, A.: Temporal planning with preferences and time-dependent continuous costs. In: International Conference on Automated Planning and Scheduling (2012)
2. Cashmore, M., Coles, A., Cserna, B., Karpas, E., Magazzeni, D., Ruml, W.: Situated planning for execution under temporal constraints. In: Learning, and Execution for Goal Directed Autonomy, AAAI Spring Symposium on Integrating Representation, Reasoning (2018)
3. Cashmore, M., et al.: ROSPlan: planning in the robot operating system. In: International Conference on Automated Planning and Scheduling, pp. 333–341 (2015)
4. Chanel, C.P.C., Lesire, C., Teichteil-Königsbuch, F.: A robotic execution framework for online probabilistic (re)planning. In: Proceedings of ICAPS (2014)
5. Chrpa, L., Pinto, J., Ribeiro, M.A., Py, F., Sousa, J., Rajan, K.: On mixed-initiative planning and control for autonomous underwater vehicles. In: IROS, pp. 1685–1690 (2015)
6. Coles, A.J., Coles, A., Fox, M., Long, D.: Forward-chaining partial-order planning. In: ICAPS, pp. 42–49 (2010)
7. Crosby, M., Petrick, R: Temporal multiagent planning with concurrent action constraints. In: ICAPS Workshop on Distributed and Multi-Agent Planning (DMAP) (2014)
8. De Weerdt, M., Ter Mors, A., Witteveen, C.: Multi-agent planning: an introduction to planning and coordination. In: Handouts of the European Agent Summer. Citeseer (2005)
9. Della Penna, G., Magazzeni, D., Mercorio, F.: A universal planning system for hybrid domains. Appl. Intell. **36**(4), 932–959 (2012)
10. Eyerich, P., Mattmüller, R., Röger, G.: Using the context-enhanced additive heuristic for temporal and numeric planning. In: Towards Service Robots for Everyday Environments, pp. 49–64 (2012)
11. Fernandez-Gonzalez, E., Williams, B., Karpas, E.: ScottyActivity: mixed discrete-continuous planning with convex optimization. JAIR **62**, 579–664 (2018)

12. Fox, M., Long, D.: PDDL2.1: an extension to PDDL for expressing temporal planning domains. JAIR **20**, 61–124 (2003)
13. Ingham, M., Ragno, R., Williams, B.C.: A reactive model-based programming language for robotic space explorers. In: Proceedings of ISAIRAS-01 (2001)
14. Marques, T., Pinto, J., Dias, P., de Sousa, J.T.: MvPlanning: a framework for planning and coordination of multiple autonomous vehicles. In: OCEANS-Anchorage, pp. 1–6 (2017)
15. McDermott, D., et al.: PDDL - the planning domain definition language (version 1.2). Technical report CVC TR-98-003/DCS TR-1165, Yale Center for Computational Vision and Control (1998)
16. McGann, C., Py, F., Rajan, K., Thomas, H., Henthorn, R., McEwen, R.: A deliberative architecture for AUV control. In: IEEE International Conference on Robotics and Automation, pp. 1049–1054 (2008)
17. Muscettola, N., Dorais, G.A., Fry, C., Levinson, R., Plaunt, C.: IDEA: planning at the core of autonomous reactive agents. In: NASA Workshop on Planning and Scheduling for Space (2002)
18. Nunes, E., Gini, M.L.: Multi-robot auctions for allocation of tasks with temporal constraints. In: AAAI, pp. 2110–2116 (2015)
19. Nunes, E., McIntire, M., Gini, M.: Decentralized multi-robot allocation of tasks with temporal and precedence constraints. Adv. Robot. **31**(22), 1193–1207 (2017)
20. Piotrowski, W., Fox, M., Long, D., Magazzeni, D., Mercorio, F.: Heuristic planning for hybrid systems. In: AAAI, pp. 4254–4255 (2016)
21. Ponda, S., Redding, J., Choi, H.-L., How, J.P., Vavrina, M., Vian, J.: Decentralized planning for complex missions with dynamic communication constraints. In: American Control Conference, pp. 3998–4003 (2010)
22. Quigley, M., et al.: ROS: an open-source Robot Operating System. In: ICRA Workshop on Open Source Software (2009)
23. Schillinger, P., Bürger, M., Dimarogonas, D.V.: Simultaneous task allocation and planning for temporal logic goals in heterogeneous multi-robot systems. Int. J. Robot. Res. **37**, 818–838 (2017)
24. Tran, T.T., Vaquero, T., Nejat, G., Beck, J.C.: Robots in retirement homes: applying off-the-shelf planning and scheduling to a team of assistive robots. JAIR **58**, 523–590 (2017)
25. Veloso, M.M., Biswas, J., Coltin, B., Rosenthal, S.: CoBots: robust symbiotic autonomous mobile service robots. In: IJCAI, p. 4423 (2015)
26. Zhang, Z., Wang, J., Xu, D., Meng, Y.: Task allocation of multi-AUVs based on innovative auction algorithm. In: Proceedings of ISCID, vol. 2, pp. 83–88. IEEE (2017)
27. Hawes, N., et al.: The strands project: long-term autonomy in everyday environments. IEEE Robot. Autom. Mag. **24**(3), 146–156 (2017)

An Optimal Approach to Anytime Task and Path Planning for Autonomous Mobile Robots in Dynamic Environments

Cuebong Wong[1]([⊠]) [iD], Erfu Yang[1] [iD], Xiu-Tian Yan[1] [iD], and Dongbing Gu[2] [iD]

[1] Department of Design, Manufacture and Engineering Management,
University of Strathclyde, Glasgow, UK
{cuebong.wong,erfu.yang,x.yan}@strath.ac.uk
[2] School of Computer Science and Electronic Engineering,
University of Essex, Colchester, UK
dgu@essex.ac.uk

Abstract. The study of combined task and path planning has mainly focused on feasibility planning for high-dimensional, complex manipulation problems. Yet the integration of symbolic reasoning capabilities with geometric knowledge can address optimal planning in lower dimensional problems. This paper presents a dynamic, anytime task and path planning approach that enables mobile robots to autonomously adapt to changes in the environment. The planner consists of a path planning layer that adopts a multi-tree extension of the optimal Transition-based Rapidly-Exploring Random Tree algorithm to simultaneously find optimal paths for all movement actions. The corresponding path costs, derived from a cost space function, are incorporated into the symbolic representation of the problem to guide the task planning layer. Anytime planning provides continuous path quality improvements, which subsequently updates the high-level plan. Geometric knowledge of the environment is preserved to efficiently re-plan both at the task and path planning level. The planner is evaluated against existing methods for static planning problems, showing that it is able to find higher quality plans without compromising planning time. Simulated deployment of the planner in a partially-known environment demonstrates the effectiveness of the dynamic, anytime components.

Keywords: Robotics · Autonomous systems · Task planning ·
Path planning · Combined task and motion planning ·
Dynamic planning

1 Introduction

Many practical applications for robots to date still rely on human-in-the-loop control [1], which is costly and inefficient for remote operation or long-duration missions. Embedding intelligence into robotic systems can provide robots with the required autonomy to plan their actions to achieve the desired goals. However, this remains an ongoing challenge due to the existence of uncertainty in

© Springer Nature Switzerland AG 2019
K. Althoefer et al. (Eds.): TAROS 2019, LNAI 11650, pp. 155–166, 2019.
https://doi.org/10.1007/978-3-030-25332-5_14

the real-world. Robots must be capable of dynamically adapting to changes and recovering from failures to operate reliably and safely without human intervention. The study of dynamic task planning and path planning is therefore an important aspect in the development of autonomous robotics.

Task planning is the process of finding a sequence of high-level actions to accomplish defined objectives. Generally, the task planning domain is represented using symbolic language and solved by searching a finite set of discrete states. Geometric relationships of objects are abstracted to reduce the size of the state space. In contrast, path planning (a purely geometric motion planning problem [2]) solves for a low-level motion path in $\mathbb{R}^d$ space to move a robot from a start configuration to a goal configuration. Extensive work exist in literature for task planning and path planning, but they have mostly been conducted in isolation. While various problems such as fruit harvesting [3] and component disassembly [4] can be solved using a decoupled approach to planning, solving more complex or larger scale problems often demands a more seamlessly coupled approach. Applying a decoupled approach in these cases may produce sub-optimal plans or, in the worst case, lead to an intractable problem. Various authors have begun to address complex manipulation problems by integrating task and motion planning. Notable examples include FFRob [5], an integrated planner that extends the *FastForward* heuristics used in symbolic planning to consider geometric details in the task planner, and the TM-Kit [6], a probabilistically complete, general-purpose framework for combined task and motion planning. However, these work focused on feasibility planning due to the high dimensionality of manipulation planning problems. When applied to robotic navigation, a coupled planning approach can improve the optimality of long mission plans, or adapt task plans in response to observable failures or perceived changes in the world.

Several authors have explored this avenue in the context of mobile robots. For example, the UP2TA framework [7] provides optimal plans for exploration mission planning. However, the authors did not consider general cost spaces or aspects of re-planning. The authors in [8] addressed multi-robot planning for partially-known environments and considered minimisation of robot resources. Their approach enables adaptation of the plan as new obstacles are detected, but possesses a number of limiting characteristics, such as being unable to consider task dependencies, requiring several hundred seconds to plan for single robot problems, and performing a needless number of re-planning instances as each update to a planned path triggers an instance of task planning. Motivated by these ongoing challenges, the contributions of this work is two-fold: (i) we present a base planner that integrates task and path planning to enable optimal task planning in continuous cost spaces using a multi-tree T-RRT* (Transition-based Rapidly-exploring Random Tree) algorithm [9] and compare it to existing methods, and (ii) we extend the base planner with dynamic, anytime capabilities to enable efficient high and low level re-planning in partially known or dynamic environments. We collectively refer to the proposed planner as the Dynamic, Anytime Task and Path Planner (DA-TPP)[1].

---

[1] This paper is an invited extension to the work presented in [10].

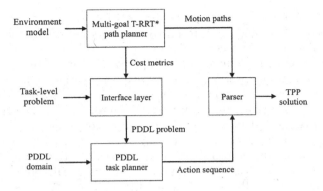

Fig. 1. Base planner architecture

2 Problem Definition

This paper addresses Task and Path Planning (TPP) problems consisting of a robot in $\mathbb{R}^2$ space and a set of landmarks L. L represents locations in space where a robot must perform a set of domain-specific actions. The robot navigates the environment by performing movement actions corresponding to motions between any pair of landmarks $l_a, l_b \in L$. A valid planning problem contains an initial landmark l_{init}, where the robot starts from, and a set of goals describing the tasks that must be performed at each landmark. A goal landmark l_{goal} for which the robot must be located at the end of the plan may optionally be specified. In our experiments we assume that for any initial planning problem the robot must begin and end at a root landmark $l_{init} = l_{goal} = l_0$ (the *robot base*) and there exist tasks that must be completed at every landmark (note, however, that our approach is equally applicable when these are not true). As re-planning takes place during execution, l_{init} is updated to reflect the new robot location. A valid TPP solution then consists of a sequence of movement actions and corresponding motion paths that guide the robot from l_{init} to l_{goal} through a route that enables the completion of all tasks while accumulating the lowest cost.

3 The DA-TPP Approach

The base planner of the DA-TPP (Fig. 1) employs a path planning layer to find an optimal path for all valid movement actions. The corresponding path costs are then linked to the discrete movement action costs for optimal task planning through an interface layer such that true path plans are used to guide the task planner. Given a continuous cost space mapping function, c, from which a cost value can be derived for all robot configurations, we define the path cost function, c_p, of a path σ as a weighted sum of integral cost and path length:

$$c_p(\sigma) = f(\sigma)\left(\frac{w_a}{n}\sum_{k=1}^{n} c\left(\sigma\left(\frac{k}{n}\right)\right) + w_b\right) \tag{1}$$

where n is the number of subdivisions of σ, $f()$ is the path length, w_a and w_b are weight factors for c and $f(\sigma)$, respectively, and k represents the point along σ. This formulation enables consolidation of both the cost function and path length as a weighted sum multi-objective optimisation problem.

When a termination criteria is met, the planner returns the best set of paths found for each of these movement actions ($c_p = \infty$ if no solution is found). A satisfactory TPP solution exists when all landmarks associated with the task objectives are connected in a reachability graph containing l_{init}, where each vertex represents a landmark and each edge is a valid motion path. That is, the robot can reach and return from any landmark by traversing through the vertices of the graph. The task planning layer employs PDDL representation [11], and is solved using Local Planning Graphs (LPG-td) [12]. We chose to represent the planning problem in PDDL due to its wide acceptance as a standard for representing classical symbolic planning problems. This enables interchangeable use of other heuristic planners (such as Metric-FF [13]) and provides generality to the planner to include new actions and treat task dependencies etc.

3.1   Anytime Extension

Anytime planning supports a request for an initial solution after a fixed allotted time, which minimises idle time at the start of a task. During execution of an existing plan, the planner continues to iterate the path planning algorithm to improve the solution at subsequent requests. Suppose that the path cost for an action a is c_p. Like the work in [14], an upper cost bound C_s^+ is defined as

$$C_s^+ = (1 - \eta_a) \cdot c_p(\sigma). \tag{2}$$

where η_a is a constant. When the path planning layer finds a new path σ' for a with $c_p(\sigma') < C_s^+$, a new instance of task planning is called. This mechanism guarantees that the task planning layer is called only when a guaranteed improvement to an action cost is found. During execution, it is also necessary to consider the goals that have been met thus far. This is addressed by updating the initial state of the planning problem at each planning instance to reflect the next state of the world after executing the current action of the latest plan.

3.2   Dynamic Anytime Extension

The complete DA-TPP architecture is shown in Fig. 2. The key extensions are a local path correction modeul and a global re-planner. Each time an obstruction to a currently executed path is detected, the local path correction algorithm finds a new optimal path to the goal configuration. The DA-TPP then determines whether an instance of global re-planning should be called using a heuristically-defined lower cost bound C_s^- shown in (3). Letting c_p' be the path cost of the remaining segments of the original path, C_s^- is given by

$$C_s^- = (1 + \eta_d) \cdot c_p'(\sigma). \tag{3}$$

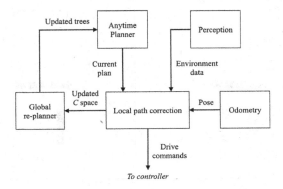

Fig. 2. Dynamic anytime planner architecture

where η_d is a constant. When $c_p(\sigma') > C_s^-$, global re-planning takes place. This permanently updates all planning trees with the detected obstruction and a new optimal sequence of movement actions is generated.

By applying the heuristic cost bound defined in (3), the DA-TPP provides the following behaviours in dynamic environments. When minor obstructions are encountered, only local adjustments are made to the currently executed path. This, in general, does not affect the optimality of the task plan from a high-level perspective. It is sufficient then to correct paths locally each time the same obstruction is encountered without initiating a global re-planning procedure, thus limiting the number of task-level re-planning instances. However, in situations where an obstruction causes significant diversion for a particular traverse (e.g. from road blockages), the likelihood of the obstruction affecting the optimality of the task plan is high. This is due to the increased cost of the current path and possible extended effects on other planned paths. In these situations the planner updates the entire plan (including all motion paths) to maintain optimality.

4   Path Planning

The path planning layer of the base planner is implemented following the multi-T-RRT* approach described in [9], which simultaneously searches for all optimal paths between landmarks by iteratively growing trees rooted at each landmark to explore the configuration space. Readers are directed to this initial work for a detailed description of the algorithm.

4.1   Local Path Correction

The local path re-planner corrects any single path according to procedures based on elements of the RRT^X algorithm [15]. At the start of any movement action, a new tree T_{new} is generated from two trees T_0 and T_g corresponding to the start

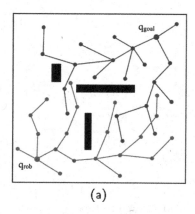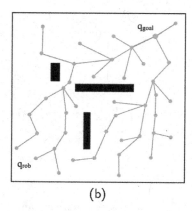

(a)   (b)

Fig. 3. (a) Trees T_0 (red), rooted at q_{rob}, and T_g (blue), rooted at q_{goal}, grown across the configuration space. (b) The resulting tree T_{new} (green) resulting from the merge function applied on T_0 and T_g. (Color figure online)

Algorithm 1. localPathCorrection

Input: Merged tree T_{new}, current path σ and robot configuration q_{rob}
Output: Updated path σ'
  1: $O_{new} \leftarrow getObstacles()$
  2: **if** $collision(\sigma, O_{new})$ **then**
  3:     $invalidNodes(T_{new}, O_{new})$
  4:     $updateOrphans(T_{new})$
  5:     $rewireTree(T_{new})$
  6:     $\sigma' \leftarrow updatePath(T_{new}, q_{rob})$
  7: **end if**

---

and goal landmarks l_0 and l_g, respectively (Fig. 3). T_{new} is rooted at the goal configuration q_g and consists of all the vertices of T_0 and T_g rewired to minimise path cost according to the new tree root. This speeds up dynamic re-planning later tree root does not need to be updated as the robot advances along the path. As new obstacles are detected during execution, the remaining segments of a traversed path are checked for collision. If these obstacles invalidate any part of this path, Algorithm 1 is called to update the path.

The algorithm invalidates vertices that lie in the collision region of new obstacles. All valid descendant vertices are then updated as orphans. This closely resembles the *propagateDescendants* function in [15]. The algorithm then updates the branches of the tree by iterating through a queue of vertices consisting initially of the neighbours of orphans (see *reduceInconsistency* function in [15]). For each of these vertices, the algorithm updates its parent, and then runs a rewiring procedure on its neighbouring vertices. Any vertices that are rewired at this step are then added to the queue. This continues until no further improvements can be made. Finally, a new path from the tree root to the robot configuration q_{rob} is found by attempting to connect q_{rob} to neighbouring vertices.

Algorithm 2. globalReplanning

Input: Set of all planning trees T, new obstacles O_{new} and robot configuration q_{rob}
Output: Set of updated planning trees T and set of path solutions Σ_{best}

1: **for all** $T_k \in T$ **do**
2:    $invalidNodes(T_k, O_{new})$
3:    $updateOrphans(T_k)$
4:    $rewireTree(T_k)$
5: **end for**
6: $\Sigma_{best} \leftarrow updatePaths(T)$
7: $\Sigma_{best} \leftarrow pathsFromRobotToLandmarks(\Sigma_{best}, T, q_{rob})$

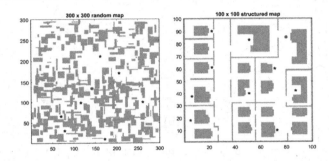

Fig. 4. Example planning problems used to compare planners. Blue markers represent the robot base and black stars represent all other landmarks. (Color figure online)

4.2 Global Re-Planning

When the condition in (3) is met, a new action-motion sequence is determined by updating the costs of all movement actions. This is achieved by updating the solutions of the path planning layer using Algorithm 2. The algorithm first updates every tree by invalidating infeasible vertices, updating orphaned vertices and propagating a rewiring cascade, as in Sect. 4.1. New optimal paths between landmarks are obtained by finding new connecting vertices between corresponding pairs of trees. The set of best paths Σ_{best} are updated accordingly. A temporary landmark l_{temp} is then inserted into the TPP problem at q_{rob}. An attempt to find an optimal path from each original landmark to l_{temp} is made by testing connections from neighbouring vertices of each tree to the root of l_{temp}. Σ_{best} is then expanded to include these paths.

5 Experimental Evaluation

5.1 Base Planner Comparison

The base planner is benchmarked across a number of randomly generated cluttered and structured environments varying between 50×50, 100×100 and 300×300 in dimensions (examples shown in Fig. 4). The cost function c in (1) for

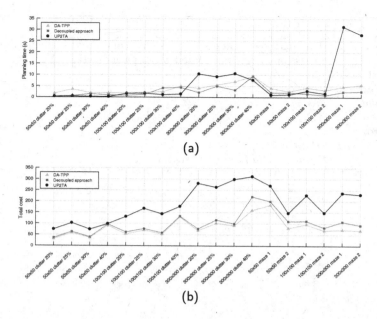

Fig. 5. Performance comparison between basic task planning, DA-TPP and UP2TA methods over 100 trials. (a) mean planning time for initial solution, (b) mean plan cost for initial solution. Simulations were conducted on an Intel® Xeon® CPU E3-1270 v3.

any configuration q is given by $c = 1/\delta^2$, where δ is the distance to the nearest obstacle. Thus c describes the 'closeness' of q to the nearest obstacle. w_a and w_b were set to 0.97 and 0.03, respectively.

We compared the performance of the DA-TPP base planner with a decoupled planning approach and UP2TA [7]. The decoupled approach solves for an optimal action sequence by using the Euclidean distances between landmarks as movement action costs. A single instance of path planning was subsequently called for each movement action to obtain the TPP solution. For consistency across the comparison, we used a bi-directional equivalent of the multi-T-RRT* algorithm for path planning. Our implementation of the UP2TA framework consisted of a greedy search algorithm to approximate the cost metrics for each possible movement action. The LPG-*td* planner was then used to solve the task planning problem (the original authors used the *FastForward* planner, but for consistency we applied the same PDDL planner as in our work). Finally, a second path planning layer that employs the graph search-based *Theta** algorithm [16] was used to obtain the true paths for each movement action.

The results generated from a PC with an Intel® Xeon® CPU E3-1270 v3 (3.50 GHz) are provided in Fig. 5. We observe that the UP2TA fails to consider cost spaces and consequently performs notably worse than other planners in terms of path cost. Planning times also highlight a key deficit of grid-based approaches: as the size of the problem increases, their performance decreases

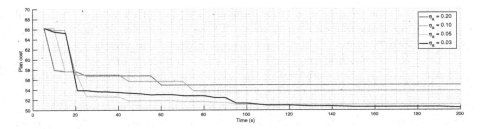

Fig. 6. Anytime planning - plan cost steadily decreases as more computation time is allowed. Step-like cost reductions indicate task-level improvements to the plan.

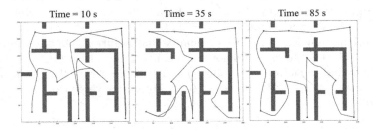

Fig. 7. Example of anytime plan evolution at selected time instances.

rapidly, as observed for environments of size 300×300. The decoupled approach scales better with the size of the problem and maintains a low computational cost across all trials. However, this approach finds solutions with overall costs that are generally greater than the DA-TPP approach, particularly for structured, maze-like environments. This is an expected observation as the task planning layer is ill-informed by misleading action costs. Without knowing the geometric relationships of objects in the world, costly movement actions are unknown to the symbolic planner. Thus DA-TPP consistently finds the lowest cost plans in all test cases. Although this sacrifices computational efficiency slightly, the proposed planner scales well with the size of the problem and indeed finds a solution faster than UP2TA in almost all cases for 300×300 environments. Finally, the quality of DA-TPP solutions may be further improved over time as a result of anytime planning, as discussed below.

5.2 Anytime Evaluation

The behavior of the anytime component of DA-TPP was assessed in the following way. An initial solution was first obtained using the base planner. Starting from this same initial solution each time, the planner described in Sect. 3.1 was run four times with η_a set to 0.2, 0.1, 0.05 and 0.03, respectively. For each run, a request for the current solution was made at the defined time instances shown in Fig. 6. Sample plans obtained over the trial durations are provided in Fig. 7.

In general, the quality of a plan improves at the path level and task level as further computation time is allowed. These correspond to small progressive cost decreases and larger *step* changes observed in Fig. 6, respectively. Task level improvements take place only when sufficient improvements to a local path changes the optimality of the global task plan. These occurred only 3–4 times over the duration of 200 s for all runs. Hence it is often unnecessary to re-plan an entire action-motion sequence for small local path changes. This provides motivation for the use of the update criteron defined in (3) for global re-planning. Finally, we observe that the value of η_a controls the rate of convergence and optimality of the planner. For larger values of η_a, the planner spends less time re-planning the task sequence as it is triggered only when more significant improvements to local paths are found, thus converging faster (60 s for $\eta_a = 0.20$ vs 95 s for $\eta_a = 0.05$). However, this in turn dismisses small, steady cost reductions that lead to a better quality final solution. On the other hand, with $\eta_a = 0.03$, the solution does not reach convergence after 200 s, yet the planner is able to find the lowest cost solution across the four runs. In the subsequent experiment we set $\eta_a = 0.05$ based on its balanced convergence and optimality characteristics.

5.3   Dynamic Anytime Evaluation

Finally, the complete DA-TPP approach was assessed through simulations in a 30×30 m partially-known environment shown in Fig. 8. The robot begins executing a plan after an initial solution is obtained. We simulate real-time execution on the Gazebo simulator using a Clearpath Husky. Perception of the environment is achieved using a laser scanner with a range of 30 m, while η_d is set to 0.05 (chosen based on an analysis similar to the selection for η_a).

Figure 8 shows global re-planning instances where actions belonging to a previously optimal plan (e.g. traversing from landmark 5 to landmark 6) are avoided on detection of significant blockage, while only local path corrections take place for smaller obstructions. Furthermore, we draw particular attention to the observation that the robot visits landmark 7 twice in the executed set of paths, which showcases the behaviour of the planner when a direct path between two landmarks do not exist. After running the global re-planning procedures triggered by the detection of obstacles C and D, a feasible path between landmarks 5 and 6 was no longer found. Nevertheless, a multi-segment path consisting of two movement actions (paths 7 and 8) enabled the robot to reach landmark 6. In this way the planner is able to identify infeasible actions through the inference from the path planning layer.

The solutions of DA-TPP may be subject to local minima according to the limitations of the heuristic planner used in task planning. For example, LPG-*td* may provide locally-optimal task plans but is always able to return solutions quickly. Other planners such as Metric-FF can provide globally-optimal solutions at the expense of lower efficiency. Conversely, the path planning layer maintains the asymptotic optimality property of RRT* and thus always converges towards globally-optimal solutions if sufficient time is allowed.

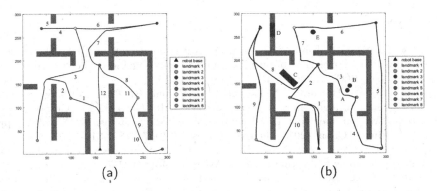

(a)   (b)

Fig. 8. (a) Initial plan for a mobile robot located at *robot base*. Motion sequence is indicated by numerical sequence. (b) True executed paths at runtime (detected obstacles shown in blue). (Color figure online)

6 Conclusion

The DA-TPP is an anytime task and path planner for autonomous mobile robots with re-planning capabilities. The base planner uses the Multi-T-RRT* algorithm to find optimal paths for all movement actions in relation to the continuous cost space. The corresponding path costs are linked to discrete movement actions in the task planning layer, which is solved using off-the-shelf planners. In our results, we show that the planner is competitive in terms of scalability and the quality of solutions obtained. The anytime extension enables a sub-optimal solution to be found quickly, and any further computation time given to planning continues to improve the quality of the task plan by a bounded degree of improvement. A local path correction algorithm updates individual paths during execution, while the global re-planner updates the structures of all trees in the path planning layer to maintain global optimality when large changes are observed. In this way the DA-TPP possesses the flexibility to adapt both individual paths and entire plans accordingly depending on the significance of observed changes in the environment. One of the limiting factors on the computational performance of the DA-TPP in large planning problems is the population size of nodes that make up each planning tree in the path planning layer. One improvement for future work includes the removals of useless nodes and branches that provide zero contribution to the search for more optimal paths over existing ones. This is similar to the *branch-and-bound* technique applied in [17], but an admissible heuristic to assess each node against all goals is necessary.

Acknowledgements. Funded by the Engineering and Physical Sciences Research Council (EPSRC) under its Doctoral Training Partnership Programme (DTP 2016–2020 University of Strathclyde, Glasgow, UK).

References

1. Wong, C., Yang, E., Yan, X.-T., Gu, D.: Autonomous robots for harsh environments: a holistic overview of current solutions and ongoing challenges. Syst. Sci. Control Eng. **6**(1), 213–219 (2018)
2. Gasparetto, A., Boscariol, P., Lanzutti, A., Vidoni, R.: Path planning and trajectory planning algorithms: a general overview. In: Carbone, G., Gomez-Bravo, F. (eds.) Motion and Operation Planning of Robotic Systems. MMS, vol. 29, pp. 3–27. Springer, Cham (2015). https://doi.org/10.1007/978-3-319-14705-5_1
3. Nguyen, T.T., Kayacan, E., De Baedemaeker, J., Saeys, W.: Task and motion planning for apple harvesting robot. IFAC Proc. **46**(18), 247–252 (2013)
4. Friedrich, C., Csiszar, A., Lechler, A., Verl, A.: Efficient task and path planning for maintenance automation using a robot system. IEEE Trans. Autom. Sci. Eng. **15**(3), 1205–1215 (2018)
5. Garrett, C.R., Lozano-Pérez, T., Kaelbling, L.P.: FFRob: an efficient heuristic for task and motion planning. In: Akin, H.L., Amato, N.M., Isler, V., van der Stappen, A.F. (eds.) Algorithmic Foundations of Robotics XI. STAR, vol. 107, pp. 179–195. Springer, Cham (2015). https://doi.org/10.1007/978-3-319-16595-0_11
6. Dantam, N.T., Chaudhuri, S., Kavraki, L.E.: The task-motion kit: an open source, general-purpose task and motion- planning framework. IEEE Robot. Autom. Mag. **25**(3), 61–70 (2018)
7. Muñoz, P., R-Moreno, M.D., Barrero, D.F.: Unified framework for path-planning and task-planning for autonomous robots. Robot. Auton. Syst. **82**, 1–14 (2016)
8. Woosley, B., Dasgupta, P.: Integrated real-time task and motion planning for multiple robots under path and communication uncertainties. Robotica **36**(3), 353–373 (2018)
9. Wong, C., Yang, E., Yan, X.-T., Gu, D.: Optimal path planning based on a multi-tree T-RRT* approach for robotic task planning in continuous cost spaces. In: 12th France-Japan and 10th Europe-Asia Congress on Mechatronics, pp. 242–247 (2018)
10. Wong, C., Yang, E., Yan, X.-T., Gu, D.: Dynamic anytime task and path planning for mobile robots. In: UK-RAS19 Conference on Embedded Intelligence: Enabling & Supporting RAS Technologies, pp. 36–39 (2019)
11. McDermott, D.: The PDDL planning domain definition language. In: AIPS-98 Planning Competition Community (1998)
12. Gerevini, A., Saetti, A., Serina, I., Toninelli, P.: LPG-TD: a fully automated planner for PDDL2.2 domains. In: 14th International Conference on Automated Planning and Scheduling International Planning Competition (2004)
13. Hoomann, J.O.: The Metric-FF planning system: translating 'ignoring delete lists' to numeric state variables. J. Artif. Intell. Res. **20**, 291–341 (2003)
14. Ferguson, D., Stentz, A.: Anytime RRTs. In: Proceedings of the 2006 IEEE/RSJ International Conference on Intelligent Robots and Systems, pp. 5369–5375 (2006)
15. Otte, M., Frazzoli, E.: RRT^X: asymptotically optimal single- query sampling-based motion planning with quick replanning. Int. J. Rob. Res. **35**(7), 797–822 (2016)
16. Daniel, K., Nash, A., Koenig, S., Felner, S.: Theta*: any-angle path planning on grids. J. Artif. Intell. Res. **39**, 533–579 (2010)
17. Karaman, S., Walter, M.R., Perez, A., Frazzoli, E., Teller, S.: Anytime motion planning using the RRT*. In: IEEE International Conference on Robotics and Automation, pp. 1478–1483 (2011)

A Self-organizing Network with Varying Density Structure for Characterizing Sensorimotor Transformations in Robotic Systems

Omar Zahra[✉] and David Navarro-Alarcon

Department of Mechanical Engineering,
The Hong Kong Polytechnic University, Hung Hom, Kowloon, Hong Kong
omar.zahra@connect.polyu.hk, dnavar@polyu.edu.hk

Abstract. In this work, we present the development of a neuro-inspired approach for characterizing sensorimotor relations in robotic systems. The proposed method has self-organizing and associative properties that enable it to autonomously obtain these relations without any prior knowledge of either the motor (e.g. mechanical structure) or perceptual (e.g. sensor calibration) models. Self-organizing topographic properties are used to build both sensory and motor maps, then the associative properties rule the stability and accuracy of the emerging connections between these maps. Compared to previous works, our method introduces a new varying density self-organizing map (VDSOM) that controls the concentration of nodes in regions with large transformation errors without affecting much the computational time. A distortion metric is measured to achieve a self-tuning sensorimotor model that adapts to changes in either motor or sensory models. The obtained sensorimotor maps prove to have less error than conventional self-organizing methods and potential for further development.

Keywords: Self-organizing maps · Sensorimotor models ·
Associative learning · Adaptive systems · Robot manipulators ·
Motor babbling

1 Introduction

Among the many interesting cognitive abilities of animals and humans is the motor babbling process that leads to the formation of the sensorimotor map. Many theories have been introduced about how these behaviors develop since prenatal stages [1]. This sensorimotor adaptation paradigm has proven to be useful in robotics for relating motor commands with sensory outputs when

This work is supported in part by the Research Grants Council (RGC) of Hong Kong under grant number 14203917, and in part by PROCORE-France/Hong Kong Joint Research Scheme sponsored by the RGC and the Consulate General of France in Hong Kong under grant F-PolyU503/18.

© Springer Nature Switzerland AG 2019
K. Althoefer et al. (Eds.): TAROS 2019, LNAI 11650, pp. 167–178, 2019.
https://doi.org/10.1007/978-3-030-25332-5_15

prior/exact knowledge of its model is unavailable (which is common in practice). A robot with changes to its mechanical structure (e.g. due to damage) or perceptual system (e.g. due to sensor decalibration) is generally not able to properly coordinate its motions without updating such sensorimotor relations. Drawing inspiration from the adaptive properties of living organisms, artificial neural systems can be developed to cope with these uncertainties. The development of computational sensorimotor models with adaptation properties can lead to the emergence of valuable self-calibrating behaviors. Additionally, these could help to (safely) verify theories about the internal workings of the human brain, but with machines.

Previous studies with primates have concluded a topographic arrangement in areas dedicated to motor and sensory processing, where adjacent body parts tend to have an adjacent representation in the brain cortex [2,3].

Thus, to represent perceptual computing units in a biologically inspired manner, such topologically preserving property was considered.

Topographic models are useful for characterizing sensory and motor spaces in robots. Yet, to co-relate how a particular motion/configuration produces a sensory stimuli, additional associative properties must be considered. One common model for linking different brain areas based on shared activity patterns is the so-called Hebbian rule [4]. It states that if two neuronal regions are persistently activated together, the connection between them is strengthened; the connection is weakened if no simultaneous activity is present. Topographic and associative properties are the basis for the sensorimotor adaptive method that we propose in this paper.

In the literature, many efforts have been placed to model human sensorimotor abilities with methods based on self-organizing maps (SOM) [5–7]. Most of these works use SOMs as a topography-preserving and dimension-reducing tool, to map several sensor readings with motor actions.

In [6], an SOM is used to form a sensory map with visual feed. However, the learning process to form a sensorimotor map takes place mainly through gradient-descent rule which makes it less biologically plausible. In [5], two dynamic SOMs (DSOM) [8] representing head and arm of a humanoid robot were used to achieve visuo-motor coordination. Yet, that model suffered from a degradation in performance when perturbations were added to motor commands. In [7], the sensorimotor coordination is achieved by utilizing bi-directional neural modularity such that motor output can be predicted from sensory input and vice versa. For the proposed method in this paper, the learning paradigm allows for the development of reciprocal correlations inherently while maintaining high accuracy.

In this study, we propose a new method for representing sensorimotor transformations of robotic systems. The neuro-inspired method combines self-organizing and associative properties to model continuously adapting relations between sensory and motor spaces. Compared to previous works, our new method proposes a varying density SOM (VDSOM) that reduces the transformation error that is typically present at the periphery of standard SOMs. This is done by automatically adjusting a parameter that controls the density of neighboring nodes at regions with large transformation errors. In case of changes in either motor or sensory models, a distortion metric is measured to readjust the formed sensorimotor map to suit these changes. The resulting computational model can effectively reduce the mean error over the whole map, while coping with changes in the original sensorimotor model. Several cases of study (such as transformation accuracy, amputation, limb extension) are presented to thoroughly evaluate the proposed method.

The rest of this paper is organized as follows: Sect. 2 describes the computational model; Sect. 3 presents its quantitative evaluation; Sect. 4 gives final conclusions.

2   Methods

2.1   A Biologically-Inspired Sensorimotor Model

Human bodies have different morphologies which develop over years (from birth to death) and even subject to drastic changes as in the case of amputations. However, the brain somehow always manages to find or re-adapt such mappings between sensory feedback and motor actions. In infants, for example, motor babbling helps to adaptively obtain these sensorimotor relations, where by performing motions covering the workspace, the brain is able to correlate bodily configurations with its corresponding motor actions [9,10].

It is also clear from recent studies that in both sensory and motor areas in the brain, adjacent body parts have also contiguous representations [11]. Moreover, many of these areas are connected together by some synapses which develop connections based on their joint activity. Among these rules is the well-known Hebbian learning rule [4].

To represent such learning paradigm, a model for human sensorimotor mapping is constructed using SOM (modeling topographically arranged brain areas) and Hebbian learning rules (modeling connections among these areas). Both of these models have clear biologically-inspired properties as they can represent topographic organization of neurons and modulation of strength of synaptic connections, respectively.

SOM are built upon the underlying rules of development of cognitive functions, as they encode competition, cooperation and adaptation [12]. The nodes (neurons) of the SOM compete against each other such that only one becomes the best matching neuron (BMU) for a given input. However not only the BMU contribute to the output, but also the neighboring neurons as well, such that the closer to the BMU the greater would be the contribution to the output. This represents the lateral interaction between neurons in a network. Adaptation by modulation of weights of BMU (and neighborhood nodes) occurs to enhance the chance of the BMU to represent the input vector and act as the BMU again for a similar input.

The Hebbian learning rule wires the SOMs representing the sensory space and motor space together, such that neurons active on both sides at the same time have the strength of the synaptic connection in between increased proportional to the magnitude of activity of both the pre-synaptic and post-synaptic neurons.

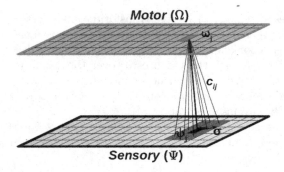

Fig. 1. Motor space (Ω) connected to Sensory space (Ψ) through Hebbian connections (c_{ij}). As learning process proceeds, active nodes in Ω (ω_i) have the connections to active ones in Ψ reinforced (ψ_j and neighborhood within a radius of σ).

These connections achieve sensorimotor correlation between the motor actions and the corresponding sensory input that happen to be active at the same time.

2.2   Modeling Sensory and Motor Spaces

The SOM is formed of a 2 dimensional lattice of M neurons (nodes), each of them associated with a weight vector (w_i) of dimension as each vector in the input space (X). These weights are initially set to random values, then, data training points are introduced in a random fashion to the SOM. When a vector of data x is introduced to the SOM, the node with least Euclidean distance between its weights and the input vector is chosen to be the best matching unit (winning neuron) based on:

$$i = \arg\min_{j} \|w_j - x\| \qquad (1)$$

where i the denotes the index of the BMU. The weights of all the neurons in the neighborhood around the BMU are updated to give a closer approximation of the input vector x. This node is computed with the following update rule:

$$w_j(t + 1) = w_j(t) + \alpha(t)h_{ji}(t)(x - w_j(t)) \qquad (2)$$

where h_{ji} is the neighboring function, which is computed with the following Gaussian function:

$$h_{ji}(t) = \exp\left(\frac{-\|r_j - r_i\|^2}{2\sigma^2(t)}\right) \qquad (3)$$

where r_i and r_j are the positions of the BMU and the neighboring jth node within the lattice, respectively. The learning rate α and neighborhood radius σ are set to decrease exponentially with time such that:

$$\sigma(t) = \sigma_{init}\exp\left(\frac{-t}{T}\right), \ \alpha(t) = \alpha_{init}\exp\left(\frac{-t}{T}\right) \qquad (4)$$

where t is the time of current iteration, T is the desired time constant of decrease, α_{init} and σ_{init} are the initial values of the learning rate and neighborhood radius, respectively. By tunning the adequate parameters for the learning process, the weights of the nodes are updated to give an adequate mapping for both sensory and motor states within the identified robot workspace.

2.3   Formation of Sensorimotor Mapping

To provide a correlation between activity of each node in motor space a_i to sensory space a_j back and forth as shown in Fig. 1, the Hebbian Oja learning rule [13] is applied by applying the equation:

$$c_{ij}(t+1) = c_{ij}(t) + \eta \left(a_i a_j - c_{ij}(t)a_j^2\right) \tag{5}$$

where c_{ij} represents the strength of the connection between the pre and post synaptic nodes, while η is the learning rate. Nodes from both maps that happen to be active at the same time tend to have high correlations and thus stronger synaptic connection between these nodes. The first term in the parenthesis ensures applying Hebbian learning rule to achieve the correlation. The second term guarantees the stability of the learning process where a forgetting term is included such that in case some nodes are not active for a long time the strength of the connection is attenuated.

The activity a_j of each node is calculated by applying the following Gaussian kernel for the Euclidean distance between the weights of the nodes and the input vector:

$$a_j(t) = \exp\left(\frac{-\|w_j(t) - x\|^2}{\sigma^2(t)}\right) \tag{6}$$

This expression gives rise of a one-to-one mapping between the nodes of the two SOMs (that respectively model the motor and sensory spaces). The resulting connections are reciprocal (i.e. bidirectional). This means that they can be used to either predict the sensory states based on a given motor action, or to compute the required motor actions to achieve a certain sensory state [14].

2.4   Varying Density Structure

The sensorimotor mappings can be achieved by combining SOM and Oja-Hebbian learning rules, as described above. However, the naive use these method results in regions (e.g. the periphery of the lattice) with large transformation errors. Two initial hypothesis were assumed to cause this problem. The first is that having a small number of training points at these regions may cause that problem. The second one is that having comparatively low number of neurons near the boundaries to represent the sensorimotor correlations may the culprit (e.g. having fewer neurons affect the accuracy of the estimated values). Such problem at the boundaries is one of the drawbacks of the SOM mentioned in the literature [15].

For the former hypothesis, training data with higher density at the lattice boundaries was used, however, it did not improve the mapping accuracy. A viable solution was to increase the density of the neurons near the problematic regions such as the boundaries of both the sensory and motor maps to give a better representation at these points. To achieve this behavior, the SOM update rule was modified by proposing a different neighborhood function that gives the required variable density of nodes. This is done by calculating the summation of the norm of the weights of the BMU to each node in the lattice then applying the Gaussian function. The *node density coefficient* ρ is computed as follows:

$$\rho = \exp\left(-\sum_{i \in O} \|w_{bmu} - w_i\|^2\right) \tag{7}$$

for O as the local neighborhood surrounding the neuron. This function aims to give a smooth gradient effect of contribution of proximal nodes.

The coefficient ρ can be used to quantitatively determine neurons with a small number of neighbors. More neurons can be attracted to these nodes to have a denser population and therefore give a better approximation of corresponding values in the sensorimotor map. The resulting map is characterized by having a variable density (even when using uniform training data) that controls the number of nodes in a region based on ρ; we call this network a varying density SOM (VDSOM). The additional term ρ shall have a minimal effect in the formation of the network at the beginning and increase as the learning process proceeds. On the other hand, if it increases at a slow rate the exponential decay term of the neighborhood radius would make the effect of that term minimal.

To achieve this effect, the new neighborhood is defined as follows:

$$h(t) = \left(\frac{t}{\rho T}\right)^4 \exp\left(\frac{-t}{\sigma^2(t)T}\right) \tag{8}$$

where the new term was chosen to be of the fourth order to have adequate values without disturbing the dynamics of the learning process.

By adding that term, the lattices formed for both the sensory and motor spaces are more dense at the boundaries. This helps to reduce the transformation errors that occurs in these regions without the need to increase the total number of neurons in the network. This density regulation concept may not (yet) have some proof from a neuro-biological perspective, however, varying densities of neurons is certainly present in many different areas of the brain and within each area. For example, in the primary visual cortex, the central region has a higher density of neurons relative to the peripheral regions. In most primates, the central vision area is the main region of interest when observing a scene [16]. Additionally, the proposed mechanism to automatically increase the number of neurons agrees with studies in which high neuronal density is observed for processing hand and face fine motions [17]. Although this study focuses on VDSOM, the same concept can be applied to vary the structure of a Growing Neural Gas(GNG) network [18] to obtain the optimal number of nodes to represent the same sensorimotor model.

2.5 Adaptation to Changes in the Sensorimotor Model

Note that in case of changes in body morphology (e.g. generated by attaching of an external limb or amputation) or changes in the perceptual system (e.g. by wearing vision inverting goggles [19]) the computed sensorimotor model is no longer representative. For this situation, both, sensory and motor maps should be updated accordingly, as well as the inter-connections representing the transformations between these spaces. However, in traditional SOM, once the learning process reaches the specified number of iterations, changes in input data—corresponding to sensory/motor information—will not modify the networks structure. This results in a model that no longer adapts, and therefore is not able to represent the new (and actual) sensory/motor configurations.

To overcome this drawback, a distortion metric ζ is incorporated into the method. If the ζ is found to exceed a give (arbitrary) threshold value after the mapping is established, the neighborhood radius σ is reset to an adequate value to be able to re-adapt the network's structure. Such distortion metric is computed as:

$$\zeta = \frac{1}{n} \sum_{i=1}^{n} \sum_{x \in X} \|x - w_i\|^2 \tag{9}$$

where n is the number of data vectors x available in the data set X. The new neighborhood radius σ_r is set to be initially equal to $\sigma(\tau)$, when the distortion metric after the perturbations occur is equal to that. Then, the value of $\sigma_r(t)$ can be calculated from the equation:

$$\sigma_r(t) = \sigma_{init} exp\left(\frac{-(t + \tau)}{T}\right) \tag{10}$$

If the value of distortion after perturbations is higher than that at the beginning of the learning process, then the radius is set to the maximum value which is the radius of the SOM. On the other hand, a modified version of Oja-Hebbian connections is used to adapt better to these changes.

$$c_{ij}(t + 1) = c_{ij}(t) + \eta(a_i a_j - \beta c_{ij}(t) a_j^2) \tag{11}$$

The additional term allows to control the *forgetting rate* of the already formed connections.

Thus the values of the additional term β and the learning rate η are set to allow for new connections to be formed in a faster manner. These terms

Table 1. Mean and maximum errors for forward and inverse mappings using SOM and VDSOM.

Error	X (mm)	Y (mm)	θ_1 (°)	θ_2 (°)
	Mean (Max)	Mean (Max)	Mean (Max)	Mean (Max)
SOM	2.6 (26.0)	2.9 (29.0)	0.37 (3.45)	0.61 (6.70)
VDSOM	1.15 (11.7)	1.26 (15.0)	0.31 (2.25)	0.44 (5.36)

Table 2. Mean and maximum errors for forward and inverse mappings using VDSOM with different number of nodes.

Error	X (mm)	Y (mm)	θ_1 (°)	θ_2 (°)
	Mean (Max)	Mean (Max)	Mean (Max)	Mean (Max)
VDSOM (30×30)	4.16 (36.3)	3.93 (21.1)	0.91 (4.60)	1.53 (7.62)
VDSOM (50×50)	2.13 (13.5)	2.11 (15.3)	0.52 (2.80)	0.80 (5.05)
VDSOM (70×70)	1.15 (11.7)	1.26 (15.0)	0.31 (2.25)	0.44 (5.36)

are assigned high values that decrease exponentially based on the following expressions:

$$\beta(t) = \beta_{init} \exp\left(\frac{T-t}{T}\right), \quad \eta(t) = \eta_{init} \exp\left(\frac{T-t}{T}\right) \tag{12}$$

3   Results

3.1   Setup

A simulation for the computational model of the sensorimotor mapping was built using Tensorflow library [20] on a PC with i7-6500 16 GB RAM. Both the system without and with the modifications were simulated for 2D lattice SOMs with square grid of 30×30, 50×50 and 70×70 nodes.

A kinematic model of two link robotic arm was used as the prototype system. The end-effector task space is assumed to be measured with an external positions sensor (e.g. a camera). In our sensorimotor model, the joint space is represented with motor SOM, whereas the task space is represented with a sensory SOM. Random joint angles within certain ranges were used to generate end-effector positions. L_1 and L_2 denote the lengths of first and second link, respectively, θ_1 and θ_2 the joint angles of first link relative to the horizontal axis and joint angle of second link relative to the first link. The forward kinematics relation can be simply computed as:

$$X = L_1 \cos(\theta_1) + L_2 \cos(\theta_1 + \theta_2)$$
$$Y = L_1 \sin(\theta_1) + L_2 \sin(\theta_1 + \theta_2) \tag{13}$$

The connections between both joint space and task space SOMs were developed, as described above, based on the Oja-Hebbian learning rule. As can be seen from Table 1 that both the mean and the maximum error values were drastically reduced after applying the proposed solution to the SOM for forward and inverse mappings. It can also be concluded from Table 2 that as the number of nodes increases the error decreases at the expense of increasing the computational time required to build the network and establish the connections.

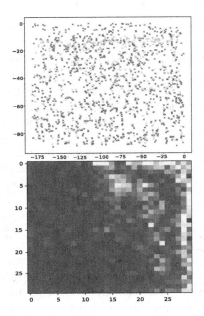

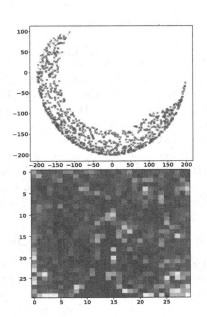

Fig. 2. Motor SOM with heatmap representing error at each node when it was chosen as a BMU. (Color figure online)

Fig. 3. Sensory SOM with heatmap representing error at each node when it was chosen as a BMU. (Color figure online)

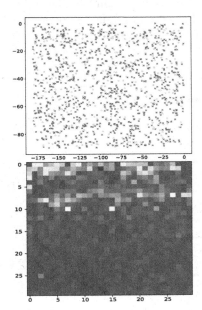

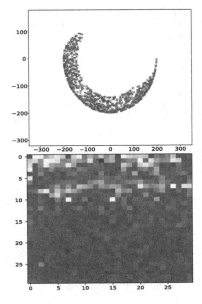

Fig. 4. Motor VDSOM with error heatmap.

Fig. 5. Sensory VDSOM with error heatmap.

3.2   Enhanced Accuracy

Figures 2 and 3 show the final SOMs developed after running several trials to obtain the most adequate parameters for each SOM. As shown in Fig. 3, the original SOM covers the whole workspace uniformly but less dense at the peripherals. It can be observed from the error plot in Figs. 2 and 3 that higher error values occur at these areas, where the dark blue color and the dark red color represent low error and high error, respectively. The effect of the added factor ρ can be noticed in Figs. 4 and 5 where higher density can be observed at the contour of the workspace, and less error in these areas in both forward and inverse mappings. Although the introduced method have an error that is relatively high compared to conventional control methods, it takes one step forward in the formation of biologically-inspired sensorimotor maps.

3.3   Adaptation to Changes in Morphology

The robot morphology was altered to simulate attaching and removing a tool from the end effector. To allow the system to detect such changes, the ζ is calculated based on Eq. (9) and compared with a threshold value. Consequently, when such changes are predicted to occur, the learning process is reset to update the mapping. In case of limb length extension, it can be concluded from Figs. 6 and 7 that the map adapts to re-accommodate for that change and decreases the distortions detected in the computed maps. The connections between the sensory and motor maps are updated to represent the new configuration. Similarly, in the case of limb length reduction, as shown in Figs. 8 and 9, the distortion is measured. The change in distortion value, triggers the adaptation mechanism that allows for the maps to be recomputed.

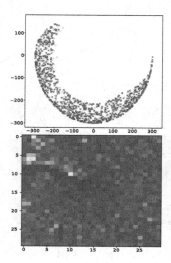

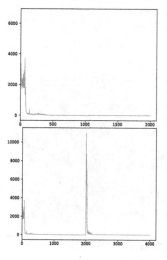

Fig. 6. Sensory VDSOM after stretching the links with error heatmap.

Fig. 7. Distortion in sensory map before and after stretching the links.

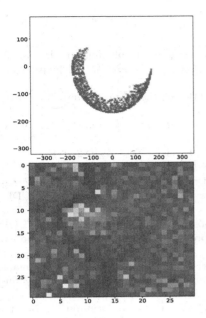

Fig. 8. Sensory VDSOM after shortening a link with error heatmap.

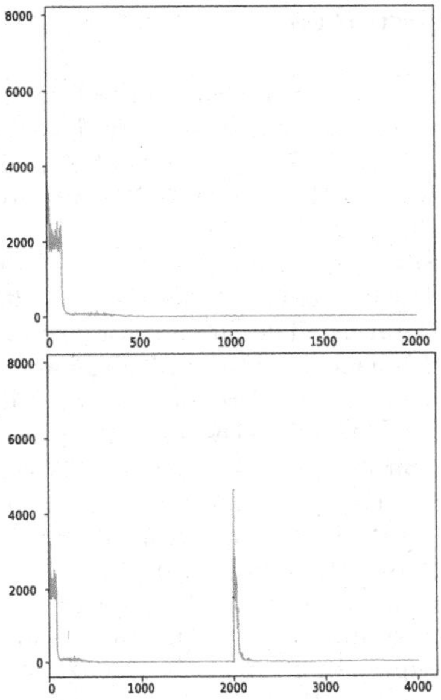

Fig. 9. Distortion in sensory map before and after shortening the link length.

4   Conclusions

A sensorimotor map was built to correlate sensory and motor spaces in a discretized form with bidirectional connections. This solution relies on collecting data samples by motor babbling, thus it is adequate to be used for various robotic manipulators without any prior information about robot kinematics. Using the SOM introduced by Kohonen with Oja-Hebbian learning rules the mapping was achieved with noticeable error values at the contour of the SOM -and thus the workspace-. A new neighborhood function was proposed to increase the density of nodes at the contour to give better approximation for the corresponding values. The proposed neighborhood increases the density of the nodes wherever the distance between the weights of the BMU and the neighboring nodes has small values. Finally, a perturbation was introduced to simulate a change in either sensory or motor map. A distortion metric was used to assess the state of the robot and reset the learning parameters to adequate values in case of changes in the morphology. Thus adaption process takes place to update the sensorimotor map, by allowing for changes in both the formed VDSOMs and connections.

Concerning the current limitations of this method, these maps can only be used for coarse control. A large number of nodes would be needed for fine discretization of the workspace which is computationally inefficient. Additionally, an extended study is needed to utilize the dimension reduction properties of SOM to be fit for robots with higher degrees of freedom.

References

1. Zoia, S., et al.: Evidence of early development of action planning in the human foetus: a kinematic study. Exp. Brain Res. **176**(2), 217–226 (2007). https://doi.org/10.1007/s00221-006-0607-3
2. Kaas, J.H.: Topographic maps are fundamental to sensory processing. Brain Res. Bull. **44**(2), 107–112 (1997)
3. Silver, M.A., Kastner, S.: Topographic maps in human frontal and parietal cortex. Trends Cogn. Sci. **13**(11), 488–495 (2009)
4. Hebb, D.: The Organization of Behavior, 1949. Wiely, New York (2002)
5. Schillaci, G., Hafner, V.V., Lara, B.: Online learning of visuo-motor coordination in a humanoid robot a biologically inspired model. In: 2014 Joint IEEE International Conferences on Development and Learning and Epigenetic Robotics (ICDL-Epirob), pp. 130–136. IEEE (2014)
6. Kumar, S., Premkumar, P., Dutta, A., Behera, L.: Visual motor control of a 7DOF redundant manipulator using redundancy preserving learning network. Robotica **28**(6), 795–810 (2010)
7. Buessler, J., Kara, R., Wira, P., Kihl, H., Urban, J.: Multiple self-organizing maps to facilitate the learning of visuo-motor correlations. In: IEEE International Conference on Systems Man and Cybernetics, vol. 3, pp. 470–475 (1999)
8. Rougier, N., Boniface, Y.: Dynamic self-organising map. Neurocomputing **74**(11), 1840–1847 (2011)
9. Piaget, J., Cook, M.T.: The origins of intelligence in children. International Universities Press, New York (1952)
10. Von Hofsten, C.: Eye-hand coordination in the newborn. Dev. Psychol. **18**(3), 450 (1982)
11. Penfield, W., Boldrey, E.: Somatic motor and sensory representation in the cerebral cortex of man as studied by electrical stimulation. Brain **60**(4), 389–443 (1937)
12. Kohonen, T.: Self-organizing Maps. Springer Series in Information Sciences, p. 502. Springer, Heidelberg (2001). https://doi.org/10.1007/978-3-642-56927-2
13. Oja, E.: Simplified neuron model as a principal component analyzer. J. Math. Biol. **15**(3), 267–273 (1982). https://doi.org/10.1007/BF00275687
14. Saegusa, R., Metta, G., Sandini, G., Sakka, S.: Active motor babbling for sensorimotor learning. In: International Conference on Robotics and Biomimetics, pp. 794–799, February 2009
15. Kohonen, T.: Essentials of the self-organizing map. Neural Netw. **37**, 52–65 (2013)
16. Collins, C.E., Airey, D.C., Young, N.A., Leitch, D.B., Kaas, J.H.: Neuron densities vary across and within cortical areas in primates. In: Proceedings of the National Academy of Sciences, vol. 107, no. 36, pp. 15927–15932 (2010)
17. Young, N.A., Collins, C.E., Kaas, J.H.: Cell and neuron densities in the primary motor cortex of primates. Front. Neural Circuit. **7**, 30 (2013)
18. Fritzke, B.: A growing neural gas network learns topologies. In: Advances in Neural Information Processing Systems, pp. 625–632 (1995)
19. Kohler, I.: Experiments with goggles. Sci. Am. **206**(5), 62–73 (1962)
20. Abadi, M., et al.: TensorFlow: large-scale machine learning on heterogeneous systems (2015). http://tensorflow.org/

Watchman Routes for Robot Inspection

Stefan Edelkamp[(✉)] and Zhuowei Yu

Department of Informatics, King's College London, London, UK
{stefan.edelkamp,zhuowei.yu}@kcl.ac.uk

Abstract. Inspection is a hot topic of robotics recently, and there are many different ways to solve the inspection problem. In this paper, we propose a new framework for a robust and efficient inspection of the entire workspace in a watchman route based on automatically generated waypoints. The framework architecture design includes several relevant technologies and refines algorithms such as medial axis transformation, shortest path approximation, and Monte-Carlo search for finding tours. This framework is evaluated in a client-server system: the simulation of the robot is run on Unity, while data processing is executed in a Python server. Experimenting with this approach, the measured inspection coverage of the workspace on random terrains was at least 99.6%.

1 Introduction

With the development of technology, robots are playing an increasingly important role in industries. Mobile robots are widely used in national defense, education, culture and many other application areas. An autonomous mobile robot generally refers to a system, which can sense the environment and its own state through sensors like cameras, and autonomously move towards the target via computed motions. Based on the tremendous effects mobile robots have in industry, solving the inspection problem is a crucial prerequisite for planning its tours. We propose a framework able to establish a collision-free and dynamically feasible trajectory in order to inspect the entire workspace, a process, which is denoted as finding a watchman route. It involves computing a short path entirely inside a polygon so that any point inside this polygon is visible from the points on the path [1]. As the robot is not idealized as being point-wise, however, full coverage cannot be achieved. Generally, the solution of the robot inspection problem is to use continuous sensors such as cameras to generate the trajectory. Different from this method, we generate waypoints from scanned input scenarios as bitmap images. After the generation of the waypoints, the system then computes the trajectory and cost of the path of the robot that inspects most of the entire workspace (see Fig. 1[1]). This paper provides an efficient and robust solution for solving the watchman route problem for robot inspection, starting from the given environment and ending in a simulation of the tour. The first challenge is to generate the waypoints, for which we used a skeleton that approximates the

---

[1] For a video see https://youtu.be/9ZnxsA5db7w.

© Springer Nature Switzerland AG 2019
K. Althoefer et al. (Eds.): TAROS 2019, LNAI 11650, pp. 179–190, 2019.
https://doi.org/10.1007/978-3-030-25332-5_16

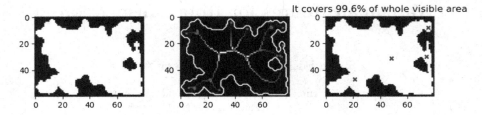

Fig. 1. The left part is the bitmap of the scenario. The middle one shows the waypoints (red points) generated from the skeleton of the bitmap. The right one is the minimized set of waypoints which covers 99.6% of the visible area. These waypoints (blue points) in the left figure is filtered from the waypoints (red points) in the middle one (figures best be viewed in colors on screen). (Color figure online)

medial axis for the robot to follow. Waypoints are filtered intersections and leaves of the skeleton. The details of the skeleton construction and waypoint filtering are illustrated. The next challenge is to define the visibility of each waypoint and calculate the distance of each waypoint pair. By using Alkhir's recursive shadow casting procedure [20], the visibility of each waypoint can be generated and act as a prerequisite of the calculation of the distance of the waypoints. Another challenge is to fetch the optimal sequence of waypoints based on the pairwise distance of waypoints. This process can be simplified as a traveling salesman problem. Last but not the least, the sequence of waypoints is used to generate the watchman tour. In the simulation, this tour has to be collision-free, which is validated using Unity.

Outline. We first describe relevant background theories of the framework, which includes the definition of the watchman tour, followed by the theory of skeletonization within morphology. Moreover, it provides the algorithms of waypoints filtering, and Monte Carlo search for solving the TSP. Next, we illustrates the specification design of the algorithms for waypoint and tour path generation. Moreover, this section also specifies the design of the client-server software architecture, consisting of a server side for the waypoints and tour generation and a client side for simulation. Then, we justify the methodology to implement the system. Besides, the detailed process of development, the problems encountered during the implementation and the relevant solutions will be described. Later on, we will not only present the results achieved with the implementation, but also discuss the impact of these results. Furthermore, we will analyze the advantages and disadvantages of this implementation. Finally, we summarize the achievements gained from the design and implementation of the whole framework. In addition, we elaborate on future research avenues.

2   Background Theories

Previous work mainly solves the watchman route for a simple polygon, which has limited application as such polygons cannot be arbitrarily (e.g., star-) shaped. Moreover, the algorithm stimulates the continuous movement between two endpoints by performing the movement of a point in the watchman route and sliding it via this reflection [8]. The algorithm, however, may not perform well when applied to more complicated scenarios such as polygons with holes. Moreover, the waypoints generated by the algorithm for the watchman route are usually on or in close proximity to the vertices of the polygon, which imposes difficulties to the smooth motion of the robot, given that its motion path has to be collision-free. Although there are algorithms to solve the complicated scenario [4], there is an easier method to compute the tour combined by the extracted waypoints in a bitmap, which have the same effect as this traditional watchman route algorithm in a polygon. We adhere to the formal setting of [3], and (additional to a different simulation environment) give alternative implementations that improve its robustness and efficiency. On the efficiency side, we avoid computing NP-hard hitting sets that are used in [3], and approximate shortest paths that are cumbersome to compute exactly, especially in highly detailed images; and, on the robustness side, we avoid deterioration of the medial axis in bitmaps that has been observed in [3].

Definition 1. *Given a desired inspection quality* $0 < \alpha \leq 1$, *an environment* W *consisting of regions* $\mathcal{R} = \{\mathcal{R}_1, \ldots, \mathcal{R}_n\}$ *with obstacles* $\mathcal{O} = \{\mathcal{O}_1, \ldots, \mathcal{O}_m\}$, *an unoccupied area* $\mathcal{U} = \mathcal{W} \setminus \mathcal{O}$, *a start point* $d \in \mathcal{U}$, *and a robot model with states* S, *compute a set of inspection points* $P = \{p_1, \ldots, p_l\} \subseteq \mathcal{W}$ *where* $\mathrm{Vis}(\mathcal{W}, d, p_1, \ldots p_l, d) \geq \alpha$, *a TSP tour* $[d, p_1, \ldots, p_l, d]$, *starting and ending at* d, *a collision-free and dynamically-feasible trajectory* $\phi\{1, \ldots, T\} \rightarrow S$ *which connects the inspection points in the order defined by* $[d, p_1 \ldots, p_l, d]$. *The objective is to reduce the number of inspection points and the travel distance by the robot.*

This definition does not attach colors to the waypoints to impose additional ordering constraints, leading to a clustered or generalized version of the underlying TSP [3]. We kick off with the concept of medial axis transformation.

Skeletonization via Medial-Axis-Transform. The process of skeletonization is to extract the skeletal remnant from the foreground region, which preserves the character of the original region [9]. Skeletonization has been proposed around the 1950s to compress the original letters to thinner ones while preserving all the key features. After applying this method successfully for character recognition, it was moved to many other fields. For instance, in computer graphics, skeletonization has be used to reconstruct the (e.g., ribbon-like) shapes, because the skeleton preserves the topological information of the object. In our case, skeletonization is applied to a binary image. There are slight differences between the skeleton and medial axis transform. As a result of skeletonization, we generate a binary image which shows the simple skeleton; while the medial axis transform generates a gray level image

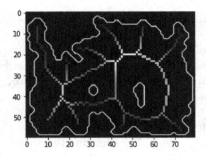

Fig. 2. Skeleton of scene computed with MAT and hit-and-miss transform.

which not only shows the skeleton but also the distances of the points of the skeleton to the nearest boundary (e.g as its intensity) [9]. Thinning refers to an operator which is applied to a binary image to maintain the original region connectivity which is similar to the operator erosion or opening in mathematical morphology [10]. The hit-and-miss transform is used in the thinning operator. It is one of basic morphological operation which can abstract the particular patterns of foreground and background pixels, and it usually needs a binary image and a structure element as its input; its output is also a binary image [11].

Through the hit-and-miss transform, we determine all pixels which have the same feature. More precisely, the hit-and-miss transform extracts the corner pixels, which have the same patterns as the structure elements.

A gray-level image, whose intensity represents the distance to the nearest boundary is also generated from the bitmap. As the binary image and gray-level image can be operated like a two-dimensional matrix, and the result can be calculated from the dot product of the binary image of the skeleton and the gray-level image which represents the closest distance. The result is also a gray-level image, where only the pixel on the skeleton show the closest distance to the boundary as its intensity; if a pixel is off the skeleton, the intensity of that pixel is zero. The next step for the waypoints generation and filtering is based on the result (gray-level image) of the skeleton generator.

Waypoint Generation and Filtering. If an agent follows the skeleton, it can inspect almost the entire workspace. However, if the scenario is complicated, the skeleton would have many branches, which would lead to the higher computational overhead, given that all pixels on the skeleton are considered. Therefore, it is necessary to filter the points on the skeleton which preserve the character of the skeleton, which means that if an agent follows these waypoints, its effect is similar to if were to follow the skeleton. Figure 2 shows a scenario's skeleton.

The intersections on the skeleton have the important feature that they cover a more extensive area than other points on the skeleton. Moreover, the end points on the skeleton also provide essential visibility information. Therefore, the first step is to identify the intersection points and the end points as candidate

Algorithm Waypoint Generator
Input: List to store the skeleton
Output: A waypoint list

for each point p in the skeleton
  $a \leftarrow$ mean dist. to neighbors of p
  if $a > thresh$ **and** $a < high$ **continue**
  add point p to waypoint list
return waypoint list

Algorithm Waypoint Filter
Input: A waypoint list
Output: The minimal waypoint list

CCVA $\leftarrow$ current combined visible area
if CCVA $> thresh$ **return** min-waypoints list
find point p with largest visible area
append p to the min. waypoint list
CCVA $\leftarrow$ CCVA $\cup$ visible area of p
remove p from the waypoint list
start new iteration

Fig. 3. Pseudo-code for waypoint generation (left) and filtering (right).

waypoint on the skeleton. Because the distance of adjacent points to the nearest boundary are close to the distances of their intersections, the latter can be identified from the illumination function, defined as the average illumination of neighbor points. Similarly, end points are found. The waypoint generator algorithm is shown in Fig. 3(left).

As the algorithm shows, for all points in the skeleton, they will calculate the average of their eight neighbors and compare them with the value from the function of high threshold and low threshold respectively. If the average of the eight neighbors is larger than the *high* threshold, it is probably a cross-point which is appended into the list. If the average of the eight neighbors is less than the *low* threshold, the point is likely an end-point, which also needs to be appended into the list. The next step is to compute a minimized set of waypoints, which jointly inspect the largest workspace.

Waypoint filtering is another important process to reduce the number of candidates of the recursive shadowcasting procedure. Briefly, the idea of the waypoint filtering is to find a minimized set of waypoints whose visible area can be combined to cover almost the entire workspace. The most straightforward algorithm to achieve this goal is to search the waypoints that have the largest visible area at each iteration and combine their visible area to reach the threshold. After that, the minimized waypoint list is created. The waypoints filtering algorithm is shown in Fig. 3(right). In recursive shadow casting a scan in each octant start from the closest point to the start point and the scan rule for the octants [13].

Nested Monte Carlo Search and Policy Adaption. Through the success of Alpha-Zero in reaching and exceeding state-of-the-art chess, shogi and go play, Monte-Carlo is a prominent randomized search and reinforcement learning methods, that trades exploration with exploitation.

Nested Monte-Carlo with policy adaptation (NRPA) is a single-player optimization Monte-Carlo search variant, which uses gradient ascent to improve the policy towards the best solution sequence [14]. The details of the algorithm, which combines the policy adaptation with rollouts are shown in Fig. 4. We see

Algorithm NRPA
Input: recursion l, policy pol
Output: best $score$ and TSP $tour$
if $l = 0$
    $n \leftarrow root()$, $j \leftarrow 0$, $tour \leftarrow []$
    while children of $n > 0$ **do**
        $tour[j] \leftarrow$ child i with prob. $e^{pol[n,i]}$
        $n \leftarrow tour[j]$; $j \leftarrow j + 1$
    return $(score(n), tour)$
$best \leftarrow \infty$
for N iterations **do**
    $(res, new) \leftarrow$ NRPA$(l - 1, pol)$
    if $res < best$
        $best \leftarrow result$; $tour \leftarrow new$
        $pol \leftarrow$ Adapt(pol, seq)
return $(best, tour)$

Algorithm Adapt
Input: policy pol, TSP $tour$
Output: updated policy pol'
$n \leftarrow root()$, $pol' \leftarrow pol$
for $j = 0, \ldots, length(tour) - 1$ **do**
    $pol'[n, tour[j]] = pol'[n, tour[j]] + 1$
    $z \leftarrow \sum_i e^{pol[n,i]}$
    for children i of n **do**
        $pol'[n, i] \leftarrow pol'[n, i] - e^{pol[n,i]}/z$
    $n \leftarrow tour[play]$
return pol'

Fig. 4. Nested rollout search with policy adaption for the TSP.

that the current recursion level and the number of iterations at a node determine the number of rollouts in level 0. In each level a policy is maintained and modified in case a better solution is backed up.

One of the most important issues is to quickly and efficiently find the shortest tour based on the distance matrix of the waypoints. This problem is a typical TSP for which NRPA provides an elegant and general solution, applicable to many TSP variants that may be of interest.

3   Framework Design

We designed a framework system, which simulates the robot to inspect the entire workspace. The system can be divided easily into two parts. One part is generating the random scenarios for inspection and displaying the simulation of the robot inspection, while the other part consists of completing the data processing, which includes skeleton generation, optimal closed path-finding, waypoint generation and filtering. Another reason to divide the system into two parts is that there are many libraries and tools for data processing in Python, while Unity is a more efficient and useful platform for robot simulation. Hence, one side in the framework uses the Python packages and libraries for fast algorithms and data structures, and the other side for running the Unity platform to generate scenarios and to display the simulation.

For the framework to be efficient, we imposed a client-server architecture. Data processing is executed on the server side, while the client-side generates scenarios and simulates the robot (Fig. 5).

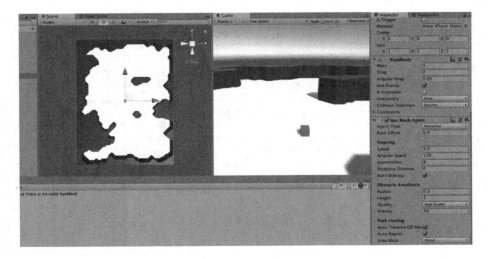

Fig. 5. Simulation of watchman tour following in Unity.

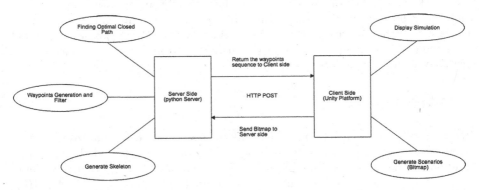

Fig. 6. Client-server architecture of robot motion planning framework to inspect the entire workspace. The system splits into two parts: one part is to generate the random scenarios for inspection and to display the simulation of the robot inspection while the other part is to complete the data processing, which includes skeleton generation, optimal closed path-finding and waypoint generation and filtering.

Through the client-server architecture, the tasks are assigned more clearly, and the resource consumption of the system is also reduced. Figure 6 illustrates the overall design of the framework and structure.

A distance matrix of the waypoints whose elements represent the distance between itself and other waypoints is a prerequisite of the TSP solver. For the distance matrix of the traveling salesman we avoid computationally expensive calculations of the shortest paths by using the skeleton.

Algorithm Distance-Matrix-Generation
Input: A minimal waypoint list
Output: A distance matrix

for each point p in the waypoint list
   for each point q (excluding p) in list
     if p and q see each other
       $DT(p,q) \leftarrow \|p - q\|$
     else
       $P \leftarrow$ Path-Search (p,q)
       $DT(p,q) \leftarrow$ sum of dist. on path P
return DT

Algorithm Path-Search
Input: Source p and destination q
Output: List of interm. points from p to q

search visible area of point p
if all intermediate point lists considered
   return list with min. distances
if point q in the visible area of point p
   calculate dist $\|p - q\|$ based on list
   if $dist < minidist$
     $dist \leftarrow minidist$
else
   select point p_{next} in visible area of p
   add Path-Search (p_{next}, q) to path

Fig. 7. Simplified path search using intermediate points.

Therefore, a new algorithm to generate the distance matrix is designed (see Fig. 7). The difficulty of the problem is that if two waypoints are invisible to each other, how to calculate the distance between the two "invisible" points. Our solution find the shortest path to the destination via the waypoints generated from the previous stage, and taking the distance of the ones on the path as the distance of the two invisible waypoints.

4 Experiments

In Fig. 1 we have already shown one random scenario used to analyze the effectiveness of the framework system. Besides this one, we generated three further randomly generated scenarios to evaluate the system. We employed a contemporary Laptop computer to validate our setup (CPU: Intel Core i7-4710HQ; CPU Clock Frequency: 2.5 GHz, 8 GB RAM). The scenario generator is based on the Unity tutorial *Procedural Cave Generation tutorial* [18,21]. There are two requirements for scenario generation. The first one is to ensure the randomness of the generated map to test in different scenarios. The other one is to maintain the connectivity of the map to ensure that there are no isolated blocks which the robot cannot reach to inspect.

It is cumbersome to extract the polygons from the (random) bitmap, so we used the skeletonization and medial axis transform presented above to compute the waypoints.

The mechanism of collision-free path-finding in Unity is applied in the specific scenarios in the last section and has been verified by monitoring the simulation. Through the verification, we obtain that the robot patrols the environment in an optimized collision-free path.

As Table 1 shows, the mean process time on the server side is 4.4 s which is acceptable for this system. For these three scenarios, in the average, the computational time on server side account for 5.79% of the CPU time which means the data processing on the server side is reliable and efficient (Figs. 8, 9, 10).

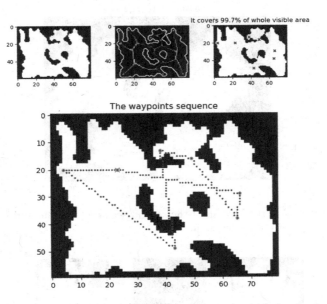

Fig. 8. The top left part is the bitmap of the scenario which is obtained from the client side. The top middle one shows the waypoints (red points) generated from the skeleton of the bitmap which is introduced before. The right one is the minimized set of waypoints which covers 99.7% of the visible area. The bottom image illustrates the established ordering of the waypoints in the tour. (Color figure online)

Table 1. Performance of the system.

Scen.	Coverage	Inspection time	Server time	Total
1	99.7%	73.436 s	5.308 s	7.23%
2	99.7%	71.165 s	4.217 s	5.93%
3	99.8%	85.159 s	3.781 s	4.44%
Average	99.73%	76.587 s	4.435 s	5.79%

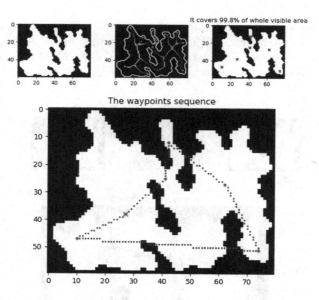

Fig. 9. The left part is the bitmap of the second scenario. The minimized set of way-points cover 99.8% of the visible area.

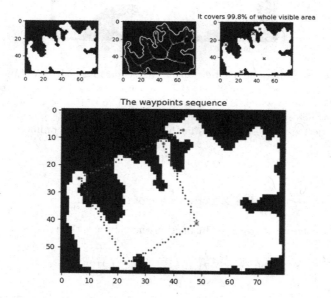

Fig. 10. The left part is the bitmap of the third scenario. The minimized set of way-points cover 99.7% of the visible area.

5   Conclusion and Discussion

This paper proposed a framework for a mobile robot to inspect the entire workspace in a collision-free closed path. Instead of traditional art gallery algorithms, which only apply to simplified scenes with polygons, we used skeletonization via medial-axis transformation to run the system on (randomly generated) bitmaps. We refined the shortest path computation, as well as the waypoint generator and filter based on the generated skeleton. Moreover, we used Unity on the client side to display simulation and to generate scenarios; as well as Python on the server side for fast data processing to combine the advantages on both sides. In addition, the framework implementation improved the performances of existing algorithms and comes with the scenario generator code.

In difference to [3] the approach relied on the more robust medial axis transform instead of the grassfire transform, it also bypasses extensive work for the all-pairs shortest path computation. Moreover, we compute the inspection tour once before the simulation In terms of dynamical adaptation to external events, the approach in [3] incrementally expands a motion tree, whose branches correspond to collision-free and dynamically-feasible motions. Each vertex is associated with a collision-free state and the region that contains the state To facilitate the motion-tree expansion, the motion tree is partitioned into equivalence classes based on the inspection points. The discrete solver guides the search by providing tour length as heuristics.

For the future we plan to automatically generate a virtual reality based on 360-degree camera scans. The general idea is generate a tour in virtual buildings, while feeling the same as being in the real one. We successfully experimented with a RGB-D camera mounted on a Turtlebot. So far is was operated with a remote controller on a manually taped path, but we plan to use a PID/fuzzy controller for path following based on sensor information that computes the location error. By simple modifications to the shadow-casting method, a limited visibility range of the camera can be supported. An extension of the approach to 3D is also available using voxels instead of pixels (supported by Unity).

References

1. Li, F., Klette, R.: An approximate algorithm for solving the watchman route problem. In: Sommer, G., Klette, R. (eds.) RobVis 2008. LNCS, vol. 4931, pp. 189–206. Springer, Heidelberg (2008). https://doi.org/10.1007/978-3-540-78157-8_15
2. ChvÃ¡tal, V.: A combinatorial theorem in plane geometry. J. Comb. Theory Ser. B **18**(1), 39–41 (1975)
3. Edelkamp, S., Secim, B.C., Plaku, E.: Surface inspection via hitting sets and multi-goal motion planning. In: Gao, Y., Fallah, S., Jin, Y., Lekakou, C. (eds.) TAROS 2017. LNCS (LNAI), vol. 10454, pp. 134–149. Springer, Cham (2017). https://doi.org/10.1007/978-3-319-64107-2_12
4. Edelkamp, S., Gath, M., Cazenave, T., Teytaud, F.: Algorithm and knowledge engineering for the TSPTW problem. In: 2013 IEEE Symposium on Computational Intelligence in Scheduling (CISched), Singapore, pp. 44–51 (2013)

5. Asano, T., Ghosh, S.K., Shermer, T.C.: Visibility in the plane. In: Sack, J.-R., Urrutia, J. (eds.) Handbook of Computational Geometry, pp. 829–876. Elsevier, Amsterdam (2000)
6. Simple polygon. Math Wiki (2018). http://math.wikia.com/wiki/Simple_polygon. Accessed 07 Jun 2018
7. Polygon. Math.ucdavis.edu (2018). https://www.math.ucdavis.edu/~latte/background/countingLecture/poly/poly/index.php. Accessed 10 June 2018
8. Carlsson, S., Jonsson, H., Nilsson, B.: Finding the shortest watchman route in a simple polygon. Discrete Comput. Geom. **22**(3), 377–402 (1999). https://doi.org/10.1007/PL00009467
9. Morphology - Skeletonization/Medial Axis Transform (2018). Homepages.inf.ed.ac.uk. https://homepages.inf.ed.ac.uk/rbf/HIPR2/skeleton.htm. Accessed 19 Jun 2018
10. Morphology - Thinning (2018). Homepages.inf.ed.ac.uk. https://homepages.inf.ed.ac.uk/rbf/HIPR2/thin.htm. Accessed 20 Jun 2018
11. Morphology - Hit-and-Miss Transform (2018). Homepages.inf.ed.ac.uk. https://homepages.inf.ed.ac.uk/rbf/HIPR2/hitmiss.htm. Accessed 22 Jun 2018
12. Morphology - Distance Transform (2018). Homepages.inf.ed.ac.uk. https://homepages.inf.ed.ac.uk/rbf/HIPR2/distance.htm. Accessed 26 Jun 2018
13. FOV using recursive shadowcasting - RogueBasin (2018). Roguebasin.com. http://www.roguebasin.com/index.php?title=FOV_using_recursive_shadowcasting. Accessed 26 Jun 2018
14. Rosin, C.D.: Nested rollout policy adaptation for Monte Carlo tree search. In: International Joint Conference on Artificial Intelligence, Barcelona, Spain, pp. 649–654 (2011)
15. Cazenave, T.: Nested Monte-Carlo search. In: International Joint Conference on Artificial Intelligence, Barcelona, Spain, pp. 456–461 (2009)
16. Flask. Pallets (2018). https://www.palletsprojects.com/p/flask. Accessed 03 Jul 2018
17. Nms.kcl.ac.uk (2018). https://nms.kcl.ac.uk/stefan.edelkamp/lectures/pi1/programs/TSPTW.java. Accessed 20 Jul 2018
18. Cellular Automata - Unity. Unity (2018). https://unity3d.com/cn/learn/tutorials/projects/procedural-cave-generation-tutorial/cellularautomata?playlist=17153. Accessed 20 Jun 2018
19. Scrum Alliance - Learn About Scrum. Scrumalliance.org (2018). https://www.scrumalliance.org/why-scrum. Accessed 20 Apr 2018
20. Akhier/Py-RecursiveShadowCasting. GitHub (2018). https://github.com/Akhier/Py-RecursiveShadowCasting. Accessed 17 Jul 2018
21. SebLague/Procedural-Cave-Generation. GitHub (2018). https://github.com/SebLague/Procedural-Cave-Generation. Accessed 18 Jul 2018

Semantic Path Planning for Indoor Navigation and Household Tasks

Nico Sun[1], Erfu Yang[1(✉)], Jonathan Corney[1], and Yi Chen[2(✉)]

[1] Department of Design, Manufacture and Engineering Management,
University of Strathclyde, Glasgow, UK
{nico.sun,erfu.yang,jonathan.corney}@strath.ac.uk
[2] Industry 4.0 Artificial Intelligence Laboratory, School of Computer Science and
Network Security, Dongguan University of Technology, Dongguan 523808, China
leo.chen@ieee.org

Abstract. Assisting people with daily living tasks in their own homes
with a robot requires a navigation through a cluttered and varying environment. Sometimes the only possible path would be blocked by an
obstacle which needs to be moved away but not into other obstructing
regions like the space required for opening a door. This paper presents
semantic assisted path planning in which a gridded semantic map is used
to improve navigation among movable obstacles (NAMO) and partially
plan simple household tasks like cleaning a carpet or moving objects
to another location. Semantic planning allows the execution of tasks
expressed in human-like form instead of mathematical concepts like coordinates. In our numerical experiments, spatial planning was completed
well within a typical human-human dialogue response time, allowing for
an immediate response by the robot.

Keywords: Semantic path planning · Robotics · Semantic map ·
Navigation among movable obstacles

1 Introduction

Today's autonomous mobile robots navigate on a binary map, often scan
their surrounding environment using Simultaneous Localization and Mapping
(SLAM) techniques [1], dividing the work-space into free space and fixed obstacles. Some algorithms explored Navigation Among Movable Obstacles (NAMO)
[9], creating a ternary map (fixed obstacles, movable obstacles and free space).
But robots operating in a human environment need to have a more comprehensive understanding of their complex environment for autonomous navigation due
to random temporary obstacles being placed in their way (e.g. chairs, bags) and
it is frequently not possible to re-plan a new path (e.g. apartments with only
one corridor).

Humans can easily identify what obstacles are movable and require the least
effort to clear a path. However, obstacles are not always moved to a position

© Springer Nature Switzerland AG 2019
K. Althoefer et al. (Eds.): TAROS 2019, LNAI 11650, pp. 191–201, 2019.
https://doi.org/10.1007/978-3-030-25332-5_17

which would require the least amount of effort, because this position would block another path which would need clearing at another time e.g. a doorway or a hazardous location (like right behind a corner). While a corridor traditionally is empty space in navigation it isn't suitable to place an obstacle there because other people need to move through it. Perhaps the most dramatic example is a fire escape. This space needs to be kept free.

The main focus in robotic navigation has been getting from point A to point B. Rather than moving to a specific (x, y) coordinate humans move close to an object which has a dimension and a region around them as a valid goal location. Navigational planners could emulate this behaviour by checking the dimensions of a region on a semantically annotated map.

This paper is an invited extension of an extended abstract presented at the UK-RAS 2019 [7]. The remainder of this paper is structured as follows: Sect. 2 gives an overview of the related work in navigation and semantic mapping. Section 3 describes our semantic detection method for navigational planning. Section 4 presents our experimental results. Section 5 discussion is made. Finally we conclude our findings in Sect. 6.

2   Semantic Path Planning

Semantics have been used in robotics to create a knowledge base to relate objects to other objects or to regions e.g. 'milk located in the fridge' and 'fridge located in the kitchen' [8,12]. Objects can have a function as well e.g. 'fridge keeps milk fresh'. Using Semantics for path planning is still largely unexplored because only recently have SLAM algorithms with the help of neural networks been able to create a dense pixel by pixel encoded semantic map [5,11]. These semantic slam algorithms still don't output the required quality for semantic path planning, but with a visualisation tool, a human user could correct misclassifications where needed.

With semantic path planning it's possible to detect during planning which region the algorithm is currently in. This means the state space isn't only divided into free space and obstacle space, it can have any identity such as 'on the carpet'. Combined with logical expressions such as 'if identity is' or 'if identity is not' a planner is able to avoid certain regions, never leave a specific region or stop planning when it reaches a region. One usage example of this function is the manipulation of obstacles known as Navigation Among Movable Objects (NAMO). Unlike a road network, a home often has only one path to a goal eliminating the possibility of re-planning. If the path is obstructed by an obstacle a robot has to move it in order to clear the path. Existing NAMO algorithms can deal with numerous obstacles [9], but don't consider any function of space like the one required to open a door. This space can't be encoded as an obstacle because the robot has to move through it and it can't be encoded as free space because if an obstacle is placed into it it's impossible to open the door. Semantics can treat this space as free for the robot and free to move through with an obstacle, but not valid as a position to leave an obstacle.

Another usage of semantics path planning is for "Task and motion planning" (TMP). For household tasks moving objects from one region to another benefit from semantic segmentation of the search space. Small objects require a centimetre or even millimetre precision for grasping and when moving them to another room several meters away it's very inefficient to perform a multi-dimensional motion planning for the entire path at the grasping precision. Navigating between two different rooms only requires two dimensions with at most centimetre precision. The high dimensional and precise manipulator's motion planning to place an object only needs to be performed when the robot arm is within the reach of the objects start or goal position. There has been previous work bringing objects to another location but didn't implement a division of the path into sub-paths with different resolutions and dimensions [2].

3   Proposed Method

In order to encode different functions in a home environment, we utilize three layers for a 2D floor map, visualized as an RGB image with some predefined pixel by pixel encoded semantics. One layer for objects and obstacles, one for dynamic entities (humans, pets) and one for the room property or function. For intelligent navigation, all semantic values are combined with a dictionary which contains the semantic map value, a keyword which is close human understanding and a property. Objects have the movable or unmovable property and regions have keepfree or usable for placing obstacles. The general format is shown in (1) and (2).

$$'object' = [semantic map value, unmovable/movable] \tag{1}$$

$$'region' = [semantic map value, keepfree/usable] \tag{2}$$

For the robot pathfinding (start to goal) we use a bi-directional rapidly-exploring random tree (Bi-RRT) algorithm with a 5% goal bias. Bi-RRT is a variant of the simple RRT [4]. Due to the nature of a home robot environment – the interaction with humans. A solution should be found close to the typical response time of a human-human dialogue [10]. This requirement gave preference for simple RRT over RRT*. RRT* generates shorter paths but at a significant running time increase [3]. Previous robots have been found to be too slow and unresponsive [6]. After a solution is found we employ local path smoothing to reduce the path cost and for a more natural motion. The semantic detection of objects for the planner is done with OpenCV by finding the specified semantic value on the map and extracting its dimensions (contours). Thus all objects positions and dimensions are part of the map and not stored in a separate system. During path planning in the RRT algorithms, the semantic detection checks the map with the bounding box of the robot or movable obstacle and disregards a point when the bounding box is in contact with another obstacle. When the robot path is blocked by an obstacle the semantic NAMO RRT, a simple modification to the RRT algorithm searches for a new collision free position that doesn't obstruct the robot's path or collide with other obstacles. The improvement of NAMO quality is done by excluding regions encoded on the semantic map as valid goal positions. This semantic check is only done after a new node is added to the RRT and not every time a node is checked against permanent obstacles. In our tests, for example, we excluded doorways as valid goal positions.

In the first household task the scenario is: "clearing a region of objects". The semantic detection only allows the RRT algorithm to end if a node would place the object completely outside the specified region.

The second household task scenario: "moving objects to another region". The planner first checks if all objects fit into the goal region before attempting to find a path towards the region. After a new position for all specified objects was found in the goal region, a bi-directional RRT is calculated between the centre of the start region and centre of the goal region. During the path smoothing the planner returns the location adjacent to each region as the start and end position instead of the region centre.

4   Numerical Evaluation

We performed the evaluation in Python 3.6 and single threaded on an AMD 2700X. RAM usage was just 10 MB for the 1000 × 800 three-layer test map. During path planning, an additional 10 MB was used for the computation of the robot path and new obstacle positions. The map resolution was 1 cm/pixel, hence representing an apartment of 10 m × 8 m. The spatial semantic knowledge data was stored in NumPy arrays and visualized with matplotlib as an RGB image. After an object is moved the map gets automatically updated (old position encoded as free space in object layer and new location encoded with the value of the object) For a better illustration of the skills we use the unused green layer (dynamic entities) to enhance the contrast between the objects original and new position and dimensions. As expected, checking a point against a list of semantic values takes longer than checking against a single value representing all obstacles. In our tests with 1000 known semantic values, the calculation time increased by a factor of 15–30: from 0.213 s for 1M single value to 3.1–6.7 s for the same number of multiple value checks. So any path planning algorithm should still perform single value collision detection against unmovable obstacles to reduce the number of slower semantic checks.

The path cost is defined by:

$$C_r = d \tag{3}$$
$$C_o = (1 + A_o/A_r) * d \tag{4}$$

where, $C_r = $ Cost of moving robot, $d = $ distance,
$C_o = $ Cost of moving obstacle, $A = $ Area

Algorithm 1. Use of semantics during pathplanning
_____

1: **Map definitions**
2: Op = permanent obstacles
3: Om = movable obstacles
4: Rf = keepfree regions
5: Ru = usable regions
6: map = SemanticMap(Op,Om,Rf,Ru)
7:
8: **Task: Move to region**
9: goal(x,y) = SemanticMap(regionvalue)
10: find path
11: **if** smoothed path node in SemanticMap(regionvalue) **then**
12:     path end
13: **if** smoothed path node in SemanticMap(Om) **then**
14:     do Task move obstacles
15:
16: **Task: move obstacles**
17: **if** path node in SemanticMap(Op) **then**
18:     discard node
19: **if** path node in robotpath or in SemanticMap(Rf) **then**
20:     continue search
21: **else**
22:     end search
23:
24: **Task: Clear a Region of Objects**
25: **if** path node in SemanticMap(Op) **then**
26:     discard node
27: **if** node in SemanticMap(regionvalue) **then**
28:     continue search
29: **else**
30:     end search
31:
32: **Task: Moving objects to another region**
33: startnode(x,y) = SemanticMap(regionvalue)
34: **if** path node in SemanticMap(regionvalue) **then**
35:     continue search
36: **else**
37:     discard node
38: **if** path node in SemanticMap(Om) **then**
39:     continue search
40: **else**
41:     end search
42: do Task Move to Region
_____

The obstacle movement cost includes the cost of moving the robot and the relative size of the object compared to the robot. Small objects will have a negligible cost and large objects will have a high cost of moving. The performance metrics: running time and path cost have been calculated over 1000 sample runs for each test. Due to the random nature of the RRT algorithm the standard deviation of our results are quite high.

In the following subsections we show some common navigational tasks for a household.

4.1   Clear a Region of Objects

In order to vacuum a carpet, it first needs to be cleared of all obstacles. Otherwise, part of it remains dirty and develops discoloured edges around obstacles. The algorithm can exclude other regions as valid obstacle positions like the task in Fig. 3 (Fig. 1, Table 1).

Table 1. Performance analysis for the task "Clear a region of objects (o)". t = time in ms, C = path cost

Metric	t_o	C_o
Average	61	263
Standard deviation	34	13

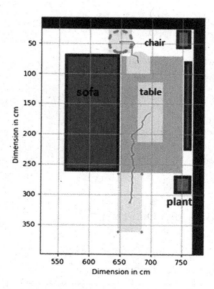

Fig. 1. Robot skill: "clearing a region": Clearing a carpet (beige) of all movable obstacles, light blue: former obstacle positions, purple dots: new obstacle positions (Color figure online)

4.2 Moving Objects to Another Region

When moving many small objects compared to the robot's size, the objects don't need additional collision detection. With the previously shown path cost calculation it's possible to calculate when it's more efficient to move the objects individually or to get a known container from a nearby place and move multiple objects at the same time. The semantically encoded map already includes the location and dimension of the goal region, therefore eliminating the need to compute a path for each individual object between its origin and goal position. Instead, the algorithm only needs to compute one path for the robot between the two regions and a short path fsor each object from the goal region to the objects final position (Table 2).

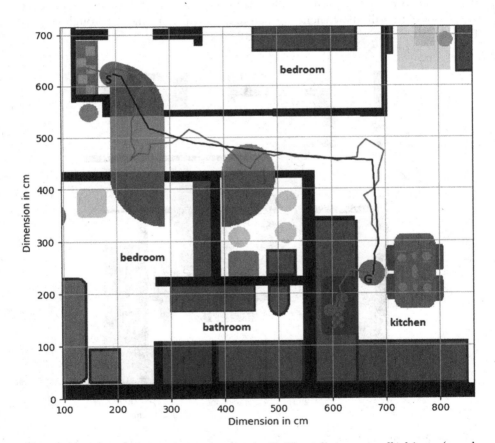

Fig. 2. Robot skill: "move objects to a region". The robot moves all objects (purple dots) from the shelf (brown) in the bedroom to the sink (green) in the kitchen. The black line shows the smoothed robot path. (Color figure online)

Table 2. Performance analysis for moving 5 objects from the shelf to the sink. t = time in ms

Metric	t_r	t_o
Average	112	8
Standard deviation	85	1

4.3 Move to a Region or an Object

As shown in Fig. 2 the robot is able to plan a path to another object encoded into the semantic map instead of fixed coordinates. When moving obstacles out of the way to clear the path the algorithm also considers the regions adjacent to the doors to still allow them to open and the robot to move through (Fig. 3, Table 3).

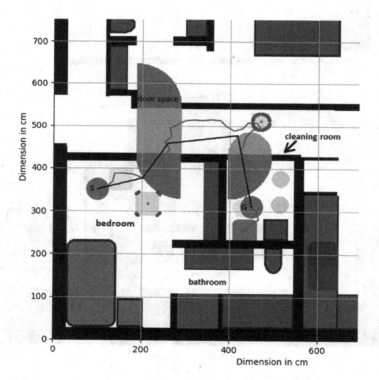

Fig. 3. Robot skill: "Move to region/object" The robot (grey) moves from the bedroom to the washing machine (orange) in the cleaning room. The red line shows the raw robot path and the black line shows the smoothed path. In light blue are the original obstacle positions and the purple dots outline the new positions for any moved obstacle. (Color figure online)

Table 3. Performance analysis for the task "move to region". For our two-obstacle example the planning time for the obstacles (o) is the same as for the robot (r) path finding. t = time in ms, C = path cost

Metric	t_r	t_o	C_r	C_o
Average	82	90	580	364
Standard deviation	84	28	14	115

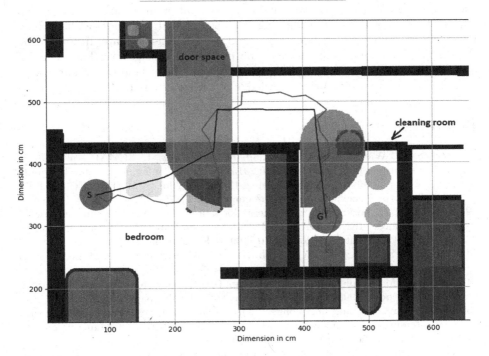

Fig. 4. Obstacle placement from task in Fig. 3 without considering semantics.

5   Discussion

Our test showed that consideration of semantics during path planning can enhance the navigation capability of robots. The pre-defined semantic map assumed a perfect semantic classification which isn't possible yet with existing semantic mapping methods. However, a simple user interface displaying the semantic map would allow a person to improve it by reducing noise and marking clear borders. A real household robot would greatly benefit from a 3D semantic map, especially when able to place small objects on top of others instead of only next to each other in two dimensions. The performance of our current un-optimized 2D representation was still well within human reaction time and an optimized version has the potential to work in 3D within reasonable human reaction time as well to ensure a desired quick response by a robot.

6   Conclusion

We have presented a semantic detection method during path planning for a gridded semantic map and how it can be used in a cluttered home with movable obstacles to avoid regions which should be kept free. With execution times of a tenth of a second in an apartment, the semantics consideration can improve the navigation quality without adding significant computation time. By combining the planning for object placement and robot navigation into one system it solved partly the task and motion planning problem needed for practical household tasks, which are not yet well developed and needed in health care. In the future, these spatial planning tasks have to be combined with general knowledge of object functions and their usage/grasping to create household tasks that can be executed without specific prior knowledge of the exact environment.

References

1. Deeken, H., Wiemann, T., Lingemann, K., Hertzberg, J.: SEMAP - a semantic environment mapping framework. In: 2015 European Conference on Mobile Robots (ECMR), pp. 1–6. IEEE, September 2015. https://doi.org/10.1109/ECMR.2015.7324176. http://ieeexplore.ieee.org/document/7324176/
2. Kaelbling, L.P., Lozano-Pérez, T.: Hierarchical task and motion planning in the now. In: Proceedings - IEEE International Conference on Robotics and Automation, pp. 1470–1477 (2011). https://doi.org/10.1109/ICRA.2011.5980391
3. Karaman, S., Frazzoli, E.: Sampling-Based Algorithms for Optimal Motion Planning, May 2011. http://arxiv.org/abs/1105.1186
4. LaValle, S.M.: Rapidly-exploring random trees: a new tool for path planning. Technical report (1998). http://msl.cs.uiuc.edu/~lavalle/papers/Lav98c.pdf
5. Li, R., Gu, D., Liu, Q., Long, Z., Hu, H.: Semantic scene mapping with spatio-temporal deep neural network for robotic applications. Cognitive Comput. **10**(2), 260–271 (2018). https://doi.org/10.1007/s12559-017-9526-9
6. Martinez-Martin, E., del Pobil, A.P.: Personal robot assistants for elderly care: an overview. In: Costa, A., Julian, V., Novais, P. (eds.) Personal Assistants: Emerging Computational Technologies. ISRL, vol. 132, pp. 77–91. Springer, Cham (2018). https://doi.org/10.1007/978-3-319-62530-0_5
7. Sun, N., Yang, E., Corney, J., Y.C., Ma, Z.: Semantic enhanced navigation among movable obstacles in the home environment. In: Embedded Intelligence: Enabling & Supporting RAS Technologies, pp. 68–71 (2019). https://www.ukras.org/wp-content/uploads/2019/03/UKRAS19-Proceedings-Final.pdf
8. Petr Masek, M.R.: A task planner for autonomous mobile robot based on semantic network in advances. Adv. Intell. Syst. Comput. **393**, 634–639 (2016)
9. Stilman, M., Kuffner, J.J.: Navigation among movable obstacles: real-time reasoning in complex environments. Technical report. https://smartech.gatech.edu/bitstream/handle/1853/36417/stilman-ijhr2005.pdf
10. Strömbergsson, S., Hjalmarsson, A., Edlund, J., House, D.: Timing responses to questions in dialogue. In: Proceedings of the Annual Conference of the International Speech Communication Association, INTERSPEECH, pp. 2584–2588 (2013)

11. Sun, H., Meng, Z., Ang, M.H.: Semantic mapping and semantics-boosted navigation with path creation on a mobile robot. In: 2017 IEEE International Conference on Cybernetics and Intelligent Systems (CIS) and IEEE Conference on Robotics, Automation and Mechatronics (RAM), pp. 207–212. IEEE, November 2017. https://doi.org/10.1109/ICCIS.2017.8274775. http://ieeexplore. ieee.org/document/8274775/

12. Tenorth, M., Kunze, L., Jain, D., Beetz, M.: KNOWROB-MAP - knowledge-linked semantic object maps. In: 2010 10th IEEE-RAS International Conference on Humanoid Robots, pp. 430–435. IEEE, December 2010. https://doi.org/10.1109/ ICHR.2010.5686350. http://ieeexplore.ieee.org/document/5686350/

A Vision-Based Assistance Key Differenciator for Helicopters Automonous Scalable Missions

Rémi Girard[1,2]([✉]), Sébastien Mavromatis[1], Jean Sequeira[1], Nicolas Belanger[2], and Guillaume Anoufa[3]

[1] Aix Marseille University, CNRS, LIS, Marseille, France
remi.girard@lis-lab.fr
[2] Airbus, Marignane, France
[3] Capgemini, Paris, France

Abstract. In the coming years, incremental automation will be the main challenge in the development of highly versatile helicopter technologies. To support this effort, vision-based systems are becoming a mandatory technological foundation for helicopter avionics. Among the different advantages that computer vision can provide for flight assistance, navigation in a GPS-denied environment is an important focus for Airbus because it is relevant for various types of missions. The present position paper introduces the different available SLAM algorithms, along with their limitations and advantages, for addressing vision-based navigation problems for helicopters. The reasons why Visual SLAM is of interest for our application are detailed. For an embedded application for helicopters, it is necessary to robustify the VSLAM algorithm with a special focus on the data model to be exchanged with the autopilot. Finally, we discuss future decisional architecture principles from the perspective of making vision-based navigation the 4th contributing agent in a wider distributed intelligence system composed of the autopilot, the flight management system and the crew.

Keywords: Visual SLAM · Vision-based navigation · Helicopters · Autonomous · Pose estimation · 3D reconstruction

1 Introduction

Autonomous navigation has become one of Airbus Helicopters' top priorities. Helicopter missions are extremely varied in nature, including freight transport, medical evacuation, search and rescue, logistics support, police operations, and aerial work.

Autonomous helicopter control will enhance the performance and security of these missions. Helicopter operations can take place in urban areas, in mountains, in hostile areas, at low altitude, at night, etc. Most of the time, only helicopters are able to operate in these types of conditions. These missions are often dangerous, and all of the following factors, among others, can contribute to the occurrence of adverse events:

© Springer Nature Switzerland AG 2019
K. Althoefer et al. (Eds.): TAROS 2019, LNAI 11650, pp. 202–210, 2019.
https://doi.org/10.1007/978-3-030-25332-5_18

- Loss of visibility during Visual Flight Rules (VFR) navigation
- Loss of GPS during Instrument Flight Rules (IFR) navigation
- Loss of the autopilot
- Loss of engine

Accidents can be caused by difficult flight conditions, the malfunctioning of a flight instrument or undetected drift. If not detected by the crew, such an occurrence may mislead them into improperly guiding the helicopter. Controlled Flight Into Terrain (CFIT) is a common type of accident most often caused by the failure of the pilot to know at all times what the position of his or her craft is and how that actual position relates to the altitude of the surface of the Earth below and immediately ahead along the flight course. Hence, missions could be made more secure thanks to our vision-based piloting system.

2   Vision-Based Piloting Assistance

Our work focuses on the design of a system aiming to improve the safety of operations without directly acting on the control of the helicopter. Our system should have the following capabilities:

- To compute the helicopter's pose in real time considering the environment in which the helicopter is moving. An estimated trajectory should be computed from consecutive poses and compared to the pre-established path.
- To be independent from the helicopter flight instruments. Indeed, a standalone system would add redundancy, resulting in more secure flight.

The computation of the helicopter's pose in real time would enable the detection of an error in the trajectory without the aid of the flight instruments in cases of GPS loss or undetected drift. Being able to detect such errors and make them deterministic could aid in the detection of unplanned trajectories, thus drastically reducing the number of crashes. Our decision-making system should warn the autopilot in cases of trajectory errors. Such an autonomous device embedded in a helicopter could directly influence the mission strategy. The intent is for our device to become a real mission assistance system.

Decisions can be of several types depending on the magnitude of the error and the type of undesirable event: go back, compute a new path, perform an emergency landing, continue the mission, return to base, stop, stay hovering, etc.

The device must operate autonomously and constantly exchange information with the helicopter's autopilot, as our system is not intended as a navigation device but as autopilot assistance. The exchange with the autopilot will need to be reliable. Simultaneous Localization And Mapping (SLAM) is a method for the simultaneous estimation of the state of a system and reconstruction of an environment map. Localization refers to the computation of the system's pose in the reconstructed environment, from which its position in the real environment can be deduced. Mapping refers to the representation of the environment and the interpretation of the data provided by sensors. Our system must be able to simultaneously process these two interdependent phases. The different available state-of-the-art SLAM methods will be detailed below.

In addition to its primary purpose, the system could also be used for environmental reconstruction. Such 3D reconstruction is interesting for the following purposes:

- Identifying terrain characteristics (e.g., slope or ground flatness).
- Identifying eligible landing zones as the mission progresses. These landing zones would be recorded in a database accessible by the autopilot.

Computer vision algorithms make it possible to analyze, process and understand an environment from images acquired by a camera system. The use of a camera is particularly interesting for cases of landing zone identification. However, a disadvantage of using a camera is the lack of a scale factor. This can be corrected by associating the camera with other sensors. Our decision-making system must be able to perceive the environment in which the helicopter is moving up to 1500 meters away. Furthermore, it will be embedded in helicopters; thus, it must be as small as possible. Therefore, our decision-making system will use a camera as its main sensor. The implementation of SLAM with cameras is known as Visual SLAM.

The following section presents an overview of the state of the art with regard to SLAM for vision-based piloting assistance. The end of this paper is devoted to our recommendations for system development.

3   SLAM for Autopilot Support

In this section, we discuss the literature on SLAM and Visual SLAM.

3.1   History

SLAM first emerged in the 1980s. Smith, Cheeseman [20] and Durrant-Whyte [6] defined a relation between the position of a sensor and the structure of the environment. Durrant-Whyte was the representative individual addressing the SLAM problem during the first 20 years. Throughout this period, the issue was seen as a probabilistic and statistical problem. The first approaches to SLAM were based on filters: the extended Kalman filter (EKF), Rao-Blackwell's particle filters, and maximum likelihood estimation. The filter-based approaches were summarized by Durrant-Whyte and Bailey in [5] and [1].

In 1990, Smith *et al.* [19] proposed an EKF-based method and presented the concept of a stochastic map. They used the EKF to compute a state vector comprising the positions of the points of interest within an estimated map. The uncertainty of the estimates was represented by a probability density. These methods have several constraints: the state vector increases linearly with the size of the map, and the computational complexity is usually quadratic. These limitations have led to the development of more advanced SLAM methods, such as the work of Montemerlo *et al.* [14], who proposed the FastSLAM algorithm. FastSLAM is also based on a filtering approach. Maps are generated with the EKF, while the robot's position is represented by distributions of set of particles, where each particle represents a trajectory. This method reduces the complexity of the algorithm, but the position estimates are not accurate, especially for long trajectories.

A graph-based approach has also been used to solve the SLAM problem. In this approach, the landmarks on the map and the poses of the robot are represented by nodes in a graph. Graph-based methods have the advantage of being applicable to much larger maps than EKF approaches. During the initial period of SLAM development (1986–2004), termed the classical age by [3], the sensors used mainly consisted of radars, lidars and sonars.

A new period of development for SLAM algorithms emerged when researchers became interested in information contained in images from cameras. The corresponding approach is known as Visual SLAM (monocular when only one camera is used and stereo when two cameras are used).

3.2   Visual SLAM

The main steps of a feature-based VSLAM algorithm are as follows:

1. extracting a set of salient image features from each keyframe,
2. defining each feature by means of a descriptor,
3. matching the features using the feature descriptors,
4. using epipolar geometry to compute both the camera motion and structure, and
5. using optimization methods, e.g., BA or loop closure, to refine the pose.

An interesting comparison of recents open-sources VSLAM and VO algorithms can be found in Table 1 at the end of this section.

Five types of methods can be identified from the Visual SLAM (VSLAM) literature.

Feature Based - Filtering Methods: The first SLAM system working in real time using a single camera (MonoSLAM) was presented in 2007 by Davison *et al.* [4]. 6 Degree of freedom (DoF) camera motion and 3D positions of feature points are represented as a state vectorin EKF. Further work was inspired by Davison's work. Building on the work of the classical age, the first algorithms for VSLAM were mainly based on filters. These techniques have several disadvantages, such as long computation times, the propagation of linearization errors and the inability to function properly during sudden motion. In large environments, the size of a state vector increases because the number of feature points is large. EKF-SLAM maps are of very poor density, making them suitable for localizing a camera only within a very small environment. Other VSLAM algorithms later emerged that were better suited for operating in real time and in larger environments.

Feature Based - Keyframe Methods: In 2007, Klein and Murray proposed a new real-time visual SLAM system (PTAM [12]). They introduced the idea of separating the computation of the camera's pose and the mapping of the environment into two different threads. One thread deals with the camera pose estimation and the selection of keyframes, while the other creates and updates a 3D map. This parallelization enabled the use of bundle adjustment (BA) techniques [25] on a set of keyframes. BA techniques are optimization methods based on the minimization of the reproduction error. One of the significant contributions of PTAM is to introduce the use of keyframe. Strasdat et al. [21] demonstrated that for the same computation time, a VSLAM algorithm based on keyframes and BA optimization is more accurate than filtering methods. Compared to MonoSLAM, the system can handle thousands of features points by splitting the tracking and the mapping into two threads on CPU. However, PTAM does not detect large loops, and relocalization is based on the correlations between low-resolution thumbnails of the keyframes, resulting in a low invariance to viewpoint. When a loop closure is detected, this information is used to reduce the error drift in both the camera path and the map. Subsequent works improved the PTAM algorithm, particularly for use in large environments [13,22]. Strasdat et al. [21] have shown that it is necessary to preserve as many points of interest as possible while conserving nonredundant keyframes. To improve an accuracy of VSLAM, it is important to increase the number of feature points in a map. In 2017, Mur-Artal et al. proposed ORB-SLAM2 [15] based on their earlier algorithm named ORB-SLAM [16]. This VSLAM algorithm can operate in real time, in any environment, in monocular, RGB-D or stereovision mode. ORB-SLAM2 is divided into 4 modules: tracking, reconstruction, position optimization and loop detection. These four phases are executed in three different threads. In contrast to PTAM, ORB-SLAM2 achieves robustness under challenging conditions by inserting keyframes as quickly as possible and removing the most redundant images. ORB-SLAM2 is based on the main ideas of PTAM, the place recognition work of Galvez-López and Tardos [11], the scale-aware loop closing of Strasdat et al. [23], and the use of covisibility information for large-scale operation.

Direct Methods: In contrast to feature-based methods, direct methods estimate structure and motion based directly on the pixel-level intensities in images. The Stereo Large-Scale Direct SLAM (LSD-SLAM) method presented by Engel et al. [8] is a semidense direct approach that minimizes photometric error in image regions with high gradients. This method is expected to be relatively robust to motion blur or poorly textured environments, they are also called featureless approaches.

Semidirect Methods: The Semidirect monocular Visual Odometry (SVO) [9] algorithm is a visual odometry method based on the semidirect approach. It is a hybrid method with a combination of the characteristics of the previous two types of methods. The tracking is done by feature point matching, the mapping is done by the direct method. It inherits some of the drawbacks of direct methods and discards the optimization and loop detection steps.

Visual Odometry: The concept of visual odometry (VO) has been summarized by Davide Scaramuzza and Friedrich Fraundorfer in [18] and [10]. The term VO was first introduced by Nister *et al.* [17]. The aim of VSLAM is to compute a global, consistent estimate of the system path, while the goal of VO is to calculate the path incrementally, pose by pose. VO can be used as one part of a complete SLAM algorithm.

$$VSLAM = VO + global\ map\ optimization$$

All VSLAM works described in the literature show that detecting and processing all points of interest in the entire image in every frame is not possible, particularly in the case of embedded systems.

Table 1. Comparison of recents open-sources VSLAM and VO algorithms.

Algorithm	Method	Scene type	Map density	GO	LC
MonoSLAM [4] www.doc.ic.ac.uk/~ajd/ Scene/index.html	Feature	Small and ind.	Sparse	No	No
PTAM [12] www.robots.ox.ac.uk/~gk/ PTAM/download.html	Feature	Small	Sparse	Yes	No
LSD-SLAM [8] www.github.com/tum-vision/lsd_slam	Direct	Small or large	Semi-dense	Yes	Yes
SVO [9] www.github.com/uzh-rpg/ rpg_svo	Semi-direct	Repetitive and h.f.t	Sparse	No	No
ORBSLAM2 [15] www.github.com/ raulmur/ORB_SLAM2	Feature	Small or large	Sparse	Yes	Yes
DSO [7] www.github.com/ JakobEngel/dso	Direct	Small or large	Sparse	No	No

Abbreviations: Global Optimizations (GO), Loop Closure (LC), hight-frequency texture (h.f.t) and indoor (ind.).

3.3 Vision-Based Navigation

The vast majority of vision-based navigation work has been implemented on micro aerial vehicles (MAVs) or small helicopters. However, these implementations also rely on inertial data most of the time. Vision-based navigation systems for flying vehicles must be capable of estimating an agent's pose from aerial views of the ground. Extracting and matching features from images acquired in a large and poorly textured environment at high speed is extremely challenging, especially for an embedded system with low computation capabilities. The authors of [24,26] embedded LSD-SLAM and SVO algorithms, respectively, in micro aerial vehicles using monocular cameras. Recently, Bayard *et al.* [2] developed an alternative approach based on velocimetry for navigation on Mars. As noted by [3], we have now entered a new period of SLAM development, which the cited authors term the robust perception age. The robustification of existing SLAM algorithms to enable real applications is the major issue at stake.

4   Discussion and Positioning

In this paper, an overview of SLAM methods for vision-based navigation is presented. Full SLAM solutions are challenging for real-time applications embedded in helicopters due to their computation-intensive filter-based state estimations. Our device will be an intermediary system between the pilot, the autopilot and the flight management system (FMS). In this mindset, we do not intend to implement the most powerful possible VSLAM algorithm. Instead, our main contribution will arise from the capability to construct a multiagent distributed intelligence system in which the VSLAM algorithm engages in the best possible dialogue with the other agents to support incremental navigation decisions all along the route. Our VSLAM system will have the ability to provide relevant navigation indicators based on image regions of interest to the autopilot to maintain a low error ratio. At the end of the day, the autopilot must be able to rely on this system as a basis for making decisions. Therefore, our most challenging task will be to robustify and format the output data of our VSLAM application.

References

1. Bailey, T., Durrant-Whyte, H.: Simultaneous localization and mapping (SLAM): part II. IEEE Robot. Autom. Mag. **13**(3), 108–117 (2006). https://doi.org/10.1109/MRA.2006.1678144
2. Bayard, D.S., et al.: Vision-based navigation for the NASA mars helicopter. In: AIAA Scitech 2019 Forum. American Institute of Aeronautics and Astronautics (2019). https://doi.org/10.2514/6.2019-1411. https://arc.aiaa.org/doi/abs/10.2514/6.2019-1411
3. Cadena, C., et al.: Past, present, and future of simultaneous localization and mapping: toward the robust-perception age. IEEE Trans. Robot. **32**(6), 1309–1332 (2016). https://doi.org/10.1109/TRO.2016.2624754
4. Davison, A.J., Reid, I.D., Molton, N.D., Stasse, O.: MonoSLAM: real-time single camera SLAM. IEEE Trans. Pattern Anal. Mach. Intell. **29**(6), 1052–1067 (2007). https://doi.org/10.1109/TPAMI.2007.1049
5. Durrant-Whyte, H., Bailey, T.: Simultaneous localization and mapping: part I. IEEE Robot. Autom. Mag. **13**(2), 99–110 (2006). https://doi.org/10.1109/MRA.2006.1638022
6. Durrant-Whyte, H.F.: Uncertain geometry in robotics. IEEE J. Robot. Autom. **4**(1), 23–31 (1988). https://doi.org/10.1109/56.768
7. Engel, J., Koltun, V., Cremers, D.: Direct sparse odometry. IEEE Trans. Pattern Anal. Mach. Intell. **40**, 611–625 (2018)
8. Engel, J., Schöps, T., Cremers, D.: LSD-SLAM: large-scale direct monocular SLAM. In: European Conference on Computer Vision (ECCV) (2014)

9. Forster, C., Pizzoli, M., Scaramuzza, D.: SVO: fast semi-direct monocular visual odometry. In: 2014 IEEE International Conference on Robotics and Automation (ICRA), pp. 15–22, May 2014. https://doi.org/10.1109/ICRA.2014.6906584

10. Fraundorfer, F., Scáramuzza, D.: Visual odometry: Part II: Matching, robustness, optimization, and applications. IEEE Robot. Autom. Mag. **19**(2), 78–90 (2012). https://doi.org/10.1109/MRA.2012.2182810. https://graz.pure.elsevier.com/en/publications/visual-odometry-part-ii-matching-robustness-optimization-and-appl

11. Galvez-López, D., Tardos, J.D.: Bags of binary words for fast place recognition in image sequences. IEEE Trans. Robot. **28**(5), 1188–1197 (2012). https://doi.org/10.1109/TRO.2012.2197158

12. Klein, G., Murray, D.: Parallel tracking and mapping for small AR workspaces. In: 2007 6th IEEE and ACM International Symposium on Mixed and Augmented Reality, pp. 225–234, November 2007. https://doi.org/10.1109/ISMAR.2007.4538852

13. Konolige, K., Agrawal, M.: Frameslam: from bundle adjustment to real-time visual mapping. IEEE Trans. Robot. **24**, 1066–1077 (2008). https://doi.org/10.1109/TRO.2008.2004832

14. Montemerlo, M., Thrun, S., Koller, D., Wegbreit, B.: FastSLAM: a factored solution to the simultaneous localization and mapping problem. In: Proceedings of the AAAI National Conference on Artificial Intelligence, pp. 593–598. AAAI (2002)

15. Mur-Artal, R., Tardós, J.D.: ORB-SLAM2: an open-source SLAM system for monocular, stereo, and RGB-D cameras. IEEE Trans. Robot. **33**(5), 1255–1262 (2017). https://doi.org/10.1109/TRO.2017.2705103

16. Mur-Artal, R., Montiel, J., Tardos, J.: ORB-SLAM: a versatile and accurate monocular SLAM system. IEEE Trans. Robot. **31**, 1147–1163 (2015). https://doi.org/10.1109/TRO.2015.2463671

17. Nister, D., Naroditsky, O., Bergen, J.: Visual odometry. In: Proceedings of the 2004 IEEE Computer Society Conference on Computer Vision and Pattern Recognition, 2004, CVPR 2004, vol. 1, pp. I-652–I-659, June 2004. https://doi.org/10.1109/CVPR.2004.1315094

18. Scaramuzza, D., Fraundorfer, F.: Tutorial: visual odometry. IEEE Robot. Autom. Mag. **18**(4), 80–92 (2011). https://doi.org/10.1109/MRA.2011.943233. https://graz.pure.elsevier.com/en/publications/tutorial-visual-odometry

19. Smith, R., Self, M., Cheeseman, P.: Estimating uncertain spatial relationships in robotics. In: 1987 IEEE International Conference on Robotics and Automation Proceedings, vol. 4, p. 850, March 1987. https://doi.org/10.1109/ROBOT.1987.1087846

20. Smith, R.C., Cheeseman, P.: On the representation and estimation of spatial uncertainly. Int. J. Rob. Res. **5**(4), 56–68 (1986). https://doi.org/10.1177/027836498600500404

21. Strasdat, H., Montiel, J.M.M., Davison, A.J.: Real-time monocular SLAM: why filter? In: 2010 IEEE International Conference on Robotics and Automation, pp. 2657–2664, May 2010. https://doi.org/10.1109/ROBOT.2010.5509636

22. Strasdat, H., Davison, A.J., Montiel, J.M.M., Konolige, K.: Double window optimisation for constant time visual SLAM. In: Proceedings of the 2011 International Conference on Computer Vision, ICCV 2011, pp. 2352–2359. IEEE Computer Society, Washington (2011). https://doi.org/10.1109/ICCV.2011.6126517

23. Strasdat, H., Montiel, J.M.M., Davison, A.J.: Scale drift-aware large scale monocular SLAM. In: RSS 2010 (2010). https://doi.org/10.15607/RSS.2010.VI.010

210   R. Girard et al.

24. Stumberg, L.v., Usenko, V., Engel, J., Stückler, J., Cremers, D.: From monocular
    SLAM to autonomous drone exploration. In: 2017 European Conference on Mobile
    Robots (ECMR). pp. 1–8, September 2017. https://doi.org/10.1109/ECMR.2017.
    8098709
25. Triggs, B., McLauchlan, P.F., Hartley, R.I., Fitzgibbon, A.W.: Bundle adjustment—
    a modern synthesis. In: Triggs, B., Zisserman, A., Szeliski, R. (eds.) IWVA 1999.
    LNCS, vol. 1883, pp. 298–372. Springer, Heidelberg (2000). https://doi.org/10.
    1007/3-540-44480-7_21
26. Yang, T., Li, P., Zhang, H., Li, J., Li, Z.: Monocular vision SLAM-based UAV
    autonomous landing in emergencies and unknown environments. Electronics 7(5),
    73 (2018). https://doi.org/10.3390/electronics7050073. https://www.mdpi.com/
    2079-9292/7/5/73

Random Walk Exploration for Swarm Mapping

Miquel Kegeleirs$^{(\boxtimes)}$ (ID), David Garzón Ramos$^{(\boxtimes)}$ (ID), and Mauro Birattari$^{(\boxtimes)}$ (ID)

IRIDIA, Université Libre de Bruxelles, Brussels, Belgium
{mkegelei,dgarzonr,mbiro}@ulb.ac.be

Abstract. Research in swarm robotics has shown that robot swarms are effective in the exploration of unknown environments. However, little work has been devoted to port the exploration capabilities of robot swarms into the context of mapping. Indeed, conceiving robot swarms that can map an unknown environment in a robust, scalable, and flexible way is an open issue. In this paper, we investigate a swarm mapping method in which robots first individually map the environment by random walk and then, we merge their maps into a single, global one. We focus on five variants of random walk and we compare the quality of the maps that a swarm produces when exploring the environment using these variants. Our experiments with ten e-puck robots show that, despite the individual maps being incomplete by themselves, it is possible to collectively map the environment by merging them. We found that the quality of the map depends on the exploration behavior of the individuals. Our results suggest that one of the variants of random walk, the ballistic motion, gives better mapping results for closed environments.

Keywords: Swarm mapping · Exploration · Random walk

1 Introduction

A robot swarm can collectively accomplish tasks that an individual robot could not accomplish alone. By its own nature, a robot swarm is a self-organizing system that operates autonomously without relying on a leader robot or on external infrastructure. In addition, it possesses desirable properties such as scalability, flexibility, and fault-tolerance [4] due to redundancy and locality of sensing and communication. Because of these properties, robot swarms are ideal candidates to perform missions that require to explore and map unknown environments in which the risk that individual robots fail or are lost is high. Yet, no well-defined methodology exists for swarm mapping (i.e. for exploring and mapping with robot swarms).

All experiments were performed by MK and DGR. The article was drafted by MK and DGR and revised by the three authors. The research was directed by MB.

The original version of this chapter was revised: The given name and the family name of the second author has been corrected. The correction to this chapter is available at https://doi.org/10.1007/978-3-030-25332-5_50

K. Althoefer et al. (Eds.): TAROS 2019, LNAI 11650, pp. 211–222, 2019.
https://doi.org/10.1007/978-3-030-25332-5_19

Mapping has been largely explored [23] in the last decades and it is usually the first task that a robot performs when it operates in an unknown environment. Most of the mapping methods have been designed to be general, platform independent, and use-case independent. However, they have been developed mostly for single robots and they cannot be directly adopted by centralized multi-robot systems and robot swarms.

State-of-the-art methods for mapping often conflict with some characteristics of robot swarms such as locality and the absence of global knowledge [4]. First, these methods usually require external infrastructure to ensure inter-robot communication or localization (a single point of failure that hinders fault tolerance). Second, either one or a small number of robots is used, and they are expensive and heavily equipped. This condition implies that the loss of a single robot seriously affects the whole system. As a result, adapting the research on mapping to swarm robotics is not straightforward and little attention has been devoted to close the gap between the two fields.

Some important questions still need to be addressed before effective swarm mapping can be achieved: How should the swarm explore and gather information on the environment? How should the robots share and spread the information gathered? How should the information be retrieved and used to produce maps? Our work aims to shed further light on the first of these questions. More precisely, we investigate the possibility of using random walk as a strategy to explore and gather information on the environment.

We are particularly interested in using random walk exploration in swarm mapping because random walk is a simple behavior that can be easily implemented in a robot swarm. Indeed, by its own nature, random walk is flexible, scalable and robust as it does not rely on localization or communication. For these reasons, though many different exploration strategies have been proposed for single robot and centralized multi-robot systems [9,18], random walk is still the most commonly adopted behavior for exploring with robot swarms [3,5,8].

In this paper, we evaluate five different variants of random walk on swarm mapping: Brownian motion, correlated random walk, Lévy walk, Lévy taxis, and ballistic motion. In our experiments, each robot individually maps the environment, driven by a random walk. Later on, the individual maps are merged to produce a single, global map of the environment. We assess the ability of the robot swarm to map the environment through the quality of the global map produced. The main original contribution we make in the paper is the evaluation of different variants of random walk in the context of swarm mapping. Moreover, to the best of our knowledge, this is the first paper in which random walk exploration, the *GMapping* algorithm [11,12], and the *multirobot_map_merge* algorithm [13] are used together to achieve swarm mapping.

The paper is structured as follows. In Sect. 2, we discuss related work in exploration and mapping with multi-robot systems. In Sect. 3, we present the swarm mapping method that we investigate in the paper. In Sect. 4, we describe the experimental setup. In Sect. 5, we illustrate the results of the experiments. In Sect. 6, we conclude the paper and we sketch future research.

2   Related Work

Traditionally, mapping with multi-robot systems has been addressed separately in the form of two sub-problems: multi-robot simultaneous localization and mapping (multi-robot SLAM) and multi-robot exploration [22].

Multi-robot SLAM concerns the collective production of maps. The work of Saeedi et al. [23] provides a review of the methods that have been proposed on this topic. The review describes advantages, problems, and challenges of widely used methods based on the Extended Kalman Filter (EKF-SLAM), particle filters (PF-SLAM), and map merging, among others. Though current SLAM methods could be implemented in robot swarms, they would introduce constrains that would affect the flexibility of the system: centralized mechanisms or complex inter-robot interactions. The issues that one can encounter by adopting SLAM on robot swarms are described by Barca et al. [1].

The literature on multi-robot mapping often assumes an existent multi-robot exploration and oversights the relationship between exploration and SLAM. Rone et al. [22] described different exploration methods used in multi-robot mapping and their characteristics. The review presents some exploration methods that could be easily implemented in robot swarms such as potential field exploration, greedy mapping, and diffusion mapping, the last two relying on random walk behaviors.

Recent work on swarm robotics has brought attention to the impact of using different variants of random walk. For example, Dimidov et al. [3] studied the performances of different variants of random walk while exploring and searching for a static target in the environment. Schroeder et al. [24] conducted a similar research and compared different variants of random walk to cover the environment. The results of these studies highlight the relationship between the performance on the task and the ability of the swarm to explore the environment with a particular variant. Our hypothesis is that the same differences in performance should appear while performing swarm mapping with different variants of random walk. To corroborate our hypothesis, we investigate the mapping performance of a robot swarm that explores by using five different variants.

Mapping with a robot swarm has already been reported by Ramachandran [20], who evaluates the efficiency of the so-called Informed Correlated Lévy Walk (i.e. a variant of random walk). However, our research differs in both the method and objectives. First, Ramachandran proposed a method that computes the global maps online in which robots know their absolute position and communicate thanks to external infrastructure. In our method, the global maps are produced offline at the end of the experiment, the robots estimate their own position, and they do not need to communicate while exploring and mapping the environment. Second, in the experiments of Ramachandran, the code was modified when ported from simulation to the real robots. In our case, we use the same code in both. Finally, Ramachandran only evaluated the performances of Lévy walk and Informed Correlated Lévy walk. As mentioned before, we evaluate four more variants in addition to Lévy walk.

3   Swarm Mapping Method

The swarm mapping method we propose integrates three algorithms: random walk exploration, *GMapping* [11,12], and *multirobot_map_merge* [13]. First, random walk exploration defines the behavior that the robots use for exploring the environment. Then, each robot uses the *GMapping* algorithm to gather information and produce an individual map of the area it has explored. Finally, *multirobot_map_merge* is used to merge the individual maps and to produce a global map of the environment.

We developed the swarm mapping method for a swarm of e-puck [15] robots. The random walk behaviors are implementations based on models previously proposed in the literature. *GMapping* and *multirobot_map_merge* are default implementations that we adopted from the Robot Operating System (ROS) [19]. In the following, we provide a brief description of the algorithms and their contribution to the swarm mapping method.

3.1   Random Walk Exploration

The first component of the swarm mapping method concerns the behavior that drives the robots to explore the environment.

In our study, we consider five variants of random walk: Brownian motion [6], correlated random walk [21], Lévy walk [25], Lévy taxis [16] and ballistic motion. We selected these variants because they have been reported as completely random, specialized in *intensification* (i.e., intensive exploration of a small area of the environment), and/or specialized in *coverage* (i.e., moderate exploration of a large area of the environment). Indeed, we are interested in studying the differences between intensification-oriented and coverage-oriented exploration in swarm mapping.

Despite their different exploration abilities, Brownian motion, correlated random walk, Lévy walk, and Lévy taxis share the same mathematical model [3,16]. They can be described within a general behavior: the robot selects a direction at random and moves towards it until a new direction is selected. The characteristics of the movement for each variant are defined by the parametrization of the model. In particular, the aforementioned variants differ in the ρ and μ parameters: the former associated to the turning angle when the robot selects a direction at random, and the later associated to the time the robot keeps moving along that direction. In our implementations, we used the parametrization described as optimal by Pasternak et al. [16] and Dimidov et al. [3] as shown in Table 1. Figure 1a describes the general behavior of Brownian motion, correlated random walk, Lévy walk and Lévy taxis.

In addition to the four variants described above, we included the ballistic motion behavior used by Francesca et al. in AutoMoDe-Vanilla [8]. The ballistic motion used in the exploration module of Vanilla drives the robots with a constant straight motion, only changing their direction when an obstacle is detected. We consider here the ballistic motion as a random walk behavior because the robots select the new direction at random. Figure 1b describes the general behavior of the ballistic motion.

Table 1. Step length, turning angle, and specialty for the variants of random walk

Variant	Step length	Turning angle	Specialty
Brownian motion	$\mu = 3$	$\rho = 0$	None
Correlated random walk	$\mu = 3$	$\rho = 0.05$	Intensification
Lévy walk	$\mu = 2.8$	$\rho = 0$	Coverage
Lévy taxis	$\mu = 2.8$	$\rho = 0.05$	Mix of coverage/intensification
Ballistic motion	N/A	N/A	Coverage

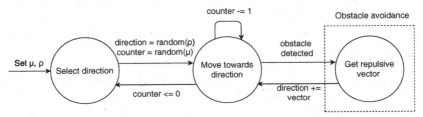

(a) Brownian motion, correlated random walk, Lévy walk and Lévy taxis

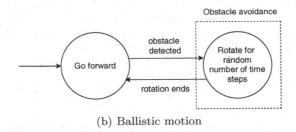

(b) Ballistic motion

Fig. 1. Finite state machines of the variants of random walk

Figures 1a, b also show that the five variants of random walk include a basic obstacle avoidance behavior. Brownian motion, correlated random walk, Lévy walk, and Lévy taxis integrate a repulsive force model [2] that drives the robots away from any object in their detection range. In the case of the ballistic motion, the obstacle avoidance is an intrinsic property of the behavior and it allows the robots to avoid objects in the same range as the others.

3.2 Individual Mapping

The second component of the swarm mapping method concerns the ability of the robots to gather information and to individually map different areas of the environment.

We use the *GMapping* algorithm to produce an individual map for each robot in the swarm. *GMapping* is a single-robot, SLAM algorithm that takes sensor information and produces a two-dimensional occupancy grid of the environment.

In our method, we consider a model of robot that explores, computes its own odometry (i.e. an estimation of its own displacement), and detects and locates objects in a short range. This information is sufficient for *GMapping* to produce a map that describes the empty and obstructed areas,that the robot finds.

The odometry on each robot is first initialized with the deployment position of the robot. Then, the robot continuously estimates its position in open loop by integrating the movement commanded by the random walk behavior. Providing the robots with knowledge about their starting position does not have any effect on their ability to produce the individual maps. The information was included in order to enable the merging of the individual maps in the following step of the swarm mapping method.

3.3   Global Mapping

The third component of the swarm mapping method concerns the combination of the individual contribution of each robot in the swarm into a single global map of the environment.

In our swarm mapping method, we merge the individual maps produced by each robot into a single map by using the *multirobot_map_merge* algorithm. *Multirobot_map_merge* is originally intended for merging an arbitrary number of individual maps at run time. The maps are merged only when the robots have finished the exploration of the environment. We chose *multirobot_map_merge* because it has been used in previous research [13] to merge individual maps produced by multi-robot systems and *GMapping*.

Multirobot_map_merge has two merging modes that differ on whether the initial position of the robots is known or not, the former being more robust. On the one hand, providing the algorithm with no positioning information is a closer approach to the self-organizing nature of the robot swarms. On the other hand, we consider reasonable that the initial relative position of the robots could be known *a priori* when the robots are deployed in a fixed location. We consider both cases in our swarm mapping method.

4   Experimental Setup

We evaluate the swarm mapping method with a swarm of e-pucks mapping a closed environment. The robots operate in an hexagonal closed environment referred to as the arena. The time available to the robots for mapping the arena is 180 s. The arena comprises an area of $2.30\,\mathrm{m}^2$ and it is surrounded by walls of 0.94 m in length. On a per-experiment basis, the arena could contain none or five rectangular obstacles of $0.02\,\mathrm{m}^2$. We expect that differences in the object density in the arena should have an effect on the ability of the swarm to explore the environment, and therefore, in the quality of the global map. The deployment position of the robots in the arena is fixed in all the experiments: the robots are aligned along the west wall of the arena with 0.10 m between their center and the wall, and 0.09 m between each other's center.

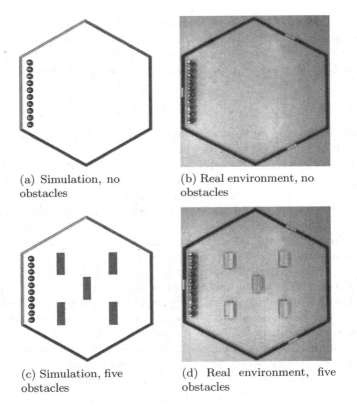

(a) Simulation, no obstacles

(b) Real environment, no obstacles

(c) Simulation, five obstacles

(d) Real environment, five obstacles

Fig. 2. Arenas used in the experiments and starting position of the robots

Figure 2 shows the arenas and robots in their deployment position for both the simulated and real environments. All the simulations are performed using ARGoS3, beta 48 [17]. In the following, we describe the reference model of the robots and the protocol we used in our experiments.

4.1 Robot

We consider an extended version of the e-puck [10, 15]. The e-puck is a differential wheeled mobile robot with a 0.08 m diameter and maximum velocity of $0.12\,\mathrm{m\,s^{-1}}$ It is equipped with an embedded computer and a set of eight infrared proximity sensors. The proximity sensors are distributed around the robot and they detect objects in a range of 0.10 m. We configured the robots to avoid objects in a range of 0.08 m to let them map obstacles before avoiding them.

For the purpose of this study, we integrated ROS Indigo into the embedded computer of the robot. We developed a ROS-based controller that drives the robot by using the variants of random walk described in Sect. 3.1. The controller transforms the desired direction of movement into appropriate velocity commands for the e-puck. In parallel, the controller also computes the odometry of the robot and receives the readings from the proximity sensors. This information is passed to *GMapping* at runtime to enable the robot mapping.

4.2 Protocol

We evaluate the five variants of random walk along with our swarm mapping method, both in simulation and real environment.

We consider a swarm of 10 e-puck robots mapping the arena described in Sect. 4. In all experiments, we execute our method for swarm mapping to produce one global map of the arena. In simulation, the swarm mapping is executed 30 times for each variant. In the real robot experiments, the swarm mapping is executed 10 times for each variant. We repeated the experiments in the two arena configurations: with and without obstacles. We report the individual and global maps obtained in a per-experiment basis.

We assess the quality of the global maps by visual inspection. For the purpose of our experiments, the quality metric represents the completeness and representativeness of the maps when compared to a reference map. In this case, the reference map is the ideal map to be produced if the robots map perfectly the environment. We consider visual inspection a sufficient metric to qualitatively assess the exploration abilities of the robots in swarm mapping. A well-established methodology for quantitative assessment is still missing and should be the objective for future work.

5   Results

We present the qualitative analysis of the results for both simulated and real experiments. In addition, we communicate the experiences made and the insights gained while adopting *GMapping* and *multirobot_map_merge* in swarm mapping. Individual and global maps, demonstrative videos, code, and ROS parameter files are available in [14]. Figure 3 shows a sample of the maps produced in swarm mapping for each variant of random walk.

With each variant, the robot swarm explores similarly the arena both in simulation and real environment. The main difference between simulation and real environment lies on the sensitivity of the proximity sensors: in real environment, robots are more sensitive and tend to detect and avoid obstacles from a further distance. As a result, then tend to cover more the environment. The maps created in simulation match the areas of the arena explored by the swarm, and provide usable information about its content. The maps obtained with real e-pucks, on the contrary, do not reflect the explored areas and are hardly useful. We compared the performance of the variants on the basis of the results obtained in simulation.

The results show that the ballistic motion provides maps with a better quality than the other variants. Indeed, robots using the ballistic motion tend to cover better the arena while the other variants focus more on intensification.

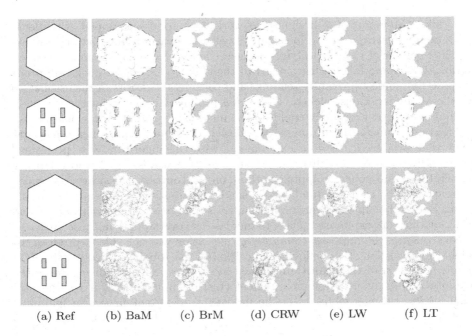

| (a) Ref | (b) BaM | (c) BrM | (d) CRW | (e) LW | (f) LT |

Fig. 3. Swarm mapping results in simulation (above) and real robot experiments (below): (a) Reference map; (b) Ballistic motion; (c) Brownian motion; (d) Correlated random walk; (e) Lévy walk; (f) Lévy taxis.

The ballistic motion is able to provide (nearly) complete maps while the maps produced with the other variants are mostly half-complete. In both cases, the exploration behavior was not affected by the presence of obstacles in the arena. We acknowledge that these observations are however only valid in the context of closed space experiments. It is easy to convince oneself that the ballistic motion cannot work in an open space without a high risk of loosing robots.

We also found that Brownian motion, correlated random walk, Lévy walk and Lévy taxis performed similarly. In overall, the maps produced with these variants do not differ neither in completeness or representativeness. As a matter of fact, we did not find substantial differences in the coverage and intensification abilities of these behaviors. The four variants responds to the same mathematical model and hence, their behavior does not differ considerably. In this sense, we argue that the parametrization of the model considered as optimal in previous research [3] cannot be generalized and it is not optimal for the e-pucks.

We successfully integrated *GMapping* and *multirobot_map_merge* in swarm mapping. The results in simulation show that, despite their limited resources, a swarm of e-pucks performing ballistic motion can map its environment. Still, we think that porting algorithms from single robot and centralized multi-robot systems is not necessarily the best approach to achieve swarm mapping.

First, *GMapping* was designed to work with robots equipped with dense long-range sensors and good localization systems; swarm robots like the e-pucks provide neither of them. Although we succeeded in obtaining the maps in simulation, *GMapping* failed when ported to the real robots. Real e-pucks are prone to have more noisy proximity readings and considerable errors in the estimation of the odometry. Consequently, *GMapping* produced noisy and erroneous individual maps that eventually could not be merged in good quality global maps.

Second, *multirobot_map_merge* was designed to merge maps regardless how they were produced. Previous experiments with this algorithm were performed with individual maps with a higher number of features and few overlapping areas [13]. In our swarm mapping method, on the contrary, the swarm succeeded in mapping due to the redundancy of small contributions from each individual map. Each robot in the swarm only maps a small area of the environment and the random walk exploration leads to increase the overlapping in those areas. As a consequence, the *multirobot_map_merge* algorithm was not able to produce the global map without the deployment position of the robots. Moreover, the ROS implementation of the algorithm crashed in some experiments disregarding the exploration behavior or the environment (real or simulated). Our results show that *multirobot_map_merge* could be used to some extent in swarm mapping, however a more suitable option should be explored in future work.

6   Conclusions

Robot swarms are suitable for the exploration and mapping of unknown environments. Still, swarm mapping is a field under development and no well-defined methodology exists to achieve it. In this article, we investigated the possibility of using random walk exploration with *GMapping* and *multirobot_map_merge* as a method to achieve swarm mapping. The robots explored and individually mapped the environment by random walk, and then the individual maps were merged to produce one single, global map. The redundancy of the individual maps contributes to obtain a good quality representation of the environment. This method can be ported with minimal effort to other ROS-based robot swarms since it does not require complex interactions between robots.

We conducted experiments, both in simulation and real environment, with a robot swarm mapping a closed environment while using five variants of random walk: Brownian motion, correlated random walk, Lévy walk, Lévy taxis, and ballistic motion. The robot swarm was able to successfully map the environment in simulation. However, experiments in real environment were less satisfying and highlighted the necessity to find strategies to better transfer the control software from simulation to real environment. Results in simulation showed that ballistic motion produces the best maps due to the better ability of the swarm to cover the environment. Yet, these results are only valid for closed environments and could not be extended to open ones. The other variants, on the contrary, showed a dominant intensification behavior that provided mostly half-complete maps.

We conclude that the selection and parametrization of the appropriate random walk behavior for swarm mapping is a topic that requires further research.

Future work will be devoted to use modular automatic design methods like Auto-MoDe [8] for this purpose. We expect a twofold contribution from AutoMoDe: first, it would provide a framework to assess the selection and parametrization of the behaviors in different environments; second, it would allow to port better the control software from simulation to the real robots. With regards to the mapping method, we will investigate the possibility of adopting concepts of distributed mapping [7] into swarm mapping. Indeed, merging individual maps centralizes the mapping process and, to some extent, affects the flexibility of the system. We expect that distributed mapping will provide alternatives to produce and retrieve useful partial maps in a fully distributed way.

Acknowledgements. The project has received funding from the European Research Council (ERC) under the European Union's Horizon 2020 research and innovation programme (grant agreement No 681872). Mauro Birattari acknowledges support from the Belgian Fonds de la Recherche Scientifique – FNRS. David Garzón Ramos acknowledges support from the Colombian Administrative Department of Science, Technology and Innovation – COLCIENCIAS.

References

1. Barca, J.C., Sekercioglu, Y.A.: Swarm robotics reviewed. Robotica **31**(3), 345–359 (2013)
2. Borenstein, J., Koren, Y.: Real-time obstacle avoidance for fast mobile robots. IEEE Trans. Syst. Man Cybern. **19**(5), 1179–1187 (1989)
3. Dimidov, C., Oriolo, G., Trianni, V.: Random walks in swarm robotics: an experiment with kilobots. In: Dorigo, M., et al. (eds.) ANTS 2016. LNCS, vol. 9882, pp. 185–196. Springer, Cham (2016). https://doi.org/10.1007/978-3-319-44427-7_16
4. Dorigo, M., Birattari, M., Brambilla, M.: Swarm robotics. Scholarpedia **9**(1), 1463 (2014)
5. Dorigo, M., et al.: a novel concept for the study of heterogeneous robotic swarms. IEEE Robot. Autom. Mag. **20**(4), 60–71 (2013)
6. Feynman, R.P., Leighton, R.B., Sands, M.L.: The Feynman Lectures on Physics Volume 1: Mainly Mechanics, Radiation, and Heat. Basic Books, New York (2011)
7. Fox, D., Ko, J., Konolige, K., Limketkai, B., Schulz, D., Stewart, B.: Distributed multirobot exploration and mapping. Proc. IEEE **94**(7), 1325–1339 (2006)
8. Francesca, G., Brambilla, M., Brutschy, A., Trianni, V., Birattari, M.: AutoMoDe: a novel approach to the automatic design of control software for robot swarms. Swarm Intell. **8**(2), 89–112 (2014)
9. Galceran, E., Carreras, M.: A survey on coverage path planning for robotics. Rob. Auton. Syst. **61**(12), 1258–1276 (2013)
10. Garattoni, L., Francesca, G., Brutschy, A., Pinciroli, C., Birattari, M.: Software infrastructure for e-puck (and TAM). Technical report. TR/IRIDIA/2015-004, IRIDIA, Université libre de Bruxelles, Belgium (2015)
11. Grisetti, G., Stachniss, C., Burgard, W.: Improving grid-based slam with rao-blackwellized particle filters by adaptive proposals and selective resampling. In: Proceedings of the 2005 IEEE International Conference on Robotics and Automation. pp. 2432–2437. IEEE Press (2005)
12. Grisetti, G., Stachniss, C., Burgard, W.: Improved techniques for grid mapping with rao-blackwellized particle filters. IEEE Trans. Rob. **23**(1), 34–46 (2007)

13. Hörner, J.: Map-merging for multi-robot system. Master's thesis, Univerzita Karlova (2016)
14. Kegeleirs, M., Garzón Ramos, D., Birattari, M.: Random walk exploration for swarm mapping: supplementary material (2019). http://iridia.ulb.ac.be/supp/ IridiaSupp2019-003/index.html
15. Mondada, F., et al.: The e-puck, a robot designed for education in engineering. In: Gonçalves, P., Torres, P., Alves, C. (eds.) Proceedings of the 9th Conference on Autonomous Robot Systems and Competitions. Instituto Politécnico de Castelo Branco, pp. 59–65, Portugal (2009)
16. Pasternak, Z., Bartumeus, F., Grasso, F.W.: Lévy-taxis: a novel search strategy for finding odor plumes in turbulent flow-dominated environments. J. Phys. A Math. Theoret. **42**(43), 434010 (2009)
17. Pinciroli, C., et al.: ARGoS: a modular, parallel, multi-engine simulator for multi-robot systems. Swarm Intell. **6**(4), 271–295 (2012)
18. Portugal, D., Rocha, R.: A survey on multi-robot patrolling algorithms. In: Camarinha-Matos, L.M. (ed.) DoCEIS 2011. IAICT, vol. 349, pp. 139–146. Springer, Heidelberg (2011). https://doi.org/10.1007/978-3-642-19170-1_15
19. Quigley, M., et al.: ROS: an open-source robot operating system. In: ICRA Workshop on Open Source Software. vol. 3, p. 5. IEEE Press (2009)
20. Ramachandran, R.K.: Exploration, mapping and scalar field estimation using a swarm of resource-constrained robots. Ph.D. thesis, Arizona State University (2018)
21. Renshaw, E., Henderson, R.: The correlated random walk. J. Appl. Probab. **18**(02), 403–414 (1981)
22. Rone, W., Ben-Tzvi, P.: Mapping, localization and motion planning in mobile multi-robotic systems. Robotica **31**(1), 1–23 (2013)
23. Saeedi, S., Trentini, M., Seto, M., Li, H.: Multiple-robot simultaneous localization and mapping: a review. J. Field Rob. **33**(1), 3–46 (2016)
24. Schroeder, A., Ramakrishnan, S., Kumar, M., Trease, B.: Efficient spatial coverage by a robot swarm based on an ant foraging model and the lévy distribution. Swarm Intell. **11**(1), 39–69 (2017)
25. Zaburdaev, V., Denisov, S., Klafter, J.: Lévy walks. Rev. Mod. Phys. **87**(2), 483–530 (2015)

Visual and Thermal Data for Pedestrian and Cyclist Detection

Sarfraz Ahmed[1]($\boxtimes$), M. Nazmul Huda[1], Sujan Rajbhandari[1], Chitta Saha[1],
Mark Elshaw[1], and Stratis Kanarachos[2]

[1] School of Computing, Electronics and Mathematics, Coventry University,
Coventry CV1 5FB, UK
`ahmed157@uni.coventry.ac.uk`
[2] School of Mechanical, Aerospace and Automotive Engineering, Coventry University,
Coventry CV1 5FB, UK

Abstract. With the continued advancement of autonomous vehicles and their implementation in public roads, accurate detection of vulnerable road users (VRUs) is vital for ensuring safety. To provide higher levels of safety for these VRUs, an effective detection system should be employed that can correctly identify VRUs in all types of environments (e.g. VRU appearance, crowded scenes) and conditions (e.g. fog, rain, night-time). This paper presents optimal methods of sensor fusion for pedestrian and cyclist detection using Deep Neural Networks (DNNs) for higher levels of feature abstraction. Typically, visible sensors have been utilized for this purpose. Recently, thermal sensors system or combination of visual and thermal sensors have been employed for pedestrian detection with advanced detection algorithm. DNNs have provided promising results for improving the accuracy of pedestrian and cyclist detection. This is because they are able to extract features at higher levels than typical hand-crafted detectors. Previous studies have shown that amongst the several sensor fusion techniques that exist, Halfway Fusion has provided the best results in terms of accuracy and robustness. Although sensor fusion and DNN implementation have been used for pedestrian detection, there is considerably less research undertaken for cyclist detection.

Keywords: Pedestrian detection · Cyclist detection · Sensor fusion · Deep Neural Networks

1 Introduction

Recently, there has been a strong research focus on protecting vulnerable road users (VRUs), such as pedestrians, cyclists and motorcyclists [22]. This is because approximately half of the deaths on road accidents involve VRUs [34]. Of these VRUs, pedestrians and cyclists are at most risk as they do not have any form of special protection. And, although pedestrian detection techniques have been

© Springer Nature Switzerland AG 2019
K. Althoefer et al. (Eds.): TAROS 2019, LNAI 11650, pp. 223–234, 2019.
https://doi.org/10.1007/978-3-030-25332-5_20

widely studied, cyclist detection has not received the same attention [10,29]. This can be viewed as a concern as cyclists are also a part of the VRUs group, and can are just as susceptible to road traffic-related accidents. Also, it should be noted that cyclists typically travel with higher speeds than pedestrians, which can lead to increased chances of road traffic-related incidents [29]. Therefore, when designing a detection system, both pedestrians and cyclists should be considered.

A number of approaches have been proposed for increasing the safety of pedestrians and cyclists. These approaches are becoming more relevant and necessary as autonomous vehicles are being used and tested on public roads. A major motivation for the development and advancement of autonomous vehicles has been to reduce the number of traffic accidents and thereby increase the safety of other road users [18]. To achieve this, various aspects of the design of the autonomous vehicle is being researched. One area that is being studied is sensor fusion. This is because the sensors are a vital part of the autonomous vehicle. They provide information, allowing the vehicle to sense its environment and detect objects within that environment. Using the information collected by the sensors, the vehicle is able to react and manoeuvre in an optimal and safe fashion [18]. By increasing the number of sensors, the perception of the vehicle can be increased in reliability and robustness.

Autonomous vehicles use various sensors, typically visual/thermal cameras, RADAR and LIDAR to sense its surrounding. For pedestrian and cyclist detection, visual sensors (i.e. cameras) are used as they produce high-resolution scene data [11]. Visual sensors have already been successfully applied for traffic sign detection and lane detection and are low cost to implement [21].

Pedestrian and cyclist detection have been a computer vision problem that has been widely explored due to its applications in autonomous vehicles, surveillance and tracking. Although there has been significant improvements made in the field of pedestrian/cyclist detection, it is yet to reach the levels to that of human perception [1,24,39]. The challenges that hinder the performance of these vision-based systems include occlusion, cluttered backgrounds and low-resolution images. Current detector designs use visual light spectrum cameras, which can provide high-resolution images in good lighting conditions. However, the quality of the images can be significantly reduced in poor lighting situations (i.e. night-time, evening) [24], decreasing the overall performance of the system. Visual (VS) and thermal-infrared (TIR) images have been fused for pedestrian detection to increase the robustness of the detection system [14,24,33].

Deep Neural Networks (DNNs) were implemented to further improve the effectiveness of general object detection, proving the effectiveness of DNNs for pedestrian detection [13,24]. For example, a DNN-based detection technique yielded a mean average precision (mAP) of 53.7% when evaluated on PASCAL VOC 2010 in [13]. In a similar detection technique was proposed in [31], however, without the use of DNNs. The technique achieved an overall 35.1% mAP. However, it is still unclear which method(s) of fusion of sensor data that will provide the optimal results for pedestrian and cyclist detection using DNNs.

The primary purpose of this paper is determining the optimal method of sensor information fusion for pedestrian and cyclist detection based on DNNs. Although research in the field has been undertaken for pedestrian detection, there are relatively fewer studies for cyclist detection. Therefore, there is still a need to study sensor fusion for cyclist detection as well as pedestrian detection. Based on previous works, DNNs should be able to provide more accurate results when compared to traditional methods of detection. The DNN is trained using multispectral data so that it can successfully extract features from both visible and infrared spectrums. This will aid in designing a detector that is more robust and accurate than the ones that currently exist for both pedestrian and cyclist detection. This will ultimately be a part of the prediction system for anticipating the behaviours of the pedestrian/cyclist for collision avoidance.

2   Pedestrian and Cyclist Detection

Although vision sensors have been widely researched for pedestrian detection in recent years, it remains a challenging problem that needs to be solved before human-like detection level is reached. The challenges are caused by the unpredictability of appearance of pedestrians due to occlusion, cluttered environment and pose. The cyclist detection problems are further complicated by multiple viewpoints of cyclist [22]. That is because cyclists, unlike pedestrians, can be perceived in a number of orientations. This causes difficulties as each orientation would have a different aspect ratio. The similarity between pedestrian and cyclists also poses another challenge. To overcome some of these challenges, a technique is proposed for detecting both pedestrians and cyclists [22]. The method uses the upper bodies (UB), which is similar for both pedestrians and cyclists.

3   Detection Systems for Autonomous Vehicles

It is vital that autonomous vehicles have a detection system that provides high levels of reliability while also being robust under various conditions (e.g. during both day and night, weather conditions). This is crucial to address safety concerns as more than 50% of accidents involving pedestrians occurs during night-time [2,9]. To reduce this figure, thermal infrared (TIR) sensor-based cameras have been employed. Unlike visual (VS) light spectrum-based cameras, the TIR camera is not dependent on an external light source, rather it uses heat signatures of objects for detection and localization. This makes TIR more effective at low light conditions, such as at night-time [2]. Both VS and TIR sensors will be discussed in the next sections. Whether using VS and TIR images together or independently, the process used for detection consists of at least feature extraction and classification. Some features that are collected during the daytime can be used for detection at night-time [2]. This is true when using the local binary pattern (LBP) technique, which was introduced for use with VS cameras. Features extracted using the LBP method only provide pixel intensity, which is the only channel of information for TIR cameras.

A common technique for feature extraction for pedestrian detection is the histogram of oriented gradient (HOG) [7]. The HOG technique extracts the gradient information for colour images and does not include information for the intensity channel. HOG is widely used as it is robust. Considerable research was undertaken resulting in many variations of the approach. Thermal position intensity HOG (TPIHOG) works for the intensity information obtained via TIR sensors [2].

Once features are extracted, they are classified into classes. A commonly implemented classifier is the linear support vector machine (SVM) due to its decent performance and speed [3,28,37]. Several variations of SVM also exist. However, more recently, deep learning techniques have been used for general object detection as well as pedestrian detection. Classifiers based deep learning require large annotated datasets to be trained, which takes a longer time than other methods of classification [4]. However, deep learning improves accuracy and speed. The convolutional neural network (CNN) has also been widely adopted for pedestrian and cyclist detection.

4 Sensors

The detection of objects such as pedestrians, cyclists and vehicles are achieved through sensors. Sensors such as VS, IR, LIDAR and RADAR sensors, allow the autonomous vehicle to recognize objects in its environment. A single type of sensor approach cannot provide necessary levels of performance required of such a crucial and integral part of an autonomous vehicle [19] and therefore, sensor fusion can provide improved information. The focus of this study is fusion of VS and TIR sensors (i.e. cameras) used for pedestrians and cyclist detections.

4.1 Visible Light Sensors

Vision-based object detection has been widely studied, in particular pedestrian detection, but still remains a challenging task. VS cameras have been used with various methods of detection such as histograms of oriented gradient (HOG) with support vector machines (SVM) and adaptive boosting (AdaBoost) [7,21,22,25,30,32]. The main concern using a VS-based pedestrian/cyclist detection is the performance susceptible to environmental conditions such as shadowing, uneven illumination, the decline in performance during low-light conditions (e.g. night-time, evening) and sensitivity to abrupt changes in illumination (e.g. going through a tunnel). They are also less effective due to occlusions caused by cluttered backgrounds or shape, size and pose of a pedestrian/cyclist. For this reason, multispectral (i.e. combined VS and TIR) data for sensor fusion have been introduced to overcome the shortcomings of the visible camera.

Even with these drawbacks of VS-based pedestrian detection, the majority of the research that has been undertaken has been based in the visible spectrum. This is due in part that the large datasets available are based on the visible spectrum [1]. These datasets are required for training DNNs to detecting desired objects.

4.2 Thermal Infrared Sensors

The spectral band of the TIR does not require an external light source, allowing it to overcome the shortcomings of the VS sensor. The far infrared (FIR) is the typical TIR sensor that is used for pedestrian detection [2]. The emitted radiation of human peaks in the FIR spectrum, making it an ideal TIR for pedestrian detection [40]. The images produced with FIR sensors are unaffected by variation in illumination. However, the performance of the thermal camera is affected by the high temperature [19]. For example, it is more difficult to detect a pedestrian or cyclist during hot days, as the background temperatures affect its resolution. Pedestrians and cyclists may also appear brighter or darker, depending on the outdoor temperatures [15]. It should be noted that FIR images include only one channel of information, which is intensity. This means that the images do not possess the same level of information provided though VS sensor cameras.

Thermal cameras have been successfully implemented for pedestrian detection [12,20,26,27] with various detection methods such as HOG [5,20,23,26]; shape and appearance-based detection [6] and contour saliency map (CSM) [8].

Visual and thermal data have been shown to be complementary [24], resulting in improved performance of the detection system in terms of accuracy and working conditions (i.e. different times of the day and under various weather conditions). To achieve an effective system, exploration of the ideal sensor fusion techniques is required.

4.3 Dual Sensor System

Combing two sensors could provide improved results whilst overcoming their individual drawbacks. With the effectiveness of TIR cameras for low-light conditions (i.e. night-time, evening) and the high level information provided by the visible cameras for well-illuminated environments.

A visible and thermal camera were combined for human tracking in an indoor environment [17]. The experiments, however, does not demonstrate the effects of outdoor influences, such as uneven lighting and shadowing. Night time pedestrian by combining visible and thermal cameras was demonstrated in [38]. This study, however, does not demonstrate the effects of high day temperatures on the thermal camera. A dual camera based on visible and thermal cameras for pedestrian detection that can function under various environmental conditions and during all times of the day was demonstrated in [19].

5 Sensor Fusion

Development of sensor fusion techniques for automotive purposes has been on the rise in recent years. This is because these techniques have been able to provide a higher level of accuracy in detection [35]. Multispectral pedestrian and cyclist detection can be one of three categories: pixel-level (Early Fusion) (see Fig. 1(a)), feature-level (Halfway-Fusion) or decision-level (Late Fusion) (Fig. 1(b)). Halfway Fusion is achieved by fusing the information after Early Fusion stage but before the Late Fusion stage. The categories are abstraction levels based on the layers of the DNN (typically a CNN-based approach) [33].

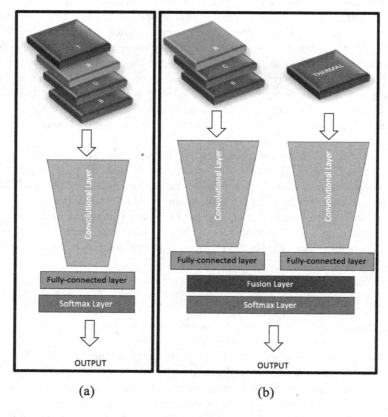

(a)　　　　　　　　　　　(b)

Fig. 1. Sensor fusion using DNNs (a) early fusion (b) late fusion

Large amounts of labelled data is required for training of DNNs, which has been limited due to the costs associated with generating these large datasets. Therefore, pre-training using a large auxiliary dataset (such as ImageNet) has become rather popular [33]. This is because there is limited combined visible and thermal image datasets. Therefore, existing visible data was used for pre-training of the DNNs. In [2], the fusion techniques (with and without pre-training) is compared with ACF+T+THOG technique, a state-of-the-art solution for use of multispectral (visible and thermal) data [16] as a baseline. The LateFusion+PreTraining approach has shown to outperform the ACF+T+THOG baseline as well as the other fusion methods [33], see Fig. 2. LateFusion+PreTraining improved by approximately 6% and approximately 10% when compared to the baseline. Further, it illustrates that pre-training results in higher performance. It was also observed that the Early Fusion architecture was unable to improve on the baseline. It was speculated that it could be due to limited data in the KAIST dataset for the Early Fusion architecture without pre-training [33]. Overall, this means that Early Fusion approaches may not have learned meaningful features.

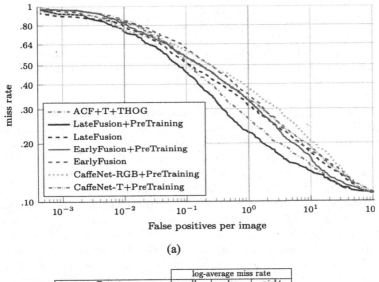

(a)

Detector	log-average miss rate		
	all	day	night
ACF+T+THOG	50.48 %	51.27 %	47.40 %
LateFusion+PreTraining	**43.80 %**	**46.15 %**	**37.00 %**
LateFusion	51.30 %	55.27 %	41.58 %
EarlyFusion+PreTraining	53.94 %	50.90 %	51.76 %
EarlyFusion	57.96 %	58.22 %	57.78 %
CaffeNet-RGB+PreTraining	56.52 %	53.51 %	63.40 %
CaffeNet-T+PreTraining	54.67 %	59.77 %	42.09 %

(b)

Fig. 2. Performance comparison of fusion techniques with ACF+T+THOG as a baseline and log-average miss rate during various times of the day (a) miss rate (b) log-average miss rate [33]

According to [24], the detector using fused data typically has enhanced performance when compared to a detectors based single sensor data. The single sensor approach, for example, vision sensors, may perform well during certain hours of the day, but that performance decreases as illumination decreases towards the evening and night-time. This is the case with some of the single sensor approaches in Fig. 3. (e.g. FasterRCNN-C and FasterRCNN-T).

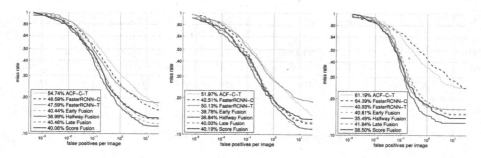

Fig. 3. Detection results (MR/false positives per image) comparison with average of daytime and night-time (left), daytime (middle) and night-time (right) [24]

For the fusion models, a CNN-based was implemented for comparison of the performance of fused data and single data approaches (see Fig. 3). Four sensor fusion techniques were employed, Early Fusion, Late Fusion, Halfway Fusion and Score Fusion, in which Halfway fusion was the most effective technique. It had the lowest miss-rate (MR) (37%), 3.5% lower when compared with the other fusion methods. It is speculated that the Halfway Fusion technique was most effective as the various levels of the DNN is able to extract the most useful information from both VS and TIR data without reducing the high quality from the VS data [24]. This is not the case with Early Fusion (pixel-level), where low-level features are fused, features that may be irrelevant. Late Fusion and Score fusion meanwhile fuses only high-level features and confidence scores, respectively. This could make it difficult for the model to eliminate noise created during the fusion.

Overall the Halfway fusion outperformed the single sensor approaches, reducing the overall MR by approximately 11%. The approach is also more effective in low-light conditions and created fewer false alarms [24]. The experiment used the KAIST for evaluation, a dataset for pedestrian detection consisting of both visible and thermal spectra.

The study in [36], proposes the use of two DNNs for pedestrian detection based on visual and thermal data, the Cross-Modality Transfer CNN (CMT-CNN). The first DNN is used to learn the relationship between the RGB and thermal images. These learned relationships are then transferred to a second DNN for detection using RGB images only. This novel approach means that thermal data is not required for detection and is suitable for various illumination conditions. This method was compared to state-of-the-art pedestrian detection techniques on both the KAIST and the Caltech datasets.

As seen in Fig. 4, the CMT-CNN architecture's performance is better than that of the best baseline (ACF-RGBT+HOG) for the KAIST dataset by approximately 5%. It should be noted that the CMT-CNN architecture only requires the RGB images, whereas the ACF-RGBT+HOG uses both RGB and thermal images. The approach also demonstrates that the approach would be very effective under low-light conditions.

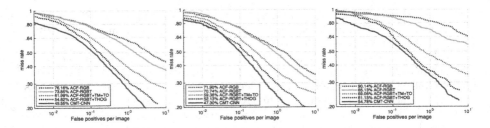

Fig. 4. Detection results (MR/false positives per image) comparison with average of daytime and night-time (left), daytime (middle) and night-time (right) [36]

6   Conclusions

Although there has been an significant increase in research conducted for pedestrian detection using multispectral data, there is an considerable lack of work undertaken for cyclist detection using multispectral data. Sensor fusion is a challenge that has yet to be overcome for both pedestrian and cyclist detection. Therefore, future works should focus on sensor fusion for concurrent pedestrian and cyclist detection based on DNNs.

Majority of the research discussed in this paper found that the Halfway fusion technique provided the most effective empirical results when compared to a baseline detector. A state-of-the-art solution, ACF+T+THOG, has been used as a baseline to measure the performance of the sensor fusion techniques employed.

The Faster R-CNN seems to be used for pedestrian/cyclist detection due to its speed and reliability. Therefore, it would sensible to use this architecture to evaluating sensor fusion techniques for pedestrian and cyclist detection. The KAIST dataset was utilised as it encompasses a large number of colour and thermal images in varying times throughout the day. It was also shown that an approach of pre-training a late fusion model can significantly outperform the baseline. However, early fusion fails in producing comparable results with the baseline. A reason for this failure could be that the approach could not learn significant abstract features from the multispectral data.

References

1. Angelova, A., Krizhevsky, A., Vanhoucke, V., Ogale, A., Ferguson, D.: Real-time pedestrian detection with deep network cascades. In: Proceedings of the British Machine Vision Conference, pp. 1–12 (2015). https://doi.org/10.5244/C.29.32
2. Baek, J., Hong, S., Kim, J., Kim, E.: Efficient pedestrian detection at nighttime using a thermal camera. Sens. (Switz.) **17**(8), 1850 (2017). https://doi.org/10.3390/s17081850
3. Bertozzi, M., Broggi, A., Caraffi, C., Del Rose, M., Felisa, M., Vezzoni, G.: Pedestrian detection by means of far-infrared stereo vision. Comput. Vis. Image Underst. **106**(2–3), 194–204 (2007). https://doi.org/10.1016/j.cviu.2006.07.016

4. Biswas, S.K., Milanfar, P.: Linear support tensor machine with LSK channels: pedestrian detection in thermal infrared images. IEEE Trans. Image Proc. **26**(9), 4229–4242 (2017). https://doi.org/10.1109/TIP.2017.2705426

5. Chang, S.L., Yang, F.T., Wu, W.P., Cho, Y.A., Chen, S.W.: Nighttime pedestrian detection using thermal imaging based on HOG feature. In: Proceedings 2011 International Conference on System Science and Engineering, pp. 694–698. IEEE (2011). https://doi.org/10.1109/ICSSE.2011.5961992

6. Dai, C., Zheng, Y., Li, X.: Layered representation for pedestrian detection and tracking in infrared imagery. In: 2005 IEEE Computer Society Conference on Computer Vision and Pattern Recognition (CVPR 2005) - Workshops. vol. 3, pp. 13–13. IEEE (2005). https://doi.org/10.1109/CVPR.2005.483

7. Dalal, N., Triggs, B.: Histograms of oriented gradients for human detection. In: 2005 IEEE Computer Society Conference on Computer Vision and Pattern Recognition (CVPR 2005), vol. 1, pp. 886–893. IEEE (2005). https://doi.org/10.1109/CVPR.2005.177

8. Davis, J., Sharma, V.: Robust detection of people in thermal imagery. In: 2004 Proceedings of the 17th International Conference on Pattern Recognition, ICPR, pp. 713–716. IEEE (2004). https://doi.org/10.1109/ICPR.2004.1333872

9. European Road Safety Observatory: Traffic Safety Basic Facts 2012. Technical report, European Road Safety Observatory (2012)

10. Gandhi, T., Trivedi, M.M.: Pedestrian protection systems: issues, survey, and challenges. IEEE Trans. Intell. Transp. Syst. **8**(3), 413–430 (2007). https://doi.org/10.1109/TITS.2007.903444

11. Gerónimo, D., López, A.M., Sappa, A.D., Graf, T.: Survey of pedestrian detection for advanced driver assistance systems. IEEE Trans. Pattern Anal. Mach. Intell. **32**(7), 1239–1258 (2010). https://doi.org/10.1109/TPAMI.2009.122

12. Gilmore, E.T., Frazier, P.D, Chouikha, M.F.: Improved human detection using image fusion. In: Proceedings of the IEEE ICRA (2009)

13. Girshick, R., Donahue, J., Darrell, T., Malik, J.: Rich feature hierarchies for accurate object detection and semantic segmentation. In: IEEE Conference on Computer Vision and Pattern Recognition (CVPR), pp. 580–587 (2014)

14. González, A., et al.: Pedestrian detection at day/night time with visible and FIR cameras: a comparison. Sens. (Switz.) **16**(6), 1–11 (2016). https://doi.org/10.3390/s16060820

15. Hurney, P., Jones, E., Waldron, P., Glavin, M., Morgan, F.: Night-time pedestrian classification with histograms of oriented gradients-local binary patterns vectors. IET Intell. Transp. Syst. **9**(1), 75–85 (2015). https://doi.org/10.1049/iet-its.2013.0163

16. Hwang, S., Park, J., Kim, N., Choi, Y., So, I.: Multispectral pedestrian detection: benchmark dataset and baseline. In: Proceedings of the IEEE Computer Society Conference on Computer Vision and Pattern Recognition, pp. 1037–1045 (2015)

17. Zhao, J., Cheung, S.C.S.: Human segmentation by fusing visible-light and thermal imaginary. In: 2009 IEEE 12th International Conference on Computer Vision Workshops, ICCV Workshops, pp. 1185–1192. IEEE (2009). https://doi.org/10.1109/ICCVW.2009.5457476, http://ieeexplore.ieee.org/document/5457476/

18. Kocic, J., Jovicic, N., Drndarevic, V.: Sensors and sensor fusion in autonomous vehicles. In: 2018 26th Telecommunications Forum (TELFOR), pp. 420–425. IEEE (2018). https://doi.org/10.1109/TELFOR.2018.8612054, https://ieeexplore.ieee.org/document/8612054/

19. Lee, J.H., et al.: Robust pedestrian detection by combining visible and thermal infrared cameras. Sens. (Switz.) **15**(5), 10580–10615 (2015). https://doi.org/10.3390/s150510580
20. Li, W., Zheng, D., Zhao, T., Yang, M.: An effective approach to pedestrian detection in thermal imagery. In: 2012 8th International Conference on Natural Computation, pp. 325–329. IEEE (2012). https://doi.org/10.1109/ICNC.2012.6234621
21. Li, X., et al.: A new benchmark for vision-based cyclist detection. In: Proceedings of IEEE Intelligent Vehicles Symposium, pp. 1028–1033 (2016)
22. Li, X., et al.: A unified framework for concurrent pedestrian and cyclist detection. IEEE Trans. Intell. Transp. Syst. **18**(2), 269–281 (2017). https://doi.org/10.1109/TITS.2016.2567418
23. Li, Z., Zhang, J., Wu, Q., Geers, G.: Feature enhancement using gradient salience on thermal image. In: 2010 International Conference on Digital Image Computing: Techniques and Applications, pp. 556–562. IEEE (2010). https://doi.org/10.1109/DICTA.2010.99, http://ieeexplore.ieee.org/document/5692620/
24. Liu, J., Zhang, S., Wang, S., Metaxas, D.N.: Multispectral deep neural networks for pedestrian detection. In: British Machine Vision Conference, pp. 1–13 (2016)
25. Mikolajczyk, K., Schmid, C., Zisserman, A.: Human detection based on a probabilistic assembly of robust part detectors. In: Pajdla, T., Matas, J. (eds.) ECCV 2004. LNCS, vol. 3021, pp. 69–82. Springer, Heidelberg (2004). https://doi.org/10.1007/978-3-540-24670-1_6
26. Neagoe, V.E., Ciotec, A.D., Bărar, A.P.: A concurrent neural network approach to pedestrian detection in thermal imagery. In: 2012 9th International Conference on Communications (COMM), pp. 133–136 (2012). https://doi.org/10.1109/ICComm.2012.6262539
27. Olmeda, D., Armingol, J.M., de la Escalera, A.: Discrete features for rapid pedestrian detection in infrared images. In: 2012 IEEE/RSJ International Conference on Intelligent Robots and Systems, pp. 3067–3072. IEEE (2012). https://doi.org/10.1109/IROS.2012.6385928, http://ieeexplore.ieee.org/document/6385928/
28. O'Malley, R., Jones, E., Glavin, M.: Detection of pedestrians in far-infrared automotive night vision using region-growing and clothing distortion compensation. Infrared Phys. Technol. **53**(6), 439–449 (2010). https://doi.org/10.1016/J.INFRARED.2010.09.006
29. Tian, W., Lauer, M.: Fast and robust cyclist detection for monocular camera systems. In: International joint Conference on Computer Vision Imaging and Computer Graphics Theory and Applications (VISIGRAPP) (2015)
30. Tian, W., Lauer, M.: Detection and orientation estimation for cyclists by max pooled features. In: Proceedings of the 12th International Joint Conference on Computer Vision, Imaging and Computer Graphics Theory and Applications, SCITEPRESS - Science and Technology Publications, pp. 17–26 (2017). https://doi.org/10.5220/0006085500170026
31. Uijlings, J.R.R., van de Sande, K.E.A., Gevers, T., Smeulders, A.W.M.: Selective search for object recognition. Int. J. Comput. Vision **104**(2), 154–171 (2013). https://doi.org/10.1007/s11263-013-0620-5
32. Viola, P., Jones, M.J., Snow, D.: Detecting pedestrians using patterns of motion and appearance. In: Proceedings of the 9th IEEE International Conference on Computer Vision, vol. 1, no. 9, pp. 734–741 (2003). https://doi.org/10.1109/ICCV.2003.1238422
33. Wagner, J., Fischer, V., Herman, M.: Multispectral pedestrian detection using deep fusion convolutional neural networks. In: European Symposium on Artificial Neural Networks (2016)

34. World Health Organisation: Global Status Report on Road Safety 2015 - Summary (2015)
35. Wu, T.E., Tsai, C.C., Guo, J.I.: LiDAR/camera sensor fusion technology for pedestrian detection. In: 2017 Asia-Pacific Signal and Information Processing Association Annual Summit and Conference (APSIPA ASC), pp. 1675–1678. IEEE (2017). https://doi.org/10.1109/APSIPA.2017.8282301
36. Xu, D., Ouyang, W., Ricci, E., Wang, X., Sebe, N.: Learning cross-modal deep representations for robust pedestrian detection. In: 2017 IEEE Conference on Computer Vision and Pattern Recognition (CVPR), pp. 4236–4244. IEEE (2017). https://doi.org/10.1109/CVPR.2017.451, http://ieeexplore.ieee.org/document/8099934/
37. Xu, F., Liu, X., Fujimura, K.: Pedestrian detection and tracking with night vision. IEEE Trans. Intell. Transp. Syst. **6**(1), 63–71 (2005). https://doi.org/10.1109/TITS.2004.838222
38. Chen, Y., Han, C.: Night-time pedestrian detection by visual-infrared video fusion. In: 2008 7th World Congress on Intelligent Control and Automation, pp. 5079–5084. IEEE (2008). https://doi.org/10.1109/WCICA.2008.4593753
39. Zhang, S., Benenson, R., Omran, M., Hosang, J., Schiele, B.: How far are we from solving pedestrian detection?. In: IEEE Conference on Computer Vision and Pattern Recognition (CVPR), pp. 1259–1267 (2016). https://doi.org/10.1109/CVPR.2016.141
40. Zhao, X., He, Z., Zhang, S., Liang, D.: Robust pedestrian detection in thermal infrared imagery using a shape distribution histogram feature and modified sparse representation classification. Pattern Recogn. **48**(6), 1947–1960 (2015). https://doi.org/10.1016/J.PATCOG.2014.12.013

Robot Path Planning Using Imprecise and Sporadic Advisory Information from Humans

Gianni A. Di Caro$^{(\boxtimes)}$ and Eduardo Feo-Flushing

Carnegie Mellon University in Qatar, Doha, Qatar
{gdicaro,efeoflus}@andrew.cmu.edu

Abstract. In environments featuring hazards (e.g., debris, holes in the ground), robot navigation can be challenging. Robot's sensors alone might be not able to guarantee timely detection of the threats. In such situations, the presence of nearby humans can be exploited to support safe robot navigation. The human can proactively provide advisory information and issue warnings. Unfortunately, verbally expressed human's inputs are usually quite imprecise or ambiguous when referring to spatial elements. We consider how to model the inherently imprecise and sporadic "human sensor" by using the formalism of imprecise probabilities, and how to use the model to build maps fusing robot sensor data and human inputs. Map information is used for path planning, searching for paths that balance survivability and efficiency (e.g., time). In a number of simulation scenarios we study the effectiveness of our approach compared to standard ways to build the map and perform path planning.

Keywords: Survivable path planning · Imprecise probabilities · HRI

1 Introduction

For mobile ground robots, the navigation in *extremely cluttered, unknown, hazardous environments* can always be a challenge. In spite of recent advances in vision and range finding devices, the detection of elements such holes, stairs, puddles, fire, transparent windows and doors, electrified wires, can still be problematic. The problem is exacerbated in scenarios such as *post-disaster* ones, where the robot has to navigate in partially collapsed or semi-destroyed buildings areas, and environmental conditions are challenging.

An option to mitigate the risk of issues during navigation consists in *leveraging the presence of nearby human agents*. In fact, humans can exploit their cognitive and sensory abilities to easily spot threats, such as a puddle, that for the robot it might be difficult to detect timely and effectively. Here we are envisaging scenarios where autonomous robots and humans will team-up performing *collaborative missions*. Applications such as search and rescue and emergency-response, seem to be first candidates for featuring such mixed teams. In these

© Springer Nature Switzerland AG 2019
K. Althoefer et al. (Eds.): TAROS 2019, LNAI 11650, pp. 235–247, 2019.
https://doi.org/10.1007/978-3-030-25332-5_21

scenarios it can be assumed that human agents will often be in the *proximity of robots* during mission deployment. Therefore, he/she can *proactively* "help" by providing information useful for path planning and navigation. At the same time, in these life-critical scenarios, humans will mostly be busy with their tasks, such as it is reasonable to state that inputs can indeed only be *sporadic*.

To these facts, we need to add up that human inputs are expected to be expressed in a *conversational language*, which is *inherently imprecise* [11]. E.g., if the robot is moving towards a target position and a puddle is in between, a nearby human may issue a warning by saying something like: "Hey, watch out, there's a puddle ahead of you!". What precisely that "ahead" means in terms of range and bearing is unspecified, as well as how large or deep the puddle is. In general, we can't really expect information being delivered in a precise form.

In this work, we start from the above types of scenarios and assumptions to address the following problem: how imprecise and sporadic humans inputs about the *spatial presence of potential hazards* for an autonomous robot can be effectively modeled and exploited to build and maintain an environment map for *safe path planning*. Humans inputs are assumed to be expressed in a *colloquial language*. Moreover, we assume that hazards might be *hardly, or not at all detectable by the robot sensors alone*. This implies that human inputs might be *necessary* to *plan* and *navigate safely*, avoiding hazards. Addressing the described problem, raises a number of general scientific questions:

- How do we model the inherently sporadic and imprecise *human sensor*?
- How do we *fuse* robot's sensors and human sensor information?
- How do we include fused, imprecise information in a *map* for *planning*?
- How do we use the map for finding paths that are *survivable* with respects to the hazards in the environment, and are *efficient* with respect to some predefined performance metric (e.g., time)?

The **contributions** of this work precisely consist in trying to provide answers to these fundamental questions, and include: modeling sporadic, verbally expressed human inputs using the formalism of *imprecise probabilities* [2]; building and updating an *imprecise probability map* that integrates robot sensory data and human inputs; a Rapidly Exploring Random Trees (RRT) algorithm specifically designed for searching for *survivable paths* on an imprecise probability map. *Performance* of proposed solutions is studied in simulation using ROS/Gazebo and compared with standard approaches. The study shows the overall effectiveness and flexibility of integrating imprecise probabilities and probabilistic maps for *survivable and efficient path planning* based on sporadic human inputs.

2   Related Work

In human-robot interaction, when it comes to communicate and model *spatial information* (e.g., the presence of an obstacle), a bulk of research works have aimed to to find methods that provide to the robot spatial information which is as precise as possible. One way to obtain this is by *multi-modality*, such as in [10,17] where gestures and speech are combined. Here we restrict ourselves to the use of *verbally and colloquially expressed information*. The motivation is twofold: we want to rely on minimal assumptions, and at the same time we aim to address scenarios such as emergency-response where humans most often have their hands busy with their tasks and do not have time or training to provide "precise" information to a robotic agent.

Imprecision is inherently rooted in colloquial expressions. Hazard warning from a human is expected to come in the form of sentences such as: "Watch out, there is a hole in the ground!", or "Watch out for the hole in the ground, which is close, in front and to the left of you!". These sentences do not provide precise metric information about relative location, shape, and dimension of the hazard. This is common when using a natural language to describe *geometric and spatial relations*. An extensive body of research is precisely devoted to these aspects (e.g. [11]), especially in the context of GIS, both outdoor and indoor, and for interactive systems [12,15]. For instance, the first sentence above expresses a purely *topological relationship*, but doesn't provide neither directional nor geometric information. These are given in the second sentence, in the form of *projective relations*, which are however still insufficient to precisely plan a survivable and efficient path. In general, the availability of qualitative spatial relations [9] might not be sufficient for performance-efficient path planning, they need to be transformed into quantitative ones, e.g., through an iterative loop of inputs capable altogether of precisely describing the spatial scene [12]. In our settings, we assume that human inputs, in addition to be imprecise are also sporadic, such that a sequence of inputs, or even a dialogue, are not contemplated. This sets our problem scenario and approach at the edges of current methods.

Scenarios featuring *hazards*, explicitly ask for performing *survivable path planning*: finding and strategically selecting the path that (at least) guarantees robot survivability with high probability. An environment presenting hidden hazards for the robot can be seen as non-strategically *adversarial*. [1] provides a survey of *adversarial robotics*, and points out that the *uncertainty* has received relatively little attention so far. In this work we emphasize that the robot has to make path planning decisions mostly based on one-shot information from the human. The uncertainty associated to this information is inherently large because of the imprecision in colloquial language, and it is also hard to model, since different humans have a different perception of spatial measures. In [8] the problem of *Safe Navigation in Adversarial Environments* is formalized. A number of algorithms and theroretical results are presented based on a game-theoretic approach on a map graph. The authors assume that relevant information about the opponent/threat can be incrementally gained over time, otherwise a generic risk-aversion approach is adopted. In our work we assume that sufficient information about the threat won't be incrementally gathered, neither from the human nor from on-board sensors. Our challenge is precisely how to strategically model and use imprecise information to balance risk minimization and performance optimization. Other works focus on multi-robot scenarios across adversarial environments, such as [13], that however are different from our scenarios since they can leverage redundancy and parallelism.

Survivability (or *traversability*) planning has been extensively studied also in general graphs, such as in the Canadian traveler problem [6], stochastic shortest path [3], and robust path optimization [4]. However, we cannot reduce our scenarios to these problems as we don't have precise probabilities between nodes, nor do the techniques for many of these problems work well practically for large and dense graphs such as occupancy grids.

To model the *uncertainty* related to human's inputs, instead of using the "typical" Bayesian approach we rely on *imprecise probabilities* [2], that are in a sense more general and reduce the requirement for setting up a probabilistic model of human's imprecision. Up to our knowledge, imprecise probabilities have found limited application in robotics. Imprecise probability maps are referred to in [5], but are grid maps with a Beta distribution to model cell occupancies, which is different from our imprecise probability map representation based on upper and lower estimates of occupancy per cell. Furthermore, these maps were not used in path planning, but to find the minimum number of inspections to certain the existence of a target. Instead, imprecise probabilities have been extensively used to model sensory information in the absence of reliable models. It's common to "approximate" imprecise probabilities by using Bayes approaches with very flat priors such as Dirichlet priors [7], instead, we face directly the issues related to lack of models for the conditional probabilities of a "human sensor".

3   Problem Scenario: Description and Challenges

We consider a generic scenario where a mixed *human-robot multi-agent team* is deployed. Each agent is given a set of tasks to deal with, together with a map that provides some (incomplete) description of the environment (i.e., maps are only partially reliable). Robotic agents are autonomous mobile robots. We don't make any particular assumption on robot's capabilities. The main point be that while navigating in the environment robot's sensors alone might be insufficient to timely and precisely detect environmental elements that constitute a *hazard* to the robot. E.g., the described scenario well-fits a post-disaster rescue mission.

The given map provides some initial support but for searching and localization, and gets dynamically updated on the field through SLAM operations. In order to reach out assigned targets on the map, a robot performs *path planning* and *local navigation* in the *partially observable and partially known environment*. Given the presence of unknown hazards, the robot face the challenge to find navigation paths that are both *survivable* and *efficient*. The notion of path survivability serves to quantify the *risk* for the robot, by specifying the probability that a selected path will be safely navigable given robot's characteristics.

In this work we aim to set up a mixed initiative system that leverages the presence of nearby humans to provide to robots information that can *complement data from on-board sensors* and can eventually help to *avoid threats*. The challenges come from the fact that we assume that humans' inputs are *sporadic*, often *one-shot* information, and are given in a rather *colloquial*, inherently *imprecise* way. In other words, we regard the human as an *imprecise, expensive, external sensor that can be accessed in a very limited way*.

Our assumptions are quite restrictive and general at the same time, and set the need to perform a conversion of the sporadic human input into *quantitative data*. More precisely, we need to define the conversion into a model that specifies distances, shapes, and so on, with some uncertainty. One obvious way of proceeding would consists in the adoption of a *Bayesian approach*: make a model of the "human sensor", start with some prior map, revise it with human input based on the human sensor model, plan based on the updated map. This is one of the standard approaches in modern probabilistic robotics [18]. One difficulty in this respect lays in the *lack of a reliable model for the generic "human sensor"* to use in Bayes' update formula. Moreover, this way of proceeding works well when repeated updates are available, such that revised, more accurate posteriors can iteratively be computed. However, we are assuming sporadic inputs from the a quite imprecise human sensor. To face these issues, here we propose to use a model based on *imprecise probabilities*, which is discussed in the next section.

4   Map Representation Using Imprecise Probabilities

We consider maps in the form of *occupancy grids*. Bayesian methods have been widely employed to create and maintain maps as probabilistic occupancy grids based on inputs from "common" sensors (e.g., range finders). Updating the map involves updating the occupancy probability of a cell in the map given a new piece of evidence. Evidence is provided by a sensor with a known probability distribution model: $P(O|S) = \frac{P(S|O)P(O)}{P(S)}$ where the random variables O represents the probability that a specific cell in the occupancy grid features the presence of an obstacle or hazard, and S is the observed value returned by the sensor.

In order to perform the update and revise the posterior conditional probability, a *probabilistic model of the sensor and of the environment* is required. In the case of a *human sensor*, how do we model it? It becomes problematic: we need a probability distribution for the observation made by the human, and a probability distribution of the human observation given the occupancy value of the cell. How do we reliably build them for a single individual accounting for the inherent imprecision and vagueness of his/her expected inputs? We need to give a precise, quantitative meaning to statements such as "in front of you", "near you, to your left", "ahead of you", "a large puddle", that do not contain (and are not expected to contain) precise statements such as "there's a hole 3.22 m 23° east your current heading, and it's shaped as a circle of 0.8 m radius".

Moreover, how do we make a model that reliably *generalize to different people*? Do the above expressions acquire a different quantitative meaning depending on the person and perception of dangers, distances, orientations? Likely, we would need to empirically build/learn a model for each different human agents the robot could interact with. This is quite unpractical and very prone to errors.

In our scenario, the robot can't neither gather multiple data from the human (one-shot input in the limit), nor get very reliable information from its own sensor (at least about hazards). Under these assumptions, the lack of a reliable sensor model in Bayesian updating can have a significant impact on the reliability of the resulting map, and therefore on path planning. A wrong model would create an initial bias that would hardly be canceled out later on, which is instead the case when multiple consecutive data inputs are made available.

In order to deal with these issues, we propose the use of *imprecise probabilities* as a replacement of Bayesian modeling. We will still have to set up *some* approximate model for human's inputs, however the impact of our approximations are expected to be less critical than using a purely Bayesian approach. Imprecise probabilities allow us to model the inherent imprecise nature of the human input by not forcing us to assign a precise probability to an event, but rather define a *range*. In the crudest sense, imprecise probabilities, can be thought of as *interval probabilities* with an upper estimated probability and a lower estimated probability associated with each event [2]. A Bayesian probability value can be thought of as the most likely value for the probability of an event as shown by the distribution curve, while the imprecise probability is a uniformly distributed uncertainty between the lower and upper probability values. Imprecise probabilities also provide us a way to automatically capture the *confidence* in the probability of an event through the range in upper and lower probability, which is not possible with Bayesian probabilities. The closer the upper and lower probabilities are to each other the more the confidence in the probability.

Imprecise probabilities are a generalization of Bayesian probability, as they converge to Bayesian probability when the upper and lower probabilities are the same. The upper probability is considered to be an estimate of the *plausibility* of a certain event, where the lower probability is considered to be the *certainty* of an event [14]. Unlike with Bayesian probabilities, where we have one value for the probability of occupancy per cell, with imprecise probabilities we make use of *two separate occupancy maps* to represent imprecise probability occupancy grids: the *belief map*, with all the lower probabilities of the cell being occupied, and the *plausibility* map with the upper probabilities of the cell being occupied. To have a consistent view of the world, the maps are updated as new sensor readings and human information arrive, which is discussed in the next section.

5   Map Updating with On-Board Sensors and Human Inputs

In our problem scenario, the main task of the robot is to perform survivable path planning and navigation, given that the environment is partially observable, partially known, and may include hazards. At this aim, the robot needs to dynamically build and update a map representation of the surrounding environment. The robot starts with a environment map which is only partially filled. The on-board sensors are used to update this map, which is in the form of a *probabilistic occupancy grid*, as well as to localize, by doing SLAM (e.g., using common ROS packages). We refer to this environment map as the *sensor map* (SM). This is the map used by the *local planner* for navigation. If/when human inputs become available, the provided information is used to create/update the *human input map* (HIM), which is an *imprecise probability map* of the environment consisting of two maps, one of upper and one of lower probabilities. Following each human input, SM and HIM are *fused* to create an *imprecise probability map* (IPM), a rich representation including both on-board and human sensory information. The IPM is further converted to a *probabilistic occupancy map for planning* (POMP), which is passed to a planning algorithm, a modified RRT, to find the most survivable path towards an assigned target pose. In the following we explain how the HIM is constructed from human inputs, which is illustrated in Fig. 1. In the next section we detail how the two maps in the HIM are fused to obtain a single POMP environment map for survivable planning.

In our model, human inputs are provided to the robot by *speech*. We can use APIs of available speech recognition systems to convert the input from natural language to a *spatial specification data structure*. In practice, we have a simple parsing system that extracts the properties of an imprecisely described hazard or obstacle and assign them as fields of a custom data structure, that includes:

- *Object*: The type and size/shape of object (e.g., large hole).
- *Range*: Distance of obstacle/hazard from the robot (e.g., close, far).
- *Direction*: Direction in which the obstacle/hazard is located with respect to robot's current orientation (e.g., left, right).
- *Message*: Additional useful information (e.g., be careful!).

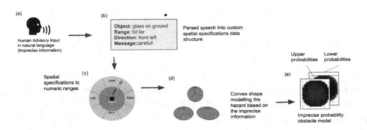

Fig. 1. Processing human inputs: (a) speech recognition, (b) parsing input to spatial specification structure, (c) quantifying imprecise inputs by given templates, (d) using convex shape to model hazard, (e) converting model to imprecise probabilities map

Spatial specifications need to be converted into numerical ranges before they can be used to update the imprecise probability maps. Conversions are performed by *template matching*. The first conversion regards the *direction* of the obstacle/hazard with respect to the robot. We have adopted a simple template with 8 slices (Fig. 1(c)). More slices can be used for increased precision, although more slices means more "priors", which is precisely what we want to avoid.

The conversion of the notion of *distance* is more problematic than that of direction, being more subjective. In an earlier contribution [16] an experimental study with 8 subjects was performed to analyze the variability of the estimated distance in relation to a moving robot. A positive correlation between the notion of "close" distance and the velocity of the robot was observed. As robot's velocity increases, the perception of a "close" distance seems to increase. Data collected during the experiment have been used to create a quantitative model for translating human's qualitative expressions of distances into numeric values.

Size and shape of the hazard are something that we cannot easily determine from the human input, especially if such information is not explicitly provided. Our approach is to model the hazard as a symmetrical shape, as our uncertainty about shape properties is high and no preferential direction of smaller uncertainty is given. Hence, we model the presence of the hazard with an *ellipsoid*, a shape that has convenient properties: it's parametric, convex, symmetric and stretchable along the two axes. The uncertainty model that we adopt has a confidence that decreases towards the edges of the hazard. To represent this, we use the lower hemisphere of the ellipsoid to model the upper probabilities and the upper hemisphere to model the lower probabilities (see Fig. 1(e)).

Once the human input has been quantified in the ellipsoid model, this is used to generate a new HIM. The SM is used by the localization algorithm to set robot's pose and where to "place" the ellipsoid in the HIM. In turn, the IPM gets updated as follows. For each environment cell, the upper probability value gets the max value between the current cell value in the SM and the corresponding cell value from the upper probability map of the HIM. The lower probabilities in the IPM are set as the min value between the cell value in SM and the corresponding cell value from the lower probability map of HIM. These updating criteria ensure consistency in the definition of imprecise probabilities and allow to consistently *fuse human and sensor inputs*.

6   Survivable Path Planning

The goal of the robot is to find the most survivable path(s) to navigate to an assigned pose. At this aim, two main steps need to be accomplished. First, create a *unified planning map*, the POMP map, from the IPM. Second, *find the most survivable paths* using the POMP. The creation of a single POMP map is motivated by the fact that doing path planning with two different sets of values (as in IPM) can quickly become cumbersome and would require a metric for survivability to be extracted from both the upper and lower probabilities of a cell, and combined somehow. Instead, having one single map representing the survivability metric for each cell makes computation faster and makes it easier to modify existing path planning algorithms to include the notion of survivability. For these reasons, we create the POMP map from the two imprecise probability maps in IPM by the following non-linear combination (for each cell in the map):

$$P = \underline{P}\Big(1 - (\overline{P} - \underline{P})\Big) \tag{1}$$

The formula defines the *survivability P of a cell* as the lower probability, which is the current belief, times the confidence in the probability values of the cell, which is given by the complement of the difference in probabilities between upper and lower probabilities. The planning map resulting from the imprecise probability map representation is published to the planner, that aims to find a path whose overall probability of crossing a hazard is acceptably low.

To find a path that is highly survivable in this respect, we modified a sampling based planning algorithm, the popular *Rapidly-exploring Random Tree* (RRT).

As preprocessing, we dilate the obstacles by the radius of the robot to define robot's configuration space. This ensures that we only sample points that the robot can safely be positioned at. Similarly, the *local planner* dilates obstacles to create a local cost map for navigation. In the RRT pseudo-code to the side, the *max risk* term denotes the max value of survivability that the planner is willing to sample before considering a cell unsurvivable. The tree T contains all the nodes that are sampled and have a survivable path to them from the current pose.

```
T.init()
currentRisk = min(Map)
While(PathNotFound):
    point = SampleMap(currentRisk, targetBias)
    If currentRisk >= maxRisk:
        break
    If point == None or iter >= maxIter:
        currentRisk += stepSize
        Iter = 0
    onTree = FindClosest(T, point)
    If Distance(point, onTree) > delta:
        point = PointInDirection(point)
    If !Collision(onTree, point):
        T.add(point, parent = onTree)
        If point == target:
            break
    Iter += 1
```

The current risk to start out is set to the lowest possible risk from the whole map. If we use up all the lowest risk cells, we will have to increase the risk by some predefined step value, until we either find a path to the target or we reach the max risk threshold. At each iteration, we first sample from the map by only looking at cells with a risk less than or equal the current risk, and use this as the random point for growing the tree. Every n samples, the random point equals the target cell, to encourage exploring towards the target. The closest node in the tree to the random point is found. If the random point is within an L2 metric distance `delta` and there's no obstacle in line of sight, the random point is added to T. If it is not a point `delta` away along the closest node, the random point vector is checked for collision with any obstacles between them, if not, it is added. Otherwise, we move onto the next iteration. If a max number of iterations is reached, the current risk level is increased, and new iterations start, so as to continue exploring the next most survivable cells.

Hence, by systematically sampling for the most survivable cells first, we can nearly guarantee (in probability) to find a path that is the most survivable. Yet, the risk level might be too high to use, which is in the end a *strategic decision*. In this case, the robot could be entitled to ask the human for *further input or better specifications*, that would help, for instance, to reduce the size of the ellipsoid modeling the hazard, or being more precise defining its eccentricity.

7   Implementation, Results, and Discussion

The described model and path planning algorithm have been implemented in ROS and evaluated in simulation using Gazebo. The Turtlebot 2, equipped with a depth camera, has been adopted as robot platform.

The implementation consists of two main components: (i) the imprecise 2D costmap IMP, which consists of two 2D costmaps – corresponding to the lower and upper probability maps – and combines the human input with the sensory data; (ii) the modified RRT planner, that uses the POMP probabilistic cost map derived from the IMP. Both components are integrated into move_base, the ROS package for mobile robots navigation. We configure move_base to use our RRT implementation as global planner, and the POMP map for global planning. Instead, the local planner uses a map equivalent to the SM one. The robot localizes itself with the depth sensor using the amcl localization driver.

The purpose of the simulation study is to evaluate *dependability* and *efficiency* of the proposed approach. The *key performance index* is quantified by the ability to find paths that guarantee robot *survivability* (facing the presence of hazards) and at the same time reach out a target pose in a *short time*.

At this aim, we have set up simulated worlds featuring relatively large obstacles randomly placed in an area of 15×15 m^2. In the *cluttered* reference scenario the density of obstacles is higher than in the *semi-cluttered* case. In both scenarios a large pile of debris is placed in the center of the world. The pile plays the role of the hazard that the robot can potentially fail to detect while moving.[1] To study path planning, four different start and end poses are defined, located at opposite corners. Each simulation begins with the robot in a start pose, and with the end pose at the opposite corner set as a navigation goal to move_base.

To assess dependability and efficiency of our approach, we have considered four different planning and navigation setups. The first three correspond to somehow *standard* approaches to the problem (including Bayesian updating), not using imprecise probabilities. The last one corresponds to our model. More specifically the setups are the following. (a) The pile of debris has been mapped and the robot uses the default move_base global planner (GlobalPlanner). (b) The pile of debris has not been mapped but, while navigating, the robot can detect it without external noise, and can update accordingly (in a Bayesian way) the local probabilistic occupancy map. (c) The pile of debris has not been mapped, frequent (0.5 Hz) but rather noisy sensory information is given to the robot, and the default move_base configuration is used with Bayesian updating (this may simulate repeated inputs from a human sensor). (d) The pile of debris has not been mapped, the robot is given one sporadic advisory information (representing the human input), and move_base is configured to use the imprecise probability framework and the RRT planner as global planner. Other navigation parameters are common to all four setups, and have been tuned accordingly.

In each simulation, the performance metric is the time it takes to arrive to the end pose. For each start and end pair, and setup, we performed 20 simulation runs to account stochasticity. Since setup (a) represents an ideal situation we use its average performance to benchmark the other setups. In the plots, setup (b) is indicated as *standard*, setup (c) as *noisy sensing*, and setup (d) as *imprecise*.

In Fig. 2 we report the observed navigation times (normalized to the ideal setup average). Results suggest that the imprecise probabilities framework achieves good performance relative to the other setups, being comparable in

---

[1] Since the pile can be actually sensed to some extent by the simulated depth sensor, we have added Gaussian white-noise for the sensor data corresponding to the pile. In this way we can simulate a situation of failure detection in the experiments.

median to the standard one and better than the noisy one. Moreover, it also lowers the variance of the navigation performance. The claim is that with sporadic inputs and imprecise probabilities modeling (supported by minimal prior models) a performance comparable if not better than methods requiring more data, and more accurate models can be achieved. Moreover, the imprecise framework can be successfully applied even when a hazard is not detectable at all by the robot, a situation that would see the other methods fail badly.

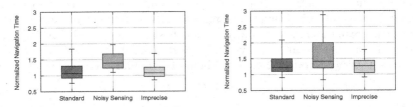

Fig. 2. Navigation results in semi-cluttered (left) and cluttered (right) environments

Figure 3 show the 2D density map of robot positions for all the simulation runs corresponding to the same setup. In these density maps we observe that the trajectories in the imprecise setup are more spread and, in general, longer with respect to other setups. Despite this apparent suboptimality, the imprecise probabilities framework allows to effectively tackle scenarios where the robot sensors would not be able to accurately spot the hazards while providing minimal performance degradation and variance reduction.

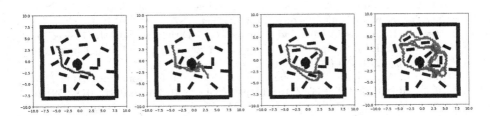

Fig. 3. Trajectories with baseline, standard, noisy, imprecise setups (from left to right)

8   Conclusions

Navigation in partly known environments featuring hazards hard to detect (e.g., post-disaster scenarios) is still a challenge for a mobile robot. We have considered how a robot can navigate avoiding hazards by exploiting inputs from a human agent. We have modeled the human as a sensor proactively providing sporadic (e.g., one-shot) and inherently imprecise information about spatial elements (e.g., hazards). To overcome difficulties adopting a Bayesian approach in this setting, we adopted the formalism of imprecise probabilities to model the human sensor and maintain an imprecise probability map where we fuse all available sensory information. The map provides the input to a modified version of the RRT planning algorithm, that finds paths that are at the same time survivable and efficient. The model and the algorithm have been implemented in ROS and studied in simulation using Gazebo considering cluttered environments featuring hazards hard to detect for the robot alone. The combination of human sensor and imprecise probabilities has shown the ability to robustly find survivable and efficient (short traveling time) paths. Our approach has also shown a systematically good performance compared to more "standard" approaches to the problem, using Bayesian updating, that however may need way more data inputs and may not be able to avoid the hazard when it is not detectable by on-board sensors (without the external help of a human).

References

1. Agmon, N.: Robotic strategic behavior in adversarial environments. In: Proceedings of IJCAI, pp. 5106–5110 (2017)
2. Augustin, T., Coolen, F.P., de Cooman, G., Troffaes, M.C.: Introduction to Imprecise Probabilities. John Wiley & Sons, Chichester (2014)
3. Bertsekas, D.P., Tsitsiklis, J.N.: An analysis of stochastic shortest path problems. Math. Oper. Res. **16**(3), 580–595 (1991)
4. Bertsimas, D., Sim, M.: Robust discrete optimization and network flows. Math. Program. **98**(1–3), 49–71 (2003). https://doi.org/10.1007/s10107-003-0396-4
5. Bertuccelli, L.F., How, J.: Robust UAV search for environments with imprecise probability maps. In: 44th IEEE Conference on Decision and Control & European Control Conference (CDC-ECC), pp. 5680–5685 (2005)
6. Fried, D., Shimony, S.E., Benbassat, A., Wenner, C.: Complexity of Canadian traveler problem variants. Theoret. Comput. Sci. **487**, 1–16 (2013)
7. Hutter, M.: Robust estimators under the imprecise Dirichlet model. In: Proceedings of 3nd International Symposium on Imprecise Probabilities and their Applications (ISIPTA), pp. 274–289 (2003)
8. Keidar, O., Agmon, N.: Safe navigation in adversarial environments. Ann. Math. Artif. Intell. **83**(2), 121–164 (2018). https://doi.org/10.1007/s10472-018-9591-0
9. Kordjamshidi, P., Hois, J., van Otterlo, M., Moens, M.F.: Learning to interpret spatial natural language in terms of qualitative spatial relations. In: Wiener, J.M., Tenbrink, T. (eds.) Representing Space in Cognition, pp. 115–146. Oxford University Press, New York (2013)
10. Lei, Z., Gan, Z.H., Jiang, M., Dong, K.: Artificial robot navigation based on gesture and speech recognition. In: IEEE SPAC, pp. 323–327 (2014)
11. Levinson, S.C.: Space in Language and Cognition: Explorations in Cognitive Diversity. Cambridge University Press, New York (2003)
12. Levit, M., Roy, D.: Interpretation of spatial language in a map navigation task. IEEE Trans. Sys. Man Cybern. Part B Cybern. **37**(3), 667–679 (2007)
13. Lyu, Y.H.: Implications of motion planning: optimality and k-survivability. Ph.D. thesis, Dartmouth College, Department of Computer Science (2016)
14. Miranda, E.: A survey of the theory of coherent lower previsions. Int. J. Approximate Reasoning **48**(2), 628–658 (2008)

15. Moratz, R., Tenbrink, T.: Spatial reference in linguistic human-robot interaction: iterative, empirically supported development of a model of projective relations. Spat. Cogn. Comput. **6**(1), 63–107 (2006)
16. Pillai, R.: A mixed initiative system for survivable path planning in unknown cluttered environments. Senior Thesis, Computer Science, CMU in Qatar (2018)
17. Skubic, M., et al.: Spatial language for human-robot dialogs. IEEE Trans. Syst. Man Cybern., Part C Appl. Rev. **34**(2), 154–167 (2004)
18. Thrun, S., Burgard, W., Fox, D.: Probabilistic Robotics. MIT Press, Cambridge (2005)

Collision-Free Optimal Trajectory
for a Controlled Floating Space Robot

Asma Seddaoui$^{(\boxtimes)}$ ⓘ and Chakravarthini M. Saaj ⓘ

University of Surrey, Guildford GU2 7XH, UK
{a.seddaoui,c.saaj}@surrey.ac.uk

Abstract. Space robots are key to the establishment of a new era of low-cost in-orbit operations. Given the complexities involved in designing and operating of a space robot, several challenges arise and developing new advanced methodologies for control and motion planning is essential. Finding an optimal trajectory for the space robot to attain an out-of-reach grasping point on the target or when the motion of the arm is restricted by singular configurations or obstacles, is a difficult task using the Degrees of Freedom (DoF) of the arm only. Hence, using the redundancy offered by the extra degrees of freedom of the spacecraft base to help the arm reach the target whilst avoiding singularities and obstacles is mission critical. In this paper, an optimal path planning algorithm using Genetic Algorithm was developed for a controlled-floating space robot that takes advantage of the controlled motion of the spacecraft base to safely reach the grasping point. This algorithm minimises several cost functions whilst satisfying constraints on the velocity. Moreover, the algorithm requires only the Cartesian location of the grasping point, to generate a path for the space robot without *a priori* knowledge of any desired path. The optimal trajectory is tracked using a nonlinear adaptive H_∞ controller for the simultaneous motion of both the manipulator and the base spacecraft. The results presented prove the efficacy of the path planner and controller and it is based on a six DoF manipulator mounted to a a six DoF spacecraft base.

Keywords: Optimal trajectory · Singularity avoidance ·
Nonlinear control · Controlled-floating space robot · Genetic Algorithm

1 Introduction

Traditionally, an orbital space robot consists of one or more robotic arms, with multiple Degrees of Freedom (DoF), mounted on a spacecraft. Such robotic manipulators can be an integral part of the International Space Station (ISS), which is a large spacecraft or they can be mounted on a smaller-sized spacecraft. The latter category has the capability to be used for a multitude of orbital missions such as the assembly of large modular telescopes [1] or the maintenance and refuelling of satellites [2]. These manipulators are known to have a large

© Springer Nature Switzerland AG 2019
K. Althoefer et al. (Eds.): TAROS 2019, LNAI 11650, pp. 248–260, 2019.
https://doi.org/10.1007/978-3-030-25332-5_22

dynamic coupling due to the smaller size of their spacecraft base compared to ISS, which makes their modelling, design and operation highly complex.

Whether the space robot is part of a large spacecraft like ISS or mounted on a small-sized platform, planning its motion is vital. Path planning for small-sized space robots is very intricate as it highly considers the impact of the dynamic coupling on the position of the end-effector. These space robots can be free-floating or free-flying [3]. Free-floating space robots have an uncontrolled base during the motion of the arm, which creates an issue with the uncontrolled unde-sired changes in the pose of the spacecraft base. Free-flying space robots have an active control for their base to cancel out the effect of the dynamic coupling and maintain a desired pose. Space robots can also be operated in the controlled-floating mode where they are referred to as Controlled Floating Space Robots (CFSRs) [4]. This mode dovetails the merits of free-flying and free-floating modes by using the extra DoFs offered by the spacecraft base to optimally reach the target whilst avoiding singularities and obstacles. Several techniques have been developed by researchers that result in minimum dynamic coupling effect and hence, minimum undesired changes in the pose of the spacecraft base, such as the Enhanced Disturbance Map (EDM) [5], Reaction Null Space (RNS) [6,7] and optimal planning [8]. Although the base of the free-flying and controlled-floating space robots actively compensates for the effect of the dynamic coupling, minimising this effect is still necessary in order to save on-board fuel as it is con-sidered a scarce resource.

When planning a path for the space robot, singularities can occur which can alter the motion of the robotic arm. Singularities in space robots are of two types: kinematic and dynamic singularities. Kinematic singularities, similar to those affecting fixed-base manipulators, are related to the geometry of the space robot. Dynamic singularities, on the other hand, are common to free-floating systems and restrain the end-effector from reaching some inertial direction [9]. In addition to singularities, the risk of collision increases drastically when obsta-cles are present in the workspace of the space robot. Avoiding these obstacles is essential for a successful and safe capture of the target. Although new method-ologies have been developed to avoid singularities and obstacles [10], research in this matter remains limited as space robots pose new challenges compared to their terrestrial counterparts.

2   Optimal Path Planning

Amongst the various techniques developed to plan the motion of a space robot, optimal path planning has gained a great deal of attention from researchers. It is based on the minimisation of one or several cost functions whilst satisfying one or several constraints. Optimal path planning for space robots often finds solutions to the optimization problem at the velocity level using the following kinematic equation [11]:

$$\begin{bmatrix} \dot{r}_e & \omega_e \end{bmatrix}' = \mathbf{J}(q)\dot{q}, \tag{1}$$

where $\dot{r}_e \in \mathbb{R}^3$ and $\omega_e \in \mathbb{R}^3$ are vectors representing the end-effector's linear and angular velocities in the Cartesian space, $\mathbf{J} \in \mathbb{R}^{6 \times N}$ is the Jacobian matrix of the system, where $N = 6+n$ represents the total DoF of a space robot consisting of an n DoF arm and 6 DoF base spacecraft and q is the vector representing the position and attitude of the spacecraft base and the joints of the arm.

For designing the motion of free-floating space robots, the main issue is the effect of the dynamic coupling on the position of the end-effector. This is due to the fact that the spacecraft base is uncontrolled. Several studies have used the Particle Swarm Optimization (PSO), in its one-objective and multi-objective forms, to minimise the effect of the dynamic coupling [12–17]. Others have utilised the Genetic Algorithm (GA) [18,19] and Differential Evolution [20] to find an optimal trajectory for a free-floating space robot. In the case of free-flying space robots, motion planning is easier as the spacecraft base is controlled to maintain one desired pose or controlled to track a desired final pose. However, finding an optimal trajectory for this category of space robots is still crucial to save fuel. Researchers have developed novel path planning algorithms using Sequential Quadratic Programming (SQR) [21], convex programming [22,23] and neural networks [24] for the motion of free-flying space robots.

All the aforementioned optimization techniques for both free-floating and free-flying space robots have either a predefined desired end-effector path or a predefined final joints angles set. In both cases the optimization algorithm has an *a priori* knowledge of a desired trajectory. Moreover, an issue arises when considering the predefined path itself i.e. the chosen path may not be an optimal one and several potentially optimal paths might exist.

3   Contribution

This paper presents a novel optimal collision-free and singularity-free trajectory planning algorithm for a CFSR. This new motion generator requires the Cartesian location of the grasping point as the only input, without *a priori* knowledge of any joint trajectory, end-effector path or desired final pose for the spacecraft base. It is based on a GA [25] that performs a constrained multi-objective optimization to find the best end-effector path. This is executed through finding optimal trajectories for the arm's joints as well as the desired position and attitude for the base spacecraft.

The singularities that can affect this system are kinematic singularities as the spacecraft base is controlled and the Jacobian matrix does not depend on the inertia parameters of the CFSR. Its motion is described with respect to the frame attached to the centre of the target for precise relative motion. Furthermore, a nonlinear adaptive H_∞ controller is utilized to track the generated trajectories in the presence of internal parametric uncertainties and external disturbances [26].

The optimization is performed at the velocity level using $\dot{q} = [\dot{r}_T \; \omega_{sc} \; \dot{\theta}]'$ as an optimization variable, with $\dot{r}_T$ and ω are vectors representing the linear and angular velocities of the spacecraft base in the target frame and $\dot{\theta}$ is the vector of joint velocities of the arm.

4 Path Optimization Using Genetic Algorithm

Designing an optimal path for the end-effector requires finding optimal trajectories for the arm as well as the spacecraft base through minimising multiple functions whilst satisfying several constraints. This is known as a constrained multi-objective optimization. This paper uses the widely-known multi-objective optimization techniques that considers constraints handling using the Genetic Algorithm and more specifically, the Non-Sorting Genetic Algorithm II (NSGAII) [25]. The optimization variable is the velocity vector at time $(t + 1)$ as the algorithm finds the next step for different configuration trajectories i.e. trajectories for the arm and the spacecraft base.

4.1 The Cost Functions

The first function is the main function that determines the Cartesian path of the end-effector and is defined as the distance between the desired final point (grasping point) r_{ef} and the next Cartesian step traveled by the end-effector $r_e(t + 1)$. The desired final point r_{ef} is the only known input for the algorithm.

The second function is the energy consumed during the motion of the arm. It is minimised to reduce the motion of the arm and hence reduce the effect of the dynamic coupling on the spacecraft base.

The third function is related to the singularity avoidance during the motion of the arm. As the configuration trajectories are found without using the inverse of the Jacobian matrix, it is not necessary to perform a classical singularity avoidance, where the Jacobian matrix is non-invertible. At the same time, the manipulability of the redundant CFSR, used in this paper, has to be maximised [27]. This is to prevent the space robot from reaching singular configurations when considering the n DoF of the arm along with the extra degree of redundancy offered by the rotation of the spacecraft base. Hence, the inverse of the manipulability M is selected as one of the cost functions in order to maximise M whilst minimising its inverse. The manipulability is calculated using the rotational part of the Jacobian $\mathbf{J_{rot}}(\boldsymbol{\phi}, \boldsymbol{\theta})$ including the arm's joints and the spacecraft base attitude.

The fourth function maintains the motion of the space robot within actuators' limits. Given the vector q_{max} representing the maximum values of r_T, $\boldsymbol{\phi}$ and $\boldsymbol{\theta}$, the difference between $q(t + 1)$ and q_{max}, denoted q_m, is to be maximised to avoid reaching the imposed limits. Hence, minimising the inverse of q_m guarantees that the saturation limits of joints and the constraints on spacecraft position and attitude are not reached.

The fifth function is the norm of the vector representing the angular velocity of the spacecraft base and the joints' velocity of the arm. This is to minimize the motion involved in the maximization of the manipulability and when only the rotational motion is needed to reach the grasping point.

The sixth function represents the norm of the linear velocity of the spacecraft base in order to minimise its linear motion.

The seventh function is only active when an obstacle is detected. It represents the inverse of the distance d_{c_i} between the CoM of the links as well as the base of the space robot and the detected obstacle r_c. This is to maximize the distance d_{c_i} whilst minimizing its inverse.

The seven cost functions involved in the optimization are grouped as follows:

$$f_1 = \|r_{ef} - r_e(t+1)\|_2, \qquad \left[r_e(t+1) \; \phi_e(t+1)\right]' = \int_t^{t+1} \mathbf{J}(q)\dot{q}(t)dt$$

$$f_2 = \tfrac{1}{2}\dot{\theta}'(t+1)\mathbf{D_m}\dot{\theta}(t+1), \; \dot{\theta} \subset \dot{q}$$

$$f_3 = \frac{1}{1+M}, \qquad\qquad M = \sqrt{det(\mathbf{J_{rot}}.\mathbf{J'_{rot}})}$$

$$f_4 = \frac{1}{1+\|q_m\|_2}, \qquad\quad q_m = \int_t^{t+1}|\dot{q}(t)dt| - q_{max}$$

$$f_5 = \left\|[\dot{\phi}(t+1)\;\dot{\theta}(t+1)]'\right\|_2, \; \dot{\phi}, \dot{\theta} \subset \dot{q}$$

$$f_6 = \|\dot{r}_T(t+1)\|_2, \qquad \dot{r}_T \subset \dot{q}$$

$$f_7 = \frac{1}{\|[d_{c_0} \dots d_{c_n}]\|_2}, \qquad \begin{cases} d_{c_0} = \|r_T(t+1) - r_c\|_2 \\ d_{c_i} = \|r_i(t+1) - r_c\|_2 \end{cases}$$

4.2   The Optimization Constraints

Minimising the cost functions may be achieved using any value of the optimization variable $\dot{q}(t+1)$ within the imposed bounds. This minimises all cost functions but does not guarantee that the resulting trajectory fits the physical requirements of the space robot. Hence, there is a crucial need to constrain $\dot{q}(t+1)$ within well-defined regions in addition to the upper and lower bounds of the velocity. In this paper, the constraints change depending on the trajectory segment where the end-effector is at time $(t+1)$. There are three different segments: the obstacle-free trajectory segment, the collision avoidance trajectory segment and the safety (final) trajectory segment.

The Obstacle-Free Trajectory. This is the segment where the algorithm finds a solution for $\dot{q}(t+1)$ without avoiding obstacles as there are none detected. There are two constraints imposed in this segment.

The first constraint is related to the velocity vector i.e. the optimization variable vector $\dot{q}(t+1)$. In this paper, the algorithm doesn't have any knowledge of a predefined desired velocity. Hence, to avoid abrupt changes in the velocity, $\dot{q}(t+1)$ is constrained to be close to the current known velocities $\dot{q}(t) \pm e_v$ depending on the sign of $\dot{q}(t)$, with e_v being a vector of small positive scalars e_v.

The other constraint prevents the spacecraft base from colliding with the target, by imposing a constraint on r_T.

The Collision Avoidance Trajectory. This is the segment where the algorithm minimises all cost function $f_1 \to f_7$, whilst satisfying several constraints similar to the obstacle-free trajectory but also another constraint to avoid obstacles. This segment is only active when one or more links of the space robot enter the sphere surrounding the obstacle, with radius d_{sphere} referred to as *the warning zone*. Computing the distance between the links and an obstacle d_{c_i} is performed using the position of the links in the target frame. The position of each link is calculated by substituting the Jacobian matrices of the links in Eq. (1).

The constraint for obstacle avoidance is then defined as:

$$d_{c_i} - d_{critical} > 0, \text{ with } \left. \begin{array}{l} d_{c_i} = \|r_i(t+1) - r_c\|_2 \\ \left[r_i \ \phi_i\right]' = \int_t^{t+1} \mathbf{J}(q)\dot{q}(t)dt \end{array} \right\}, \qquad (2)$$

where $d_{critical}$ is the radius of the *keep-out zone* surrounding the obstacle that the space robot is not allowed to enter, with $d_{critical} < d_{sphere}$.

The Safety Trajectory. As both the end-effector's velocity and the configuration velocities are not pre-defined prior to the motion of the space robot, the algorithm does not have *a priori* information on the value of these velocities at each time step. Instead, the algorithm uses the previously introduced velocity constraint to avoid abrupt changes. This constraint is enough during the obstacle-free and the obstacle avoidance trajectory segments as the velocity can take any value as long as it does not change abruptly within the imposed bounds. However, when the end-effector reaches the close proximity of the grasping point, also known as the safety distance from the grasping point, the configuration velocities have to decrease until the end-effector comes to a stop at the grasping point. This means that the algorithm has to decrease the configuration velocities depending on the remaining distance between the end-effector and the grasping point.

In this paper, a decreasing function is introduced in the velocity constraint as follows:

$$f(s) = \frac{1}{1 + \nu s^2}, \text{ with } s = \frac{d_{safe} - d(t+1)}{d_{safe}}, \qquad (3)$$

where d_{safe} is the user-defined minimum safety distance between the end-effector and the grasping point and ν is a positive scalar that defines the final value of $f(s)$.

The constraint on the velocity during the safety trajectory segment is then defined as follows:

$$\dot{q}(t+1) = (q(t+1) - q(t)) f(s), \qquad (4)$$

where $\boldsymbol{f}(s) \in \mathbb{R}^N$ is a column vector with each row representing $f(s)$.

4.3   Shortcomings of the Equality Constraints

The constraints presented so far are of two natures: equality and inequality constraints. The equality constraints are known to be computationally heavy as the optimization algorithm fails to find solutions that satisfy these constraints.

Hence, a tolerance is added to the constraints to loosen the optimization process and find a solution within the imposed tolerance. This tolerance is added when the equality constraint is transformed into an inequality constraint as follows [28]:

$$f(x) = 0, \text{ becomes } |f(x)| - e \leq 0, \tag{5}$$

where e is the user-defined tolerance. In this paper, the constraint (4) is the only equality constraint presented. Transforming this constraint into inequality constraint using (5) gives:

$$|\dot{q}(t+1) - [(q(t+1) - q(t)) f(s)]| - e \leq 0, \tag{6}$$

with $e \in \mathbb{R}^N$ is a column vector with each row representing the tolerance e and $0 \in \mathbb{R}^N$.

4.4   The Resultant Trajectory Optimization Algorithm

The collision-free and singularity-free optimal trajectory generator using GA is described by the following algorithm:

$$
\begin{aligned}
&if \quad \text{obstacle-free segment} \\
&\qquad\qquad min \; f_i(\dot{q}), \quad i = 1, 2, ..., 6 \\
&\qquad\quad s.t \\
&\qquad\qquad \dot{q}_{min} \leq \dot{q} \leq \dot{q}_{max} \\
&\qquad\qquad |\dot{q}(t+1) - \dot{q}(t)| < e_v \\
&\qquad\qquad \|r_\tau - r_f\|_2 > d_{impact} \\
&elseif \text{ obstacle avoidance segment} \\
&\qquad\qquad min \; f_i(\dot{q}), \quad i = 1, 2, ..., 7 \\
&\qquad\quad s.t \\
&\qquad\qquad \dot{q}_{min} \leq \dot{q} \leq \dot{q}_{max} \\
&\qquad\qquad |\dot{q}(t+1) - \dot{q}(t)| < e_v \\
&\qquad\qquad \|r_\tau - r_f\|_2 > d_{impact} \\
&else \qquad\qquad \text{safety segment} \\
&\qquad\qquad min \; f_i(\dot{q}), \quad i = 1, 2, ..., 6 \\
&\qquad\quad s.t \\
&\qquad\qquad \dot{q}_{min} \leq \dot{q} \leq \dot{q}_{max} \\
&\qquad\qquad |\dot{q}(t+1) - [(q(t+1) - q(t)) f(s)]| - e \leq 0 \\
&\qquad\qquad \|r_\tau - r_f\|_2 > d_{impact}
\end{aligned}
$$

The constraints imposed on the configuration velocities of the CFSR result in a motion free from abrupt changes. Nevertheless, sometimes the GA does not find a solution within the constraints, which leads to undesired and small peaks in the velocity. In order to remediate to this issue, a smoothing function, using interpolation, was introduced in this paper to guarantee smoothness of motion.

5   Simulations and Results

Simulations were conducted in Matlab to compute the optimal trajectories for the arm and the base of the CFSR. The CFSR model used for simulations consists of a 6 DOF arm coupled with a 6 DOF spacecraft base. The base of the CFSR has a mass equal to 200 kg considering 40% of it is fuel. The mass of the links of the arm from first to last link are respectively: 7 kg, 5 kg, 4 kg, 2 kg, 1 kg. The initial spacecraft base position and attitude are respectively $r_r = [1.4\,m\ 0\,m\ -0.5\,m]$ and $\phi = [0°\ 0°\ 0°]$ and the initial joints positions are $\theta = [0°\ 0°\ 0°\ 0°\ 0°\ 0°]$. The grasping point is located at $r_{ef} = [0.5\ 0\ 0.5]$. Other parameters involved in the algorithm are: $d_{safe} = d_{sphere} = 0.2\,m$, $d_{critical} = 0.1\,m$ and $\nu = 20$. The generated trajectories for the CFSR are tracked using an adaptive H_∞ controller as shown in Fig. 1. The detailed design of the adaptive H_∞ controller for a CFSR can be found in [26].

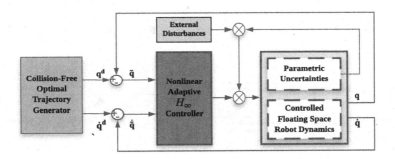

Fig. 1. Closed-loop architecture of the nonlinear adaptive H_∞ controller with the optimal trajectory generator

5.1   Motion of CFSR

Given the desired grasping point on the target, the trajectory planning algorithm presented in this paper results in smooth displacements of the arm's joints as well as the spacecraft base position and attitude. Figure 2 shows the desired and real trajectories of the arm. The desired trajectories are generated from the algorithm described in Sect. 4 and the real trajectories are a result of the closed-loop control for trajectory tracking using the nonlinear adaptive H_∞ controller. The corresponding torques that generate this arm motion are depicted in Fig. 3. The motion of the spacecraft base on the other hand is shown in Fig. 4 resulting from small applied forces and torques as shown in Fig. 5. The fluctuations exhibited by the applied forces and toques for both the arm and its base are a result of the disturbance rejection ensured by the nonlinear adaptive H_∞ controller.

The velocities of the arm's joints and the linear and angular velocities of the spacecraft base are shown in Figs. 6 and 7 respectively. It is clear from these results that the proposed optimal trajectory planning algorithm is capable of producing smooth velocities throughout the motion of the CFSR and decelerates until it comes to a stop when the grasping point is reached.

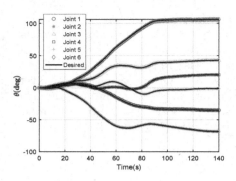

Fig. 2. Joint trajectories of arm

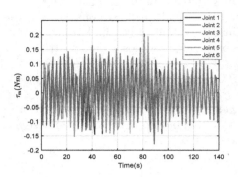

Fig. 3. Joint torques of arm

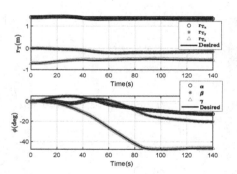

Fig. 4. Spacecraft position and attitude

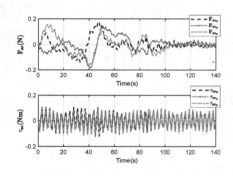

Fig. 5. Spacecraft forces and torques

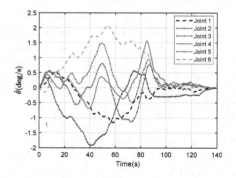

Fig. 6. Joint velocities of arm

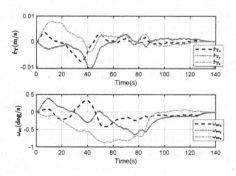

Fig. 7. Spacecraft velocities

5.2   Obstacle Avoidance

As stated in Sect. 4.2, there are two levels of avoidance of a potential obstacle. The first one is the detection of the *warning zone* defined by d_{sphere} and the second is the *keep-out zone* defined by $d_{critical}$. When the obstacle avoidance constrained optimization is active, if the links enter the *warning zone* then the algorithm drives them away to prevent collisions. This is depicted in Fig. 8. However, when the obstacle avoidance constrained optimization is not applied, the links reach the *keep-out zone* where collisions are highly likely to occur, as shown in Fig. 9.

This obstacle avoidance method can easily be applied to one or several fixed or moving obstacles as long as the relative velocity between the space robot and the obstacle is within the bounds imposed on the optimization variable.

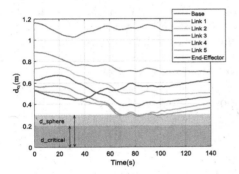

Fig. 8. Relative distance between the obstacle and the links of the CFSR including the spacecraft base with optimization

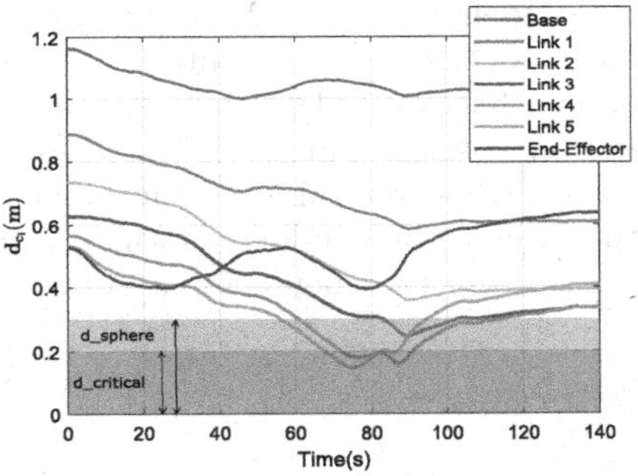

Fig. 9. Relative distance between the obstacle and the links of the CFSR including the spacecraft base without optimization

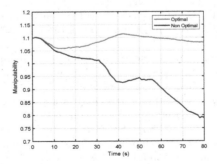

Fig. 10. Manipulability of the CFSR with and without optimization

5.3 Singularity Avoidance

The redundancy offered by the spacecraft base aids the arm to avoid singularities. As the cost function f_3 is minimised during the optimization, the manipulability is maximised to ensure that the arm is kept away from singular configurations. Figure 10 shows that when f_3 is optimized, the manipulability is higher when compared to the case where f_3 is not optimized. In the non-optimal case, the manipulability decreases and alarmingly reaches singular configurations.

6 Conclusion

This paper presents a novel collision-free and singularity-free optimal trajectory generator using a Genetic Algorithm for a space robot. The the only input is the Cartesian location of the grasping point on the target without knowledge of any predefined path whilst the space robot operates in the controlled-floating mode. As there is an infinite number of paths between the space robot and the target, this novel algorithm ensures that the chosen path is optimal. Although the collision avoidance was tested for one fixed obstacle, this algorithm can also be used when several fixed and moving obstacles are present. However, an extra study has to be conducted, when dealing with moving obstacles, regarding the relative velocity when compared to the imposed bounds of the CFSR velocities.

References

1. Eckersley, S., et al.: In-orbit assembly of large spacecraft using small spacecraft and innovative technologies. In: 69th International Astronautical Congress (IAC), Bremen, Germany, 1–5 October 2018
2. Henshaw, C.G.: The DARPA phoenix spacecraft servicing program: overview and plans for risk reduction. In: International Symposium on Artificial Intelligence, Robotics and Automation in Space (i-SAIRAS), Montreal, 17–19 June 2014
3. Flores-Abad, A., Ma, O., Pham, K., Ulrich, S.: A review of space robotics technologies for on-orbit servicing. Prog. Aerosp. Sci. 68, 1–26 (2014)
4. Seddaoui, A., Saaj, C.: Combined nonlinear H-infinity controller for a controlled-floating space robot. J. Guidance Dyn. Control (JGDC) 22, 1–8 (2019). https://doi.org/10.2514/1.G003811
5. Dubowsky, S., Torres, M.A.: Path planning for space manipulators to minimize spacecraft attitude disturbances. In: IEEE International Conference on Robotics and Automation, Sacramento, 9–11 April 1991
6. Piersigilli, P., Sharf, I., Misra, A.: Reactionless capture of a satellite by a two degree-of-freedom manipulator. Acta Astronaut. 66(1–2), 183–192 (2010)
7. Yoshida, K., Hashizume, K., Abiko, S.: Zero reaction maneuver: flight validation with ETS-VII space robot and extension to kinematically redundant arm. In: IEEE International Conference on Robotics and Automation, Seoul, South Korea, 21–26 May 2001
8. Rybus, T., Seweryn, K.: Manipulator trajectories during orbital servicing mission: numerical simulations and experiments on microgravity simulator. Prog. Flight Dyn. Guidance Navig. Control-Volume 10(10), 239–264 (2018)

9. Papadopoulos, E., Dubowsky, S.: Dynamic singularities in free-floating space manipulators. J. Dyn. Syst. Measur. Control **115**(1), 44–52 (1993)
10. Rybus, T.: Obstacle avoidance in space robotics: review of major challenges and proposed solutions. Prog. Aerosp. Sci. **101**, 31–48 (2018)
11. Seddaoui, A., Saaj, C.: H-infinity control for a controlled floating robotic spacecraft. In: International Symposium on Artificial Intelligence, Robotics and Automation in Space (i-SAIRAS), Madrid, Spain, 4–6 June 2018
12. Wei, X.-P., Zhang, J.-X., Zhou, D.-S., Zhang, Q.: Optimal path planning for minimizing base disturbance of space robot. Int. J. Adv. Robot. Syst. **13**(2), 41 (2016)
13. Wang, M., Luo, J., Walter, U.: Trajectory planning of free-floating space robot using particle swarm optimization (PSO). Acta Astronaut. **112**, 77–88 (2015)
14. Wang, M., Luo, J., Yuan, J., Walter, U.: Coordinated trajectory planning of dual-arm space robot using constrained particle swarm optimization. Acta Astronaut. **146**, 259–272 (2018)
15. Kaigom, E.G., Jung, T.J., Roßmann, J.: Optimal motion planning of a space robot with base disturbance minimization. In: 11th Symposium on Advanced Space Technologies in Robotics and Automation, Noordwijk, 12–14 April 2011
16. Zhang, L., Jia, Q., Chen, G., Sun, H.: Pre-impact trajectory planning for minimizing base attitude disturbance in space manipulator systems for a capture task. Chin. J. Aeronaut. **28**(4), 1199–1208 (2015)
17. Xu, W., Li, C., Liang, B., Liu, Y., Xu, Y.: The cartesian path planning of free-floating space robot using particle swarm optimization. Int. J. Adv. Robot. Syst. **5**(3), 27 (2008)
18. Huang, P., Chen, K., Xu, Y.: Optimal path planning for minimizing disturbance of space robot. In: 9th International Conference on Control, Automation, Robotics and Vision, Singapore, 5–8 December 2006
19. Chen, Z., Zhou, W.: Path planning for a space-based manipulator system based on quantum genetic algorithm. J. Robot. **2017**, 10 (2017)
20. Wang, M., Luo, J., Fang, J., Yuan, J.: Optimal trajectory planning of free-floating space manipulator using differential evolution algorithm. Adv. Space Res. **61**(6), 1525–1536 (2018)
21. Lampariello, R., Agrawal, S., Hirzinger, G.: Optimal motion planning for free-flying robots. In: IEEE International Conference on Robotics and Automation, Taipei, 14–19 September 2003
22. Misra, G., Bai, X.: Optimal path planning for free-flying space manipulators via sequential convex programming. J. Control Dyn. **40**(11), 3019–3026 (2017)
23. Virgili-Llop, J., Zagaris, C., Zappulla, R., Bradstreet, A., Romano, M.: Laboratory experiments on the capture of a tumbling object by a spacecraft-manipulator system using a convex-programming-based guidance. In: AAS/AIAA Astrodynamics Specialist Conference, Stevenson, 20–24 August 2017
24. Wilson, E., Rock, S.M.: Neural-network control of a free-flying space robot. Trans. Soc. Model. Simul. Int. **65**(2), 103–115 (1995)
25. Deb, K., Sundar, J.: Reference point based multi-objective optimization using evolutionary algorithms. In: Proceedings of the 8th Annual Conference on Genetic and Evolutionary Computation, Washington, 08–12 July 2006
26. Seddaoui, A., Saaj, C.M., Eckersley, S.: Adaptive H infinity controller for precise manoeuvring of a small space robot accepted. In: The IEEE International Conference on Robotics and Automation (ICRA), Montreal, Canada, 20–24 May 2019

27. Yoshikawa, T.: Dynamic manipulability of robot manipulators. Trans. Soc. Instrum. Control Eng. **21**(9), 970–975 (1985)
28. Chehouri, A., Younes, R., Perron, J., Ilinca, A.: A constraint-handling technique for genetic algorithms using a violation factor. J. Comput. Sci. Sci. Publ. **12**, 350–362 (2016)

A Cross-Landscape Evaluation of Multi-robot Team Performance in Static Task-Allocation Domains

Dingdian Zhang$^{(\boxtimes)}$, Eric Schneider, and Elizabeth Sklar

Depaerment of Informatics, King's College London, London, UK
{dingdian.zhang,eric.schneider,elizabeth.sklar}@kcl.ac.uk
http://www.kcl.ac.uk

Abstract. The performance of a multi-robot team varies when certain environmental parameters change. The study presented here examines the performance of four task allocation mechanisms, compared across a mission landscape that is defined by a set of environmental conditions. The landscape is categorised by three dimensions: (1) single-robot versus multi-robot tasks; (2) independent versus constrained task correspondence; and (3) static versus dynamic allocation of tasks with respect to mission execution. Two different task scenarios and two different starting formations were implemented with each environmental condition. Experiments were conducted on teams of simulated and physical robots, to demonstrate the portability of the results. This paper investigates the "static allocation" portion of the mission landscape, filling in a gap that has not been investigated previously. Experimental results are presented which confirm that the previous conclusion still holds: there is no single task allocation mechanism that consistently ranks best in performance when tasks are executed.

Keywords: Multi-robot team · Auction mechanism · Task allocation

1 Introduction

Distribution of tasks amongst members of a multi-robot team is a well-studied problem within the multi-agent systems and robotics communities. Most work has focused on the development of algorithms that strive to optimise *task allocation*, within restricted settings and without evaluating the effectiveness of the allocation when tasks are actually executed. Our work has pushed beyond the "allocation" stage and concentrated on a systematic and empirical study of the impact of market-based task allocation mechanisms when applied to a diverse landscape of missions and environments [21–24]. We have demonstrated, through statistically significant experimental results, that mechanisms proven optimal in the allocation of tasks lose their distinction when those tasks are actually executed by a multi-robot team. The study presented here fills in one portion of the mission landscape that was previously unexplored and confirms that our

© Springer Nature Switzerland AG 2019
K. Althoefer et al. (Eds.): TAROS 2019, LNAI 11650, pp. 261–272, 2019.
https://doi.org/10.1007/978-3-030-25332-5_23

earlier conclusion still holds: of the market mechanisms tested, there is no single mechanism that consistently ranks best in any of the task execution metrics considered.

The *multi-robot task allocation (MRTA)* problem is defined as deciding which tasks should be assigned to which robots so that the overall execution of a mission is, by some measure(s), efficient. While there are several kinds of approaches to solving MRTA problems, our work has focused on *market-based* methods of task allocation. A common kind of market-based mechanism for MRTA is an *auction*, which compares bids for resources from interested parties and awards them to the highest (or lowest) bidder according to the particular rules of a mechanism. Auction mechanisms are a good choice for MRTA problems because they are flexible, distributed, and scalable.

We define our *mission landscape* along three dimensions [3,13]: (1) *Single-Robot (SR)* vs *Multi-Robot (MR)*; (2) *Independent Tasks (IT)* vs *Constrained Tasks (CT)*; and (3) *Static Allocation (SA)* vs *Dynamic Allocation (DA)*. Single-robot tasks can be completed by one robot acting alone, while multi-robot tasks require more than one robot to complete—such as offloading packages from one robot to another. Independent tasks can be executed at any time and in any order, while constrained tasks depend on others which must be completed first—such as moving debris from blocking a robot's path. Statically allocated tasks are known *a priori* and can be assigned to robots ahead of time, before a mission starts, while dynamically allocated tasks may appear throughout a mission and must be assigned whilst robots are already executing previously assigned tasks.

The focus and contribution of the work presented here is on the assessment of *statically allocated (SA)* tasks, across the landscape of the first two mission dimensions, both environment dimensions and four task allocation mechanisms. This work fills in the remaining gap from our earlier investigations, as shown in Table 1. The remainder of this paper is organised as follows. Section 2 describes related research stemming from the multi-agent systems and multi-robot systems communities. Section 3 provides further details of our approach to this systematic investigation of the landscape outlined above, followed by experiment design in Sect. 4. Section 5 presents our experimental results. We conclude in Sect. 6 with some discussion and a summary of our contributions.

Table 1. Mission landscape and research contribution

SR-IT-SA vs SR-IT-DA	sim	TAROS 2015 [24]
SR-IT-DA vs SR-CT-DA	sim	TAROS 2016 [23]
MR-IT-DA vs MR-CT-DA	phy	
SR-IT-SA vs SR-CT-SA	sim	*contribution*
MR-IT-SA vs MR-CT-SA	phy	*here*

2 Related Work

An early example of market-based multiagent task allocation is Smith's Contract Net Protocol [26] which defined a communication model for agents to negotiate with each other to distribute tasks by advertising and honouring contracts for work. Wellman and Wurman [28] introduced ideas from economics to multiagent task allocation, where agents compute and compare private valuations, or prices, for tasks. A primary strength of market-based approaches is their reliance only on local information and/or the self-interest of agents to arrive at efficient solutions to large-scale, complex problems that are otherwise intractable [2]. Gerkey and Matarić introduced *auctions* for MRTA problems in their MURDOCH architecture [5], an extension of the Contract Net Protocol. Auctions are commonly used for distribution tasks, where resources are treated as commodities and auctioned to agents. Existing work analyses the effects of different auction mechanisms [1,2,11,30], bidding strategies [19], dynamic task re-allocation [6,16] and levels of commitment to the contracts [15] on the overall solution quality.

In domains where there is a strong synergy between items, single-item auctions can result in sub-optimal allocations [1]. In multi-robot exploration, studied here, strong synergies may exist between tasks. Combinatorial auctions remedy this limitation by allowing agents to bid on bundles of items, and minimise the total travel distance because they take the synergies between tasks into account [8]. Combinatorial auctions suffer, however, from the computational costs of bid generation and bundle valuation by the agents, and winner determination by the auction mechanism itself, all of which are NP-hard [9]. As a result, a body of work has grown up around the *sequential single-item auction* (SSI) [9], which has been proven to create close to optimal allocations, handling synergies while not suffering from the complexity issues of combinatorial auctions.

Gerkey and Matarić [3] draw major distinctions between single-robot (SR) and multi-robot tasks (MR), which require multiple robots to execute. Landen et al. [13] extend Gerkey and Matarić's taxonomy to classify settings in which tasks are either independent (IT) or have constraints, such as precedence-ordering, between them (CT), and distinguish static allocation (SA) and dynamic allocation (DA). Korsah et al. [10] define a taxonomy for multi-robot tasks that classifies tasks as atomic or compound bundles which may have inter-task dependencies or utilities.

This paper is a further contribution to the body of work around SSI [8,9,16, 25,29], extending the use of SSI and related mechanisms to task environments that are multi-robot (*MR*) and constrained (*CT*). Auction-based approaches to task allocation have been proposed for tasks with precedence [14], with temporal [7,17] constraints, and for dynamic environments [24] with single robot tasks. Environments that contain multi-robot tasks, with and without constraints, are less well investigated than their single-robot counterparts [10].

3 Approach

We use the MRTeAm framework [20,24], based on the Robot Operating System (ROS) [18], as the basis of our experimental setup. In MRTeAm, a central *auctioneer* agent coordinates the team. The auctioneer holds a list of tasks, communicates the start of an auction and allocates tasks to robots. Each robot is represented by a *robot controller*, which submits bids to the auctioneer. The auctioneer determines winner(s) in an auction and awards the tasks in turn. Tasks are allocated in this way over a number of auction *rounds*. When all tasks have been allocated, the robot controllers begin to execute their allocated tasks.

A *map* specifies the extent of a geographical space and the arrangements of free space and obstacles within it. A *team* is a set of n robots $R = \{r_0, \ldots, r_{n-1}\}$. A *starting formation*, F, specifies the location on a map of each robot in the team at the beginning of a *mission*. A *scenario* is a set of m tasks $T = \{t_0, \ldots, t_{m-1}\}$ situated on the map. A scenario may also contain ordering constraints CT, a set of pairs of tasks $(t_p, t_q), t_p, t_q \in T$ such that t_p must be completed before t_q can proceed. A *mission* comprises the map, a scenario, and a robot team with a starting formation: $M = \{map, T, R, F\}$.

We evaluate our mission environment along two dimensions: (1) *physical* vs *simulation* setting; and (2) *clustered* vs *distributed* starting formation. The simulation settings that we employ are replicas of the physical world (or "arena") that we have available for running tests with hardware platforms (i.e., "real" robots). With respect to the second mission environment dimension, we have determined that the starting formation has substantial impact on mission performance metrics. In the *clustered* formation, all the robots on the team are co-located in close proximity when the mission starts. In the *distributed* formation, the robots are spread out across the mission arena.

We compare four task allocation mechanisms that are representative of the most common mechanisms in the multi-agent systems and multi-robot systems literature on task allocation: (1) *Round Robin (RR)*; (2) *Sequential Single Item (SSI)*; (3) *Ordered Single Item (OSI)*; and (4) *Parallel Single Item (PSI)*. The baseline "round robin" mechanism merely assigns each task as it appears to robots in sequence, without considering any features of the task or robot. The sequential single-item mechanism is an auction-based strategy that offers a group of tasks to a team of robots; team members "bid" on single tasks, which are then assigned by a centralised auctioneer over a series of "rounds" in which one task is assigned in each round. The ordered single-item mechanism is a variant of SSI in which tasks are offered one at a time, in a particular order; the contrast with SSI is that, in OSI, the order is pre-determined, whereas with SSI the order of task assignment emerges as robot bids determine which tasks go first, second, etc. The parallel single-item mechanism is a further variant of SSI in which all tasks are offered in one round and robots bid on all tasks; the centralised auctioneer then assigns all tasks to robots in that one round.

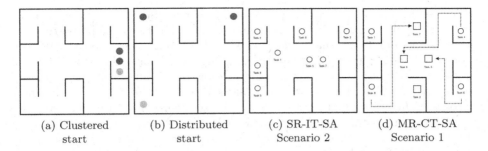

(a) Clustered start   (b) Distributed start   (c) SR-IT-SA Scenario 2   (d) MR-CT-SA Scenario 1

Fig. 1. Two different starting formations (a and b), and two different mission scenarios (c and d). Bold lines indicate the walls of the arena. In (a) and (b), the three colours indicate three different robot starting positions. In (c) and (d), circles and squares show single-robot tasks and multi-robot tasks (two robots in our experiments), respectively. A dotted line from task t_p to task t_q indicates that t_q must be completed before t_p can proceed. (Color figure online)

3.1 Metrics

To evaluate the performance of a team, we consider metrics that measure the performance of both individual robots and the team as a whole. In any work with robots, power consumption is the fundamental scarce resource that a robot possesses. Robot batteries only last for a limited time, and so, all other things being equal, we prefer task allocations and subsequent executions that minimise battery usage. As in [8,9,12,27], therefore, we measure the **distance travelled** by the robots in executing a set of tasks—both individually and as a group—since this is a suitable proxy for power consumption. Note that we compute distance not by looking at the shortest distances between the task locations, but it is (as closely as we can establish) the actual distance travelled by the robots during task execution. We collect frequent position updates, compute the Euclidean distance between successive positions, and sum these.

Time is also important, which we measure and analyse here in several ways: **deliberation time** is the time that it takes for tasks to be allocated amongst the robots; **execution phase time** is the time it takes robots to complete tasks once they have been allocated, which includes time travelling to each task location; and **idle time** is the amount of time that robots wait for others to complete tasks, having completed their own.

4 Experiments

Our physical platform is the TurtleBot3 Burger[1] (Fig. 2a), a differential drive robot with a 360° laser distance sensor and a Raspberry Pi camera. The ROS [18] navigation stack provides communication, localisation and path planning capabilities. The operating arena is a 3.2 m × 3.2 m office-like setting with a central

---

[1] http://www.robotis.us/turtlebot-3/.

corridor which connects each "room", shown in Fig. 2b. Simulation experiments were conducted using Stage [4]. Our simulated robot has the same properties as the physical robot (size, shape, sensors, actuators, etc.). The *robot controllers* are agnostic about physical and simulated settings, and behave the same in both.

Our experimental setup is almost the same as in [23], in which our physical platform is the TurtleBot2 and the arena is in a larger dimension to fit the size of the TurtleBot2 platform. However, the structure of the interior walls is exactly the same. All of the experiments reported here involve a team of $n = 3$ robots and $m = 8$ task points. In MR scenarios, four of the eight tasks are multi-robot (MR) and the rest are single-robot (SR). In CT scenarios, there are three tasks that "depend on" three other tasks. Figure 1 shows two sets of starting formations: *clustered* and *distributed*. In the *clustered* formation, all of the robots start in the same "room" (Fig. 1a). In the *distributed* formation, robots start distributed in the upper right corner, upper left corner and the lower left corner of the arena (Fig. 1b). We conducted experiments in four different parameterised environments, combining single-robot (SR) vs. multi-robot (MR) and independent task (IT) vs. constrained task (CT), with static allocation (SA) only: SR-IT-SA, SR-CT-SA, MR-IT-SA and MR-CT-SA. There were two scenarios employed to each parameterised environment. Figure 1c and d show SR-IT-SA *scenario 2* and MR-CT-SA *scenario 1*, respectively.

For the results presented here, 320 physical and 1920 simulation trials were conducted in total:

$$4 \; allocation \; mechanisms$$
$$\times \; \langle SR|MR \rangle \times \langle IT|CT \rangle \times 2 \; starting \; formations \times 2 \; scenarios$$
$$\times \; \{5 \; physical \; trials \,|\, 30 \; simulation \; trials\}$$

For each experiment, we recorded the metrics described in Sect. 3.1.

5   Results

Our experimental results are given in Figs. 3, 4, 5 and 6. We analyse these results, across our landscape and environmental conditions, in several ways: (1) **distance travelled**; (2) **deliberation time** and **execution phase time**; and (3) efficiency, i.e., evenness of workload distribution amongst robots, as measured by **idle time** and **distance travelled**. The variable we are assessing is *allocation mechanism*: RR vs OSI vs SSI vs PSI. Our analysis began by checking all our data for normality using the Shapiro-Wilk test and statistical significance using Analysis of Variance (ANOVA), for each metric, classified into samples according to allocation mechanism. For the simulation experiments, where we collected 30+ runs for each condition, all the results show statistically significant differences ($p < 0.05$) between samples for each mechanism. This is also the case for most of the physical experiments, though not all; however, we only have 5 trials for physical experiments, so no conclusion can be drawn here.

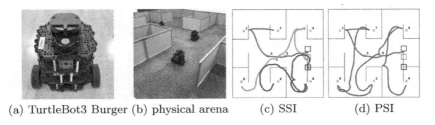

(a) TurtleBot3 Burger (b) physical arena   (c) SSI   (d) PSI

Fig. 2. Our robots and arena, and some sample trajectories.

5.1   Distance Travelled

Figure 3 shows the average **distance travelled** in all experiments. In each plot (a–h), the allocation mechanisms are ordered, from left to right: RR, OSI, SSI and PSI. In most of these settings, RR produces the longest distance travelled, except in the Clustered-Scenario1-physical conditions, where RR performs close to or better than other mechanisms. In contrast, PSI frequently produces the shortest distance. The *heatmaps* (plots i–p) summarise these results, rank ordered. These results are similar to those in [23,24] for dynamic allocation (DA).

5.2   Time

Figure 4 contains heatmaps of the physical experiments showing performance rankings among four allocation mechanisms for **deliberation time** and **execution phase time**. Unlike our previous results [23,24], the **deliberation time** values are very consistent: RR is always fastest, PSI ranks next, followed by OSI and then SSI taking the longest. In practice, these differences are negligible, since the amount of time taken by deliberating is very small compared to the time taken to execute the allocated tasks; but it is still worth measuring and comparing. The **execution phase time** results are more aligned with the **distance travelled** results illustrated in Fig. 3—there are trends, but no substantial consistency. For example, the OSI allocations are best for execution phase time for many of the SR conditions (75%), while the MR results are more varied.

5.3   Efficiency

In the context of multi-robot team performance, the notion of *efficiency* refers to how well the workload of the mission is distributed amongst the robots. If the workload is evenly distributed, then all robots are doing something most of the time, and all robots complete their individual tasks at nearly the same time. If the workload is unevenly distributed, then some robots sit idly whilst others do the work. An extreme example of this is the case where one robot is allocated all the tasks and the other two do nothing. An illustration is shown in Figs. 2c and d, where the SSI results are evenly distributed amongst the three robots, whilst the PSI results highlight that only one robot performed all the tasks.

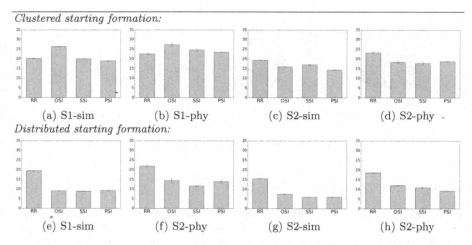

Clustered starting formation:

(a) S1-sim   (b) S1-phy   (c) S2-sim   (d) S2-phy

Distributed starting formation:

(e) S1-sim   (f) S2-phy   (g) S2-sim   (h) S2-phy

Average distance (meters) travelled in SR-IT-SA, with clustered starts. Scenarios 1 (S1) and 2 (S2) are shown, for physical (phy) and simulated (sim) robots. Mechanisms are ordered RR, OSI, SSI and PSI. These correspond plots (i) and (m) below.

Simulation

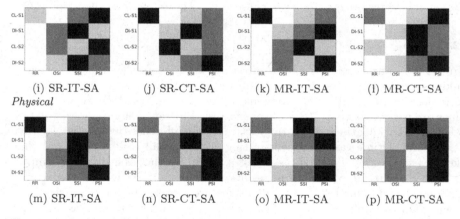

(i) SR-IT-SA   (j) SR-CT-SA   (k) MR-IT-SA   (l) MR-CT-SA

Physical

(m) SR-IT-SA   (n) SR-CT-SA   (o) MR-IT-SA   (p) MR-CT-SA

Heatmaps show rank ordering of mechanisms according to total distance travelled. In each heatmap, the four cells in a row represent each of the task allocation mechanisms; and the columns represent the two starting formations for each of the two scenarios. The darkest blocks indicate the lowest value of the metric (least distance travelled), while the lightest block indicates the highest value (most distance travelled).

Fig. 3. Results: distance travelled.

We analyse efficiency in two ways. First, we look at the **idle time** metric, which tallies how much time some robots sit idly (doing nothing) while others are executing tasks. The heatmaps shown in Fig. 5 illustrate that no mechanism is always the best with respect to fair distribution of workload, although OSI is most frequently the best (56% of the time). However, PSI stands out as the worst for every mission that starts in the clustered formation. This result fits our expectations as it was first noted in [9].

The second way in which we look at efficiency considers the distribution of distances travelled by each robot on a team. Figure 6 plots a Gaussian distribution for the distances travelled by the three robots on the team, averaged across trials for each mechanism (30+ for the simulation runs shown, so $3 \times 30 = 90$ samples). When the peaks in the plots are narrow, the standard deviation is small, indicating that the distances travelled by the individual robots are fairly evenly distributed. In contrast, when the peaks are flat, the standard deviation is large, indicating poor distribution of tasks. In the bottom four plots (Clustered starting formation), the red lines (PSI) are almost flat, highlighting how poorly

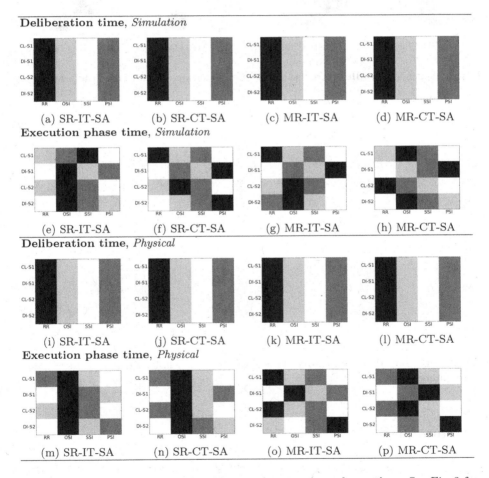

Fig. 4. Heatmaps for **deliberation time** and **execution phase time**. See Fig. 3 for explanation of how to read the heatmaps.

the tasks are distributed by this mechanism for this starting formation. In these cases, one robot does all the tasks and the others do none (or two robots, in the MR missions).

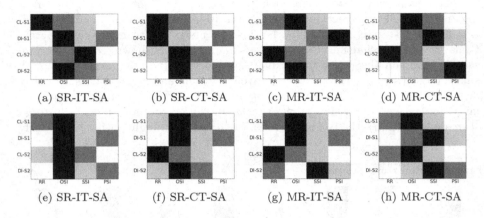

Fig. 5. Heatmaps for **idle time**. See Fig. 3 for explanation of how to read the heatmaps.

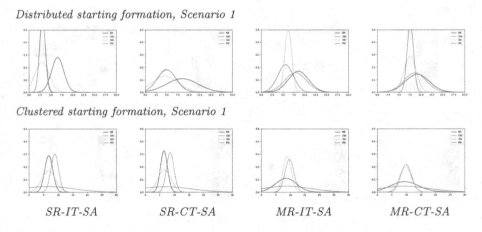

Fig. 6. Distributions of **distance travelled** from *simulation* experiments. (Color figure online)

6   Summary

Our previous work [21,22] compared the performance of four multi-robot task allocation mechanisms in a simple environment in which tasks were statically allocated and could be executed independently by single robots (SR-IT-SA).

Experimental results showed that SSI was indeed effective at producing efficient allocations that generally led to the best performance in practice, by most metrics. But an unexpected result was observed when the starting locations of robots were spread out over the map ("distributed") and the differences among the four mechanisms were diminished in terms of the time taken to execute a mission. The results of experiments in [24] showed that when the arrival times of tasks was distributed over time (SR-IT-DA), the performance differences among the mechanisms diminished further. In particular, the performance of PSI allocations during execution was indistinguishable from that of SSI while being much less expensive to compute. The experiments in [23], designed to determine if relative performance rankings of mechanisms would hold when the mechanisms were employed across multi-robot (MR), constrained (CT), *dynamic allocation* (DA) environments, showed that factors like multi-robot coordination and honouring precedence-ordering during execution of tasks make it difficult or impossible to predict performance outcomes based only on starting conditions and the expected efficiency of allocations. The results of experiments reported here support the same conclusion in static allocation (SA) variants of the same environments.

References

1. Berhault, M., et al.: Robot exploration with combinatorial auctions. In: Proceedings of IROS (2003)
2. Dias, M.B., Zlot, R., Kalra, N., Stentz, A.: Market-based multirobot coordination: a survey and analysis. Proc. IEEE **94**(7), 1257–1270 (2006)
3. Gerkey, B.P., Matarić, M.J.: A formal analysis and taxonomy of task allocation in multi-robot systems. Int. J. Robot. Res. **23**(9), 1257–1270 (2004)
4. Gerkey, B., Vaughan, R.T., Howard, A.: The player/stage project: tools for multi-robot and distributed sensor systems. In: Proceedings of International Conference on Advanced Robotics, vol. 1 (2003)
5. Gerkey, B.P., Mataric, M.J.: Sold!: Auction methods for multirobot coordination. IEEE Trans. Robot. Autom. **18**(5), 758–768 (2002)
6. Golfarelli, M., Maio, D., Rizzi, S.: A task-swap negotiation protocol based on the contract net paradigm. Technical report 005–97, DEIS, CSITE - Università di Bologna (1997)
7. Gombolay, M., Wilcox, R., Shah, J.A.: Fast scheduling of multi-robot teams with temporospatial constraints. In: Robotics: Science and Systems (2013)
8. Koenig, S., Keskinocak, P., Tovey, C.A.: Progress on agent coordination with cooperative auctions. In: AAAI (2010)
9. Koenig, S., et al.: The power of sequential single-item auctions for agent coordination. In: Proceedings of AAAI (2006)
10. Korsah, G.A., Stentz, A., Dias, M.B.: A comprehensive taxonomy for multi-robot task allocation. Int. J. Robot. Res. **32**(12), 1495–1512 (2013)
11. Kraus, S.: Automated negotiation and decision making in multiagent environments. In: Luck, M., Mařík, V., Štěpánková, O., Trappl, R. (eds.) ACAI 2001. LNCS (LNAI), vol. 2086, pp. 150–172. Springer, Heidelberg (2001). https://doi.org/10.1007/3-540-47745-4_7

12. Lagoudakis, M.G., et al.: Auction-based multi-robot routing. In: Proceedings of RSS (2005)
13. Landén, D., Heintz, F., Doherty, P.: Complex task allocation in mixed-initiative delegation: a UAV case study. In: Desai, N., Liu, A., Winikoff, M. (eds.) PRIMA 2010. LNCS (LNAI), vol. 7057, pp. 288–303. Springer, Heidelberg (2012). https://doi.org/10.1007/978-3-642-25920-3_20
14. Luo, L., Chakraborty, N., Sycara, K.: Multi-robot assignment algorithm for tasks with set precedence constraints. In: Proceedings of ICRA (2011)
15. Matarić, M.J., Sukhatme, G.S., Østergaard, E.H.: Multi-robot task allocation in uncertain environments. Auton. Robot. **14**(2–3), 255–263 (2003)
16. Nanjanath, M., Gini, M.: Repeated auctions for robust task execution by a robot team. Robot. Auton. Syst. **58**(7), 900–909 (2010)
17. Nunes, E., Gini, M.: Multi-robot auctions for allocation of tasks with temporal constraints. In: Proceedings of AAAI (2015)
18. Quigley, M., et al.: ROS: an open-source robot operating system. In: ICRA OSS Workshop (2009)
19. Sariel, S., Balch, T.: Efficient bids on task allocation for multi-robot exploration. In: Proceedings of FLAIRS (2006)
20. Schneider, E.: Mechanism selection for multi-robot task allocation. Ph.D. thesis, Univ of Liverpool, UK (2018)
21. Schneider, E., Balas, O., Özgelen, A.T., Sklar, E.I., Parsons, S.: An empirical evaluation of auction-based task allocation in multi-robot teams (extended abstract). In: Proceedings of AAMAS, May 2014
22. Schneider, E., Balas, O., Özgelen, A.T., Sklar, E.I., Parsons, S.: Evaluating auction-based task allocation in multi-robot teams. In: ARMS Workshop at AAMAS, Paris, France, May 2014
23. Schneider, E., Sklar, E.I., Parsons, S.: Evaluating multi-robot teamwork in parameterised environments. In: Alboul, L., Damian, D., Aitken, J.M.M. (eds.) TAROS 2016. LNCS (LNAI), vol. 9716, pp. 301–313. Springer, Cham (2016). https://doi.org/10.1007/978-3-319-40379-3_32
24. Schneider, E., Sklar, E.I., Parsons, S., Özgelen, A.T.: Auction-based task allocation for multi-robot teams in dynamic environments. In: Dixon, C., Tuyls, K. (eds.) TAROS 2015. LNCS (LNAI), vol. 9287, pp. 246–257. Springer, Cham (2015). https://doi.org/10.1007/978-3-319-22416-9_29
25. Schoenig, A., Pagnucco, M.: Evaluating sequential single-item auctions for dynamic task allocation. In: AI 2010: Advances in Artificial Intelligence (2011)
26. Smith, R.G.: The contract net protocol: high-level communication and control in a distributed problem solver. In: Gasser, L., Huhns, M. (eds.) Distributed Artificial Intelligence. Morgan Kaufmann Publishers Inc., San Mateo (1988)
27. Tovey, C., Lagoudakis, M.G., Jain, S., Koenig, S.: Generation of bidding rules for auction-based robot coordination. In: Parker, L.E., Schneider, F.E., Schultz, A.C. (eds.) Multi-Robot Systems. From Swarms to Intelligent Automata, vol. III. Springer, Dordrecht (2005). https://doi.org/10.1007/1-4020-3389-3_1
28. Wellman, M.P., Wurman, P.R.: Market-aware agents for a multiagent world. Robot. Auton. Syst. **24**, 115–125 (1998)
29. Zheng, X., Koenig, S., Tovey, C.: Improving sequential single-item auctions. In: Proceedings of IROS (2006)
30. Zlot, R., Stentz, A., Dias, M.B., Thayer, S.: Multi-robot exploration controlled by a market economy. In: Proceedings of ICRA, vol. 3 (2002)

Mobile Robot Trajectory Analysis with the Help of Vision System

Dinmohamed Danabek[1], Ata Otaran[1], Kaspar Althoefer[1,2],
and Ildar Farkhatdinov[1(✉)]

[1] School of Electronic Engineeeing and Computer Science,
Queen Mary University of London, London, UK
dimash97@hotmail.co.uk,i.farkhatdinov@qmul.ac.uk
[2] School of Engineering and Material Science,
Queen Mary University of London, London, UK

Abstract. We present a vision-based motion analysis method for single and multiple mobile robots which allows quantifying the robot's behaviour. The method defines how often and for how much each of the robots turn and move straight. The motion analysis relies on the robot trajectories acquired online or offline by an external camera and the algorithm is based on iteratively performed a linear regression to detect straight and curved paths for each robot. The method is experimentally validated with the indoor mobile robotic system. Potential applications include remote robot inspection, rescue robotics and multi-robotic system coordination.

Keywords: Mobile robot · Motion analysis · Visual tracking

1 Introduction

Multi mobile robotic systems can be efficiently used in exploration and inspection tasks [1–3]. Successful task completion in such applications depends on careful multi-robot control and coordination [4]. However, due to limited communication, computing and human-operator resources it is often difficult to ensure safe and reliable operation of such robotic systems. For example, in common applications it is required to know the current state of each individual robot to ensure that it follows the exploration tasks. Understanding the actual movement patterns of a group of robots is important for many reasons. Comparing the actual motion with pre-programmed behaviour can reveal potential deviations from the expected task. It can also be helpful to identify whether the remotely observed robots are teleoperated [5] or controlled autonomously [6], as well as to detect and indicate the mobile robots' operation faults, such as reduced speed due the low battery charge or mechanism jamming.

Vision-based tracking has been widely investigated and deployed for mobile robots motion analysis [7]. Video surveillance systems are used for real-time

© Springer Nature Switzerland AG 2019
K. Althoefer et al. (Eds.): TAROS 2019, LNAI 11650, pp. 273–279, 2019.
https://doi.org/10.1007/978-3-030-25332-5_24

tracking and can classify certain activities to detect unusual events of people and vehicles [8]. On-board sensory systems can also be used to measure the effectiveness of the operation of multi-robot and multi-sensors networks to estimate the robot's locations in hazardous environments [2]. Other studies have explored the trajectory tracking with adaptive vision control systems to guide mobile robots towards a desired location [9]. Camera-based environment tracking was used for obstacle avoidance in mobile robot navigation [10]. A graph-based modelling approach was used for motion analysis of a multi-robotic system [11]. Similarly, point distribution modelling trajectories analysis and comparison between several mobile robots [12]. An on-board vision based tracking system was used together with a UAV to track moving objects during the flight [13,14].

In this work, we propose to use an external visual tracking system to continuously monitor a multi-mobile robotics system and to quantify each robot's behaviour. An algorithm which analyses the trajectories of the mobile robots based on the captured top view from a video camera is the core component of the proposed methodology.

2   Motion Tracking and Analysis

Our method analyses a mobile robot's movement trajectories and classifies them into elementary motion patterns such as straight movements and turns. The proposed method assumes that the position of the mobile robot, $p(k)$, is available through an external visual tracking system. The position of the robot is defined as

$$p(k) = [x(k), \ y(k)] \in \mathcal{R}^2,$$
$$\text{for discrete time points}: k = \{1...M\}, \ M \in \mathcal{N}, \tag{1}$$

where $x(k)$ and $y(k)$ are planar coordinates in the camera frame at discrete time, $t = k$, and, M - the number of recorded points. These coordinates are estimated through visual tracking and recorded for online (on-fly) or offline analysis. In the following we describe the motion analysis steps for the online case and a similar approach can be used for the off-line analysis. Our algorithm runs simultaneously with visual tracking and at every iteration (frame) a series of recorded robot position points $\{p(k)...p(k-N)\}$, $N \in \mathcal{N}$ and $N < M$, is used to test whether the robot's trajectory can be expressed with a straight line. In other words, a linear regression analysis is done for the points $\{p(k)...p(k-N)\}$ to define straight paths of the trajectory leading to a linear fit, Y_k, at time $t = k$:

$$Y_k : \ y = \hat{\beta}_{0,k} + \hat{\beta}_{1,k}x,$$
$$\text{for } \{p(k)...p(k-N)\}, \tag{2}$$

with constant parameters, $\hat{\beta}_0$ and $\hat{\beta}_1$, to be identified. For each obtained fit Y_k, the coefficient of determination (R^2, R-squared) was calculated to define the goodness of estimation for the robot's straight movements. This is conveniently scaled between 0 and 1, where a coefficient closer to 1 indicates a straight line movement. Subsequent fits Y_k and Y_{k-1} were compared to detect turns in the robot's trajectories:

$$\textbf{turning detected if} : \varphi_k > \delta,$$

$$\text{where } \varphi_k = \text{atan}\,\beta_{1,k} - \text{atan}\,\beta_{1,k-1},$$

$$\text{or } \varphi_k = \text{atan}\,\frac{\beta_{1,k} - \beta_{1,k-1}}{1 - \beta_{1,k}\beta_{1,k-1}}, \tag{3}$$

where constant design parameter δ defines the turning detection threshold and the sign of the angle φ_k defines the direction of turning at time t_k. For example, clockwise turning (right turn) corresponds to $\varphi_k < 0$. Then, the coefficients of determinations for each fit (2) are compared at each iteration to define when turning starts and ends:

$$\textbf{turning motion} : \textbf{if } R^2_k < \delta_R,$$

$$\textbf{straight motion} : \textbf{otherwise}, \tag{4}$$

where δ_R is the design parameter defining the threshold to discriminate between straight motion (linear trajectories) and turning motion (curved trajectories). In our algorithm, δ_R was set to be 0.999. Conditions (3) and (4) were used together to define the transitions between the straight motion paths and the turnings, and total turning angle was computed for each turning action as follows

$$\Theta = \sum_{i=l}^{k} \varphi_i,$$

$$\text{where } \textbf{turning started} \text{ at time } t = l,$$

$$\text{and } \textbf{turning completed} \text{ at time } t = k. \tag{5}$$

The calculated turning angle, Θ, was recorded for each turning action in addition to the total number of turning actions for a robot. Then, the final outcome of the motion analysis described above is the turning statistics expressed as the turning frequency (distribution) function $F(\Theta)$ which specifies the turning behaviour patterns for a given mobile robot.

The proposed motion analysis method is scalable to a multi-robot case when an external vision system would track several mobile robots and the proposed motion analysis will apply to each of the robots. The statistics collected through our tracking and analysis algorithm can provide useful information about the behavioural and control patterns of the observed robots. Next section presents the experimental validation of our method.

3   Experimental Setup

We validated the proposed motion analysis algorithm in an indoor environment using three miniature mobile robots (Elisa 3 [15]) and an RGB camera-based visual tracking system (SwisTrack [16]).

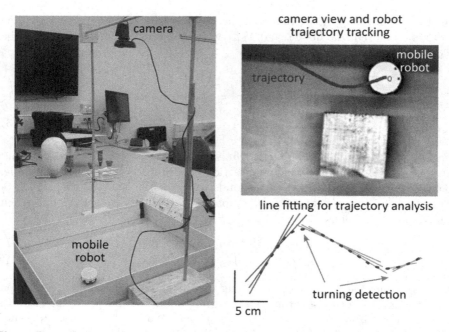

Fig. 1. General view of the experimental setup (left) and mobile robot trajectory tracking and analysis (right).

Elisa 3 miniature mobile robots are small (⌀5 cm) wheeled autonomous robots. Each robot is equipped with Atmel-Arduino compatible micro-controller, central RGB LEDs, eight infra-red obstacle range sensors, four terrain detection sensors, three infra-red emitters, accelerometers and two DC motors to actuate the wheels. The robots were pre-programmed to follow straight trajectories and navigate around the obstacles detected with the infra-red sensors. The same obstacle avoidance programme was uploaded to the controller of each robot. For testing the robots were placed on a table top (size 1 by 1 m) surrounded by a 10 cm high protection barrier as shown in Fig. 1. As a result, the robots normally moved straight and avoided collisions with the protective barrier during the tests.

Visual tracking was performed with a simple RGB-camera connected to a laptop through the USB port. The camera was fixed one meter above the robot arena to perform tracking using the top view. The robot's positions on the desktop were obtained with the help of an open-source visual tracking library SwisTrack [16]. In the experiments, the position of the robot (1) was sent by SwisTrack via a TCP/IP protocol to our motion analysis algorithm described in the previous section. The algorithm was implemented as Matlab-script. The analysis was performed online at 25 Hz.

The test involved motion analysis of a single Elisa mobile robot. 5000 data points (frames) were recorded in the test. The goal of the test was to quantify the motion of the robot.

4   Results

Figure 2A shows an example of trajectory tracking for a robot. It shows the data points acquired during visual tracking of a single robot's motion. Figure 2B shows the results of straight movement detection experiment. By detecting straight movements and turns with the proposed algorithm we could quantify the movement of the robot. For example, in this particular test there were 80 straight movements, 53 left turns and 26 right turns.

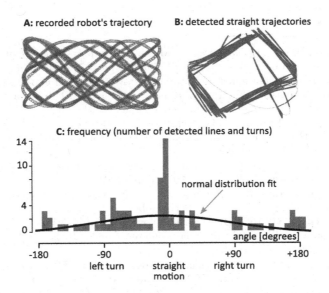

Fig. 2. Experimental results. **A:** an example of recorded robot's trajectory; **B:** linear fitting to detect straight movements; **C:** distribution of turning and straight movements for one robot.

The proposed motion analysis algorithm enabled us to describe the movement patterns for the tested robot. Figure 2C shows the results of motion analysis as frequency (distribution) plot in which the height of the bars corresponds to the number of straight movements (around angle $0°$) and turning left or right (around angles $±90°$) or half turns (around angles $±180°$).

The frequency plot of Fig. 2C can be used to quantitatively characterise the robots' behaviour. Furthermore, the data characterising the robot's behaviour can be modelled statistically by fitting the data points to normal distribution.

For example, the behaviour of the robot can be modelled with the normal distribution with mean 14.47° and the standard deviation is 92.48°. This normal distribution fit is shown in Fig. 2C. It is easily noticed that these fits do not fully capture the behaviour of the robots but they can indicate how much each robot deviates from the straight movements and the range of the turning angles. Alternatively, the frequency plots can be modelled by a combination of several normal distribution fits. For example, separate normal distribution models can be found for the data points for straight motion (around 0°) and left/right turns to form a kernel density estimate of behaviour for each robot.

Acknowledments. This work was funded by the UK EPSRC grant EP/R02572X/1 (NCNR) and in part by The Alan Turing Institute Fellowships to I. Farlkhatdinov and K. Althoefer.

References

1. Amigoni, F., Banfi, J., Basilico, N.: Multirobot exploration of communication-restricted environments: a survey. IEEE Intell. Syst. **32**(6), 48–57 (2017)
2. Schneider, F.E., Wildermuth, D., Moors, M.: Methods and experiments for hazardous area activities using a multi-robot system. In: IEEE International Conference on Robotics and Automation, New Orleans (2004)
3. Farkhatdinov, I., Ryu, J.H.: Teleoperation of multi-robot and multi-property systems. In: 2008 6th IEEE International Conference on Industrial Informatics, pp. 1453–1458 (2008)
4. Yan, Z., Jouandeau, N., Cherif, A.A.: A survey and analysis of multi-robot coordination. Int. J. Adv. Robot. Syst. **10**(12), 399 (2013)
5. Farkhatdinov, I., Ryu, J.H., Poduraev, J.: A user study of command strategies for mobile robot teleoperation. Intell. Serv. Robot. **2**(2), 95–104 (2009)
6. Sahin, E., et al.: SWARM-BOT: pattern formation in a swarm of self-assembling mobile robots. In: IEEE International Conference on Systems, Man and Cybernetics, vol. 4, p. 6, 6 October 2002
7. Masutani, Y., Mikawa, M., Maru, N., Miyazaki, F.: Visual servoing for non-holonomic mobile robots. In: IEEE/RSJ International Conference on Intelligent Robots and Systems 1994, vol. 2, pp. 1133–1140 (1994)
8. Stauffer, C., Grimson, W.E.L.: Learning patterns of activity using real-time tracking. IEEE Trans. Pattern Anal. Mach. Intell. **22**(8), 746–757 (2000)
9. Liang, X., Wang, H., Chen, W., Guo, D., Liu, T.: Adaptive image-based trajectory tracking control of wheeled mobile robots with an uncalibrated fixed camera. IEEE Trans. Control Syst. Technol. **22**(6), 2266–2282 (2015)
10. Kruise, E, Wahl, F.M.: Camera-based observation of obstacle motions to derive statistical data for mobile robot motion planning. In: IEEE International Conference on Robotics and Automation (1998)
11. Mai, C., Lian, F.: Analysis of formation control and communication pattern in multi-robot systems. In: SICE-ICASE International Joint Conference, IEEE (2006)
12. Rodiut, P., Martinoli, A., Jacot, J.: A quantitative method for comparing trajectories of mobile robots using point distribution models. In: IEEE/RSJ International Conference on Intelligent Robots and Systems (2007)

13. Dobrokhodov, V., Kaminer, I.I., Jones, K.D., Ghabcheloo, R.: Vision-based tracking and motion estimation for moving targets using small UAVs. In: American Control Conference. IEEE (2006)
14. Tokekar, P., Isler, V., Franchi, A.: Multi-target visual tracing with aerial robots. In: IEEE/RJS International Conference on Intelligent Robots and Systems (2014)
15. http://www.gctronic.com/doc/index.php/Elisa-3
16. Lochmatter, T., Roduit, P., Cianci, C., Correll, N., Jacot, J., Martinoli, A.: Swistrack-a flexible open source tracking software for multi-agent systems. In: IEEE/RSJ International Conference on Intelligent Robots and Systems (2008)

Novel Robotic Systems and Applications

Intuitive Bare-Hand Teleoperation of a Robotic Manipulator Using Virtual Reality and Leap Motion

Inmo Jang[✉], Joaquin Carrasco, Andrew Weightman, and Barry Lennox

The University of Manchester, Manchester M13 9PL, UK
{inmo.jang,joaquin.carrasco,andrew.weightman,
barry.lennox}@manchester.ac.uk

Abstract. Despite various existing works on intuitive human-robot interaction (HRI) for teleoperation of robotic manipulators, to the best of our knowledge, the following research question has not been investigated yet: Can we have a teleoperated robotic manipulator that simply copies a human operator's bare hand posture and gesture in a real-time manner without having any hand-held devices? This paper presents a novel teleoperation system that attempts to address this question. Firstly, we detail how to set up the system practically by using a Universal Robots UR5, a Robotiq 3-finger gripper, and a Leap Motion based on Unity and ROS, and describe specifically what information is communicated between each other. Furthermore, we provide the details of the ROS nodes developed for controlling the robotic arm and gripper, given the information of a human's bare hands sensed by the Leap Motion. Then, we demonstrate our system executing a simple pick-and-place task, and discuss possible benefits and costs of this HRI concept.

Keywords: Human-robot interaction · Teleoperation ·
Virtual Reality · Leap Motion

1 Introduction

Teleoperation of robotic manipulators have been widely studied for various domains [7,14]. Recently, this technology is attracting interests and considered to be promising for tasks in extreme environments, for example, glovebox operations [1,15]. Use of teleoperated robots will minimise the need for human workers to be exposed to radioactive hazardous materials and thus improve safety and reduce the operational costs in a long-term perspective.

To this end, as one of the stepping stones, this paper presents an intuitive human-robot interaction concept to teleoperate a robotic manipulator by using

This project has been supported by the RAIN Hub, which is funded by the Industrial Strategy Challenge Fund, part of the government's modern Industrial Strategy. The fund is delivered by UK Research and Innovation and managed by EPSRC [EP/R026084/1].

K. Althoefer et al. (Eds.): TAROS 2019, LNAI 11650, pp. 283–294, 2019.
https://doi.org/10.1007/978-3-030-25332-5_25

Virtual Reality and a Leap Motion (a hand tracking system). Our system does not require a human operator to have any hand-held devices, but the robotic manipulator simply and directly follows the posture and gesture of his/her bare hands. To the best of our knowledge (see more details in Sect. 2), this is the first attempt to teleoperate a robotic manipulator using bare hands in real-time manner without having neither virtual targets nor predefined hand gestures.

In this paper, we show how to practically setup the system using a 6-DOF robotic arm (Universal Robots UR5), a 3-finger gripper (Robotiq), a Leap Motion, Virtual Reality based on Unity (3D game engine) and ROS (Robot Operating System), and describe specifically what information is communicated between each other. Furthermore, we provide the details of the ROS nodes developed for controlling the robotic arm and gripper, given the information of a human's bare hands sensed by the Leap Motion. Then, we demonstrate our system executing a simple pick-and-place task, and discuss about possible benefits and costs of this HRI concept.

2   Related Work

Over the past decade, many researches have proposed human-robot interface concepts using Virtual Reality (VR) for teleoperation of robotic manipulators. Many of the works have utilised default hand-held devices [12,19], which may cause considerable long-term workload on a user's arms for time-consuming tasks. As alternative interfaces without hand-held devices, human motion capture systems such as *Kinect* (using vision) [13] and/or *Myo* (using electromyography) [11] have been also popularly used. However, the former needs a large space to capture the whole body of a user, and the location of such a sensor relative to VR should be calibrated carefully. The latter, as a wearable device, is convenient to use, but reportedly provide less accuracy than Kinect, requiring sensor fusion [3,11].

Recently, *Leap Motion* (LM), i.e. vision-based hand motion/gesture capture system, has started to be utilised along with VR for robotic teleoperation. In [2,4,18], predefined hand gestures are used to control a robotic manipulator. This HRI concept requires a human operator to map those input gestures to the desired output robot behaviours, although it is shown to be at least more efficient than using a default interface device for a robot given by its manufacturer (e.g. Teach pendant for *Universal Robots*) [18]. For better intuitiveness, some works use virtual objects [9,10] or waypoints [16], which are the spatial targets that the end effector of a robotic manipulator has to follow and reach, and a human can simply pick up and place such a virtual target within a virtual space. It is presented in [10] that manipulating virtual objects can reduce task completion time, compared with using *Moveit* interactive markers in Rviz. However, all the works use plan-and-execution concepts, which inevitably induce latency for every command.

Our work was inspired by the following research question: Can we have a teleoperated robotic manipulator that simply copies a human operator's hand posture and gesture in a real-time manner, without having neither virtual targets

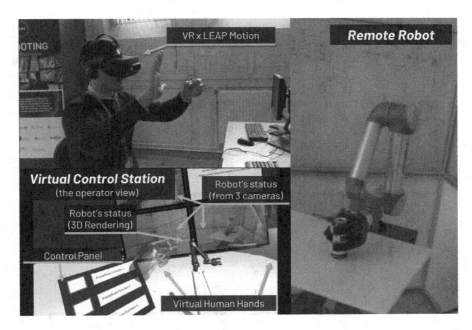

Fig. 1. The proposed teleoperation system using Virtual Reality and a Leap Motion (Up left: a user wearing a VR goggle with a Leap Motion; Bottom Left: the virtual control room; Right: the robot in a remote site)

nor predefined hand gestures nor hand-held devices? The following sections show our teleoperation system that attempts to answer this question.

3   The Proposed System

In this paper, we present a novel HRI concept where a human operator can teleoperate a robotic manipulator using his/her bare hands intuitively. In our system, as shown in Fig. 1, a human operator can be seated in a virtual control room, where there are three-view displays and a virtual robot model rendering the actual robot's status, and control panels by which the operator can give any predefined commands. The human's hands can be sensed and intuitively interact with the control panels by touching them, without any hand-held devices, via the LM attached to the outer surface of the VR goggle. More importantly, depending on control modes, i.e. *Reaching mode* or *Manipulating/Grasping mode* (see Sect. 3.2), the robot manipulator can follow the operator's bare hands sensed by the LM, which provides a high degree of intuitiveness.

3.1   System Architecture

Figure 2 shows hardware/software components comprised of our proposed teleoperation system, which uses a 6-DOF robotic manipulator (UR5), a 3-finger gripper (Robotiq), and three webcams for the slave side in a remote site, and uses a Leap Motion and a VR system (Oculus Rift) for the master side. All the devices in the remote site are communicated via *ROS* (kinetic version) running

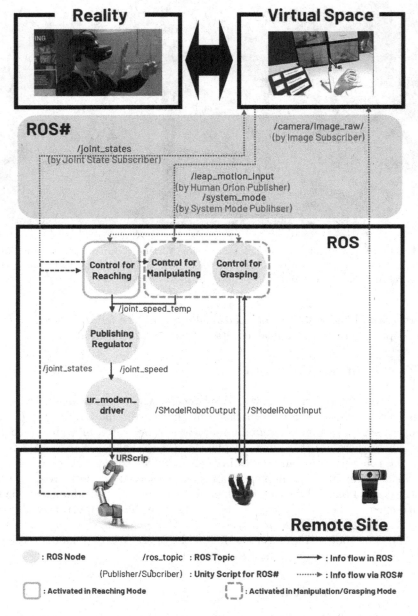

Fig. 2. System architecture of the proposed teleoperated robotic manipulator

on Ubuntu 16.04. User interface devices such as VR and LM are connected to *Unity3D* on Windows 10, and then ROS and Unity3D are linked by *ROS#*[1], which is based on *Rosbridge*[5]. Refer to [17] for more details of ROS# usage.

Unity-Side Setup: We use *Orion Beta* for LM, the recent software providing significantly better performance compared with the previous one, *V2*[2], but only available on Windows for the moment. Importantly, when Orion is used with VR, LM enables an immersive interface without hand-held devices. Compared with use of LM via ROS directly (which uses V2), Orion also gives additional information about hands such as a palm's normal and directional vectors, which are used in this work to map a user hand to the robot hand.

Furthermore, we utilise LM's Unity SDK such as *Interaction Engine*[3] to enable a user to interact with virtual objects such as the virtual control panels by simply touching them in a virtual space.

In the current teleoperation system, a user's right hand gestures are used to select a control mode, e.g. *Reaching mode* or *Manipulating/Grasping mode*, by a thumbs-up or stretching out all fingers, respectively. To this end, LM's *Detection Example*[4] is also imported.

ROS-Side Setup: ROS packages for UR5[5] and the gripper[6] are used to communicate with the devices via ROS topics such as `joint_speed` (`trajectory_msgs/ JointTrajectory.msg` (http://docs.ros.org/melodic/api/trajectory_msgs/html /msg/JointTrajectory.html), i.e. the reference velocity of each joint), `joint_sta tes` (`sensor_msgs/JointState.msg` (http://docs.ros.org/melodic/api/sensor_ msgs/html/msg/JointState.html), i.e. the current status of each joint) for UR5, and `SModelRobotOutput` (`robotiq_s_model_control/SModel_robot_output. msg` (http://docs.ros.org/hydro/api/robotiq_s_model_control/html/msg/SModel _robot_output.html), i.e. gripper function registers) for the gripper.

For UR5, `ur_modern_driver` package[7] is used as recommended for newer system versions (v3.x and up). The driver receives `joint_speed` topic as an input, then transforms it to the corresponding *URScript*, which is the programming language that controls the robot at a script level. According to the URScript manual[8], "the robot must be controlled a frequency of 125 Hz, or in other words, it must be told what to do every 0.008 s".

As shown in Fig. 2, we have two ROS nodes for controlling the UR5 and one node for the gripper, and they are activated or deactivated depending on the input signal `system_node` from the Unity side, which contains a single string value indicating the control mode selected by a user.

---

[1] https://github.com/siemens/ros-sharp/.
[2] See comparison in https://youtu.be/7HnfG0a6Gfg.
[3] https://leapmotion.github.io/UnityModules/interaction-engine.html.
[4] https://gallery.leapmotion.com/detection-example/.
[5] https://github.com/ros-industrial/universal_robot.
[6] https://github.com/ros-industrial/robotiq.
[7] https://github.com/ros-industrial/ur_modern_driver.
[8] The URScript Programming Language, ver 3.5.4, April 12, 2018.

Despite the selected control mode, either of the two nodes for UR5 generates `joint_speed_temp` topic, which has the same message type as `joint_speed` but needs to be through the publishing regulator node because ROS does not guarantee real-time capabilities. Particularly, since the two control nodes have processing burden such as inverse and forward kinematics computation within them, it is not straightforward to keep the computation time for each processing loop consistently. Due to this fact, when `joint_speed_temp` was directly input to `ur_modern_driver` node, it was easily experienced that the movement of the UR5 was not smooth but starting and stopping repeatedly. To address this undesirable behaviour, we included the publishing regulator node. Basically, this node simply subscribes `joint_speed_temp` and then publishes it as `joint_speed`, but if there is no new topic received within 0.008 sec after the previous topic, it instead publishes the previous topic again. Although this does not provide proper real-time capability as well, at least the movement of the UR5 has become much smoother.

For the gripper, the control node for grasping subscribes `leap_motion_input`, which contains the user hand's grabbing strength sensed by the LM, i.e. `grab_strength` $\in [0, 1]$, where the value of 1 represents fully-closed hand. Depending on the grabbing strength and its rate of change, `rPRA`, `rPRB`, and `rPRC` (i.e. the robotic gripper's each finger position request) and `rSPA`, `rSPB`, `rSPC` (i.e. speed request) are chosen and comprised of `SModelRobotOutput`, which is then published to the gripper.

ROS# Setup: ROS# publishes the user's input such as `system_mode` and `leap_motion_input` from the Unity side to the ROS side, while subscribing the status information from the remote site such as `joint_states` and `camera`. Here, `leap_motion_input` contains ROS message `Human_Orion.msg`, which is based on `Human.msg` of the existing ROS package for LM but modified by ourselves to have new information such as a user palm's normal and directional vectors. To implement the publishing and subscribing processing between the Unity and ROS sides, we also created the C# scripts such as `Human Orion Publisher` and `System Mode Publisher` and utilised existing ones such as `Joint State Subscriber` and `Image Subscriber`.

3.2   How Bare Hands Control the Robotic Manipulator?

As mentioned previously, there are two control modes in the current system: *Reaching mode* and *Manipulating/Grasping mode*. In Reaching mode, the three-dimensional Cartesian position of the robot end effector only follows the operator's palm position sensed via the Leap Motion only during the time when the hand is closing, which activates the movement of the robot. This activation functionality is intended to reduce excessive human concentration load during the entire operation, preventing undesirable accidents caused by the operator' possible unconscious hand gestures or movements. This section describes more details of each control mode.

Algorithm 1. ROS node: Control for Reaching

1: **while** ROS is not shutdown **do**
2:      **if** grab_strengh $\geq c_1$ and control_mode $=$ 'reaching' **then**
3:          $\theta_k \leftarrow$ joint_states
4:          ${}^6_0\mathbf{B}_k \leftarrow$ kin.forward(θ_k)
5:          $\Delta\mathbf{p} \leftarrow$ palm_position$_k$ - palm_position$_{k-1}$
6:          $\mathbf{p}^d_{k+1} \leftarrow \mathbf{p}_k + \Delta\mathbf{p}$
7:          Construct ${}^6_0\mathbf{B}^d_{k+1}$ using $\mathbf{p}^d_{k+1}$
8:          $\theta^d_{k+1} \leftarrow$ kin.inverse(${}^6_0\mathbf{B}^d_{k+1}$)
9:          $\dot{\theta}^d_{k+1} = (\theta^d_{k+1} - \theta_k)/\Delta t$
10:         joint_speed $\leftarrow \dot{\theta}^d_{k+1}$
11:         Publish joint_speed and sleep Δt.
12:     **end if**
13: **end while**

Reaching Mode: The description of this control mode is shown as Algorithm 1. Basically, the main loop runs at every computation time instant k after each sampling time $\Delta t = 0.008$ s, if a user's hand is closing (i.e. grab_strength from topic leap_motion_input is larger than a certain threshold constant c_1) as well as Reaching mode is selected (i.e. control_mode from topic system_mode). Note that we set c_1 to 0.9 because grab_strength sometimes becomes less than 1 due to the sensor noise even when a human hand is fully closed. At first, the ROS node obtains the current status of the robot arm in joint space, i.e. joint_states. It is then, by using the forward kinematics method for UR5 [6][9], transformed to the corresponding position and orientation of the end effector in Cartesian space, ${}^6_0\mathbf{B}_k \in \mathbb{R}_{4\times4}$, which is defined as

$$ {}^6_0\mathbf{B}_k = \begin{bmatrix} \mathbf{E}_k & \mathbf{p}_k \\ \mathbf{0}_{1\times3} & 1 \end{bmatrix}. \tag{1} $$

$\mathbf{E}_k = [\mathbf{u}_{X_6}, \mathbf{u}_{Y_6}, \mathbf{u}_{Z_6}] \in \mathbb{R}_{3\times3}$ indicates the orientation of the end effector, where $\mathbf{u}_{X_6}, \mathbf{u}_{Y_6}, \mathbf{u}_{Z_6} \in \mathbb{R}_{3\times1}$ are unit vectors representing each orthogonal direction of the end effector coordination frame with respect to the robot arm's base frame (i.e. the shoulder). $\mathbf{p}_k \in \mathbb{R}_{1\times3}$ is the position of the end effector in task space.

Then, it obtains the desired amount of the end effector translation, $\Delta\mathbf{p}$, using the user's palm position from topic leap_motion_input. It updates the desired position $\mathbf{p}^d_{k+1}$ and construct ${}^6_0\mathbf{B}^d_{k+1}$, which is then transformed to the desired joint states for the next instant θ^d_{k+1}. Finally, the desired joint speed for each joint $\dot{\theta}^d_{k+1}$ is computed and published.

Manipulating/Grasping Mode: In Manipulating/Grasping mode, not only the position of the end effector but also its orientation follows those of a human hand. In this mode, closing-hand gesture instead triggers grasping behaviour of the robotic gripper.

---

[9] http://wiki.ros.org/ur_kin_py.

Algorithm 2. ROS node: Control for Manipulating

1: **while** ROS is not shutdown **do**
2:     **if** control_mode = 'manipulating/grasping' **then**
3:         // *Get the current status*
4:         $\theta_k \leftarrow$ joint_states
5:         ${}^6_0\mathbf{B}_k \leftarrow$ kin.forward(θ_k)
6:         // *Position control*
7:         $\Delta\mathbf{p} \leftarrow$ palm_position$_k$ - palm_position$_{k-1}$
8:         $\mathbf{p}^d_{k+1} \leftarrow \mathbf{p}_k + \Delta\mathbf{p}$
9:         // *Orientation control*
10:        thumb_direction$_k \leftarrow$ palm_normal$_k \times$ palm_direction$_k$ (for left hand)
11:        $\mathbf{H}_k = [$palm_normal$_k,$ palm_direction$_k,$ thumb_direction$_k]$
12:        Get the transformation matrix $\mathbf{T}_{\mathbf{H}_{k-1}\to\mathbf{H}_k} \leftarrow \mathbf{H}_k \cdot \mathbf{H}^{-1}_{k-1}$
13:        $\mathbf{E}^d_{k+1} \leftarrow \mathbf{T}_{\mathbf{H}_{k-1}\to\mathbf{H}_k} \cdot \mathbf{E}_k$
14:        // *Command*
15:        Construct ${}^6_0\mathbf{B}^d_{k+1}$ using $\mathbf{p}^d_{k+1}$ and $\mathbf{E}^d_{k+1}$
16:        $\theta^d_{k+1} \leftarrow$ kin.inverse$({}^6_0\mathbf{B}^d_{k+1})$
17:        $\dot{\theta}^d_{k+1} = (\theta^d_{k+1} - \theta_k)/\Delta t$
18:        joint_speed $\leftarrow \dot{\theta}^d_{k+1}$
19:        Publish joint_speed and sleep Δt.
20:    **end if**
21: **end while**

Algorithm 2 shows how the ROS node for the robotic manipulator works in more details. Compared with Algorithm 1, additionally included are Lines 10–13 for orientation control. At first, it obtains the user hand's current orientation $\mathbf{H}_k \in \mathbb{R}_{3\times3}$ using palm_normal and palm_direction from topic leap_motion _input, and thumb_direction, which is the cross product between the two vectors. Then, it calculates $\mathbf{T}_{\mathbf{H}_{k-1}\to\mathbf{H}_k}$, the transformation matrix from the previous hand's orientation $\mathbf{H}_{k-1}$ to the current one $\mathbf{H}_k$. Using the transformation matrix, the desired orientation of the end effector $\mathbf{E}^d_{k+1}$ can be obtained. ${}^6_0\mathbf{B}^d_{k+1}$ is then constructed using $\mathbf{E}^d_{k+1}$ along with the desired position $\mathbf{p}^d_{k+1}$, and eventually transformed to the desired joint speed for each joint $\dot{\theta}^d_{k+1}$, which is then published to the robotic manipulator.

The ROS node for grasping is described in Algorithm 3. It computes the time difference of the hand grabbing position grab_speed$_k$ using the current grab_strength$_k$ from topic leap_motion_input and the one at the previous time instant. Then, grab_speed$_k$ and grab_strength$_k$ are used to set the gripper's desired position and speed (i.e. rPRA, rSPA, etc.), respectively. Since the values of rPRX and rSPX are integers from 0 to 255, it is required for grab_speed$_k$ and grab_strength$_k$ to be mapped appropriately, for which function f_P and f_S are used. Finally, those values are comprised of topic SModelRobotOutput, which is then published to the gripper.

Algorithm 3. ROS node: Control for Grasping

1: **while** ROS is not shutdown **do**
2:     **if** control_mode = 'manipulating/grasping' **then**
3:         $\text{grab\_speed}_k \leftarrow \text{abs}(\text{grab\_strength}_k - \text{grab\_strength}_{k-1})$
4:         **if** $\text{grab\_strength}_k \geq c_2$ **then**
5:             rPRA, rPRB, rPRC $\leftarrow f_P(\text{grab\_strength}_k, c_2)$
6:             rSPA, rSPB, rSPC $\leftarrow f_S(\text{grab\_speed}_k)$
7:         **else**
8:             rPRA, rPRB, rPRC, rSPA, rSPB, rSPC $\leftarrow 0$
9:         **end if**
10:        Construct and publish SModelRobotOutput and sleep Δt.
11:    **end if**
12: **end while**

In summary, the hand gestures and their resultant commands towards the robot are shown in Fig. 3.

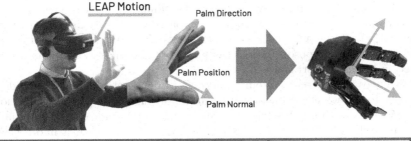

Fig. 3. How to control the robotic manipulator through hand tracking

Control Mode \ Hand gesture	Closing Hand	Moving Hand
Reaching Mode	Movement activated	Gripper moves (when activated)
Manipulating/Grasping Mode	Gripper closes	Gripper moves

4   Demonstration and Discussion

As shown in Fig. 4, we successfully demonstrated the proposed teleoperation system to pick up an empty aluminium canister[10]. Hand position and gestures can be sensed very well, which provides a high degree of intuitiveness. Thanks to this intuitiveness, it was mentioned by the test operator that the multiple plane displays were enough to perceive the remote situation and accomplish the task.

---

[10] Watch also the video: https://youtu.be/lu-0yrl9J5g.

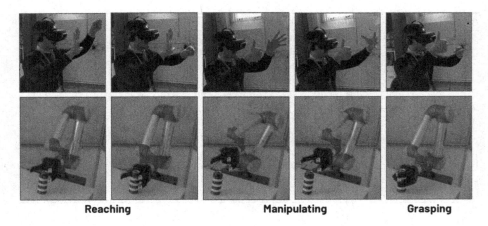

Fig. 4. Demonstration of the proposed teleoperation system: the first two subfigures present Reaching mode; the rest subfigures show Manipulating/Grasping mode

In this context, as future work, we will evaluate this HRI concept by participating through human-case studies, compared with the existing one using a virtual target object. One of our hypotheses is that, relying on multiple plane displays only, the proposed HRI concept will provide more benefits as we experienced in this demonstration.

Obviously, the current system based on LM does not inherently provide any haptic feedback, which is considered as an important feature for teleoperation in many cases. Even though we tried to use a commercial-grade exoskeleton haptic-force-feedback glove (i.e. *CyberGrasp*), according to our test, a hand wearing the haptic glove or occluded by even a small object is not able to be sensed by a LM. In this context, it will be a valuable future work to explore how to provide haptic feedback to LM users. Firstly, we might be able to use multiple LMs as in [8], where two sensors are located to view orthogonal aspects of a human hand. However, even use of this approach is challenging due to the fact that the haptic-force-feedback glove almost fully covers the back of a hand and thus the palm should be always oriented towards the auxiliary LM to be sensed clearly, which limits the user's operational range. Without such force-feedback gloves, we possibly could use virtual haptics based on visual or audio feedback. Alternatively, an artificial haptic device can be used such as *Ultrahaptics*[11], which uses ultrasound to provide mid-air haptics. Otherwise, it would be also an interesting research to design a wearable light-weight haptic device compatible to LM.

---

[11] https://www.ultrahaptics.com/products-programs/.

5   Conclusion

This paper presented a novel teleoperation system where a robotic manipulator simply and directly copies a human operator's bare hand posture and gesture in a real-time manner without having any hand-held devices. We showed how to practically setup the system using commercial-grade robots such as Universal Robots UR5 and Robotiq 3-finger gripper, and a Leap Motion and Virtual Reality, based on Unity and ROS. We demonstrated our system executing a simple pick-and-place task, and discussed about possible benefits and costs of this HRI concept.

References

1. Allspaw, J., Roche, J., Lemiesz, N., Yannuzzi, M., Yanco, H.A.: Remotely teleoperating a humanoid robot to perform fine motor tasks with virtual reality. In: Waste Management Symposium (WM 2018), Phoenix, AZ (2018)
2. Cancedda, L., Cannavò, A., Garofalo, G., Lamberti, F., Montuschi, P., Paravati, G.: Mixed reality-based user interaction feedback for a hand-controlled interface targeted to robot teleoperation. In: De Paolis, L.T., Bourdot, P., Mongelli, A. (eds.) AVR 2017. LNCS, vol. 10325, pp. 447–463. Springer, Cham (2017). https://doi.org/10.1007/978-3-319-60928-7_38
3. Chae, J., Jin, Y., Sung, Y., Cho, K.: Genetic algorithm-based motion estimation method using orientations and EMGs for robot controls. Sensors 18(2), 183 (2018). https://doi.org/10.3390/s18010183
4. Chen, S., Ma, H., Yang, C., Fu, M.: Hand gesture based robot control system using leap motion. In: Liu, H., Kubota, N., Zhu, X., Dillmann, R., Zhou, D. (eds.) ICIRA 2015. LNCS (LNAI), vol. 9244, pp. 581–591. Springer, Cham (2015). https://doi.org/10.1007/978-3-319-22879-2_53
5. Crick, C., Jay, G., Osentoski, S., Pitzer, B., Jenkins, O.C.: Rosbridge: ROS for non-ROS users. Springer Tracts Adv. Robot. 100, 493–504 (2017)
6. Hawkins, K.P.: Analytic inverse kinematics for the universal robots UR-5/UR-10 arms. Technical report, Georgia Institute of Technology (2013). https://smartech.gatech.edu/bitstream/handle/1853/50782/ur_kin_tech_report_1.pdf
7. Hokayem, P.F., Spong, M.W.: Bilateral teleoperation: an historical survey. Automatica 42(12), 2035–2057 (2006). https://doi.org/10.1016/j.automatica.2006.06.027
8. Jin, H., Chen, Q., Chen, Z., Hu, Y., Zhang, J.: Multi-LeapMotion sensor based demonstration for robotic refine tabletop object manipulation task. CAAI Trans. Intell. Technol. 1(1), 104–113 (2016). https://doi.org/10.1016/j.trit.2016.03.010. https://linkinghub.elsevier.com/retrieve/pii/S2468232216000111
9. Krupke, D., Einig, L., Langbehn, E., Zhang, J., Steinicke, F.: Immersive remote grasping: realtime gripper control by a heterogenous robot control system. In: Proceedings of the ACM Symposium on Virtual Reality Software and Technology, VRST 02–04-Nove, pp. 337–338 (2016). https://doi.org/10.1145/2993369.2996345
10. Kruusamae, K., Pryor, M.: High-precision telerobot with human-centered variable perspective and scalable gestural interface. In: Proceedings - 2016 9th International Conference on Human System Interactions, HSI 2016, pp. 190–196 (2016). https://doi.org/10.1109/HSI.2016.7529630

11. Li, C., Yang, C., Wan, J., Annamalai, A.S.S., Cangelosi, A.: Teleoperation control of Baxter robot using Kalman filter-based sensor fusion. Syst. Sci. Control Eng. **5**(1), 156–167 (2017). https://doi.org/10.1080/21642583.2017.1300109
12. Lipton, J.I., Fay, A.J., Rus, D.: Baxter's homunculus: virtual reality spaces for teleoperation in manufacturing. IEEE Robot. Autom. Lett. **3**(1), 179–186 (2018). https://doi.org/10.1109/LRA.2017.2737046
13. Makris, S., et al.: Dual arm robot in cooperation with humans for flexible assembly. CIRP Ann. **66**(1), 13–16 (2017). https://doi.org/10.1016/j.cirp.2017.04.097
14. Nuño, E., Basañez, L., Ortega, R.: Passivity-based control for bilateral teleoperation: A tutorial. Automatica **47**(3), 485–495 (2011). https://doi.org/10.1016/j.automatica.2011.01.004
15. Pancake, D., et al.: A novel and cost effective approach to the decommissioning and decontamination of legacy glove boxes - minimizing TRU waste and maximizing LLW waste - 13634. In: Waste Management Symposium (WM 2013), Phoenix, AZ (2013)
16. Peppoloni, L., Brizzi, F., Avizzano, C.A., Ruffaldi, E.: Immersive ROS-integrated framework for robot teleoperation. In: 2015 IEEE Symposium on 3D User Interfaces (3DUI), pp. 177–178. IEEE, March 2015. https://doi.org/10.1109/3DUI.2015.7131758
17. Roldán, J.J., et al.: Multi-robot systems, virtual reality and ros: developing a new generation of operator interfaces. In: Koubaa, A. (ed.) Robot Operating System (ROS). SCI, vol. 778, pp. 29–64. Springer, Cham (2019). https://doi.org/10.1007/978-3-319-91590-6_2
18. Tang, G., Webb, P.: The design and evaluation of an ergonomic contactless gesture control system for industrial robots. J. Robot. (2018). https://doi.org/10.1155/2018/9791286
19. Whitney, D., Rosen, E., Phillips, E., Konidaris, G., Tellex, S.: Comparing robot grasping teleoperation across desktop and virtual reality with ROS reality. In: International Symposium on Robotics Research, pp. 1–16 (2017)

A Robust Polyurethane Depositing System for Overcoming Obstacles in Disaster Scenario Robotics

Alec John Burns$^{(\boxtimes)}$, Sebastiano Fichera , and Paolo Paoletti

University of Liverpool, Liverpool L69 3GH, UK
{sgaburns,sebastiano.fichera,P.Paoletti}@liverpool.ac.uk

Abstract. One of the most difficult challenges for terrestrial robotic platforms in disaster scenarios is their inability to traverse highly irregular terrain. Many different robotic architectures have been proposed over recent years, each with benefits and shortfalls. In this work, we propose a Polyurethane Foam depositing system, which can be applied to any such platform and increase its ability to overcome obstacles significantly. The system proposed is inexpensive, and the way in which it overcomes obstacles allows very simple control systems for autonomy. The deposited foam has a potential expansion ratio of over $33\times$ its constituent parts and a final compressive strength exceeding $2\,\mathrm{MPa}$, final mechanical properties can be tuned on board. The system has been implemented on a two-tracked rover and its autonomous responses tested against significant objects and chasms. The results show that the amount of foam deposited can be well controlled and multiple layers can be stacked on top of each other to significantly increase altitude.

Keywords: Robotics · Disaster scenario · Polyurethane Foam · Overcoming obstacles · Search and rescue

1 Introduction

1.1 Background

Disaster scenarios consider the environment or aftermath of an area post-event; where an event can typically be considered a sudden accident or a natural catastrophe that causes great damage or loss of life. Hundreds of floods, storms, heat waves and droughts have left over 600,000 people dead and 4.1 billion injured or homeless around the world since 1995, according to a U.N. report [4].

When a disaster strikes, it is often critical to find victims as soon as possible. People stranded after an earthquake or hurricane or who are living in a war zone are often stuck for days without food, water or medicines. They are usually cut off from the world due to collapsed infrastructure, making it hard for them to receive necessities. First responders are some of the most at risk in the relief efforts [1], often entering highly unstable areas with little knowledge of the interiors.

© Springer Nature Switzerland AG 2019
K. Althoefer et al. (Eds.): TAROS 2019, LNAI 11650, pp. 295–306, 2019.
https://doi.org/10.1007/978-3-030-25332-5_26

Recent advancements in technology are revolutionizing the roles of aerial, terrestrial and maritime robotic systems in disaster relief, search and rescue and salvage operations [6]. Robots can be deployed quickly in areas deemed too unsafe for humans and can be used to guide rescuers, collect data, deliver essential supplies or provide communication services. However, taking terrestrial robotic platforms from the often predictable even surfaces of a lab, to the highly irregular terrain present in disaster zone environments, presents one of their greatest shortfalls: overcoming obstacles.

Various robot architectures have been proposed for driving and climbing on rough terrain and the models can be divided into roughly five categories [2]: single-tracked, multi-tracked, wheeled, quadruped-platforms (or biologically inspired systems) and humanoid. The unique solution of each platforms results in particular benefits when overcoming obstacles. Hybrid platforms have been proposed to maximise the pros of their constituent architectures. Such products are often costly and their added benefits limited. A comparison of tracked, wheeled, humanoid and their respective hybrids was performed in [3] and is reported in Table 1. This overlooks quadruped and biologically inspired platforms as these represent a very diverse array of systems which are difficult to generalise.

Table 1. Synthetic comparison of locomotion system features, taken from [3]. LW = Legged Wheeled, LT = Legged Tracked and WT = Wheeled Tracked

	Wheeled	Tracked	Legged	LW	LT	WT
Maximum speed	High	Med/high	Low	Med/high	Medium	Med/high
Obstacle crossing	Low	Med/high	High	Med/high	High	Medium
Step climbing	Low	Medium	High	High	High	Medium
Slope climbing	Low/med	High	Med/high	Med/high	High	Med/high
Soft terrain	Low	High	Low/med	Low/med	Med/high	High
Uneven terrain	Low	Med/high	High	High	High	Med/high
Energy efficiency	High	Med	Low	Med/high	Medium	Med/high
Mechanical complexity	Low	Low	High	Med/high	Med/high	Low/med
Control complexity	Low	Low	High	Med/high	Med/high	Medium

As can be seen from Table 1, no one platform architecture has so far proven to outperform the rest. As a result of this, projects have been put forward more recently to increase the abilities of platforms using material deposition. One such material is Polyurethane (PU).

1.2 Polyurethane Foam

PU is a synthetic resin in which the polymer units are linked by urethane groups; when combining the two part constituents (PU-5800, Polycraft), the mix quickly expands and then sets rigid. The final properties of the PU foam depend largely on the mix ratio and can be changed quite easily. Compressive strengths of over

2 MPa are possible, which can easily support the weight of a human standing thereon. Also, potential expansion ratios of over 30× the original volume means it can generate $25\,dm^3$ of final structure foam from $840\,cm^3$ of the two part liquid constituents [5]. These values depend largely on the mixing style and have been recorded through testing on the system shown in Sect. 2.1. The final form is a closed-cell and thus water-proof when set. All mix types are lighter than water, yet strong enough to support the weight of an average sized male human on the area of a foot. Additionally, these foams attach to a variety of materials including wood, iron, and concrete, among others. Based on these characteristics, this material is suitable for use in disaster scenarios in real-time. Two projects have utilised a robotic PU foam depositing system for traversing obstacles.

1.3 Related Work

The first project of this type was proposed by Napp et al. [7]. The platform utilises a mechanised syringe to deposit small amounts of two part PU to create a ramp which allowed it to traverse an object larger than its original capability. This style of deposit system provides little mixing and thus very low expansion ratio of the foam, meaning a significant amount of material extrusion was needed to create said ramp. Also, continuous deposition was required if the syringe was to remain unblocked before using all of the material. For the ramp demo shown in this project multiple syringe cartridges and mixing devices were manually replaced on the system to allow continuous usage. One final remark on this system is that the single rigid nozzle deposit system and small expansion rate resulted in a very complex build requirement, which would be difficult to implement autonomously and was thus manually controlled by a human operator.

The second project of this type is that shown by Fujisawa et al. [5]. This platform utilised an aerosol depositing system on a gimbal, with both single part and two part PU tested. This system allowed much more flexible deposition than [7], and therefore an autonomous ramping system was possible upon detecting an object. However, the use of an aerosol depositing system gives little control over the material being deposited, as the mix ratio and outlet speed are determined with mechanical design and cannot be controlled by the system once setup. Also, the use of prepackaged aerosols brings into question how well this system could be scaled.

This project proposes an on board pumping and mixing system to drive the two part liquids of PU foam to reaction, thus giving complete control over the deposition.

2 Design

2.1 Deposit System

Peristaltic pumps are used to drive PU part one and two from their separate reservoirs to a mixing chamber. This chamber, shown in Fig. 1, ensures the two parts have been thoroughly mixed without increasing the turbulence to such an extent that the parts begin reacting. This mixing is necessary as multiple outlets are required and due to the viscous nature of the individual parts, the flows would otherwise develop separate channels with no mixing, as shown in figure Fig. 2. This balance between preventing channel development and averting PU reaction is achieved through a calculated design considering three primary parameters of the mixing chamber: inlet diameters, angle between PU inlets 1 and 2 and joint configuration between inlets/outlets. Inlet diameter primarily controls the flow velocity per pump rate. The angle between PU inlets effects how likely PU parts are to form separate channels. The joint style between inlets and outlets also has an effect on this. The final inlet diameters of 2 mm, angle between inlet 1 and 2 of 120° and central spherical joints connected between a straight cylinder allowed sufficient liquid velocities and contact momentum to ensure full dispersion without initiating reaction.

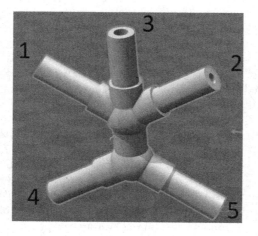

Fig. 1. Illustration of the mixing chamber designed. Labels 1 and 2 represent inlets for PU part 1 and 2 respectively. Label 3 represents the inlet for the solvent flush. Labels 4 and 5 highlight the outlets of the mix chamber, which will contain an even distribution of PU part 1 and 2 or the solvent depending on the stage.

Following the mix chamber the now combined PU is separated and passed through a static mixing nozzle (MA6.3-21S, Adhesive Dispensing Ltd.) before the outlet. A major drawback of previous systems were the blockages that occur between use, as after use residue will be left in the system and particularly the static mixing nozzles. For this a solvent (Isopropyl alcohol) is then autonomously flushed through the system to mitigate the reaction and eject any residue. This allows the system to be used multiple times without blockage or manual intervention. The whole process is illustrated in Fig. 3.

Driving the system with peristaltic pumps means that at any one time the amount of liquid being driven is equal to that in the tubing and mixing devices

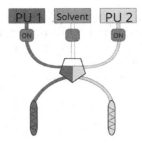

Fig. 2. Illustration of PU parts one and two not mixing, which occurs without a suitable mixing chamber.

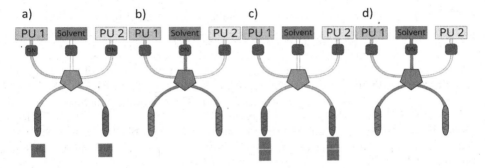

Fig. 3. Illustration of the stages of pumping PU part one and two to create PU foam and the solvent flush stages: (a) Pumping of PU part one and two to create first batch of PU foam (b) flush of solvent to ensure no blockages after use (c) Pumping of PU part one and two to create second batch of PU foam (d) flush of solvent. Peristaltic pumps are represented by red symbols, central pentagon represents the mixing chamber and crossed cylinder represent the static mixing nozzles. (Color figure online)

and is thus independent of the size of the reservoir from which it is being pulled. Unlike syringe and aerosol driven designs [5,7], this allows the system to be significantly scaled as the size of the reservoirs has no effect on the force needed to drive the depositing system.

Further, the system can control the rate of each pump independently. Altering the ratio of PU part one to PU part two alters the properties of the deposit as previously mentioned. For example, if the system required a harder deposit, it could autonomously increase the ratio of PU part one to the mix. Likewise, increasing the ratio of PU Part two would increase expansion ratio; this could be necessary if maximising the volumetric output was required. Additionally, increasing overall flow velocity increases the turbulence with which the chemicals are mixed, thus reducing the time taken to begin expansion. This has the potential to allow outputted material to be less fluid-like and more immediately sticky, where obvious applications would be to allow foam deposition on a vertical wall. However, making the deposit more liquid-like on exit allows the substance to be deposited into crevices and cracks which would not be possible for syringe or aerosol deposited systems. Increasing this rate of reaction makes the substance more likely to block the static-mixers and thus a maximum overall pump speed is set to prevent this.

Finally, the system allows two pumps to drive the liquids to two outlets, although it is possible to increase this number. The importance of this will be mentioned in Sect. 3.

2.2 Robotic Platform

As previously mentioned, this project puts forward a PU depositing system which has potential to be combined with any terrestrial robotic platform to extend its ability. For the purposes of testing, a simple low cost tracked rover was designed as follows.

Rover Design. The rover used for the test is the two-tracked vehicle, with a track height of 100 mm and a track length of 300 mm, shown in Fig. 4. The foam ratio been tested to easily support 0.42 MPa (an 85 kg human on a small section of the foot) whereas the rover in question has a pressure value of 0.02 MPa (15 kg Rover on the total surface area of its tracks). The platform is driven by two large stepper motors (RB-Phi-266, Robotshop), which would allow a 50 kg payload to be pulled along an even medium friction surface. The rover is driven by a central Arduino Mega 2560 board which controls the motor speeds via two Arduino Nanos and the pumping systems via another Arduino Mega 2560. A digital compass is connected to the central control board to feed orientation information back to the controller and positional information is estimated from motor steps. The PU Foam depositing system will be mounted on top of the rover with the two outlets positioned directly behind the tracks. As the rover moves, the foam will be deposited, forming two distinct extrusions which are aligned with the rovers tracks. Once the foam has expanded and solidified the rover can simply climb on said extrusions to increase or maintain altitude. When depositing foam in a straight line, controlling either deposit speed or rover speed allows the platform create ramp structures as will be seen in Sect. 4. This is an alternative to the complex depositing mechanism proposed in [5] and the complicated ramp structure required in [7].

2.3 Object Overcoming System

Basic ultrasonic distance sensors (HC-SR04) are utilised to determine the presence of obstacles or chasms in front of the vehicle. If an object is detected, a ramp construction procedure is initiated. Whereas, if a chasm is present, a void filling function is executed.

Fig. 4. Image of the rover platform.

Frontal Object Detection. One sensor is placed at the front of the rover, at just above half of the rover track height. It was determined through testing that if an object is detected at this height or above, the rover will not be able to overcome it independently. As the rover cannot detect whether it is meeting an object perpendicularly, once the rover detects the object it will begin to move forward at a low motor torque to align the rover front face with the straight edge of an object. Once in contact with the object it will initiate the depositing protocol. A programmed deposit rate/time sequence is utilized that will produce a ramp thus allowing the rover to overcome an obstacle at half of the rover track height. Waiting times are also predetermined based on the amount of foam deposited from previously collected set times. If the obstacle is still detected after climbing on this deposit, then the same procedure will be repeated, but with increased ramp length. The rover can overcome minor over/under expansions for frontal obstacles that may occur. A flowchart of the autonomous response to objects and respective illustrations for the responses are shown in Fig. 5.

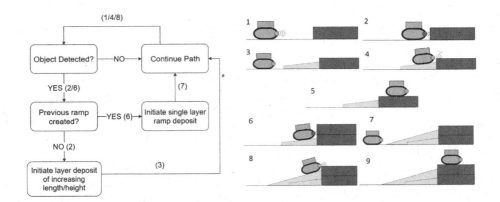

Fig. 5. Flowchart and illustration of the frontal object detection system.

Chasm Detection. The other tested scenario is chasm detection, which considers detecting large gaps in the flooring preventing path following. Two sensors are placed on the undercarriage of the chassis, facing the ground. One is positioned near the front of the rover and the other in the center. The rover can overcome chasms of up to 100 mm in length (one third of the total rover length) without falling into said gap. Therefore, if both forward and center undercarriage sensors detect a continuous gap, the rover will stop moving and initiate its void filling procedure. The rover will estimate the amount of deposit required from the depth measurements of the chasm, set values were taken heuristically. However, if it under deposited (for example if the foam expanded less than expected) then it would once again detect the chasm and repeat the filling procedure. Overdepositing typically leads to foam overflowing the chasm, but the amount is usually trivial for the rover to overcome. A flowchart of autonomous response to objects and respective illustration for the responses is shown in Fig. 6. Chasm detection is overridden when climbing a ramp produced by system 1.

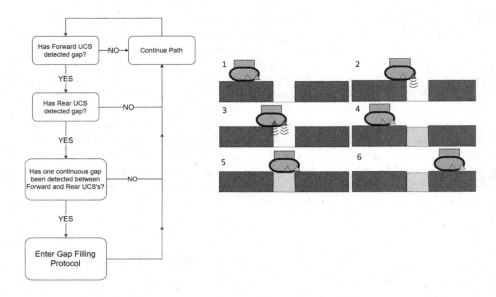

Fig. 6. Flowchart and illustration of the chasm detection system.

3   Results

Three experiments were carried out, with both detection systems being operational. The rover is given a straight line path which it is required to follow, if it detects any objects along this path it must work out how best to overcome them. All three experiments require the ability to: first, detect an obstacle that inhibits the rover's ability to follow the planned path, eject the PU foam correctly, flush the system to ensure no blockages occur, wait until the foam has cured and then overcome obstacle using the deposited foam. The first two experiments consider frontal obstacles and the third considers chasm detection. For all three tests the mix ratio of PU part one: part two was fixed at 1:1 so that it can settle within 6 min, expand around 30× and have sufficient strength to support the rover weight. All three of these obstacles have been tested to ensure that the rover could not overcome them without using the PU depositing system, with the rover toppling/not able to grip onto the material for the frontal objects and getting stuck in the chasm. Total run time is taken from the moment the object is detected until the time the object has been fully overcome (the entire rover is atop the object or passed the chasm).

3.1 Small Frontal Object Test

In this experiment a 60 mm high block was placed along the rover's path, just over half of the 100 mm rover track height. The rover detected the object, aligned itself and began the first layer ramp deposit procedure. It then waited for the foam to expand and solidify before using the deposit to continue its path; detecting no further obstacles along the way. The rover created the ramp, varying pump speed as it moved away at a constant speed with more material being deposited closer to the object as shown in Fig. 7. The total time to run this experiment was 6 min and 42 s.

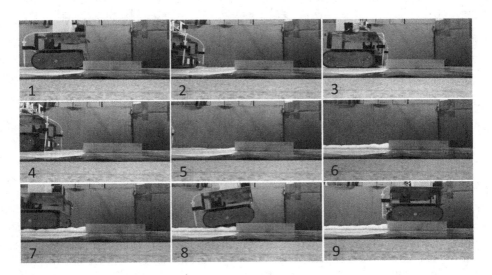

Fig. 7. Test one, the stages of the rover detecting a 60 mm high block and depositing a ramp foam to overcome said block.

3.2   Large Frontal Object Test

In this experiment a 130 mm high block was placed along the rover's path, 1.3×
the rover track height. The rover detected the object and conducted the same first
layer ramp deposit procedure as in test one. However, upon climbing the ramp,
it detects the object once more. Knowing it has previously deposited a ramp,
the rover initiates the ramping procedure but deposits foam for an increased
duration/distance over the previously created ramps. The rover then waits for
the second layer to cure and is able to overcome the object, as shown in Fig. 8.
This success of this test proves that building large, multi-layered ramp structures
is possible and that the system ensures no blockages occur between layers/uses.
Total time for this experiment was 13 min and 42 s.

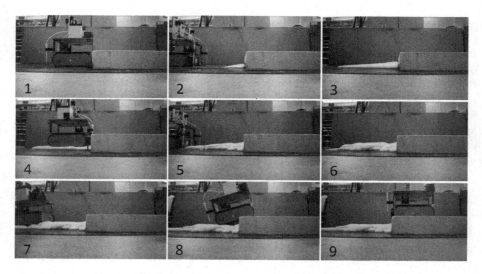

Fig. 8. Test two, the stages of the rover detecting a 130 mm high block and depositing
a ramp foam to overcome said block.

3.3   Chasm Test

In the final experiment a 160 mm long chasm was placed along the rover's path,
over half the 300 mm rover tracks length. The chasm was 80 mm deep and 400 mm
wide. The rover moves, first detecting a small gap with the frontal undercarriage
sensor, the rover then moves more slowly to ensure it has sufficient time to
either detect whether it is able or not to overcome the chasm without depositing
material. This is performed by detecting a continuous gap between the frontal
and rear undercarriage sensors. Once the rover detects that the chasm is too
long and/or deep, it begins its the gap filling procedure. The rover estimates
the amount of PU foam to be deposited using sensor depth measurements of the

chasm, performs the deposit and then waits for this to expand and cure. The rover filled the chasm sufficiently and overcame the obstacle as shown in Fig. 9. Total time for this experiment time was 5 min and 60 s.

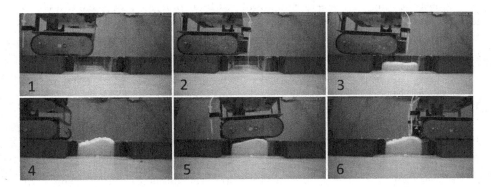

Fig. 9. Test three, the stages of the rover detecting a 160 mm long chasm and depositing to fill said gap and overcome the obstacle.

3.4   Summary of Experimental Results

A summary of the experimental results is reported in Table 2, showing that the proposed PU foam depositing system enables the rover to overcome obstacles which were previously insurmountable. In all cases expansion ratio is between $29\times$ and $32\times$ the original parts, showing the robust control over the mixing process and, hence, the final mechanical properties of the foam.

Table 2. Summary of experimental results, where H = Height, D = Depth, L = Length and Vol = Volume

	Type	Dimensions	Deposit vol	PU used	Run time
Test one	Small frontal	H: 60 mm	$2000\,\text{cm}^3$	$63\,\text{cm}^3$	6 min 42 s
Test two	Large frontal	H: 130 mm	$5000\,\text{cm}^3$	$170\,\text{cm}^3$	13 min 42 s
Test three	Chasm	D × L: 100 × 200 mm	$4000\,\text{cm}^3$	$126\,\text{cm}^3$	5 min 60 s

4   Conclusion

In this paper an inexpensive and easy-to-use PU foam depositing system is proposed. The system is designed as an independent module for existing ground robot platforms to expand their capabilities. Thanks to its design, it can be utilised without complicated control algorithms to allow systems to autonomously overcome obstacles. This system, unlike others previously proposed, allows complete control over the deposited material. Specifically, it allows the PU foams expansion ratio and final compressive strength to be tuned autonomously according to the situational requirement. The flush system embedded allows the long term use of the module without blockage, a typical drawback for such systems. Initial tests show it provides significant extension to capabilities, with no drawbacks. Work presented in this paper is an early prototype and has not been extensively tested yet. In the near future we plan to extensively test the full capabilities of the system.

References

1. Alexander, D.A., Klein, S.: First responders after disasters: a review of stress reactions, at-risk, vulnerability, and resilience factors. Prehospital Disaster Med. **24**(2), 87–94 (2009). https://doi.org/10.1017/S1049023X00006610
2. Brunner, M., Brüggemann, B., Schulz, D.: Towards autonomously traversing complex obstacles with mobile robots with adjustable chassis, May 2012. https://doi.org/10.1109/CarpathianCC.2012.6228617
3. Bruzzone, L., Quaglia, G.: Review article: locomotion systems for ground mobile robots in unstructured environments. Mech. Sci. **3**, 49–62 (2012). https://doi.org/10.5194/ms-3-49-2012
4. The Centre for Research on the Epidemiology of Disasters (CRED), The United Nations Office for Disaster Risk Reduction (UNDRR): The human cost of weather related disasters 1995–2015 (2016). https://www.preventionweb.net/files/46796_cop21weatherdisastersreport2015.pdf
5. Fujisawa, R., Nagaya, N., Okazaki, S., Sato, R., Ikemoto, Y., Dobata, S.: Active modification of the environment by a robot with construction abilities. ROBOMECH J. **2**(1), 9 (2015). https://doi.org/10.1186/s40648-015-0030-2
6. Murphy, R.R., et al.: Search and rescue robotics. In: Siciliano, B., Khatib, O. (eds.) Springer Handbook of Robotics, pp. 1151–1173. Springer, Heidelberg (2008). https://doi.org/10.1007/978-3-540-30301-5_51
7. Napp, N., Rappoli, O.R., Wu, J.M., Nagpal, R.: Materials and mechanisms for amorphous robotic construction. In: 2012 IEEE/RSJ International Conference on Intelligent Robots and Systems, pp. 4879–4885, October 2012. https://doi.org/10.1109/IROS.2012.6385718

Omni-Pi-tent: An Omnidirectional Modular Robot With Genderless Docking

Robert H. Peck$^{(\boxtimes)}$ (iD), Jon Timmis (iD), and Andy M. Tyrrell (iD)

Department of Electronic Engineering, University of York, York, UK
rp1060@york.ac.uk

Abstract. This paper presents the design and development of Omni-Pi-tent, a self-reconfigurable modular robot capable of self-repair during continuous motion. This paper outlines the design features necessary for Dynamic Self-repair experiments and how the design of Omni-Pi-tent implements them, we summarise the construction of the first prototype and discuss initial experiments testing some of its key sensors and actuators. In addition, the paper describes experiments in which empirical data from laboratory tests of sensor hardware was integrated into V-REP simulations by means of creating custom sensor models so as to reduce the reality gap.

Keywords: Omni-Pi-tent · Modular robot ·
Modular self-reconfigurable robots · Self-reconfigurable · Swarm robot ·
Genderless docking

1 Introduction

Modular robotic structures display a number of advantages over non-modular single robots [1]. They have increased versatility as they can take many forms for different tasks, while keeping costs lower by using common parts rather than requiring a specialised robot designed and built. This reuse of modules also offers the potential for robustness as damaged modules can be replaced by others.

Alongside applications in space exploration and urban disaster zone search and rescue, a field which could see great demand for modular robots is that of infrastructure monitoring. With predictions of $3407.7M being spent in 2022 on periodic inspections of civil infrastructure such as nuclear sites, bridges and tunnels and mechanical systems such as jet engines this is a field which already makes extensive use of specialised robots to access hard-to-reach places [2].

Research in modular robotics has focused on many techniques which are necessary to enable practical applications of such systems. Key focuses have been: locomotion methods for groups, docking, control strategies, and communication methods. Despite it being regarded as a grand challenge [1] in modular robotics, self-repair appears to have recieved far less attention than other aspects of modular systems.

© Springer Nature Switzerland AG 2019
K. Althoefer et al. (Eds.): TAROS 2019, LNAI 11650, pp. 307–318, 2019.
https://doi.org/10.1007/978-3-030-25332-5_27

1.1 Self-repair During Continuous Motion

This paper describes the initial hardware designs for a robot capable of performing self-repair methods which can function while the robot group maintains collective motion [3], methods henceforth referred to as Dynamic Self-repair. Our previous work [3] hypothesized that modular robots using Dynamic Self-repair will be able to complete missions faster and more effectively than using prior self-repair methods which required group actions to pause before repair or reconfiguration could take place. Dynamic Self-repair should offer major advantages: for robots in time critical situations, for example minimising radiation dose on a robot operating in a reactor; for robots which must be able to react quickly to dangers such as attempting to self-repair while performing search and rescue under rubble which may further collapse at any moment; and for robots in locations where mobility is reduced such as trying to self-repair while crossing obstacles or resisting environmental forces [3]. For the purposes of this work it is intended that the Dynamic Self-repair strategies developed be constrained to using only those systems and sensors which could be plausibly implemented in a future modular robot for infrastructure monitoring or urban search and rescue, the algorithms developed will not be able to make use of global positional information or require computing systems external to the robots. To achieve these goals a new robot, the Omni-Pi-tent modular robot platform, is being developed. It uniquely combines genderless docking, omnidirectional motion, a 2 Degree of Freedom (DoF) hinge, a full suite of the sensors needed for autonomous docking, local and global communication systems, and a central computer (Raspberry Pi Zero W) running a Linux OS.

The rest of this paper is structured as follows: Sect. 2 considers the requirements of a platform capable of Dynamic Self-repair, Sect. 3 explains the implementation of these requirements within our design, Sects. 4 and 5 discuss the hardware so far produced and some of the testing that sub-systems have undergone, before finishing with Sect. 6 and a discussion of the next steps to be taken.

2 Design Requirements

This section considers the functionality required for an individual module able to form part of a structure which will enable the testing of self-repair during continuous motion. These requirements are broadly similar to those in [2] for an infrastructure monitoring robot, albeit somewhat less constrained due to the benign environmental conditions of the laboratory as compared to the locations in which the authors of [2] envision operational uses for industrial modular robots. Key design requirements include:

- Active genderless docking: this is necessary to let robots free themselves even when the robot they are docked to fails. Mechanical links tend to be stronger and stiffer than magnetic docking making the construction of complex structures more reliable [4], they consume power only when changing between locked and unlocked states whereas electromagnetic docking uses power at all times while the connection is held. The HyMod [5] platform and the RoGenSid [6] port on ModRED provide good examples of such mechanisms.

- Omnidirectional locomotion: necessary for group locomotion. For docking to a moving structure this is especially important as doing so requires a robot to maintain a compass orientation independently of the driving direction, omnidirectional drive is also important for enabling groups of docked robots to drive together without running into situations where docked robots would encounter major resistive forces when attempting to move their companions perpendicular to their wheels. To date the only omnidirectional modular robots have been Trimobot [7] and some SYMBRION [8] modules. Robots like the two wheeled SMORES [9] or the tracked SYMBRION Scout [8] would be unsuitable for the situations robots are envisioned to encounter during Dynamic Self-repair experiments.
- Modules should contain within them all the sensors needed for autonomous docking. Many modular platforms such as SMORES [9] have had few sensors and relied on specialised sensor modules for these purposes, such modules can limit reconfiguration options and act as single points of failure.
- Joint actuators in each module: for a 3 dimensional system this is necessary to allow structures to fold up from the floor into the 3rd dimension. SMORES (4 DoF) [9], HyMod (3 DoF) [5], SYMBRION [8] (2 DoF) and Trimobot (1 DoF) [7] all have forms of these within their modules. It is considered in this work that being able to lift a chain of two modules is the minimum necessary to form interesting structures. For robots of mass M with distance between module centres r, the torque requirement is given by Eq. (1).

$$\tau = gMr\cos(\theta) + 2gMr\cos(\theta) \tag{1}$$

- Modules should each contain equipment for global communication across the swarm, and local line-of-sight communication to neighbours they are docked or docking to.
- Common robotic hardware should exist in the real-world and in simulation. The high level interfaces by which a user can program a robot's behaviour should be as similar as possible between simulation and real world hardware.

With these fundamental requirements in mind the next section provides details of how they are met by the Omnni-Pi-tent design. Given the necessary complexity of the design this section relies heavily on images and diagrams.

3   Design Features

The Omni-Pi-tent modular robot platform has been designed and constructed to enable the higher-level objectives of this research to proceed. Figure 1 introduces the design. A thorough literature search found no modular robot in existence with all of these attributes. Omni-Pi-tent's key features are further explained in Figs. 2, 3, 4, and 5.

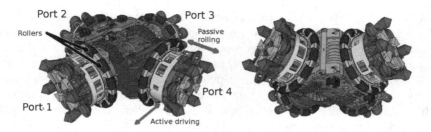

Fig. 1. The Omni-Pi-tent modular robot platform, note the rollers (dark green) around the edge of the omniwheels allowing each wheel to actively drive while also passively sliding in a perpendicular direction. Four omniwheels were used instead of 3 as this enabled the robot to be designed with 4 ports to fit a cubic lattice structure. The ports are numbered clockwise with the hinged port at the front being Port 4. On the right, the rear view reveals the worm gears (orange) which elevate the forward hinge. The module overall has a 2.5 kg mass and a lattice spacing of 29.2 cm. (Color figure online)

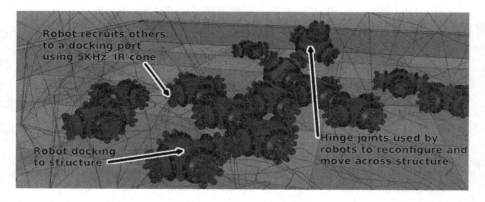

Fig. 2. A V-REP [10] simulation shows robots self-assembling into a defined structure and folding up into a 3D structure. Due to the torques necessary it is not possible to have all docking ports able to provide rotational degrees of freedom, so a SMORES or HyMod like 4 or 3 DoF system was not possible. A 2 DoF system is used in Omni-Pi-tent, however by using pitch and roll degrees of freedom it is possible to use both degrees of freedom in a single docked connection so arm like structures can be formed more easily than with SYMBRION which used a pitch DoF for the forward port and a roll DoF for the side ports. Having pitch and roll DoFs on the same port also enables a chain of two modules to form a structure which can "walk" across a surface of other modules' docking ports to traverse the structure, as SMORES and HyMod have been demonstrated to do. The torques on modules doing this are less than those involved in the two module lifting requirement outlined in Sect. 2.

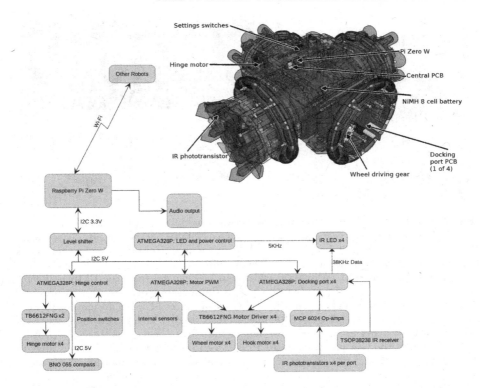

Fig. 3. A block diagram of the electronic components inside an Omni-Pi-tent module. The Pi with a Raspbian operating system runs the program which the robot is currently executing, it communicates over I2C with ATMega328P microcontrollers which handle realtime sensing, actuation and IR communication. During operation a user's controller code runs on the Raspberry Pi Zero W. Using elements of the BCM2835 library [11], we have written a C library which abstracts away the details of I2C communication with the realtime ATMega chips, actuators and sensors. Timing and expected data formats are automatically handled freeing the user to concentrate on high level multi-robot behaviours and multi-robot geometry. C programs written with our library can either be compiled and preloaded onto the Pi's MicroSD card to begin execution after the Omni-Pi-tent module is powered on, or can be transferred over ssh to the Pi. The 3D printed body provides easy access to the MicroSD slot of the Pi to enable rapid changing of cards. Status and debugging messages can be generated by a speech synthesizer and output through a speaker. The low level AVR code on the ATMega chips should typically not need changing once written to the relevant microcontrollers, due to the number of GPIO pins necessary for their roles there are not sufficient pins left for ICSP hence the use of DIP format versions of the microcontrollers to allow programming in an Arduino Uno before transferring the programmed chip to an IC socket within the robot. The physical positions of some of the elements are shown to the right, the face of Port 4 has been removed to expose the location of the docking port PCB.

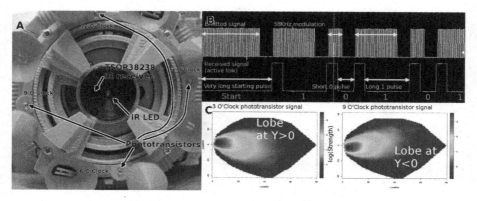

Fig. 4. Local line-of-sight communication between modules uses IR transmissions with a 38 KHz modulated carrier, this data is sent as 17 byte packets, a size chosen after testing in simulation to find which data, and how many bits of precision for continuous values within this data, needed to be exchanged between modules to perform docking. Messages are repeated at an interval which can be changed from the Pi to be longer for low priority messages, a deliberate random timing offset on this interval prevents consistent interference between multiple emitters which could occur if their delays were precisely synchronised. A 2 byte CRC checksum is used to ensure that messages corrupted by interference are ignored, allowing an emitting docking port to keep repeating a message until the user program on the Pi decides to send a different message or cease transmission entirely, without risking robots acting on any corrupted messages which they may receive during repeated transmissions. A single message takes up to 144 ms to transmit, as a pulse width encoding method is used, common for infrared communications, messages can be shorter depending on the content. A sample section of the waveform is shown in **B**. Each docking port can transmit and receive IR messages independently of the tasks taking place on other ports. There are three possible power levels for transmission allowing a robot to target messages to others within 10 cm, 40 cm or 140 cm. The 10 cm mode is especially useful for Mergeable Nervous Systems [12] inspired communication across a multi-robot structure. When a port recruits other robots to dock with it a cone of 5 KHz IR emissions is used for guidance, this frequency does not interfere with the 38 KHz messaging although the same IR LED is used. The 5 KHz signal is detected as an analogue signal by a ring of 4 phototransistors around the approaching docking port, the signal is filtered by frequency, amplified, then passed to the docking port ATMega which takes a digital strength reading. By comparing the signal strengths, plotted in **C**, on each phototransistor a module can work out its range from the recruiting port, up to 68 cm, and which direction it needs to correct in such that it can align and dock. The 5 KHz amplification system can also be used in reflection mode as a proximity sensor for ranges up to 20 cm. The use of modulation makes the IR system insensitive to sunlight and fluorescent lights. The physical positions of the IR communication and guidance components on a docking port face are shown in **A**. Global communication uses the Pi Zero W's Wi-Fi capability to exchange messages of arbitrary size across the swarm, each robot having a buffer able to hold several incoming messages. In the Dynamic Self-repair project's experiments an external router handling the Wi-Fi will be the only off-module piece of equipment required.

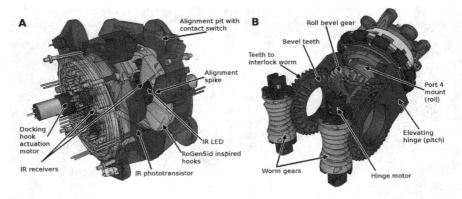

Fig. 5. A: Omni-Pi-tent has a genderless mechanical docking system actuated by an electric motor. The hooks are based on the previously tested RoGenSid [6] docking mechanism and allow single-sided disconnection by either robot in a docked pair. The spikes around the rotating centre of the docking port help guide the robots together with the proper alignment as they dock, enabling docking without the need for perfect alignment before docking begins. An IR LED and 38 KHz receiver are centrally mounted where they will remain in line-of-sight between docked modules, no electrical connection is made between modules as that would complicate docking by requiring extremely precise connection of contacts. Modular robots in future use may forego using inter-module electrical connections for similar reasons, amplified by the ways in which a harsh environment may oxidise exposed connectors. **B:** Omni-Pi-tent uses a 2 DoF hinge similar to that within SMORES modules [9], unlike SMORES worm gears are used to increase the torque of the motor by a 45:1 ratio and ensure that the hinge cannot be backdriven and hence maintains position under load without needing motor power to be applied. A key advantage of the bevel gear arrangement is that the torques of all the hinge motors can be combined for both pitch and roll motions, the different motions resulting from whether the motors are run together or in opposition. Calculations predict Omni-Pi-tent's hinge to have a stall torque of 93.6 Nm, well above the necessary torque for lifting a two module chain. During motion Port 4 remains on the surface of a spherical region, easily forming cubic lattice structures. Port 4 can pitch within a range of ±90°, although the gears could conceivably enable roll across an infinite range it is restricted to ±90° to avoid excessive tangling of the wires which connect the central PCB to the Port 4 PCB. Ports 1, 2 and 3 do not have rotational DoFs due to the space required for the 3D printed gearing necessary to produce torques useful for a robot of this size and mass.

4   Constructing the Omni-Pi-tent Prototype

The Omni-Pi-tent prototype contains 7 circuit boards, marked in Fig. 3, which are restricted to two layers for ease of fabrication, positioned in a 3D printed mechanical body. The printing was all performed with a Robox FDM printer with a 0.2 mm layer height. The motors and other electronic components are low cost off-the-shelf types. An NiMH battery fitted within the axis of the 2 DoF hinge supplies power to a central circuit board which hosts the Pi Zero W and

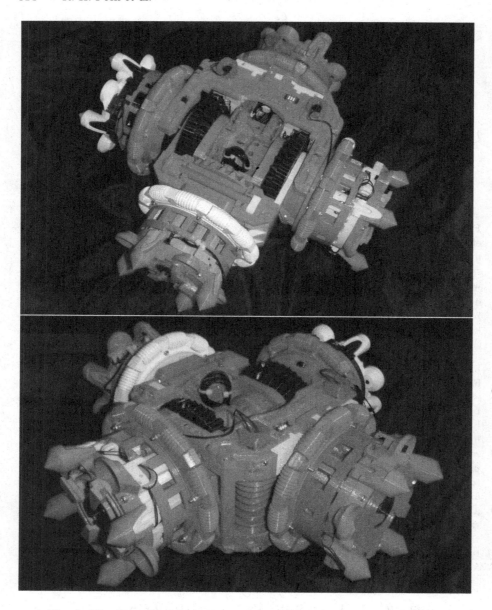

Fig. 6. The 3D printed Omni-Pi-tent prototype with sensors and motors.

hinge control microcontroller, this board connects to docking port PCBs which handle infrared strength measurement and IR communication. All components are held together with machine screws for ease of access to replace and upgrade 3D printed components. The complete robot is shown in Fig. 6.

5   Testing the Prototype

The prototype has been constructed, however testing of the fully integrated module continues, this section therefore simply outlines the earlier tests of Omni-Pi-tent's sub-systems as each of them was developed.

5.1   Testing Infrared Docking Guidance

A pair of docking ports were used to provide a proof of principle demonstration for the docking sensors and actuators. A recruiting port with an IR LED and a recruited port with phototransistors were positioned at points on a grid with a distance X between the ports and a distance Y offset from the centreline of the recruiting port's emission cone. When moving between positions the relative angles of the ports were maintained at all times as if both ports were on robots which had already matched compass orientation before trying to dock.

Data was analysed using R [13], and the plot3D, akima, pracma and spatial libraries. For each position an average and standard deviation for each phototransistor's readings across a time period was taken. Figure 7 shows the averaged values further averaged across the 4 phototransistors on the recruited port.

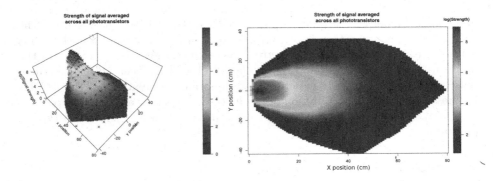

Fig. 7. Graph showing the interpolated function of the averaged, across all 4 phototransistors, signal strength (arbitrary units) across X-Y space. On the 3D plot black crosses show the actual data at the appropriate signal strength Z values and X-Y measurement locations. The graph uses a logarithmic scale to bring all the data into a conveniently viewable range.

While the averaged strengths are symmetrical about the X axis, the signal strengths on the individual phototransistors are not, Fig. 4 displays the lobes of strongest signals for the 3 O'clock and 9 O'clock phototransistors around a port. A $Z = f(X, Y)$ 5th order polynomial model was fitted using R's linear regression functionality. Figure 8 displays the model in comparison to the data.

The V-REP simulations were modified to include a customised sensor model for the guidance system based on the polynomial. A V-REP "proximity sensor" object is used to represent the cone of light from the 5 KHz IR LED, this

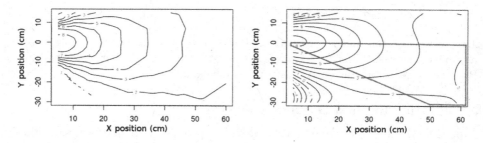

Fig. 8. On the left a contour plot of the signal strengths averaged across the 4 photo-transistors. Contour heights are logarithmic values. On the right a 5th order polynomial model fitted to the data. Note that as the data is symmetrical about the X axis, and as the illuminated cone has only a limited angle, the difference in the model from the data for positive Y values and in the lower left corner of the plot is not a problem as the model is only ever evaluated in V-REP for X-Y values within the red bordered region.

object is modified to detect "dummy objects" which represent phototransistors. In the sensing step of the V-REP simulation each object representing a photo-transistor's location has an IR strength reading, as calculated from applying our polynomial model to the relative positions of V-REP objects representing the 5 KHz LED and phototransistor, written to it as a "custom datablock". This helps reduce the reality gap and better tie the simulations to the reality of the hardware that has been developed. Simulated robots have been able to use these sensors, alongside similarly experimentally informed simulations of the 38 KHz IR messaging system, to autonomously dock to stationary and moving recruiting robots. This will be replicated in hardware as soon as a 2nd prototype is produced.

5.2   Testing the Docking System

Although the RoGenSid system from which Omni-Pi-tent's docking hooks were inspired had been previously tested, the implementation used on Omni-Pi-tent is 3D printed rather than metal and features alignment spikes and pits designed to operate at 90° intervals rather than 2 separated positions 180° apart. It was found that, when docked, forces of 59N could be withstood by a pair of ports in both tensional and shear directions. Larger loads were not available to test at the time. Actuation time to lock or unlock is 0.3 s. A gif of the docking hooks actuating is available at https://tinyurl.com/y9fnr4wj

5.3   Testing the Hinge

The prototype's 2 DoF hinge has been tested with minimal loads, testing larger weights connected to a spare docking port to find the maximum torque the hinge can supply has yet to begin. With the load of Port 4 itself the ability of the hinge to rotate the robot's fourth docking port through both pitch and roll degrees of freedom, both for independent and simultaneous motions, has been verified Fig. 9. The hinge is, as designed, not backdrivable. The motion is slow, taking 33 s to elevate by 45°, however this is as expected given the choice to use low power motors with large reduction ratio gearing. This choice saves on space, weight, component costs and power consumption, the hinge was found to draw peaks of 240 mA of current, with an average close to 220 mA, 55 mA per motor.

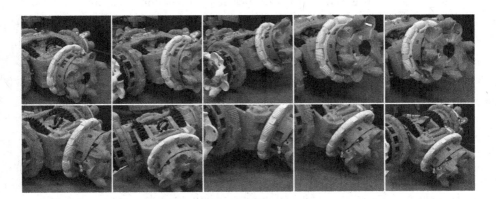

Fig. 9. Testing of the hinge system with a partly assembled module and temporary external driver circuitry. The upper series of images shows the hinge elevating Port 4's pitch to 45° then rolling Port 4 clockwise. The lower series shows the robot raising itself up by pitching the hinge downwards, even while lifting the weight of the robot currents did not rise above a 240 mA peak. A video of the test's highlights is available at https://tinyurl.com/yc96hllb

6   Conclusion and Future Work

This paper has described the design and development of the Omni-Pi-tent modular robot platform. The need for key features such as: genderless docking, joint actuators, a full suite of docking sensors and an omnidirectional drive, has been explained, and the implementation of these features described. The use of reality gap reduction techniques is also summarised. Near-future work will progress to multi-module testing including confirming the predicted torque of the main hinge and performing autonomous docking of robots to stationary and then moving recruiters, as has been previously demonstrated in simulation. Having tightened the reality gap between the simulations and hardware while testing the subsystems of the prototype, an element of future work will be further reducing the reality gap by refining the simulations based on experimental data gathered from future tests of the fully integrated hardware. Further information on the Omni-Pi-tent platform is available at https://www.york.ac.uk/robot-lab/omr/ and regular project updates are posted at http://omni-pi-tent.blogspot.com/.

Acknowledgments. The authors would like to thank Mark Hough for introducing R.H. Peck to PCB design software and principles, and EPSRC for funding R.H. Peck's studentship.

References

1. Yim, M., et al.: Modular self-reconfigurable robot systems, challenges and opportunities for the future. In: IEEE Robotics and Automation Magazine, pp. 39–45, March 2007
2. Jahanshahi, M.R., et al.: Reconfigurable swarm robots for structural health monitoring - a brief review. Int. J. Intell. Robot. Appl. **1**, 287–305 (2017)
3. Peck, R.H., Timmis, J., Tyrrell, A.M.: Towards self-repair with modular robots during continuous motion. In: Giuliani, M., Assaf, T., Giannaccini, M.E. (eds.) TAROS 2018. LNCS, vol. 10965, pp. 457–458. Springer, Cham (2018)
4. Ostergaard, E.H., et al.: Design of the ATRON lattice-based self-reconfigurable robot. Auton. Robots **21**(2), 165–183 (2006)
5. Parrott, C., Dodd, T.J., Groß, R.: HyMod: a 3-DOF hybrid mobile and self-reconfigurable modular robot and its extensions. In: Groß, R., Kolling, A., Berman, S., Frazzoli, E., Martinoli, A., Matsuno, F., Gauci, M. (eds.) Distributed Autonomous Robotic Systems. SPAR, vol. 6, pp. 401–414. Springer, Cham (2018). https://doi.org/10.1007/978-3-319-73008-0_28
6. Hossain, S.G.M., et al.: RoGenSid: a rotary plate genderless single-sided docking mechanism for modular self-reconfigurable robots. In: ASME 2013 IDETC/CIE, V06BT07A011-V06BT07A011 (2013)
7. Zhang, Y., et al.: A modular self-reconfigurable robot with enhanced locomotion performances: design, modeling, simulations, and experiments. J. Intell. Robot. Syst. **81**, 377–393 (2016)
8. Kernbach, S., et al.: Evolutionary robotics: the next-generation-platform for online and on-board artificial evolution. In: 2009 IEEE Congress on Evolutionary Computation, pp. 1079–1086. IEEE (2009)
9. Davey, J., Kwok, N., Yim, M.: Emulating self-reconfigurable robots - design of the SMORES system. In: 2012 IEEE/RSJ International Conference on Intelligent Robots and Systems, pp. 4464–4469. IEEE (2012)
10. Rohmer, E., Singh, S.P.N., Freese, M.: V-REP: a versatile and scalable robot simulation framework. In: IROS 2013, pp. 1321–1326. IEEE (2013). http://www.coppeliarobotics.com/downloads.html
11. McCauley, M.: BCM2835 library. https://www.airspayce.com/mikem/bcm2835/
12. Mathews, N., et al.: Mergeable nervous systems for robots. Nat. Commun. **8**, 439 (2017)
13. R Core Team: R: A Language and Environment for Statistical Computing. R Foundation for Statistical Computing (2016). https://www.R-project.org/

Evaluating ToRCH Structure
for Characterizing Robots

Manal Linjawi$^{(\boxtimes)}$ and Roger K. Moore

Department of Computer Science, University of Sheffield,
211 Portobello, Sheffield S1 4DP, UK
{malinjawi1,r.k.moore}@sheffield.ac.uk

Abstract. Robots are increasingly used in different scenarios, depending on the development of their capabilities and performance. The accelerating growth of robotics applications requires a tool that can comprehensively capture a wide range of robot capabilities. In this study, we evaluate robot capabilities using a structure known as "Towards Robot Characterization" (ToRCH) recently developed to meet this need. This structure defines robot capabilities and consequently enables capabilities and applications to be mapped against each other. An experiment was conducted to obtain the capabilities of two scenarios presented by the NAO robot. The method used to capture the capabilities was performed via the ToRCH structure. ToRCH implicitly illustrates the scenarios in a simple capability profile. This research assesses two aspects of the ToRCH capabilities capturing process. First, it verifies the moderate agreement level among roboticists in using ToRCH to capture the robot's capabilities. Second, it demonstrates the richness of the ToRCH structure for capturing robot capabilities compared to the Multi-Annual Roadmap (MAR) levels. This initial study evaluates the ToRCH method in extracting different capability levels and illustrating them in a robot capability profile. It therefore highlights the potential of ToRCH in classifying robots.

Keywords: Robot capabilities · Capabilities profile ·
Robot characterization

1 Introduction

If there was a general classification system it would identify a robot and enable comparisons between robots. To identify a robot, its characteristics and capabilities need to be illustrated. Although several classifications have been developed, they include only some of the ever-growing range of possible robot characteristics. For example, they cover classification by function [15], field [12], domain [13], size [4], manipulation [17] or robot intelligence [2,16]. Each of these classifications has its own list of capabilities and therefore, cannot be used to define robot capabilities in general [3].

© Springer Nature Switzerland AG 2019
K. Althoefer et al. (Eds.): TAROS 2019, LNAI 11650, pp. 319–330, 2019.
https://doi.org/10.1007/978-3-030-25332-5_28

Due to a lack of comprehensive structure in the literature, the Multi-Annual Roadmap (MAR) [13], developed to shape the European research development and innovation programme, was selected as a baseline. It provides a detailed list of possible robotic capabilities, such as perception, cognitive ability and motion ability. Each capability is presented in levels, with a higher level denoting more advanced skill in that capability. However, as the purpose of the MAR was to provide guidelines on the future development of robotic characteristics, it cannot be used as a comprehensive classification system in its current form.

A newly proposed structure to capture robot characteristics, defined in this research as "Towards Robot Characteristics" (ToRCH) [9], could fulfil this criterion. ToRCH was developed to capture robot characteristics, covering the robot's features (including hardware and software), technical capabilities and operational capabilities. The structure of ToRCH serves as an umbrella to hold these different types of capabilities in specific areas with different levels of maturity. It draws on the comprehensiveness of the MAR [13] in its development, especially since the MAR is regularly updated with new capabilities to reflect the goals of future research. ToRCH encompasses capabilities from the MAR, but also includes those missed by the MAR. For example, advanced social capabilities such as the presentation of emotional or social skills, which are becoming more prevalent in recent robotics developments [1]. The MAR presents several social and physical interactions but does not cover other types of interaction such as wearable technology [7,8,14], virtual interaction, augmented interaction or embedded interaction, used by smart devices in the Internet of Things (IoT) [10]. ToRCH's structure enables the classification of these technologies according to their capability evaluations. It is flexible enough to grow as robotics technologies develop. If a capability is not listed, the structure allows it to be added within any section of the structure according to the capability type. This gives ToRCH the ability to allocate any newly developed capabilities within its main section or subsections.

In this study, we investigate the ToRCH structure and propose it as a tool that can be used to extract the current state of a robot's capability to classify it. We focus on implementing ToRCH and utilizing it as a method to capture a robot's capabilities and distinguish it from others. The method could be used even if the capabilities were presented by the same robot. There are two aspects investigated in this research: (1) investigating ToRCH's accuracy as a classifier to define robot capabilities; (2) examining the richness of ToRCH in capturing robot capabilities and checking whether it contains an adequate list of capabilities.

2   Method

To investigate different robot capabilities, we performed an experiment using ToRCH as a method to gather robot capabilities. The proposed method evaluated the performance of a specific programmed robot using the ToRCH structure and capability levels. We chose to assess the NAO robot due to its common use in robotics research; however, ToRCH could be used for any robot. NAO robots

[5] are developed with different capabilities to satisfy specific application requirements. They can be delivered in different forms, such as full body or just a torso, and are flexible and adaptable for programming. Therefore, assessing which capabilities an NAO is programmed to perform is important in distinguishing one NAO from another. Our hypothesis states that the ToRCH method would enable users to consistently distinguish between different capabilities of the robot. The experiment also evaluated the accuracy and richness of ToRCH in extracting robot capabilities. Therefore, this experiment was performed in parts. In the first part, we used the ToRCH method to define an NAO robot's performance in two scenarios as numeric capability scores and present them in a simple capability profile. The second part of the experiment was designed to use the capability profile to assess the accuracy and richness of the method compared to the MAR.

Defining ToRCH as a Method for Capturing Robot Capabilities

ToRCH is presented hierarchically in three layers (robot features, technical capabilities and operational capabilities). These layers are structured according to their relationship to each other; for example, the features layer (hardware and software) supports the technical capabilities layer, which in turn supports the operational layer. The technical capabilities layer is categorized into sections and subsections containing capabilities. Where each capability is categorized into three types (physical, cognitive and social). Each capability type contains sub-capabilities that are presented at various maturity levels. Thus classifying a robot's capabilities using the technical layer presented in the ToRCH structure is a straightforward procedure as it follows the hierarchy of its structure. For more details see [9].

ToRCH uses a levelled capability structure derived from the MAR. The capability levels were mapped from the MAR on a quantitative basis. A capability scored at level zero indicates that the robot cannot perform that capability. At level (1), the robot would have a basic performance of the capability and at the highest level the robot would execute the capability with the highest possible performance.

Generating the Robot Capability Profile

The first step in generating the robot capability profile is to compare the textual description of the scenario with each capability under consideration. The next step is to score each capability appropriately to determine the level exhibited in the scenario. ToRCH assigns each maturity level a numeric score; for example, a robot with level (0) for a capability would achieve a score of zero, and at level (3) it would score three. The final step is to sum up the scores for all the capabilities in each scenario to obtain a capability profile. The robot capability profile is thus a numerical display of the robot's performance. The number of capabilities presented in a profile depends on the capabilities that require investigation. For the profile demonstration in this study, only 11 capabilities relevant to the scenarios were examined. These capabilities have different levels and can be found in Table 2. Other capabilities were not mentioned in the scenarios and so they were not examined or analysed.

The two scenarios presented in the experiment are defined in the following section. The robot capability profiles for scenario 1 (S1) and scenario 2 (S2) are presented in Table 1. The table includes the capabilities categories, the specified capabilities and the model score for each capability for both scenarios.

Scenario 1 (S1): The NAO robot is programmed to recognize a predefined ball on the floor among other unknown objects. The robot moves towards the ball and says to the person in the room "I found the missing ball". If the person smiles, the robot maps the facial expression to a predefined model of 'happy' and says "I found your ball". If the person does not smile, the robot says "I will dance for you".

Scenario 2 (S2): The NAO robot is programmed to recognize a predefined ball on the floor among other unknown objects. The robot recognizes an individual among the people in the room because it has a picture of that person in its database. It moves towards that individual, laughs and says "I found you and I found your ball".

Table 1. ToRCH categories, capabilities and levels according to the model answer (presented here as scores) for each of the NAO robot scenarios. The scores represent the capability maturity levels demonstrated in the robot performance. The levelling scheme for each capability was adopted from the MAR with additional capabilities augmented through ToRCH using parameters or variables related to their specifications. Capabilities that are available within each scenario will score more than zero. The scoring specifies the capability maturity level that was achieved within the scenario. The scoring depends strongly on the NAO properties and features as well as on the capabilities that are programmed in the NAO robot to perform the scenario.

Category	Capabilities	S1 score	S2 score
Physical perception	Object perception	3	3
Physical perception	Self-location perception	1	1
Social perception	Agent perception	2	4
Social perception	Emotion perception	1	0
Physical perception	Object location perception	1	0
Physical perception	Agent location perception	0	1
Physical interpretation	Object interpretation	0	0
Physical task	Unconstrained motion	1	1
Social task	Emotion expression	0	1
Social interaction	Human interaction modality	2	2
Social interaction	Interaction levels of extent	1	1

To assess the methodology of the ToRCH structure in capturing robot capabilities, several aspects were examined. For verification, we tested the accuracy

Table 2. The table contains the questions related to the capabilities in scenarios 1 and 2; whether the capability available in MAR, ToRCH or both of them; where the capabilities were used and in which of the scenarios and, in the final column, the range of the capabilities levels (the range of levels were either adopted directly from the MAR or developed and added by ToRCH using the same MAR style in presenting the capabilities; each capability level was distinguished according to the parameters or variables related to maturity of the capability).

Capability questions	Availability	Usage in the scenario	Levels
Object perception	MAR/ToRCH	Recognize the ball in S1& S2	0−12
Self-location perception	MAR/ToRCH	Moving towards something S1& S2	0−7
Object interpretation	MAR/ToRCH	Not available	0−9
Unconstrained motion	MAR/ToRCH	Movements capabilities in S1& S2	0−7
Interaction modality	MAR/ToRCH	Interaction type in S1& S2	0−6
Interaction levels of extent	MAR/ToRCH	Repeated interaction in S1& S2	0−7
Agent perception	ToRCH	Recognize a person in S1& S2	0−8
Emotion perception	ToRCH	Recognize a smile/happiness in S1	0−4
Object-location perception	ToRCH	Moving towards objects in S1	0−7
Agent-location perception	ToRCH	Moving towards agent in S2	0−7
Emotion expression	ToRCH	Expressing happy emotion in S2	0−3

of ToRCH as a classifier to measure robot capabilities. We used a questionnaire to investigate how participants would use ToRCH in capturing a robot's capabilities. We presented the two scenarios above, and asked participants to define the levels of the capabilities presented. We then performed an analysis to rate agreement between participant responses and the model scores.

Experimental Set-Up. The experiment presented two simple, controlled NAO performances, defined as scenarios within the questionnaire. Each question asked responders to rate the level of the NAO robot for each capability. ToRCH is comprehensive, containing all of the capabilities available in the MAR with additional capabilities added where MAR was found to be lacking. The experiment evaluated two scenarios, each used to sample 11 capability scores. The two scenarios therefore, covered 22 capability scores. To avoid leading the participants, the language used to describe the scenarios did not map to the capabilities or levels measured.

The capabilities and the scenarios were designed to cover some standard robot capabilities; thus only the capabilities relating directly to the scenarios were investigated as it would not have been feasible to assess all of the ToRCH capabilities within one questionnaire. Using the entire list of capabilities provided by ToRCH to evaluate the NAO scenarios would have been too time-consuming for the participants, particularly if the participants had to evaluate capabilities not present in the NAO scenarios. Therefore, only the capabilities that were relevant to the scenarios were examined. A total of six questions covered capabilities included in both the MAR and ToRCH, and a further five questions related to capabilities only available in ToRCH. The capabilities assessed in this experiment using the two NAO scenarios can be seen in Table 1. Six of the capabilities are presented in both scenarios while the other five capabilities are presented in one of the scenarios but not in both of them.

Procedure. Twelve participants volunteered from University of Sheffield Robotics Institute and Computer Science department. All of them were self-defined as NAO robot programmers or users. The study was approved by the university research ethics committee and informed consent was given. No personal or demographic information was recorded. The questionnaire was conducted through an online form. Participants were presented with a textual description for each of the scenarios followed by a set of 11 questions. Based on their knowledge of the NAO robot and their interpretation of the scenarios, participants chose the capabilities level they felt best matched the NAO performance for each capability. Depending on the capability, the maximum score a participant could give the NAO robot varied, as presented in Table 2. Participants also had the option of leaving a comment relating to their response.

The 22 scores and any corresponding comments from each participant were downloaded and extracted for analysis. Their evaluation was compared with the model scores of the scenarios, presented in Table 1, in order to assess the accuracy of ToRCH in capturing robot capabilities. This was achieved by performing an inter-rater reliability analysis [11], calculated using the Cohen's kappa measure. This measure represents the extent to which participant selections matched the model scores, as displayed in Table 1, for two NAO scenarios.

To calculate Cohen's kappa measure, the model scores of the capabilities were defined, and the agreement between the rater and model score was calculated. Each rater was compared to the model scores separately for each scenario. A mean score was then calculated for each scenario, representing the extent of agreement between the raters and the model scores. A guideline for mean kappa suggests that a value of zero indicates no agreement between the model and raters, values below 0.40 are poor, values between 0.40 and 0.75 indicate fair to good agreement, and values over 0.75 indicate an excellent agreement [6].

3 Results

3.1 Evaluating the Accuracy of ToRCH

In total, the 12 participants performed 264 robot capability assessments. Of these assessments, whether the robot possessed the capability was correctly identified 231 times and incorrectly 33 times. Most of the incorrect capability assessments were of interpretive capabilities, indicating that some capabilities need to be described in more detail to be correctly assessed. In general, robot capability assessments were performed with 88% accuracy. The experiment thus shows the accuracy of the ToRCH structure in capturing capabilities and confirms it as a useful tool for classifying robot capabilities. Differences between the level assigned by the participants and the model answer for each capability can be seen

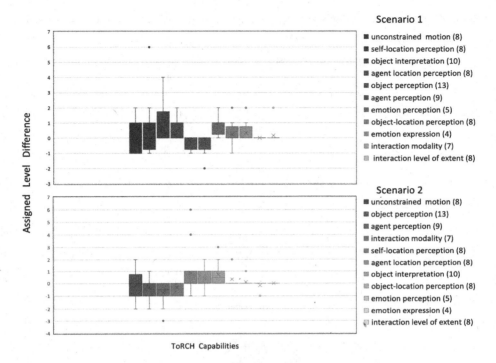

Fig. 1. This figure demonstrates the difference in level scoring from the model answer for each capability for scenario 1 and scenario 2. Zero difference indicates the participant gave the same score as the model answer. The scoring difference from the model answers is presented for each capability in inter-quartic range with a median. The number in the brackets after the capability name indicates the total number of levels available for the capability listed.

in Fig. 1. To fully verify this, the following Cohen's kappa scores were obtained. For scenario 1 the mean kappa was 0.46, representing a moderate agreement. For scenario 2 the mean kappa was 0.55, also representing moderate agreement. The overall mean kappa was 0.5, suggesting users of ToRCH would agree on its classification to a moderate extent. The Cohen's kappa results are presented in Table 3 and Fig. 2.

3.2 Evaluating the Richness of ToRCH

In this experiment, we additionally sought to demonstrate the richness of the ToRCH structure in capturing different robot capabilities. This was achieved by comparing the capabilities captured by ToRCH with those of the MAR. We investigated the efficiency of ToRCH in capturing capabilities by performing an analysis of the two different NAO robot scenarios. Each profile was distinguished by a specific set of capabilities, as presented in Table 1. For scenario 1, object

Table 3. Participant Cohen's kappa scores for each scenario, and the mean for both scenarios.

Participant	CK scoresS1	CK scoresS2	Mean S1 & S2
1	0.22	0.63	0.43
2	0.19	0.12	0.16
3	0.61	0.52	0.57
4	0.48	0.50	0.49
5	0.31	0.65	0.48
6	0.27	0.14	0.20
7	0.06	0.28	0.17
8	0.29	0.33	0.31
9	0.75	0.75	0.75
10	0.61	0.88	0.74
11	0.87	0.87	0.87
12	0.87	0.87	0.87

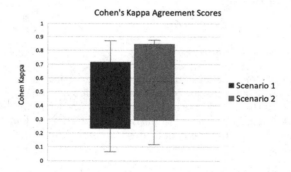

Fig. 2. The figure shows the distribution of the Cohen's kappa scores for both scenarios.

interpretation, agent location perception and emotion expression capabilities were not included as they were not relevant. For scenario 2, object interpretation, emotion perception and object location perception were excluded for the same reason. A comparison of the ToRCH profiles for scenarios 1 and 2 with the MAR profiles shows the ToRCH set of profiles present a comprehensive illustration of the robot's capabilities. We speculated that the capability levels presented through ToRCH would demonstrate the two scenarios with different robot capability profiles. As each profile presented the capabilities exhaustively, this is something that would not be captured by the MAR levels.

The model scores of the two scenarios shown in Table 1 are presented in bar graph form in Fig. 3, which shows the ToRCH and the MAR model scores for both scenarios. A comparison between the upper chart and the lower chart indicates that ToRCH is able of capturing the difference between the capabilities

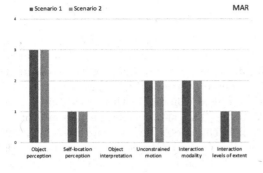

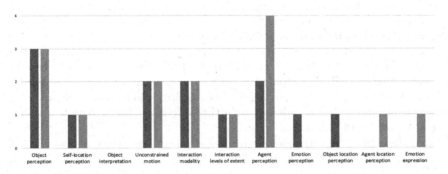

Fig. 3. The upper chart shows no difference between scenario 1 and scenario 2 while using the MAR list of capabilities. But the lower chart, presents the difference in the NAO capabilities for scenario 1 and 2 using ToRCH. The presented values are the model scores for the scenarios.

demonstrated in the NAO scenarios, whereas the MAR graphs do not capture such differences, presented in the last four bars in the ToRCH lower chart. For example, ToRCH captures the emotion perception and object location perception, in scenario 1 but not in scenario 2 and vice versa for agent location perception and emotion expression. Thus ToRCH allows the capture of more capabilities for the scenarios. This is a result of its flexibility and the number of capabilities within its structure. It illustrated the difference in the agent perception capabilities between the two scenarios. It also presented scenario 1 with emotion and object location perception, which is not presented in scenario 2. Additionally, it presented scenario 2 with agent location perception and emotional expression which are not available in scenario 1. This analysis confirms that the ToRCH structure includes more robot capabilities, and in greater detail, than the MAR. Therefore, this evaluation indicates the richness of ToRCH in capturing a robot's capabilities and its performance.

4   Discussion

The Cohen's kappa test only captures absolute agreement and disagreement between the rater and model score, it does not consider the degree of agreement. For example, the "interaction modality" has seven levels. For scenario 2, all 12 participants agreed that the NAO presented this capability; however, only eight agreed with the model score. The four who differed in their assessment were only one level away from the model score. This shows that the presence of the capability was defined correctly even if the chosen levels were not the same. The difference of levels assigned by the participants compared to the model answer can be seen in Fig. 1 where zero difference indicates the participant gave the same score as the model answer. Any number above zero indicates that the participants over-ranked the capabilities levels and below zero indicates that they underestimated the capabilities levels. The figure also highlights the outliers who have scored outside the average range of scores. These are suggestive of erroneous data and were therefore excluded from the analysis.

Analysing the mean kappa agreement scores for scenarios 1 and 2 shows there is a slight increase of agreement from scenario 1 to scenario 2. A possible explanation for this is that participants became practised in what was required for assessing the levels and in classifying robot capabilities in general. This may indicate issues around ease of usability, with the ToRCH method requiring training or instruction for initial use.

Analysing the data, the scores in "self-location perception" and "unconstrained motions" had the biggest difference from the model answer. This could be due to participants scoring the scenario based on their knowledge of a specific version of the NAO robot, not according to the version used in the scenarios. For example, the unconstrained motion capability presents levels according to the robot's movement within the environment. At level (1) the robot performed a predefine open loop motion, level (2) the robot performed a close loop motion where accuracy of these movement depends on perception abilities and level (3) the robot performed an open path motion to follow a given path accurately. In this context, an older version of the NAO robot might have a lower possible level of ability than the most advanced version, which may cause some difference in the scoring of these capabilities.

5   Limitations

In the course of this study, several limitations are acknowledged and presented: (1) The limited number of participants (12) used in the experiments can only provide a preliminary view of the utility of the ToRCH structure. (2) The textual presentation of the scenarios created uncertainty in defining the quality of the robot's capabilities. The textual format facilitated different interpretations compared to a video or direct interaction, causing the assignment of different capability levels. This would become more evident if capabilities such as dexterity or autonomy are assessed observation of which would help fine-tune the evaluation of levels. (3) The version of the NAO robot used in this study may not have been identical to the model the participants had experience with. This might have affected the capability scoring. (4) The examination of two similar scenarios one after the other by the participants might have reduced independence in the answers for the two scenarios. (5) The robotics terminology presented in the capability levels had some ambiguity that may have resulted in difficulties in scoring. (6) The participants varied in their level of experience and knowledge which might have lowered the agreement scores. (7) The presentation of the questionnaire in an online format might have increased the difficulty of the rating process as it required participants to scroll up and down to move between the questions and the scenario descriptions.

6   Conclusions

Robots are commonly used in research. Different laboratories and organizations develop robots with various capabilities to satisfy specific application requirements. Determining which robot is programmed to perform which capabilities is important for its identification and deployment. This robot identification process requires detailed description of the robot capabilities. This comprehensive representation will distinguish robots from each other and implicitly classify them. Therefore, we propose using the ToRCH structure in capturing a robot's capabilities and demonstrating them in an understandable and quantifiable format. The proposed structure contains a wide range of capabilities as they are all categorized and grouped. Each capability is presented with several levels according to the capability specifications. In this study, we established a novel procedure to capture robot capabilities by using ToRCH as a tool. The structure was able to extract robot capabilities and to present them in a numerical format defined as the 'robot capabilities profile'. We evaluated the capability profile by examining the accuracy of ToRCH in capturing robot capabilities finding 88% correct assessment thereby establishing ToRCH as the first robot capability classifying tool. Finally we illustrated the richness of the ToRCH structure by conducting a comparison between the capabilities captured by ToRCH and those captured by the MAR has demonstrated that ToRCH contains an extensive list, whereas the latter has a limited list of capabilities. The research also establishes the importance of familiarity with the ToRCH capabilities and their levels. This research has demonstrated ToRCH's potential as a robot classification method. It distinguished between two scenarios for the same robot so future research could utilize ToRCH in assessing capabilities beyond the NAO robot. As more researchers become acquainted with ToRCH its simplicity and comprehensiveness can have a positive impact on the field of robotics.

References

1. Anzalone, S.M., Boucenna, S., Ivaldi, S., Chetouani, M.: Evaluating the engagement with social robots. Int. J. Soc. Robot. **7**(4), 465–478 (2015)
2. Bhatnagar, S., et al.: Mapping intelligence: requirements and possibilities. In: Müller, V.C. (ed.) PT-AI 2017. SAPERE, vol. 44, pp. 117–135. Springer, Cham (2018). https://doi.org/10.1007/978-3-319-96448-5_13
3. Bonsignorio, F., Del Pobil, A.P., Messina, E.: Fostering progress in performance evaluation and benchmarking of robotic and automation systems [tc spotlight]. IEEE Robot. Autom. Mag. **21**(1), 22–25 (2014)
4. Dobra, A.: General classification of robots. size criteria. In: Proceedings of 23rd International Conference on Robotics in Alpe-Adria-Danube Region (RAAD), pp. 1–6. IEEE (2014)
5. Gouaillier, D., et al.: Mechatronic design of NAO humanoid. In: 2009 IEEE International Conference on Robotics and Automation, pp. 769–774, May 2009
6. Landis, J.R., Koch, G.G.: The measurement of observer agreement for categorical data. Biometrics **33**, 159–174 (1977)
7. Lee, J., Kim, D., Ryoo, H.Y., Shin, B.S.: Sustainable wearables: wearable technology for enhancing the quality of human life. Sustainability **8**(5), 466 (2016)
8. Lenzi, T., et al.: Measuring human-robot interaction on wearable robots: a distributed approach. Mechatronics **21**(6), 1123–1131 (2011)
9. Linjawi, M., Moore, R.K.: Towards a comprehensive taxonomy for characterizing robots. In: Giuliani, M., Assaf, T., Giannaccini, M.E. (eds.) TAROS 2018. LNCS (LNAI), vol. 10965, pp. 381–392. Springer, Cham (2018). https://doi.org/10.1007/978-3-319-96728-8_32
10. Rastic-Dulborough, O.: Internet of things (IoT) and human computer interaction. Technical report, University of Southampton (2014)
11. Interrater reliability. J. Consum. Psychol. **10**(1&2), 71–73 (2001)
12. Siciliano, B., Khatib, O.: Springer Handbook of Robotics. Springer, Heidelberg (2016). https://doi.org/10.1007/978-3-540-30301-5
13. SPARC Robotics, eu-Robotics AISBL, Brussels, Belgium: Robotics Multi-Annual Roadmap for Robotics in Europe, Horizon 2020 (2016)
14. Stead, L., Goulev, P., Evans, C., Mamdani, E.: The emotional wardrobe. Pers. Ubiquit. Comput. **8**(3–4), 282–290 (2004)
15. Winfield, A.: Robotics: A Very Short Introduction. Oxford University Press, Oxford (2012)
16. Winfield, A.F.T.: How intelligent is your intelligent robot? (2017). arxiv:1712.08878
17. Yousef, H., Boukallel, M., Althoefer, K.: Tactile sensing for dexterous in-hand manipulation in robotics-a review. Sens. Actuators, A **167**(2), 171–187 (2011)

Optimal Manoeuver Trajectory Synthesis for Autonomous Space and Aerial Vehicles and Robots

Ranjan Vepa[(⊠)] [iD]

School of Engineering and Material Science, Queen Mary University of London,
London E1 4NS, UK
r.vepa@qmul.ac.uk

Abstract. In this paper the problem of the synthesis of optimal manoeuver trajectories for autonomous space vehicles and robots is revisited. It is shown that it is entirely feasible to construct optimal manoeuver trajectories from considerations of only the rigid body kinematics rather than the complete dynamics of the space vehicle or robot under consideration. Such an approach lends itself to several simplifications which allow the optimal angular velocity and translational velocity profiles to be constructed, purely from considerations of the body kinematic relations. In this paper the body kinematics is formulated, in general, in terms of the quaternion representation attitude and the angular velocities are considered to be the steering inputs. The optimal inputs for a typical attitude manoeuver is synthesized by solving for the states and co-states defined by a two point boundary value problem. A typical example of a space vehicle pointing problem is considered and the optimal torque inputs for the synthesis of a reference attitude trajectory and the reference trajectories are obtained.

Keywords: Attitude manoeuvers · Optimal manoeuver trajectory ·
Trajectory optimization · Trajectory tracking

1 Introduction

The concept of using the kinematic equations of a vehicle or robot for trajectory synthesis has been around for some time, since it was introduced by several authors. (see for example Vukobratovic and Kircanski 2013). It has been successfully used for trajectory planning of drones and car-like robots. (Lagache et al. 2017 and Wolek et al. 2016). However for the case space vehicles and robots the use of the kinematic equations, particularly formulations based on quaternions and dual quaternions, is relatively new. Özgür and Mezouar (2016) have used a dual velocity representation to develop an expression for the Jacobian matrix and to perform kinematic control on a robotic arm. Using the dual velocity concept, Valverde and Tsiotras (2018) have extended the quaternion kinematic law to an equivalent formulation in terms of dual quaternions, after providing an introduction to them. The formulation developed by them reduces to a sequence of quaternion updates, which in some cases reduces further to a set scalar update equations. While the adaptive attitude control problem using dual

© Springer Nature Switzerland AG 2019
K. Althoefer et al. (Eds.): TAROS 2019, LNAI 11650, pp. 331–345, 2019.
https://doi.org/10.1007/978-3-030-25332-5_29

quaternions has only recently been solved (Filipe and Tsiotras 2014), the corresponding attitude and translational optimal trajectory synthesis problem has not received much attention.

In this paper the problem of the synthesis of optimal manoeuver trajectories for autonomous space vehicles and robots is revisited. It is shown that it is entirely feasible to construct optimal manoeuver trajectories from considerations of the only rigid body kinematics rather than the complete dynamics of the space vehicle or robot under consideration. Such an approach lends itself to several simplifications which allow the optimal angular velocity and translational velocity profiles to be constructed, purely from considerations of the body kinematic relations. In this paper the body kinematics is formulated, in general, in terms of the quaternion representation attitude and the angular velocities are considered to be the steering inputs. The optimal inputs for a typical attitude manoeuver are synthesized by solving for the. states and co-states defined by a two point boundary value problem. A typical example of a space vehicle pointing problem is considered and the optimal torque inputs for the synthesis of a reference attitude trajectory are obtained. Based on the reference trajectory and a typical tracking controller, it is shown that the reference trajectory can be successfully tracked. The approach has the added advantage that it could be generalized to deal with complex space robotic mechanisms on-board a space platform. This is done by defining decoupled attitude and orbit trajectory synthesis problems both for the vehicle and for the on-board robot manipulators.

2   Optimal Attitude Orientation Acquisition Trajectory Synthesis

To begin with the quaternion kinematics can be expressed in one of two alternate forms which are given as.

$$\frac{d\mathbf{q}}{dt} = \frac{1}{2}\mathbf{A}_\omega(\omega)\mathbf{q} = \frac{1}{2}\mathbf{\Gamma}(\mathbf{q})\omega, \tag{2.1a}$$

where, where the quaternion $\mathbf{q} = \begin{bmatrix} \varepsilon_1 & \varepsilon_2 & \varepsilon_3 & \eta \end{bmatrix}^T$, consists of a vector part,

$\varepsilon = \begin{bmatrix} \varepsilon_1 & \varepsilon_2 & \varepsilon_3 \end{bmatrix}^T$ and the scalar η so,

$$\mathbf{q} = \begin{bmatrix} \varepsilon \\ \eta \end{bmatrix} \text{ and } \mathbf{A}_\omega = \begin{bmatrix} -\mathbf{\Omega}(\omega) & \omega \\ -\omega^T & 0 \end{bmatrix}, \ \mathbf{\Omega}(\omega) = \begin{bmatrix} 0 & -\omega_3 & \omega_2 \\ \omega_3 & 0 & -\omega_1 \\ -\omega_2 & \omega_1 & 0 \end{bmatrix}. \tag{2.1b}$$

$$\mathbf{\Gamma}(\mathbf{q}) = \begin{bmatrix} \eta\mathbf{I}_{3\times3} + \mathbf{S}(\varepsilon) \\ -\varepsilon^T \end{bmatrix}, \ \mathbf{S}(\varepsilon) = \begin{bmatrix} 0 & -\varepsilon_3 & \varepsilon_2 \\ \varepsilon_3 & 0 & -\varepsilon_1 \\ -\varepsilon_2 & \varepsilon_1 & 0 \end{bmatrix}, \tag{2.1c}$$

and $\mathbf{I}_{3\times3}$ is the 3×3 unit matrix. Although Eq. (2.1a, 2.1b, 2.1c) can be generalized and both the quaternion and angular velocity can be expressed as a dual quaternion and dual angular velocity vector as outlined by Sjøberg and Egeland (2018) the dual component of the quaternion satisfies an additional constraint which is not easily implemented, in practice. Thus the dual component has effectively only three independent variables and represents the translational kinematics.

In Eq. 2.1a, 2.1b, 2.1c, the angular velocity vector is treated as a control variable and expressed as,

$$\boldsymbol{\omega} = |\boldsymbol{\omega}|_{max}\boldsymbol{u}, \tag{2.2}$$

where the direction vector $\boldsymbol{u}$ is parametrized by two angles defining the direction of the ω vector. Thus the direction vector $\boldsymbol{u}$ is expressed as,

$$\boldsymbol{u} = [\sin \alpha \cos \beta \quad \cos \alpha \cos \beta \quad \sin \beta]^T. \tag{2.3}$$

When one is interested in the problem of finding the directional control,

$$\boldsymbol{u} = \boldsymbol{u}(t), t_0 \le t \le t_f, \tag{2.4}$$

the angular velocity direction time history is sought, such that it minimizes the cost functional:

$$J = 0.5(\mathbf{q}(t) - \mathbf{q}_d)^T \mathbf{Q}_f(\mathbf{q}(t) - \mathbf{q}_d)\big|_{t=t_f} = \Phi\{\mathbf{q}(t)\}\big|_{t=t_f}, \tag{2.5}$$

subject to, Eqs. (6.1), (6.2) and (6.3). Introducing the single state vector, $\mathbf{x} = \mathbf{q}$ so the Eq. (2.1a, 2.1b, 2.1c), are expressed as,

$$d\mathbf{x}/dt = \mathbf{f}. \tag{2.6}$$

To solve the optimization problem, three Lagrangian multipliers or co-states are introduced given by the vector $\boldsymbol{\lambda}_\mathbf{q}(t)$. Following Bryson and Ho (1969), a Hamiltonian function is defined as,

$$H = \boldsymbol{\lambda}_\mathbf{q}^T(0.5\mathbf{A}_\omega(\boldsymbol{\omega})\mathbf{q}) = \boldsymbol{\lambda}_\mathbf{q}^T(0.5\boldsymbol{\Gamma}(\mathbf{q})\boldsymbol{\omega}) = \left(|\boldsymbol{\omega}|_{max}/2\right)\left(\boldsymbol{\lambda}_\mathbf{q}^T\boldsymbol{\Gamma}(\mathbf{q})\right)\boldsymbol{u}. \tag{2.7}$$

The corresponding differential equations that the co-state vector must satisfy are,

$$\frac{d}{dt}\boldsymbol{\lambda}_\mathbf{q}^T(t) = -\frac{\partial H}{\partial \mathbf{q}} = -\frac{1}{2}\boldsymbol{\lambda}_\mathbf{q}^T\mathbf{A}_\omega(\boldsymbol{\omega}). \tag{2.8}$$

The optimality conditions for the control parameters are,

$$\frac{\partial H}{\partial \alpha} = \frac{|\boldsymbol{\omega}|_{max}}{2}\boldsymbol{\lambda}_\mathbf{q}^T\boldsymbol{\Gamma}(\mathbf{q})[\cos \alpha \cos \beta \quad -\sin \alpha \cos \beta \quad 0] = 0, \tag{2.9}$$

and

$$\frac{\partial H}{\partial \beta} = \frac{|\boldsymbol{\omega}|_{max}}{2} \boldsymbol{\lambda}_{\mathbf{q}}^T \boldsymbol{\Gamma}(\mathbf{q})[-\sin \alpha \sin \beta \quad -\cos \alpha \sin \beta \quad \cos \beta] = 0. \tag{2.10}$$

Hence it follows that the c-state vector $\boldsymbol{\lambda}_{\mathbf{q}}(t)$, satisfies the relation,

$$\frac{|\boldsymbol{\omega}|_{max}}{2} \boldsymbol{\Gamma}(\mathbf{q})\boldsymbol{\lambda}_{\mathbf{q}} = \left|\frac{|\boldsymbol{\omega}|_{max}}{2} \boldsymbol{\Gamma}(\mathbf{q})\boldsymbol{\lambda}_{\mathbf{q}}\right|[\sin \alpha \cos \beta \quad \cos \alpha \cos \beta \quad \sin \beta]^T$$

$$= \left|\frac{|\boldsymbol{\omega}|_{max}}{2} \boldsymbol{\Gamma}(\mathbf{q})\boldsymbol{\lambda}_{\mathbf{q}}\right| \boldsymbol{u}. \tag{2.11}$$

Thus, the optimal control is given by,

$$\boldsymbol{u} = -\boldsymbol{\Gamma}^T(\mathbf{q})\boldsymbol{\lambda}_{\mathbf{q}}/|\boldsymbol{\Gamma}^T(\mathbf{q})\boldsymbol{\lambda}_{\mathbf{q}}| = \boldsymbol{\Gamma}(\mathbf{q})\boldsymbol{\lambda}_{\mathbf{q}}/|\boldsymbol{\Gamma}(\mathbf{q})\boldsymbol{\lambda}_{\mathbf{q}}|. \tag{2.12}$$

For the co-state boundary conditions one has,

$$\boldsymbol{\lambda}_{\mathbf{q}}(t_f) = \left.\frac{\partial \Phi\{\mathbf{q}(t)\}}{\partial \mathbf{q}}\right|_{t=t_f} = \mathbf{Q}_f(\mathbf{q}(t_f) - \mathbf{q}_d). \tag{2.13}$$

Once the control is found from Eqs. 2.12, 2.2 is used to define the angular velocity vector, which is then used to define the optimal input control torques. When implementing constraints, it is often more appropriate to use alternate representations of the quaternion such as the Euler vector and the Euler principal angle or the Gibbs vector.

3   Optimal Translational Trajectory Synthesis

The translational kinematics may be expressed as,

$$\frac{d\mathbf{r}}{dt} + \boldsymbol{\Omega}(\boldsymbol{\omega})\mathbf{r} = \mathbf{v}, \frac{d\mathbf{r}}{dt} = -\boldsymbol{\Omega}(\boldsymbol{\omega})\mathbf{r} + \mathbf{v}, \tag{3.1}$$

where, $\boldsymbol{\Omega}(\boldsymbol{\omega})$ is defined in Eq. (2.1b). Hence, with,

$$\mathbf{A_r} = \begin{bmatrix} -\boldsymbol{\Omega}(\boldsymbol{\omega}) & \mathbf{0} \\ \mathbf{0} & 0 \end{bmatrix} \text{ and } \mathbf{q_r} = \begin{bmatrix} \mathbf{r} \\ 0 \end{bmatrix}, \tag{3.2}$$

$$\frac{d}{dt}\mathbf{q_r} = \mathbf{A_r}\mathbf{q_r} + \begin{bmatrix} \mathbf{v} \\ 0 \end{bmatrix}. \tag{3.3}$$

Equation (3.3) is similar in form to the quaternion kinematics equation. It is often advantageous to use Eq. (3.3) rather than the dual quaternion formulation as the constraints are explicitly satisfied. In above equations, the linear velocity vector is treated as a control variable and expressed as,

$$\mathbf{v} = |\mathbf{v}|_{max}\boldsymbol{u}, \tag{3.4}$$

where the direction vector $\boldsymbol{u}$ is parametrized by two angles defining the direction of the $\mathbf{v}$ vector. Thus the direction vector $\boldsymbol{u}$ is expressed as,

$$\boldsymbol{u} = [\sin \alpha \cos \beta \quad \cos \alpha \cos \beta \quad \sin \beta]^T. \tag{3.5}$$

When one is interested in the problem of finding the directional control,

$$\boldsymbol{u} = \boldsymbol{u}(t), t_0 \le t \le t_f, \tag{3.6}$$

the angular velocity direction time history is sought, such that it minimizes the cost functional:

$$J = 0.5(\mathbf{r}(t) - \mathbf{r}_d)^T \mathbf{Q}_{rf}(\mathbf{r}(t) - \mathbf{r}_d)\big|_{t=t_f} = \Phi_r\{\mathbf{r}(t)\}\big|_{t=t_f}, \tag{3.7}$$

subject to, Eq. (3.1). Introducing the single state vector, $\mathbf{x} = \mathbf{r}$ so the Eq. (3.1), are expressed as,

$$d\mathbf{x}/dt = \mathbf{f}. \tag{3.8}$$

To solve the optimization problem, three Lagrangian multipliers or co-states are introduced given by the vector $\boldsymbol{\lambda}_{\mathbf{r}}(t)$. Following Bryson and Ho (1969), a Hamiltonian function is defined as,

$$H = -\boldsymbol{\lambda}_{\mathbf{r}}^T(t)\boldsymbol{\Omega}(\boldsymbol{\omega})\mathbf{r}(t) + \boldsymbol{\lambda}_{\mathbf{r}}^T(t)\boldsymbol{u}. \tag{3.9}$$

The corresponding differential equations that the co-state vector must satisfy are,

$$\frac{d}{dt}\boldsymbol{\lambda}_{\mathbf{r}}^T(t) = -\frac{dH}{d\mathbf{r}} = \boldsymbol{\lambda}_{\mathbf{r}}^T(t)\boldsymbol{\Omega}(\boldsymbol{\omega}). \tag{3.10}$$

The optimality conditions for the control parameters are,

$$\frac{\partial H}{\partial \alpha} = |\mathbf{v}|_{max}\boldsymbol{\lambda}_{\mathbf{r}}^T[\cos \alpha \cos \beta \quad -\sin \alpha \cos \beta \quad 0] = 0, \tag{3.11}$$

and

$$\frac{\partial H}{\partial \beta} = |\mathbf{v}|_{max}\boldsymbol{\lambda}_{\mathbf{r}}^T[-\sin \alpha \sin \beta \quad -\cos \alpha \sin \beta \quad \cos \beta] = 0. \tag{3.12}$$

Hence it follows that the co-state vector $\boldsymbol{\lambda}_{\mathbf{r}}(t)$, satisfies the relation,

$$|\mathbf{v}|_{max}\boldsymbol{\lambda}_{\mathbf{r}} = ||\mathbf{v}|_{max}\boldsymbol{\lambda}_{\mathbf{r}}|[\sin \alpha \cos \beta \quad \cos \alpha \cos \beta \quad \sin \beta]^T = ||\mathbf{v}|_{max}\boldsymbol{\lambda}_{\mathbf{r}}|\boldsymbol{u}. \tag{3.13}$$

Thus, the optimal control is $\mathbf{v} = |\mathbf{v}|_{max}\boldsymbol{u}$, $\boldsymbol{u}$ where is given by,

$$u = \lambda_{\mathbf{r}}/|\lambda_{\mathbf{r}}|. \tag{3.14}$$

For the co-state boundary conditions one has,

$$\lambda_{\mathbf{r}}(t_f) = \left.\frac{\partial \Phi_r\{\mathbf{r}(t)\}}{\partial \mathbf{r}}\right|_{t=t_f} = \left.\mathbf{Q}_{rf}(\mathbf{r}(t) - \mathbf{r}_d)\right|_{t=t_f}. \tag{3.15}$$

Once the control is found from Eq. 3.14, the attitude kinetics equations are used, to define the angular velocity vector, which is then used to define the optimal input control torques.

4 Translational Kinematics of an Aerospace Robotic Platform

Consider a 3-1-3 sequence of Euler angles, where the angles are θ the longitude, a 90° rotation about the "1" axis and ϕ the latitude. The corresponding transformations are,

$$T_3(\theta) = \begin{bmatrix} \cos\theta & \sin\theta & 0 \\ -\sin\theta & \cos\theta & 0 \\ 0 & 0 & 1 \end{bmatrix}, T_1(90°) = \begin{bmatrix} 1 & 0 & 0 \\ 0 & 0 & 1 \\ 0 & -1 & 0 \end{bmatrix},$$

$$T_3(\phi) = \begin{bmatrix} \cos\phi & \sin\phi & 0 \\ -\sin\phi & \cos\phi & 0 \\ 0 & 0 & 1 \end{bmatrix}. \tag{4.1}$$

The Earth-fixed to body fixed transformation is given by,

$$T_{BE} = T_3(\theta)T_1(90°)T_3(\phi), T_{BE} = \begin{bmatrix} \cos\theta\cos\phi & \cos\theta\sin\phi & \sin\theta \\ -\sin\theta\cos\phi & -\sin\theta\sin\phi & \cos\theta \\ \sin\phi & -\cos\phi & 0 \end{bmatrix}. \tag{4.2}$$

Combined with the radial position r, θ the longitude and ϕ the latitude, constitute a set of spherical coordinates. The angular velocity components for the above 3-1-3 sequence are:

$$\omega = \begin{bmatrix} \dot\theta\sin\phi & \dot\theta\cos\phi & \dot\phi \end{bmatrix}^T. \tag{4.3}$$

Now let γ be the flight path angle, ψ be the heading or yaw angle and v the magnitude of the vehicle's velocity. Then the kinematic equations relating the velocity components to the rate of change of position in the spherical coordinates are,

$$\dot{r} = v\sin\gamma, r\dot\phi = v\cos\gamma\sin\psi, r\cos\phi\,\dot\theta = v\cos\gamma\cos\psi. \tag{4.4}$$

The Eq. (4.4) are non-singular as long as the variable ϕ satisfies $-\pi/2 < \phi < \pi/2$; i.e. the vehicle does not overfly the poles.

5 Translational Kinetics of an Aerospace Robotic Platform

For completeness the translational kinetics of the platform orbiting the Earth in a low Earth orbit is also briefly presented. Consider first a non-rotating planet. The local acceleration due to gravitation, positive down, which is also the negative radial component may be defined as,

$$g = \mu/r^2. \tag{5.1}$$

The kinetic equations are expressed as,

$$\dot{v} = a_s - g \sin \gamma, \tag{5.2}$$

$$v \cos \gamma \, \dot{\psi} = a_w - \frac{v^2}{r}\cos^2 \gamma \cos \psi \tan \phi, \tag{5.3}$$

$$v\dot{\gamma} = a_n - \left(g - \frac{v^2}{r}\right) \cos \gamma, \tag{5.4}$$

$$\dot{m} = -T/v_e, \tag{5.5}$$

Equation (5.5) represents the rate of change of mass of the vehicle due to the expulsion of mass with relative velocity v_e by the propulsion system. In Eqs. (5.2) to (5.4) the aerodynamic forces in the tangential, normal and bi-normal directions are respectively defined by,

$$ma_s = T \cos \alpha - D, ma_w = (L+T \sin \alpha) \sin \phi_r, ma_n = (L+T \sin \alpha) \cos \phi_r. \tag{5.6}$$

In Eq. 5.6, ϕ_r is the bank angle, T is the body fixed thrust, L is the aerodynamic lift which is linearly dependent on the elevator angle, D is the aerodynamic drag, α is the angle of attack, which is equal to the pitch plus the flight path angles, $\alpha = \theta_p + \gamma$. The Euler angles defining the attitude of the vehicle are ψ, θ_p, ϕ_r (yaw, pitch roll or 3-2-1 sequence) which can be obtained from the quaternion components. Given the Euler parameters or quaternion components,

$$\eta = \cos(\phi/2); \boldsymbol{\varepsilon} = [\varepsilon_1 \quad \varepsilon_2 \quad \varepsilon_3]^T = \mathbf{n} \sin(\phi/2), \tag{5.7}$$

the transformation relating an orbiting reference frame to a body fixed frame is given by,

$$\mathbf{T}_{BR}(\mathbf{q}) = \{T_{ij}\} = \begin{bmatrix} \eta^2 + \varepsilon_1^2 - \varepsilon_2^2 - \varepsilon_3^2 & 2(\varepsilon_1\varepsilon_2 + \varepsilon_3\eta) & 2(\varepsilon_1\varepsilon_3 - \varepsilon_2\eta) \\ 2(\varepsilon_1\varepsilon_2 - \varepsilon_3\eta) & \eta^2 - \varepsilon_1^2 + \varepsilon_2^2 - \varepsilon_3^2 & 2(\varepsilon_2\varepsilon_3 + \varepsilon_1\eta) \\ 2(\varepsilon_1\varepsilon_3 + \varepsilon_2\eta) & 2(\varepsilon_2\varepsilon_3 - \varepsilon_1\eta) & \eta^2 - \varepsilon_1^2 - \varepsilon_2^2 + \varepsilon_3^2 \end{bmatrix}. \tag{5.8}$$

Thus it follows that,

$$t = Trace(T_{ij}) = 3\eta^2 - \varepsilon_1^2 - \varepsilon_2^2 - \varepsilon_3^2 = 4\eta^2 - 1; r = \sqrt{1+t} = 2\eta; \eta = r/2 = \sqrt{1+t}/2;$$
$$s = 1/2r = 1/(4\eta); \varepsilon_1 = (T_{23} - T_{32})s, \varepsilon_2 = (T_{31} - T_{13})s, \varepsilon_3 = (T_{12} - T_{21})s.$$

$$(5.9)$$

Hence the quaternion components may be related to the 3-2-1 Euler angle sequence components from the elements of the attitude transformation matrix.

In the case of a rotating planet with the atmosphere rotating with it, one has,

$$\dot{v} = a_s + g_s + cf_v, \dot{m} = -T/v_e, \tag{5.10}$$

$$v \cos \gamma \, \dot{\psi} = a_w + g_w - \frac{v^2}{r} \cos^2 \gamma \cos \psi \tan \phi + \left(cf_\psi + v \cos \gamma \, co_\psi\right), \tag{5.11}$$

$$v\dot{\gamma} = a_n + \left(g_n + \frac{v^2}{r}\right) \cos \gamma + \left(cf_\gamma + vco_\gamma\right). \tag{5.12}$$

The centrifugal (cf) and coriolis (co) terms due to the planets rotation rate (Ω) are:

$$cf_v = \Omega^2 r \cos \phi(\sin \gamma \cos \phi - \cos \gamma \sin \phi \sin \psi), \tag{5.13}$$

$$cf_\psi = -\Omega^2 r \sin \phi \cos \phi \cos \psi, \tag{5.14}$$

$$cf_\gamma = -\Omega^2 r \cos \phi(\cos \gamma \cos \phi + \sin \gamma \sin \phi \sin \psi), \tag{5.15}$$

$$co_\psi = 2\Omega(\tan \gamma \cos \phi \sin \psi - \sin \phi), co_\gamma = 2\Omega \cos \phi \cos \psi. \tag{5.16}$$

6 Optimal Translational Trajectory Synthesis for an Aerospace Robotic Platform

Generally when constraints need to applied to the kinematic variables it is often convenient to express the kinematics in a frame where the constraints reduce to equality relations applied to the variables. In deriving the optimal control input, corresponding to Eq. 3.15, for the translational kinematic equations in Sect. 4, Eq. 4.4 are often used in place of Eq. 3.1. Thus the Hamiltonian is defined by,

$$H = \lambda_r v \sin \gamma + \lambda_\theta \frac{v \cos \gamma \cos \psi}{r \cos \phi} + \lambda_\phi \frac{v \cos \gamma \sin \psi}{r}. \tag{6.1}$$

The differential equations that the co-states must satisfy are,

$$\dot{\lambda}_r = -\frac{\partial H}{\partial r} = \lambda_\theta \frac{v \cos \gamma \cos \psi}{r^2 \cos \phi} + \lambda_\phi \frac{v \cos \gamma \sin \psi}{r^2}, \tag{6.2}$$

$$\dot{\lambda}_{\theta} = -\frac{\partial H}{\partial \theta} = 0, \dot{\lambda}_{\phi} = -\frac{\partial H}{\partial \phi} = -\lambda_{\theta}\frac{v \cos \gamma \cos \psi}{r(\cos \phi)^2}\sin \phi. \qquad (6.3)$$

The control input is expressed in terms of the fixed magnitude $v = |\mathbf{v}|_{\max}$ and the direction of the velocity vector. Thus the optimality conditions for the control parameters are,

$$\frac{\partial H}{\partial \gamma} = \lambda_r v \cos \gamma - \lambda_{\theta}\frac{v \sin \gamma \cos \psi}{r \cos \varphi} - \lambda_{\varphi}\frac{v \sin \gamma \sin \psi}{r} = 0, \qquad (6.4)$$

$$\frac{\partial H}{\partial \psi} = -\lambda_{\theta}\frac{v \cos \gamma \sin \psi}{r \cos \varphi} + \lambda_{\varphi}\frac{v \cos \gamma \cos \psi}{r} = 0. \qquad (6.5)$$

Hence co-states satisfy the relation,

$$v[\lambda_r \quad \lambda_{\theta} \quad \lambda_{\varphi}] = |v[\lambda_r \quad \lambda_{\theta} \quad \lambda_{\varphi}]|[\sin \gamma \quad r \cos \phi \cos \gamma \cos \psi \quad r \cos \gamma \sin \psi]. \qquad (6.6)$$

Thus, the optimal control parameters defining the direction of the velocity vector are given by,

$$[\sin \gamma \quad \cos \gamma \cos \psi \quad \cos \gamma \sin \psi]^T = \begin{bmatrix} 1 & 0 & 0 \\ 0 & r \cos \phi & 0 \\ 0 & 0 & r \end{bmatrix}^{-1}\frac{[\lambda_r \quad \lambda_{\theta} \quad \lambda_{\varphi}]^T}{||[\lambda_r \quad \lambda_{\theta} \quad \lambda_{\varphi}]||}. \qquad (6.7)$$

For the co-state boundary conditions one has,

$$\lambda_r(t_f) = (r(t) - r_d)|_{t=t_f}, \lambda_{\theta}(t_f) = (\theta(t) - \theta_d)|_{t=t_f}, \lambda_{\phi}(t_f) = (\phi(t) - \phi_d)|_{t=t_f}. \qquad (6.8)$$

7   Extension to an on-Board Robot Manipulator

In the presence of an on-board manipulator, to be able compute the trajectories of the manipulator links, it is essential to include the joint kinematics. In general, it is possible to assume that the manipulator joints have a single degree of freedom and are either revolute or prismatic joints. Under these circumstances, in many situations, the joint kinematics are given by scalar, uncoupled equations of the form, $\dot{\theta}_i = \omega_i$ for the ith revolute joint and $\dot{d}_i = v_i$ for the ith prismatic joint. Following Yakimenko (2000), the optimal trajectories in these cases are expressed by eighth order polynomials in a scaled arc-length parameter where the coefficients are determined by the maximum bounds on the jerk, jerk-rate, acceleration and velocity as well as boundary conditions on the scale factor, position and acceleration at the two end points. The method has been adapted also by Cowling et al. (2006), Lukacs and Yakimenko (2007), Etchemendy (2007) and is discussed in some detail by Vepa (2016) in section 14.13. The method integrating such a trajectory segment into the complete motion plan is discussed by Dugar et al. (2017).

Once the velocity profile over a time frame is known from the co-state equations and the boundary conditions, the optimum forces and torques acting on the vehicle as well as the optimum torques acting the manipulator joints may be determined.

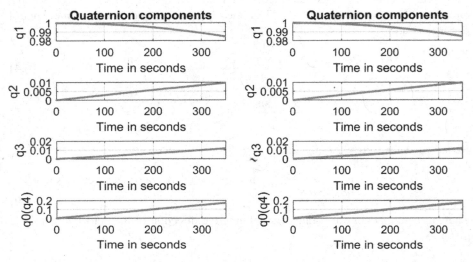

Fig. 1. The synthesized quaternion reference trajectory

Fig. 2. The actual quaternion trajectory tracked by the vehicle

8   Typical Simulation Examples

The first example considered is one where the quaternion attitude needs to smoothly change from its current initial value $\left(\eta = 0, \varepsilon = [1\,0\,0]^T\right)$ to final desired value, which involves a small but high precision change in the attitude. Figure 1 illustrates the synthesized trajectory while Fig. 2 illustrates the actual quaternion trajectory components as a space vehicle tracks the reference trajectory. In the Fig. 1, η is shown as $q_0(q_4)$ while $\varepsilon = [q_1 \quad q_2 \quad q_3]^T$. The estimated maximum error between the plots in Figs. 1 and 2 is less than 3% always. Figure 3 illustrates a typical set angular velocity time histories required to achieve the desired attitude.

In Fig. 4 are shown the corresponding torques, including the gravity gradient torques for a typical CUBESAT type space vehicle. The torques are provided by an electric magnetic actuation system. The two-point boundary value problem was solved by using the MATLAB m-file, bvp4c.m. The maximum magnitude of the angular velocity is restricted to 0.001 rad/s. When this method is applied to a robotic manipulator with three or more degrees of freedom, once the reference quaternion time histories are obtained, the joint angles are found from the solutions for the inverse kinematics.

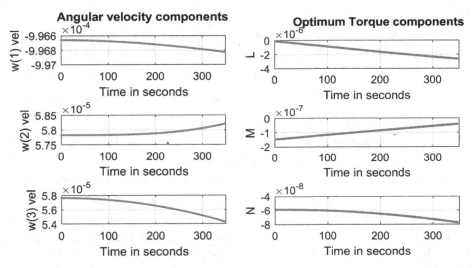

Fig. 3. The corresponding reference angular velocity time histories

Fig. 4. The corresponding torque (in Nm) time histories

The second example considered defines the trajectory of a low Earth orbiting vehicle. The vehicle translational kinematics is defined by Eqs. 4.3 and 4.4. In Fig. 5 are shown the position or altitude, longitude and latitude as it travels towards a destination longitude and latitude while slowly losing altitude. In Fig. 6 are shown the position or altitude, longitude and latitude as it travels towards a destination longitude and latitude while holding the altitude fixed. To achieve the fixed altitude the corresponding co-state variable is set equal to zero. In both these figures the altitude is normalized and the initial altitude is set at 1.3.

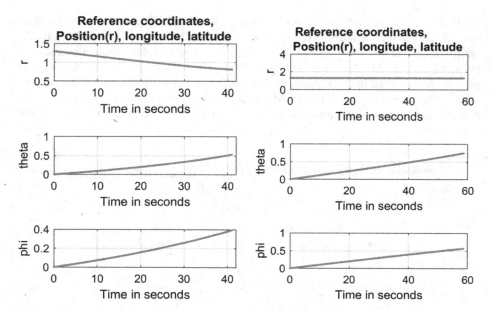

Fig. 5. The time histories of the position longitude and latitude

Fig. 6. The time histories of the position, which is fixed, longitude and latitude

The final example is a UAV such as a quadcopter which is modelled as a body rather than as a point mass. The attitude kinematics continues to be given by Eq. 2.1a, 2.1b, 2.1c

$$\frac{d\mathbf{q}}{dt} = \frac{1}{2}\mathbf{A}_\omega(\boldsymbol{\omega})\mathbf{q} = \frac{1}{2}\boldsymbol{\Gamma}(\mathbf{q})\boldsymbol{\omega}. \tag{8.1}$$

The position kinematics is given by,

$$\dot{\mathbf{r}} = \mathbf{T}_{BI}^T(\mathbf{q})\mathbf{v}_b, \tag{8.2}$$

where $\mathbf{v}_b = \begin{bmatrix} u & v & w \end{bmatrix}^T$ is the velocity of the vehicle in body fixed coordinates while $\mathbf{T}_{BI}(\mathbf{q})$ is the transformation from an inertial of space fixed frame to the body fixed frame. It may be expressed in terms of the components of the quaternion vector.

The Hamiltonian in this case is:

$$H = \boldsymbol{\lambda}_\mathbf{q}^T \frac{1}{2}\mathbf{A}_\omega(\boldsymbol{\omega})\mathbf{q} + \boldsymbol{\lambda}_\mathbf{r}^T \mathbf{T}_{BI}^T(\mathbf{q})\mathbf{v}_b = \boldsymbol{\lambda}_\mathbf{q}^T \frac{1}{2}\boldsymbol{\Gamma}(\mathbf{q})\boldsymbol{\omega} + \boldsymbol{\lambda}_\mathbf{r}^T \mathbf{T}_{BI}^T(\mathbf{q})\mathbf{v}_b, \tag{8.3}$$

$$\frac{d}{dt}\boldsymbol{\lambda}_\mathbf{q}^T(t) = -\frac{\partial H}{\partial \mathbf{q}}, \frac{d}{dt}\boldsymbol{\lambda}_\mathbf{r}^T(t) = -\frac{\partial H}{\partial \mathbf{r}} = 0. \tag{8.4}$$

Thus one may choose, $\lambda_\mathbf{r}^T(t) \equiv 0$ and $\mathbf{v}_b = \mathbf{v}_{b,\text{max}} = [\,u_{\text{max}} \quad v_{\text{max}} \quad w_{\text{max}}\,]^T$ is a constant vector. Hence, it follows that,

$$\frac{d}{dt}\lambda_\mathbf{q}^T(t) = -\frac{\partial H}{\partial \mathbf{q}} = -\frac{1}{2}\lambda_\mathbf{q}^T \mathbf{A}_\omega(\boldsymbol{\omega}). \qquad (8.5)$$

The angular velocity vector is treated as a control variable and expressed as, $\boldsymbol{\omega} = |\boldsymbol{\omega}|_{\text{max}}\boldsymbol{u}$, where $\boldsymbol{u}$, may continue to be chosen in accordance with Eq. 2.12. Thus the problem reduces to one where the optimal attitude variation only need to be computed using the methodology outlined in Sect. 2. For the translational trajectories, in the body frame a relatively simple approach is to relate the velocity vector to the applied specific thrust vector (thrust vector per unit mass) and the net drag or lift forces. Ignoring the gravity forces, the equation relating the velocity vector $\mathbf{v}_b$, to the specific thrust magnitude and to the position vector in the body frame $\mathbf{r}_b$, are assumed to be given by,

$$\dot{\mathbf{v}}_b + \boldsymbol{\omega} \times \mathbf{v}_b = T\mathbf{u} - \mathbf{K}_{ld}. \times \mathbf{v}_b. \times \mathbf{v}_b, \dot{\mathbf{r}}_b + \boldsymbol{\omega} \times \mathbf{r}_b = \mathbf{v}_b, \qquad (8.6)$$

where T is the magnitude of the specific thrust, $\mathbf{K}_{ld}$ is a vector of constants relating the lift or drag to the square of the velocity component and '.×' is the elementwise product of two vectors. The reference velocity and reference position components may then be obtained with $\boldsymbol{\omega} = 0$ in steady state. Typical non-dimensional plots of the position and velocity components in the body frame obtained in this way are shown in Figs. 7 and 8 respectively. They may then be transformed to the space fixed frame by using the

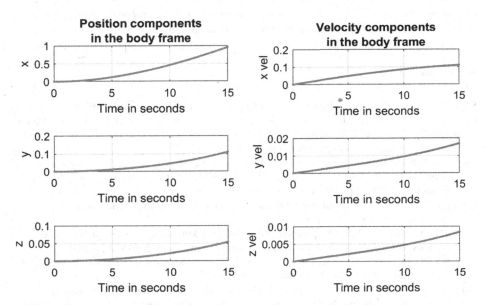

Fig. 7. The time histories of the position components in the body frame

Fig. 8. The time histories of the velocity components in the body frame.

transformation $\mathbf{T}_{BI}(\mathbf{q})$ obtained from the reference quaternion components. In this case a model of the vehicle dynamics is used and the trajectory synthesis is not purely based on kinematic relations.

9 Discussion and Conclusions

In this work the feasibility of using a quaternion formulation of the attitude kinematics to develop the attitude acquisition trajectory using small changes in the angular velocity components has been successfully demonstrated. The application of the methodology to the translational kinematics is also demonstrated. The usefulness of this work is in its application to space robotic manipulators where the change in pose can be defined as a set of sequential changes in the attitudes of serially connected links with several revolute and some prismatic joints. Although the change in pose may be conveniently defined by a set of dual quaternions, the actual attitude acquisition problem is formulated as a sequence of vector attitude optimal synthesis problems similar to the form considered in this paper. When a set of manipulator links are serially connected with only revolute joints, the synthesis problem reduces to the simultaneous synthesis of attitude time histories of these links. When a finite number of prismatic joints are present, the problem reduces to a set of independent synthesis problems. The complete pose is found by accumulating the attitudes with alternate representations of the other vectors. It is demonstrated succinctly that the methodology may be applied, with minimal use of the dynamics, to actual space and aerial robotic manipulators attached to a vehicle in flight, a planetary rover (Vepa 2019) or a robotic vehicle, where the attitude of the vehicle and the pose of the manipulator links or vehicle itself must be obtained. Apart from the simplicity, the fact they are non-dimensional implies that they could be used in variety of different physical solutions, by appropriate re-scaling.

References

Bryson Jr., A.E., Ho, Y.C.: Applied Optimal Control. Ginn & Co., Waltham (1969)

Cowling, I.D., Whidborne, J.F., Cooke, A.K.: Optimal trajectory planning and LQR control for a quadrotor UAV. In: Proceedings of the International Conference Control-2006, Glasgow, Scotland, 30 August–11 September 2006

Dugar, V., Choudhury, S., Scherer, S.: A κITE in the wind: smooth trajectory optimization in a moving reference frame. In: 2017 IEEE International Conference on Robotics and Automation (ICRA), pp. 109–116 (2017)

Etchemendy, M.: Flight Control and Optimal Path Planning for UAVs, MSc Thesis, School of Engineering, Cranfield University, August 2007

Filipe, N., Tsiotras, P.: Adaptive position and attitude-tracking controller for satellite proximity operations using dual quaternions. J. Guid. Control Dyn. 38(4), 566–577 (2014)

Lagache, M.-A., Serres, U., Andrieu, V.: Minimal time synthesis for a kinematic drone model. Math. Control Relat. Fields 7(2), 259–288 (2017)

Lukacs, J.A, Yakimenko, O.A.: Trajectory-shape-varying missile guidance for interception of ballistic missiles during the boost phase. In: AIAA Guidance, Navigation and Control Conference and Exhibit, Hilton Head, South Carolina, 20–23 August 2007

Özgür, E., Mezouar, Y.: Kinematic modeling and control of a robot arm using unit dual quaternions. Robot. Autom. Syst. **77**, 66–73 (2016)

Sjøberg, A.M., Egeland, O.: Kinematic feedback control using dual quaternions. In: Proceedings of the 26th Mediterranean Conference on Control and Automation. IEEE, Zadar, Croatia, 19–22 June 2018. https://doi.org/10.1109/med.2018.8442800

Valverde, A., Tsiotras, P.: Spacecraft robot kinematics using dual quaternions. Robotics **7**(64), 1–24 (2018)

Vepa, R.: Nonlinear Control of Robots and Unmanned Aerial Vehicles: An Integrated Approach. CRC Press, Boca Raton (2016)

Vepa, R.: Dynamics and Control of Autonomous Space Vehicles and Robotics. Cambridge University Press, New York (2019)

Vukobratovic, M., Kircanski, M.: Kinematics and Trajectory Synthesis of Manipulation Robots. Springer, Heidelberg (2013). https://doi.org/10.1007/978-3-642-82195-0

Wolek, A., Cliff, E.M., Woolsey, C.A.: Time-optimal path planning for a kinematic car with variable speed. J. Guid. Control Dyn. **39**(10), 2374–2390 (2016)

Yakimenko, O.A.: Direct method for rapid prototyping of near-optimal aircraft trajectories. J. Guid. Control Dyn. **23**(5), 865–875 (2000)

MRComm: Multi-Robot Communication Testbed

Tsvetan Zhivkov, Eric Schneider$^{(\boxtimes)}$, and Elizabeth Sklar$^{(\boxtimes)}$ (iD)

Department of Informatics, King's College London, London, UK
{tsvetan.zhivkov,eric.schneider,elizabeth.sklar}@kcl.ac.uk
http://www.kcl.ac.uk

Abstract. This work demonstrates how dynamic robot behaviour that responds to different types of network disturbances can improve communication and mission performance in a *Multi-Robot Team (MRT)*. A series of experiments are conducted which show how two different network perturbations (i.e. packet loss and signal loss) and two different network types (i.e. wireless local area network and ad-hoc network) impact communication. Performance is compared using two MRT behaviours: a baseline versus a novel dynamic behaviour that adapts to fluctuations in communication quality. Experiments are carried out on a known map with tasks assigned to a robot team at the start of a mission. During each experiment, a number of performance metrics are recorded. A novel dynamic *Leader-Follower (LF)* behaviour enables continuous communication through two key functions: the first reacts to the network type by using signal strength to determine if the robot team must commit to grouping together to maintain communication; and the second employs a special task status messaging function that guarantees a message is communicated successfully to the team members. The results presented in this work are significant for real-world multi-robot system applications that require continuous communication amongst team members.

Keywords: Multi-robot team · Behaviour-based control · Dynamic roles

1 Introduction

In a *Multi-Robot Team (MRT)*, providing correct and current information to team members are two of the critical functions that depend on networked communication facilities. Reliable communication is such an important aspect in robotics that it prompted a fundamental change in the communication middleware used in the Robot Operating System (ROS1) [13] from *Publisher-Subscriber (Pub-Sub)* to the open source *Data Distributed Service (DDS)* that is being integrated into ROS2 [5,6]. As home automation and mobile technologies grow, the

This work was partially supported by a King's College London Graduate Training Scholarship and by the ESRC under grant #ES/P011160/1.

© Springer Nature Switzerland AG 2019
K. Althoefer et al. (Eds.): TAROS 2019, LNAI 11650, pp. 346–357, 2019.
https://doi.org/10.1007/978-3-030-25332-5_30

potential applications for MRTs also expand [1, 11, 19]. Furthermore, robots are often deployed in mission scenarios that are unsuitable or dangerous for human operators and which often have poor or crippled network infrastructure, such as urban search-and-rescue (USAR) [12, 18, 19], humanitarian de-mining or nuclear plant monitoring. Even state-of-the-art deployment of telecommunication networks and research that addresses latency and outage issues may experience poor routing, network congestion, channel interference or packet dropping, which can have significant impact on robot systems that rely on timely and accurate mission critical information, as noted by Caccamo [4] and Kashino *et al.* [9].

In earlier work [20], we employed the ROS-based *MRTeAm (Multi-Robot Task Allocation)* framework [15] as the basis for a study in which we applied a probabilistic message loss function to one message "topic"[1] that is shared amongst the robot team members. The affected topic, *AmclPose*[2], comprises messages that receive and send data about a robot's position in a known map. We ran a series of experiments to measure the impact on mission performance metrics when *AmclPose* messages were lost at increasingly frequent rates. Our results showed non-linear degradation in performance as message loss probability grew from 0% to 75%. Although limited, these results gave us an initial understanding of how a multi-robot team is affected by lowering communication quality. Here, the probabilistic message loss function is applied to two message topics, *AmclPose* and *TaskStatus*. Moreover, we expand the experiment configuration to include network types, network perturbations, new performance metrics, message functionality and behaviours. We demonstrate experimentally the range of effects that various network perturbations have on multiple aspects of team performance and how this changes with different network types. To facilitate our empirical investigation, we have developed the **MRComm** (Multi-Robot Communication) testbed that allows for control of communication for individual message topics and thus subsequently experimental analysis by topic. Though the results here are for all message topics. MRComm makes use of a novel, dynamic *Leader-Follower (LF)* behaviour inspired by the concept of infrastructure-less (i.e. ad-hoc) networks, which is used to respond to real-time fluctuations in network connectivity. Moreover, we employ a novel messaging function that does not require any changes to the underlying pub-sub communication middleware while offering a best effort to verify acknowledgement of message transmission. Our results show that the LF behaviour and the new message function maintain continuous communication regardless of the network type and network perturbation that effects the communication quality. This is a crucial step for multi-robot research toward acquiring the tool set needed to assess and adapt to unreliable communication and maintain continuous connectivity. Our long-term aim is to improve message passing capabilities in MRTs, by providing adaptive behaviours that respond to different network problems which arise during a mission.

---

[1] A "topic" in a Publisher-Subscriber (Pub-Sub) communication system refers to a category of related messages that are defined and grouped together when the applied system is engineered.

[2] Adaptive Monte Carlo localisation (position estimation) for mobile robots [7].

The remainder of the paper is structured as follows. In Sect. 2, we review related work. Section 3 briefly describes the approach, the architecture of our system and expansion of our framework, MRComm. Section 4 outlines the experimental setup for performing the set of experiments, which are designed to analyse performance of communication between the baseline and novel behaviours. In Sect. 5 we present our experimental results and discussion. Finally, we close in Sect. 6 with a brief summary and directions for ongoing and future research.

2   Related Work

The motivation to analyse, react and mitigate the effects of degrading communication quality in MRTs started in the mobile device domain. Although research on communication networks in the mobile device domain is plentiful, this is not the case for the MRT domain. However, an overlap exists between these domains as shown by Witkowski et al. [18] and Lujak et al. [11]. These works investigate different outcomes but use similar methods for communication, i.e. mobile ad-hoc network (MANET) or leverage smart devices for communication. When looking at research on the effects of communication networks in only the Robot and MRT domains, it is clear that it is still in its early stages and there are many aspects to be still considered. In work by Murphy et al. [12] a remote controlled robot is used to perform triage on a victim in a search-and-rescue scenario and they examine the impact of different sensors on communication (e.g., audio and video). Zadorozhny and Lewis [19] look at autonomous MRT collaboration with human assistants to perform search and rescue of victims in a simulated environment. The work by Kashino et al. [9] looks at optimal predetermined delivery of static-sensor networks using MRTs to cover an area to enable complete communication. This work shows motivation from the need to create network infrastructure in an infrastructure-less environment. The notion of using ad-hoc networks for communication in multi-robot systems isn't thoroughly covered. However, some works such as Takahashi et al. [17] investigate, in simulation, MRT formations with the aim of using an ad-hoc network. Furthermore, Witkowski et al. [18] looks at reestablishing infrastructure using robot teams and ad-hoc networks in disaster zones. Finally, Caccamo et al. [4] demonstrate a novel robot navigation planner, in simulation, that is communication-aware. We look at one of the initial works on behaviour based control for MRTs by Balch and Arkin [3]. Their work is focused on the interaction among lower level systems (e.g., navigation and obstacle avoidance) and formation control, and on analysing the strengths and weaknesses of different formation patterns; however, it is not inspired by MRT communication. Although we draw insight from [3], our behaviour based on the leader-follower paradigm does not directly interact with the lower level systems or adopt any particular formation control, which is explained in *Robot Behaviours* Sect. 3.1. We combine the analysis of communication issues of shared messages between robots, different network parameters and the use of behaviour-based control of MRTs into one testbed, MRComm, which we present here. The ROS platform is originally designed for single robot academic experiments, with no real-time requirements and an assumption that wireless local area network connectivity is available and good. Research and real use-cases now extend the use of MRTs into a number of different environments where connectivity is poor or no network infrastructure exists at all. However, while it is possible to create multi-robot systems using ROS, there is no standardised approach. Moreover, there are works such as [2] and MRTeAm [15] that provide the tools to create MRS.

3 Approach

Our overall line of work on multi-robot teams examines various problems related to *coordination*, with the ultimate goal of developing strategies that guarantee efficient and effective mission completion. We have produced a number of metrics that capture detailed aspects of team performance, these are discussed further in Sect. 5. The contribution described here builds upon this exploration of the multi-robot team coordination domain and specifically investigates the importance of reliable communication within this domain. While our earlier work studied the impact of different market-based mechanisms to distribute tasks amongst team members [15], in the setup employed here, messages are passed which: (1) directly assign tasks to robots instantaneously and sequentially; (2) provide location information about robots' positions, as input to the task distribution process and to facilitate collision-free movement; and (3) report task completion status, possibly accompanied by sensor data acquired as part of the task. The robots are given tasks by an assigner agent (i.e., robot, remote or virtual agent) which initiates messages of topic 1, and the assigned robots initiate the other message topics (2 and 3). Our previous investigation into the impact of poor communication in multi-robot teams only considered failure of message topic 2. Here, we consider failure of message topics 2 and 3, which constitutes *AmclPose* (team position messages) and *TaskStatus* respectively.

3.1 MRComm Testbed

Here, we describe our MRComm testbed, which is built on MRTeAm, the software framework mentioned earlier which we designed for conducting research on multi-robot task allocation [14–16]. Both layers rely on ROS [13] and employ two main types of components: a centralised agent that distributes tasks to robots and multiple robot controller agents for executing the tasks. Furthermore, our simulated experiments are conducted in the mobile robot simulator Stage[3]. In MRComm, the "auctioneer" is replaced by an *assigner* agent, as we shift our research emphasis from task allocation (in MRTeAm) to team communication (in MRComm)—assigning tasks directly to robots using a fixed distribution that is defined *a priori* as part of a mission configuration. The robot controller agent is extended as discussed below, to be able to respond dynamically when communication problems arise. The assigner agent used in MRComm is responsible for

---

[3] http://wiki.ros.org/stage.

loading a mission configuration and assigning tasks to all team members sequentially. The assigner also acts as a recording agent, without interfering, recording received experiment and team messages. The MRComm testbed defines a failed task when the recording agent does *not* receive a SUCCESS message after a mission has been completed. The robot controller is initialised with parameters for behaviour, scenario, network perturbation and network type at the start of an experiment. Thereafter, it receives tasks from the assigner agent and begins to execute them.

Network Type. The network type is the communication network used in experiments: *WiFi* via either a wireless local area network (WLAN) or an *ad-hoc* (AH) network[4]. To create the AH network, devices connect directly to one robot and rely on the close proximity of neighbouring devices to maintain connectivity. Devices can also leave and join the network freely without issues; however, shared information is only available as long as connections are maintained. The characteristics of the AH network are: no infrastructure, quick dissemination of information and distributed control (i.e., no single point of failure). We impose network limitations to make our problem tractable by assuming specific WLAN and AH network conditions. For the simulation experiments presented here, we modelled the limitations of our ad-hoc network using Turtlebot2 robots[5] and the type of IEEE 802.11n/ac wireless network cards that come standard with that platform. We measure the signal strength at a high resolution and take over thirty readings per resolution in order to construct a realistic model for our experiments, as shown in Fig. 1. From Fig. 1, we conclude that the AH network limit for communication is $\approx 8.0\,\mathrm{m}$. After this limit, the signal becomes oversaturated or too weak and as a result drops consistently below $-70\,\mathrm{dBm}$, which makes predicting distance impossible. Moreover, for both WLAN and AH, it is assumed that *signal-to-noise-ratio* (SNR) experiences uniform loss and SNR interference from other devices (not our robots) is negligible. Additionally for WLAN, we assume uniform radial coverage of the operational environment.

Network Perturbations. In our experiments, we apply a network perturbation mechanism to disrupt the quality of communication. We analyse the effects on team performance of two such mechanisms: *simulated packet-loss (SPL)* and *simulated signal loss threshold (SLT)*. The SPL mechanism impacts communication quality by dropping a certain percentage, such as $\{0\%, 25\%, 50\%, 75\%\}$, of the shared messages (i.e., topics 2 and 3, as mentioned above). The SLT mechanism shows the effect that limited signal strength has on the MRT. The threshold distance used for SLT is 6.0 m. The SLT mechanism is only employed in experiments with the AH network; given our assumptions, made above, about the WLAN network coverage hold, the implementation of SLT within a WLAN environment is meaningless.

Robot Behaviours. We compare two different robot behaviours: a baseline *no-behaviour* (NB) and our novel *Leader-Follower* (LF) behaviour, which is designed

---

[4] Currently the ad-hoc network is simulated.

[5] https://www.turtlebot.com/turtlebot2/.

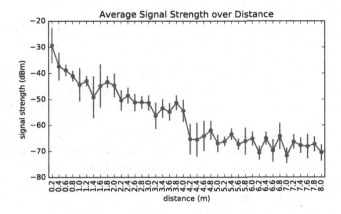

Fig. 1. Signal strength vs distance. Average values over 30 readings.

to respond to and maintain communication regardless of network type or perturbation. In NB mode, robot team members do not adjust their behaviour based on network quality. They attempt to complete their assigned tasks, disregarding network parameters or loss of communication, and perform standard navigation and obstacle avoidance behaviours. The LF behaviour is inspired by the AH network type, in which change in signal strength (communication quality), modelled as a function of distance, is detected as the robot team move away from each other, triggering the action of "regrouping" to maintain communication. In order to regroup, LF has its own signal strength threshold limit, which is approximately 5.0 m as depicted in Fig. 4(b). In LF mode, no experiments are executed using the WLAN network type; as we expect our complete and uniform radial coverage assumption to hold. The action of regrouping can be translated easily to react to dynamic change in network type as well, for example from WLAN to AH and back again.

When the robot agents use LF behaviour, they assume one of three roles: *not assigned (NA)*, *leader* or *follower*. Initially all robots start with the NA role. Upon the team detecting a loss of connection from any member, the robots dynamically assign themselves to either the *leader* or *follower* role, based on a The utility score, u, is defined as follows:

$$u = d\_score * num\_incomplete * recently\_completed$$

where:

- d_score = distance score, computed as $1/distance\_to\_goal$ (task location);
- $num\_incomplete$ = number of incomplete tasks remaining on the robot's agenda[6], which is computed as the total number of tasks assigned less the number of tasks completed;

---

[6] The "agenda" is the list of tasks a robot has been allocated by the assigner agent.

- *recently_completed* = 0.5 if the robot has just completed a task or 1.0 if it has not (this value is reset with every change in role and/or completion of a task).

This last factor acts to balance out the priorities of tasks amongst the teammates. This is because the *follower* behaviour prioritises staying in communication with teammates over completing its allocated tasks, whereas the *leader* robot prioritises completing its tasks. In effect it prevents a deadlock in roles from occurring, for example having the same robot as leader. Effectively, this factor ensures that all tasks are given priority at some point during the mission. The robot with the highest u value is selected as *leader*. In our simulation, the leader is a proxy for the robot that initialises the ad-hoc network in a physical setup. Then the followers connect to this new network. The final stage of the behaviour clears all robots of their roles, i.e., NA, which we denote as *switching*.

The switching behaviour helps mitigate communication loss when using the AH network and the SLT network perturbation. The unique message function, implemented in LF, helps mitigate communication loss when using the AH network with the SPL network perturbation. The rationale for using our message function over other communication methods is because *TaskStatus* messages are of light load, do not require internal processing and can easily be analysed for communication quality. A status message sent using the message function includes a Boolean value, which is initially set to false. Once a robot sends a status message, it and any other robot that receives the message, will periodically re-send it. This continues until each robot *knows* that everyone in the team has received the message. This process is achieved by checking that the total number of robots that have re-sent the message is equal to the size of the team, which implies that all robots have received the message. The final step of the message function is to set the Boolean value to true and re-send the message, as illustrated in Fig. 2.

4   Experiments

The experiments are defined as:

$$F_i = \{WLAN, AH\} \times \{SPL, SLT\} \times \{S_x\} \times \{NB, LF\}$$

where

- F_i is an experiment setup with $i \in \mathbb{N}$;
- the network types $WLAN$ and AH represent wireless local area network (standard infrastructure) and ad-hoc network (no infrastructure) respectively (details described earlier);
- network perturbation SPL is simulated packet-loss where $\{SPL0, SPL25, SPL50, SPL75\}$ denote $\{0, 25, 50, 75\}$ percent of messages that are dropped respectively[7];

---

[7] The 2 message topics effected by SPL are *TaskStatus* and team members' *AmclPose*.

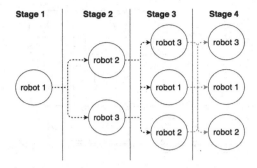

Fig. 2. Message propagation is shown by dotted lines in the diagram. In stage 1 a status message is sent; in stage 2 all team members have received the message; in stage 3 the entire team *knows* that the message has been received, Boolean value is set to true (i.e., this is further indicated by the blue dotted lines between stage 3 and 4); in stage. 4 the message is sent with Boolean set to true and communication ends successfully. (Color figure online)

- S_x is a task scenario where $x \in \gg$ is associated to specifically defined scenario containing sub-parameters n and m, which refer to the size of the team and number of tasks, respectively, described in [8,10,15,16]; and
- the robot behaviours NB and LF denote our standard no-behaviour and our leader-follower behaviour, respectively.

For our experiment scenario, we have chosen 3 robots to perform 7 exploration tasks starting in a clustered formation, where each task is independent from the next and requires a single robot to complete it. We have purposefully chosen difficult task locations in narrow spaces and poor starting locations for the robot team (illustrated in Fig. 3). Tasks T_R are assigned to each robot R (see Fig. 3), and the assignments are fixed for all our experiments. The legend in Fig. 4 Sect. 5, consists of three tables that list the set of experiment configurations. For WLAN, we compared the four different SPL network parameters. For AH, in addition to the four SPL network parameters, we also compare SLT.

Each experiment is performed 30 times. We collect a number of different metrics during each experiment. The most relevant metrics discussed here are: *number of successful tasks, distance travelled, movement time, minimum and maximum separation distance, overall near collisions* and *idle time*. We expect that the number of successful tasks will decrease when the network is perturbed or when the network type is AH, except when employing the LF behaviour, which attempts to maintain connectivity. However, we expect an increase in distance travelled, time spent moving and overall near collisions by robots with the LF behaviour. The LF's action of assigning roles and regrouping means that the robots are always busy moving and relatively close to each other in order to remain connected, which causes an increase in these three metrics. We predict that minimum and maximum separation distance among team members will be very small and the time spent idle after robots are done with their agenda is going to be reduced with LF compared to NB.

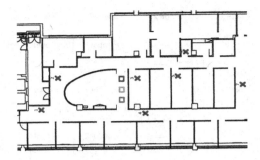

Fig. 3. Office setting for experiments, crosses represent task locations and squares robots (based on actual floor plan of building). Robot_1 (red square) is assigned tasks $T_1 = \{1, 4, 7\}$, robot_2 (green square) $T_2 = \{2, 5\}$ and robot_3 (blue) $T_3 = \{3, 6\}$. (Color figure online)

5 Results and Discussion

The legend in Fig. 4 is split into three tables in the same way as the resulting plots (a), (b), (c), (d), (e) and (f) to better highlight the changes in the performance metrics. The first set of results in plots (a) and (b) of Fig. 4 present the positive outcomes of using LF over NB for the MRT. Figure 4(a) presents the successful communication of task status messages for LF. However, NB increasingly fails to maintain successful communication as SPL increases and practically fails when the AH network type is used. Figure 4(b) demonstrates the minimum and maximum separation between team members throughout the duration of an experiment, which highlights an important dynamic between the two behaviours. As a result of LF's grouping capability, the minimum separation distance is approximately 0.35 m and the maximum is never greater than approximately 7.0 m. This is perfect for allowing communication when the AH network is used, although it is the primary reason for the increase that is observable in Figs. 4(c), (d) and (e). In NB mode, the minimum separation is approximately 0.40 m and the maximum is approximately 23.0 m. Thus connection fails in NB mode after the limits for communication, applied to AH and SLT (i.e., 8.0 m and 6.0 m, respectively), are reached. The next set of results in plots (c) and (d) in Fig. 4 demonstrate the distance travelled and the time spent moving by the robots to be about three times greater for LF compared to NB. This is the expected result due to LF's current design, which is depicted more clearly by the movement time plot, Fig. 4(d). Figure 4(d) shows the different design of LF's movement time, which is made up of three parts, namely NA, Leader and Follower movement time. For NB, movement time is made up of only NA movement time. The overall near collisions metric is much greater for LF than it is for NB. The reason for this is due to the grouping behaviour performed by LF, which is further established by Fig. 4(b). As the robots navigate the environment while performing grouping behaviour, in LF mode, the act of manoeuvring in close proximity creates a higher likelihood of a near collision, hence the performance seen in Fig. 4(e).

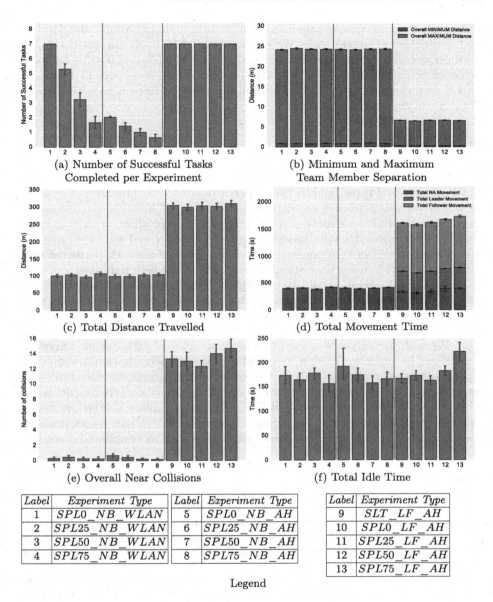

Fig. 4. Results show mean and standard deviation over 30 simulation trials for each experimental condition.

On the other hand, since NB performs no grouping, hence the MRT spread-out (i.e., maximum separation is very high), there is a lower likelihood of a near collision, i.e., Fig. 4(e). The idle time in Fig. 4(f), is the time accumulated after a robot has completed all the tasks in their agenda and is either waiting for the rest of the team to complete their tasks or waiting to detect communication loss and is assigned a follower role. We expected that LF, in its current design, to perform worse and thus have an increased idle time. However, both behaviours achieved similar results in Fig. 4(f). Our results for SLT show very little impact on LF performance. As we expand SLT in future work, to be used with NB and WLAN, we expect this to change.

6 Summary

We have presented MRComm, a testbed, which utilises behaviours to deal with different network types and network perturbations. We present our results, in which certain performance metrics are used to evaluate how communication impacts MRT awareness and mission success. We show promising early results of our novel dynamic Leader-Follower behaviour and message function, which achieve perfect communication with a test set of network perturbations. The baseline MRT using only standard navigation and collision avoidance (NB behaviour) shows poor results in comparison. Our immediate next step is to demonstrate that MRComm can easily reproduce the same results in a physical environment. Furthermore, it is inevitable that in the real world, environments are dynamic and conditions change, including the type of network and perturbation. We wish to analyse how the LF behaviour can deal with dynamic network conditions. In future work, we will expand the network perturbation to simulated signal strength degradation and effective signal strength applied to physical robot experiments. We believe this will have a different impact on experiments using SLT and/or WLAN parameters. Finally, we hope to explore if other strategies improve the performance of the dynamic behaviour which can be particularly important for time-critical environments/missions such as search-and-rescue.

References

1. Al-Akkad, A., Raffelsberger, C., Boden, A., Ramirez, L., Zimmermann, A.: Tweeting when online is off? Opportunistically creating mobile ad-hoc networks in response to disrupted infrastructure. In: 11th International ISCRAM Conference Proceedings. Theme 13 - Social Media in Crisis Response and Management, May 2014
2. Andre, T., Neuhold, D., Bettstetter, C.: Coordinated multi-robot exploration: out of the box packages for ROS. In: Published in IEEE Globecom Workshops (GC Wkshps), Austin, TX, USA (2014)
3. Balch, T., Arkin, R.C.: Behaviour-based formation control for multirobot teams. IEEE Trans. Robot. Autom. **14**, 926–939 (1998)
4. Caccamo, S., Parasuraman, R., Freda, L., Gianni, M., Ögren, P.: RCAMP: a resilient communication-aware motion planner for mobile robots with autonomous repair of wireless connectivity. In: International Conference on Intelligent Robots and Systems (IROS) (2017)
5. Dąbrowski, A., Kozik, R., Macias, M.: Evaluation of ROS2 communication layer. ROSCon, Seoul, Korea (2016)

6. Fernandez, E., Foote, T., Woodall, W., Thomas, D.: Next-generation ROS: building on DDS. ROSCon, Chicago, US (2014)
7. Fox, D., Burgard, W., Dellaert, F., Thrun, S.: Monte carlo localization: efficient position estimation for mobile robots. In: Published in Proceedings of the Association for the Advancement of Artificial Intelligence (AAAI) (1999)
8. Gerkey, B.P., Mataríc, M.J.: A formal analysis and taxonomy of task allocation in multi-robot systems. Int. J. Robot. Res. **23**(9), 939–954 (2004)
9. Kashino, Z., Nejat, G., Benhabib, B.: A multi-robot sensor-delivery planning strategy for static-sensor networks. In: International Conference on Intelligent Robots and Systems (IROS), Vancouver, BC, Canada (2017)
10. Landén, D., Heintz, F., Doherty, P.: Complex task allocation in mixed-initiative delegation: a UAV case study. In: Desai, N., Liu, A., Winikoff, M. (eds.) PRIMA 2010. LNCS (LNAI), vol. 7057, pp. 288–303. Springer, Heidelberg (2012). https://doi.org/10.1007/978-3-642-25920-3_20
11. Lujak, M., et al.: Towards robots-assisted ambient intelligence. In: Belardinelli, F., Argente, E. (eds.) EUMAS/AT -2017. LNCS (LNAI), vol. 10767, pp. 490–497. Springer, Cham (2018). https://doi.org/10.1007/978-3-030-01713-2_34
12. Murphy, R., et al.: Interacting with trapped victims using robots. In: International Conference on Technologies for Homeland Security, HST (2013)
13. Quigley, M., et al.: ROS: an open-source robot operating system. In: ICRA Workshop on Open Source Software (2009)
14. Schneider, E., Sklar, E.I., Parsons, S.: Mechanism selection for multi-robot task allocation. In: Gao, Y., Fallah, S., Jin, Y., Lekakou, C. (eds.) TAROS 2017. LNCS (LNAI), vol. 10454, pp. 421–435. Springer, Cham (2017). https://doi.org/10.1007/978-3-319-64107-2_33
15. Schneider, E., Sklar, E.I., Parsons, S.: Evaluating multi-robot teamwork in parameterised environments. In: Alboul, L., Damian, D., Aitken, J.M.M. (eds.) TAROS 2016. LNCS (LNAI), vol. 9716, pp. 301–313. Springer, Cham (2016). https://doi.org/10.1007/978-3-319-40379-3_32
16. Schneider, E., Sklar, E.I., Parsons, S., Özgelen, A.T.: Auction-based task allocation for multi-robot teams in dynamic environments. In: Dixon, C., Tuyls, K. (eds.) TAROS 2015. LNCS (LNAI), vol. 9287, pp. 246–257. Springer, Cham (2015). https://doi.org/10.1007/978-3-319-22416-9_29
17. Takahashi, T., Kitamura, Y., Miwa, H.: Organizing rescue agents using ad-hoc networks. In: Pérez, J., et al. (eds.) Highlights on Practical Applications of Agents and Multi-Agent Systems. Advances in Intelligent and Soft Computing, vol. 156. Springer, Heidelberg (2012). https://doi.org/10.1007/978-3-642-28762-6_17
18. Witkowski, U., et al.: Ad-hoc network communication infrastructure for multi-robot systems in disaster scenarios. In: Proceedings of IARP/EURON Workshop on Robotics for Risky Interventions and Environmental Surveillance, Benicassim, Spain (2008)
19. Zadorozhny, V., Lewis, M.: Information fusion for USAR operations based on crowdsourcing. In: Proceedings of the 16th International Conference on Information Fusion, Istanbul, Turkey (2013)
20. Zhivkov, T., Schneider, E., Sklar, E.I.: Measuring the effects of communication quality on multi-robot team performance. In: Gao, Y., Fallah, S., Jin, Y., Lekakou, C. (eds.) TAROS 2017. LNCS (LNAI), vol. 10454, pp. 408–420. Springer, Cham (2017). https://doi.org/10.1007/978-3-319-64107-2_32

Autonomous Air-Hockey Playing Cobot Using Optimal Control and Vision-Based Bayesian Tracking

Ahmad AlAttar[(✉)][iD], Louis Rouillard[iD], and Petar Kormushev[iD]

Robot Intelligence Lab, Imperial College London, London, UK
{a.alattar19,louis.rouillard-odera17,p.kormushev}@imperial.ac.uk
https://www.imperial.ac.uk/robot-intelligence/

Abstract. This paper presents a novel autonomous air-hockey playing collaborative robot (cobot) that provides human-like gameplay against human opponents. Vision-based Bayesian tracking of the puck and striker are used in an Analytic Hierarchy Process (AHP)-based probabilistic tactical layer for high-speed perception. The tactical layer provides commands for an active control layer that controls the Cartesian position and yaw angle of a custom end effector. The active layer uses optimal control of the cobot's posture inside the task nullspace. The kinematic redundancy is resolved using a weighted Moore-Penrose pseudo-inversion technique. Experiments with human players show high-speed human-like gameplay with potential applications in the growing field of entertainment robotics.

Keywords: Air hockey · Cobot · Bayesian tracking ·
Analytic Hierarchy Process · Autonomous robot ·
Entertainment robotics

1 Introduction

Robots are expanding from strictly industrial applications to closer interactions with humans. Two major applications of such close encounters are in home-care robotics [5] and entertainment robotics [10], which naturally raises the question of how to make user interaction with robots both enjoyable and safe. In this paper, we focus on air hockey which is a challenging example of an arcade game where humans can physically play against robots. An air-hockey table is a constrained 2D environment which is ideal for testing high-speed robot motion planning. However, strategies to master the game involve trajectory prediction, high puck speed, and uncertainty management. Therefore, air hockey presents an easy-to-learn yet hard-to-master task for robots to perform effectively against a skilled opponent.

In this work, we program a Panda collaborative robot (cobot) arm, hereinafter referred to as the *Panda arm*, to play air hockey, as shown in Fig. 1. This cobot is relatively new to robotics research, only released in 2017 by

© Springer Nature Switzerland AG 2019
K. Althoefer et al. (Eds.): TAROS 2019, LNAI 11650, pp. 358–369, 2019.
https://doi.org/10.1007/978-3-030-25332-5_31

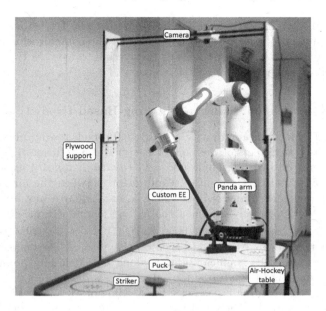

Fig. 1. General setup for the air-hockey task. A Sony PlayStation Eye camera is fixed on top of the table using a plywood structure. The puck and striker are colored with bright tones for ease of filtering. The Panda arm stood at the far side of the table with its custom-made end effector.

Franka Emika GmbH [6]. Recent works have implemented robotic entertainment applications using different approaches and other robotic arms. In [10], a dual system composed of a tactics layer governing patterns of gameplay and a skill layer governing individual shots is introduced with a custom robotic arm. In [8], a Barett WAM arm is used with a three-layer system: motion control, short-term strategy and long-term strategy - adapting its playstyle to the opponent. Other studies also used various control strategies such as learning from movement primitives [1], task-switching [2], with fuzzy control [14], using weak points of the human vision [9], and more recently using Deep Reinforcement Learning [12].

This paper proposes a novel architecture for air-hockey playing cobots using Bayesian filtering for perception, nullspace-based posture optimization for robot motion, and a combined Analytic Hierarchy Process (AHP) and probabilistic tactical framework for human-like behavior. The proposed architecture comprises two layers: (1) a tactical layer, implementing the high-speed perception, motion prediction, and strategy planning; and (2) an active layer, implementing the robot movement execution via optimal control. The two layers are introduced in Sects. 2 and 3, followed by experimental results in Sect. 4.

2   Tactical Layer: Determination of Cobot Actions

In a competitive game, the puck can cross the entire length of the air-hockey table in a mere hundred milliseconds, which is similar in speed to the human vision reflex [13]. A human player needs to predict the trajectory of the puck using the movement of the opponent's striker and the configuration of the table, which is implemented for the cobot using a Bayesian framework that mimics the decision-making process of humans [4,16].

2.1 Computer Vision: Kalman Filtering-Based Predictive Approach

A Sony PlayStation Eye camera with a (320×240) pixels resolution and a $187\,Hz$ frame rate is used to detect the position of the puck at a high speed. The 2D table frame is represented by a rectangle $(W \times L)$ $(width \times length)$ associated with a Cartesian coordinate system (x, y). Calibration between the air-hockey table frame and the camera frame is done using a least-squares method. Moreover, a 2D affinity that optimally matched the (x^c, y^c) camera frame to the (x^r, y^r) cobot frame is obtained, having the form $\begin{bmatrix} x^r\ y^r\ 1 \end{bmatrix}^T = S \begin{bmatrix} x^c\ y^c\ 1 \end{bmatrix}^T$ where S is a homogeneous transform. A method based on the Moore-Penrose pseudo inverse is used to determine the coefficients of S along with training points from the camera frame and the cobot frame [7].

A flowchart representing the general functioning of the tactical layer is shown in Fig. 2. Positions of the puck and the human player's striker (hereon referred to as the *striker*) are obtained using color filtering and contouring. The striker and the puck are tracked to be able to predict the puck trajectory before it is hit by the human player, so that the cobot has a longer time window to move before the puck arrives at a position within its reach. For this matter, Kalman filtering [11] is used as it provides a simple framework to deal with state prediction and uncertainty under a Gaussian assumption:

$$\overrightarrow{X_\mu} = \begin{bmatrix} x\ y\ v_x\ v_y \end{bmatrix}^T, \quad C = \begin{bmatrix} 1\ 0\ 0\ 0 \\ 0\ 1\ 0\ 0 \end{bmatrix}, \quad \overrightarrow{Y} = C\overrightarrow{X_\mu}$$

Where x, y is Cartesian position, v_x, v_y is Cartesian speed, $\overrightarrow{X_\mu}$ is the object's state vector expected value, C is the measurement transition matrix and $\overrightarrow{Y}$ is the measurement vector. Along with $\overrightarrow{X_\mu}$, the state of the object is associated with the co-variance matrix Σ. Both define a normally distributed random variable. Acceleration is ignored as it is modified frequently and non-linearly by external sources (mainly human and cobot actions). At any given time in the future, the predicted position of the object can be obtained by repetitively applying the operations:

$$\overrightarrow{X_\mu}(t + dt) = A\overrightarrow{X_\mu}(t) \tag{1}$$
$$\Sigma(t + dt) = A\Sigma(t)A^T \tag{2}$$

where dt is the time-step since the last measurement and A is the state transition matrix. Equation (1) returns a position in $\mathbb{R}^2$ that neglects puck bounces against the table walls. For those bounces, we make the assumption of a perfectly elastic model with infinite inertia for the walls compared to the puck.

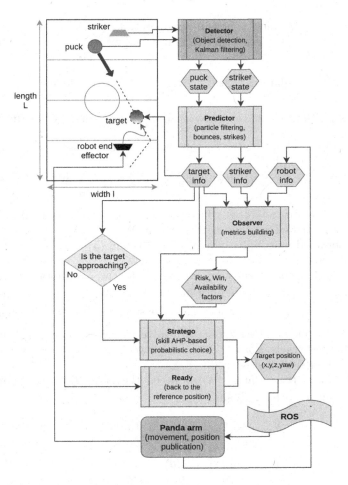

Fig. 2. General tactical layer flow chart.

The table is modelled with two walls at $y = 0$ and $y = W$. For a single bounce on the $y = W$ wall, for example, this results in these equations:

$$\overrightarrow{X_\mu} \leftarrow \begin{bmatrix} 1 & 0 & 0 & 0 \\ 0 & 0 & 0 & 0 \\ 0 & 0 & 1 & 0 \\ 0 & 0 & 0 & -1 \end{bmatrix} \overrightarrow{X_\mu} + \begin{bmatrix} 0 \\ 2W - y \\ 0 \\ 0 \end{bmatrix} \tag{3}$$

$$\Sigma \leftarrow \begin{bmatrix} 1 & 0 & 0 & 0 \\ 0 & 1 & 0 & 0 \\ 0 & 0 & 1 & 0 \\ 0 & 0 & 0 & -1 \end{bmatrix} \Sigma \begin{bmatrix} 1 & 0 & 0 & 0 \\ 0 & 1 & 0 & 0 \\ 0 & 0 & 1 & 0 \\ 0 & 0 & 0 & -1 \end{bmatrix}^T \tag{4}$$

Equation (3) introduces a non-linear operation, which is not suitable for the Kalman framework. To deal with this limitation, we use a variant of the particle filter [3] as follows:

- We sample a population $\overrightarrow{X_i}$, $i = 1..N$, $N > 1000$ from the normal distribution defined by $\overrightarrow{X_\mu}$ and Σ
- For each particle $\overrightarrow{X_i}$ we repetitively apply Eqs. (1) and (3) for future predictions
- The future state expected value and co-variance can be obtained as:

$$\overrightarrow{X}_{\mu\,fut.\,st.} = \frac{1}{N}\sum_{k=0}^{N}\overrightarrow{X_i} = \overrightarrow{X'}, \quad \Sigma_{fut.\,st.} = \frac{1}{N}\sum_{k=0}^{N}(\overrightarrow{X_i} - \overrightarrow{X'}) * (\overrightarrow{X_i} - \overrightarrow{X'})^T$$

Estimates for future states when the puck is close to the table limits are theoretically improved by this method when $N \to \infty$. A quicker estimate can always be obtained by simply applying Eqs. (3) and (4) to the expected value of the state at time $(t + n \times dt)$ for $n > 0$.

To deal with puck-striker contacts, we make the assumption of an infinite striker inertia compared to the puck inertia. With $\overrightarrow{X}_{puck}$ and Σ_{puck} referring to the puck's state and $\overrightarrow{X}_{striker}$ referring to the striker's state we reason as follows:

- We have the puck and striker states evolve with Eqs. (1) and (2) until either a time limit is reached or the distance between puck and striker is inferior to the sum of their respective radii;
- If the latter is true, the surface between the two objects is defined by its normal unit vector $[\cos(\theta)\ \sin(\theta)]^T$:

$$\overrightarrow{X}_{puck}^{s.\,ref} = \overrightarrow{X}_{puck} - \overrightarrow{X}_{striker}, \quad \theta = \text{atan2}(\overrightarrow{X}_{puck}^{s.\,ref}[1], \overrightarrow{X}_{puck}^{s.\,ref}[0])$$

$$R_\theta = \begin{bmatrix} \cos(\theta) & -\sin(\theta) & 0 & 0 \\ \sin(\theta) & \cos(\theta) & 0 & 0 \\ 0 & 0 & \cos(\theta) & -\sin(\theta) \\ 0 & 0 & \sin(\theta) & \cos(\theta) \end{bmatrix}$$

- The puck then elastically bounces on the surface:

$$M = R_\theta * \begin{bmatrix} 1 & 0 & 0 & 0 \\ 0 & 1 & 0 & 0 \\ 0 & 0 & -1 & 0 \\ 0 & 0 & 0 & 1 \end{bmatrix} * R_\theta^{-1}$$

$$\overrightarrow{X}_{puck} \leftarrow \overrightarrow{X}_{striker} + M * \overrightarrow{X}_{puck}^{s.\,ref}, \quad \Sigma_{puck} \leftarrow M * \Sigma_{puck} * M^T$$

By combining all the previous points, we update the estimated puck state vector using camera measurements. Using this updated state, we then predict the puck's future state expected value and co-variance matrix at any given time by taking into account bounces on the walls and human player's potential strikes. This provides an effective online state-estimate filtering framework, with measures of uncertainty in future predictions which is useful for strategy-making.

2.2 Strategy-Making: AHP-Based Probabilistic Behavior

The filtered state and equations specified in the previous section are sufficient to determine the set of future positions and velocities for the puck up to a certain point. Performing a Principal Component Analysis (PCA) on the co-variance matrix of the puck's position determines the first principal component: the corresponding eigenvalue is taken as a measure of the uncertainty of the prediction, and the eigenvector is taken as the Cartesian direction of maximum uncertainty. Combining those elements, among the set of future puck positions, we find the closest to the current cobot end-effector position $\vec{x}_{cobot}$. We name this optimal position $\vec{x}_{target}$ and its corresponding speed $\vec{v}_{target}$. We also determine the corresponding time of arrival, how uncertain that prediction is, and the safest axis on which we maximize the probability to reach the puck, i.e. the direction defined by the aforementioned eigenvector. This set of variables is hereon referred to as the *target*. To obtain diverse gameplay, following the methods of [10] we built a set of skills, standard actions that depend on the cobot and puck relative positions. This ensemble is hereon referred to as the *skillset*:

- Ready: the cobot returns to its own goal position;
- Defend: the cobot moves to $\vec{x}_{target}$ and stops;
- Stop: the cobot intercepts the puck at $\vec{x}_{target}$ with a speed $0.5\,\vec{v}_{target}$
- Counter: the cobot intercepts the puck at $\vec{x}_{target}$ with a speed $-2\,\vec{v}_{target}$
- Cut: the cobot intercepts the puck at $\vec{x}_{target}$ from $\vec{x}_{cobot}$
- Smash: the cobot strikes the puck at $\vec{x}_{target}$ towards the opponent's goal
- Rally: the cobot strikes the puck at $\vec{x}_{target}$ towards the human player's goal with a bounce on one of the walls

Once this skillset is defined, we then specify at any point during the game what kind of event should trigger the execution of a skill by the cobot. For this purpose, we explored different possible trigger events, for instance human player's strikes, bounces on the walls, and time elapsed. Most of them resulted in an erratic behavior for the cobot, either not reacting to an obvious incoming shot or continuously triggering inconsistent skills. We thus settle on a simple event: when $\vec{x}_{target}$ is predicted to be on the cobot's side of the table with a speed not indicating a movement towards the other side. Once the cobot decides that an action needs to be taken, we then specify a way to discriminate the skills in the skillset to select the most relevant. We do not systematically select the most relevant skill to provide the cobot's gameplay with some unpredictability. To discriminate between the skills, we combine the frameworks of [8] and [10]:

- We define three normalized metrics continuously updated during the game by combining at any given time the target, cobot, and striker information: risk factor $\mathcal{R}$ (assessing the risk for the cobot to concede a goal), win factor $\mathcal{W}$ (assessing the possibility to score a goal) and availability factor $\mathcal{A}$ (assessing how easy it is to reach the target and how much the prediction can be trusted). For each factor, 0 indicates a bad context for the cobot and 1 a good context.

– As in [8], using an AHP [15], we define a static Pairwise Comparison Matrix (PCM), describing the relative preference for a skill compared to another one according to a given criteria ($\mathcal{R}$, $\mathcal{W}$ or $\mathcal{A}$). In our case, we define three (7×7) matrices Φ_R, Φ_W, Φ_A respectively associated to the (7×1) normalized first principal components $\vec{\varphi}_R$, $\vec{\varphi}_W$, $\vec{\varphi}_A$.

– When an event triggers the choice for a skill at time t, each skill is assigned to a probability specified by the (7×1) probability vector $\vec{\mathbb{P}}$ as follow:

$$\mathcal{S}(t) = \mathcal{R}(t) + \mathcal{W}(t) + \mathcal{A}(t)$$

$$\mathcal{R}'(t) = \frac{\mathcal{R}}{\mathcal{S}} \quad \mathcal{W}'(t) = \frac{\mathcal{W}}{\mathcal{S}} \quad \mathcal{A}'(t) = \frac{\mathcal{A}}{\mathcal{S}}$$

$$\vec{\mathbb{P}}(t) = \begin{bmatrix} \vdots & \vdots & \vdots \\ \vec{\varphi}_R & \vec{\varphi}_W & \vec{\varphi}_A \\ \vdots & \vdots & \vdots \end{bmatrix} \begin{bmatrix} \mathcal{R}' \\ \mathcal{W}' \\ \mathcal{A}' \end{bmatrix}$$

– As in [10], a skill is then randomly sampled from the skillset according to $\vec{\mathbb{P}}$ and executed by the cobot. The skill is stopped when the predicted time of arrival of the puck at the target is reached. If the puck now moves towards the human's side of the table, the cobot performs a Ready skill, otherwise a trigger event runs the previous steps again.

This framework uses the rich information provided by the target to select a skill in a considered yet randomized way among several possibilities. The uncertainty management and unpredictability resulting from this approach mimic human behavior [4,16], creating an interesting and variable gameplay.

3   Active Layer: Implementation of Cobot Actions

The active layer in the proposed architecture implements the robot movement execution via optimal control. The main goal is to maximize the end-effector velocity without exceeding the individual joint-level speed limits. Compared to setups in [10] or [14], the usage of a 7-DoF robot may be suboptimal since the workspace is only a 2D plane. However, the Panda arm's safe interaction with users makes it a suitable option for safe gameplay in close human proximity. Note that the z-dimension (normal to the air-hockey table) and the roll, pitch and yaw orientations are not constrained by design and need to be dealt with inside the controller.

3.1   Software Implementation: Translation of PD Commands into Joint Velocities

Desired cobot end-effector (EE) Cartesian positions are sent by the tactical layer through ROS at a frequency of 500 Hz. A real-time Linux kernel was used to minimize the control latency. Four dimensions are being controlled as described in the next section. These dimensions represent the (x_d, y_d) desired position in the air-hockey table frame, the z_d dimension that needs to be fixed so that the EE stays in contact with the table, and the orientation of the EE in the table frame that is equivalent to its $yaw = \alpha_d$ angle.

The Panda arm's library allows the return of a (4×4) transformation matrix T_{EE}^0, linking the EE frame to the cobot reference frame. Using this matrix, the cobot current position $(x_c, y_c, z_c, \alpha_c)$ is:

$$x_c = T_{EE}^0[0,3], \quad y_c = T_{EE}^0[1,3], \quad z_c = T_{EE}^0[2,3], \quad \alpha_c = \text{atan2}(T_{EE}^0[1,0], T_{EE}^0[0,0])$$

The difference between desired and current Cartesian position serves as an input to a PD controller to obtain a desired Cartesian acceleration $\overrightarrow{\ddot{\mathbb{X}}}$. Using a custom symmetric positive definite weighting matrix W we then construct the equivalent Cartesian impedance matrix Λ and the Jacobian Moore-Penrose weighted pseudo inverse $J_4^\dagger$ [7]:

$$\Lambda = (J_4 W J_4^T)^{-1}, \quad J_4^\dagger = W J_4^T \Lambda$$

Where J_4 is a (4×7) EE Jacobian matrix with the four (x, y, z, α) dimensions. Supposing that we know the (7×1) joint velocity vector $\overrightarrow{\dot{\mathbb{Q}}}$ at the previous timestep, we can derive the joint acceleration $\overrightarrow{\ddot{\mathbb{Q}}}$ minimizing the equivalent kinetic energy using W as a mass matrix [7]:

$$\overrightarrow{\dot{\mathbb{X}}} = J_4 \overrightarrow{\dot{\mathbb{Q}}} \implies \overrightarrow{\ddot{\mathbb{X}}} = \dot{J}_4 \overrightarrow{\dot{\mathbb{Q}}} + J_4 \overrightarrow{\ddot{\mathbb{Q}}}, \quad \overrightarrow{\ddot{\mathbb{Q}}}_{move} = J_4^\dagger (\overrightarrow{\ddot{\mathbb{X}}} - \dot{J}_4 \overrightarrow{\dot{\mathbb{Q}}})$$

Compared to a situation where we control all six Cartesian dimensions to operate a movement on the (x, y, z, α) dimensions, using the custom weight matrix W and the three redundant DoF of the Panda arm allows a better distribution of the joint speed, further away from upper limits that would cap the EE movement velocity.

However, this local optimization process can result in long movements, such as drifting of the arm joint positions (for instance towards positions minimizing the gravitational potential energy), that ultimately reach joint limits, thus stopping the process. To prevent this drifting, given the arm joint positions $(q_1, ..., q_7)$, we implement a gradient descent optimization with damping on the cost function Ω inside the three DoF nullspace:

$$\Omega = \frac{1}{2} \sum_{i=1}^{7} (q_i(t) - q_i^0)^2, \quad \overrightarrow{\nabla}\Omega = \begin{bmatrix} q_1 - q_1^0 \\ \vdots \\ q_7 - q_7^0 \end{bmatrix}, \quad \overrightarrow{\dot{\Psi}} = -\mathcal{P}_n \overrightarrow{\nabla}\Omega - \mathcal{D}_n \overrightarrow{\nabla}\dot{\Omega}$$

where $(q_1^0, ..., q_7^0)$ are chosen so that the arm kept a straight position as much as possible, and that $\mathcal{P}_n$, $\mathcal{D}_n$ created a slow, non-oscillating, non-overshooting movement inside the nullspace, disturbing as less as possible the EE movement.

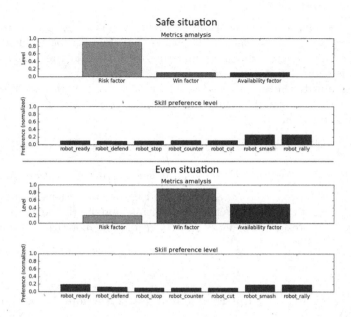

Fig. 3. Comparison of skillset weighing in a typically safe (top) and more even (bottom) gamewise situation. The skill weighing varies in the 2 situations yet we can observe a rather equal distribution in both cases, which guarantees an unpredictable gameplay.

3.2 Hardware Implementation: Universal-Joint Based Striker

As explained in the previous section, we choose to limit the EE control to the four (x, y, z, α) dimensions. To maximize the cobot EE Cartesian speed with a capped set of joint velocities, we choose to build a custom, partially 3D-printed EE that transformed a typical six DoF "full-body" movement into a four DoF "wrist-like" movement as detailed in Fig. 4. To linearly multiply the EE speed at a given joint rotation speed, we base our design around a 46 cm-long carbon fiber rod. The tip of the rod, considered as the EE, is linked to the flange frame by the transformation matrix T_{EE}^{flange}.

The transformation T_{EE}^{flange} can be passed (along with a mass and inertia matrix) to the Panda arm internal models to automatically adapt kinetic and dynamic functions (notably for the Jacobian calculations used in the previous section). With this design, by slightly orienting and translating the flange of the Panda arm, we obtained an amplified EE movement at the tip of the rod. Moreover, to transmit $\alpha = yaw$ movements on the cobot striker (to orient it inside the air-hockey table frame), we use a 3D-printed combination of a striker with a universal joint (see Fig. 4B): rotations around the carbon rod axis are fully transmitted to the cobot striker's α while keeping *roll* and *pitch* dimensions free. The latter are mechanically constrained by the design to always keep the cobot striker's surface parallel to the air-hockey table. As the z dimension of the cobot EE is fixed in the controller, and with a rather large flat surface for the striker,

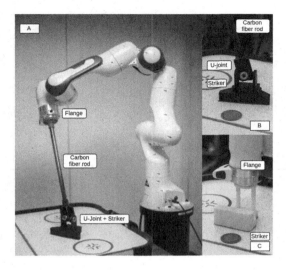

Fig. 4. Overview of the custom end effector. (A) General view of the Panda arm. (B) Close view on the universal joint/striker combination. (C) For comparison purpose, close view on a "full body motion" striker prototype linked to the Panda flange: the whole Panda arm mass has to be moved to displace the striker.

the system naturally adapted its *roll* and *pitch* to the controlled *yaw* dimension. This mechanical design helps the software minimize the joint velocity for a given Cartesian EE speed by delegating some dimensions' control to the mechanics, therefore liberating DoF for the software optimization.

4 Experimentation Results and Analysis

During the experimentation phase, the cobot demonstrates robust gameplay, able to adapt to a majority of situations[1]. The main limitations lie in the hardware side and include difficulty to perform EE impulsive movements necessary for strong strikes and vibrations of the actuators at very high frequency due to constant small re-adaptations of the desired EE position. The efficacy of some of the frameworks introduced in this work is assessed in this section.

4.1 Strategy Making: Evolution of Skillset Usage with Game State

The combination of the AHP framework with a probabilistic choice help create a varied yet logical gameplay as represented in Fig. 3. We deliberately choose not to implement any pairwise strong difference in the *PCM* matrices, as this can create a rather deterministic gameplay, but this factor can be tuned to adjust the

---

[1] A video demonstration of the system is available at: https://www.imperial.ac.uk/robot-intelligence/videos/.

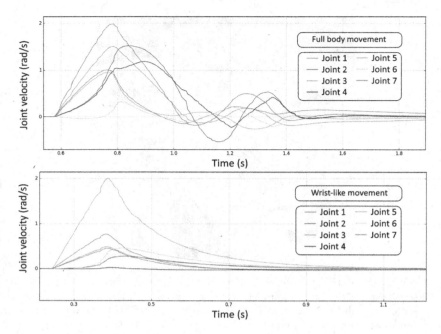

Fig. 5. For a given arm +30 cm translation on the y axis, comparison of joint velocity between (top) a fully constrained "full-body" motion and (bottom) a partially freed "wrist-like" movement. "Wrist-like" movement allows for a more evenly distributed joint velocity, preventing some joints to reach their velocity limit.

efficiency of the cobot. This result validates the similar approach performed in [10] by showing a comparable evolution of skill choice weighing depending on the game situation. We, however, propose AHP as a more unified and transparent way to assign probability weights regarding different criteria.

4.2   Active Layer: Preparation of Joint Velocity

The combination of the custom universal-joint based EE hardware and the software weighted Moore-Penrose technique yield a better distribution of the joint velocities as shown in Fig. 5. For the "wrist-like" movement, we can observe that the majority of the joint speed is limited to small values away from joint limits, with no unnecessary compensation of rotation between different joints. This gives rise to a higher potential for faster more complex movements of the EE without risking any instability or process breaking issues.

5   Conclusion

In this work, an air-hockey playing cobot, both safe and challenging for human opponents, is introduced. Inherent uncertainties in the predictions, as a by-product of Kalman filtering, induced a more natural process of state prediction. Along with the AHP-based probabilistic technique that is used for skill selection, this architecture is a step forward towards a more human-like gameplay in the expanding field of entertainment robotics. Throughout this research, we found that the limited joint speeds of the arm combined with the constrained environment were two limitations hard to overcome for a high-speed high-frequency application such as air hockey. Nonetheless, this research highlights the potential application of cobots, such as the Panda arm, for *safe* human interactions in entertainment robotics.

References

1. Bentivegna, D.C., Atkeson, C.G.: A framework for learning from observation using primitives. In: Kaminka, G.A., Lima, P.U., Rojas, R. (eds.) RoboCup 2002. LNCS (LNAI), vol. 2752, pp. 263–270. Springer, Heidelberg (2003). https://doi.org/10.1007/978-3-540-45135-8_20
2. Bishop, B., Spong, M.: Vision-based control of an air hockey playing robot. IEEE Control Syst. Mag. **19**(3), 23–32 (1999)
3. Djuric, P.M., et al.: Particle filtering. IEEE Signal Process. Mag. **20**(5), 19–38 (2003)
4. Ernst, M.O., Banks, M.S.: Humans integrate visual and haptic information in a statistically optimal fashion. Nature **415**, 429 EP (2002)
5. Falck, F., Doshi, S., Smuts, N., Lingi, J., Rants, K., Kormushev, P.: Human-centered manipulation and navigation with Robot DE NIRO. In: IROS 2018 Workshop: Towards Robots that Exhibit Manipulation Intelligence, IEEE/RSJ International Conference on Intelligent Robots and Systems (IROS), Madrid, Spain, October 2018
6. Franka Emika GmbH: Panda arm (2017). https://www.franka.de/
7. Nakamura, Y.: Advanced Robotics: Redundancy and Optimization, 1st edn. Addison-Wesley Longman Publishing Co., Inc., Boston (1990)
8. Namiki, A., Matsushita, S., Ozeki, T., Nonami, K.: Hierarchical processing architecture for an air-hockey robot system. In: 2013 IEEE International Conference on Robotics and Automation, pp. 1187–1192. IEEE (2013)
9. Ogawa, M., et al.: Development of air hockey robot improving with the human players. In: IECON 2011, pp. 3364–3369 (2011)
10. Shimada, H., Kutsuna, Y., Kudoh, S., Suehiro, T.: A two-layer tactical system for an air-hockey-playing robot. In: 2017 IEEE/RSJ International Conference on Intelligent Robots and Systems (IROS), pp. 6985–6990. IEEE (2017)
11. Sorenson, H.: Kalman Filtering Techniques, Advances in Control Systems, vol. 3. Elsevier, Amsterdam (1966)
12. Taitler, A., Shimkin, N.: Learning control for air hockey striking using deep reinforcement learning. In: 2017 International Conference on Control, Artificial Intelligence, Robotics Optimization (ICCAIRO), pp. 22–27 (2017)
13. Thorpe, S., Fize, D., Marlot, C.: Speed of processing in the human visual system. Nature **381**, 520 EP (1996)
14. Wang, W.J., Tsai, I.D., Chen, Z.D., Wang, G.H.: A vision based air hockey system with fuzzy control. In: Proceedings of the International Conference on Control Applications, vol. 2, pp. 754–759 (2002)
15. Whitaker, R.: The analytic hierarchy process - what it is and how it is used. Math. Model. **9**, 161–176 (1987)
16. Wolpert, D.M., Flanagan, J.R.: Motor prediction. Curr. Biol. **11**(18), R729–R732 (2001)

Development and Evaluation of a Novel Robotic System for Search and Rescue

Andrea Cachia[1], M. Nazmul Huda[1(✉)], Pengcheng Liu[2],
Chitta Saha[1], Andrew Tickle[1], John Arvanitakis[1],
and Syed Mahfuzul Aziz[3]

[1] Coventry University, Coventry, UK
ab9467@coventry.ac.uk
[2] Cardiff Metropolitan University, Cardiff, UK
[3] University of South Australia, Adelaide, Australia

Abstract. Search and Rescue robotics is a relatively new field of research, which is growing rapidly as new technologies emerge. However, the robots that are usually applied to the field are generally small and have limited functionality, and almost all of them rely on direct control from a local operator. In this paper, a novel wheeled Search and Rescue robot is proposed which considers new methods of controlling the robot, including using a wireless "tether" in place of a conventional physical one. A prototype is then built which acts as a proof of concept of the robot design and wireless control. The prototype robot is then evaluated to prove its mobility, wireless control and multi-hop networking. The experimental results demonstrate the effectiveness of the proposed design incorporating the rocker-bogie suspension system and the multi-hop method of "wireless tethering".

Keywords: Search and rescue robot · Rocker-bogie system · Wireless control · Multi-hop network

1 Introduction

Disaster scenes such as a collapsed skyscraper, an earthquake in a densely-populated area or a collapsed tunnel are not exclusively fatal at the time the disaster strikes. Search and rescue (SAR) services must operate quickly and efficiently, as the first full day immediately after poses numerous risks to life from unstable rubble to fires spreading through ruins. This is not only dangerous for the potential survivors but also for the rescue workers [4].

Many robots have been proposed over the past years into the field of SAR to reduce the risk to human life, but these robots face many limitations; cost of repair or replacement if damaged, scenarios where GPS location is unavailable, unsuitable traction method for a specific type of terrain, poor communications with base station, and general efficiency of conducted search [23].

Searching under rubble for survivors is often a battle against time but is crucial to survival of any person trapped in voids under rubble. However, there is no single tactic that is efficient enough to employ on any given disaster scenario that ensures a

© Springer Nature Switzerland AG 2019
K. Althoefer et al. (Eds.): TAROS 2019, LNAI 11650, pp. 370–382, 2019.
https://doi.org/10.1007/978-3-030-25332-5_32

thorough search, given the complexity and uniqueness of building collapse patterns. The prevailing methods for localising trapped people remain physical searching, audible calling-out, search cameras and fibre optics/borescopes, thermal imaging, electronic listening devices and canine searching [24]. These methods have advantages and disadvantages, but the main problem is the need for rescue workers to stand in the proximity of or on unstable debris. This poses risk to both survivor and rescuer.

Extensive research has been done to implement robotics into SAR to help the trapped people survive in hazardous environments. However, the choice of SAR depends on the nature of disaster [13]. Natural disasters generally affect a wide area and the victims are largely dispersed. Unmanned Aerial Vehicles (UAVs) and Unmanned Surface Vehicles (USVs) have the potential to be employed in such scenarios.

Manmade disasters, however, pose different challenges; they are generally more concentrated, and thus the focus is often less on surveying the full extent of the damage but rather to search the remaining rubble or wreckage. Damaged infrastructure such as electricity and gas are important to monitor due to their risk to the life of buried survivors. Unmanned Ground Vehicles (UGVs) are likely to be the most useful form of robotic rescue vehicle, due to the small and enclosed nature of voids remaining in rubble after a major collapse [23].

The motivation for this paper stems from the need to reduce human loss in a major crisis, both for survivors of such incidents and for the rescue workers. Also, the speed of recovery time is important for survival time. In theory, robotics can solve these problems by replacing rescue workers in hazardous situations and in large numbers to find survivors more quickly, however, in practice, few such robots have been consistently used in the field. Thus, this paper aims to develop a novel robot that can bridge the gap between the development stage and field use, and thus help to save more lives. This paper presents (i) a literature review on the current methods and robots used/proposed in SAR in collapsed disaster scenarios, and on multihop wireless networking; (ii) a design of a SAR robot system; (iii) development of a prototype for the proposed robot system; and (iv) experimentation and control of the proposed robot system to demonstrate the effectiveness.

2 Related Works

Canine units were heavily used for search and rescue during the 9/11 incident due to their ability to detect human presence through scent [1, 24]. However, this is detrimental to the health of both dog and handler [6]. Human cognition on its own is not reliable enough to adequately detect human remains or live, buried persons when seen by a typical small-scale robot which has only a camera on it and is purely user controlled. Instead, robots must be redesigned to provide intelligent assistance, including the ability to tell the robot's orientation, surrounding temperature and some level of image processing [2].

Several kinds of UGV were deployed to the world trade centre (WTC) on 9/11 such as Inuktun micro-VGTV, Inuktun micro-tracks, Foster-Miller Solem, Foster-Miller Talon, iRobot Packbot etc. [19]. They were used largely to investigate voids that were 1 m in diameter, too small for human and dog to fit, and voids with a 2 m diameter that were still burning. One robot was lost in the rubble when it lost wireless communications and stopped, and the safety tether broke on retrieval. It was noted that thermal imaging was unusable in the WTC rubble due to the overall heat from the fires of the surroundings [19, 23]. The main problems were poor communications inside the rubble, difficulty recovering robots and thus the need for a safety tether, waterproofing, and lack of usability of thermal imaging. These vehicles were deployed at other disaster scenes, and it was found that the ultimate cause of failure for them was poor track design (particularly on the smaller micro-UGV) [19, 23].

Robots for SAR should be small enough to fit small voids of ~ 1 m diameter and it must be mobile and flexible. On the other hand, it needs to be large enough to traverse debris and obstacles present in a disaster site. Further, selection of SAR robots depends on the available logistic support as large robots require large vehicles to transport it to the disaster site whereas small robots can be carried on cars or by people [19].

Researchers have proposed various types of robots that could be evaluated for SAR applications. The examples include wheeled robot, tracked robot [29], legged robot [28], capsule-type robots [9, 10], robot with visco-elastic joint [15], hybrid legged-wheeled robot [12, 17, 30], hybrid legged-capsule robot [31], snake-like robot [20], crawler-robot [11, 25], swarm robots etc.

Many off-the-shelf tracked vehicles [7, 21] are widely used such as in bomb disposal but legged and snake-like robots show promise. Wheeled platforms' [16] capability in SAR is limited, due to the inability to overcome obstacles and steep ramps [23]. Arm-like manipulators [21] are a common addition and allow interaction with the environment, as well as the possibility for different camera angles. This addition, however, has its drawback that it increases the likelihood of damaging the robot due to added complexity. Serpentine [20] robots have a sophisticated structure to implement and legged [28] robots are challenging in their design compared to wheeled or tracked robot; however, their mimicry of biometric principles make them very effective at traversing difficult terrain [23].

For decades now, the NASA Mars Exploration Rover has been utilising a tried and tested wheeled platform, the rocker-bogie suspension system [3, 18, 22]. They are designed to overcome rough terrain, and they must function for long periods of time without failure.

The research was also done on wireless communications, particularly on multihop wireless networking for robot control. Tardioli [26] proposed a multihop solution to solve the problem of poor point-to-point wireless control of a robot. The nodes for the mesh network were pre-placed, in such a way that when a robot equipped with a SLAM device for mapping follows a path around a square corridor [26]. This work is a proof-of-concept of the usability of multihop networking for the direct control of a robot, as well as real-time processing of telemetry received from the robot.

Timotheou and Loukas [27] presented a scenario where a multihop network was established using multiple robots as nodes, creating a wireless network for the robots to communicate and to create a communication link at the surface for the trapped survivors. [27]. Here each node is attached to a robot and some robots are forced to remain close to the base station to provide the connectivity between the base and the rest of the network. Thus, the utility of the robots providing the backbone of the network is drastically reduced since they are forced to remain stationary to maintain connectivity.

The main points taken from this literature review are (i) SAR robot is a relatively new research area, and there is currently little in the way of standardised design; new designs and research is welcomed and needed. (ii) Robots are needed where rescue workers and canine units cannot access for health and safety or logistical reasons [6]. (iii) The use of robotic SAR can reduce the number of on-scene rescue workers, which will reduce the number of people with respiratory problems due to rescue tasks [23]. (iv) Robot designs that are useful for SAR have a small form factor, must be weatherproof and suitable for loose and hazardous terrain including high-temperature tolerance, have a camera with a feed to operators, and are ideally easy to set up and use [23]. (v) A big problem with robots searching rubble is communications; limited wireless signal under fallen debris and a tether can limit the travel of robot and potentially catch on debris or break [23]. (vi) Rocker-bogie suspension is designed to be simple and durable as well as able to overcome significant obstacles, and thus may be a better alternative to tracked vehicles which have more points of failure [3, 18, 22]. (viii) Multi-hop networking is a viable method of wireless communications with SAR robots. (ix) The use of swarm robotics with multihop networking can result in robots forced to remain largely stationary nodes to maintain connectivity, thus the utility of these robots is greatly reduced compared to their potential, and the resources put into making these "tether" robots could be saved by instead using small, simple repeater nodes that are dropped in the wake of a single robot [27].

3 Design of the Search and Rescue Robot System

3.1 Proposed Overall Design

In this paper, we consider a wheel-based UGV robot, wirelessly controlled utilizing multi-hop, with a rocker-bogie suspension system. This is a new approach to SAR robotics. Block diagram of the complete system is shown in Fig. 1(a).

The robot utilises multi-hop networking to overcome the obstacle of poor wireless connectivity in collapsed rubble, particularly involving reinforced concrete structures. This paper presents a functioning mobile rocker-bogie robot and implementation of multi-hop nodes for wireless communication. Wireless control of the robot is performed using a MATLAB user interface.

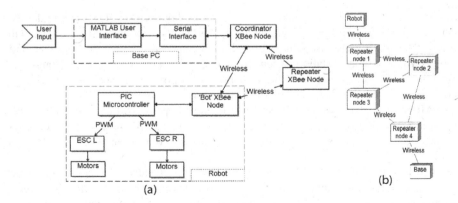

Fig. 1. (a) Block diagram of the complete system (b) Network model for multi-hop network

3.2   Robot Body Design

The robot body (Fig. 2(a)) was designed in a 3D CAD software DesignSpark Mechanical and then it was 3D printed. The robot body features a box-shaped body, left hollow for housing the electronics and battery, and a door that swivels around a pivot mounted on the top. The two halves of the robot body were designed to be held together using the main axle holder on either side of the body, which serves the dual purpose of holding the body together and strengthening the holes in the body through which the main axle passes. On the top of the body is the bar which differentially connects the arms of the robot on either side, a key component of the rocker-bogie suspension. Finally, the arms themselves are made up of three-wheel mounts (which clamp onto the motor for each wheel), the 'shoulder' which mounts onto the main axle and has a mount to connect to the differential bar, the pivot for the rocker and the rocker itself. The robot body design is inspired by the design of EPFL's Space Rover [5] and NASA Mars Exploration Rover and rocker-bogie suspension system [14].

The key design specifications for the robot design were that it should be small, specified as no larger than half a metre in any dimension, and have a sizable ground clearance so as not to snag on large debris. The robot occupies an area of 37 × 27 cm and has a ground clearance of 8 cm with the 9 cm diameter soft wheels fitted. This ground clearance could be further increased by fitting larger diameter wheels.

(a)   (b)

Fig. 2.   (a) Design of the Robot Body (b) Prototype of the Search and Rescue Robot

3.3   Multi-hop Networking

Multi-hop networking is constructed by having the robot drop small repeater nodes as it roams deeper into the rubble, providing a wireless "tether" for the signal to return to the surface through. It increases both the signal quality and the chances of a signal making it from robot to base station when compared with the point-to-point long-range transmission. This also removes the limitations of a physical tether, by removing the possibility of catching the tether and thus trapping the robot.

UML of Fig. 1(b) shows the concept of multi-hop networking, showing how a signal is received by the base station from the robot even if the robot has no direct connection to the base, and even if some nodes are also out of range of the base or the robot.

ZigBee was selected for the network protocol as it natively supports mesh networking. It has better range than Bluetooth but less range than wifi. However, it consumes less power than wifi and is more geared towards embedded systems.

4 Development of the Robot

The first part of the development of the robot was printing the outer shell. The full body (Fig. 2(b)) was 3D printed out of ABS, except for the pipes between the motor mount points and the rocker/bogie and shoulder joint, which were cut out of PVC plastic piping to save cost and for ease of cutting.

A PIC microcontroller is used to handle incoming commands and control the motor circuits. The code and embedded circuit for the PIC was designed in Proteus, allowing for the code to be written and tested without the need for building test circuits, eliminating any potential faults caused by circuitry for debugging code. ZigBee was chosen for low power multi-hop networking. The specific type of XBee module which supports ZigBee mesh networking natively is the series 2 line of modules.

The motors were chosen to suit the purpose of the robot; 133 rpm geared motors with a gear ratio of 1:75 was selected for their high torque. This is an advantage when the wheels are intended for use in a rocker-bogie suspension system, as the key method of surmounting obstacles is using the torque of the motors to push the robot against the obstacles and force the front most wheels up and over. This means that the motors are likely to be at risk of reaching their stall current often. The specific model of motor selected has a 5.5 A stall current rating and given that there are 3 motors per side the current consumption was likely to be very high. Thus, a pair of high current Electronic Speed Controllers (ESCs) were selected with a max output current of 45 A and includes a Battery Elimination Circuit which supplies a 5.6 V, 2 A output for powering the control circuit and thermal protection.

The XBee modules were configured to implement the ZigBee mesh network. For XBee modules to work together effectively, there are several important parameters to check and configure. Firstly, they must all be series 2 XBee modules, as only series 2 modules support mesh networking. Secondly, they must all support use of the same protocol.

5 Experiments and Evaluation

The completed prototype robot can move forward, reverse, and turn. Two types of wheels are used: foam wheels and rubber wheels where rubber wheels have higher friction coefficients. The rocker and bogie mechanisms rotate freely, even with the weight and wires of the motors in them, and the addition of a damper on the bogie prevents it from hyper-rotating, helping it to keep a grip on the ground with all six wheels. Following subsections, A to E presents various experiments.

5.1 Free Standing, Small Obstacles Test

The robot is capable of surmounting flat obstacles of 8 cm height with little difficulty. Due to having six powered wheels and a great range of motions for each rocker arm, if the undercarriage of the body was caught on an obstacle at or under this height there was always at least 1 wheel in contact with the ground to push/pull the robot off the obstacle.

With the rubber wheels, the robot is more likely to grip loose obstacles and go over them than to simply push them as with foam wheels. This is beneficial as pushing loose obstacles can exasperate further obstacles or create insurmountable piles.

Lots of loose small debris is likely to be scattered around collapsed or partially collapsed buildings, so being able to handle small loose obstacles without pushing or slipping is an important capability.

5.2   Slope Test

The robot was tested (Fig. 3(a)) with two types of wheels (foam and rubber) and with varying slopes. A successful climb is defined as the robot reaching the top of the slope and not sliding down. The experimental results are provided in Table 1.

Table 1. Experimental results for slope test (Yes = Successful climb and No = failed to climb)

	Foam wheels		Rubber wheels	
Slope	Low speed (0.5 m/s)	High speed (1 m/s)	Low speed (0.5 m/s)	High speed (1 m/s)
20°	Yes	Yes	Yes	Yes
25°	Yes	No	Yes	Yes
30°	No	No	Yes	No
35°	No	No	No	No

The slope test demonstrates that grip strength of wheels contributes towards the performance of the robot. The robot has better performance with rubber wheel compared to the foam wheel as rubber wheel has a higher friction coefficient. It demonstrates that a low speed combined with a high torque of the motor is an efficient way to enable the robot to climb without slipping, as reinforced by the NASA study of a rocker-bogie system [8]. It demonstrates the ability of the robot to function in non-flat scenarios, a high likelihood in unstable/collapsed structures. It also demonstrates that the grip of the wheels failed before the robot was unbalanced enough to tip over backwards.

5.3   Obstacle Test: Loose Rubble/Outdoor Environment

The robot was tested in a variety of outdoor scenarios, including over loose rubble, over plant material and over a single large step. Every scenario was tested forwards and backwards, to highlight the difference between using either end of the rocker-bogie system as the front.

The first test was over the loose stone and plant debris on an uneven surface (Fig. 3(a)). The debris was made up of loose rocks on the ground, of a maximum of approx. 8 cm in diameter. The plant debris was made up of long sticks (approx. 60 cm max). The robot was able to pass over the uneven surface in both directions. The loose rubble was also surpassed in both directions; however, the longer twigs were susceptible to beaching the robot by trapping it between wheels. In some, but not all attempts, moving the robot back and forth dislodges it. A standard brick was added to the rubble. The robot was unable to traverse the brick head-on without maneuvering carefully either around it or so that only one leg of the rocker-bogie mounted it. On a direct approach, the robot was beached on the leading edge of the brick.

The next test was over plant material, over a low carpet of long grass (Fig. 3(b)). The robot managed to go a short distance in the long grass, however, it never managed to fully traverse the terrain without getting beached as the soft leaves were pushed down away from the wheels. The wheels also failed to grip the soft leaves. The main conclusion drawn from this test was that the wheels used are too slick for softer, moist terrain.

The final outdoor test was over a single, large step in outdoor conditions (Fig. 3(c)). The step was initially 8 cm in height, increased to 10 cm using two wooden boards. The robot succeeded in scaling the step in the forward direction at 8, 9 and 10 cm heights; however, in the reverse direction, it failed at scaling the 10 cm height.

The conclusion from these outdoor tests show that the rocker-bogie system behaves as designed, and the motors can provide enough torque; however, the robot needs larger, grippier wheels to keep it further off the ground and grip the floor better.

5.4   Obstacle Test: Staircase

Steps of the stairs are 14 cm (Fig. 3(e)). The robot can pull itself up onto the step, but when rearmost wheels contact the step, the robot loses its balance and tips backwards. Attempts to add counterweights to the front were not enough to prevent this (as shown in Fig. 3(e), the robot is seen with counterbalances on the front, at the point of tipping) and this combined with the slipping backwards on the slope test demonstrate balancing issues with the robot design. The robot was tested at faster and slower speeds in both directions to confirm that this was the case, and in each test, the same result occurred. In the reverse direction, the robot tipped quicker and was unable to scale the leading wheel over the step. Revision of current design should see the main axle mounted closer towards the centre of the body.

Stair climbing is a critical ability for search and rescue reconnaissance robots, as partially collapsed or even completely collapsed buildings are likely to have a completely or partially intact stairwell, and with no human intervention possible the robot must be able to overcome such an obstacle with ease and stability. Stairs are regularly used as a test bench for SAR robots and this problem must be overcome before the chassis design can be considered for more rough terrain testing.

Fig. 3. (a) Slope test setup (b) Loose Rubble used for testing (c) Long grass used for testing (d) Step used for testing (e) Staircase obstacle test

5.5   Testing the Multi-hop Network

Three nodes were used to demonstrate the multi-hop network. The hardware version of the nodes was XBee24-ZB (Fig. 4(a)). Each node was loaded with the latest ZigBee firmware version. Each node was set up to be able to recognise each other and talk on the same local area network. ZigBee protocol uses a PAN ID to define the local area network; a coordinator establishes the PAN, and routers search for PANs nearby, joining if they are set up to have a matching PAN ID and the coordinator is not gatekeeping other nodes from joining. When the network was tested, all three nodes could join the same PAN.

Once all three nodes were set up in API mode, a test set up was created to ensure that the nodes would be forced to utilize multi-hop networking for the coordinator to reach the 'bot' node. First, the coordinator and router node, which have RPSMA connectors for high-gain antennas, had their antennas removed to shorten their range for the test.

The 'bot' node uses a whip antenna, which has a shorter range than the other two by default. The ranges for each node type was measured by transmitting a broadcast message repeatedly with only 2 nodes connected until no more messages were received. This test was done in an open space with line-of-sight between nodes, in a room containing computers and desks. The reliable range of an RPSMA node (without antenna) to the whip antenna was found to be roughly 8.5 m, and between 2 RPSMA nodes were within 2 m. The nodes were then placed so that the router was in the range of both nodes, but the coordinator was not in range of the 'bot' node. The connectivity of the network was checked using XCTU's Network Working Mode, which allows each node to scan the network and draw a graphic map showing the connectivity and even signal strength between nodes (Fig. 4(b)).

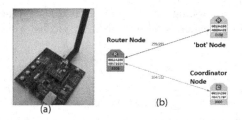

Fig. 4. (a) XBee node with RPSMA connector with antenna (b) Screenshot from XCTU Network View

The network view (Fig. 4(b)) confirmed that the nodes were connected in the proper configuration. To ensure that multi-hop routing was being used, the router node was turned off and a transmit request frame was created in the XCTU terminal at the coordinator node. The frame was sent in a repeating pattern, with the 'bot' node set as the destination address. With the router off, the frames were not received by the 'bot' node. When the router was turned on, the 'bot' node began receiving frames, thereby proving that the protocol had automatically routed the frame through the router (Fig. 4 (b)).

5.6   Power Consumption of the Robot

The robot was powered by an 11.1 V 1000 mAh Li-Po battery, typically used and designed for radio-controlled hobby vehicles. This was chosen for its ability to handle high current outputs, and its compatibility by design with the selected ESCs. Each motor has a no-load current of 0.35 A, so 2.1 A for the wheel system in total, thus consuming 23 W of power. The stall current for the motors is 5.5 A at 8.8 kg/cm of torque, resulting in peak power consumption of 366.3 W at the stall. On very rough terrain or aggressive climbs each motor can consume 2 A each on average, so 12 A in total, which is 133.2 W of power. The ESCs have a max continuous current of 45 A, and a max burst current of 340 A, so the motors are effectively unlimited in their current consumption.

This reflects the motor usage at top speed. The upside of using ESCs is that they reduce power consumption at lower speeds, and as it drives the motors using PWM pulses it is more efficient than regulating the output voltage.

Typically, the robot is used at half of its top speed to better navigate the terrain, so it can roughly double the battery life this way. Finally, the PIC micro has a typical run current of 11 uA and the Zigbee of 150 mA when transmitting, consuming 55 uW and 495 mW respectively. Thus, accounting for a small amount of current to power the ESCs the robot does not consume much energy and will run for approximately 5 h on a 1000 mAh battery when stationary.

The robot's battery life was tested by placing it on a pedestal where the wheels did not contact the ground with a fully charged battery, and the motors are driven at full speed continuously until their performance was severely degraded. The robot lasted just under 30 min, which reflects the no-load current of just over 2 A total when supplied by a 1 Ah battery. Hence, for long term use in inaccessible conditions where the battery cannot be replaced, Li-Po batteries of 3000 mAh or greater would be optimal.

6 Conclusions

In this paper, a new perspective on SAR robotics was presented through research into the field. A robot design was proposed and built, which drew its influence from other fields of robotic exploration, namely interplanetary exploration. The developed prototype robot based on Rocker-bogie system works and moves as intended. The experimental results show that Rocker-bogie system is viable for surmounting smaller obstacles and dramatic slopes, but the performance was hindered by grip strength of wheels, positioning of the robot's centre of balance. Thus, the robot must be rebalanced by shifting the main axle and re-examined before it can be tested on more rugged obstacle tests. Rubber-based, larger wheels perform better than firmer, slicker, smaller foam wheels. Bigger, more grippy wheels and lower speeds are the best methods to ensure the robot can surmount most obstacles it encounters.

The proposed robot incorporates multi-hop networking, with a method of distributing repeater nodes behind the robot as it travels to form a wireless "tether" replacing a hard cable tether. This multi-hop network has the capacity as is the nature of ZigBee for other router nodes to be added, thus in theory expanding the network to be as big as the coordinator node can handle.

Overall, the work done in this paper is a proof of concept of the full proposed design, and a good base for future work to expand on and grow towards a possible solution to making the use of SAR robots more affordable, streamlined and efficient, and thus increase chances of discovering survivors earlier with less risk to rescue workers' lives.

References

1. Alvarez, J., Hunt, M.: Risk and resilience in canine search and rescue handlers after 9/11. J. Trauma. Stress **18**(5), 497–505 (2005)
2. Casper, J., Murphy, R.R.: Human-robot interactions during the robot-assisted urban search and rescue response at the world trade center. In: IEEE Transactions on Systems, Man, and Cybernetics, Part B (Cybernetics), vol. 33, no. 3, pp. 367–385 (2003)
3. Choi, D., et al.: A new mobile platform (RHyMo) for smooth movement on rugged terrain. IEEE/ASME Trans. Mechatron. **21**(3), 1303–1314 (2016)
4. Coburn, A.W., et al.: Factors determining human casualty levels in earthquakes: mortality prediction in building collapse. In: Proceedings of the 10th World Conference on Earthquake Engineering, pp. 5989–5994 (1992)
5. Estier, T., et al.: An innovative space rover with extended climbing abilities. Robotics **2000**, 333–339 (2000)
6. Fitzgerald, S.D., et al.: Pathology and toxicology findings for search-and-rescue dogs deployed to the September 11, 2001, terrorist attack sites: initial five-year surveillance. J. Vet. Diagn. Invest. **20**(4), 477–484 (2008)

7. Guizzo, E.: Japan Earthquake: More Robots to the Rescue. https://spectrum.ieee.org/automaton/robotics/industrial-robots/japan-earthquake-more-robots-to-the-rescue
8. Harrington, B.D., Voorhees, C.: The challenges of designing the rocker-bogie suspension for the mars exploration rover. In: NASA Jet Propulsion Laboratory (2004)
9. Huda, M.N., et al.: Behaviour-based control approach for the trajectory tracking of an underactuated planar capsule robot. IET Control Theory Appl. 9(2), 163–175 (2014)
10. Huda, M.N., Yu, H.: Trajectory tracking control of an underactuated capsubot. Auton. Robot. 39(2), 183–198 (2015)
11. Ito, K., Maruyama, H.: Semi-autonomous serially connected multi-crawler robot for search and rescue. Adv. Robot. 30(7), 489–503 (2016)
12. Kim, Y.S., et al.: Wheel transformer: a wheel-leg hybrid robot with passive transformable wheels. IEEE Trans. Robot. 30(6), 1487–1498 (2014). https://doi.org/10.1109/TRO.2014.2365651
13. Lima, P.U.: Search and rescue robots: the civil protection teams of the future. In: Third International Conference on Emerging Security Technologies, pp. 12–19 IEEE (2012)
14. Lindemann, R.A., et al.: Mars exploration rover mobility development. IEEE Robot. Autom. Mag. 13(2), 19–26 (2006)
15. Liu, P., et al.: A self-propelled robotic system with a visco-elastic joint: dynamics and motion analysis. Eng. Comput. (2019)
16. Liu, S., Sun, D.: Minimizing energy consumption of wheeled mobile robots via optimal motion planning. IEEE/ASME Trans. Mechatron. 19(2), 401–411 (2014)
17. Ma, Z., Duan, H.: Structural design and performance analysis for a novel wheel-legged rescue robot. In: 2016 IEEE International Conference on Robotics and Biomimetics (ROBIO), pp. 868–873 (2016)
18. Mori, Y., et al.: Development of an omnidirectional mobile platform with a rocker-bogie suspension system. In: 42nd Annual Conference of the IEEE Industrial Electronics Society, pp. 6134–6139 (2016)
19. Murphy, R.R.: Trial by fire [rescue robots]. IEEE Robot. Autom. Mag. 11(3), 50–61 (2004)
20. Neumann, M., et al.: Snake-like, tracked, mobile robot with active flippers for urban search-and-rescue tasks. Ind. Robot Int. J. 40(3), 246–250 (2013)
21. Qinetic: Bomb & Explosive Ordnance Disposal - Robotics & Autonomy - What we do – QinetiQ. https://www.qinetiq.com/What-we-do/Robotics/Bomb-and-Explosive-Ordnance-Disposal
22. Setterfield, T.P., Ellery, A.: Terrain response estimation using an instrumented rocker-bogie mobility system. IEEE Trans. Robot. 29(1), 172–188 (2013)
23. Siciliano, B., Khatib, O.: Springer Handbook of Robotics. Springer, Cham (2016). https://doi.org/10.1007/978-3-319-32552-1
24. Statheropoulos, M., et al.: Factors that affect rescue time in urban search and rescue (USAR) operations. Nat. Hazards 75(1), 57–69 (2015)
25. Suzuki, N., Yamazaki, Y.: Basic research on the driving performance of an autonomous rescue robot with obstacles. In: IEEE International Conference on Robotics and Biomimetics, pp. 982–987 (2015)
26. Tardioli, D.: A proof-of-concept application of multi-hop robot teleoperation with online map building. In: 9th IEEE International Symposium on Industrial Embedded Systems, pp. 210–217. IEEE (2014)
27. Timotheou, S., Loukas, G.: Autonomous networked robots for the establishment of wireless communication in uncertain emergency response scenarios. In: Proceedings of the 2009 ACM symposium on Applied Computing, pp. 1171–1175. ACM (2009)
28. Wang, P., et al.: The nonfragile controller with covariance constraint for stable motion of quadruped search-rescue robot. Adv. Mech. Eng. 6, 917381 (2014)

29. Wang, W., et al.: Development of search-and-rescue robots for underground coal mine applications. J. Field Robot. **31**(3), 386–407 (2014)
30. Wang, X., et al.: Dynamic analysis for the leg mechanism of a wheel-leg hybrid rescue robot. In: UKACC International Conference on Control, pp. 504–508 (2014)
31. Yu, H., et al.: Travelling capsule with two drive mechanisms (2013)

Payload Capabilities and Operational Limits of Eversion Robots

Hareesh Godaba[1,3]($\boxtimes$), Fabrizio Putzu[2,3], Taqi Abrar[1,3],
Jelizaveta Konstantinova[1,3], and Kaspar Althoefer[1,2,3]

[1] School of Electronic Engineering and Computer Science,
Queen Mary University of London, London, UK
h.godaba@qmul.ac.uk
[2] School of Engineering and Materials Science, Queen Mary
University of London, London, UK
[3] Centre for Advanced Robotics @ Queen Mary, Queen Mary
University of London, London, UK

Abstract. Recent progress in soft robotics has seen new types of actuation mechanisms based on apical extension which allows robots to grow to unprecedented lengths. Eversion robots are a type of robots based on the principle of apical extension offering excellent maneuverability and ease of control allowing users to conduct tasks from a distance. Mechanical modelling of these robotic structures is very important for understanding their operational capabilities. In this paper, we model the eversion robot as a thin-walled cylindrical beam inflated with air pressure, using Timoshenko beam theory considering rotational and shear effects. We examine the various failure modes of the eversion robots such as yielding, buckling instability and lateral collapse, and study the payloads and operational limits of these robots in axial and lateral loading conditions. Surface maps showing the operational boundaries for different combinations of the geometrical parameters are presented. This work provides insights into the design of eversion robots and can pave the way towards eversion robots with high payload capabilities that can act from long distances.

Keywords: Eversion robots · Soft robots · Inflated beams ·
Timoshenko beam theory · Failure modes · Operational limits ·
Design parameters

1 Introduction

Recent years have seen huge strides in the field of soft robotics with a variety of actuation mechanisms improving the maneuverability, range of actuation and offer novel functionalities. Soft actuation mechanisms are based on different principles such as electroactuation [1, 2], shape memory effect [3], swelling of gels [4], tendon based actuation [5], pneumatic [6] and hydraulic actuation [7]. Pneumatic actuation has been very popular due to its ease of fabrication, low cost and inherent compliance of the materials. Earlier works predominantly utilized hyperelastic materials molded into soft structures and then inflated with air to cause deformation in the soft robotic bodies.

© Springer Nature Switzerland AG 2019
K. Althoefer et al. (Eds.): TAROS 2019, LNAI 11650, pp. 383–394, 2019.
https://doi.org/10.1007/978-3-030-25332-5_33

However, further developments have seen the introduction of new materials, such as paper, plastics and fabrics [8–11]. In contrast to hyperelastic materials which harness large extensions in their bodies to generate actuation, these elastic materials utilise topological changes such as bending, folding or unfolding to generate actuation. This principle has been used to develop fabric based actuators that can exhibit linear elongations and bending, pouch type actuators that can contract and robots that can grow in length through eversion [8, 9, 12].

Hawkes et al. utilized a polyethylene sheet to develop an apically extending soft robot that grows by everting material from its tip [12]. In this eversion robot, a long tubular sock of polyethylene was prefabricated, and one end of the tube was sealed. The sealed end was folded inwards and passed back through the center of the tube and fed into a spool. When pressure is exerted through the open end of the tube, the pressure pushes the material out of the tip and the robot grows in an everting fashion. The eversion robots have been demonstrated to be steerable and can extend at rates of up to 10 m/s to tens of meters in length. Different applications such as surveillance and monitoring, reconfigurable antennas, a soft burrowing device, soft artificial muscles and manipulators for minimally invasive surgery have been demonstrated using the eversion principle [12–15]. Furthermore, by embedding sensing technologies, bioinspired control techniques can be implemented to control eversion robots and track complex trajectories due to their high maneuverability [16].

However, there has been minimal work on developing and characterizing eversion robots that can deliver payloads. Putzu et al. developed a pneumatic actuator based on the eversion principle in which a payload of 3N was suspended using a tendon attached to the sealed end of the membrane [15]. With the large range of actuation and interesting maneuvering capabilities of eversion robots, the subsequent goals would be to equip the eversion-based robots with sensing and manipulation capabilities by attaching sensors and effectors to the tip of the robot. This requires the eversion robots to have sufficient payload capabilities to carry these components and execute manipulation tasks. The slender form factor of the eversion robots presents us with challenges such as low flexural rigidity and susceptibility to instabilities. Towards the goal of developing payload capabilities in eversion robots, we conduct here a modelling study to investigate the achievable forces under different loading conditions. We make use of analytical models of inflatable beams based on the Timoshenko beam theory to find the different failure modes and operation limits of eversion robots. 3D maps showing the operational limits and modes of failure for axial and lateral loading conditions are presented. This work lays a foundation for more exciting applications of eversion robots with high payload capabilities.

The rest of the paper is organized as follows. In Sect. 2, we develop the analytical model for an eversion robot and describe the stresses in the robot. In Sect. 3, we discuss the various failure modes of the eversion robots and present 3D surface maps showing the operational capabilities of the eversion robot subject to different failure modes.

2 Analytical Modelling

An eversion robot is made of a thin elastic membrane preformed into a long tubular sock. The tubular sock is folded inwards and housed inside the robot body. When a pressure is applied through the open end, the material folded inwards begins to evert from the tip increasing the length of the eversion robot. A tendon is attached to the tip of the tubular sock and can be utilized to exert forces on the tip. Tension can be applied to the tendon to exert larger pressure to the eversion robot and increase its stiffness. Figure 1 shows a schematic of the eversion robot. The thickness of the membrane is denoted by **t**. It is generally much smaller compared to the radius of the robot. This is to ensure a low flexural stiffness of the membrane so that it can attain high curvatures and facilitate eversion. In this paper, we model the eversion robot as an inflated beam made of a thin elastic membrane. The proximal end of the eversion robot is fixed, and a pressure denoted by P is applied through this opening. The force exerted by a tendon (attached to the distal, sealed end of our eversion robot), denoted by F_{tendon}, and the external force, F_{ext}, act on the sealed end of the beam, as shown in Fig. 1. We consider the quasi static equilibrium in the eversion robot of a given radius to calculate the forces exerted by the robot at different pressures and everted lengths. Since, the thickness of the membrane is much smaller than the radius of the eversion robot and the stresses are assumed to not vary along the thickness direction of the membrane. The lengths of the robot considered are much larger as compared to the radii of the robot so that small deformation approximations can be applied.

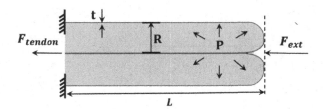

Fig. 1. Free body diagram of eversion actuator. An eversion robot of radius, R, wall thickness, t and everted length, L is fixed at one end. It is subject to an internal pressure, P, external force, F_{ext} and a force, F_{tendon}, is exerted by the tendon at the tip.

2.1 Force Equilibrium

When the robot is pressurized and the tip is unobstructed, the robot grows while everting. The rate of growth is given by the following equation [17, 18]:

$$r = \varphi(P - Y)^n, \tag{1}$$

where P and Y are the internal pressure and the threshold pressure required for eversion, φ is the extensibility of the system and n is a power term that relates the degree of change of rate of extension to internal pressure.

When the robot is in a static equilibrium with respect to external forces, the force analysis simplifies to a static force equilibrium problem for the system. Figure 1 shows the schematic of an eversion robot showing the forces acting on the robot in the case of equilibrium. The external force, F_{ext} is balanced by the force pulling on the tendon, F_{tendon} and the internal pressure acting on the robot body. Assuming that the cross section of the tip is circular with an effective radius, R, the force balance is given by:

$$P(\pi R^2) = F_{ext} + F_{tendon}. \tag{2}$$

As we can see from the equation above, the maximum external force (or payload) is achievable when the force in the tendon is zero, i.e., the tendon is slack. So, from this point, we consider $F_{tendon} = 0$, in our analysis concerning the maximum achievable forces.

2.2 Longitudinal and Circumferential Stresses

In an eversion robot, the membrane forming the robot body should be very thin and flexible in order to allow the tip to evert. Typically, the thickness of the membrane to the radius ratio is extremely small. Due to this, the membrane does not experience radial stresses when pressurized and only experiences longitudinal (or axial) and circumferential (or hoop's) stresses [19]. These stresses are denoted by σ_L and σ_θ respectively. Figure 2 shows the longitudinal and axial cross sections of an eversion robot with an everted length, L, showing the longitudinal and circumferential stresses.

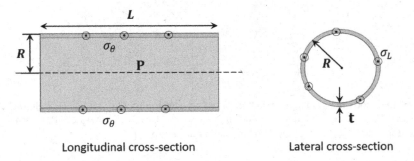

Fig. 2. Longitudinal and lateral cross-sections showing the circumferential stress, σ_θ and longitudinal stress, σ_L, respectively.

In the longitudinal direction, the forces exerted by the internal pressure on the tip of the eversion robot are balanced by the longitudinal stresses in the robot body. When the thickness of the membrane is much smaller than the radius of the eversion robot, the force equilibrium in the longitudinal direction is given by:

$$\sigma_L(2\pi R t) = P(\pi R^2),\tag{3}$$

and the longitudinal stress in the body is given by

$$\sigma_L = PR/2t.\tag{4}$$

The robot everts from a fixed end that is annular in cross-section. Close to the fixed boundary, there may be boundary inhomogeneities. However, away from the fixed boundary, we consider that the circumferential stresses are uniformly distributed along the length of the eversion robot. Along a longitudinal cross section, the force balance is given by:

$$\sigma_\theta(2Lt) = P(RL).\tag{5}$$

The circumferential or hoop's stress is given by:

$$\sigma_\theta = \frac{PR}{2t}.\tag{6}$$

The expressions for the stresses in the membrane are similar to those of a thin-walled cylinder subject to internal pressure. The circumferential and longitudinal stresses should always be non-negative for the robot to be in operation.

3 Results

In this section, we discuss the various failure modes of the eversion based. The payload capability of the eversion-based robot depends on various factors such as the type of loading, the geometric parameters such as the radius, thickness of the membrane and the everted length, as well as the material properties. In this work, we consider the payload capabilities in the longitudinal and lateral loading of the eversion robot. These quantities indicate the amount of forces that the robot can deliver while operating in a given state. In the axial loading, we are mainly concerned about two main modes of failure: (1) yielding and (2) buckling due to compression. In the case of lateral loading, we consider the lateral collapse of the robot due to loss of tension along the longitudinal direction.

In this simulation, we consider low density polyethylene (LDPE) as the material for the eversion-based robot. This has been chosen as the subject material because of its use in previous works and also due to its easy processability and fabrication. The various material and geometric parameters used in the simulation are shown in Table 1 [20].

Table 1. Material and geometric parameters of the eversion robot for modelling.

Parameter	Symbol	Value	Unit
Young's modulus	E	110	MPa
Thickness	t	100	μm
Yield stress	σ_y	40	MPa
Shear modulus	G	66	MPa
Density	ρ	925	kg/m^3

3.1   Failure Due to Yielding

The membrane fails by yielding (or bursting) when the circumferential stresses, σ_θ in the membrane reach the yield stress of the material. The circumferential stress is considered for the failure criterion because, at maximum payload capability, the longitudinal stresses in the membrane tend to zero since the external forces acting on the robot are fully balanced by the internal pressure. The failure criterion for yielding is given by [21]:

$$\sigma_\theta = \sigma_y, \tag{7}$$

where σ_y denotes the yield stress of the material. We consider an eversion robot of radius, $R = 2.5$ cm and a length of 1 m. Figure 3(a) shows the circumferential stress in the robot body as a function of pressure. The black cross (x) in Fig. 3(a) shows the pressure at which the circumferential stress in the robot reaches the yield stress, indicating the yielding pressure. The corresponding force, F_{ext} that would be exerted by the robot is given by $F_{ext} = \pi P R^2$ and is plotted in Fig. 3(b).

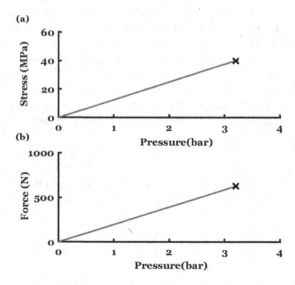

Fig. 3. (a) The circumferential stresses generated in the robot body upon inflation by internal pressure; (b) Blocked forces of the eversion robot as a function of internal pressure. The black crosses (x) in both the plots indicate failure due to yielding.

3.2 Failure Due to Buckling

When the eversion robot is actuated against a load, compressive forces are generated on the robot. Due to the long lengths of eversion robots and the low radius to length ratio, the eversion robots are prone to buckling. An eversion robot buckled under compression when it encounters a rigid obstacle is shown in Fig. 4(a).

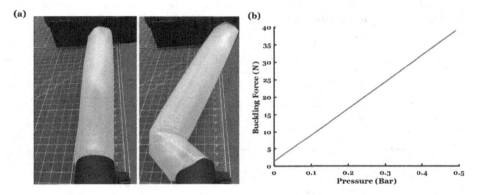

Fig. 4. (a) An eversion robot encounters a rigid obstacle and undergoes buckling; (b) Calculated critical buckling load for an eversion robot of radius 2.5 cm and length of 1 m at different internal pressure levels.

Under the assumptions that the cross-sections of the eversion robot along the length do not change, and in the limit of small strains, the critical load for buckling is given by [22]:

$$F_{cr} = \frac{\left(E + \frac{P}{S}\right)I\Omega^2}{1 + \Omega^2 \frac{I}{S} + \Omega^2 \frac{\left(E + \frac{P}{S}\right)I}{P + kGS}}, \tag{8}$$

where S denotes the cross-sectional area of the eversion robot, I refers to the second moment of area about the central axis, Ω corresponds to the mode shape of the buckled beam given by $\Omega L = (2n - 1)\pi/2$ and the primary mode of buckling is obtained by substituting $n = 1$. The constant k is the correction shear factor and is equal to 0.5 for circular tubes [23].

Eversion robots are generally made of very thin sheets or fabrics to facilitate the eversion mechanism, the effective shear modulus is generally low, and the effect of the pressure dominates the buckling behavior. When the internal pressure is zero and the shear modulus of material is low, the critical force for buckling recovers a value close to that of the Euler buckling load of a classical beam. However, the eversion robot cannot operate at zero pressure as this causes the longitudinal stresses in the membrane to disappear and even the smallest force will crush the robot. Figure 4b shows the critical buckling load at different internal pressures for an eversion robot of a length of 1 m and a radius of 2.5 cm. The calculated buckling load at zero pressure is 1.328N.

3.3   Lateral Collapse Force

The eversion robots may also be applied to carry loads in the lateral direction. For example, sensors mounted at the tip of a horizontally extending robot are subject to a lateral force due to gravity. A free body diagram of an eversion robot with a concentrated load applied laterally at its tip is shown in Fig. 5(a). Very long eversion robots may also experience large moments at the fixed end due to their own weight. These loads cause bending in the lateral direction. However, beyond a threshold, the eversion robot collapses with a kink in its surface as shown in Fig. 5(b).

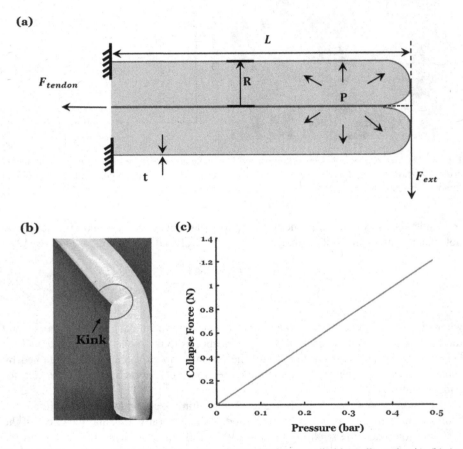

Fig. 5. (a) Free body diagram of an eversion robot with force applied laterally at the tip, (b) An eversion robot collapses laterally with a kink when the lateral force exceeds the critical limit; (c) Calculated critical buckling load for an eversion robot of radius 2.5 cm and length of 1 m at different internal pressures.

Since the membrane making up an eversion robot is very thin, they cannot resist any compression and the longitudinal stress in all parts of the membrane along the length need to be non-negative. The condition for collapse of the eversion robot when a moment, M is applied, is given by:

$$\sigma_L = \frac{M}{I}R > 0. \tag{9}$$

For a concentrated force, F applied at the tip of the eversion robot inflated with a pressure P and balanced at equilibrium length, L by the tendon, Eq. (9) can be evaluated to give the condition for lateral collapse of the robot as follows [24]:

$$F_{collapse} = \frac{\pi R^3 P}{2L}. \tag{10}$$

Figure 5(c) shows the change in the critical force for lateral collapse of the eversion robot. The critical force at zero pressure is zero as expected and the lateral load bearing capacity increases with the increase in pressure.

3.4 Operational Limits

The geometrical parameters of the eversion robot play an important role in determining the payload capabilities and the mode of failure encountered by the robot when loaded axially and laterally. Since eversion robots grow in length during their operation, the mechanical design should keep in mind the evolution of operation limits with changes in the everted length. To aid in this procedure, we calculate the maximum obtainable payloads in the axial and lateral directions before the robot encounters yielding, buckling or lateral collapse.

Figure 6 shows a 3D map of the maximum axial payload capability for different combinations of radius and everted lengths. The pressure for the critical points has been abstracted and only the maximum achievable forces for the combinations of radii and everted lengths have been plotted. The pink surface shows the maximum force considering yielding as the failure criterion and the green surface shows the maximum load at which buckling occurs for the given combination of radius and everted length. The plot for failure due to buckling shows a very nonlinear pattern and cannot be obtained as a closed form solution. This is because both the axial force that can be generated by the robot and the critical force for buckling vary with pressure. When the axial force generated by the robot becomes equal to the critical load for buckling for the given pressure, the robot undergoes buckling.

As the radius of the eversion robot is increased, the payload capability always increases for the same material at a given everted length of the robot. The dynamic variation of payload capability with the change in length of the eversion robot can also be noted from the figure. When the radius of the robot is large, the maximum force does not vary with the length and is dependent only on the yield strength of the material that the robot is composed of. However, beyond a particular length, the robot becomes prone to buckling and the payload capability rapidly decreases. The maximum achievable axial payload at an everted length of 2 m for a radius of 5 cm is 2.95N as compared to 23.34N achievable for a radius of 10 cm.

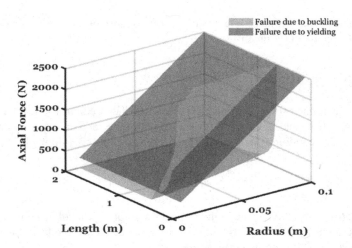

Fig. 6. Operational limits of eversion robots with different radii and everted lengths. The pink and green surfaces show the maximum axial force considering yielding and buckling as the failure criterion respectively. (Color figure online)

The distribution of the lateral payloads before collapse for different radii and everted lengths of the robot is shown in Fig. 7. From Eq. (10), we see that the lateral payload linearly increases with the internal pressure. It is evident that the maximum lateral payload would be attained at the maximum possible internal pressure which occurs at the yield limit of the robot. From Eqs. (6–7), we get the maximum pressure at yield as, $P_{max} = 2t\sigma_y/R$. This internal pressure can be achieved at any everted length by applying force to the tendon. However, within the limit of small deformations, we assume that the tendon does not affect the lateral load bearing capability as it remains in the neutral plane of the eversion robot. By substituting P_{max} in Eq. (10), the maximum possible lateral force is given by:

$$F_{lateral} = \frac{\pi R^2 \sigma_y t}{L}. \tag{11}$$

Equation (11) is evaluated for different radii and everted lengths and shown as a 3D surface in Fig. 7. The maximum achievable lateral payload at an everted length of 2 m for a radius of 5 cm is 15.71N as compared to 62.83N achievable for a radius of 10 cm. We observe from Figs. 6 and 7 that the critical load for axial buckling is more sensitive to changes in length and reduces at a faster rate as compared to the critical load for lateral collapse.

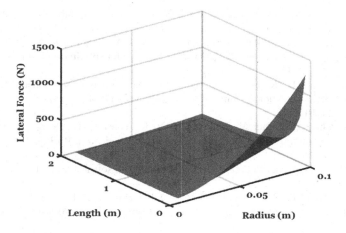

Fig. 7. Operational limits of eversion robots with different radii and everted lengths. The blue surface shows the maximum lateral force beyond which the robot collapses. (Color figure online)

4   Conclusions

In this paper, we present an analysis to determine the payload capabilities of eversion robots. We have investigated the effects of the radius of the robot and the everted length on the axial and lateral payload bearing capabilities of the robots. We studied yielding, buckling due to compression and collapse due to lateral loading as the main modes of failure. The results show an interplay of these failure modes and suggest that the mechanics and the intended actuation ranges should be kept in mind to optimize the payload of the eversion robots. The analysis presented in this paper can aid in designing eversion robots with different payload capabilities and lays the foundation for high payload eversion robots.

Acknowledgements. This work was supported in part by the EPSRC National Centre for Nuclear Robotics project (EP/R02572X/1), and the Innovate UK project WormBot (104059).

References

1. Shintake, J., Rosset, S., Schubert, B., Floreano, D., Shea, H.: Versatile soft grippers with intrinsic electroadhesion based on multifunctional polymer actuators. Adv. Mater. **28**, 231–238 (2015)
2. Godaba, H., Li, J., Wang, Y., Zhu, J.: A soft jellyfish robot driven by a dielectric elastomer actuator. IEEE Robot. Autom. Lett. **1**, 624–631 (2016)
3. Behl, M., Kratz, K., Noechel, U., Sauter, T., Lendlein, A.: Temperature-memory polymer actuators. Proc. Natl. Acad. Sci. **110**, 12555–12559 (2013)
4. Liu, Z., Calvert, P.: Multilayer hydrogels as muscle-like actuators. Adv. Mater. **12**, 288–291 (2000)

5. Althoefer, K.: Antagonistic actuation and stiffness control in soft inflatable robots. Nat. Rev. Mater. **3**, 76 (2018)
6. Shepherd, R.F., et al.: Multigait soft robot. Proc. Natl. Acad. Sci. **108**, 20400–20403 (2011)
7. Marchese, A.D., Katzschmann, R.K., Rus, D.: A recipe for soft fluidic elastomer robots. Soft Robot. **2**, 7–25 (2015)
8. Niiyama, R., Rus, D., Kim, S.: Pouch motors: printable/inflatable soft actuators for robotics. In: 2014 IEEE International Conference on Robotics and Automation (ICRA), pp. 6332–6337. IEEE (2014)
9. Liang, X., Cheong, H., Sun, Y., Guo, J., Chui, C.K., Yeow, C.-H.: Design, characterization, and implementation of a two-DOF fabric-based soft robotic arm. IEEE Robot. Autom. Lett. **3**, 2702–2709 (2018)
10. Li, J., Godaba, H., Zhang, Z.Q., Foo, C.C., Zhu, J.: A soft active origami robot. Extrem. Mech. Lett. **24**, 30–37 (2018)
11. Abrar, T., Putzu, F., Althoefer, K.: Soft wearable glove for tele-rehabilitation therapy of clenched hand/fingers patients. In: Workshop on Computer/Robot Assisted Surgery, London (2018)
12. Hawkes, E.W., Blumenschein, L.H., Greer, J.D., Okamura, A.M.: A soft robot that navigates its environment through growth. Sci. Robot. **2**, eaan3028 (2017)
13. Blumenschein, L.H., Gan, L.T., Fan, J.A., Okamura, A.M., Hawkes, E.W.: A tip-extending soft robot enables reconfigurable and deployable antennas. IEEE Robot. Autom. Lett. **3**, 949–956 (2018)
14. Naclerio, N.D., Hubicki, C.M., Aydin, Y.O., Goldman, D.I., Hawkes, E.W.: Soft robotic burrowing device with tip-extension and granular fluidization. In: 2018 IEEE/RSJ International Conference on Intelligent Robots and Systems (IROS), pp. 5918–5923. IEEE (2018)
15. Putzu, F., Abrar, T., Althoefer, K.: Plant-inspired soft pneumatic eversion robot. In: 2018 7th IEEE International Conference on Biomedical Robotics and Biomechatronics (Biorob), pp. 1327–1332. IEEE (2018)
16. Althoefer, K.A.: Neuro-fuzzy motion planning for robotic manipulators (1997)
17. Lockhart, J.A.: An analysis of irreversible plant cell elongation. J. Theor. Biol. **8**, 264–275 (1965)
18. Blumenschein, L.H., Okamura, A.M., Hawkes, E.W.: Modeling of bioinspired apical extension in a soft robot. In: Mangan, M., Cutkosky, M., Mura, A., Verschure, P.F.M.J., Prescott, T., Lepora, N. (eds.) Living Machines 2017. LNCS (LNAI), vol. 10384, pp. 522–531. Springer, Cham (2017). https://doi.org/10.1007/978-3-319-63537-8_45
19. Timoshenko, S.P., Gere, J.M.: Theory of Elastic Stability (1961)
20. Jordan, J.L., Casem, D.T., Bradley, J.M., Dwivedi, A.K., Brown, E.N., Jordan, C.W.: Mechanical properties of low density polyethylene. J. Dyn. Behav. Mater. **2**, 411–420 (2016)
21. Timoshenko, S.: Strength of Materials Part 1. D. Van Nostrand Co., Inc. (1940)
22. Le Van, A., Wielgosz, C.: Bending and buckling of inflatable beams: some new theoretical results. Thin-walled Struct. **43**, 1166–1187 (2005)
23. Cowper, G.R.: The shear coefficient in Timoshenko's beam theory. J. Appl. Mech. **33**, 335–340 (1966)
24. Comer, R.L., Levy, S.: Deflections of an inflated circular-cylindrical cantilever beam. AIAA J. **1**, 1652–1655 (1963)

The Impact of the Robot's Morphology in the Collective Transport

Jessica Meyer[(✉)]

Osnabrück University, Osnabrück, Germany
`jessy.meyer@gmail.com`

Abstract. The idea of this research is to evolve the shape of robots within a swarm, in order for them to work better as a whole. Small robots are not so powerful individually, but when cooperating with each other, by physically hooking together forming a larger organism for example, they may be able to solve more complex tasks. The shape each robot has influences the way they physically interact and, taking advantage of the morphological computation phenomenon, I show that evolving the robots' morphology in a swarm makes it more efficient for the task of transporting objects, even in comparison to evolving the robot's controller. In order to fulfill this objective, I have evolved the shape of arm-like structures for the robots' bodies and their controller separately, and compared the results with control experiments.

Keywords: Swarm robotics · Morphological evolution ·
Collective transport

1 Introduction

The idea of the research is to have small autonomous robots that work as a swarm and, if and when needed, they can physically cooperate in order to better perform the given task; this might be by physically interacting with each other to temporarily form a larger organism [13]. The robots should be able to evolve as a swarm for the task, therefore it was created the possibility of forming new body shapes for the individuals of the swarm such that when several robots physically interact their shapes are optimized for the collective, cooperative task.

The aim of this work is to demonstrate that the morphology of robots in charge of group transportation plays a vital role in their performance, and furthermore that a more complex body shape can assume part of the computation that would have to be attributed to the controller otherwise and even outperforms a more complex controller with simple morphology.

Two controllers were used in the experiments, the simpler one makes the robots move forwards and, if they exert enough force as a swarm, results in the pushing of any object placed in their way. The more complex controller has the behavior of attracting the robots to the object to be transported. On both controllers the interaction between the robots is solely due to the robots'

© Springer Nature Switzerland AG 2019
K. Althoefer et al. (Eds.): TAROS 2019, LNAI 11650, pp. 395–408, 2019.
https://doi.org/10.1007/978-3-030-25332-5_34

(a)   (b)   (c)

Fig. 1. (a), (b) Simulation of the e-pucks with their new evolved body parts (represented in blue) cooperating to push an object to a determined location. Being (a) one of the most successful morphology of the experiment with a simpler controller, (b) with a more complex controller and (c) the control experiment without arms. (Color figure online)

morphology. This way, part of the computation that the controller would have to perform - for example being aware of the other robots in the swarm and deliberately computing their interaction - is being attributed to the robot's body instead, taking advantage of the morphological computation phenomenon [17], in which it is suggested that controllers may be simpler, relying on their physical shapes [2] to compute more sophisticated interactions.

The morphological computation theory is relatively recent, and focuses on reducing computational effort or complexity in robots, by using their physical properties to generate and control behavior automatically [6]. The G. Dodig-Crnkovic's article argues that morphological computation is not simply an analogy or metaphor, but it is a computational model of physical reality.

In [1], Bongard remarks that researchers are starting to see intelligence as more than abstract algorithms, attributing it also to the physical properties of neurons and body. In embodied cognition the robot's physical shape is already being recognized as a major role player in its intelligence, and cannot be ignored.

Also [16] affirms that it has become increasingly evident that the morphology of a robot affects its control requirements, not only determining the possible behaviors as well as the amount of control required to perform them. The morphology plays even more important role when the robot's behavior is a direct result of the interaction of its body with the environment. As physical interactions result in computation, it is possible for the dynamics of the morphology to have a computational presence in the system, absorbing part of the control.

Several studies have been made in the area of swarm robotics transporting an object and the main reasons to study it are the low cost of manufacture, high robustness, high failure tolerance, and high flexibility, which are valuable properties desired in a robotic system [7]. Instead of using one powerful robot to transport the object, the task can be accomplished by the cooperation of a group of simple robots.

Deneubourg et al. [5] suggest that even though each robot could be simple and inefficient in itself, a swarm of these robots could show complex and efficient behaviors. They propose self-organized approaches in order to move objects in unpredictable environments.

Most of the research mentioned uses non-evolving robots behaving as a swarm to push a large object, most commonly controlled by a Finite State Machine or Neural Networks. None of the papers cited used Genetic Algorithms to evolve the body of the robots, some however did evolve the controller in order to optimize the swarm's performance for the given task.

In the experiments [3], Gross et al. used e-pucks to push a tall object to a specific target location. For that they position the robots around the object in a way that the robots would not be able to see the target. The robots keep moving to always be behind the object in relation to the target, so that if they push while in that position the object will move towards the target. Gross et al. used a Finite State Machine to control the robots, and there is no evolution either of the controller or of the robot's morphology.

Some papers from Dorigo and Gross on the other hand, use Neural Networks to control the robots for the task of pushing a large object collectively, usually shaping the network through artificial evolution, like in [7–9].

In the first case [8], they evolved neural networks to control two simple robots for the task of pulling or pushing a cylindrical object as far as possible in an arbitrary direction; with one of their main findings being about the density of robots around the object: increasing the weight of the object and the number of robots, reduced the performance, but increasing the weight, diameter and number of robots maintained the performance at around the same level, what was consistent with the research from [12].

In the second case [7], they use up to sixteen simple autonomous robots for the task of cooperative transporting heavy objects of different shapes and sizes. The robots are supposed to self-assemble into structures which pull or push the object towards a target location. One interesting characteristic of this research was that the controllers evolved for a small swarm could be applied to larger groups, making it possible to transport heavier objects.

On the latter case [9], they claim that group transport has become a canonical task in multi-robot systems for studying cooperation. They aim to investigate whether robots that are capable of self-assembling may overcome the lack of flexibility and scalability that limits the practical value of current group transport systems. In contrast to their previous work, the robots were provided with advanced acting and cognitive abilities and at the same time the neural network was allowed to exploit all aspects of these abilities. This strategy has as advantage that it places relatively few constraints on the evolved solutions, enabling a variety of complex group behaviors to emerge; the disadvantage being that the solution search space is relatively complex and large, making the evolutionary process very computationally demanding. Based on their findings, they suggested that these systems might benefit from a tight coupling between behavior and morphology, as also mentioned in [15, 17].

Their system performed what they considered fairly robustly with respect to the object's geometry and could cope well with sudden changes in the target location. In relation to the scalability it was shown that the system would be applicable to the transport of heavier objects by larger groups, but with loss of performance with the increase of the group size.

Considering the state of the art, between the two main approaches for the transport of objects by multi-robot systems, and since the controllers are meant to be untouched during the morphological evolution experiments, it was decided to use in this research Finite State Machine controllers. Given the proposed hypothesis, simple controllers will show clearly the differences between a swarm formed by the original robots and the ones formed by the robots with evolved morphology; besides, using Finite State Machine controllers are straightforward to distinguish their complexity by considering their number of states.

The experiments gather valuable data in the areas of evolutionary robotics and morphological computation, answering some pending questions. Both of these fields are gaining more ground recently and further research is needed to better establish them in the scientific community. Besides the crucial fact that they are both uncharted territory for swarm robotics with the collective transportation task.

The longer-term impact of the proposed research will be to open up the possibility of robots able to physically evolve and adapt themselves to be able to collectively operate in an unknown or changing environment without human intervention, like for instance in disaster scenarios or planetary exploration.

2   Research Setup

This section presents the tools selected and the environment modeled for the research.

2.1   Robots: E-pucks

The default e-pucks have no effectors other than its wheels [4], they are only capable of interacting with the environment by pushing objects around with their cylindrical bodies, making it difficult for them to interact with the surrounding environment and with other robots. With the proposed new body members - see Fig. 1, the e-pucks gain actual effectors, molded specifically to their needs, facilitating not only the interaction with a fellow robot but also with the whole surrounding world.

2.2   Simulation: Webots

The work in this paper has been conducted in simulation, using the well know multi-robot simulator Webots [4]. Webots already integrates the e-puck basic prototype, serving as a simulation software for programming, simulation and remote control of the real robots.

2.3   Scenario: Collective Transport

The idea of giving the e-pucks arm-like structures is to enable them to interact better with each other and with the environment surrounding them, making them more useful, giving them extra functionalities. The action of moving an object to another location creates the right opportunities to evaluate the robots and their new body parts, since they will undeniably use the arms to get in contact with the object, as can be seen in Fig. 1. And as [9] says, collective transport task has become a canonical task for studying cooperation in multi-agent systems. Hamann also states in [10] that collective transport is a good scenario for an actual swarm effect to appear, since a few robots may not be able to move certain object at all but crossing a threshold in the swarm size, the group can then move it for an unlimited distance.

2.4 Genetic Algorithm

With arm-like structures, the e-pucks are able to hook themselves together, combining their small bodies to form a larger structure, more suitable to solve certain tasks, like in the case of collective transportation. And, to find out how these new structures should be modeled, I designed a Genetic Algorithm to optimize these structures, based on the task the robots face. Therefore, the environment in which the robots find themselves in is what shapes their bodies, making them more able to perform the task with the passage of time.

A set of ten trials was conducted for each experiment, running for fifty generations. The swarm is composed of six robots and the population of ten genomes.

2.4.1 Genome

The choice of the parameters of the new body structure that are to be evolved tried to reflect nature's evolution. This way, the size of the arms and their number in the body are the most noticeable ones to vary and those variations should give perceptible behavior outcomes. The robot's arm is divided into fore and upper arms. As the arms are static, the position of the fore and upper arms should be predefined; and, also the amount of arms the robots should have. These are characteristics that commonly vary in animals. Therefore, the chosen parameters to be evolved are: the length of the forearm (lf), the length of the upper arm (lu), the angle between the fore and upper arms (a) and the number/position of arms (n), as illustrated in Fig. 2. These parameters form the genetic code - genome - of the robots responsible for their physical shapes.

For the behavioral evolution the idea is to evolve the parameters responsible for the transitions of the controller: the target color amount (tca), the middle size (ms), the time stuck (ts), the time reverse (tr) and the speed (s). The controller is presented in the next section.

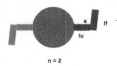

Fig. 2. Model of the e-puck showing the proposed parameters to be evolved.

2.4.2   Fitness

The fitness measure is the distance that the swarm is able to move the object from the original location in a determined amount of time. Since the only changes in the swarm between one simulation and the other is the robot's genotype, the difference of performance can be directly related to the genome used in the run.

In order to know how well the swarm was performing, a maximum fitness was estimated. The e-puck speed in the experiments of the simulation is 2.58 cm/s, each run lasts for 60 s, therefore, the object would not be able to be moved more than 1.55 m in this case. This is a perfect case scenario where the robots would push the object, moving at maximum speed for the whole duration of the run, what is clearly impossible to be reached as the robots are not positioned in contact with the object and need to run a certain distance before coming in contact with the target. This means the 100% fitness is unreachable, but this utopic maximum fitness allows the comparison between the experiments. The exact maximum fitness is unknown as it depends on several variables, not all being possible to be determined. The relative fitness is calculated as the percentage of the achieved fitness over the maximum fitness.

2.4.3   Selection

The population is ranked by fitness and the two best individuals are preserved, two are created through the crossover of the two best individuals, three are formed through a mutation of the three best individuals and three are formed through migration.

2.4.4   Mutation

In order to avoid the local maximum problem, a uniformly distributed random variation is set to form three individuals for the new population based on the three best individuals of the old population.

All the genes may suffer mutation, varying by a random factor between 0.85 and 1.15 of their original values for the morphological evolution and between 0.5 and 1.50 for the behavioral evolution.

The only exception is the gene related to the number/position of arms, which varies by randomly selecting one of the possible values.

2.4.5   Crossover

Two of the new genomes are formed by a crossover of the two best genomes from the population. It was chosen a uniform crossover with mixing ratio of 0.5, where all the genes are mixed. If the generated genomes are the same as the three best individuals or as the previous crossed over genome, then these two genomes are created by the mutation of the best individual instead.

2.4.6   Migration

Two of remaining three genomes of the new population are randomly chosen, by the same method the first population is aleatoryly formed. The last genome is formed by conserving the morphological genes of the best individual and randomly choosing the behavioral genes. This mechanism was introduced to mimic a migration, where new individuals are randomly introduced to the population, helping the avoidance of the local maximum.

3 Experiments

A set of experiments was made to prove the hypothesis, there was a control group where no evolution happened, a group that suffered behavioral evolution and a group that was exposed to morphological evolution. Co-evolution was also performed as part of a larger research.

3.1 Controllers

Two Finite State Machine controllers with different number of states were selected in an effort to show that a simpler controller with a better shaped robot can be more successful than a more complex controller with simpler shaped robots, even if their controller is being evolved. This assumption exploits the principle of morphological computation [19], which has not been tested in swarm robotics tasked with collective transport, to the best of my knowledge.

3.1.1 Forwards Walk
This is a trivial controller that sets the angular speed of both wheels at the beginning of the simulation, making the robots always move straight forward if they do not encounter any opposing force. In each following time step of the simulation, the robots do not receive any new command: they follow the original motor command until the simulation reaches its end. It is a Finite State Machine with only one state: *Forwards*.

3.1.2 Object Attraction
In this controller, the e-pucks are attracted to the object from the start of the fitness test.

In Fig. 3 the controller structure is represented as a Finite State Machine. As it can be seen, the controller starts checking how much of the target color the robots can see, to choose between a *searching* or a *following* behavior.

If in the *Search* state, the robot turns until it can find the object, but if it keeps turning for a certain amount of time there's a failsafe mechanism that makes it run backwards for some time - the *Backwards* state. This mechanism was designed to avoid the robots to get physically stuck to each other, making them change their behavior to facilitate them get untangled; nevertheless it showed itself to be useful for the search state as well, since it changes the proximity of the robots to the object enabling them to get the object back into view distance in some situations. Once the e-puck can see the object, it changes to the *Follow* state.

The *Follow* state is divided into three different sub-states according to the position of the object on the robot's vision field. If the object is on the robot's left, the robot should turn *Left* by stopping the movement of the left wheel; if the object is on the robot's right, the robot should turn *Right* by stopping the movement of the right wheel; and if the object is the middle of the robot's vision field, then the robot should go *Forwards* toward the object.

If the robot repeats an action for a certain amount of time though, besides going forwards, the backwards mechanism is activated as a failsafe device, making the robot enter the *Backwards* state.

Once the robot loses the object from sight it returns to the *Search* state.

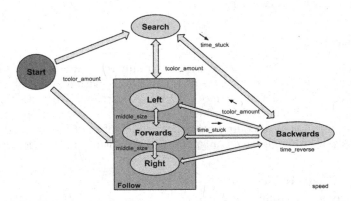

Fig. 3. Finite State Machine of the most complex controller, showing the states, transitions and their conditions.

3.2 Results

The experiments demonstrate that different robot's shapes result in different performance of the swarm, being possible to optimize the robot's morphology to increase the swarm fitness. As far as I am aware, this is the first time morphological evolution has been used to optimize swarms with an object transportation task.

3.2.1 No Arms with Simpler Controller
This is the control group which uses the *Forward Walk* controller, the simplest of the two presented.

As can be seen in Table 1, the best averaged individual and the averaged population from this experiment had fitness of 21.03%, both 4.5% less effective than the control group with more complex controller, with probability of it being due to chance of only 3E-121% according to the Student's t-Test. This means that the control experiment with the more complex controller performed better than with the simpler controller, the opposite of what is seen with the morphological evolution experiments, where the one with simpler controller performed better than the one with more complex controller.

This is believed to be because the most efficient controller for robots with more complex morphology would be the one that makes the robots move less (increasing the occurrence of the Forwards state and decreasing of the other states), since it would mean that the robots need to spend less time and energy with positioning themselves to push the object and more time actually pushing the object. The morphology evolves to a shape that makes the robots act as a single organism, connecting themselves with each other as soon as possible in order to move forwards the most they can, combining their forces in one direction, as seen in Figs. 1(a) and (b). The simpler controller already makes the robots go Forwards all of the time, and the morphological evolution steps in to make the robot's shape also efficient for that controller, resulting in a good combination. For robots without arms, there is no morphological enhancement, so the robots cannot work as a single organism and end up needing more position adjustments to better transport the object - hence the more complex controller being more effective for this case. Therefore, it is concluded that a more complex morphology performs better (Table 1) as it reduces the need for a more complex controller, exploiting instead the morphological computation phenomenon.

3.2.2   No Arms with More Complex Controller

In order to compare how much morphological evolution improved the original swarm and if a more complex controller with a simple morphology would perform better than a simpler controller with a more complex morphology, a set of experiments was run with the robots not having any arms - their original morphology - and with no evolution. This is the control group that uses the *Object Attraction* controller, which is the most complex of the two presented.

Comparing the data on Table 1, it is seen that the evolution of the morphology increased the performance of the swarm in both cases: with the more complex controller and even with the simpler one, being possible to confirm the advantages of the morphological evolution for the group transport task.

The Student's t-Test also corroborates that the difference of the best averaged fitness between this experiment without arms is statistically relevant compared to all other experiments that have been made with morphological evolution; therefore, the null hypothesis should be rejected in those cases, since the probability of it being due to chance being smaller than 0.05%.

As there is no evolution in these control experiments, the fitness remains the same for all of the runs, generating a fitness graphics that is represented by a constant horizontal line at 25.53% in this case, as it can be seen in Fig. 4.

In Fig. 1(c), it is possible to see that the e-pucks without arms surround the object wasting their forces as their vectors are not combined into the same direction as happens with evolved arms. In Figs. 1(a) and (b), the resulting morphology ensures that all robots point in the same direction, increasing the resulting force and, consequently, improving their performance.

3.2.3 No Arms with Evolvable Controller

For the swarm without arms, a behavioral evolution was able to improve their performance in 9.48% from the swarm with the more complex controller and 13.98% in comparison to the swarm with the simpler controller. Therefore, the controller evolution alone increased the fitness of the original shaped swarm in 11.73%, considering both tested controllers. This is a significant improvement, but between the morphological evolution and the controller evolution, the morphological evolution was able to reach circa six times better results, having the biggest impact in the swarm.

In Fig. 4, it is possible to see the constant fitness growth of this experiment throughout the generations.

3.2.4 Evolvable Morphology with Simpler Controller

The four genes - as in Fig. 2 - are being simultaneously evolved and the robots are using the *Forwards Walk* controller, outlined in the previous subsection.

This controller, although simple, resulted in a good fitness for the averaged best individual - average of ten trials of the generation with best fitness - with 90.85% of efficacy on pushing the object, as seen on Table 1.

Figure 4 shows an initial fast increase of fitness, with smooth convergence throughout evolution, where the fitness was improved at every generation, but slowed down at the end. This indicates that if the evolution continued further, the fitness could be increased even more, but was already getting closer to its peak.

The evolved shape of the robots converged to four long arms with acute angle between fore and upper arms, as can be seen in Fig. 1(a).

3.2.5 Evolvable Morphology with More Complex Controller

The four genes - as in Fig. 2 - are being simultaneously evolved and the robots are using the *Object Attraction* controller, where they use vision to look for the object and move towards it.

This more complex controller resulted also in a good fitness, with the averaged best individual very close to the previous experiment with 89.55% of efficacy, as seen on Table 1. The population fitness was slightly lower though with 71.80% of efficacy, a decrease of 4.36% compared to the one with simpler controller. Even though the difference between their best individual was only of 1.30%, it is statistically significant according to the Student's t-Test, with only 0.0004% that it was due to chance.

Figure 4 shows an excellent convergence rate, with the fitness improving at most of the generations and having a smooth convergence. This indicates that if the evolution continued further, the fitness could also be increased, though convergence rate was slowing down getting closer to its peak.

The evolved shape of the robots converged to four long arms with obtuse angle between fore and upper arms, as can be seen in Fig. 1(b).

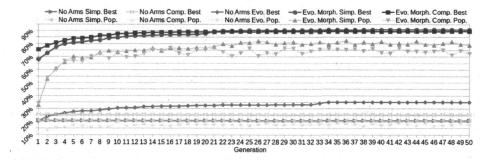

Fig. 4. Fitness graphics of the experiments for both best individual and population.

Table 1. Fitness values of the experiments for both best individual and population.

No.	Experiment	Best ind.	Pop. avg.
3.2.1	No Arms Simple	21.03%	21.03%
3.2.2	No Arms Complex	25.53%	25.52%
3.2.3	No Arms Evolvable	35.01%	17.39%
3.2.4	Evo. Morph. Simple	90.85%	76.16%
3.2.5	Evo. Morph. Complex	89.55%	71.80%

4   Conclusions

It was expected that the robot's morphology would impact on the performance of
the swarm, and that the morphology could then be improved through evolution.
Given the obtained results, it is shown for the first time that the evolution of
the robot's shape can improve the swarm performance for the task of collective
transport. The robots in their original shape performed worse than the robots
with an evolved morphology, independently of the controller's complexity.

The experiments show that the complexity of the controller can be decreased
(3.2.5 to 3.2.4) and still achieve good results if there is morphological evolution,
thus exploiting the morphological computation phenomenon in the transport
of objects by multi-robot systems. A more complex controller with a simple
morphology (3.2.2 and 3.2.3) does not perform as well as a simpler controller
with an evolvable morphology (3.2.4).

It was observed that the evolved robots act as a single organism, they connect
with each other almost instantly and combine their forces in the most efficient
way, i.e. without creating opposing forces within the swarm. The arms facilitate
the connection with the object, making one of the robots touch it, while the
other robots connect with one another pushing in unison in the same direction,
thus increasing their performance. The morphological evolution was responsible for most of the improvements, with the robots performing better due to

the morphological computation. The hypothesized computational savings in the controllers open up possibilities for new improvements in the robot's minds that would not be possible otherwise.

Furthermore, the Morphological Evolution (3.2.4 and 3.2.5) had a greater impact in the optimization of the swarm than the Behavioral Evolution (3.2.3).

5   Future Work

It would be possible to implement an even more advanced version of the controller, where the robots would communicate with each other. This new approach would increase the controller's complexity and would give interesting new insights in the swarm cooperation.

An instantiation of the experiments into the real world would be straightforward, there is a simple interface between Webots and the MakerBot 3D printer and the transfer of the robot's controller from Webots to the real robots is direct.

In order to save time, there is also a possibility of using a high definition 3D printer to pre-print several arm shapes that could be attached to the robots body as Lego® pieces. I have already done some work towards it and a prototype set of the arms was printed as seen in the pictures 5(a), (b) and (c).

(a)   **(b)**   **(c)**

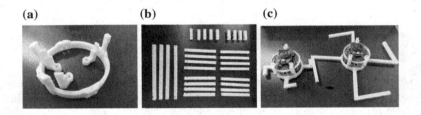

Fig. 5. (a), (b), (c) Arms printed by an HD 3D printer.

In the future, with High-Performance Computing (HPC) more available, the processing of the evolution could be run in parallel in simulation, being inspired by Surrogate Models [11], in a continual adaptive process. Controller, morphology and simulation could be co-evolved to address a reality gap between the real world and the simulator [14]. This way, the real robots would be able to adapt to the unforeseen scenarios almost immediately, making them susceptible to evolution in an accelerated pace. It would give the robots a way to predict what could happen and therefore better prepare themselves. A combined technique setup like this could give the robots a sense of ethics as they could simulate the outcome before acting [18], being able to know if their actions would be safe for humans, acquiring what could be called the first steps towards a conscience. The combination of this research with HPC and these new techniques would make the robots as real as they could get while not being biologically alive. They would be able to predict, reflect, adapt, evolve their entire selves, not only based on nature, but faster.

References

1. Bongard, J.: Embodied cognition: the other morphology. Neuromorphic Eng. (2008). https://doi.org/10.2417/1200812.1420
2. Bongard, J.: Taking a biologically inspired approach to the design of autonomous, adaptive machines. Commun. ACM **56**(8), 74–83 (2013). https://doi.org/10.1145/2493883
3. Chen, J., Gauci, M., Groß, R.: A strategy for transporting tall objects with a swarm of miniature mobile robots. In: IEEE International Conference on Robotics and Automation (ICRA), pp. 863–869 (2013). https://doi.org/10.1109/ICRA.2013.6630674
4. Cyberbotics Ltd., Michel, O., Rohrer, F., Heiniger, N., Wikibooks Contributors: Cyberbotics' Robot Curriculum. Wikibooks (2010)
5. Deneubourg, J., Goss, S., Sandini, G., Ferrari, F., Dario, P.: Self-organizing collection and transport of objects in unpredictable environments. In: Japan-USA Symposium on Flexible Automation, pp. 1093–1098 (1990)
6. Dodig-Crnkovic, G.: The info-computational nature of morphological computing. In: Müller, V. (ed.) Philosophy and Theory of Artificial Intelligence, vol. 5, pp. 59–68. Springer, Heidelberg (2013). https://doi.org/10.1007/978-3-642-31674-6_5
7. Groß, R., Dorigo, M.: Cooperative transport of objects of different shapes and sizes. In: Dorigo, M., Birattari, M., Blum, C., Gambardella, L.M., Mondada, F., Stützle, T. (eds.) ANTS 2004. LNCS, vol. 3172, pp. 106–117. Springer, Heidelberg (2004). https://doi.org/10.1007/978-3-540-28646-2_10
8. Groß, R., Dorigo, M.: Evolving a cooperative transport behavior for two simple robots. In: Liardet, P., Collet, P., Fonlupt, C., Lutton, E., Schoenauer, M. (eds.) EA 2003. LNCS, vol. 2936, pp. 305–316. Springer, Heidelberg (2004). https://doi.org/10.1007/978-3-540-24621-3_25
9. Groß, R., Dorigo, M.: Towards group transport by swarms of robots. Int. J. Bio-Inspired Comput. **1**(1/2), 1–13 (2009). https://doi.org/10.1504/IJBIC.2009.022770
10. Hamann, H.: Swarm Robotics: A Formal Approach. Springer, Cham (2018). https://doi.org/10.1007/978-3-319-74528-2
11. Jin, Y.: Surrogate-assisted evolutionary computation: recent advances and future challenges. Swarm Evol. Comput. **1**, 61–70 (2006). https://doi.org/10.1016/j.swevo.2011.05.001
12. Kube, C., Bonabeau, E.: Cooperative transport by ants and robots. Robot. Auton. Syst. **30**, 85–101 (2000). https://doi.org/10.1016/S0921-8890(99)00066-4
13. Levi, P., Kernbach, S. (eds.): Symbiotic Multi-Robot Organisms: Reliability, Adaptability Evolution. Springer, Heidelberg (2010). https://doi.org/10.1007/978-3-642-11692-6
14. O'Dowd, P., Winfield, A., Studley, M.: The distributed co-evolution of an embodied simulator and controller for adaptive swarm behaviours. In: IEEE/RSJ International Conference on Intelligent Robots and Systems (IROS), pp. 4995–5000 (2011). https://doi.org/10.1109/IROS.2011.6094600
15. O'Grady, R., Groß, R., Christensen, A.: Performance benefits of self-assembly in a swarm-bot. In: IEEE/RSJ International Conference on Intelligent Robots and Systems (IROS), pp. 2381–2387 (2007). https://doi.org/10.1109/IROS.2007.4399424
16. Paul, C.: Morphological computation - a basis for the analysis of morphology and control requirements. Robot. Auton. Syst. **54**, 619–630 (2006). https://doi.org/10.1016/j.robot.2006.03.003

17. Pfeifer, R., Bongard, J.: How the Body Shapes the Way We Think: A New View of Intelligence. The MIT Press (2006). https://doi.org/10.7551/mitpress/3585.001. 0001
18. Winfield, A.F.T., Blum, C., Liu, W.: Towards an ethical robot: internal models, consequences and ethical action selection. In: Mistry, M., Leonardis, A., Witkowski, M., Melhuish, C. (eds.) TAROS 2014. LNCS (LNAI), vol. 8717, pp. 85–96. Springer, Cham (2014). https://doi.org/10.1007/978-3-319-10401-0_8
19. Zambrano, D., Cianchetti, M., Laschi, C.: The morphological computation principles as a new paradigm for robotic design. In: Opinions and Outlooks on Morphological Computation, Chap. 19, pp. 214–225 (2014). https://doi.org/10.13140/2.1. 1059.4242

System Design and Control
of a Di-Wheel Rover

John Koleosho$^{(\boxtimes)}$ and Chakravarthini M. Saaj

Surrey Space Centre, Department of Electrical and Electronic Engineering,
University of Surrey, Guildford, Surrey GU2 7XH, UK
john.koleosho@hotmail.co.uk, c.saaj@surrey.ac.uk

Abstract. Traditionally, wheeled rovers are used for planetary surface exploration and six-wheeled chassis designs based on the Rocker-Bogie suspension system have been tested successfully on Mars. However, it is difficult to explore craters and crevasses using large six or four-wheeled rovers. Innovative designs based on smaller Di-Wheel Rovers might be better suited for such challenging terrains. A Di-Wheel Rover is a self - balancing two-wheeled mobile robot that can move in all directions within a two-dimensional plane, as well as stand upright by balancing on two wheels.

This paper presents the outcomes of a feasibility study on a Di-Wheel Rover for planetary exploration missions. This includes developing its chassis design based on the hardware and software requirements, prototyping, and subsequent testing. The main contribution of this paper is the design of a self-balancing control system for the Di-Wheel Rover. This challenging design exercise was successfully completed through extensive experimentation thereby validating the performance of the Di-Wheel Rover. The details on the structural design, tuning controller gains based on an inverted pendulum model, and testing on different ground surfaces are described in this paper. The results presented in this paper give a new insight into designing low-cost Di-Wheel Rovers and clearly, there is a potential to use Di-Wheel Rovers for future planetary exploration.

Keywords: Di-Wheel rover · Inverted pendulum · Control system ·
Planetary exploration

1 Introduction

Robotics and Autonomous Systems (RAS), and Space Engineering are listed amongst the eight great technologies announced by the UK government [1]. One of the interesting applications discussed within the theme of RAS for extreme and challenging environments is planetary exploration. A well-designed rover is key to the success of any planetary exploration mission as the rover is expected to traverse rugged and unknown terrains with minimal inputs from the ground station. Rover chassis designs may include multi-legged systems (e.g. the Ambler legged robot [2]), multi-wheeled rovers (e.g. the Mars Sojourner, Spirit, Opportunity, Curiosity rovers [3]), or mono-wheeled rovers (e.g. the Gyrover [4]).

© Springer Nature Switzerland AG 2019
K. Althoefer et al. (Eds.): TAROS 2019, LNAI 11650, pp. 409–421, 2019.
https://doi.org/10.1007/978-3-030-25332-5_35

Commonly used planetary exploration rovers are ones consisting of multiple wheels. The Mars Sojourner rover which landed on Mars, in July 1997, adopted a chassis structure made up of six wheels [3]. Although this micro-rover mission was successful, the follow-on missions (e.g. NASA's Spirit, Opportunity and Curiosity rovers) were all based on larger multi-wheeled mobility systems. However, conventional large rovers have inherent limitations in traversing steep craters and crevasses [5]. Thus, there is a rise in interest to design agile micro-rovers to explore such challenging terrains that are otherwise inaccessible to larger rovers [6].

The field of terrestrial wheeled mobile robots is far more advanced than its Space counterpart. In addition to the advancements in the field of multi-wheeled robots, there are various interesting developments in the field of Di-Wheeled robots for terrestrial applications. A dynamically-stabilized Di-Wheeled scooter, capable of being ridden by a single person at speeds of up to 20 km/h, and a robotic platform have been patented by DEKA Products, Manchester, New Hampshire, USA, and are being marketed commercially by Segway Inc, Delaware [7]. These products are shown in Fig. 1. The stabilization system uses a solid-state angular rate sensor. These vehicles are not fitted with any form of suspension and rely on tyre pressure to provide ride comfort. More recently, successful cross-country trials have been conducted with the manned version of the vehicle fitted with resilient-rimmed, solid-tyre wheels, which have been jointly developed by JPL and Michelin. However, adapting this technology for designing a two-wheeled micro-rover for planetary exploration is not a straight forward exercise.

(a)   (b)

Fig. 1. The commercially-available gyro-stabilized Di-Wheeled scooter and platform: (a) Segway cross-country explorer [7], (b) Segway robotic mobility platform.

In recent years, there have not been many well-known planetary rovers that have adopted a two-wheeled structure. One two-wheeled rover that has been developed for lunar exploration is the JALURO lunar robot developed within a lunar competition [8]. This rover, however, has its chassis underslung between its wheels, which allows for immediate static stability, and has independently controlled motors useful for drive and steering manoeuvres. This rover is shown in Fig. 2.

This paper looks specifically into the design engineering aspects and control of a two-wheeled micro-rover (i.e. a Di-Wheel Rover) that adopts an overhead chassis

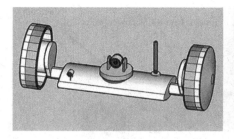

Fig. 2. JALURO Lunar robot by Team FREDNET: (a) CAD Model [8] (b) Prototype designed for the Google Lunar X Prize competition.

structure. With an overhead chassis, the Di-Wheel Rover has no immediate static stability, however, its onboard chassis components are less prone to crashing into obstacles due to higher ground clearance.

Seeing as there is no immediate static stability with the Di-Wheel Rover discussed in this paper, the engineering problem of obtaining a statically stable rover in its vertically upright position is an important part of the control of the Di-Wheel Rover. Given that the rover can only tilt and fall in the forward or backward directions (i.e. in one-plane), this problem can be modelled using the two-dimensional inverted pendulum model. An example of this model can be found in citation [9].

The overhead chassis of the rover represents the pendulum by being the part of the rover that is free to tilt/fall in the fore/aft directions. The DC motors represent the big wheels located at the bottom of the structure. The DC motors move the overall rover forwards or backwards, which counteracts any possible tilting thereby allowing for a statically stable rover in its vertical position. This paper is organised as follows: Sect. 2 includes an extensive design engineering exercise that shows the evolution of the Di-Wheel Rover chassis structure and its prototypes. More details on experimental testing, validation and simulation-based analysis are presented in Sect. 3, followed by concluding remarks in Sect. 4.

2   Chassis Design of Di-Wheel Rover

The design engineering exercise for developing the chassis structure went through several iterations and the different views of the Di-Wheel Rover's structure can be seen in Figs. 3 and 4. A well-designed Di-Wheel Rover will have the ability to self-balance, and move in all directions in the two-dimensional frame, (i.e. forwards, backwards, left, and right). Although the Di-Wheel Rover movement is controlled by a wireless remote, shown in Fig. 4(a), the self-balancing feature of the rover is automated.

The Di-Wheel Rover consists of four different sub-systems which are as follows: the Drive sub-system, the Steering Control sub-system, the Wireless Communication sub-system, and the Balancing Control sub-system. Figure 5 shows the sub-system layout for all the rover's onboard sub-systems. The HC-05 and L298 N refer to the Bluetooth modules used, and the motor module used respectively.

412   J. Koleosho and C. M. Saaj

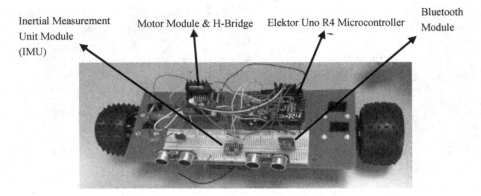

Fig. 3. Overall structure of the Di-Wheel Rover prototype.

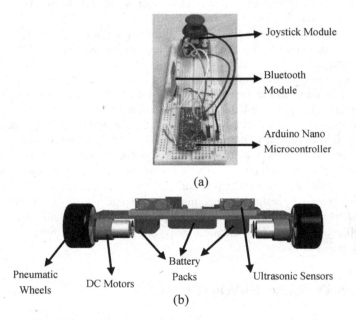

Fig. 4. Extra Di-Wheel Rover components: (a) remote controller (b) annotated CAD model of the Di-Wheel Rover showing components under the frame.

This Di-Wheel Rover prototype has its wheels positioned horizontally beside each other, taking on-board a similar structure to a Segway [7]. The wheels used are pneumatic wheels with rubber spikes located on its surface area; this is used to provide extra friction for the tyres. These tyres are controlled by normal brushless DC motors with a rated speed of 320 rpm.

The Balancing Control sub-system proved to be the most challenging sub-system to implement. This is because it involved implementing and adapting the same concepts used in the inverted pendulum model to different operating conditions such as different floor surfaces, and different voltage-level outputs from the batteries (i.e. power supply).

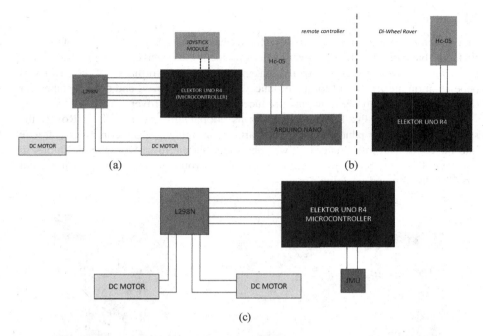

Fig. 5. Di-Wheel Rover sub-system layouts: (a) Drive and Steering Control sub-system, (b) Wireless Communications sub-system, (c) Balancing Control sub-system.

3 Experimental Analysis and Results

This section of the paper discusses in detail the key experiments undertaken within this study, the results, and the validations made from subsequent testing. In-depth experimentation was mainly done on the Balancing Control sub-system of the Di-Wheel Rover. A Proportional-Derivative (PD) controller was designed for balancing this Di-Wheel Rover, however, a Proportional (P) controller was designed and used for experimentation purposes. The control signal is fed to the actuators based on the error signal; in this case, the microcontroller will be sending Pulse-Width Modulation (PWM) signals to the DC motors (i.e. the actuators) via an H-bridge circuit and based on the magnitude of the error signal. In this way, the actuators will move at the correct speed and direction in order to maintain good balancing performance and a stable Di-Wheel Rover.

3.1   Structural Analysis

The structure of the Di-Wheel Rover chassis has been a key feature in obtaining a perfectly balanced Di-Wheel Rover. After conducting extensive testing with different physical structures, it was discovered that the balancing performance of the rover was dependent on the amount of torque produced by the tilting rover, and the time taken for the motors to react to the moments produced by the tilting rover.

Figure 6 shows the first structural forms adopted by the Di-Wheel Rover; the spacing between the panels are 12 cm apart. Upon uploading the controller software into the rover with this structure, it was observed that the rover would avoid falling to the ground for only roughly two seconds. The rover would attempt to balance itself, but would generally end up falling over.

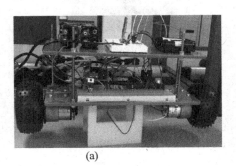

(a)   (b)

Fig. 6. First structural forms of the Di-Wheel Rover (a) Rover Structure with batteries on the top panel; (b) Rover structure with batteries on the bottom panel.

The conclusion drawn about this structure, in reference to the points mentioned above, is that the rover's motors could not react quickly enough to the tilting effects of the rover with the given moment (turning force about the centre of the wheel) provided by this structural form. Due to the constant height of the rover with this particular structure, there is a specific moment attached to it. It is important to note that the moment value actually changes dynamically as the rover falls or rises; as the rover is falling/tilting the moment of the rover about the wheels increases.

The amount of torque produced by the DC motors was compatible with the magnitude of the moment (turning force) produced by the rover about its wheels when tilting, however, the DC motors could not provide the required torque for the rover quickly enough when it initially starts to tilt. As a result, the rover begins to tilt more, which in turn increases the tilting moment (turning force) of the rover about its wheels. At this point, the turning force of the rover becomes so high that it becomes incompatible with the torque (turning force) produced by the rover's DC motors.

In order to give the rover more time to react to the initial and slow tilts it makes, a tall Di-Wheel Rover structure, which takes longer to fall over, was experimented on. This is shown in Fig. 7(a). The spacing between the panels for this structure is 50 cm.

Upon uploading the controller software into the rover with this structure, it was observed that the smallest displacement of the rover about its vertical position would result in the rover tilting and falling over. The experimental results with this structure showed no reactions to the rover tilting whatsoever.

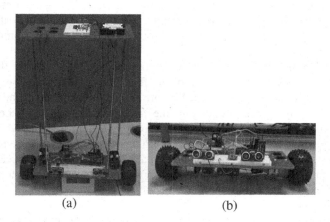

(a)   (b)

Fig. 7. Alternative structural forms of the Di-Wheel Rover (a) Tall structure (b) Flat structure

The conclusion drawn from this Di-Wheel Rover structure was that the motors could not provide the sufficient torque needed for the rover to react to itself tilting and therefore keep itself from falling over. Effectively the new distance between the pivot point of the rover (i.e. the centre of the wheels) and the tallest part of the rover is over 50 cm. This new height creates a much bigger moment (turning force) when the rover is tilting, which therefore means that much more torque is required from the motors in order to balance out the magnitude of the tilting moments and thereby make the rover stable in an upright and vertical position.

This led to adopting a Di-Wheel Rover structure with a shorter height and lower weight, as it was also predicted that a Di-Wheel Rover with a lower weight could increase the time needed for the motors to react. From these predictions, the Di-Wheel Rover structure shown in Fig. 7(b) was constructed and further experimented on. This shows the evolution of the structure previously introduced in Fig. 3 and it is the successful structure used for the Di-Wheel Rover in this paper.

Upon uploading the controller software into the Di-Wheel Rover in Fig. 7(b), it was noticed that the rover never fell to the ground. If the rover tilts in one direction (e.g. forwards), the motors would instantly move the rover in the forward direction in order to act against the forward tilt. The same process applied for the backward tilt that the rover had made. As a result, the rover with this structure swung forwards and backwards infinitely, and it never fell to the ground. The infinite swinging of the rover is explained through the proportional controller software, which was initially uploaded to the rover. With this structure, the motors were able to provide the torque required to act against the tilting rover and were also able to provide this torque in good time which ensured a quick reaction time for the rover when it began to tilt.

3.2 Controller Type

Once the correct Di-Wheel Rover structure was obtained, the other major experiment carried out with the Di-Wheel Rover involved assessing the controller used within the microcontroller. The types of controller that were implemented for this study were P- Proportional gain controller and PD- Proportional Derivative gain controller. Software for these controllers was constructed in the Arduino IDE and was written in C++. They were then uploaded to the Arduino microcontroller, via a serial communications port available within the PC.

PID-Proportional Integral and Derivative controller was not used in this study as the I-Integral gain was purposefully avoided. The integral gain has the property of reducing steady-state error to zero, which in turn decreases the speed of the controller's response [10]. Applying this property to the rover would mean that the rover will undergo increased fore/aft oscillations until the displacement from the vertical axis is precisely at zero degrees. Being precisely at zero degrees is not a major requirement, as the rover can still be stationary and stable with a tolerance of ±2°. A quicker response is more important than the accuracy of the rover's angular position, which makes using the I-Integral gain less favourable as they are known to reduce the speed of the controller's response.

The P-Proportional gain controller was the first controller that was experimented on during extensive testing of the Balance Control sub-system. By using this controller, the resulting motion of the Di-Wheel Rover involved a constant swinging of the Di-Wheel Rover in the fore/aft directions. This is the same movement discussed in the latter part of the Structural Analysis section of this paper (i.e. the part referring to the flat single layer structure of the Di-Wheel Rover). A graphical illustration of the movement can be seen in Fig. 8.

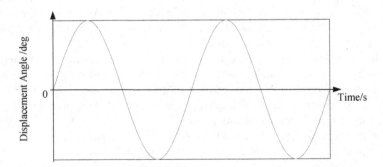

Fig. 8. Graphical representation of Rover movement with only a P-controller

A system which only uses a P-Proportional gain controller with the appropriate gains will reach stability due to the size of the oscillations being big enough to keep the system stable, i.e. keep the rover from falling over in this case. However, the system will never reach a steady state condition, which is what is seen by the rover constantly swinging in the fore/aft directions and not being able to stand and remain still.

By carrying out extensive tests on the Balancing Control sub-system using the PD-Proportional-Derivative controller, the motion of the Di-Wheel Rover resulted in some initial oscillations, which then reduced over time. After some time had passed, the oscillations ceased to exist and the Di-Wheel Rover stood in an upright position that had a slight offset to the vertical axis. Occasionally when the offset was too big, the rover would slip back into oscillating again, however, it then soon came to a standstill with much less of an offset than its previous standstill state. A graphical illustration of this phenomenon can be seen in Fig. 9. The result obtained with this controller is the desired outcome required for the Di-Wheel Rover. This controller has a relatively quick response time and it performs well in having the rover reach a steady state with a slight error in the vertical position.

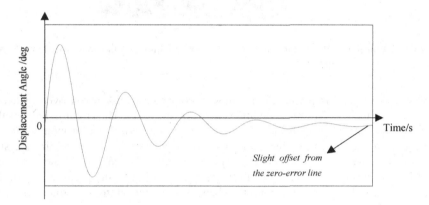

Fig. 9. Graphical representation of Rover movement with a PD controller

3.3 Ground Surfaces

Once the structure and the controller type for the Di-Wheel Rover were selected, a fully self-balancing Di-Wheel Rover was obtained, however different performances of the balancing action were observed with different ground/floor surfaces.

Experimentation of the Di-Wheel Rover was undertaken on three different ground surfaces shown in Fig. 10. One surface consisting of relatively thick carpet, one surface consisting of fairly light carpet, and one surface which was made out of smooth lino. After obtaining a Di-Wheel Rover capable of self-balancing, the rover was tested on these three ground surfaces and the resulting self-balancing motion was compared for each ground surface.

The resulting self-balancing motion proved to be most stable (i.e. reduced oscillation amplitude) on the thick carpet, and the steady state condition (i.e. the rover being able to stand still and upright), was achieved the quickest on thick carpet. This was followed by light carpet ground and then followed by smooth lino where the self-balancing motion was least stable and it took the longest time for the Di-Wheel Rover to reach a steady state.

Fig. 10. Di-Wheel Rover on different floor surfaces (a) Smooth Lino floor (b) lightly-dense carpet floor (c) thick carpet floor.

The thick carpet ground applied the most friction to the Di-Wheel Rover's wheels, which reduces the speed of the oscillations made by the rover. This, in turn, reduces the size of the oscillations, which improves its stability and steady-state response. On the other hand, smooth ground surfaces will have the opposite effect by increasing the size of the oscillations, due to less friction, thereby reducing the stability of the rover.

The most important inference from this experiment is that the performance of the Balancing Control system varies with the changes in the wheel-ground contact friction.

3.4   Electrical Characteristics

During this study, experimentation was carried out in order to observe the behaviour of key quantities such as the DC motor current, DC motor voltage and the DC motor rpm. Two sets of tests were carried out in order to observe the electrical behaviour when using fully charged new batteries, and partly-charged batteries. The results in Fig. 11 were based on a healthy battery supply voltage of 12 V to the DC motors.

The PWM signals are basically numbers ranging between 0–255. They determine how much voltage is supplied to the DC Motors. The higher the PWM signal, the higher the voltage across the DC motors due to the linear relationship existing between these two quantities.

From Fig. 11(a), it can be seen that the overall current through the DC motors increases as the PWM signals increase. These two quantities possess a linear relationship up to a PWM value of 100 and thereafter, the current starts to saturate; this shows that the biggest change in current takes place at PWM values below 100. The graph in Fig. 11(a) takes a very similar shape to the graph in Fig. 11(b), which is the variation of motor speed vs PWM signals. From this similarity, it can be deduced that the current through the DC motors and rpm of the motors share a linear relationship. In practice, the maximum rpm value obtained from the DC motors is just below 250, as seen in Fig. 11 (b); this is different to the rated value of the DC motors which is 320 rpm.

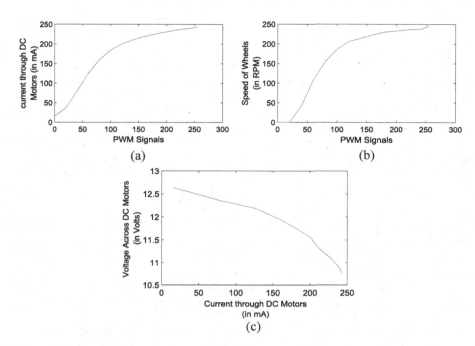

Fig. 11. Fully charged batteries: graphs showing the relationship between (a) DC Motor Current vs PWM signal value (b) Wheel Speed vs PWM value (c) Voltage across DC Motors vs Current through DC Motors

Figure 11(c) shows the voltage variation across the DC motors as the current through them increases. From this graph, we see that the voltage drop across the DC motors is roughly 1.9 V when the maximum current is drawn from the batteries and fed through the DC motors. The relatively small voltage drop shows that a high voltage of roughly 11 V–12 V, required for the optimum performance of the DC motors, is still obtainable with high current. The result proves that a good electrical performance is obtained with new healthy batteries.

The graphs in Fig. 12 show the electrical characteristics of the Di-Wheel Rover when using old and worn out batteries. The voltage supplied to the DC motors from these batteries is only 8.6 V. The experiment which investigated the rpm of the wheels with respect to the PWM signals could not be carried out, with this voltage, due to the rpm of the wheels being too slow to be detected accurately by the available tachometers.

From Fig. 12(a), it is observed that the maximum current obtained through the DC motors is roughly 160 mA, which is significantly less than the 240 mA obtained with healthy batteries. It is also interesting to note that the current through the DC motors start to drop as the PWM signals increase beyond the value of 180, which is after the current is saturated. From this, it can be deduced that current drawn from old and used

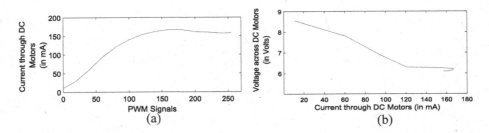

Fig. 12. Partially charged batteries: graphs showing the relationship between (a) Current through DC Motors vs PWM value (b) Voltage Across DC Motors vs Current through DC Motors.

batteries can only be increased to a specific value, in this case, this value is roughly 160 mA. Trying to increase the current beyond this value will end up in reduced current drawn from the DC motors. This is a different case with new batteries, which keeps the maximum current drawn at its value.

As evident from Fig. 12(b), the voltage drop across the DC motors is slightly higher (~ 2.5 V) with older batteries than with new batteries (~ 1.9 V) as the current increases. With older batteries this voltage drop happens for low increases of current, e.g. in Fig. 12(b), the most change/drop in voltage takes place when the current is increased to only 120 mA. This differs from the prolonged voltage drop/change seen with new batteries which completes the voltage drop when the current is increased to roughly 240 mA. This shows the incapability of older batteries to provide sufficient current for the DC motors when they require higher current (i.e. when higher motoring speeds are required).

It is also interesting to note from Fig. 12(b) that when the current starts decreasing from its maximum point, the voltage decreases which gives a fold-back effect in the graph. It can be deduced that this is due to the reduced power the old batteries are capable of supplying.

4   Conclusions

In this paper, the design engineering of a Di-Wheel Rover and its sub-systems are addressed. The different structural designs, useful for the Balancing Control of the rover, have been evaluated to optimise its chassis design. The self-balancing controller design has also been evaluated, along with a preliminary assessment on indoor ground surfaces which best optimise Di-Wheel Rover performance. The electrical characteristics of the rover were also analysed for periods of high and low input voltage values. Having all these conditions looked into and configured towards a specific application, a Di-Wheel Rover for planetary exploration could be feasible. The next phase of the test campaign would involve field trials and the new results will be published separately.

Further enhancements to a Di-Wheel Rover for space applications are protective armour and bumpers for the chassis. Based on all the experiments discussed in this paper, there are some limitations with the Di-Wheel Rover design. One of these limitations is based around the structural design for the rover. It has been observed that the DC motors used in the rover need to be ones that can provide sufficient torque for any tilting movements, and they also need to have a quick reaction time for the tilting movements in the fore/aft directions. Since the fore/aft tilting movements of the rover are dependent on the height and weight of the structure, the DC motors and the structural design of the rover need to match each other well in order to achieve a good balancing performance. This makes the Di-Wheel Rover harder to use when particular payloads onboard the rover may be added or removed, as this will alter the Di-Wheel Rover structure and weight. Having the Balancing Control sub-system tested on Earth means that it is only compatible with moments (turning forces) felt under the Earth's gravity. The Di-Wheel Rover design would need to be able to cope with a variety of environmental challenges that it may experience on other planets. Finally, the Di-Wheel Rover would also need a Balancing Control sub-system capable of maintaining a good balancing performance on ground surfaces that vary in friction.

Acknowledgements. A special thanks to the University of Surrey lab technicians John Mouat, Alexander Todd, Steve Mills, and Andy Walker for their help and assistance with obtaining the equipment required for this study.

References

1. Willetts, D.: Eight great technologies, GOV.UK (2013). https://www.gov.uk/government/speeches/eight-great-technologies. Accessed 22 Apr 2019
2. Krotkov, E., Simmons, R., Whittaker, W.: Ambler: performance of a six-legged planetary rover. Acta Astronaut. **35**(1), 75–81 (1995)
3. "Mars Pathfinder – NASA Facts", Jpl.nasa.gov. https://www.jpl.nasa.gov/news/fact_sheets/mpf.pdf. Accessed 22 Apr 2019
4. Ferreira, E., Tsai, S., Paredis, C., Brown, H.: Control of the Gyrover: a single-wheel gyroscopically stabilized robot. Adv. Robot. **14**(6), 459–475 (2000)
5. Matson, J.: Unfree spirit: NASA's mars rover appears stuck for good. Sci. Am. **302**(4), 16 (2010)
6. Comin, F.J., Saaj, C.M.: Models for slip estimation and soft terrain characterization with multilegged wheel–legs. IEEE Trans. Rob. **33**(6), 1438–1452 (2017)
7. Kamen, D.L., et al.: Personal mobility vehicles and methods. US Patent 6,367,817, filed on 10 August 2000 and patented on 9 April 2002. Asignee: DEKA Products, Limited Partnership, Manchester, New Hampshire
8. Christensen,B.: Meet Jaluro, A Two-Wheeled Open-Source Lunar Rover, Space.com (2004). https://www.space.com/6359-meet-jaluro-wheeled-open-source-lunar-rover.html. Accessed 22 Apr 2019
9. Khaled, M., Ibraheem, M., Omar, A., Moukarrab, R.: Balancing a two wheeled robot. Minia University, Faculty of Engineering, Computers and Systems Dept., pp. 11–12 (2009)
10. "How Does a PID Controller Work? – Structure & Tuning Methods", *ElProCus – Electronic Projects for Engineering Students.* https://www.elprocus.com/the-working-of-a-pid-controller/. Accessed 22 Apr 2019
11. Franklin, G., Powell, J., Emami-Naeini, A.: Feedback Control of Dynamic Systems, pp. 182–212. Pearson, Upper Saddle River (2006)

An Auto-Correction Teleoperation Method for a Mobile Manipulator Using Gaze Tracking and Hand Motion Detection

Junshen Chen[1], Ze Ji[1(✉)], Hanlin Niu[1], Rossitza Setchi[1],
and Chenguang Yang[2]

[1] School of Engineering, Cardiff University, Cardiff CF24 3AA, UK
jiz1@cf.ac.uk
[2] Bristol Robotics Laboratory, University of the West of England,
Bristol BS16 1QY, UK

Abstract. Situational awareness in remote environments is crucial for human operators to teleoperate mobile manipulators confidently and reliably. Visual feedback is the most common way for environment perception, providing rich information to human operators. This paper proposes an intuitive teleoperation method by combining gaze tracking and hand motion detection to teleoperate a mobile manipulator. A camera is fixed on the end-effector of the mobile robot's arm to provide visual feedback, acting as the eye of the teleoperator. Rather than direct remote control of the robot, an adaptive auto-correction mechanism is introduced for helping human operators to achieve better hand-eye coordination of the teleoperation experiences. The mobile manipulator can adjust its behaviours, such as speed, while gaze and hand movements of the operator are in different states. The experiments carried out demonstrated the effectiveness of the proposed algorithm and the survey evaluation verified the practical application value of the system.

Keywords: Teleoperation · Hand-eye coordination ·
Mobile manipulator

1 Introduction

Telerobotics has been widely applied in both research and industrial fields. Teleoperated robots, also known as telerobots, are often compared with fully automated control robots. Automated robots are often used to perform fixed tasks,

This work is supported by the Advanced Sustainable Manufacturing Technologies (ASTUTE) 2020 and ASTUTE East projects. We would like to thank the visiting MSc students from INSA-Strasbourg, France, for their previous work on the Smart Eye system

K. Althoefer et al. (Eds.): TAROS 2019, LNAI 11650, pp. 422–433, 2019.
https://doi.org/10.1007/978-3-030-25332-5_36

while telerobots are designed to work in more unstructured environments and collaborate with humans on more diverse tasks.

A mobile manipulator is a system consisting of a mobile robot mounted with one or more robotic manipulators. There are a diverse range of applications of tele-operated mobile manipulators, ranging from large-scale outdoor applications, such as the Mars Rovers [9] for space exploration and military operations, to indoor domestic environments, such as home-care and health-care applications [8].

There are various modalities nowadays allowing human operators to interact with robots, including voice recognition, human body gestures, joystick, gaze tracking, hand gestures, and combinations of them. This work aims to investigate the performance of combining gaze tracking and hand gesture recognition to provide an intuitive and natural interactive modality for mobile manipulators.

Nowadays, gaze-tracking and hand-tracking systems are manifold, and the applications keep on increasing. Video games and virtual reality are two examples of general public usage. In the scientific community, new interfaces using such technologies are being researched and developed, in particular, for human-computer interactions, and notably for human-robot interactions. A gaze tracking teleoperation method was proposed in [11], and it also offered a 2-D mapping-based calibration method for a user's head movement. In [4], experiments were taken out for letting human operators teleoperate a robot arm to write and draw by using their gaze. An interface designed in [7] enables the user to teleoperate the robot using his hands' motion. The user can make an online adjustment for the autonomy of the robot. Another hand movements teleoperation system was introduced in [3]. In [5], it presented a robot teleoperation platform that used a user interface based on eye-gaze tracking that users can navigate a teleoperated mobile robot using their eyes. Interval Kalman filter and improved particle filter are applied to realise a markerless and contactless teleoperation interface.

However, for a hand-eye combined system of teleoperation, as developed in this work, hand-eye coordination is an important factor to gain better teleoperation experience. Eye-hand coordination, or hand-eye coordination, is the ability to simultaneous use of eyes and hands to fulfil tasks, much like an activity that uses the visual information to guide movements of hands. For example, drivers are required to constantly use hand-eye coordination that visual information needs to be translated into actions executed by hands on the steering wheels, in order to keep the car in the middle of the lane to avoid accidents.

In [10], the perspective of uncalibrated hand-eye coordination has been studied on a humanoid robot. Online image Jacobian matrix was identified by using Kalman filter. A microsurgery system used in minimally invasive surgery, which requires a high level of hand-eye coordination, was introduced in [6]. To eliminate the changing orientation of the object from visual feedback, a disorientation auto-recovery algorithm was applied to calibrate the rotation angle in real time. This helps to simplify manual dexterity among surgeons. However, no related researches have been carried out for enhancing hand-eye coordination while tele-operating mobile manipulators.

In this work, an intuitive teleoperation method for remote controlling a mobile manipulator is developed by combining gaze tracking and hand motion recognition. A camera is fixed on the end-effector of the mobile robot's arm to provide visual feedback, acting as the eye of the teleoperator. Rather than direct remote control of the robot, an adaptive auto-correction method is introduced for helping human operators to gain better hand-eye coordination of the teleoperation experience. The mobile manipulator is able to adjust its behaviours, especially its speed, while gaze and hand movements of the operator are in different states. These methods will help to gain better experience while teleoperating a mobile manipulator using hand motion and gaze simultaneously. Also, it helps to minimise distractions while teleoperating, as well may help operators with poor hand-eye coordination.

2   System Description

To enhance teleoperation experience, in this paper, a gaze tracking and hand motion detection combined method is used for teleoperating a KUKA Youbot. The Youbot is an omnidirectional mobile robot platform with a 5 Degree of Freedoms (DoFs) robot manipulator and a 2-finger gripper. A Smart Eye® system is used to track a human user's gaze, which is associated to the behaviours of the Youbot's manipulator in this work, mainly involving the rotational motions or orientations of the Youbot's manipulator. A camera is attached to the robot arm's end-effector, and allows visualisation to the users of the environment, such as obstacles, from the robot's perspective during teleoperation. User's hand motion is detected by a Leap Motion® sensor. The gestures of the right hand are translated to the Youbot's base behaviours for teleoperation, with the same direction as the operator's hand positioned over the sensor. The combined system provides the user an intuitive experience while operating the telebot.

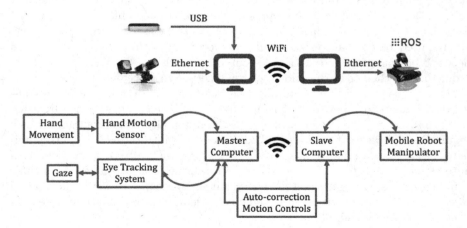

Fig. 1. The overall control system structure.

In addition, the speed of Youbot has corrected adaptively according to the current states of the gaze tracked and hand motion. When the user is looking forward and pointing forward, the system will consider that the user has full attention on the robot so that the robot would run in full speed on its base. When the operator is looking and pointing to the same side, the speed of Youbot's base will be reduced. The movement of the robot's manipulator will also slow down until the direction of gaze and hand motion are both pointing forward again. The robot will gradually slow down to stationary when the user is looking and pointing in two different sides. The overall communications system is shown in Fig. 1.

(a) SmartEye camera and IR flash. (b) Leap Motion device. (c) Youbot mobile manipulator.

Fig. 2. Sensors and robot used for the teleoperation system.

2.1 Gaze Control with Smart Eye

The device used for this application is the Smart Eye Pro from the company Smart Eyes. It consists of two infra-red projectors and three high-quality cameras. The third camera is used to improve robustness and accuracy by creating redundant data. Figure 2(a) shows one of the cameras and an infra-red projector. The system is combined with a desktop computer, whose screen is used to display video streams broadcasted from the embedded camera on the robot.

The device is provided with a specific piece of software called *Smart Eye*, which requires a two-phase calibration before use and also can be used to monitor gaze behaviours of operators. Those data can be stored in a log file or sent in real time to third-party software.

The Smart Eye system is a stereoscopic device, which requires a first calibration step to determine the relative position and orientation of the three cameras and the IR flashes. The calibration is done using a chessboard, which is monitored by all the cameras at the same time. The extrinsic parameters are stored and should not change for the duration of the experimentation.

The result of camera calibration can be evaluated by a calibration verification process. By presenting again the chessboard to the cameras, the SmartEye software computes and displays the average difference in pixels between its model and the reality. The calibration is considered accurate, when the value displayed is sub-pixelic. Otherwise, a new calibration phase will be repeated.

The origin and the orientation of the 3D-world have also to be done by defining a world coordinate system. The origin of the head's roll, pitch and yaw and the intersection between the sight and the screen depends on how precisely the world coordinate system has been established.

The second calibration phase is to improve the performance of eye tracking by estimating and correcting the errors caused by the differences of each individual user. By asking the user to stare at four pre-defined targets on the screen, the Smart Eye system can compute the differences between the estimated coordinates of users' attention on the screen and the desired coordinates at the four pre-defined targets. The errors are compensated to make a correction for gaze tracking of each individual user. The direction of the sight is computed in real time. Figure 3 shows the graphical interface of the gaze tracking system.

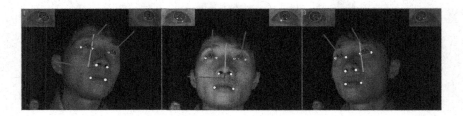

Fig. 3. User gaze tracking calibrated results.

2.2 Hand Detection with Leap Motion

The tracking device used is the *Leap Motion*®, which captures hands and fingers' motions as input, providing a low-cost structured light based motion capture system. Compared to a mouse, no contact or touching is required here. The device has been conceived to be embedded into a virtual reality headset, but also to be used as a standalone for various applications.

The device illustrated in Fig. 2(b) is a small module of size 80 mm × 30 mm × 11.25 mm. It is composed of two cameras and three infra-red lights. Those cameras track the interactions in an area shaped like an inverted pyramid in which field of view is 120° × 150° for a depth of approximately 600 mm. According to the manufacturer, the accuracy of the Leap Motion is about 0.7 mm inside this zone.

2.3 Youbot

The *Youbot* (Fig. 2(c)) is an omnidirectional mobile manipulator designed by the German robotic company *KUKA*. It was conceived for research and education purposes [1]. This robot is composed of two parts: A rectangular-shaped mobile base moving in the plan using four Swedish wheels; A robotic arm made of five degrees of freedom. A gripper is located at the tip of the arm, as well as a bracket intended to fix a camera.

Some applications already use gaze to control mobile robots. In this work, the particularity of the Youbot, which is to combine the assets of mobile robots and robotic arm, will be fully exploited to develop the system. Indeed, as the camera is set at the tip of the arm, the whole kinematic chain of the robot is used to control precisely the pose of the camera as the user requires it.

3   Method

This section describes the strategies of how user gestures are linked to the behaviours of the robot. The joint angles $\underline{q}$ of the robot can be described as

$$\underline{q} = f^{-1}(\underline{X}) \tag{1}$$

where $\underline{q} \in R^5$ is the joint angles of the manipulator, $\underline{X}$ is the end-effector coordinate, represented as $\underline{X} = [X_E, Y_E, Z_E, \phi, \Omega, \psi]'$ and X_E, Y_E and Z_E are the corresponding positions on the X, Y and Z axes of the end effector, whereas ϕ, Ω and ψ are the roll, pitch and yaw of the end effector, respectively.

Controlling the robot using hand gestures is straightforward. Figure 4(a) shows the relationship between the left hand gesture and the robot end-effector, and Fig. 4(b) illustrates the relationship between the right hand gesture and robot displacement. The right hand controls the base movement in all directions, by translating the relative pose between the hand and the sensor to speed control commands for the robot, where the distance from the hand to the sensor is proportional to the robot speed. The left hand controls the end-effector; however, it only deals with its coordinate, (X_E, Y_E, Z_E), rather than orientations (β, θ_1), which are controlled by the gaze gestures.

3.1   Impact of Gaze Commands

The arm receives three values from the user intended to orientate the end-effector: x_{screen}, y_{screen} and $head_{roll}$, where x_{screen} represents the horizontal position of the sight on the screen. 0 means that the user is looking at the left edge of the screen, 0.5 at the middle and 1 at the right edge, y_{screen} represents the vertical position of the sight on the screen. 0 means that the user is looking at the bottom edge of the screen, 0.5 at the middle and 1 at the top edge and $head_{roll}$ represents the user's head roll in radian. A positive angle means that the user is bending its head to the left and a negative means that the head bends to the right.

Considering that the screen displays in real-time the images captured by the camera, Fig. 5 illustrates the relationship between the field of view of the camera (horizontal here) and the computer screen, where:

- L_x represents the width of the computer screen.
- θ_{FOVx} represents the horizontal camera field of view.
- α_x is equal to x_{screen}.

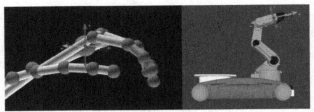

(a) Left hand motion control and end-effector displacement

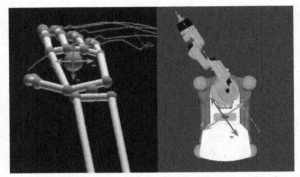

(b) Right hand motion control and robot base displacement

Fig. 4. Hand motion control and robot displacement

- $\theta_{\alpha x}$ is the output angle corresponding at the angular displacement of the camera.
- D is a variable which represents the virtual focal of the system represented.

According to the Fig. 5, the following equations can be written:

$$\begin{cases} \tan\theta_{FOVx} = \frac{L_x}{2D} \\ \tan\theta_{\alpha x} = \frac{L_x \alpha_x - L_x/2}{D} \end{cases} \tag{2}$$

which leads easily to the relation:

$$\theta_{\alpha x} = atan[(2\alpha_x - 1)tan\theta_{FOVx}] \tag{3}$$

Likewise, the following equation can be obtained:

$$\theta_{\alpha y} = atan[(2\alpha_y - 1)tan\theta_{FOVy}] \tag{4}$$

where θ_{FOVy} represents the vertical camera field of view, α_y is equal to y_{screen}, $\theta_{\alpha y}$ is the output angle corresponding at the angle displacement of the camera.

Therefore, $\theta_{\alpha x}$ and $\theta_{\alpha y}$ are the angular variation of the end-effector, with respect to x_{screen} and y_{screen}. Equations (3) and (4) describe the calculations of $\theta_{\alpha x}$ and $\theta_{\alpha y}$ that will be used to control the movement of the camera to the desired position of the sight, hence producing a natural way to move the robot arm.

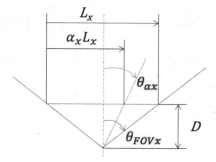

Fig. 5. Orientation of the camera according to the sight.

Moreover, the *arctangent* form of Eqs. (3) and (4) produces a smoothing of commands which will reduce the high amplitude sight motion and will bond the maximal motion amplitude to the field of view of the camera. The user is then assured of controlling the camera motion easily.

3.2 Adaptive Speed Control

The speed control algorithm for the Youbot's base unit is explained in Algorithm 1, and is further explained and visualised in Fig. 7(a). It should be noted that only the right hand is considered in the context of adaptive base speed control. When the hand is pointing forward, and eyes are looking at the forward direction at the same time, the robot will also go forward in full speed. In Fig. 7(b), when the operator is looking and pointing to the same side, the speed of Youbot's base is reduced. The movement of the robot's manipulator also slows down until the direction of gaze and hand motion are pointing forward both again. The robot gradually slows down to stationary when the user is looking and pointing in two different sides, as shown in Fig. 7(c).

4 Experiments

From a user point of view, it is intuitive for an operator to manipulate the robot using the proposed teleoperation system. Once the calibrations phases are completed with the Smart Eye software, users, either skilled or unskilled, are expected to be able to control the robot within negligible learning time.

The gaze tracking device, however, introduces some noticeable noises with its measurements. To understand the noise characteristics of gaze tracking, three tests were carried out with one user performing three tasks, namely eye moving from centre to the right horizontally, eye moving from centre to the left, and staring at one fixed point. As shown in Fig. 6, the left column shows the trajectories of eye movements in three tests. The right column shows the statistical distributions respectively. The first two show the distributions of robot

Algorithm 1. Speed control algorithm of a mobile robotic arm.

Input: D_e: direction of user's gaze; D_h: direction of user's hand; k_a and k_b: control gain of robot arm speed and base speed;

Output: optimal movement speed of robot's arm V_a; optimal movement speed of robot's base V_b;

1: initial $k_a = k_b = 1$;
2: **repeat**
3:     compute difference of directions $D' = D_e - D_h$;
4:     **if** $D' \le \frac{\pi}{2}$ **then**
5:         let base follow arm $k_a = 0.5$, $k_b = 0.7$;
6:     **end if**
7:     **if** $D' > \frac{\pi}{2}$ **then**
8:         let base wait arm $k_a = 0.7$, $k_b = 0$;
9:     **end if**
10: **until** $D_e = D_h = Forward$
11: set back $k_a = k_b = 1$.

orientation motions in the vertical axis ($\theta_{\alpha y}$ in radian), calculated from the raw measurement in the image pixel space using Eq. (4), and the third one shows the distribution of robot motions in both directions ($\theta_{\alpha x}$ in Eq. (3), and $\theta_{\alpha y}$ in Eq. (4). The figures shown are the results after applying a simple moving average (MA) filter with 20 samples for each window. Thanks to the averaging effects from both the MA filter and also the latency introduced by the robot controllers, the robot motions are not as jerky as the raw measurement and look satisfactorily smooth.

The TCP client/server between the subsystems works correctly, and no problems were noticed during the user commands transmissions. Images are transmitted with a latency of approximately 200 ms, which was small enough to control the arm correctly. During the tests, a user could control the robot with his/her hand gestures and gaze while monitoring the reactions of the arm in real time. The auto-correction system would step in automatically to help the user gain better hand-eye cooperation during teleoperation.

The method was implemented and tested with nine untrained operators. The task was to navigate the robot around the laboratory. All participants were given a brief introduction of how the gaze and hand motion control interface works. Each participant was asked to complete a survey for evaluating the system performance. The survey used is a System Usability Scale (SUS) survey designed by [2]. Users were asked to evaluate the system based on 10 statements, to rate them from 1 to 5 (will be scaled to 0 to 4 for calculating the final score).

Figure 8 presents the average scores of the survey results. 10 questions were grouped into 5 sets to demonstrate different characteristics of the system [5]. And the final SUS score was calculated as an average of 69.8, out of 100. Taking both the average scores from Fig. 8 and the final SUS survey score into account, it can be concluded that the proposed teleoperation method has been proved to be usable and acceptable to general users. However, more user trials will be needed with more complex scenarios.

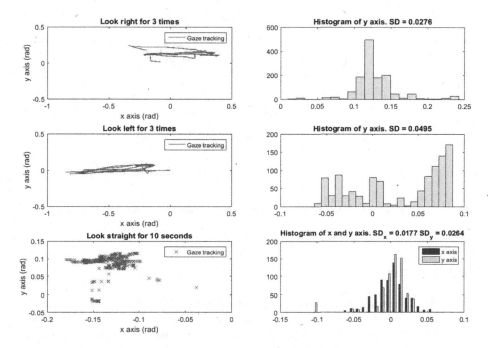

Fig. 6. Gaze tracking input data with their corresponding standard deviations (SD) in three different scenarios.

(a) Teleoperating while user pointing forward and looking forward.

(b) Teleoperating while user pointing and looking in same directions.

(c) Teleoperating while user pointing and looking in different directions.

Fig. 7. The illustration of auto-correction teleoperation method. Photos captured from the video of tests.

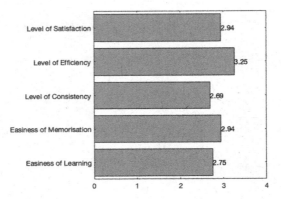

Fig. 8. Average scores of SUS survey results. 10 questions was grouped into 5 different characteristics.

5   Conclusion

This paper presents a combination method of using gaze tracking and hand motion detection to teleoperate a mobile manipulator. A camera was attached to the robot manipulator's end-effector to provide the user with visual feedback. To allow the user to control the robot in a more natural way, gaze tracking is used to orientate the camera, providing an intuitive method of interaction with the robot. The right hand motion tracking is used for moving the robot base on the ground and the left hand motion controls the translation of the manipulator end-effector. This combination method offers the operator to view the robot's workspace from a first-person perspective to operate the robot intuitively. Also, the operator can manipulate the orientations of the robot's end-effector through intuitive head motions. Hand-eye coordination was enhanced during multi-sensor teleoperation with the applied algorithm. The proposed system was validated with tests on a KUKA Youbot and demonstrated the improved performance of the designed auto-correction teleoperation method. User experience survey was carried out to prove the feasibility of the system. Future works can be developed based on the survey to further improve the robot teleoperation experience for unskilled operators.

References

1. Bischoff, R., Huggenberger, U., Prassler, E.: KUKA youBot-a mobile manipulator for research and education. In: 2011 IEEE International Conference on Robotics and Automation (ICRA), pp. 1–4. IEEE (2011)
2. Brooke, J., et al.: SUS-a quick and dirty usability scale. In: Jordan, P.W., Thomas, B., Weerdmeester, B.A., McClelland, I.L. (eds.) Usability Evaluation in Industry, pp. 4–7. CRC Press, London (1996)

3. Du, G., Zhang, P., Liu, X.: Markerless human-manipulator interface using leap motion with interval kalman filter and improved particle filter. IEEE Trans. Industr. Inf. **12**(2), 694–704 (2016). https://doi.org/10.1109/TII.2016.2526674

4. Dziemian, S., Abbott, W.W., Faisal, A.A.: Gaze-based teleprosthetic enables intuitive continuous control of complex robot arm use: writing amp; drawing. In: 2016 6th IEEE International Conference on Biomedical Robotics and Biomechatronics (BioRob), pp. 1277–1282, June 2016. https://doi.org/10.1109/BIOROB.2016.7523807

5. Ggo, D., Carreto, C., Figueiredo, L.: Teleoperation of a mobile robot based on eye-gaze tracking. In: 2017 12th Iberian Conference on Information Systems and Technologies (CISTI), pp. 1–6, June 2017. https://doi.org/10.23919/CISTI.2017.7975673

6. Li, X., et al.: Active cannula robot with misorientation auto-recovery camera: a method to improve hand-eye coordination in minimally invasive surgery. In: 2013 13th International Conference on Control, Automation and Systems (ICCAS 2013), pp. 276–280, Oct 2013. https://doi.org/10.1109/ICCAS.2013.6703908

7. Peppoloni, L., Brizzi, F., Avizzano, C.A., Ruffaldi, E.: Immersive ROS-integrated framework for robot teleoperation. In: 2015 IEEE Symposium on 3D User Interfaces (3DUI), pp. 177–178, March 2015. https://doi.org/10.1109/3DUI.2015.7131758

8. Qiu, R., et al.: Towards robust personal assistant robots: experience gained in the SRS project. In: 2012 IEEE/RSJ International Conference on Intelligent Robots and Systems, pp. 1651–1657, Oct 2012. https://doi.org/10.1109/IROS.2012.6385727

9. Tunstel, E., Maimone, M., Trebi-Ollennu, A., Yen, J., Petras, R., Willson, R.: Mars exploration rover mobility and robotic arm operational performance. In: 2005 IEEE International Conference on Systems, Man and Cybernetics, vol. 2, pp. 1807–1814. IEEE (2005)

10. Xiang, Z., Su, J., Ma, Z.: Uncalibrated hand-eye coordination based HRI on humanoid robot. In: Proceedings of the 33rd Chinese Control Conference, pp. 8438–8443, July 2014. https://doi.org/10.1109/ChiCC.2014.6896416

11. Yu, M., Wang, X., Lin, Y., Bai, X.: Gaze tracking system for teleoperation. In: The 26th Chinese Control and Decision Conference (2014 CCDC), pp. 4617–4622, May 2014. https://doi.org/10.1109/CCDC.2014.6852997

A Novel Wireless Measurement While Drilling System for the Detection of Deeply Buried Unexploded Bombs (UXBs)

Moutazbellah Khater[1]([⊠]), Waleed Al-Nauimy[2], and Asger Eriksen[3]

[1] Deep Sea Electronics, Hunmanby, North Yorkshire, UK
moutaz_k@hotmail.com
[2] University of Liverpool, Liverpool, UK
[3] Zetica Ltd., Witney, Oxfordshire, UK

Abstract. The problem of Unexploded Ordnance/Bomb (UXO/UXB) affects most big cities in UK and Europe. It is estimated that 10% of aerially dropped bombs failed to explode. The heavy weight of the bombs allowed them to penetrate the ground to a depth that may exceed 14 m. The disturbance of these bombs could result in fatal explosion and represents a serious danger to construction and foundations workers. Current methods for deep bomb detection include predrilled and pushed methods. The pushed method is the preferred technique but it cannot penetrate hard ground. The alternative is the predrilled method that employs a more powerful rotary drilling method to drill and scan the borehole in stages. However, it is very time-consuming and costly. This paper describes the development of an instrument equipped into a rotary drilling rig, which captures, transmits and records earth magnetic field wirelessly while drilling. The proposed system allows UXO detection in real time whilst drilling in various types of ground conditions and provides faster, safer and cheaper method of UXO detection overcoming the limitations of the existing methods. In order to further improve the safety of deeply buried UXB clearance in hazardous environment, this solution can be attached to an autonomous vehicle or robot while data can be remotely collected. Hence, this work focuses on designing a sensor system that can identify deeply buried underground bombs and can be integrated into a mobile robotic system.

Multiple challenges are associated with the development of the proposed solution, mainly: strong magnetic noise interference caused by surrounding metal on the measurements, real time data transmission and the very harsh and noisy drilling environment. This paper addresses the telemetry challenge.

Keywords: UXB · Down-hole telemetry · MWD · Waveguide theory

1 Threat of UXO

During the Second World War, thousands of bombs were dropped across UK and Europe [1, 2]. Throughout UK, cities, towns, ports, military sites and traffic and rail infrastructures were targeted and heavily bombed. For many reasons, a large percentage of those bombs failed to function as expected and did not explode. According to

© Springer Nature Switzerland AG 2019
K. Althoefer et al. (Eds.): TAROS 2019, LNAI 11650, pp. 434–446, 2019.
https://doi.org/10.1007/978-3-030-25332-5_37

governmental statistics, every day from September 21, 1940, to July 5, 1941 an average of 84 bombs fell on civilian targets and failed to explode [3]. In general, it is estimated that 10% of all aerially delivered bombs and military exercises munitions have failed to explode [1].

Figure 1 shows an unexploded bomb risk map for part of London (East Central - produced by Zetica [4]). It shows the potential distribution and the densities of air-delivered UXB within that area. Apparently, the high density in central area suggests that UXO represent a serious hazard to people, infrastructure and the environment.

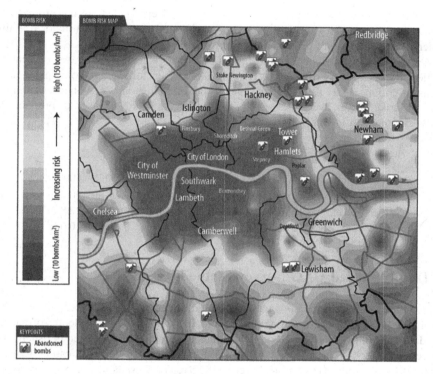

Fig. 1. London - East Central bomb risk map

According to the Construction Industry Research and Information Association CIRIA [1], from 2006 to 2009, over 15,000 items of ordnance were found in construction sites in the UK. In recent years, several accidents have been reported, more recently, three people were killed and six injured in a construction site in Germany in the town of Goettingen when a WWII 500 kg bomb exploded [5].

2 Deeply Buried UXO

Deeply buried unexploded bombs, the subject of this study, are most likely to be airdropped. In the UK, German WWII aerially delivered bombs represent the main source of deeply buried UXBs. The majority of air bombing attacks on the UK were considered to be high-level attacks (height > 5000 m), and from such altitude, a typical bomb velocity will be in the range of 300 to 360 m/s and the typical strike angle is about 10°–15° from the vertical line [1]. These bombs vary in weight from 50 kg up to 1800 kg. The aerodynamic shapes of the bombs alongside to their heavy weight and their velocity have allowed the unexploded ones to deeply penetrate the ground to a depth that can exceed 14 m in some scenarios. Ground geology has a major role that influences the final depth of the bomb.

Zetica Ltd. has developed a multi-layer UXB depth calculator [4] based on analytic solution. It uses ministry of defence (UK) guidance tables for average bomb penetration depths in common UK soil, and rock types for different bomb sizes and assuming a range of strike angles and strike speed. This calculator has been used to produce the results summarised in Table 1.

Table 1. Average bomb penetration depths

Bomb weight (kg)	50 kg	100 kg	500 kg	1000 kg	2000 kg	4000 kg
Soft clay/loose sand	7.4 m	9.2 m	18.2 m	21.4 m	24.4 m	30.4 m
Stiff clay/chalk	5.6 m	6.9 m	13.6 m	16.0 m	18.3 m	22.8 m
Gravel/weak rock	2.4 m	3.0 m	6.0 m	7.1 m	8.1 m	10.0 m

3 Deeply Buried UXO Survey Methods

Surface-based detection methods cannot be used to detect objects at depths exceeding few meters. Instead, a drilling system is used to drill a borehole to the depths of interest and data are collected using a borehole magnetometer. Magnetometer is usually the choice as it offers larger detection radius and it is relatively small so it can be lowered down into a borehole. UXO typically contain ferrous materials to improve robustness and to gain strength. However, all ferrous materials are magnetic materials, thus ferrous UXO will distort/interfere with the earth magnetic field resulting in an anomaly/change that can be detected using a magnetometer. Current techniques for deep bomb detection include predrilled borehole method and pushed method. Those types of surveys are usually used prior to piling and foundation activities, deep excavation and ground investigation boreholes.

3.1 Pushed Method (Cone Penetration Test-CPT)

In the industry, this method is also known as MagCone as it involves using a magnetometer equipped inside a cone, which is pushed into the ground under hydraulic pressure using a CPT rig. Data are collected in real time while the cone is pushed into the ground. The collected data are transmitted over a cable that runs through the string to the logging device/computer located inside the CPT truck [6].

The main advantage of MagCone is that it provides an in-situ real time measurement for detecting deeply buried objects. Furthermore, it is safe as it provides real time data. Limitations of this method are ground conditions, surface and subsurface obstructions such as made ground, hard strata or hardcover may prevent penetration of the cone to the required depth of investigation in which it is necessary to employ a more powerful drilling method in order to reach the required depth of investigation.

3.2 Predrilled Borehole Method

Borehole method involves drilling a borehole in stages and lowering a magnetometer manually. The borehole is usually drilled using a suitable rotary drilling method. The drilling of the borehole is carried out in stages, typically 1 m at each stage. The drilling string is withdrawn from the borehole and a suitable nonmagnetic casing is installed to prevent the borehole from collapsing, after that, a borehole magnetometer is lowered down manually and the data are collected. Once the section is cleared, the casing will then be taken out and the drilling process continued to the next level. This process is repeated until the required depth of investigation is reached. When hard ground is experienced, plastic non-magnetic casing cannot be pushed directly into the drilled borehole. In these circumstances, a normal steel casing is advanced first and a plastic casing is introduced inside it, then the steel case is pulled back to a level that does not interfere with the sensor readings (1.5–2 m). After that, the sensor is lowered down to clear that section. The sensor and the casings are then withdrawn and the borehole is advanced to the next stage. The main advantage of this method is that it can penetrate hard underground layers and most soil conditions. However, in terms of productivity, it is very time-consuming method when compared to pushed method. It is also more dangerous as it involves drilling the borehole in stages. In addition, data collected using predrilled method usually suffer from magnetic interference caused by the casing of the borehole and this may affect the detection radius of the sensor.

3.3 The Role of Geology in Selecting a Suitable Detection Technique

The geology of the ground must be considered as it affects the selection of the clearance technique. London geology is extremely complex and includes several areas that are not suitable for pushed method clearance technique. Figure 2 shows a simplified map for the geology of Greater London, this map is based on British Geological Survey information and it provides a general guidance on what technique should be used. The complex geology has been reduced into three main areas: Areas that are suitable for drilling based techniques (which include gravel) are shown in pink, green areas are suitable for pushed methods and they include clay or alluvium. Areas that include chalk are shown in grey. As we can see in Fig. 2, pushed method cannot be employed in more than 40% of Greater London. Currently, the only other option for deep bomb detection is predrilled boreholes methods, as they can penetrate hard ground, though they are slow, costly and unsafe.

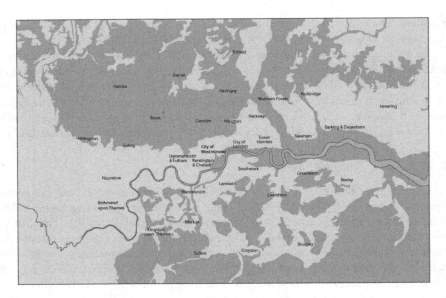

Fig. 2. Geology of Greater London (Color figure online)

4 Proposed Real Time Measurement While Drilling System

The development of a real time measurement while drilling system that consists of a rotary drilling rig equipped with an onboard magnetometer would provide a quick method that can penetrate most soil types overcoming the limitations of the current deep bomb detection techniques. In addition, it will improve the quality of data collected and provide a safer detection method.

One of the major challenges associated with the development of the proposed measurement system is the data transmission, where the data needs to be transmitted from the bottom of the borehole up to the surface while drilling in real time. This telemetry system needs to be wireless due to the nature of the drilling procedure and the rotation of the drill string.

It is obvious that the material of the drill string has to be nonmagnetic in order not to interfere with the magnetic measurements. However, In order to come up with a commercially viable and practical solution, there has to be a compromise between cost, low magnetic permeability, and hardness. This implies that the solution should be able to compensate for magnetic interference caused by the magnetisation of the drill string. As well as any variation in the magnetisation the drill string may gain through storage, transportation and drilling activity. The very harsh and noisy drilling environment has made the development of a practical and reliable system even more difficult. The choice and the protection of the magnetometer and the downhole electronics have significant implication on cost and the reliability of the solution. In order to utilise a cost effective magnetometer, the solution shall consider the effect of rotating the magnetometer and its internal errors on the measured magnetic field. Numerous challenges are expected in the development of the proposed system. This paper addresses the data transmission challenge. The quantification and compensation for the magnetic interference caused by the drill string and the rotation of the magnetometer will be covered in future publications.

In order to further improve the safety of deeply buried UXB clearance, the proposed solution can be mounted on mobile robotics systems, which can be autonomous or remotely operated. Mobile robots fitted with rotary drilling systems are used for ground, underwater and space application [7, 8]. In addition, robotics systems are widely employed for de-mining activities [9]. The suggested system can be combined with these robotics technologies to offer an efficient and safe survey method for deeply buried UXBs detection.

4.1   Auger - The Selected Drilling Method

A suitable rotary drilling method needs to be identified taking into consideration that the measurement instrument has to be installed inside the drilling column. Auger drilling is the most suitable drilling method for the proposed system. Auger drilling is a rotary drilling method done with a helically continuous flights column(s) (Archimedes screw) which is driven into the ground with rotation [10]. The borehole is drilled by simultaneously rotating and axially advancing the auger column into the ground. The cutter head of the auger break up and drill the materials, while the auger flights act as a screw conveyor to move the cuttings from the bottom of the hole. The dry mechanism of cutting removal and the hollow stem allow the electronics to be easily fitted inside the stem and this also simplifies the communication with the surface. Moreover, auger drilling provides rapid ground penetration with relatively low levels of shock and vibrations and this reduce the complexity of the design.

4.2   Existing Wireless Telemetry Systems Used in the Oil and Gas Industry

Measurement while drilling (MWD) provides the oil and gas exploration operators with real time information while the borehole is being drilled. It can take measurements of downhole formation properties, borehole geometry alongside with other useful parameters and this allows for more efficient and safer drilling. The main wireless telemetry method used in the oil and gas industry is the mud pulse telemetry; other less frequently used solutions include electromagnetic telemetry and acoustic telemetry. Mud pulse telemetry is the most common technique used in commercial measurement while drilling systems. Mud pulse telemetry is accomplished by using a downhole valve which modulates the digital information into pressure pulses or continuous pressure wave that can propagate through the drilling fluid (mud) up to the surface [11, 12]. At the top of the drill pipe, the pulses are detected by a pressure sensor and then processed and displayed. The data rate can reach up to 40 bits per second (bps) [13] and decreases as the length/depth of the well increases. The average bit rate is usually less than 10 bps.

Electromagnetic telemetry employs extremely low frequency electromagnetic waves (<10 Hz) to transmit downhole data through the ground; it uses the drill pipe as a dipole to transmit the modulated low frequency electromagnetic wave into the ground. On the surface, the signal can be detected by a small voltage drop between the drill pipe and small electrodes driven into the ground away from the drill pipe. This system generally offers data rates comparable to mud pulse telemetry [14] and is limited by the conductivity of the formation and the depth of the borehole.

Acoustic telemetry uses modulated sound waves propagated through the dill pipe. Acoustic telemetry is a very promising technology that can provide a relatively high bit rate of up to 100 bps. However, the acoustic noise in the drill string is high leading to severe propagation losses. The acoustic noise has prevented the development of a commercially viable solution for the last 50 years, but in the recent years, acoustic MWD has been made commercial.

Common MWD systems used in oil and gas are usually complex and very expensive. They have been designed to operate at deep depths (thousands of metres), However proposed UXO detection only needs to reach 20 m. In addition, the very limited bandwidth will reduce the quality of the collected data and increase the complexity of the system. Therefore, in order to provide a cost effective telemetry solution, two custom solutions will be considered. The first is based on the infrared communication technology and the second employs waveguide theory.

4.3   The Infrared (IR) Option

For a narrow beam signal such as infrared, transmission along the metal pipe is possible as long as line of sight is maintained. In fact, the darkness inside the auger string may improve the sensitivity of the infrared receiver. The IR solution is able to provide a reasonable bit rate (20 kbits/s), however the main drawback of the IR link is the limited range. Ideally, commercially available IR receiver can achieve a communication range up to 20 m (e.g. TSOP7000 [15]). This communication range should be enough for the proposed system. However, this range will be highly attenuated by the dust and mud; those may penetrate into the auger stem under certain drilling conditions. Though infrared signal can propagate through the auger string, from the previous discussion, one can conclude that the infrared solution do not provide a reliable telemetry system for the proposed high risk measurement system.

4.4   The Auger as a Waveguide

This solution is based on waveguide theory. The auger is made out of conductive metal and is hollow. Therefore, if carrier frequency is carefully chosen, electromagnetic waves can propagate along the metal auger. In previous publication [16] this telemetry system was introduced which utilises the hollow stem of the auger as a circular waveguide. It was found that, the majority of available auger sizes allow propagation at the standard unlicensed 2.4 GHz frequency. Table 2 lists typical range auger diameters and the corresponding cutoff frequency for the TE_{11} mode which is the dominant mode for a circular waveguide. Depending on the size of the auger, more than one propagation mode may exist. The total power will be distributed between the excited modes. The overall attenuation constant depends on the power radiated in each mode, which in turn depends on the antenna radiation characteristics, antenna orientation and position inside the auger, waveguide cross sectional area and operating frequency [17]. The auger is not an ideal waveguide, the corrosion of the auger's internal wall and the antenna coupling loss are the main contributor to the total loss. Other losses include multiple reflections form terminated ends and loss due to auger joints.

Table 2. Typical Auger sizes with corresponding TE$_{11}$ cutoff frequency

Auger internal diameter (mm)	Outside (flights) diameter (mm)	Weight (kg)	TE$_{11}$ cutoff frequency
57.2	136.5	20.9	3.07 GHz
82.6	187.3	37.2	2.13 GHz
100	200	40	1.76 GHz
111	215.9	50	1.58 GHz
168.3	273.1	57.2	1.04 GHz
209.5	314.3	67.1	839.2 MHz
260.3	368.3	114.8	675.4 MHz
311.2	419.1	134.7	564.9 MHz

Analysis of similar propagation conditions do exist in the literature, The most relevant study was done by a group of researchers where indoor radio wave propagation using heating, ventilation and air conditioning duct (HVAC ducts) was proposed and studied in details [18–20]. Niktin and others proposed [20] a simple analytical propagation model for straight duct, the proposed model accounts for mode excitation, reflections from terminated ends but it requires knowledge of mode-dependent antenna impendence. Tonguz and others [21] presented an empirical model to predict path loss inside a HVAC duct operating in the 2.4–2.5 GHz, experimental measurements were used to determine attenuation loss and antenna coupling loss for HVAC duct of 0.3 m diameter, the attenuation loss was found to be 0.16 dB/m, while the antenna coupling loss was found to be 14.8 dB.

4.5 Concept Demonstration

A simple test was conducted to validate the concept of using the auger as a communication channel. The test was performed with an auger string of 3.2 m length and 100 mm diameter (two auger sections), the test setup is depicted in Fig. 3a. Two IEEE 802.1.5.4 2.4 GHz wireless transceivers modules have been used to establish communication inside the auger string [22]. The transceiver used has the option of adjusting the output power from a minimum of −38.75 dBm up to a maximum of 0 dBm in steps of 1.25 dB. It also provides a measure for the received signal strength with an accuracy of ±5 dBm. The centre frequencies of the 16 supported channels were tested with transmit power of −38.75 dBm. Figure 3b shows the frequency response obtained by varying the operating frequency and calculating the average signal attenuation/loss. Figure 3b shows two curves. The first curve represents the measurements obtained with both ends of the auger are open, this condition simulate a matched load as there is no reflection from the ends. The second curve is for the measurements obtained while the ends of the auger are terminated by a conductive metal sheet, this simulates a short circuit condition in which reflections from both ends are expected. It can be noticed that, loss due to reflections from the terminated ends is quite small. This agrees with the results achieved by other researchers [20, 21]. Among the frequency range of interest, the average of overall loss is 12 dB. The attenuation constant of the waveguide is expected to be very low, for the HVAC duct, 0.12 dB/m was reported by stencil [19] and 0.16 dB/m reported by Ozan [21]. It is believed that, the majority of the loss mainly comes from Antenna coupling. An antenna coupling loss of 14.8 dB was reported by Ozan [21] for a monopole antenna radiating inside a HVAC duct. Stencil [19] also estimated an antenna coupling loss of 20 dB. If we ignore losses due to joints and conservatively assume a 25 dB coupling loss, 0.2 dB/m waveguide loss and 10 dB error margin, then, for a transceiver with 0 dBm transmit power capability and −80 dBm receive sensitivity, the communication range would be 225 m. Therefore, the minimum 20 m can be easily achieved. In order to assess the reliability and the quality of the communication through the auger, 1000 messages were transmitted from the first transceiver to the second transceiver at the other side of the auger, the number of the received messages was counted. This experiment was repeated for the 16 tested channels and there was no messages loss at all. The results obtained from this test confirm that the auger can be employed as a reliable communication channel for the proposed telemetry system.

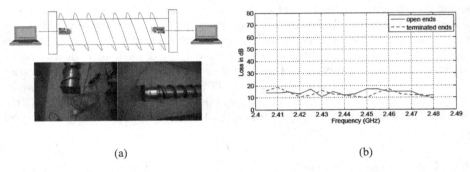

(a)   (b)

Fig. 3. (a) Test setup for measuring the frequency response of the auger. (b) Frequency response measured inside an Auger of 3.2 m length and 100 mm diameter

5   Implementations and Field Testing

A prototype of the measurement system has been produced. Figure 4 shows a block diagram for the system. The system consists of two wireless channels; a high frequency channel intended to provide communication inside the auger, and a high-power external channel that provide communication externally between the logging computer, the magnetic measurement system and the rig instrumentation system. The logging computer control the operation of the system by regularly requesting magnetic and drilling data. Magnetic data are delivered from the downhole unit inside the auger to the logging unit through the relay unit. Drilling parameters including the depth of the borehole are provided by a rig instrumentation system fitted on the drill rig. The output of this instrumentation system can connect directly to the logging computer using a serial cable and can also connect wirelessly through the wireless interface unit. The logging computer runs the application software which buffers, processes and presents the data to the operator in real time. The housing of the downhole and the relay units has been designed in a way that reduces the effect of shock and vibration as well as providing good thermal insulation.

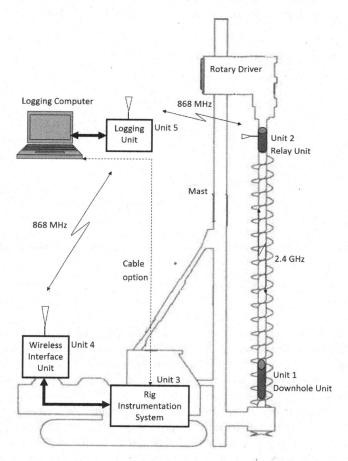

Fig. 4. Magnetic measurement system block diagram

The prototype system allowed field drilling tests to be conducted to demonstrate and evaluate the system in actual drilling environment. The system was mounted on a drill rig and several boreholes were drilled around a dummy steel target (1 m steel tube) buried approximately at a depth of 6 m below ground. Augers with standard 100 mm – diameter were used to drill boreholes of 8 m depths. Figure 5a depicts two magnetic profiles for one borehole located at 0.7 m from the dummy steel object; the solid profile was collected using the developed real time measurement system, the dotted profile was collected manually after the borehole has been drilled and a plastic casing was inserted. The strong correlation between both profiles suggests that the developed system is reliable and able to produce satisfactory data. Figure 5b shows the received signal strength measured during the drilling of the borehole, as expected, the received signal strength is high. The high frequency transceiver in units 1 and 2 were configured to transmit at 0 dBm power. The maximum value that can be measured by the internal received signal strength indicator (RSSI) of the transceiver is −20 dBm, hence, the received signal strength measured in Fig. 5b is capped at −20 dBm.

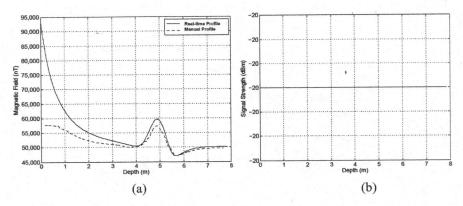

(a)   (b)

Fig. 5. (a) Magnetic profiles collected in the vicinity of dummy metal object. (b) Received signal strength measured during the drilling of the borehole

6 Conclusion

Deeply buried bombs represent a serious risk to the construction industry, especially during foundation work and pilling activities. A review of the current survey methods for deeply buried UXO leads to the conclusion that there is great need for a real time measurement while drilling system to improve the efficiency and the safety of the survey process. This paper introduced a novel downhole telemetry method for the detection of deeply buried unexploded bombs. The method is based on guiding the electromagnetic waves inside the drill string. The proposed method has been implemented and successfully tested in the field. The ability of the measurement system to monitor the earth's magnetic field in real time during the drilling process has been demonstrated. Robotics systems with drilling capabilities can utilise the presented telemetry system for the detection of deeply buried UXBs and metal objects.

Acknowledgment. I wish to express my sincere thanks to Zetica Ltd. and the Knowledge Transfer Partnership programme UK (KTP) for supporting this work.

References

1. Stone, K., Murray, A., Cooke, S., Foran, J., Gooderham, L.: Unexploded ordnance (UXO), a guide for the construction industry. Technical report C681, Construction Industry Research and Information Association (CIRIA), London, UK (2009)
2. Britain sitting on a time-bomb. BBC news, September 1998. http://news.bbc.co.uk/1/hi/uk/179387.stm
3. British Army Defuses Giant WWII-Era Bomb in London. Fox news, June 2008. https://www.foxnews.com/story/british-army-defuses-giant-wwii-era-bomb-in-london
4. Zetica Ltd. - company website. http://www.zeticauxo.com
5. World War II bomb kills three in Germany. BBC news, June 2010. http://www.bbc.co.uk/news/10212890
6. Brouwer, J.: In-situ Soil Testing. Lankelma Ltd., East Sussex, UK (2007). http://www.conepenetration.com/
7. Beji, L., Benchikh, L.: A method of drilling a ground using a robotic arm. Int. J. Mech. Aerosp. Ind. Mechatron. Manuf. Eng. 11(11), 1821–1826 (2017). International Science Index 131
8. Glass, B., Thompson, S., Paulsen, G.: Robotic planetary drill tests. In: Proceedings of 13th International Symposium on Artificial Intelligence, Robotics and Automation in Space, pp. 464–470 (2010)
9. Baudoin, Y., Habib, M.K., Doroftei, I.: Mobile robotics systems for humanitarian de-mining and risky interventions. In: Using Robots in Hazardous Environments. Woodhead Publishing (2011)
10. England, B., Morris, R., Wakeling, R.: Drilling Technology. British Drilling Association, Essex (1992)
11. Baker Hughes INTEQ's Guide To Measurement While Drilling, Baker Hughes INTEQ's, Houston, Texas, September 1997
12. Tubel, P., Bergeron, C., Bell, S.: Mud pulser telemetry system for down hole measurement-while-drilling. In: Proceedings of 9th IEEE Instrumentation and Measurement Technology Conference (IMTC 1992), Metropolitan, New York, vol. 2, pp. 219–223, May 1992
13. Wassermann, I., Kaniappan, A.: How high-speed telemetry affects the drilling process. J. Pet. Technol. 61(6), 26–29 (2009)
14. Murphy, D.: Advances in MWD and formation evaluation for 2003. World Oil 224(3) (2003)
15. TSOP7000 - IR Receiver for High Data Rate PCM at 455 kH - data sheet. Vishay Semiconductors, Heilbronn, Germany
16. Khater, M., Al-Nuaimy, W.: A novel wireless measurement while drilling system for geotechnical and geophysical applications. In: Proceedings of 2nd UK-RAS Conference, Loughborough, UK, pp. 104–107, January 2019
17. Nikitin, P.V., et al.: Antennas in a waveguide propagation environment. In: Antennas and Propagation Society International Symposium, vol. 2, pp. 1181–1184. IEEE, June 2003
18. Andersson, H., Larsson, P., Wikstrom, P.: The use of HVAC ducts for WCDMA indoor solutions. In: 2004 IEEE 59th Vehicular Technology Conference, VTC 2004-Spring, vol. 1, pp. 229–233, May 2004
19. Stancil, D.D., Tonguz, O.K., Xhafa, A., Cepni, A., Nikitin, P., Brodtkorb, D.: High-speed internet access via HVAC ducts: a new approach. In: Global Telecommunications Conference, GLOBECOM 2001, vol. 6, pp. 3604–3607. IEEE (2001)

20. Nikitin, P.V., Stancil, D.D., Cepni, A.G., Tonguz, O.K., Xhafa, A.E., Brodtkorb, D.: Propagation model for the HVAC duct as a communication channel. IEEE Trans. Antennas Propag. **51**(5), 945–951 (2003)
21. Tonguz, O.K., Xhafa, A.E., Stancil, D.D., Cepni, A.G., Nikitin, P.V., Brodtkorb, D.: A simple path-loss prediction model for HVAC systems. IEEE Trans. Veh. Technol. **53**(4), 1203–1214 (2004)
22. MRF24J40MA 2.4 GHz IEEE Std. 802.15.4 RF Transceiver Module. Data sheet, Microchip Technology Inc. (2008)

Short Papers

Making the Case for Human-Aware Navigation in Warehouses

Manuel Fernandez Carmona$^{(\boxtimes)}$, Tejas Parekh, and Marc Hanheide

School of Computer Science, University of Lincoln, Lincoln LN6 7TS, UK
{mfernandezcarmona,tparekh,mhanheide}@lincoln.ac.uk

Abstract. This work addresses the performance of several local planners for navigation of autonomous pallet trucks in the presence of humans in a simulated warehouse as well as a complementary approach developed within the ILIAD project. Our focus is to stress the open problem of a safe manoeuvrability of pallet trucks in the presence of moving humans. We propose a variation of ROS navigation stack that includes in the planning process a model of the human robot interaction.

Keywords: Logistics · Human-aware navigation

1 Introduction

Autonomous Guided Vehicles (AGV) operating on virtual rails are evolving towards true Autonomous Mobile Robots (AMR) moving freely without any specific infrastructure or extra safety guards in warehouses. This trend raises concerns about the safety and comfort of sharing the space with humans as co-workers. Of course, obstacle-aware navigation itself has been in the focus of research for several decades already and has

Fig. 1. The ILIAD robot, a Linde CitiTruck modified for autonomous operation

matured ever since, also dealing with dynamic obstacles safely. But it has been confirmed by many previous works that the aspect of *human*-aware navigation [5] demands often distinct approaches that consider also the implicit intention communicated by motion itself [4,6] and the negotiation of space for navigation.

In this paper, we focus at the case of an autonomous pallet truck (see Fig. 1), developed to operate in infrastructure-free (no beacons, magnetic strips or other infrastructure to facilitate navigation and localisation) in the context of the H2020 ILIAD project[1].

---

[1] http://iliad-project.eu.

This work was supported in part by EPSRC under grant EP/R02572X/1 (NCNR) and in part by EU H2020 project No. 732737 (ILIAD).

K. Althoefer et al. (Eds.): TAROS 2019, LNAI 11650, pp. 449–453, 2019.
https://doi.org/10.1007/978-3-030-25332-5_38

Specifically, the objectives of this paper are to appraise the suitability of two classical variants of the general `move_base`[1] navigation frameworks for navigation of pallet trucks in the presence of humans in a simulated warehouse setting as well as a complementary approach developed within the ILIAD project; and to suggest an extension to these frameworks to address challenges of human-aware navigation.

2   Problem Statement and Analysis

Classical Robot Navigation in Warehouses. Safety is one of the highest priorities in any working environment. However, even though safety itself may be guaranteed by safety lasers, human *perceived* safety is a completely different matter [6]. Sudden stops or abrupt changes on speeds are usually perceived as threads by humans and have also detrimental effects on robot performance.

Aim for our work is therefore to minimise safety stops induced by a safety device itself, and maximise comfort of humans in vicinity of the robot (perceived safety), while maintaining effective and efficient operational characteristics. We will perform tests using three planning algorithms to illustrate how "classical" approaches (that do not treat humans different from other obstalces) handle human presence: *Dynamic Window Approach (DWA)*, a local planner based on an online collision avoidance strategy developed originally by Fox et al. in [3]. *Timed Elastic Bands (TEB)*, first proposed in [9], it dynamically optimizes running time and guarantees kinodynamic compliance in global trajectories. *ILIAD planner*: a real-time, lattice-based planner for non holonomic vehicles developed by Andreasson et al. in [1].

Analysis. In order to test the performance of these three classical navigation approaches, we defined five different simulation scenarios in the Gazebo simulator[2]:

- *Base Scenario:* Robot travels towards a goal 6.5 straight ahead, undisturbed.
- *Cross L-R:* Human crosses the robot's path from its left side.
- *Cross R-L:* Human crosses the robot' path from its right side.
- *Overtake:* Robot is overtaken by a human.
- *Pass-by:* Human is walking towards the robot and passes it.

Results in *Base* scenario are presented in Table 1, to be compared with results in the other scenarios. Each combination of scenarios and navigation algorithms was tested 6 times (3× *slow* moving human, 3× fast moving human, timed to collide with robot if not actively avoided). Table 2 highlight how in case of the fast human motion collisions cannot be avoided.

---

[1] http://wiki.ros.org/move_base.
[2] http://gazebosim.org.

Discussion. The simulation experiments give an indication of the problems of human presence in robot navigation (as also discussed in details in [5]). In alignment with expectations, presence of humans has an immediate impact on the trajectory length, and, consequently, on the completion times.

The TEB planner outperforms DWA in all our test cases, likely due

Scenario	Base		
Planner	DWA	TEB	ILIAD
∅ time to compl.	37.38	32.62	**31.98**
∅ path length	6.55	**6.5**	6.67
∅ robot speed	0.17	0.2	**0.21**

Table 1. Performance results of three classical navigation approaches in base scenario.

to its ability to better plan with the Ackermann constraints of the robot's kinematics. Both motion controllers (TEB & DWA) are liable to failure due to collision, and inefficiency (time, paths) due to constant replanning of trajectories due to the dynamic motion. On the other hand, *ILIAD* planner is always capable of handling crossings by just stopping (implementing the preferred model of [6]). Although it is a very accurate planner, it does not change its trajectory in presence of obstacles/humans, but instead slows down and even stops if an obstacle happens to be too close. In crossing scenarios, this crossing is so narrow that fully stops the robot, notifying an early finish of the plan, but safe after all. This policy is clearly insufficient in the event of an obstacle that is heading towards the robot, like in scenario *pass-by*. As a conclusion, strong commitment to a robot's original path (and slowing the execution of the trajectory in the presence of humans), like offered by the ILIAD planner, can indeed show better performance than continuous replanning (TEB & DWA), in specific scenarios. More generally, a motion planner must actively avoid humans, but a certain level of commitment to its global reference path is expected to provide a good trade-off.

3 Proposed Approach and Conclusion

As the experiments have indicated, an operational "sweet spot" may exist between the full commitment to a global trajectory (current ILIAD planner) and

Table 2. Performance results in 3 scenarios (∅ of 6 runs at 2 different human speeds, ∅ computed on successful runs only).

Scenario	Cross L-R			Cross R-L			Overtake			Pass-by		
Planner	DWA	TEB	ILIAD	DWA	TEB	ILIAD	DWA	TEB	ILIAD	DWA	TEB	ILIAD
∅ time to compl.	40.07	35.14	**28.22**	38.99	35.5	**27.61**	37.95	34.88	**31.26**	48.86	**41.75**	-
∅ path length	6.59	6.54	**4.54**	6.56	6.52	**5.41**	6.55	**6.53**	6.66	**6.85**	7.20	-
∅ robot speed	0.16	**0.18**	0.17	0.17	0.18	**0.19**	0.17	0.18	**0.21**	0.13	**0.16**	-
∅ min. h-r dist.	1.43	1.47	**1.85**	**2.0**	1.96	1.65	0.78	0.78	0.78	0.44	**0.53**	-
#Collisions	3	3	-	3	3	-	-	-	-	3	3	6

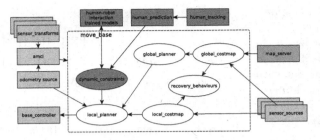
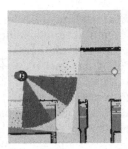

(a) Classical navigation architecture with proposed additional modules (yellow).

(b)   QTC-generated constraints for DWA.

Fig. 2. Architectural overview and example QTC-generated constraint [2] (Color figure online)

the continuous replanning approach of the classical motion controllers. Hence, we propose an extension to the classical ROS move_base stack, depicted in Fig. 2(a), to incorporate additional constrains into the local planning. This concept shall allow the robot to flexibly switch between very strong commitment to a (global) reference trajectory provided by narrow constraints, and to give freedom to flexibly avoid humans in other situations.

Current implementation can track humans around the robot [7] and plan accurate global reference trajectories [1]. Relative motion between human and robot is represented as a sequence of Qualitative Trajectory Calculus (QTC) states, as in [2]. This way, different situations will be trained and represented in a Markov model, allowing to learn and predict suitable, situation-dependent dynamic constraints (see Fig. 2(b) for an example). This work will be extended towards a more flexible and ROS-compatible framework, allowing the dynamic incorporation of local constraints, based on trained models. Other deep learning navigation algorithms, such as [8] will be also taken into consideration as candidates for enhancement with human aware constraints.

References

1. Andreasson, H., Saarinen, J., et al.: Fast, continuous state path smoothing to improve navigation accuracy. In: 2015 IEEE ICRA, pp. 662–669, May 2015. https://doi.org/10.1109/ICRA.2015.7139250
2. Dondrup, C., Bellotto, N., et al.: A computational model of human-robot spatial interactions based on a qualitative trajectory calculus. Robotics 4(1), 63–102 (2015). https://doi.org/10.3390/robotics4010063. http://www.mdpi.com/2218-6581/4/1/63/
3. Fox, D., Burgard, W., et al.: The dynamic window approach to collision avoidance. IEEE Robot. Autom. Mag. 4(1), 23–33 (1997). https://doi.org/10.1109/100.580977
4. Huettenrauch, H., Eklundh, K.S., Green, A., Topp, E.A.: Investigating spatial relationships in human-robot interaction. In: IEEE International Conference on Intelligent Robots and Systems (2006). https://doi.org/10.1109/IROS.2006.282535

5. Kruse, T., Pandey, A.K., Alami, R., Kirsch, A.: Human-aware robot navigation: a survey. Robot. Auton. Syst. **61**(12), 1726–1743 (2013). https://doi.org/10.1016/j.robot.2013.05.007
6. Lichtenthaler, C., Lorenzy, T., Kirsch, A.: Influence of legibility on perceived safety in a virtual human-robot path crossing task. In: Proceedings of IEEE International Workshop on Robot and Human Interactive Communication (2012). https://doi.org/10.1109/ROMAN.2012.6343829
7. Linder, T., Breuers, S., et al.: On multi-modal people tracking from mobile platforms in very crowded and dynamic environments. In: 2016 ICRA (2016)
8. Pfeiffer, M., Shukla, S., et al.: Reinforced imitation: sample efficient deep reinforcement learning for mapless navigation by leveraging prior demonstrations. IEEE Robot. Autom. Lett. **3**(4), 4423–4430 (2018)
9. Rösmann, C., Feiten, W., et al.: Efficient trajectory optimization using a sparse model. In: 2013 European Conference on Mobile Robots. pp. 138–143, September 2013. https://doi.org/10.1109/ECMR.2013.6698833

The Third Hand, Cobots Assisted Precise Assembly

Mohammad Safeea[1,2] , Pedro Neto[1](✉) , and Richard Béarée[2]

[1] Department of Mechanical Engineering, University of Coimbra, Coimbra, Portugal
ms@uc.pt, pedro.neto@dem.uc.pt
[2] Arts et Métiers, LISPEN, Lille, France
richard.bearee@ensam.eu

Abstract. Collaborative robots (Cobots) are indispensable tools in the factories of the future. Owing to their safety centered design, Cobots are allowed to work side by side with humans, making their use as an assistive third hand appealing for tedious assembly tasks. Consequently, we propose a robot that can be hand-guided to lift and hold parts in place while the human performs assembly tasks. Such functionality reduces the risk to workers (falling components for example), provides precision, allows lifting heavier parts, and increases productivity by allowing human workers to focus on more value-added tasks.

Keywords: Collaborative robots · Smart assembly · Hand-guiding

1 Methodology

One of the least automated tasks on the factory floor are assembly works. This fact is more evident in high-tech production facilities, as in aerospace industry. For example, during aircraft and satellite assembly, where in the last scenario the product is specifically customized to client's requirements. In such situation, assembly tasks are mainly done by human workforce, making them prone to delays and human errors. In this study, we investigate the integration of collaborative robots [1] as assistants to human coworkers for performing precise assembly tasks. We test our solution on a satellite dummy, where it is required to assemble sensitive equipment in the roof of the dummy. Traditionally, such task requires at least two workers (depending on the instrument's weight). Thus our idea of using a collaborative robot as a third hand, allowing one worker to do the task and reducing the risk of fallen parts. Due to their safety centered design, collaborative robots can work side by side with humans safely [2]. Consequently, in our solution the coworker utilizes hand-guiding for performing the assembly works. Two operation modes are made available, the hand-guiding at the joints level, which is suitable for performing rapid and long displacements of the robot. On the other hand, the worker can switch to our precise hand-guiding

K. Althoefer et al. (Eds.): TAROS 2019, LNAI 11650, pp. 454–457, 2019.
https://doi.org/10.1007/978-3-030-25332-5_39

application [4] for performing the precise motion. To guarantee precision, in our application the robot is hand guided at its end-effector (EEF) level, where the motion of the robot is divided into three different groups:

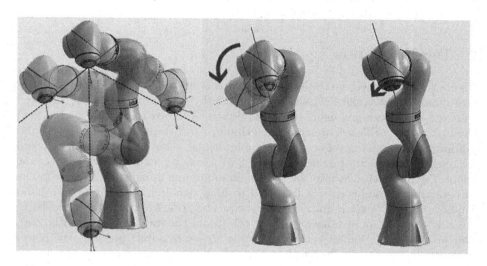

Fig. 1. First motion group (Left). Second motion group (Middle). Third motion group (Right).

1. First motion group, Fig. 1 at left: in this case the operator can move the EEF on a line along the axes of the robot base frame, while the orientation of the EEF is kept unchanged during the motion.
2. Second motion group, Fig. 1 in the middle: in this case the operator can orient the EEF in space by applying a moment, the position of the EEF is kept fixed.
3. Third motion group, Fig. 1 at right: in this case the user can rotate the EEF of the robot round its axis, the position of the EEF is kept fixed, and the orientation of the EEF's axis is also kept fixed.

Our solution offers various advantages over the traditional way of positioning robot's EEF using the teach-pendant (a handheld device that allows the user to control the robot), which suffers various drawbacks:

1. Unlike the hand-guiding, when using the teach-pendant the user does not have a feel of the force applied between the instrument and its surrounding in case of a contact. Accidents could happen and the user might over press the sensitive instrument against the surrounding without noticing.
2. When using the teach-pendant to position the EEF in Cartesian space, the user has to keep a track of the orientation of the robot base, this could become confusing even for the experienced worker (especially if the robot is mounted on a mobile platform).

3. For adjusting EEF's orientation, most teach-pendants use Euler rotation angles convention. This way for describing the orientation is not intuitive for humans.
4. The override control to change the velocity of the robot while performing the positioning operation is not convenient.

2   Demonstration

Figure 2 shows a demonstration of the third hand application. The collaborative manipulator Kuka iiwa was used in the demonstrator, while the required software was developed using the Kuka Sunrise Toolbox (KST) [3]. In Fig. 2(a) the instrument is picked up using the gripper. Afterwards in Fig. 2(b), the hand guiding at the joints level is used for rapid displacement of the instrument, and for rough adjustment of its position Fig. 2(c). Using a button on the flange of the robot, the user switches into the precise hand guiding application Fig. 2(d). The integrated LED lights switch from red to blue signaling that the precise hand guiding at EEF level is initiated. Consequently, the worker moves the object steadily towards its installation site at the top of the satellite dummy Fig. 2(e). Our proposed solution gives the worker the ability to adjust precisely the placement of the instrument in its place Fig. 2(f), allowing him to apply the fixture (bolts).

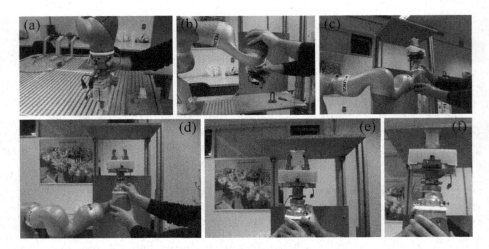

Fig. 2. Demonstrator of the third hand application. (a–c) Rapid motion using hand-guiding at joints level. (d) Switching to precise hand-guiding application. (e–f) Precise adjustment of the position of the instrument.

Acknowledgments. This research was partially supported by Portugal 2020 project DM4Manufacturing POCI-01-0145-FEDER-016418 by UE/FEDER through the program COMPETE 2020, and the Portuguese Foundation for Science and Technology (FCT) SFRH/BD/131091/2017 and COBOTIS (PTDC/EME-EME/32595/2017).

References

1. Hirzinger, G., Sporer, N., Schedl, M., Butterfaß, J., Grebenstein, M.: Torque-controlled lightweight arms and articulated hands: do we reach technological limits now? Int. J. Robot. Res. **23**(4–5), 331–340 (2004)
2. Neto, P., Simão, M., Mendes, N., Safeea, M.: Gesture-basedhuman-robot interaction for human assistance in manufacturing. Int. J. Adv. Manuf. Technol. **101**(1), 119–135 (2019). https://doi.org/10.1007/s00170-018-2788-x
3. Safeea, M., Neto, P.: KUKA sunrise toolbox: interfacing collaborative robots with MATLAB. IEEE Robot. Autom. Mag. **26**(1), 91–96 (2019). https://doi.org/10.1109/MRA.2018.2877776
4. Safeea, M., Bearee, R., Neto, P.: End-effector precise hand-guiding for collaborative robots. In: Ollero, A., Sanfeliu, A., Montano, L., Lau, N., Cardeira, C. (eds.) ROBOT 2017. AISC, vol. 694, pp. 595–605. Springer, Cham (2018). https://doi.org/10.1007/978-3-319-70836-2_49

Towards a Swarm Robotic System for Autonomous Cereal Harvesting

Alan G. Millard[1]([⊠]), Roopika Ravikanna[2], Roderich Groß[2], and David Chesmore[3]

[1] School of Computing, Electronics and Mathematics, University of Plymouth, Plymouth, UK
alan.millard@plymouth.ac.uk
[2] Sheffield Robotics, The University of Sheffield, Sheffield, UK
roopikaravi@gmail.com, r.gross@sheffield.ac.uk
[3] Department of Electronic Engineering, University of York, York, UK
david.chesmore@york.ac.uk

Abstract. Swarm robotics is an emerging technology that has the potential to revolutionise precision agriculture by coordinating fleets of small autonomous vehicles to minimise soil damage, increase farming resolution, lower the cost of automation, and provide solutions that are intrinsically safer and more sustainable than large monolithic systems. Here, we propose a novel swarm robotic system for autonomous harvesting of cereal crops such as wheat and barley. In contrast to existing agricultural swarm robotic systems, we intend to use small autonomous versions of traditional agricultural vehicles, in an attempt to narrow the skills gap for future end-users.

1 Introduction

With the world population predicted to reach 10 billion by the year 2050, there is a pressing need to feed the masses with fewer resources. To achieve this, farmers must make more effective use of their land by reducing waste, increasing yield, and improving sustainability. In order to cope with rising demand, and labour shortages that are leaving crops unharvested, some food producers are turning to robotic automation. However, existing solutions are often so large that they lack precision, resulting in waste; so heavy that they cause serious soil compaction, limiting yield; or prohibitively expensive for small farms.

Swarm robotics [5] is an emerging technology that has the potential to overcome these issues and revolutionise precision agriculture by coordinating fleets of smaller autonomous vehicles to minimise soil damage, increase farming resolution, lower the cost of automation, and provide solutions that are intrinsically safer and more sustainable than large monolithic systems. The benefits of this technology have already been explored in the context of automated seeding as part of the Mobile Agricultural Robot Swarms (MARS) project [2], which used

This work is supported by N8 AgriFood.

K. Althoefer et al. (Eds.): TAROS 2019, LNAI 11650, pp. 458–461, 2019.
https://doi.org/10.1007/978-3-030-25332-5_40

cloud-based path-planning and supervision to manage different fleet sizes, field shapes, and seeding patterns, while preventing collisions and repeated work. In addition, the Swarm Robotics for Agricultural Applications (SAGA) project [1] experimented with fleets of drones for autonomous weed detection, demonstrating that a decentralised system of UAVs could be scaled to different farm sizes without loss of performance.

Here, we propose a novel swarm robotic system for autonomous harvesting of cereal crops such as wheat and barley. We have chosen cereal harvesting as a case study, as cereals are the most cultivated staple crops in the UK [6], and because the task has yet to be automated with small vehicles in a fault-tolerant manner. In contrast to existing agricultural swarm robotic systems, we intend to use small autonomous versions of traditional agricultural vehicles, in an attempt to narrow the skills gap for future end-users.

2 Autonomous Multi-vehicle Cereal Harvesting

Cereal harvesting is typically carried out using combine harvesters (agricultural vehicles that mechanically separate the grain from the rest of the plant) that drive through fields of crops in a predictable pattern. The harvested grain collects in an on-board tank that must be periodically emptied into the trailers of tractors that drive alongside the harvester, which then transport the grain to a nearby silo. A combine harvester will be forced to stop harvesting when its grain tank becomes full, so multiple unloading tractors and trailers are required to ensure an uninterrupted harvest. Due to changeable weather conditions, there may only be a short time window during which the harvest can be completed, so maximising the rate at which crops are harvested is essential.

Many agricultural vehicles are already semi-autonomous, thanks to auto-steer technology and GPS localisation, and can be programmed to repeatably follow paths defined by virtual waypoints. Centimetre-level accuracy can even be achieved via Real-Time Kinematic (RTK) positioning, through the addition of an on-farm base station. An autonomous cereal harvesting system has recently been prototyped as part of the Hands Free Hectare Project[1]—a two-vehicle system comprising an autonomous tractor that offloads cereals on-the-go from an autonomous combine harvester (shown in Fig. 1). These vehicles are significantly smaller and lighter than those typically used on large farms, thus reducing soil compaction and improving sustainability. However, the vehicles are relatively unintelligent—they both follow predefined paths, and their on-board sensors simply bring the system safely to a halt if an obstacle is detected.

Path planning for fleets of combine harvesters and unloading tractors is a relatively well-studied subject, and is often modelled as a Vehicle Routing Problem [3] (a generalisation of the travelling salesman problem). The challenge of minimising the time wasted when turning in headlands has also largely been solved [4], and established methods exist for planning efficient field coverage in

---

[1] http://www.handsfreehectare.com.

Fig. 1. Hands Free Hectare autonomous harvest using a Sampo Rosenlew 130 combine harvester and an Iseki compact tractor retrofitted with GPS autopilot hardware.

complex field shapes [8]. Unfortunately, the solutions found using these algorithms can be brittle, as they often assume fixed fleet sizes and static environments, so cannot cope with unexpected events occurring at run-time, such as mechanical failure in one (or more) of the vehicles.

3   A More Flexible Swarm Robotic System

To better cope with such eventualities, we propose a swarm robotic approach to autonomous cereal harvesting that employs local sensing and decentralised control, to achieve a more flexible and scalable system. Farms of the future will require autonomous vehicles with on-board sensors for navigation and obstacle avoidance, as well as the capacity for real-time inter-vehicle communication and coordination, rather than machines that simply follow pre-planned routes. This will enable effective coordination between autonomous combine harvesters and unloading tractors, allowing them to adapt their behaviour in response to changes in system status and the environment.

We envisage automated fleets of small commercial tractors and combine harvesters, similar to systems already used in projects such as Robot Fleets for Highly Effective Agriculture and Forestry Management [7] and Hands Free Hectare, which feature limited storage capacity to minimise vehicle weight and size. Relay chains of autonomous tractors will offload each combine harvester, with multiple autonomous harvester/tractor teams operating on the same farm. The allocation of offloading trailers to harvesters will not be predefined, rather they will be dynamically reallocated in response to changing demand. Harvesters will signal to nearby tractors when their grain tank is reaching capacity and needs unloading, and inter-vehicle communication between unloading tractors will be used to prevent congestion around the harvesters and grain silos.

The proposed swarm robotic harvesting system will first be implemented in the V-REP robot simulator [9], to explore its potential benefits before implementation in hardware. We will evaluate the efficacy of the proposed solution by investigating how parameters of the system affect total harvest time and levels of simulated soil compaction. The system will be parameterised by the grain tank capacity and harvesting rate of the combine harvesters, the trailer size of unloading tractors, the time required to offload grain from one vehicle to another, the speed of the vehicles, and the distance between the farmland and the nearest grain silo. Through a series of simulation studies, we will determine the optimal number of unloading tractors per harvester and storage capacity of the vehicles, such that both soil compaction and harvest time are minimised.

References

1. Albani, D., Nardi, D., Trianni, V.: Field coverage and weed mapping by UAV swarms. In: IEEE/RSJ International Conference on Intelligent Robots and Systems (IROS), pp. 4319–4325. IEEE (2017)
2. Blender, T., Buchner, T., Fernandez, B., Pichlmaier, B., Schlegel, C.: Managing a mobile agricultural robot swarm for a seeding task. In: 42nd Annual Conference of the IEEE Industrial Electronics Society (IECON), pp. 6879–6886 (2016)
3. Bochtis, D., Sørensen, C.G.: The vehicle routing problem in field logistics: Part I. Biosyst. Eng. **104**(4), 447–457 (2009)
4. Bochtis, D., Vougioukas, S.: Minimising the non-working distance travelled by machines operating in a headland field pattern. Biosyst. Eng. **101**(1), 1–12 (2008)
5. Brambilla, M., Ferrante, E., Birattari, M., Dorigo, M.: Swarm robotics: a review from the swarm engineering perspective. Swarm Intell. **7**(1), 1–41 (2013)
6. Department for Environment: Food & Rural Affairs: Agriculture in the United Kingdom 2017 (2017)
7. Emmi, L., Gonzalez-de Soto, M., Pajares, G., Gonzalez-de Santos, P.: New trends in robotics for agriculture: integration and assessment of a real fleet of robots. Sci. World J. **2014**, 404059 (2014)
8. Oksanen, T., Visala, A.: Coverage path planning algorithms for agricultural field machines. J. Field Robot. **26**(8), 651–668 (2009)
9. Rohmer, E., Singh, S.P., Freese, M.: V-REP: a versatile and scalable robot simulation framework. In: 2013 IEEE/RSJ International Conference on Intelligent Robots and Systems, pp. 1321–1326. IEEE (2013)

Boundary Detection in a Swarm
of Kilobots

Yingyi Kuang[1,2(✉)], Yuri Kaszubowski Lopes[1,3], and Roderich Groß[1]

[1] Sheffield Robotics, The University of Sheffield, Sheffield, UK
`r.gross@sheffield.ac.uk`
[2] Engineering and Applied Science School, Aston University, Birmingham, UK
`180205312@aston.ac.uk`
[3] Department of Software Engineering, Federal University of Technology – Paraná
(UTFPR), Dois Vizinhos, Brazil
`yurilopes@utfpr.edu.br`

Abstract. This paper presents a distributed boundary detection method for a swarm of robots. It employs the cyclic-shape algorithm together with a local coordinate identification, thereby allowing boundary detection without bearing measurements. Each robot can communicate with, and estimate the distance to, its neighbouring robots. The method is validated using swarms of up to 45 Kilobot robots.

Many tasks require swarms of robots to cover vast areas, for example, exploration, inspection, and search and rescue. A related problem is for the robots of the swarm to detect the boundary of their formation [4,5]. Boundary detection can provide information about the extent to which an area is covered, including possible omissions, for example, caused by a sub-optimal distribution of robots or by inaccessible regions of the environment. Boundary detection is also relevant in other contexts, including sensor networks [3]. Topological approaches [1,2,8] estimate whether a node (e.g., a robot) is near the boundary without bearing or distance measurements. However, they often make strong assumptions about the distribution of nodes, and typically require computational and communication resources that exceed those found in swarms of miniature robots. To overcome these limitations, McLurkin and Demaine [6] proposed the cyclic-shape algorithm. Each robot determines whether its neighbours are interconnected. If they are—effectively forming a loop around the focal robot—the latter is considered as an interior node of the formation; otherwise, it is considered as a boundary node. One assumption of the cyclic-shape algorithm is that each robot can obtain distance and bearing measurements, and therefore has full information about the relative positions of nearby robots.

In this paper we present a local coordinate identification method that makes it possible for the cyclic-shape algorithm to be used on nodes that have distance but no bearing measurements. This makes it possible to perform distributed

---

The first author conducted the conceptual and experimental work while with The University of Sheffield. She is currently with Aston University.

K. Althoefer et al. (Eds.): TAROS 2019, LNAI 11650, pp. 462–466, 2019.
https://doi.org/10.1007/978-3-030-25332-5_41

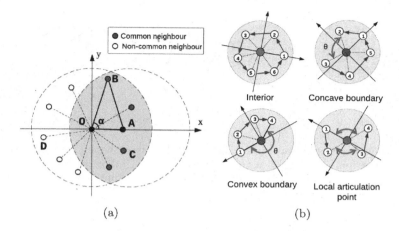

(a)   (b)

Fig. 1. Distributed boundary detection method. (a) The focal node (robot O) determines successively: the closest neighbour, A, defining the x-axis; furthest neighbour, B, that O and A have in common, defining the positive direction of the y-axis; other common neighbours, C; and non-common neighbours, D. (b) The focal node is of one of four possible types: it is interior (number of missing sectors $n = 0$), part of a concave boundary ($n = 1$ and $\theta < 180°$) or convex boundary ($n = 1$ and $\theta \geq 180°$), or it is a local articulation point ($n > 1$), that is, a node connecting multiple networks.

boundary detection on a physical swarm of Kilobots [7], which is a swarm robotics platform with exceedingly simple capabilities. Kilobots can exchange infra-red messages when nearby. They can use the signal strength to estimate the distance (but not the bearing) of other robots in their neighbourhood. In the following, we describe the identification method and report a series of systematic trials on a physical swarm demonstrating the feasibility of our solution.

The local coordinate identification method is based on the assumption that all robots in the swarm have a unique ID, can share a few bytes of information, and all have the same communication range. Each robot begins broadcasting its own ID. As the robot receives messages from its neighbours, it will store for every neighbour i, the corresponding ID and distance, d_i. In the second phase, the robot (hereafter also called O) seeks to establish its own local coordinate system [see Fig. 1(a)]. It identifies the closest neighbour, A, and places it at $(d_{OA}, 0)$, where d_{OA} is the distance between O and A. Then it identifies all neighbours it has in common with A, and chooses the one that is furthest to itself, neighbour B, as shown in Fig. 1(a). The robot assumes that the triangle formed by O, A and B is not degenerate, and uses B to define the positive direction of the y-axis. In other words, B is located in either the first or second quadrant. To obtain B's coordinates, the robot calculates angle α, as shown in Fig. 1(a), using trigonometry from d_{OA}, d_{OB} and d_{AB}, the latter being provided by A. The coordinates of B are then given as $(d_{OB} \cos \alpha, d_{OB} \sin \alpha)$. In the third phase, the robot calculates the coordinates of the remaining common neighbours.

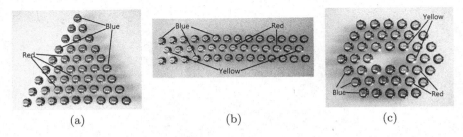

Fig. 2. Kilobot robots densely arranged in one of three base shapes: (a) regular triangle, (b) narrow stripe, (c) hexagon with internal hole. Each robot displays the detection result using its on-board LEDs (red = interior, blue = convex boundary, yellow = concave boundary). (Color figure online)

A common neighbour, C, forms a triangle with O and A. The first estimate of C's coordinates is obtained in the same way as for neighbour B. Robot C could be located on the same side of the x-axis as robot B (positive y-coordinate) or on the opposite side (negative y-coordinate). If B is outside of C's neighbourhood, or if the measured distance between B and C differs substantially from the predicted one, assuming they are located on the same side of the x-axis, the robot infers that B and C are located on opposite sides. In the final phase, the robot calculates the coordinates of the non-common neighbours. The robot chooses iteratively any non-common neighbour that forms a triangle with itself and any other neighbour for which the coordinates are already established, and then obtains the position information analogous to the aforementioned procedure. The robot assumes that the nodes are spaced sufficiently dense such that all positions can be estimated using this process.

Once the coordinates of its neighbourhood have been identified, the robot searches counter-clockwise through all its neighbours. It checks if each neighbour can communicate with the next one, that is, whether they are connected via an edge in the communication graph. The angles between pairs of subsequent connected neighbours are determined and summed up. If there exists no edge between subsequent neighbours, a *missing sector* has been detected. The cyclic-shape algorithm determines the number of missing sectors, n, and, if $n = 1$, the corresponding angle (θ). The procedure is illustrated in Fig. 1(b).

To validate the boundary detection method on a real system, experiments with swarms of 41–45 Kilobot robots were conducted. The Kilobots were placed in an open environment, assuming one of three regular base shapes (see Fig. 2). The robots were either placed in a "dense" (30 to 40 mm spacing) or "sparse" (45 to 55 mm spacing) setting; they were calibrated to have a communication range of 70 mm. Each of the six settings was tested 15 times. In other words, 90 trials were performed in total.

Figure 3 shows the classification accuracy for all six formations. The accuracy is defined as the percentage of robots that identify their boundary type correctly. It is between 83% and 89%, depending on the formation. Irregular shapes were tested too, and led to a decreased accuracy, in between 20% and 70%.

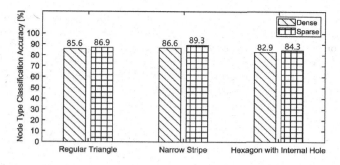

Fig. 3. Experimental results. Node type classification accuracy (mean over 15 trials per box) for different shapes with the robots either densely or sparsely distributed.

Further analysis showed that the interior nodes had a lower classification accuracy compared to the boundary nodes (around 15% less on average). We further investigated the coordinates, obtained via a serial port from robots with incorrectly classified type. Errors were mainly caused by inaccuracies of distance measures and the non-detection of neighbours. Future work will address these uncertainties, for example, by using filtering algorithms or allowing robots to exchange information about their respective boundary types. This could make the system more robust to variations in shape, sensing noise, and dropped messages.

Acknowledgements. This research was supported by the Engineering and Physical Sciences Research Council (grant No. EP/J013714/1).

References

1. Fekete, S.P., Kröller, A., Pfisterer, D., Fischer, S., Buschmann, C.: Neighborhood-based topology recognition in sensor networks. In: Nikoletseas, S.E., Rolim, J.D.P. (eds.) ALGOSENSORS 2004. LNCS, vol. 3121, pp. 123–136. Springer, Heidelberg (2004). https://doi.org/10.1007/978-3-540-27820-7_12
2. Funke, S.: Topological hole detection in wireless sensor networks and its applications. In: Proceedings of the 2005 Joint Workshop on Foundations of Mobile Computing, pp. 44–53. ACM (2005)
3. Khan, I., Mokhtar, H., Merabti, M.: A survey of boundary detection algorithms for sensor networks. In: Proceedings of the 9th Annual Postgraduate Symposium on the Convergence of Telecommunications, Networking and Broadcasting. Liverpool John Moores University (2008)
4. Lee, S.K., Kim, D., Shin, D.S., Jang, T., McLurkin, J.: Distributed deformable configuration control for multi-robot systems. In: 2016 IEEE/RSJ International Conference on Intelligent Robots and Systems (IROS), pp. 5347–5354. IEEE (2016)
5. Lee, S.K., McLurkin, J.: Distributed cohesive configuration control for swarm robots with boundary information and network sensing. In: 2014 IEEE/RSJ International Conference on Intelligent Robots and Systems, pp. 1161–1167. IEEE (2014)
6. McLurkin, J., Demaine, E.D.: A distributed boundary detection algorithm for multi-robot systems. In: 2009 IEEE/RSJ International Conference on Intelligent Robots and Systems (IROS), pp. 4791–4798. IEEE (2009)

7. Rubenstein, M., Ahler, C., Nagpal, R.: Kilobot: A low cost scalable robot system for collective behaviors. In: 2012 IEEE International Conference on Robotics and Automation (ICRA), pp. 3293–3298. IEEE (2012)
8. Wang, Y., Gao, J., Mitchell, J.S.: Boundary recognition in sensor networks by topological methods. In: Proceedings of the 12th Annual International Conference on Mobile Computing and Networking, pp. 122–133. ACM (2006)

Towards Generating Simulated Walking Motion Using Position Based Deep Reinforcement Learning

William Jones[1]([✉]), Siddhant Gangapurwala[2], Ioannis Havoutis[2], and Kazuya Yoshida[1]

[1] Space Robotics Laboratory, Department of Aerospace Engineering, Tohoku University, Sendai, Japan
william@dc.tohoku.ac.jp, yoshida@astro.mech.tohoku.ac.jp
[2] Oxford Robotics Institute, Department of Engineering Science, Oxford University, Oxford, UK
{siddhant,ioannis}@robots.ox.ac.uk

Keywords: ANYmal · Reinforcement learning · Walking robot · Proximal Policy Optimization

1 Introduction

Much of robotics research aims to develop control solutions that exploit the machine's dynamics in order to achieve an extraordinarily agile behaviour [1]. This, however, is limited by the use of traditional model-based control techniques such as model predictive control and quadratic programming. These solutions are often based on simplified mechanical models which result in mechanically constrained and inefficient behaviour, thereby limiting the agility of the robotic system in development [2]. Treating the control of robotic systems as a reinforcement learning (RL) problem enables the use of model-free algorithms that attempt to learn a policy which maximizes the expected future (discounted) reward without inferring the effects of an executed action on the environment.

RL has recently proven effective for the generation of walking motion for legged robots, both in simulation and in the real world [3]. However, there has been little investigation into model free RL where reward is given based on position rather than velocity. In this work, we show that a reward function based on position is able to train a legged robot to walk, which has potential application in a goal based motion planning problem.

2 Deep Reinforcement Learning

2.1 Definition

The RL problem can be introduced in the framework of Markov Decision Process (MDP) which is a discrete time stochastic control process in which, at each time

© Springer Nature Switzerland AG 2019
K. Althoefer et al. (Eds.): TAROS 2019, LNAI 11650, pp. 467–470, 2019.
https://doi.org/10.1007/978-3-030-25332-5_42

step, the process is in a state s, and an action a is chosen from the available actions A. The process then shifts to a new state s' with a probability given by the state transition function $P(s, s') = Pr\{s_{t+1} = s' \mid s_t = s, a_t = a\}$, returning a corresponding reward $R(s, s')$. In our work, we define an MDP tuple $(S, A, \{P_{sa}\}, \gamma, R, \rho_0)$, where

- S is a finite set of states given by the robot's centre of mass (COM) pose, joint torques and joint angles.
- A is a 12-dimensional set of actions representing joint-position commands.
- $P_{sa}\left(s'\right)$ is the state transition probability of landing at state $s' : P\left(s, a, s'\right)$ upon taking the action a at state s.
- $\gamma \in [0, 1)$ is the discount factor.
- $R : S \to \mathbf{R}$ is the reward function.

We defined the reward function of the RL framework in such a way as to encourage smooth movement of the robot body along the y axis, by giving reward for increasing y position, whilst punishing deviation from the y axis, joint torque use, and body orientation deviation from the nominal;

$$R = b_y - 0.1||b_x||^2 - 0.001\tau - 0.1\phi - 0.1\theta - 0.1\psi \tag{1}$$

where b_y and b_x is the projection of the COM of the robot's body on the y and x axis, τ is the sum of all joint torques per step, and ϕ, θ, and ψ is the body roll, pitch and yaw respectively.

- $\rho_0 : S \to \mathbf{R}$ is the state distribution of the initial state s_0
- $\rho_\pi : S \to \mathbf{R}$ is the discounted visitation frequencies

2.2 Learning Algorithm

In our work we decided to use the Proximal Policy Optimization (PPO) algorithm [4]. Based on Trust Region Policy Optimization, given as,

$$\underset{\theta}{\text{maximize}} \quad L_{\theta_0}(\theta) - C\bar{D}_{KL}\left(\pi_0||\pi\right)$$
$$\text{subject to} \quad \bar{D}_{KL}\left(\pi_{\theta_0}||\pi_\theta\right) \leq \delta$$

PPO skips the computation created by constrained optimization by proposing a clipped surrogate objective function as described in Algorithm 1 [5].

3 Experimental Setup

3.1 Simulation Environment

The simulation platform used in this framework is V-REP, an integrated development environment using a distributed control architecture [6]. The remote API V-REP scene, as shown in Fig. 1, was converted into an OpenAI Gym environment and used in conjunction with a tensorflow based policy. The robot model used was ANYmal, a 12 DoF, torque controlled robot weighing 33 kg, developed by ANYbotics [7].

Algorithm 1. Proximal Policy Optimization using Actor-Critic Method

---

for iteration=1,2,... **do**
    for actor=1,2,...,N **do**
        Run policy $\pi_{\theta_{old}}$ in environment for T timesteps
        Compute advantage estimates $\hat{A}_1, ..., \hat{A}_T$
    end for
    Optimize surrogate L wrt θ, with K epochs and minibatch size $M \leq NT$;
    $\theta_{old} \leftarrow \theta$
    end for

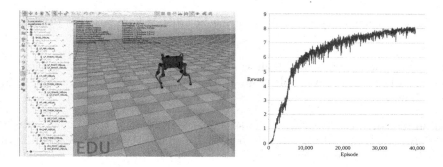

Fig. 1. *Left*: ANYmal model in V-REP. *Right*: Reward curve.

4 Current Result

Using the implementation of PPO from [4] and the reward function (1), we obtained the reward curve shown in Fig. 1. All training was done on commodity hardware without a specialist GPU architecture, resulting in a relatively long training time of over 2 weeks. The aim of this work though, was not to investigate the training time of reinforcement learning algorithms, but to demonstrate effective learning with a positional reward function. A new GPU based simulator can drastically reduce training time, and will be used in future work, as the software becomes available [8].

At the time of writing, training of the policy has not yet finished. This can be seen in Fig. 1, where the gradient of the curve is positive at its end point, indicating that the trained policy has not yet converged to an optimal one. This is also visible in the video associated with Fig. 2, where toward the end of the episode, the legs the left of the robot become outstretched and the gait pattern that can be seen emerging initially is lost.

4.1 Future Work

In future, we will extend this work to vision based locomotion by including depth map obtained using an RGBD sensor into the state space. The policy network will be modified to include a convolutional neural network (CNN) block

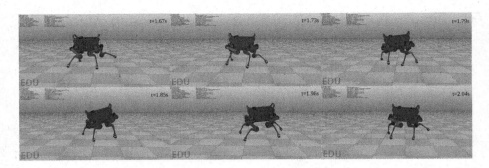

Fig. 2. Walking Sequence. Video available at https://youtu.be/4DFKBevlVbs

to process vision data. This will allow us to investigate a path planning based RL problem where the robot is able to guide itself to a goal state in more challenging environments.

Acknowledgments. This research is supported by the UKRI and EPSRC (EP/R026084/1, EP/R026173/1, EP/S002383/1) and the EU H2020 project MEMMO (780684). This work has been conducted as part of ANYmal Research, a community to advance legged robotics.

References

1. Gangapurwala, S., et al.: Generative adversarial imitation learning for quadrupedal locomotion using unstructured expert demonstrations (2018)
2. Mastalli, C., et al.: Trajectory and foothold optimization using low-dimensional models for rough terrain locomotion (2017)
3. Hwangbo, J., et al.: Learning agile and dynamic motor skills for legged robots. Sci. Robot. **4**(26), eaau5872 (2019). https://doi.org/10.1126/scirobotics.aau5872
4. Schulman, J., Wolski, F., Dhariwal, P., Radford, A., Klimov, O.: Proximal policy optimization algorithms (2017)
5. Schulman, J., Levine, S., Abbeel, P., Jordan, M., Moritz, P.: Trust region policy optimization. In: International Conference on Machine Learning, pp. 1889–1897, 1 June 2015
6. Rohmer, E., Singnh, S. P. N., Freese, M.: V-REP: a versatile and scalable robot simulation framework. In: IEEE/RSJ International Conference on Intelligent Robots and Systems (2013)
7. Hutter, M., et al.: ANYmal - a highly mobile and dynamic quadrupedal robot. In: 2016 IEEE/RSJ International Conference on Intelligent Robots and Systems (IROS), Daejeon, pp. 38–44 (2016). https://doi.org/10.1109/IROS.2016.7758092
8. Liang, J., et al.: GPU-accelerated robotic simulation for distributed reinforcement learning. CoRL (2018)

Improved Safety with a Distributed Routing Strategy for UAVs

William D. Bonnell[✉]

University of Bristol, Bristol BS8 1TH, UK
wb17716@bristol.ac.uk

Abstract. This paper presents a routing strategy for UAVs that can be applied in conjunction with lower level collision avoidance methods. The strategy allows individual UAVs to route themselves in 2D space in order to avoid areas of high-density traffic. The proposed approach is explored in simulation. The results demonstrate a safer system operation when the routing strategy is used, compared with just a simple collision avoidance method.

Keywords: UAV · Distributed · Routing

1 Introduction

This paper demonstrates that by implementing higher level routing on top of simple navigation algorithms, we can ensure Unmanned Aerial Vehicles (UAVs) fully exploit airspace capacity. We present the routing algorithm and simulation results for a 2D system, as a near-term model of likely UAV operations. In future, the model will be extended to 3D.

There are numerous methods for navigating a robot. Some of these methods involve developing a path from the robot to the end goal and then following it [2]. Others produce motion based on the robot's environment [1,3,6], usually toward some goal and away from obstacles.

Many of these methods were first developed with static environments in mind, though [2] and [6] account for dynamic obstacles. However, in both cases the focus is still on navigating one robot, along the shortest path, to its goal.

For moving large ensembles of robots much work has been done in the field of swarm robotics. In [4] swarm ideas are used to display flocking behaviour in UAVs in confined spaces. For this sort of method to work however it assumes a degree of cooperation between robots as well as a shared purpose which is not necessarily the case with commercial UAVs undertaking deliveries, for example.

The rest of this paper is divided in to three sections. Section 2 describes the routing method along with details of the underlying collision avoidance scheme. Section 3 describes the simulation implementation. Section 4 presents the results from a representative traffic scenario for a variety of simulation parameters.

This work was supported by an EPSRC grant EP/R0047571 and by Thales SA.

K. Althoefer et al. (Eds.): TAROS 2019, LNAI 11650, pp. 471–475, 2019.
https://doi.org/10.1007/978-3-030-25332-5_43

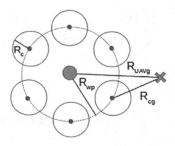

Fig. 1. Schematic of UAV routing.

2   Methods

We begin with a brief overview of the underlying navigation and collision avoidance (CA) scheme. The UAVs move using a method inspired by the SFM, comprised of two parts. The first part causes the UAV to move toward its goal with a desired velocity. In the second part, UAVs accelerate away from one another with a magnitude that is inversely proportional to their separation.

The routing developed for this paper was inspired by [5], a routing algorithm for cars. In order to extend this to 2D space, each UAV generates candidate intermediary waypoints, and then chooses one to travel toward. This enables the routing method to be layered on top of any individual CA regime, as each waypoint becomes the goal of that particular section of the journey. Also, as each UAV generates and ranks its own waypoints, this allows the UAV to operate without centralised control.

The routing method works by first generating a set number of candidate waypoints at a distance R_{wp} away from the UAV, see Fig. 1. Each candidate waypoint, c, is then assigned a dimensionless score Q_{c} according to

$$Q_{\mathrm{c}} = N_{\mathrm{c}} + (R_{\mathrm{cg}} - R_{\mathrm{UAV_g}})\gamma, \tag{1}$$

where N_{c} is the number of other UAVs within a distance R_{c} of the candidate waypoint, R_{cg} and $R_{\mathrm{UAV_g}}$ are the distances from the candidate waypoint and the UAV to the end goal respectively, and γ is a parameter with units m^{-1}. All distances in Eq. 1 have units m. The candidate with the smallest score Q_{c} is then chosen as the next waypoint. Once the UAV reaches that waypoint, it generates new candidate waypoints and chooses again. If the end goal is within R_{wp} of the UAV then it is also added to the list of candidate waypoints.

The waypoint that has the least traffic in its local vicinity and is closest to the end goal is therefore chosen according to Eq. 1. The parameter γ can be used to decide which of these two factors is more important. A UAV with a high γ will prioritise heading toward their end goal while a UAV with a small γ will prioritise avoiding areas with lots of other UAVs present. For this paper, γ is the same for all UAVs throughout a simulation run, but this could be relaxed in future work.

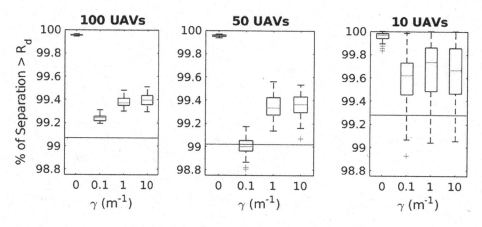

Fig. 2. Safety metric for several system parameters.

3   Simulation Procedure

In order to ensure that the routing method was tested in a scenario with high traffic density, all the UAVs share an end goal in the centre of the simulation, modelling an a depot or similar landing area that all UAVs converge upon. The UAVs simulated in this paper are quadcopter-like (they can hover). As such there is a certain minimum desired separation R_d that UAVs should try to maintain in order to not adversely affect one another. This defines the idea of a conflict, when two UAVs have a separation that is less than the desired minimum.

4   Results

Using the concept of the conflict as described in Sect. 3, the percentage of recorded UAV separations that are greater than or equal to the desired minimum separation, R_d, provides a metric to understand the safety of each simulation. If the percentage is 100%, then no conflicts are recorded for that particular run (perfect safety).

This metric is recorded in Fig. 2 for a variety of values of γ and number of UAVs. The solid line shows the average percentage for that number of UAVs when there is no routing. There are two main results to note. Firstly, in almost all scenarios the average percentage of UAV separations compliant with the minimum separation increases for all values of γ compared with the average for simulations where no routing is used. Thus, the system is safer when the routing method is implemented. Secondly, the system becomes safer as γ increases from $0.1\,\mathrm{m^{-1}}$ to $10\,\mathrm{m^{-1}}$. This is the opposite of the expected behaviour as smaller values of γ should correspond to traffic that prioritises avoiding areas of higher density.

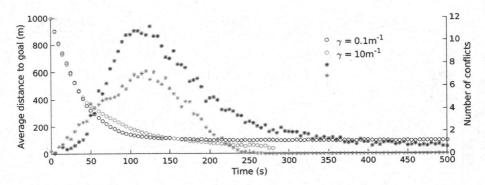

Fig. 3. Average distance to goal (o) and number of conflicts (*). Averaged over 50 simulations.

To explore this unexpected behaviour, Fig. 3 shows two metrics for 50 UAVs with two different values of γ. These metrics are the average distance to the end goal and number of conflicts, both over time and averaged over the 50 simulations. The number of conflicts in both cases rises at each time step to a peak level before declining. In every simulation where γ was $10\,\mathrm{m}^{-1}$, all UAVs landed by 300 s; thus there are no data points for the average distance to target after this point.

When γ is $0.1\,\mathrm{m}^{-1}$ however not every UAV landed in the 500 s simulation time. Figure 3 shows that the average distance to the goal, in this case, stabilises to around 100 m. However, the number of conflicts decreases throughout the simulation after this stabilisation. This seems to suggest that the UAVs are self organising in to an orbiting behaviour.

References

1. Helbing, D., Molnár, P.: Social force model for pedestrian dynamics. Phys. Rev. E **51**(5), 4282–4286 (1995). https://doi.org/10.1103/PhysRevE.51.4282. https://link.aps.org/doi/10.1103/PhysRevE.51.4282
2. Otte, M., Frazzoli, E.: RRTX: asymptotically optimal single-query sampling-based motion planning with quick replanning. Int. J. Robot. Res. **35**(7), 797–822 (2016). https://doi.org/10.1177/0278364915594679
3. Van Den Berg, J., Guy, S.J., Lin, M., Manocha, D.: Reciprocal n-body collision avoidance. In: Pradalier, C., Siegwart, R., Hirzinger, G. (eds.) Robotics Research. Springer Tracts in Advanced Robotics, vol. 70, pp. 9–19. Springer, Heidelberg (2011). https://doi.org/10.1007/978-3-642-19457-3_1
4. Vásárhelyi, G., Virágh, C., Somorjai, G., Nepusz, T., Eiben, A.E., Vicsek, T.: Optimized flocking of autonomous drones in confined environments. Sci. Robot. **3**(20), eaat3536 (2018). https://doi.org/10.1126/scirobotics.aat3536. http://robotics.sciencemag.org/lookup/doi/10.1126/scirobotics.aat3536

5. Wedde, H.F., et al.: A novel class of multi-agent algorithms for highly dynamic transport planning inspired by honey bee behavior. In: 2007 IEEE Conference on Emerging Technologies and Factory Automation (EFTA 2007), pp. 1157–1164, September 2007. https://doi.org/10.1109/EFTA.2007.4416912
6. Woods, A.C., La, H.M., Member, S.: A novel potential field controller for use on aerial robots. IEEE Trans. Syst. Man Cybern. Syst. 49(4), 665–676 (2019). https://doi.org/10.1109/TSMC.2017.2702701

Exploration: Do We Need a Map?

Mohamed Osama Idries[✉], Matthias Rolf, and Tjeerd V. olde Scheper

Oxford Brookes University, Oxford, UK
{midries,mrolf,tvolde-scheper}@brookes.ac.uk

Abstract. Exploration is one of the fundamental problems in mobile robotics. Efforts to address this problem made over the past two decades divide into two approaches: reactive approaches, that make only instantaneous decisions, and map-based approaches involving e.g. grid, metric, or topological representations. Comparative studies have so far largely focused on comparing different map-based algorithms, while no common framework to compare them to purely reactive approaches currently exists. This paper aims at creating a framework to simulate, evaluate, and compare exploratory algorithms as different as reactive and map-based approaches. Preliminary results are demonstrated for two reactive algorithms, random walk and wall follower, and one map based approach, pheromone potential field, have been implemented. Measurements of navigation success, time to success, as well as computational and memory usage reveal a dominance of simple wall-following over the map-based potential field approach, and a distinct load/efficacy trade off for random walks. These preliminary results challenge the common assumptions that maps are needed for successful and efficient exploration and navigation.

Keywords: Robot · Navigation · Reactive exploration

1 Introduction

Robotic exploration is a field that is well studied and has matured to the point where we can explore and map complex environments in real-time, specifically indoors. A large number of algorithms have been proposed to solve this problem. These algorithms can be divided into reactive and map based approaches. Comparisons in reactive algorithms show that the choice of algorithm largely depends on the robot's mission and choice of environment [5]. Surveys into map-based exploration [1,2,6] result also in comparisons showing the difference in criteria including representation, uncertainty, and ability to map static environments. However, little efforts have been made in comparing those types of approaches.

This paper aims at comparing those approaches by asking the question: "When would we need a map?". To answer that question a framework is developed to compare reactive, and map-based approaches in simulation and evaluating it's results.

© Springer Nature Switzerland AG 2019
K. Althoefer et al. (Eds.): TAROS 2019, LNAI 11650, pp. 476–479, 2019.
https://doi.org/10.1007/978-3-030-25332-5_44

2   Methodology

2.1   Exploration Strategies

The framework developed to evaluate the need of a map compares a number of different types of exploration algorithms. These algorithms represent the simplest implementation for each type of approach and were chosen for that reason.

Random walk, a reactive strategy based of a Brownian motion, is an algorithm where the robot moves randomly till it sees it goals at which point it moves towards it. At each step a random direction (north, west, south, or east) is chosen and, provided it won't collide with a wall, a single step forwards to the neighbouring cell is taken.

Wall Follower, a reactive strategy based of a Braitenberg vehicle, is an algorithm where the robot moves forward until it finds a wall. It continues then to follow the wall counter-clockwise until it sees the goal at which point it moves towards it. Each step, after initially finding the wall, it will turn right and step forward if there is no wall on it's right, step forward if there is no collision ahead, or turn left if there is a collision ahead.

Pheromone potential field, a simple map-based strategy, is an extension of normal potential fields [3] where the robot moves depending on the attractive and repulsive forces acting on it. The attractive force originates from the goal, and the repulsive fields originate from the walls within range, and the pheromone trail it leaves behind.

2.2   Environmental Setup

The environment used to run the trials is 400 by 400 arbitrary units, divided in two equal parts by an artificial wall. The robot is spawned randomly on the left side of the wall, while the goal spawned randomly at the right side of the wall. The length of the wall is variable to add different levels of complexity to the environment by increasing the distance between robot and goal (Fig. 1).

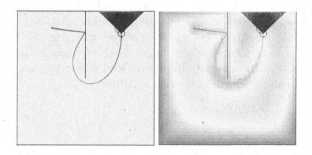

Fig. 1. A sample trial of the Pheromone Potential Field algorithm (left). The state of a current sections (right) is shown as range from repulsive (red) through neutral (white) to attractive (green). (Color figure online)

The simulator generates 100 different combinations of robot and goal locations and evaluates each of the explorations strategies across a total of 10 different wall sizes ranging from no length to almost blocking. Running through each of the algorithms and evaluating them on two main attributes; exploration time and the associated energy cost. The exploration time is calculated as a measure of time required to either complete the task or hit the maximum number of iterations. The energy cost is a combination of the CPU usage, memory usage and distance covered. It's presumed that the robot has object recognition built in and can detect the goal when in sensory range.

3   Results

The approach described has been implemented with sample results shown in Fig. 2. The robot's path is indicated by a coloured trail starting from blue until red. The goal is shown with a red circle.

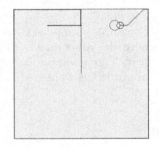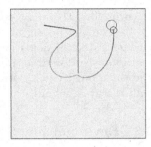

Fig. 2. A sample run displaying the random walk (left), the wall follower (center), and the Pheromone Potential Field (right) (Color figure online)

Evaluating all of the associated attributes (see Fig. 3) we can see that given this environment the wall follower reactive algorithm actually outperforms a map-based approach. It consumes significantly less time, CPU, or memory consuming than the map-based approach while only having a slightly higher failure rate. The Random walk was too costly in time consumption, and distance covered.

Using a simple energy cost-function where we sum all the normalized attributes we can determine the cost associated with each algorithm for this environment. This function is only indicative and depending on the application different weights can be assigned to each attribute.

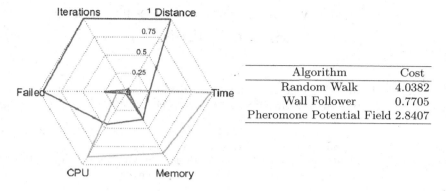

Algorithm	Cost
Random Walk	4.0382
Wall Follower	0.7705
Pheromone Potential Field	2.8407

Fig. 3. The radar plot shows the normalized resource usage of each algorithm. (Random walk - blue, Wall Follower - red, and Pheromone Potential Field - yellow). The sum of these values are indicative of the algorithms performance for this environment. This clearly display the efficiency of the Wall Follower in this scenario. Different weights can be assigned to resources depending on the application. (Color figure online)

4 Conclusions

In this paper we set out to answer the question: "Do we need a map?". While it's presumed that map-based approaches outperform purely reactive ones, our preliminary results show that this is not the case and that the environment truly plays a major role in dictating the necessary approach.

It is difficult to imagine fully autonomous exploration in a dynamic world where one approach would continuously outperform. To achieve this, it is advised to generate a model of the current environment, and then dynamically switch to the favourable approach(es) for that environment. Future research aims at determining an efficient approach by considering more environments, and approaches (reactive, map-based, and learning-based [4]). This approach would consider the environment and the cost of running specific algorithms on this environment to determine the change of algorithm.

References

1. Aulinas, J., Petillot, Y., Salvi, J., Lladó, X.: The SLAM problem: a survey. Technical report
2. Juliá, M., Gil, A., Reinoso, O.: A comparison of path planning strategies for autonomous exploration and mapping of unknown environments. Auton. Robot. **33**(4), 427–444 (2012). https://doi.org/10.1007/s10514-012-9298-8
3. Koren, Y., Borenstein, J.: Potential field methods and their inherent limitations for mobile robot navigation (May 1991), pp. 1398–1404 (2002)
4. Mishkin, D., Dosovitskiy, A., Koltun, V.: Benchmarking classic and learned navigation in complex 3D environments (2019)
5. Russell, R.A., Bab-Hadiashar, A., Shepherd, R.L., Wallace, G.G.: A comparison of reactive robot chemotaxis algorithms. Robot. Auton. Syst. **45**(2), 83–97 (2003)
6. Thrun, S.: Others: robotic mapping: a survey. In: Lakemeyer, G., Nebel, B. (eds.) Exploring Artificial Intelligence in the New Millennium, vol. 1, pp. 1–35. Morgan Kaufmann, Burlington (2002)

The Downsizing of a Free-Flying
Space Robot

Lucy Jackson[1](✉), Chakravarthini M. Saaj[1](✉), Asma Seddaoui[1](✉),
Calem Whiting[2](✉), and Steve Eckersley[2](✉)

[1] Surrey Space Center, University of Surrey, Guildford GU2 7XH, UK
{l.jackson,c.saaj,a.seddaoui}@surrey.ac.uk
[2] Surrey Satellite Technology Ltd., Tycho House, Guildford GU2 7YE, UK
{c.whiting,s.eckersley}@sstl.co.uk

Abstract. Robotic technologies have been long-serving in space, and
are still an active and ever-growing field of research. Satellite mounted
manipulators allow more ambitious tasks to be carried out in a safer
and more timely manner, by limiting the need for astronaut intervention during task execution. Downsizing these free-flying space robots will
expand their potential by increasing their versatility, allowing task sharing between multiple systems, as well as further lowering mission costs
and timescales. Limited research has been done in assessing the practical challenges involved in downsizing a space robot and its consequences
on overall performance. This paper presents a system level analysis into
deciding the optimum dimensions for a manipulator mounted on a small
free-flying spacecraft. Simulation results show the effect of downsizing
on the efficiency of the manipulator and the overall system.

Keywords: Space robot · Small satellites · Free-flying mode ·
Robot arm

1 Introduction

Space robots were first introduced with the aim of utilizing an agile system
with robotic capabilities for rendezvous and docking. This was achieved by
the Experimental Test Satellite (ETS-VII) and the Orbital Express mission,
launched in 1997 and 2007 respectively [1,2]. Recently, there has been a surge
in the demand for missions with servicing objectives. RemoveDEBRIS successfully demonstrated debris capture, and Restore-L, designed to service satellites,
has passed its preliminary design review [3,4]. Missions with on-orbit assembly
objectives, such as AAReST, RAMST and GOAT, have also been proposed [5–7];
opening a market for a small free-flying system capable of assembly components
in-orbit. The commercial appeal for downsizing these systems comes from an

Supported by Surrey Satellite Technology Ltd. and the Engineering and Physical Sciences Research Council.

increase in their capabilities, a reduction in the required launch vehicle volume, shorter mission time scales, and a fall in overall cost. Smaller systems are also easier to relocate in space, with a change of orbit requiring less fuel; thus enabling multi-mission use for a single space robot. Here, multi-mission use refers to the ability of one space robot to remain in orbit for an extended period of time and aid a number of different missions. While no smaller missions have flown some are in the planning stages, with the lightest proposed system being NASA's Tendon-Actuate Lightweight In-Space MANipulator (TALISMAN), weighing 36.2 kg [8].

This research is focused on designing a small space robot equipped with a robotic manipulator. Issues with downsizing the manipulator stem from trying to maintain dexterity while minimizing mass and power requirements. Preserving dexterity is paramount for assembly missions since they involve the connection of joints, a demanding task; yet to be carried out by a space robot in-orbit [9]. Discussed here is the downsizing of a robotic manipulator, currently modeled as operating off a 12U free-flying spacecraft with a dedicated attitude control system. The system is 3-axis stabilized, and the manipulator can be modeled as if mounted on a fixed base in the absence of gravity.

2 Manipulator Design

The process of designing a downsized manipulator started from the requirement on reachability (~ 0.5 m) and specified link/joint configuration: 3 links and 5 Degrees of Freedom (DoF) [10]. Since most mass is concentrated in the joints, joints 1 and 2 have been combined to lower the mass while maintaining dexterity (Fig. 1). Analysis was then carried out into optimizing the link dimensions. Three different options were identified (Table 1) based on the following specifications: (i) Link $0 = 0$ m, due to the combination of joints 1 and 2, (ii) Link 3 is shortest to increase end effector accuracy, (iii) Total link length $= 0.5$ m.

The total attitude confined workspace of each configuration was calculated and it was found that option 3 provided the smallest reachable area; 17% smaller than option 1 and 9% smaller than option 2. The end effector accuracy was then investigated and compared for all options. A simple Proportional Integral Derivative controller was used to make each option track 10 trajectories; pre-defined using random joint angles and a 5th order polynomial. The final error and maximum path deviation were calculated based on the simulation results.

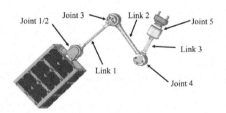

Fig. 1. Proposed link/joint configuration of the 12U space robot [10]

Table 1. Design options for arm configurations

Option	Link 0 (m)	Link 1 (m)	Link 2 (m)	Link 3 (m)	Total length (m)
1	0	0.2	0.2	0.1	0.5
2	0	0.25	0.15	0.1	0.5
3	0	0.3	0.15	0.05	0.5

Fig. 2. Tracking error between desired trajectory and actual trajectory for one simulation scenario (a) x-axis (b) y-axis (c) z-axis

The maximum path deviation is of interest since the successful completion of mission objectives will be dependent on the path accuracy as well as the final position. It was found that the maximum error with configuration 3 was consistently smallest across all three axis (Fig. 2); and on average it was 0.1 mm smaller than the option with the largest error, which varied between options 1 and 2. The same analysis was carried out for the torque required at each joint (Fig. 3). A smaller torque is preferable as it lowers the overall power requirements. Configuration 3 required the smallest torque across all 10 trajectories for all joints.

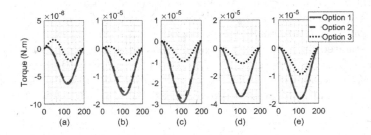

Fig. 3. Torque required to actuate each joint tracking one out of ten trajectories (a) Joint 1 (b) Joint 2 (c) Joint 3 (d) Joint 4 (e) Joint 5

3   Conclusion and Further Work

The extensive simulation based trajectory tracking exercise showed that there is a clear trade-off between the manipulator's workspace, joint torques and tracking accuracy. Design option 3 had the lowest error and required least torque but also has the smallest workspace. This means a rigid recommendation cannot be made as mission specifics may call for a larger workspace at the expense of the power requirements. Nevertheless, the presented information should be applied to mission concepts whose requirements have been outlined, allowing an informed recommendation to be made. Carrying on from this, the analysis will be expanded in relation to user defined mission concepts. Research will then be carried out into the optimal sizing of the base spacecraft onto which the manipulator will be mounted to ensure the optimum operating levels of the system. At this stage, further investigation will be carried out into the other operating modes of the base spacecraft, in particular the controlled-floating mode.

References

1. Oda, M.: Space robot experiments on NASDA's ETS-VII satellite - preliminary overview of the experiment results. In: IEEE International Conference on Robotics and Automation, vol. 1–4, pp. 1390–1395 (1999)
2. Friend, R.B.: Orbital express program summary and mission overview. In: Sensors and Systems for Space Applications II, vol. 6958 (2008)
3. Forshaw, J.L., et al.: RemoveDEBRIS: an in-orbit active debris removal demonstration mission. Acta Astronaut. **127**, 448–463 (2016)
4. Reed, B.B., Smith, R.C., Naasz, B.J., Pellegrino, J.F., Bacon, C.E.: The restore-1 servicing mission. In: AIAA Space, Long Beach, California (2016)
5. Underwood, C., Pellegrino, S., Lappas, V.J., Bridges, C.P., Baker, J.: Using cubesat/micro-satellite technology to demonstrate the autonomous assembly of a reconfigurable space telescope (AAReST). Acta Astronaut. **114**, 112–122 (2015)
6. Eckersley, S., et al.: In-orbit assembly of large spacecraft using small spacecraft and innovative technologies. In: 69th International Astronautical Congress, Bremen, Germany, October 2018
7. Saunders, C., Lobb, D., Sweeting, M., Gao, Y.: Building large telescopes in orbit using small satellites. Acta Astronaut. **141**, 183–195 (2017)
8. Doggett, W.R., Dorsey, J.T., Jones, T.C., King, B.: Development of a tendon-actuated lightweight in-space MANipulator (TALISMAN). In: 42nd Aerospace Mechanisms Symposium, vol. 405. NASA Goddard Space Flight Center, May 2014
9. Roa, M., Nottensteiner, K., Wedler, A., Grunwald, G.: Robotic technologies for in-space assembly operations. In: Advanced Space Technologies in Robotics and Automation, June 2017
10. Jackson, L., Saaj, C., Seddaoui, A., Whiting, C., Eckersley, S., Ferris, M.: Design of a small space robot for on-orbit assembly missions. In: 5th International Conference on Mechatronics and Robotics Engineering, Rome, Italy, February 2019

Preliminary Investigation on Visual Finger-Counting with the iCub Robot Cameras and Hands

Alexandr Lucas[1]([⊠]), Carlos Ricolfe-Viala[2], and Alessandro Di Nuovo[1]

[1] Sheffield Hallam University, Sheffield S1 1WB, UK
A.Lucas@shu.ac.uk
[2] Universitat Politecnica de Valencia, 46022 Valencia, Spain

Abstract. This short paper describes an approach for collecting a dataset of hand's pictures and training a Deep Learning network that could enable the iCub robot to count on its fingers using solely its own cameras. Such a skill, mimicking children's habits, can support arithmetic learning in a baby robot, an important step in creating artificial intelligence for robots that could learn like children in the context of cognitive developmental robotics. Preliminary results show the approach is promising in terms of accuracy.

Keywords: Developmental robotics · Finger-counting · Faster R-CNN · iCub

1 Introduction

This paper presents preliminary results of an ongoing investigation to identify fingers using computer vision with a humanoid robotics platform in the context of cognitive developmental robotics. Even if it is one of the first ability that children learn, visually counting the fingers is not an easy task in computer vision. In one of the few previous works in robot hand detection using Machine Learning methods [7], Cartesian Genetic Programming for Image Processing algorithm was trained to detect the iCub hands and fingertips. Although the results were announced as competitive, no comparison was given due to the lack of suitable datasets at that time. A combined approach of estimating the iCub hand pose using proprioception, stereo vision and 3D model of the robot was presented in [10], with a comparison of silhouette segmentation vs edge extraction techniques. However, to the best of our knowledge, the problem of reliably identifying the number of fingers being shown in the finger-counting scenario has not been addressed yet. The importance of acquiring the skill of visually counting fingers is crucial for supporting cognitive developmental robotics models of number cognition and basic arithmetic [6, 8], which are envisioned by the EPSRC project NUMBERS. Indeed, fingers have a significant influence on the development of our counting system, with some suggesting that we likely use a base 10 system due to the number of fingers on our hands [3]. Moreover, recent studies suggest that fingers, being natural tools, play a fundamental role at many stages of maths learning, from developing a sense of numbers to acquiring proficiency in the basic arithmetic processing [4, 5, 9].

K. Althoefer et al. (Eds.): TAROS 2019, LNAI 11650, pp. 484–488, 2019.
https://doi.org/10.1007/978-3-030-25332-5_46

Application of these concepts to robotics formed what is now known as Cognitive Developmental Robotics (CDR), defined as the "interdisciplinary approach to the autonomous design of behavioural and cognitive capabilities in artificial agents (robots) that takes direct inspiration from the developmental principles and mechanisms observed in natural cognitive systems (humans)" [1, 2].

2   Materials and Methods

2.1   Setup

As our research platform, we used the iCub humanoid robot provided by Sheffield Robotics (Fig. 1). iCub is one of the most advanced child-like robotics platforms available, featuring 41 actuated DOF and tendon-driven joints. Particularly important for this work are fully functional five-fingered hands, closely emulating the human hand. The setup comprised a legless iCub fixed on a platform, with a greenscreen board positioned in the background, in such a way that the board fully covered the field of view of iCub's eye cameras looking directly forward. Gaze direction and head pose were fixed to minimise background variance. For image segmentation algorithm to produce a hand silhouette of good quality, illumination control, and uniform background are necessary. Green was chosen as the background colour because it is the most distinct from the colours of the robot's hand and its covers.

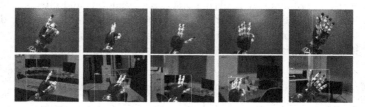

Fig. 1. Sheffield robotics' iCub

Fig. 2. iCub counting against a green background (top row). These images were used to produce the DNN model dataset (bottom row) (Color figure online)

iCub was programmed to count from one to five using fingers on the left hand. From a range of different finger-counting styles representing numbers from one to five, we chose the American Sign Language, as being most convenient given specific hardware implementation of iCub's hands (shared actuator for the ring and little fingers).

2.2   Image Data Collection

In the initial data collection, for each number shown the hand cycled through slightly different orientations using the wrist pro/sup, pitch, and yaw joints, sequentially, with all other hand joints being fixed. The angle (min, max, step) values of the wrist pro/sup joint were set to be $(-55, 55, 15)$, for the wrist pitch joint to be $(-50, 25, 15)$ and for the wrist yaw joint to be $(-20, 25, 10)$. For each hand pose, the robot would take a picture using both its left and right camera with 640×480 pixels resolution. This resulted in 200 pictures for each number of fingers shown from 1 to 5, totalling 1000 images for each of the two cameras. Settings for both cameras were adjusted manually at the beginning to find the optimum values of gain, shutter speed, exposure, brightness, and white balance. The top row of Fig. 2 contains a sample image from each class. However, some poses where found to be looking ambiguous, with fingers occluding each other and not clearly visible. This effect increased with the number of fingers shown. Removing ambiguous images from the database reduced its size to 619 images for the left camera and 562 for the right.

2.3   Extracting the Hand Silhouettes

For extraction of regions of interest containing the hand with fingers silhouettes from each image, we utilised TensorFlow Object Detection API library, which in turn makes use of OpenCV routines. The labelling process was as follows:

1. The images are converted to HSV space to highlight hand pixels. Detection of contours in RGB space was found to be ineffective, due to noise and a bright light source directly over the robot's head causing glare.
2. One image with just the green background without the hand is used to detect the threshold values for pixel segmentation.
3. Noise is removed by applying a series of dilations and erosions.
4. Detection of contours of the biggest object (hand), which is then drawn separately with a polygonal approximation (see Fig. 2, bottom row).
5. ROI coordinates for each image are saved in a .xml file.

2.4   A Deep Neural Network Model for Fingers Detection

For validating the collected image database, we trained a DNN model to identify the number of fingers being shown. Due to a large amount of time it takes to train and tune a model from scratch, we chose to utilise the Faster R-CNN Inception Resnet image classification model pre-trained with COCO dataset from the TensorFlow Model Zoo[1] as a base model for further re-training. The out-of-the-box model parameters were used with no changes during the training. With the primary goal to test the feasibility of the approach, Faster R-CNN model was chosen as being more accurate, albeit slower than SSD models, for example. Training and testing datasets (1000 and 200 images, correspondingly) were compiled by composing random office backgrounds with the hand pixels extracted from the original images using corresponding silhouettes. 100K training steps were performed, which amounts to 100 epochs given batch size of 1 image. A checkpoint was saved every hour (approx. 3K steps). Since the training was

---

[1] https://github.com/tensorflow/models/blob/master/research/object_detection/g3doc/detection_model_ zoo.md.

done for fixed number of steps and no parameter-tuning was performed, the testing set also acted as the validation set.

3 Results

The model was evaluated at different checkpoints on a validation set of 200 images (40 for each class). Classification accuracy peaks at about 26K steps and then drops because of overfitting (Fig. 3). Confusion matrix for this checkpoint (step 26581) is given in Table 1, with most errors due to 'fours' classified as 'fives'.

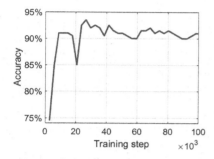

Fig. 3. The progress of classification accuracy with the test dataset

Table 1. Confusion matrix for the model with the best accuracy on the test dataset. Rows—actual values, columns—predicted values.

%	One	Two	Three	Four	Five
One	100.0	0.0	0.0	0.0	0.0
Two	0.0	100.0	0.0	0.0	0.0
Three	0.0	5.0	95.0	0.0	0.0
Four	2.5	0.0	0.0	75.0	22.5
Five	0.0	0.0	0.0	2.5	97.5
Sensitivity	100.0	100.0	95.0	75.0	97.5
Precision	97.6	95.2	100.0	96.8	81.2

Further work will focus on expanding the hand image dataset, improving the silhouette extraction and preventing miss-classification for images showing occlusion and finger overlap (such as 5-as-4).

Acknowledgments. This work has been supported by the EPSRC through the grant no. EP/P030033/1 (NUMBERS). Authors are grateful to the NVIDIA Corporation for donating GeForce GTX TITAN X that has been used to accelerate the computation.

References

1. Asada, M., et al.: Cognitive developmental robotics as a new paradigm for the design of humanoid robots. Robot. Auton. Syst. **37**(2–3), 185–193 (2001)
2. Cangelosi, A., Schlesinger, M.: Developmental Robotics: From Babies to Robots. MIT Press, Cambridge (2015)
3. Dantzig, T.: Number-The Language of Science. Free Press, New York (1954)
4. Fischer, M.H., et al.: Finger Counting and Numerical Cognition. Front. Psychol. **3**, 108 (2012)
5. Goldin-Meadow, S., et al.: Gesture's role in learning arithmetic. In: Edwards, L.D., et al. (eds.) Emerging Perspectives on Gesture and Embodiment in Mathematics, pp. 51–72. Information Age Publishing, Charlotte (2014)

6. De La Cruz, V.M. et al.: Making fingers and words count in a cognitive robot. Front. Behav. Neurosci. **8**, 12 pages (2014)
7. Leitner, J. et al.: Humanoid learns to detect its own hands. In: 2013 IEEE Congress Evolutionary Computation, CEC 2013, pp. 1411–1418 (2013)
8. Di Nuovo, A., Jay, T.: The development of numerical cognition in children and artificial systems: a review of the current knowledge and proposals for multi-disciplinary research. IET Cogn. Comput. Syst. **1**, 2–11 (2019)
9. Soylu, F., et al.: You can count on your fingers: the role of fingers in early mathematical development. J. Numer. Cogn. **4**(1), 2363–8761 (2018)
10. Vicente, P., et al.: Robotic hand pose estimation based on stereo vision and GPU-enabled internal graphical simulation. J. Intell. Robot. Syst. **83**(3–4), 339–358 (2016)

Modular, Underactuated Anthropomorphic Robot Hand with Flexible Fingers and Twisted String Actuators

Muhammad Faiz Rahman$^{(\boxtimes)}$(iD), Kaiqiang Zhang(iD), and Guido Herrmann(iD)

Mechanical Engineering, University of Bristol, Bristol, UK
g.herrmann@bristol.ac.uk

Abstract. For general grasping, a strong lightweight and compact robot hand needs to be designed as a robot end effector. This paper describes the design of a 3D printed anthropomorphic robot hand that actuates flexible fingers using Twisted String Actuators (TSAs). A total of 6 of these actuators were fitted within a limited confined space, the palm of the hand. This gives the hand 6 Degrees of Freedom (DOFs) 2 in the thumb and 1 in each of the other fingers. A simple modular design was used which allows for rapid prototyping of different finger designs with respect to different requirements at low cost. In this paper, only power grasping is considered for simplicity. The hand is capable of performing both spherical and cylindrical grasps whereby the flexible nature of the fingers allows for forming around the geometry of a target object. The maximum holding load of the hand was found to be 10 kg in performance tests.

Keywords: Twisted string actuators · Additive manufacturing · Flexible fingers · Anthropomorphic robot hand

1 Introduction

From studies, tendon based transmission is one of the most commonly used actuation methods for robot hands [1]. This method of actuation is intuitive to implement and allows compact arrangements. However, the inherent compliance introduced by the flexibility of the tendons consequently requires complicated control methods for accurate position control [2]. The need of complicated control methods would be dependent on the design requirements, such as in the case of an industrial robot in car manufacturing where accurate position control is required.

In this paper, the design of a 3D printed anthropomorphic robot hand with flexible compliant fingers actuated by Twisted String Actuators (TSAs) [3] is proposed. The objective is to create an effective end effector that is cheap, light, strong, and compact. The efficacy of this hand will be defined by its performance

© Springer Nature Switzerland AG 2019
K. Althoefer et al. (Eds.): TAROS 2019, LNAI 11650, pp. 489–492, 2019.
https://doi.org/10.1007/978-3-030-25332-5_47

in load carrying and its adaptability to grasp different shaped objects. This paper is structured as follows: The design considerations for the hand will be elaborated on in Sects. 2, 3 describes the tests and their results and Sect. 4 talks about the conclusions and future work.

2   Design Considerations

For this paper, each TSA consists of 1 Permanent Magnet DC(PMDC motor) [4] attached to 2 tendons. The motor is paired with an encoder to measure the rotations of the shaft for control. This actuation method in particular was adopted as it is relatively cheap, easy to manufacture, compact, and is capable of handling very high loads [3]. To fit the actuation system in a compact space, a total of 6 actuators were used and fitted into the palm of the hand, in particular, 2 in the thumb and 1 in each of the other fingers as shown in Fig. 1(b). This results in the hand itself having 6 Degrees of Freedoms (DOFs) 2 for the thumb and 1 each for the remaining fingers. Having 2 DOFs for the thumb makes it opposable, as a result it allows the thumb to move in 2 planes of motion. This allows for more dexterous grasping to accommodate for geometrically different objects. Additionally, the hand weighs 235 g which is approximately half the weight of an average human male hand [5]

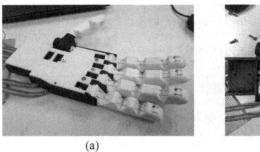
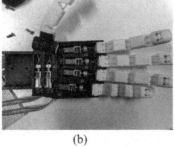

(a)   (b)

Fig. 1. (a) Overview of the hand (b) Actuation system in the palm

A challenge of using this actuation method is the limited durability of the tendons used as opposed to their strength [6]. This is due to the fact that repetitive twisting of the tendons causes wear. From previous studies performed on different materials for TSAs, Dyneema, which is a type of Ultra High Molecular Weight Polyethylene (UHMWP), was adopted for its high durability [6].

The hand is made of polylactic Acid (PLA) [7] which has been chosen for its durability and low cost. NinjaFlex, [8] which is a type of 3D printable flexible plastic, is used as the material for the fingers. A workpiece printed with this material is flexible at thin cross sections and stiff at thick cross sections. This allows for each finger to be 3D printed as an individual workpiece. From this, production time can be significantly reduced as compared to a standard robot finger which consists of multiple components. In addition, due to the inherent elastic nature of the material, the finger has sufficient elasticity to return to its initial shape after deformation. Therefore, antagonistic actuation is not required to fully actuate a finger, after releasing the tension from the actuators.

The hand was designed to be modular, which allows for rapid prototyping of different designs of fingers to be easily changed based on different design requirements. This is especially important for future work to allow for fingers with different inbuilt sensors to be tested without having the need to rebuild the entire hand. In addition, the compliancy of the fingers could be changed depending on their design and materials used.

3   Grasping and Load Test

Different grasps were tested with the hand on different shaped objects. Motivated to present the success of the hand design, the performance tests were carried out for power grasping in this paper. Only power grasping [9] is considered as it is simpler to implement and does not require a high amount of accuracy to implement. As shown in Fig. 2, benefiting from the opposable thumb design, the hand is capable of both cylindrical and spherical based grasping. This confirms that the compliant nature of the fingers allows the fingers to form around objects of different geometries, in particular a human brain model as shown in Fig. 2(b).

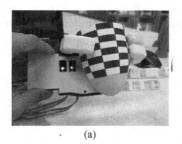
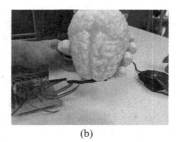

(a)   (b)

Fig. 2. (a) Cylindrical grasp (b) Spherical grasp

To investigate the strength of the hand, varying loads were lifted by the hand until failure. Here, the measured strength refers to the maximum holding load of the hand. These tests were carried out by enclosing the fingers around the handles of kettlebells such that the TSAs have reached their limits in rotations. The hand was then lifted off the ground and held in the air for 10 s, before placing the kettlebell safely back on the ground as shown in Fig. 3(a).

From Fig. 3(b), the maximum holding load was found to be 10 kg. Over this weight, the fingers are unable to hold on to the handle while carrying the kettlebell. This is due to the compliancy of the finger design, primarily the flexibility of the material.

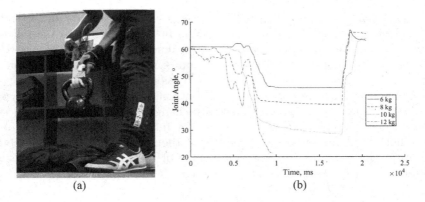
(a)   (b)

Fig. 3. (a) The hand holding up a 10 kg kettleball (b) Average joint angle response for differing loads

4   Conclusion

This paper presents the design of a compact and light-weight humanoid hand for potential use as an effective end effector. The design, which comprises of compliant fingers and TSA actuating mechanisms, enables power grasping of objects in various shapes and the carrying of heavy loads. The design allows for rapid manufacturing of a powerful compliant gripper at low cost. Future work will focus on the incorporation of complex control methods for more precision based pinch grasps. In addition, different finger designs that incorporate force sensing can be implemented to improve feedback control ability.

References

1. Alba, D., Armada, M., Ponticelli, R.: An introductory revision to humanoid robot hands. In: Armada, M.A., de Santos, P.G. (eds.) Climbing and Walking Robots. Springer, Heidelberg (2005). https://doi.org/10.1007/3-540-29461-9_69
2. Chang, S.-L., Lee, J.-J., Yen, H.-C.: Kinematic and compliance analysis for tendon-driven robotic mechanisms with flexible tendons. Mech. Mach. Theory **40**(6), 728–739 (2005). https://doi.org/10.1016/j.mechmachtheory.2004.11.003
3. Kremer, S.R.: Twisted Cord Actuator. US Pat. 4843921, 4 July 1989, filed 18 April 1988
4. Micro Metal Gearmotor HPCB 6V with Extended Motor Shaft. https://www.pololu.com/product/3075. Accessed 5 Nov 2018
5. Body Segment Data. https://exrx.net/Kinesiology/Segments. Accessed 5 Nov 2018
6. Godler, I., Sonoda, T., Miyamoto, H.: Twisted Strings Based Robotic Hand and Eyes. http://www-lar.deis.unibo.it/people/gpalli/TwistedString_Workshop/Godler-IROS2016.pdf
7. PLA MSDS. ampolumer.com
8. NinjaTek: NinjaFlex Safety Data Sheet 2016
9. Cutkosky, M.R.: On grasp choice, grasp models, and the design of hands for manufacturing tasks. IEEE Trans. Robot. Autom. **5**(3), 269–279 (1989)

A Quest Towards Safe Human Robot Collaboration

Mohammad Safeea[1,2] , Pedro Neto[1](✉) , and Richard Béarée[2]

[1] Department of Mechanical Engineering, University of Coimbra, Coimbra, Portugal
ms@uc.pt, pedro.neto@dem.uc.pt
[2] Arts et Métiers, LISPEN, Lille, France
richard.bearee@ensam.eu

Abstract. In the upcoming industrial revolution (Industry 4.0) automation and robotics play a central role. Humans and robots are expected to share the same workspace and work safely side by side. Consequently, various collaborative robots have been introduced to the market. Nevertheless, those robots are still limited in their reactions. In some cases they are restricted to reducing their working speed as a response to the proximity of humans or they initiate an emergency stop, particularly if a contact is detected. In this paper, our work on real-time human robot collision avoidance is presented. Unlike the existing solutions, in our method the robot is provided with agile reactivity to human presence. The system is engineered to achieve natural collision avoidance behavior. As a result, the robot acts with smooth avoidance motion upon the proximity of human, giving him/her the space required to do his/her work in shared tasks between a human co-worker and robot.

Keywords: Human robot safe collaboration · Safe coexistence · Industry 4.0

1 Methodology

We are living in a dynamic and competitive world where change is touching every aspect of our lives, including industry. The paradigm of manufacturing is shifting towards flexible production. In such a case, multi-functional programmable machines (mainly robots) along with skilled manpower offer this flexibility, by combining the cognitive power of humans with robots' ability to perform tedious and repetitive tasks. To achieve this quest humans and robots are required to work with proximity, sometimes in the same workplace collaborating with each others. In such a case, having safe human robot collaboration poses both safety and technological challenge to existing solutions. Yet, the field of human-robot collaboration is still in its infancy. Most industrial robots are still posing safety risks to humans, such that they are confined behind steel fences on the factory floor. To tackle this issue, collaborative robots are introduced into the market,

© Springer Nature Switzerland AG 2019
K. Althoefer et al. (Eds.): TAROS 2019, LNAI 11650, pp. 493–495, 2019.
https://doi.org/10.1007/978-3-030-25332-5_48

due to their safety-centered design they are allowed to work side by side with humans. Those machines are provided with advanced mechatronic components, but their full potentialities are not fully realized. Existing collaborative solutions tend to reduce robot's velocity with human's proximity, or to stop the robot altogether [1]. Such behaviors seem un-natural and cause interruptions when human and robots are performing shared tasks. For example, the existence of robot in the workspace might deny acceptability to the worker, reducing the robot's velocity or stopping it might not solve this issue. One solution is to give the robot an ability to perform safe collision avoidance motion, by endowing the robot with human like reflexes and more autonomy. In our proposed solution, the robot senses the proximity of the human through external sensors attached to his/her body [2]. Then, sensors data are used to capture the configuration of the human (approximated by capsules), the structure of the robot is also approximated by capsules. The minimum distance between both, human and robot, is calculated using the method in [3], that is used as an input to our custom collision avoidance algorithm based on the potential fields method [4].

2   Tests and Results

Figure 1 shows the experimental setup used for testing the proposed real-time collision avoidance system. The robot used is an industrial collaborative manipulator KUKA iiwa 7 R800. An external computer is also used to implement the control algorithm and to process sensors data in real-time. The robot was controlled from MATLAB through TCP/IP connection using the KUKA Sunrise Toolbox KST [5].

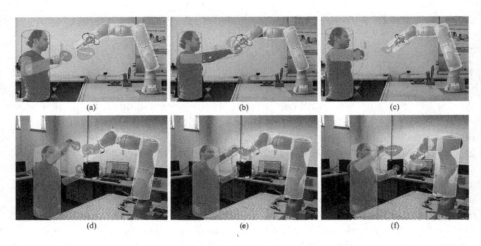

Fig. 1. Human robot collision avoidance, the human is trying to touch the robot causing the robot to maneuver in a collision avoidance motion.

In the proposed experiment a human is performing random motions around the robot with the two arms, causing a reactive motion of the robot as it avoids collision with him/her. Figure 2 at the left shows various data recorded during the experiment regarding the end-effector (EEF), its velocity and position in Cartesian coordinates, as well the minimum distance (d1 and d2) between each human arm and the robot. Figure 2 at the right shows the path of the EEF in 3D space during the maneuvering motion. The results demonstrated that the robot avoids collisions by reacting quickly and smoothly. Such behavior was achieved due to accurate sensing, efficient calculation of minimum distance and fast computations of collision avoidance algorithm which allow controlling the robot at a frequency of 275 Hz. A video demonstrating the experiment is available in [6].

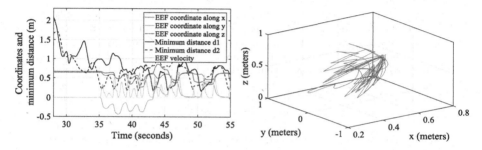

Fig. 2. Minimum distance, EEF velocity and position (Left). Collision avoidance path of EEF in 3D space (Right).

Acknowledgments. This research was partially supported by Portugal 2020 project DM4Manufacturing POCI-01-0145-FEDER-016418 by UE/FEDER through the program COMPETE 2020, and the Portuguese Foundation for Science and Technology (FCT) SFRH/BD/131091/2017 and COBOTIS (PTDC/EME- EME/32595/2017).

References

1. Mohammed, A., Schmidt, B., Wang, L.: Active collision avoidance for human-robot collaboration driven by vision sensors. Int. J. Comput. Integr. Manuf. **30**(9), 970–980 (2017)
2. Safeea, M., Neto, P.: Minimum distance calculation using laser scanner and imus for safe human-robot interaction. Rob. Comput. Integr. Manuf. **58**, 33–42 (2019)
3. Safeea, M., Neto, P., Bearee, R.: Efficient calculation of minimum distance between capsules and its use in robotics. IEEE Access **7**, 5368–5373 (2019)
4. Khatib, O.: Real-time obstacle avoidance for manipulators and mobile robots. Int. J. Rob. Res. **5**(1), 90–98 (1986)
5. Safeea, M., Neto, P.: Kuka sunrise toolbox: interfacing collaborative robots with matlab. IEEE Robot. Autom. Mag. **26**(1), 91–96 (2019)
6. Video segment demonstrating the experiment. https://youtu.be/eh5s8PTe5VM. Accessed 30 Jan 2019

Wheelchair Navigation: Automatically Adapting to Evolving Environments

Tomos Fearn$^{(\boxtimes)}$ ⓘ, Frédéric Labrosse ⓘ, and Patricia Shaw ⓘ

Department of Computer Science, Aberystwyth University, Aberystwyth, Wales
{tof7,ffl,phs}@aber.ac.uk

Abstract. Power wheelchairs can increase independence by supporting the mobility of their users. However, severe disabilities of users can render controlling the wheelchair difficult, if not impossible, especially over longer periods of time. This paper describes a proposal for research into techniques that would improve the experience and quality of life of wheelchair users by reducing the cognitive burden introduced by repetitive and complicated navigation tasks and manoeuvres. This will be achieved by sharing the control between the user and an autonomous controller. A number of techniques will be used to achieve this aim. Simultaneous Localization and Mapping (SLAM) and topological mapping will be used for navigation between rooms while Computer Vision techniques will allow the (semi) automatic recognition of places in the user's home, based on the detection and categorization of objects. Finally, medium to high level automation will be provided. This includes automatic and transparent assistance with tasks such as navigating through doorways but also autonomous navigation to specific locations using high level constructs ("take me to the kitchen table").

Keywords: Wheelchair · Computer vision · SLAM · Shared control · Middleware

1 Introduction

A power wheelchair is an option available to users with a mobility impairment. An abundance of wheelchair interfaces exist to control the power wheelchair to cater for a variety of disabilities. The joystick is most commonly fitted to power wheelchairs. Clinicians found that 40% of power wheelchair users considered it difficult or impossible to manoeuvre within tight spaces such as offices or doorways [1]. These issues arise when the wheelchair user has more severe disabilities.

Several factors impede on a wheelchair user's participation in day-to-day life [2]. Major factors include inaccessible locations and uneven surfaces, which are challenging to navigate for the healthiest of wheelchair users.

© Springer Nature Switzerland AG 2019
K. Althoefer et al. (Eds.): TAROS 2019, LNAI 11650, pp. 496–500, 2019.
https://doi.org/10.1007/978-3-030-25332-5_49

2   Background and Motivation

During the last two decades many research projects have created and developed prototype "smart wheelchairs" [3]. Although prototypes have been developed, there are no commercially available wheelchairs that offer "smart features" that aid navigation and obstacle avoidance. Past research shows that the smart wheelchairs previously developed focused on a few areas, described below.

2.1   Shared Control and User Intentions

Not all users possess the ability to accurately control their wheelchair to perform common manoeuvres, such as following a corridor or navigating through a doorway. A smart wheelchair known as 'Sharioto' [4] provides a working example of human computer interaction or *shared control*, where the user dictates their intentions to the autonomous controller on-board the wheelchair via their preferred interface. Once the wheelchair recognizes what the user's intentions are, it takes perceptions from sensors into account to decide how it should traverse to the goal.

One of the most important aspects of shared control is switching between different modes of operation; the 'Sharioto' wheelchair requires the user to make the high-level planning, while utilising LIDAR and Sonar sensors for obstacle avoidance and a behaviour based framework to act upon common wheelchair manoeuvres, such as docking at a table or navigating a doorway.

2.2   Global Navigation

Simultaneous Localisation and Mapping is a well-defined method of localising a robot while navigating in the environment. Many existing software frameworks exist to perform SLAM and path planning. A "smart wheelchair" developed in California [5] utilises the Robotic Operating System (ROS) to unite SLAM and shared control. They use a deliberative control system that enables the wheelchair to navigate its environment, based on an occupancy grid populated by on-board LIDAR data. Given the improvements and developments in the field of computer vision, using low cost cameras and sophisticated algorithms has achieved a viable solution to aid in the wheelchair navigation process. Using an omnidirectional camera that provides a panoramic view of the environment, objects can be detected. In [6], a prototype smart wheelchair uses an omnidirectional camera to capture images at regular intervals. Localisation can be achieved using epipolar geometry, the captured images and odometry data (including speed and distance travelled). Another example of vision-based navigation is shown in [7], where a Microsoft Kinect is used to calculate distances between the wheelchair and obstacles. This enables the wheelchair to determine safe docking locations.

3   Proposed System

We describe in this section the novel aspects of the proposed system.

3.1   Object Segmentation and Recognition

Many algorithms allow for object detection using deep neural networks, pre-trained on large datasets of annotated objects in images. We aim to automatically detect the type of room the wheelchair is in by performing object recognition. Because every home is different, we propose to complement the database of objects by allowing the automatic detection of new objects and asking the user what these are. This is done using stereo cameras to perform depth segmentation on objects unrecognized by the wheelchair. In Fig. 1(a) we show a mug and refrigerator as recognised objects, and a kettle in the foreground as an unrecognized object, using the MobileNetV2 architecture and OpenCV. MobileNetV2 is used due to its accuracy and efficiency, valuable for running on small, energy efficient, embedded computers on board wheelchairs. Figure 1(b) shows the first step of the segmentation process; a depth map is generated from stereo cameras. This enables the objects (e.g. kettle and mug) at the forefront of the image to be segmented using the OpenCV vision library. Figure 1(c) shows that once the image has been segmented, the user can be asked to provide a label for the unrecognized object (kettle) and the deep neural network would be further trained using the Tensorflow software.

(a) Object detection using MobileNetV2   (b) Depth map from a stereo camera

(c) Segmented objects from depth map

Fig. 1. Example of object detection

We aim to assist the identification of unknown objects by analysing the context of the environment using other identifiable items; for example, if a refrigerator and an oven are detected, the scene is likely to be a kitchen. This can help narrow down the detected object as one normally found in a kitchen, such as a kettle. The user then confirms what the object is, resulting in the development and customization of the wheelchair for the user.

The system will be evaluated by comparing the confidence level in detecting new objects compared to objects the system was originally trained for (using the COCO dataset).

3.2   Localisation and Path Planning

For the wheelchair to traverse to its desired location, the tools associated with ROS, such as Cartographer for mapping and Wavefront for path planning, provide a viable solution to performing global navigation. ROS is a widely used framework, where libraries and drivers for a variety of sensors exist. ROS is also compatible with the Gazebo simulator, enabling us to test the wheelchair extensively before trialling the wheelchair with users. We aim to predict the type of location (i.e. kitchen or bedroom) based on the categorisation of the detected objects within the environment. This might require confirmation from the user in case of ambiguity. The wheelchair can then adapt its behaviour, for example, by reducing its speed and docking at a table in the kitchen. Secondly the wheelchair will build a topological map of the home that will allow high-level planning and navigation, recording the important locations as nodes and the type of control along the edges linking the nodes.

The system will be evaluated using a number of scenarios, first in simulation, then using tame testers and finally selected real users. Feedback will be collected to gather evidence about the performance, specifically about incorrect behaviours, such as avoiding the object the chair is supposed to dock to.

4   Conclusions

We have described in this paper a proposal for a system that will provide power wheelchair users more autonomy while keeping them involved in the control of the wheelchair as much as possible.

The system will automatically learn a map of the home of the user, involving the user in the process by asking the user to confirm or correct choices made by the system ("I can see a kettle and a refrigerator, are we in the kitchen?"). This will be based on automatically recognizing objects as well as detecting unrecognized ones, again asking the user what these might be, therefore progressively adapting to the environment of the user.

Although only a proposal at this stage, our informal tests and evaluations of existing technologies allow us to believe that such a system can be researched and developed.

References

1. Fehr, L.: Adequacy of power wheelchair control interfaces for persons with severe disabilities. J. Rehabil. Res. Dev. **37**(3), 353–360 (2000)
2. Jensen, J.: User perspective on assistive technology: a qualitative analysis of 55 letters from citizens applying for assistive technology. J. World Fed. Occup. Therapists Bull. **69**(1), 42–45 (2014)

3. Leaman, J., La, H.M.: A comprehensive review of smart wheelchairs: past, present and future. IEEE Trans. Hum.-Mach. Syst. **47**(4), 486–499 (2017)
4. Vanhooydonck, D., Demeester, E., Nuttin, M., Van Brussel, H.: Shared control for intelligent wheelchairs: an implicit estimation of the user intention. In: Proceedings of the ASER, 1st International Workshop on Advances in Service Robotics, pp. 176–182 (2003)
5. Grewal, H., Matthews, A., Tea, R., George, K.: LIDAR-based autonomous wheelchair. In: IEEE Sensors Applications Symposium (SAS) (2017)
6. Yassine, N., Vauchey, V., Khemmar, R., Ragot, N., Sirlantzis, K., Ertaud, J.: ROS-based autonomous navigation wheelchair using omnidirectional sensor. Int. J. Comput. Appl. **133**(6), 12–17 (2016)
7. Jain, S., Argall, B.: Automated perception of safe docking locations with alignment information for assistive wheelchairs. In: 2014 IEEE/RSJ (IROS), pp. 4997–5002 (2014)

Correction to: Random Walk Exploration for Swarm Mapping

Miquel Kegeleirs[iD], David Garzón Ramos[iD], and Mauro Birattari[iD]

Correction to:
Chapter "Random Walk Exploration for Swarm Mapping"
in: K. Althoefer et al. (Eds.): *Towards Autonomous*
***Robotic Systems*, LNAI 11650,**
https://doi.org/10.1007/978-3-030-25332-5_19

In the metadata ("Cite this chapter as" section) of the originally published XML version and the author index of the volume the name of the second author was incorrectly stated as "Ramos, David Garzón". The name has been corrected to "Garzón Ramos, David".

The updated version of this chapter can be found at
https://doi.org/10.1007/978-3-030-25332-5_19

K. Althoefer et al. (Eds.): TAROS 2019, LNAI 11650, p. C1, 2019.
https://doi.org/10.1007/978-3-030-25332-5_50

Author Index

Printed in the United States
By Bookmasters